The Victoria History of the Counties of England

EDITED BY WILLIAM PAGE, F.S.A.

A HISTORY OF

STAFFORDSHIRE

VOLUME I

THE
VICTORIA HISTORY
OF THE COUNTIES
OF ENGLAND
STAFFORDSHIRE

PUBLISHED FOR

THE UNIVERSITY OF LONDON

INSTITUTE OF HISTORICAL RESEARCH

REPRINTED FROM THE ORIGINAL EDITION OF 1908

BY

DAWSONS OF PALL MALL

LONDON

1968

Issued by
Archibald Constable and Company Limited
in 1908
Reprinted for the University of London
Institute of Historical Research
by
Dawsons of Pall Mall
16 Pall Mall, London, S.W.I.
1968

SBN : 7129 0308 9

Reprinted in Belgium by Jos. Adam, Brussels

INSCRIBED
TO THE MEMORY OF
HER LATE MAJESTY
QUEEN VICTORIA
WHO GRACIOUSLY GAVE
THE TITLE TO AND
ACCEPTED THE
DEDICATION OF
THIS HISTORY

THE ADVISORY COUNCIL
OF THE VICTORIA HISTORY

GENERAL ADVERTISEMENT

The Victoria History of the Counties of England is a National Historic Survey which, under the direction of a large staff comprising the foremost students in science, history, and archaeology, is designed to record the history of every county of England in detail. This work was, by gracious permission, dedicated to Her late Majesty Queen Victoria, who gave it her own name. It is the endeavour of all who are associated with the undertaking to make it a worthy and permanent monument to her memory.

Rich as every county of England is in materials for local history, there has hitherto been no attempt made to bring all these materials together into a coherent form.

Although from the seventeenth century down to quite recent times numerous county histories have been issued, they are very unequal in merit; the best of them are very rare and costly; most of them are imperfect and many are now out of date. Moreover, they were the work of one or two isolated scholars, who, however scholarly, could not possibly deal adequately with all the varied subjects which go to the making of a county history.

In the VICTORIA HISTORY each county is not the labour of one or two men, but of many, for the work is treated scientifically, and in order to embody in it all that modern scholarship can contribute, a system of co-operation between experts and local students is applied, whereby the history acquires a completeness and definite authority hitherto lacking in similar undertakings.

The names of the distinguished men who have joined the Advisory Council are a guarantee that the work represents the results of the latest discoveries in every department of research, for the trend of modern thought insists upon the intelligent study of the past and of the social, institutional, and political developments of national life. As these histories are the first in which this object has been kept in view, and modern principles applied, it is hoped that they will form a work of reference no less indispensable to the student than welcome to the man of culture.

THE SCOPE OF THE WORK

The history of each county is complete in itself, and in each case its story is told from the earliest times, commencing with the natural features and the flora and fauna. Thereafter follow the antiquities, pre-Roman, Roman, and post-Roman; ancient earthworks; a new translation and critical study of the Domesday Survey; articles on political, ecclesiastical, social, and economic history; architecture, arts, industries, sport, etc.; and topography. The greater part of each history is devoted to a detailed description and history of each parish, containing an account of the land and its owners from the Conquest to the present day. These manorial histories are compiled from original documents in the national collections and from private papers. A special feature is the wealth of illustrations afforded, for not only are buildings of interest pictured, but the coats of arms of past and present landowners are given

HISTORICAL RESEARCH

It has always been, and still is, a reproach that England, with a collection of public records greatly exceeding in extent and interest those of any other country in Europe, is yet far behind her neighbours in the study of the genesis and growth of her national and local institutions. Few Englishmen are probably aware that the national and local archives contain for a period of 800 years in an almost unbroken chain of evidence, not only the political, ecclesiastical, and constitutional history of the kingdom, but every detail of its financial and social progress and the history of the land and its successive owners from generation to generation. The neglect of our public and local records is no doubt largely due to the fact that their interest and value is known to but a small number of people, and this again is directly attributable to the absence in this country of any endowment for historical research. The government of this country has too often left to private enterprise work which our continental neighbours entrust to a government department. It is not surprising, therefore, to find that although an immense amount of work has been done by individual effort, the entire absence of organization among the workers and the lack of intelligent direction has hitherto robbed the results of much of their value.

In the VICTORIA HISTORY, for the first time, a serious attempt is made to utilize our national and local muniments to the best advantage by carefully organizing and supervising the researches required. Under the direction of the Records Committee a large staff of experts has been engaged at the Public Record Office in calendaring those classes of records which are fruitful in material for local history, and by a system of interchange of communication among workers under the direct supervision of the general editor and sub-editors a mass of information is sorted and assigned to its correct place, which would otherwise be impossible.

THE RECORDS COMMITTEE

SIR EDWARD MAUNDE THOMPSON, K.C.B.   C. T. MARTIN, B.A., F.S.A.
SIR HENRY MAXWELL-LYTE, K.C.B.   J. HORACE ROUND, M.A., LL.D.
W. J. HARDY, F.S.A.   S. R. SCARGILL-BIRD, F.S.A.
F. MADAN, M.A.   W. H. STEVENSON, M.A.
                    G. F. WARNER, M.A., F.S.A.

CARTOGRAPHY

In addition to a general map in several sections, each History contains Geological, Orographical, Botanical, Archæological, and Domesday maps; also maps illustrating the articles on Ecclesiastical and Political Histories, and the sections dealing with Topography. The Series contains many hundreds of maps in all.

ARCHITECTURE

A special feature in connexion with the Architecture is a series of ground plans, many of them coloured, showing the architectural history of castles, cathedrals, abbeys, and other monastic foundations.

In order to secure the greatest possible accuracy, the descriptions of the Architecture, ecclesiastical, military, and domestic, are under the supervision of Mr. C. R. PEERS, M.A., F.S.A., and a committee has been formed of the following students of architectural history who are referred to as may be required concerning this department of the work :—

ARCHITECTURAL COMMITTEE

J. BILSON, F.S.A., F.R.I.B.A.
R. BLOMFIELD, M.A., F.S.A., A.R.A.
HAROLD BRAKSPEAR, F.S.A., A.R.I.B.A.
PROF. BALDWIN BROWN, M.A.
ARTHUR S. FLOWER, M.A.
GEORGE E. FOX, M.A., F.S.A.

J. A. GOTCH, F.S.A., F.R.I.B.A.
W. H. ST. JOHN HOPE, M.A.
W. H. KNOWLES, F.S.A., F.R.I.B.A.
ROLAND PAUL, F.S.A.
J. HORACE ROUND, M.A., LL.D.
PERCY G. STONE, F.S.A., F.R.I.B.A.

H. THACKERAY TURNER, F.S.A.

The general plan of Contents and the names among others of those who are contributing articles and giving assistance are as follows :—

Natural History

Geology. CLEMENT REID, F.R.S., HORACE B. WOODWARD, F.R.S., and others

Palæontology. R. LYDEKKER, F.R.S., F.L.S., F.G.S.

Flora
Fauna { Contributions by G. A. BOULENGER, F.R.S., H. N. DIXON, F.L.S., G. C. DRUCE, M.A., F.L.S., WALTER GARSTANG, M.A., D.Sc., F.L.S., HERBERT GOSS, F.L.S., F.E.S., R. I. POCOCK, REV. T. R. R. STEBBING, M.A., F.R.S., etc., B. B. WOODWARD, F.G.S., F.R.M.S., etc., and other Specialists

Prehistoric Remains. SIR JOHN EVANS, K.C.B., D.C.L., LL.D., W. BOYD DAWKINS, D.Sc., LL.D., F.R.S., F.S.A., GEO. CLINCH, F.G.S., JOHN GARSTANG, M.A., B.LITT., F.S.A., and others

Roman Remains. F. HAVERFIELD, M.A., LL.D., F.S.A., and others

Anglo-Saxon Remains. C. HERCULES READ, F.S.A., REGINALD A. SMITH, B.A., F.S.A., and others

Domesday Book and other kindred Records. J. HORACE ROUND, M.A., LL.D., and other Specialists

Architecture. C. R. PEERS, M.A., F.S.A., W. H. ST. JOHN HOPE, M.A., HAROLD BRAKSPEAR, F.S.A., A.R.I.B.A., and others

Ecclesiastical History. R. L. POOLE, M.A., and others

Political History. PROF. C. H. FIRTH, M.A., LL.D., W. H. STEVENSON, M.A., J. HORACE ROUND, M.A., LL.D., PROF. T. F. TOUT, M.A., PROF. JAMES TAIT, M.A., and A. F. POLLARD

History of Schools. A. F. LEACH, M.A., F.S.A.

Maritime History of Coast Counties. SIR JOHN K. LAUGHTON, M.A., M. OPPENHEIM, and others

Topographical Accounts of Parishes and Manors. By Various Authorities

Agriculture. SIR ERNEST CLARKE, M.A., Sec. to the Royal Agricultural Society, and others

Forestry. JOHN NISBET, D.Œc., and others

Industries, Arts and Manufactures
                                              } By Various Authorities
Social and Economic History

Ancient and Modern Sport. E. D. CUMING, the REV. E. E. DORLING, M.A., and others
    Cricket. SIR HOME GORDON, BART.

Steel Works, Bilston.

W Hyde

THE
VICTORIA HISTORY
OF THE COUNTY OF
STAFFORD

EDITED BY
WILLIAM PAGE, F.S.A

VOLUME ONE

PUBLISHED FOR
THE UNIVERSITY OF LONDON
INSTITUTE OF HISTORICAL RESEARCH

REPRINTED BY
DAWSONS OF PALL MALL
LONDON

CONTENTS OF VOLUME ONE

CONTENTS OF VOLUME ONE

LIST OF ILLUSTRATIONS

LIST OF ILLUSTRATIONS

LIST OF MAPS

★ *Not reproduced in this edition owing to technical difficulties*

∘ *Reproduced in black and white in this edition*

PREFACE

STAFFORDSHIRE has from an early date attracted the attention of the topographer. In 1593 Sampson Erdeswicke began his *View and Survey of Staffordshire*, which he left unfinished at his death in 1603. What became of the original manuscript of his work is unknown, but several copies exist, and although they were referred to by subsequent writers, none of them was printed till 1717 when Curll issued the *Survey*, together with a letter written in 1669 from Sir Simon Degge, setting out the condition of the county at that date. The next to interest himself in the county was Robert Plot, who settled in Oxford for a time after taking his degree, and in 1677 published *The Natural History of Oxfordshire*. Upon the reputation he acquired from this volume he was invited by Walter Chetwynd of Ingestry to undertake a similar work for Staffordshire, and in 1686 *The Natural History of Staffordshire* was issued. Under the term natural history Plot included the archaeological remains of the county, and it is for the record of these that his work is most valuable. In the unfinished *History and Antiquities of Staffordshire*, published in 1798, the Rev. Stebbing Shaw made use of Erdeswicke's collections, and added much from the manuscript sources at the British Museum and elsewhere. He only completed his history up to the first part of the second volume and died in 1802. William Pitt published *A Topographical History of Staffordshire* in 1817, which is largely based on the work of the earlier historians of the county, particularly that of Robert Plot. The history of Staffordshire, however, will always be associated with the name of William Salt, who, although not claiming to be an historian, yet collected the material upon which all future work on the topography of the county must be largely based. Shortly after his death in 1863 his collections were housed at Stafford and form a remarkable memorial of his industry. The work which he began is being continued and expanded by 'The William Salt Archaeological Society,' whose volumes have added much valuable material for the history of the county.

The Editor has to regret that Professor Haverfield was unable to undertake the article on the Roman Remains of the county owing to the pressure of other engagements. The Editor, however, wishes to express his thanks to Professor Haverfield for reading the proofs of this article and to Mr. Charles Lynam, F.S.A., for the information and great assistance afforded on the same subject. He also desires to acknowledge his indebtedness to Mr. Josiah Wedgwood, M.P., for reading some of the proofs and for advice generally on the volume, and to Mr. E. Howarth and the Society of Antiquaries for illustrations.

TABLE OF ABBREVIATIONS

Abbrev. Plac. (Rec. Com.)   Abbreviatio Placitorum (Record Commission)
Acts of P.C. . .   Acts of Privy Council
Add.. . . . .   Additional
Add. Chart. . .   Additional Charters
Admir. . . . .   Admiralty
Agarde . . . .   Agarde's Indices
Anct. Corresp.. .   Ancient Correspondence
Anct. D. (P.R.O.) A 2420   Ancient Deeds(Public Record Office) A 2420
Ann. Mon.. . .   Annales Monastici
Antiq. . . . .   Antiquarian or Antiquaries
App. . . .   Appendix
Arch. . . . .   Archæologia or Archæological
Arch. Cant. . .   Archæologia Cantiana
Archd. Rec. . .   Archdeacons' Records
Archit. . . . .   Architectural
Assize R. . . .   Assize Rolls
Aud. Off. . . .   Audit Office
Aug. Off. . . .   Augmentation Office
Ayloffe . . .   Ayloffe's Calendars

Bed.. . . . .   Bedford
Beds . . . .   Bedfordshire
Berks . . . .   Berkshire
Bdle. . . . .   Bundle
B.M. . . . .   British Museum
Bodl. Lib. . . .   Bodley's Library
Boro. . . . .   Borough
Brev. Reg.. . .   Brevia Regia
Brit.. . . . .   Britain,British, Britannia, etc.
Buck. . . . .   Buckingham
Bucks . . . .   Buckinghamshire

Cal.. . . . .   Calendar
Camb. . . .   Cambridgeshire or Cambridge
Cambr. . . . .   Cambria, Cambrian, Cambrensis, etc.
Campb. Chart.. .   Campbell Charters
Cant. . . . .   Canterbury
Cap.. . . . .   Chapter
Carl. . . . .   Carlisle
Cart. Antiq. R. .   Cartæ Antiquæ Rolls
C.C.C. Camb.. .   Corpus Christi College, Cambridge
Certiorari Bdles. (Rolls Chap.)   Certiorari Bundles (Rolls Chapel)
Chan. Enr. Decree R.   Chancery Enrolled Decree Rolls
Chan. Proc. . .   Chancery Proceedings
Chant. Cert. . .   Chantry Certificates (or Certificates of Colleges and Chantries)
Chap. Ho. . . .   Chapter House
Charity Inq. . .   Charity Inquisitions
Chart. R. 20 Hen. III. pt. i. No. 10   Charter Roll, 20 Henry III. part i. Number 10

Chartul.. . . .   Chartulary
Chas. . . . .   Charles
Ches. . . . .   Cheshire
Chest. . . . .   Chester
Ch. Gds. (Exch. K.R.)   Church Goods (Exchequer King's Remembrancer)
Chich. . . . .   Chichester
Chron. . . . .   Chronicle, Chronica, etc.
Close . . .   Close Roll
Co. . . . . .   County
Colch. . . . .   Colchester
Coll. . . . .   Collections
Com. . . . .   Commission
Com. Pleas . . .   Common Pleas
Conf. R. . . .   Confirmation Rolls
Co. Plac. . . .   County Placita
Cornw.. . . .   Cornwall
Corp. . . . .   Corporation
Cott. . . . .   Cotton or Cottonian
Ct. R. . . . .   Court Rolls
Ct. of Wards . .   Court of Wards
Cumb. . . . .   Cumberland
Cur. Reg. . . .   Curia Regis

D. . . . . .   Deed or Deeds
D. and C. . . .   Dean and Chapter
De Banc. R. . .   De Banco Rolls
Dec. and Ord . .   Decrees and Orders
Dep. Keeper's Rep.   Deputy Keeper's Reports
Derb. . . . .   Derbyshire or Derby
Devon . . . .   Devonshire
Dioc. . . . .   Diocese
Doc. . . . .   Documents
Dods. MSS. . .   Dodsworth MSS
Dom. Bk. . . .   Domesday Book
Dors. . . . .   Dorsetshire
Duchy of Lanc. .   Duchy of Lancaster
Dur. . . . .   Durham

East. . . . .   Easter Term
Eccl. . . . .   Ecclesiastical
Eccl. Com. . .   Ecclesiastical Commission
Edw. . . . .   Edward
Eliz. . . . .   Elizabeth
Engl. . . . .   England or English
Engl. Hist. Rev. .   English Historical Review
Enr. . . . .   Enrolled or Enrolment
Epis. Reg. . . .   Episcopal Registers
Esch. Enr. Accts. .   Escheators Enrolled Accounts
Excerpta e Rot. Fin. (Rec. Com.)   Excerpta e Rotulis Finium (Record Commission)
Exch. Dep. . .   Exchequer Depositions
Exch. K.B. . .   Exchequer King's Bench
Exch. K.R. . .   Exchequer King's Remembrancer
Exch. L.T.R. . .   Exchequer Lord Treasurer's Remembrancer

TABLE OF ABBREVIATIONS

Exch. of Pleas, Plea R.	Exchequer of Pleas, Plea Roll
Exch. of Receipt .	Exchequer of Receipt
Exch. Spec. Com. .	Exchequer Special Commissions
Feet of F. . . .	Feet of Fines
Feod. Accts. (Ct. of Wards)	Feodaries Accounts (Court of Wards)
Feod. Surv. (Ct. of Wards)	Feodaries Surveys (Court of Wards)
Feud. Aids . .	Feudal Aids
fol.	Folio
Foreign R. . .	Foreign Rolls
Forest Proc. . .	Forest Proceedings
Gaz.	Gazette or Gazetteer
Gen.	Genealogical, Genealogica, etc.
Geo.	George
Glouc. . . .	Gloucestershire or Gloucester
Guild Certif. (Chan.) Ric. II.	Guild Certificates (Chancery) Richard II.
Hants	Hampshire
Harl.	Harley or Harleian
Hen.	Henry
Heref. . . .	Herefordshire or Hereford
Hertf.	Hertford
Herts	Hertfordshire
Hil.	Hilary Term
Hist.	History, Historical, Historian, Historia, etc.
Hist. MSS. Com. .	Historical MSS. Commission
Hosp.	Hospital
Hund. R. . . .	Hundred Rolls
Hunt.	Huntingdon
Hunts	Huntingdonshire
Inq. a.q.d. . . .	Inquisitions ad quod damnum
Inq. p.m. . . .	Inquisitions post mortem
Inst.	Institute or Institution
Invent.	Inventory or Inventories
Ips.	Ipswich
Itin.	Itinerary
Jas.	James
Journ.	Journal
Lamb. Lib. . .	Lambeth Library
Lanc.	Lancashire or Lancaster
L. and P. Hen. VIII.	Letters and Papers, Hen. VIII.
Lansd. . . .	Lansdowne
Ld. Rev. Rec. . .	Land Revenue Records
Leic.	Leicestershire or Leicester
Le Neve's Ind. .	Le Neve's Indices
Lib.	Library
Lich.	Lichfield
Linc.	Lincolnshire or Lincoln
Lond.	London
m.	Membrane
Mem.	Memorials

Memo. R. . . .	Memoranda Rolls
Mich.	Michaelmas Term
Midd.	Middlesex
Mins. Accts. . .	Ministers' Accounts
Misc. Bks. (Exch. K.R., Exch. T.R. or Aug. Off.)	Miscellaneous Books (Exchequer King's Remembrancer, Exchequer Treasury of Receipt or Augmentation Office)
Mon.	Monastery, Monasticon
Monm.	Monmouth
Mun.	Muniments or Munimenta
Mus.	Museum
N. and Q. . . .	Notes and Queries
Norf.	Norfolk
Northampt. . .	Northampton
Northants . . .	Northamptonshire
Northumb. . . .	Northumberland
Norw.	Norwich
Nott.	Nottinghamshire or Nottingham
N.S.	New Style
Off.	Office
Orig. R. . . .	Originalia Rolls
O.S.	Ordnance Survey
Oxf.	Oxfordshire or Oxford
p.	Page
Palmer's Ind. . .	Palmer's Indices
Pal. of Chest. . .	Palatinate of Chester
Pal. of Dur. . .	Palatinate of Durham
Pal. of Lanc. . .	Palatinate of Lancaster
Par.	Parish, parochial, etc.
Parl.	Parliament or Parliamentary
Parl. R.	Parliament Rolls
Parl. Surv. . . .	Parliamentary Surveys
Partic. for Gts. .	Particulars for Grants
Pat.	Patent Roll or Letters Patent
P.C.C.	Prerogative Court of Canterbury
Pet.	Petition
Peterb.	Peterborough
Phil.	Philip
Pipe R.	Pipe Roll
Plea R.	Plea Rolls
Pop. Ret. . . .	Population Returns
Pope Nich. Tax. (Rec. Com.)	Pope Nicholas' Taxation (Record Commission)
P.R.O.	Public Record Office
Proc.	Proceedings
Proc. Soc. Antiq. .	Proceedings of the Society of Antiquaries
pt.	Part
Pub.	Publications
R.	Roll
Rec.	Records
Recov. R. . . .	Recovery Rolls
Rentals and Surv. .	Rentals and Surveys
Rep.	Report
Rev.	Review
Ric.	Richard

TABLE OF ABBREVIATIONS

Roff.	Rochester diocese
Rot. Cur. Reg. .	Rotuli Curiæ Regis
Rut.	Rutland
Sarum	Salisbury diocese
Ser.	Series
Sess. R.	Sessions Rolls
Shrews.	Shrewsbury
Shrops	Shropshire
Soc.	Society
Soc. Antiq. . . .	Society of Antiquaries
Somers.	Somerset
Somers. Ho. . .	Somerset House
S.P. Dom. . . .	State Papers Domestic
Staff.	Staffordshire
Star Chamb. Proc.	Star Chamber Proceedings
Stat.	Statute
Steph.	Stephen
Subs. R. . . .	Subsidy Rolls
Suff.	Suffolk
Surr.	Surrey
Suss.	Sussex
Surv. of Ch. Livings (Lamb.) or (Chan.)	Surveys of Church Livings (Lambeth) or (Chancery)

Topog.	Topography or Topographical
Trans.	Transactions
Transl.	Translation
Treas.	Treasury or Treasurer
Trin.	Trinity Term
Univ.	University
Valor Eccl. (Rec. Com.)	Valor Ecclesiasticus (Record Commission)
Vet. Mon. . . .	Vetusta Monumenta
V.C.H.	Victoria County History
Vic.	Victoria
vol.	Volume
Warw.	Warwickshire or Warwick
Westm.	Westminster
Westmld. . . .	Westmorland
Will.	William
Wilts	Wiltshire
Winton. . . .	Winchester diocese
Worc.	Worcestershire or Worcester
Yorks	Yorkshire

A HISTORY OF
STAFFORDSHIRE

GEOLOGY

JUST as the county of Staffordshire is situated toward the centre of England, so the geological formations met within its boundaries occupy a similar position in the geological scale. Tracing the well-known orderly ascending sequence of rocks from the oldest in Wales to the newest in the eastern counties, we find in the Triassic formation of the midlands the central link between these two extremes.

The rocky ridges which characterise the older formations on the Welsh borderlands, when traced eastward, pass gradually beneath a mantle of red Triassic sandstones and marls, until in Staffordshire the latter form the commonest features of the landscape. Rising as islands out of them much older formations appear at the surface in the north and south, where by their bolder scenic aspects they afford a sharp contrast to the monotonous and softer outline of the red rocks ; and since the minerals essential to modern civilization are found in these older strata their presence is indicated by the great centres of population whose natural wants have been largely supplied from the rich grazing lands and vast reservoirs of pure underground water existing in the enveloping newer formation. The study of the geology of the county therefore forms the natural prelude to its history.

Extending as they do over by far the larger part of the county, the red Triassic rocks, which have been aptly compared to a solidified sea, afford a datum to which the other stratified deposits may be conveniently referred. This great spread of one formation has been brought about by the dying away, ere it reaches the centre of the county, of the great Pennine uplift, which further north divides the Trias into an eastern and western portion. Thrown into wide gentle undulations where the major Pennine movement has died away, the formation naturally covers a wide expanse ; but these red rock waves may be said to have piled themselves up and broken against two ancient ridges : first, in North Staffordshire against the carboniferous offshoot of Derbyshire ; secondly, against the carboniferous uplift in South Staffordshire. In this way the conspicuous island character of these older deposits has arisen. Further, in the highest summits of the South Staffordshire island we recognize in the Dudley Hills and Sedgley Beacon the unburied peaks of Silurian strata, standing as lonely outposts of the Silurian territory to the west.

It will be gathered from this that the formations represented are few in number. Of the three main divisions into which geologists have separated the stratified rocks, only the later portion of the great Palæozoic, the early stages of the Mesozoic and latest phases of the

Kainozoic eras are met with. The history of the formations present is however replete with interest, for not only are they grandly developed, but they have attracted the attention of some of the most celebrated observers in British geology, and conclusions which have revolutionized the science have been arrived at from investigations of these rocks in the laboratory or in the field.

In the following tables giving the classification and sub-divisions of the Staffordshire rock formations in descending order the results of recent investigation and re-surveys have been embodied; where the age of certain groups remains under discussion the published opinions of the latest authorities have been adhered to.[1]

TABLE OF STRATA IN STAFFORDSHIRE

Period	Formation	Character of Material	Approximate thickness in feet
Recent	Alluvium, Peat. . . .	Mud, silt, gravel, peat; bordering streams, rivers and in hollows . . .	up to 15
Pleistocene	Old River Drift . . .	Gravel, sand, loam, etc., of ancient river terraces	up to 40
	Glacial Deposits . . .	Pebbly loam (Ratchel), sand, gravel, clay, cave earth	up to 130
Keuper	Rhætic	Grey marl and black shales	up to 125
	Keuper Marl	Red marls with thin sandstones (skerries), beds of rock salt and gypsum .	up to 2,000
	Waterstones and Lower Keuper Sandstone	Red and white sandstones, building stones and false-bedded red sandstones.	up to 400

[1] For more detailed information the following works should be consulted : *Memoirs of the Geological Survey*, 'The Geology of the South Staffordshire Coalfield,' by J. Beete Jukes (1859) ; *The Iron Ores of Great Britain*, pts. ii. and iv., by Sir W. W. Smyth (1862), for a description of the ironstones and for a list of fossils by J. W. Salter ; *The Geology of the country round Stockport, Macclesfield, Congleton and Leek*, by E. Hull and A. H. Green (1866) ; *The Triassic and Permian Rocks of the Midland Counties of England*, by E. Hull (1869) ; *The Geology of the country round Stoke-upon-Trent*, by W. Gibson and C. B. Wedd (1902); *The Geology of the Cheadle Coalfield*, by G. Barrow (1903) ; *Summaries of Progress of the Geological Survey from 1899 to 1902*. *A Sketch of the Geology of the Birmingham District*, by Prof. C. Lapworth, Geologists' Association, 1898, gives a concise account of the stratified deposits of South Staffordshire, also a short description of the igneous rocks by Prof. W. W. Watts, and a brief summary of the ancient glaciers of the midland counties, by W. J. Harrison ; there is in addition a useful list of bibliographical references. A full account of the organic remains of the North Staffordshire Coalfield has been published by John Ward in *Trans. North Staff. Inst. Min. Eng.* vol. x. (1890) ; while the order and nature of the ironstones and coals are given by C. J. Homer in the *Proc. Iron and Steel Inst.* (1875). Several important papers treating of the local geology are scattered through the *Trans. Birm. Philos. Soc.*, *The Midland Naturalist*, and the *Trans. North Staff. Field Club*. The last-mentioned society publishes from time to time a bibliography by John Ward.

The county includes the following maps of the Geological Survey on the scale of one inch = one mile : Sheets (Old Series)—62, N.E. Lichfield, Tamworth ; 62, N.W. Cannock Chase ; 62, S.E. Sutton Coldfield, Birmingham, Coleshill ; 62, S.W. Wolverhampton, Walsall, Dudley ; 72, N.W. Hanley, Stoke-on-Trent ; 72, N.E. Ashbourne ; 72, S.W. Stafford, Stone ; 72, S.E. Burton-on-Trent, Tutbury ; 72, S.E. Market Drayton, Eccleshall. Sheets (New Series)—123, Stoke-upon-Trent ; 110, Macclesfield.

GEOLOGY

Period	Formation	Character of Material	Approximate thickness in feet
Bunter	Upper Mottled Sandstone	False-bedded red sandstones	up to 300
	Pebble Beds.	Red pebbly sandstones with beds of shingle .	up to 500
	Lower Mottled Sandstone	False-bedded red sandstones	up to 300
Permian	Upper Red Sandstones and Marls of Enville	Marls, sandstone and a band of breccia . . .	up to 150
	Middle Red Sandstone and Marls of Enville	Sandstone, marls, conglomerates and 'trappoid breccia'	up to 550
	Keele Sandstones and Marls, Lower Red Sandstones and Marls of Enville	Red sandstones and marls, thin beds of earthy limestone, occasional thin seams of coal (N. Staffs).	over 800
	Newcastle - under - Lyme Series and Halesowen Sandstones	Grey sandstones and marls, thin coals and two thin limestones at the base .	up to 400
Carboniferous	Etruria Marls and Oldhill Brick Clays	Red marls with thin beds of earthy limestone, ashy green grits and conglomerates	up to 1,100
	Blackband Series of North Staffordshire	Grey marls and sandstones, thin seams of coal and beds of laminated ironstones (N. Staffs), and bands of earthy limestone	up to 450
	Middle Coal Series . .	Grey and black shales with numerous coals; beds of grit and ironstone . .	up to 1,200
	Lower Coal Series. . .	Grey and black shales, bands of sandstone ; numerous seams of coal	up to 4,000
	Millstone Grits and Pendleside Series	Grits, sandstones, shales ; thin seams of coal and beds of dark impure limestone	up to 2,000
	Carboniferous Limestone .	Compact highly fossiliferous limestone	Great, but undetermined
Silurian	Ludlow Shales and Limestones	Grey shales and beds of limestone	up to 1,050
	Wenlock Limestone and Shales	Grey shales and beds of limestone	up to 1,600
	Woolhope Beds . . .	Limestone	up to 80
	Upper Llandovery or May Hill Sandstone	Sandstone and grits . .	not known

3

SILURIAN SYSTEM

In the adjoining county of Shropshire the Pre-Cambrian, Cambrian, Ordovician and Silurian formations follow each other in natural consecutive order. Of these only the Silurian emerges in Staffordshire, from under the intervening Red Rocks, on the crests of the three anticlines of Sedgley Beacon, Dudley Hills and Walsall.

The complete sequence of the sediments composing this essentially marine deposit, the oldest of the county, does not occur in any one of the three localities ; yet by piecing together the information obtained in one district with that in another it is found that, excepting the initial stages represented by the Lower Llandovery sub-formation and that of the final close of the period (*Ludlow Passage Beds*), there is present, in the heart of the South Staffordshire Coalfield, a typical development of that most famous of British formations—the Silurian. In one of its stages, that of the Wenlock, the district of Dudley has become especially celebrated both on account of its furnishing Murchison with material for his great work on the Silurian system and also for the abundance of typical fossils, excellently preserved.

Upper Llandovery or May Hill Sandstone.—The first deposits of the Silurian seas indicate shallow water conditions. They afford a very limited exposure, and that only in the Walsall area, where they consist of pale yellow, brown, or occasionally white sandstones poorly representing the littoral and sub-littoral deposits of the Upper Llandovery or May Hill Sandstone of the Welsh borderland. Among other fossils the characteristic brachiopods—*Stricklandinia lens*, *S. lirata*, and the trilobite *Encrinurus punctatus* are not uncommon.

Barr Limestone.—The May Hill Sandstone is closely followed by a band of richly fossiliferous limestone, well known to local geologists from its containing at Hay Head, in the parish of Barr, fine examples of a trilobite—*Ilænus barriensis*—a fossil characteristic of the Woolhope Limestone of other Silurian regions, and to which the Barr Limestone, as it is locally known, corresponds. The limestone was formerly extensively quarried, but little opportunity of obtaining fossils now exists.

Wenlock Limestone and Shale.—The next overlying sub-division consists of slightly consolidated dark blue and grey mudstones and shales about 800 feet thick, at the summit of which lie two bands of limestone (*Wenlock Limestone*) separated by about 800 feet of shale. The lower shales are inclined at gentle angles in the Walsall area, and consequently cover a considerable extent of ground. They are not well exhibited in sections, but abundant fossils—chiefly brachiopods and corals—can be obtained in the railway cutting at Five Lanes. The limestones occur only in the western extremity of the inlier and are exposed in the railway cuttings within the town of Walsall and in some old quarries in the neighbourhood. In the Dudley Castle Hills and Wren's Nest the Wenlock strata are bent up into an elongated dome dislocated by faults. The core of the hills consists of the lower shales ; the flanks of the two beds of limestone with their intervening shales and overlying Ludlow Snales. Owing to their purity and excellence as a flux, their proximity to the blast furnaces, and to the high inclination rendering the extraction of the stone a cheap and simple process, the limestones have been quarried for many centuries. This industry was sufficiently striking to attract the attention of Dr. Plot in 1686, who also unmistakably figures some of the common fossils. At the present day the underground excavations extend for great distances and to considerable depths into the heart of the hills, beneath which they form vast gloomy caverns, through which there wanders a long canal used in the transportation of the quarried stone.

Fossils abound, some thin layers of the limestone being crowded with organic remains—corals, brachiopods, bryozoa. The district has become especially famous for the extremely beautiful and extensive series of crinoids (stone-lilies) and for the excellent preservation and large number of trilobites which have not only enriched several local collections, but have found their way into many cabinets abroad.

Ludlow Shales and Aymestry Limestone.—At Walsall the Wenlock limestones are succeeded immediately by the unconformable Coal-measures, but around Dudley Castle they pass up into bluish grey shales belonging to the Ludlow sub-division, which in turn become covered up by Coal-measure strata. In the Sedgley inlier the upward sequence is further continued. Here, at Hurst Hill, a sharp anticline brings up the Wenlock limestones with some overlying calcareous shales—1,000 feet thick—and the fossil contents indicate an horizon equivalent to the Lower Ludlow Shales. To these succeeds a bed of limestone 25 feet thick, locally known as the Sedgley Limestone. It is not so pure as the Wenlock Limestone, and burns into a greyish variety of lime locally distinguished as 'black lime,' that made from the Wenlock Limestone being termed 'white lime.' The commonest fossil is *Pentamerus knightii*, which stamps it at once as the equivalent of the Aymestry Limestone of Shropshire.

Upper Ludlow Shales.—Whenever present in full sequence the Silurian deposits indicate a piling up of sediments on an oscillating sea floor until, towards the summit, the accumulations, assisted by gentle uprisings, gradually approached the surface of the sea. The commencement only of these conditions is met with in Staffordshire, and this in the Sedgley area alone, where a mere fragment of the lower portion of the Upper Ludlow Shales has been preserved in the centre of a syncline under a capping of Coal-measure sandstone, which has prevented its destruction by denudation. In sinking the Manor Pits near Halesowen, it is stated that somewhat higher beds containing fossils of the Passage beds into the Old Red Sandstone were entered beneath the Coal-measures, but nowhere has any undoubted Old Red Sandstone been met with, and the formation next succeeding is separated by a great interval of time from the highest Silurian strata exposed on Sedgley Beacon.

A HISTORY OF STAFFORDSHIRE

CARBONIFEROUS SYSTEM

We have seen that the geological history of Staffordshire presents, in the absence of the Old Red Sandstone, one of those tantalizing breaks so frequent in the imperfect record of the rocks. The missing chapters are found in Worcestershire, Herefordshire, and in South Wales, where the lacustrine deposits of the Old Red Sandstone indicate an elevation of the Silurian sea floor and the subsequent formation of large fresh-water lakes. So great was the time represented by the missing period that the fauna of the Carboniferous strata—the next group met with —has a totally distinct aspect : many new orders, many new genera make their appearance, while the species differ from those of the Silurian seas ; the vertebrata have increased in numbers and are very much more highly organized.

The Carboniferous system commences abruptly with the marine conditions of the richly fossiliferous Mountain Limestone of North Staffordshire, when the ocean waters were warm and clear, and coral reefs, on which flourished a prolific marine fauna, extended their fringes along the coast line. A large river then appears to have entered the sea driving away the corals and many other life forms, and laying down first the muds and grits of the Pendleside Series, and then the grits and shales of the Millstone Grit period. Ultimately a delta appears to have been formed in which, or along its margins, the muds, shales, sandstones and numerous seams of coal constituting the Coal-measures, were deposited.

The Carboniferous rocks stand out boldly above the Triassic plain in the North and South Staffordshire Coalfields. Though separated from each other by the intervening red strata, it is now almost beyond dispute that these isolated coalfields are connected underground. Local inter-ruptions there may be, such as are shown at the surface in the Silurian hills of Dudley and Walsall, but recent borings and shaft-sinkings to the east and west of the present outline of the South Staffordshire Coalfield prove conclusively the extension of the Coal-measures in these directions; while the identity of the Coal-measure sequence as a whole in North and South Staffordshire is strongly in favour of the sediments having been deposited in the same basin.

The exact nature of the pre-carboniferous floor has not been ascertained, but the thinning away and final disappearance of the individual members of the system, when traced from the north-north-west to the south-south-east, shows it to have sloped rapidly upwards to the south-south-east, and at a still greater rate due south. Thus the southern area appears to have lain above water during the long period represented by the great thicknesses of the Carboniferous Limestone, Pendleside Series and Millstone Grits of the north, and not to have been submerged until Coal-measure times.

The filling up of the basin and its submergence does not appear to have been a simple process, for a study of the Carboniferous rocks of the Midlands, especially in North Staffordshire, clearly shows that the period was marked by minor earth movements temporarily raising one area and depressing a closely contiguous one. Therefore, in the important search for coal underneath the red rocks, it will long remain uncertain what particular member of the Carboniferous System will be encountered or what its thickness will be.

Differences in the distribution of the fossils have been taken to mark out the Carboniferous System into an Upper and a Lower portion, but authorities are at variance as to where the divisional line should be drawn. The plants and fishes indicate a change at the top of the so-called Yoredales (Pendleside Series) of Staffordshire ; the mollusca on the other hand show no such differences, but many of the marine forms continue from the base of the Pendleside Series to high up in the Coal-measures. In a short sketch however it is out of place to enter into a discussion of this vexed question ; whatever floral and faunal changes may ultimately be found to differentiate the various stages, stratigraphically, as Ramsay always contended, the Carboniferous System can be regarded as a unit.

CARBONIFEROUS OR MOUNTAIN LIMESTONE

The celebrated scenery of Dovedale and the beautiful valley of the Manifold owe their charms to the rocks of this important sub-division. Excavated into deep gorges and pinnacles of fantastic shapes, enhanced by the soft verdure of peculiar vividness and the delicacy of outline of numerous limestone-loving plants, threaded with caves and mysterious underground water channels, the Carboniferous Limestone country ever exerts a strong impression on the mind.

The Carboniferous Limestone, which, as previously mentioned, only occurs in the north of the county, consists of an undivided mass of pale grey, white or blue limestone of great but undetermined thickness. The quality of the rock varies from place to place ; that at Caldon Low in the Weaver Hills is of exceptional purity, and thousands of tons are annually quarried for use as a flux in the iron furnaces of Staffordshire and for the production of alkalies and lime for various purposes. The pipes and hollows traversing the rocks have also yielded large quantities of copper and lead, the famous mines at Ecton being considered, towards the commencement of the eighteenth century, to be the richest copper mines in Europe.

The outcrop of limestone in the Weaver Hills and the Manifold Valley forms a southerly extension of the large *massif* of the Carboniferous Limestone of Derbyshire, and similarily owes its existence to a strong anticlinal uplift bringing it to the surface from under the denuded cover of the shales and grits of the Pendleside Series. The convolutions visible in the Staffordshire lobe of the Derbyshire limestone west of the Dove are doubtless continued, underneath the folded Pendleside strata, to the west of the main limestone outcrop in the Weaver Hills. This is shown to be the case by the small mass of limestone which comes to the surface at Mixon on the crest of a long oval-shaped dome that is bent into a large number of lesser anticlines and synclines, and threaded with mineral lodes containing ores of copper and lead. The top beds are also brought up on another sharp fold in an old quarry near Congleton Edge, close to the county border, west of Biddulph. In this section the highest thin bands of limestone are intercalated with layers of tuffs, fragments of lava and ashy fossiliferous limestone, thus denoting the presence of volcanic action during the deposition of the strata.[1] Such evidences of igneous or volcanic activity during or closely subsequent to the deposition of the limestone are abundant in Derbyshire, but do not actually occur within the county.

A curious bed made up of rolled shells and fragments of waterworn limestone has been traced by Dr. Wheelton Hind in the valley of the Manifold, from Apes Tor to Ecton Bridge and Warslow. It occurs at or near the summit of the limestone, a position it occupies in several places in Derbyshire, notably near Castleton.

The Carboniferous Limestone abounds in fossils, including genera and species of corals, brachiopods, lamellibranchs, gasteropods, crustaceans and cephalopods, and other invertebrates. The prolific trilobite fauna of the Silurian and Devonian seas is however represented by only three genera—*Brachymetopus*, *Griffithides* and *Phillipsia*—forms distinct from those of the preceding formations. Fish remains are not abundant within the Staffordshire area, but numerous specimens have been obtained at Park Hill in Derbyshire, just across the county border, including types with pavement teeth such as would be adapted for grinding and crushing corals. Attempts have been made, but with little success, to distinguish one part of the massive limestone from another by means of the fossils. Dr. Wheelton Hind regards the limestone as one big zone, of which *Productus giganteus*, *P. cora*, *Chonetes papilionacea*, *Amplexus coralloides* constitute the zonal forms, and have a general distribution throughout the deposits of the period.

PENDLESIDE SERIES

The clear waters of the limestone seas became ultimately charged with silts and muds brought down by a large river which spread its deposits not only over North Staffordshire but also over a wide area in mid-England, and which possibly reached the Isle of Man.[2]

With this change of conditions the varied marine fauna of the Carboniferous Limestone seas vanished and was replaced by a few mud-loving molluscs, some of which are found attached to pieces of timber floated out into the turbid waters. Muds ceased at times to be borne seaward, enabling a marine fauna to establish itself. These periods of comparatively clear water, of which the fauna is abundantly preserved on Congleton Edge in the strata exposed in a quarry to the east of the limestone inlier,

[1] W. Gibson and W. Hind, 'On Agglomerates and Tuffs in the Carboniferous Limestone Series of Congleton Edge,' *Quart. Journ. Geol. Soc.* p. 548 (1899).
[2] W. Hind, *Quart. Journ. Geol. Soc.* lvii. 374 (1901).

were of brief duration and of sparse recurrence, for the series consists essentially of clays, shales, muds and sandstones of a united thickness of many hundreds of feet. Occasionally the quantity of vegetable matter floated down was in excess of any other material, and a mass of decaying vegetable débris accumulated, to be ultimately converted into a seam of coal, or it may be the carbonaceous matter collected in swamps lying at or near sea level.

The Pendleside Series occurs in two areas to the east and west of Leek, being brought into this position by two major folds separated by the trough enclosing the Coal-measures of the Cheadle and Shaffalong Coal-fields with their enveloping Millstone Grits. The major folds are made up of minor convolutions, frequently of great complexity, of which a striking illustration is afforded by a section in Badgers Clough near Pye-Clough. The extensive quarries on the anticline of Gun Hill, west of Meerbrook, also forcibly illustrate, in the bent and shattered Pendleside grits and shales, the violent nature of the disturbances and the amount of compression the strata have undergone ; nor is this to be wondered at, seeing that these sections lie well within the influence of the Great Pennine uplift—the dominant structural feature of mid-England.

With the exception of deep dingles or gorges like those of the Dane Valley system and Churnet Valley the scenery is tame, consisting for the most part of open grassy moorland. This is due chiefly to the preponderance of soft shales, but also in part to the frequent low inclination of the strata. Whenever ridges such as Catsedge, Gun Hill and Morridge relieve this monotony they are found to be composed of sandstone or grit, of which the harder and more siliceous varieties are known as Crowstones, when they are extensively quarried for rough road metal. Coal smuts, thin seams of coal with fireclays, occasionally underlie these grits, and were formerly worked to a limited extent.

Fossils are comparatively rare and poorly preserved. They occur in certain restricted bands in the shales, but are more abundant and better preserved in some thin layers and nodules (bullions) of dark earthy lime-stones clearly exposed in the banks of the Dane south of Wincle. They include several species of *Goniatites* (*Glyphioceras*), *Posidonomya Becheri*, *Pterinopecten papyraceus*, *Posidoniella lævis*, fossils Messrs. Hind and Howe find characterizing a similar set of strata above the Mountain Limestone in adjacent counties, especially on Pendle Hill (Lancashire), from which the series derives its name.

The river system which transported the sediments of the Pendleside Series is considered by Dr. Hind to have flowed from the east and north-east. He observes the series to be thickest over Lancashire, where the succeeding Millstone Grits are also at their maximum development, while from this centre the beds thin out in all directions ; thus North Staffordshire lay towards the southern margin, South Staffordshire wholly beyond it.

These strata have for long been regarded as the southern equivalent of the thick bands of white limestone and interbedded shales of Yoredale, whence they were termed ' Yoredale Rocks,' the change from this supposed northern type being considered to take place in the neighbourhood of the great Craven faults. According to Messrs. Hind and Howe the Yore-dales of Yorkshire are the equivalents of the undivided massive limestone of Derbyshire, which splits up in the north into several bands separated by inter-bedded shales. The Pendleside Series they regard as occupying a superior position, and containing a fauna distinct from the Carboniferous Limestone of Derbyshire and the Yorkshire Yoredales.[1]

MILLSTONE GRIT SERIES

This sub-division lithologically resembles the Pendleside Series, differing chiefly, as the name implies, in the greater prevalence of gritty material, aggregated into bands of considerable thickness separated by black and grey shales. While a definite band of grit (First Grit or Rough Rock) happens to separate the sub-division from the Coal-measures above, no such well marked or persistent bed indicates its junction with the Pendleside Series, to which it is allied in the closest possible stratigraphical manner.

Conspicuous objects in the landscape, the different bands of grit follow each other in consecutive order with their separating bands of shale, and have been named from above downward : *First Grit* (Rough Rock or Farewell Rock of the miner), *Second Grit* (Haslingden Flags of Lancashire), *Third Grit* (Roaches Grit), *Fourth* and *Fifth Grits* (Kinderscout Grits). These constitute in the north and north-east portion of the county grit bands of singular persistency, but traced southward they are found to decrease gradually till around the Pottery and Cheadle Coalfields only the First and Third Grits remain.

Some distance below the Kinderscout Grits and separated from them by shales there lies an impersistent bed of grit, sometimes known as the ' Yoredale Grit,' which has been regarded in Derbyshire as the base of the series, though avowedly an artificial datum line.[2]

Throughout nearly the whole length of their outcrop the Millstone Grits can be recognized almost at a glance by the distinctive features to which they give rise. The splendid escarpment of the Roaches and ' The Rocks,' the crags of Ipstones and the numerous ' Edges '—Axe Edge, Ladderedge, Brown Edge, Congleton Edge—and other less marked but still conspicuous ridges have been carved by denudation out of the various bands of grit whose broad sheets of heather-clad rocks end in rugged crags standing boldly out in the air, while the flanks and valleys lying at their feet have been fashioned out of the interbedded shales. These bold, bare, rocky ridges impressed early writers and seem to

---

[1] For a full account of the Pendleside Series the reader is referred to the paper by W. Hind and J. A. Howe, ' The Geological Succession and Palæontology of the Beds between the Millstone Grit and the Limestone Massif of Pendle Hill, and the equivalents in certain other parts of Britain,' *Quart. Journ. Geol. Soc.* lvii. 347 (1901).

[2] ' The Carboniferous Limestone, Yoredale Rocks and Millstone Grits of North Derbyshire ' (*Mem. Geol. Survey*), p. 8 (1887).

have exerted a powerful influence on the ancient inhabitants, appearing to them as something above the common and therefore fit burial places for their chiefs. Many of the stream-cut gorges are strikingly deep and gloomy; while elsewhere the rocks have been opened out into curious chasms, such as the impressive cleft of Ludchurch—100 yards long, 30 to 40 feet deep, and 6 to 10 feet wide—south of the Castle Cliff Rocks.

The Millstone Grits are arranged in lesser or greater synclinal folds completely or partially surrounding the coalfields; frequently, as in the small elongated trough of Goldsitch Moss with perfect symmetry. Denudation has removed vast masses of material, thus severing the outcrops and forming detached areas, of which the outlier of the Third or Roaches Grit on the summit of Sheen Hill is the most remote.

Seams of coal which are rare in the Pendleside Series become of greater frequency and are usually present a few feet above or lying directly on the grit bands. The most persistent is a seam above the Third Grit, which was formerly worked to a considerable extent in the Roaches and Ipstones areas. Another seam, known as the Feather Edge Coal, lying above the First Grit, also proved to be workable around parts of the Goldsitch Moss Coalfield, though the seam should more properly be included in the Coal-measures. The commercial value of the sub-division however mainly consists in the fairly good quality of the building stones afforded by the First and Third Grits, both of them, but especially the latter, being extensively quarried.

The fossils of the 'grits' consist of the remains of plants—*Calamites*, *Lepidodendron*. Plant remains are also met with in the shales, but the most interesting fossils are the marine organisms—*Pterinopecten papyraceus, Posidoniella lævis, Goniatites*—which occur in abundance in certain dark bands of impure limestone lying in muddy shales between the First and Third Grits, of which the banks of the Trent to the east of Knypersley Reservoir afford an excellent section.

COAL MEASURES

The detritus-bearing currents—now swift, now gentle—which deposited the grits and shales of the Pendleside Series and Millstone Grits continued to carry their burden seaward long after the First Grit was laid down. The pauses in sedimentation however became more prolonged, the sea was frequently excluded, and the floor, owing to constant deposition aided by local elevation, was even raised above sea-level. The lower portion of the Coal-measure formation, with its great thicknesses of shales, clays, sandstone and intercalated coal seams, ironstones and marine bands, demands some such varied conditions of origin. During the later stages of the period the pauses became brief and a large body of sediment was deposited, but now under new conditions. A land-locked area appears to have been formed upon whose continuously sinking floor mainly red sediments thickly accumulated. The end of the story however is not known; the record is lost or buried deep under the overlying Triassic rocks with their history of a new order of events.

We know however that before the commencement of the Trias era the Carboniferous strata were intensely folded, fractured and extensively denuded, resulting in their more or less complete isolation, so that in North Staffordshire we find the four detached coal basins of the Potteries, Cheadle, Shaffalong and Goldsitch Moss, while the South Staffordshire Coalfield is separated from the northern field by a wide expanse of Triassic rocks.

Though the coalfields of the north and south possess many points in common the northern area presents the type development and will therefore be described first.

THE NORTH STAFFORDSHIRE COALFIELD

Lower and Middle Coal-measures.—Situated on the line of the great Pennine uplift or along its western margin it is not surprising to find this coal-bearing region complicated by numerous faults and folds. The folds trend in a general north and south direction, and enclose the four separate coalfields mentioned above. The Cheadle, Shaffalong and Pottery Coalfields may be connected under the Trias of Caverswall, but the small coalfield of Goldsitch Moss is sunk deep in a fold of Millstone Grits, and removed several miles from its sister coalfields. The important coalfield of the Potteries can be further naturally divided into a central synclinal region and a western anticlinal portion. In the latter the coal seams are frequently vertical and occasionally bent on themselves; in the former the coals are sometimes highly inclined but never vertical. The faults, the majority of which trend north and south, are not only many but of very great throw; one, known as the Apedale Fault, traversing the central portion of the Pottery Coalfield in a north and south direction exceeds 600 yards in vertical displacement, while an even larger dislocation extends along the western margin of the coalfield. The faults have exerted a strong influence on the physiography of the district. Thus the Apedale Fault lets in a strip of barren measures in the heart of the coalfield so that the ancient town of Newcastle-under-Lyme lies in a pleasant agricultural district, while immediately east and west there extends the usual grimy landscape of a coal-mining district; again, on the west a large fault suddenly introduces unproductive measures, when the mining industry abruptly ends.

The Coal-measures have been sub-divided into *Lower*, *Middle* and *Upper*; but the exact horizons at which the dividing lines should be drawn have not been definitely settled. Whatever scheme is adopted the lower and middle sub-divisions constitute the storehouse of the chief seams, of which the most important, commencing with the Winpenny Coal, about 1,200 feet above the First Grit, are grouped together. Above this coal there are no less than thirty recognized seams, making a total thickness of over 140 feet of coal. A seam towards the middle, known as the Ash Coal, has been taken by some geologists as the base of the middle sub-division, while another seam—Bassey Mine Coal—has been chosen as the base of the upper sub-division. The unequal rate of deposition of the Coal-measures is accentuated in the Pottery Coalfield, where the strata between the Bassey Mine and Winpenny Coals approximate to 1,200 yards at Shelton, whereas at Apedale, 4 miles to the west, they are under 800 yards thick, from which the rate of diminution can be calculated to be about 1 in 17, equivalent to a gradient of over 3 degrees.

Below the Winpenny the coal seams are of small value, but one called the Crabtree Coal, a few yards above the First Grit, is well known from its shale roof, yielding in all four areas abundant specimens of *Goniatites*, *Pterinopecten* and *Lingula*. The strata below the Winpenny occur in all the four areas, while they constitute the entire measures of the small basin of Shaffalong and a considerable portion of that of Cheadle and Goldsitch Moss.

The strata enclosing the coals and ironstones consist of clays, marls, fireclays and shales with an occasional band of sandstone very impersistent and of no great thickness. The colour is generally a dull grey excepting a few bands of intensely black shales or an occasional impersistent stratum of a red colour. The absence of any great mass of hard rocks is reflected in the scenery, which is tame and uninteresting, but whenever a ridge breaks the monotony it is almost certainly found to consist of one of the bands of sandstone, and inasmuch as the sandy material is more prevalent in the north so the ridgy character of the coalfield, as in the Norton district, becomes more pronounced.

The numerous coal seams between the Ash and Winpenny Coals constitute the chief seams of the Pottery Coalfield. They include varieties suitable for house purposes, for making gas and coke, for raising steam, or for use in the arts and manufactures of the district. The only ironstone at present raised is the Burnwood Stone of the variety known as semi-blackband. In the adjacent Cheadle Coalfield there are also several valuable coal seams, but they have not been satisfactorily identified with those of the Pottery Coalfield. A peculiarity in the distribution of the coals in the Pottery area is the fact that certain easily recognized seams, which are gas or coking coals in the western area, rapidly lose a large quantity of their bituminous matter when traced eastward, until they become house or steam coals.

The commonest fossils are molluscs, of which the most abundant belong to the genus *Carbonicola* (*Anthracosia*), regarded as a freshwater, mud-loving animal. They occur in great profusion in the ironstones and shales overlying the Cockshead, Ten-feet and other coals, forming the so-called 'mussel or cockle bands' of the miner. In comparison with the Middle Coal-measures, fish remains may be said to be rare; of great interest are fragments of various parts of the skeleton of the amphibian *Loxomma*, met with in the shale overlying the Cockshead Coal at Adderley Green. Within recent years a number of thin bands of shales and calcareous nodules containing marine organisms have been brought to light at no less than seven widely separated horizons; the lowest, as previously mentioned, is the one above the Crabtree Coal ; the highest occurs only a few yards below the Ash Coal, while the remainder are found at intervals. In the highest band—that above the Gin Mine Coal—Mr. John Ward collected over twenty different species ; in the other bands *Goniatites, Lingula, Pterinopecten, Posidoniella* occur most frequently, and include some of the species of the Pendleside Series. As might be expected plant remains are not infrequent, though met with most abundantly on certain definite horizons. Among these *Neuropteris heterophylla, Alethopteris lonchitica* indicate, according to Mr. R. Kidston, a low horizon throughout the Coal-measures of Great Britain.[1]

The strata between the Ash and Bassey Mine Coals (*Middle Coal-measures*) by their strict resemblance in colour, texture, composition and by their stratigraphical conformity to the rocks below denote the continuation of similar conditions. The coal seams number over fourteen, representing a collective thickness of nearly 50 feet of coal. The quality however is inferior to the seams of the lower sub-division, though they are of great value to the potter in baking his wares, and being near the surface over a large portion of the area are in great request. The Middle Coal-measures contain several bands of ironstone, but of these only the semi-blackband, laminated Chalkey Mine Ironstone is raised in any quantity. The number and variety of fish remains is extraordinary, especially in the shales associated with the Winghay or Knowles Ironstone of Longton and Fenton ; with them the remains of amphibia are sparingly associated. The mollusca are abundant in the lower portion, but become gradually rarer towards the summit. The flora, notably on the horizon of the Great Row Coal, is particularly rich.

The strata above the Bassey Mine Coal (*Upper Coal-measures*) belong to a different class of sediments, being made up chiefly of red sandstones and marls, among which grey rocks retain a definite but quite subordinate position. Coal seams are thin and lie on widely separated horizons, but bands of earthy limestone, crowded with Entomostraca and very rare in the inferior sub-divisions, become a marked constituent. Four distinct groups of rock individualize the Upper Coal-measures.

In the lowest (*Blackband Series*) the material remains much the same as in the Middle Coal-measures, but there is a tendency for red marls to be developed along definite horizons. Several bands of Blackband ironstones frequently exceeding 4 feet in thickness, readily calcined and rich in metallic iron, render the group of great economical importance ; while the associated grey marls, along whose outcrop the pottery towns have gradually extended, may be said to have initiated the pottery trade. Even now, when clays foreign to the district have come into general use,

---

[1] The organic contents as a whole have been fully dealt with by John Ward, *Trans. North Staff. Inst. Mining Engineers,* vol. x. (1890), and *Proc. North Staff. Field Club* (1893–4). For the plants see R. Kidston, *Trans. Roy. Soc. Edin.* vol. xxxv. (1891) and *Proc. Royal Physical Society Edin.* vol. xii. (1893–4). The Lamellibranchs are described by Wheelton Hind, *Palæontographical Society,* vols. xlviii.–l. For a recent account of the marine beds the reader may consult J. T. Stobbs, *Trans. North Staff. Field Club,* vols. xxxv., xxxvi. and *Trans. Fed. Inst.* xxii. 229 (1902).

the local marls continue to furnish the material for the vessels in which the pottery is baked in the kilns in addition to being extensively used for other purposes. The fauna indicates the conditions under which the strata were deposited ; for, excepting Entomostraca, which constitute three or more thin bands of impure limestone, and a few fishes, the animal life consisted of the delicate thin valved mollusc *Anthracomya phillipsi*, met with in countless numbers in the Blackband Ironstones. The flora, occasionally rich in species and numbers, partakes, according to Mr. Kidston, of a transitional character between Middle and Upper Coal-measures, thus further illustrating the gradual passage of one stage into the other.

The *Etruria Marls*, which succeed, consist almost exclusively of red and mottled marls exceeding 1,000 feet in thickness in the central area. Thin bands of green grits, apparently derived in great part from the breaking down of igneous rocks, are interstratified at intervals. Only one locally developed coal seam has been met with, and excepting two thin beds of limestone containing the serpula *Spirorbis* the entire group consists of practically unstratified red marls.

The Newcastle-under-Lyme Series conformably overlying the Etruria Marls shows, as far as the colour and nature of the material is concerned, a return to the conditions of the Blackband group. Grey sandstones and shales, in which lie four thin seams of coal, constitute almost the entire bulk. Plant remains are numerous, including the characteristic Upper Coal-measure fossil, *Pecopteris arborescens*, but associated with others of Middle Coal-measure age. Two thin bands of limestone with Entomostraca and a minute shell (*Anthracomya calcifera*) which are exposed in the marl pits between Etruria and Longport, invariably commence the sequence.

In the *Keele Series*,[1] into which these grey strata graduate upward, we again find rocks of a brilliant red colour, mainly red sandstones with intercalated red marls, among which at intervals thin beds of limestone with Entomostraca are interstratified. The flora, though badly preserved, as in most red rocks, contains species having a wide range throughout the Coal-measure period. For how long the Carboniferous period continued beyond the record contained in these red rocks remains uncertain, since the strictly unconformable Triassic rocks conceal the top beds of the Keele Series or whatever strata may elsewhere succeed, and thus the legend in North Staffordshire abruptly terminates.

THE SOUTH STAFFORDSHIRE COALFIELD

The Carboniferous strata of this coalfield are arranged in a dome possessing a length of about 23 miles and a breadth of 6 miles. This main anticline, broken by three subsidiary folds, constitutes the Dudley,

---

[1] This group was formerly placed in the Permian System. The reasons for the classification here adopted will be found in a paper by the author, *Quart. Journ. Geol. Soc.* lvii. 256 (1901), and in the 'Geology of the Country around Stoke-upon-Trent' (*Mem. Geol. Survey*), pp. 45–7 (1902).

Barr and Netherton anticlines, between which lie the faulted synclines of Bilston, Corngreaves and Pensnett. The coalfield is completely surrounded by the unconformable Triassic rocks, underneath which it slopes gradually on the south and north, and against which it is faulted on the east and west by the great 'Boundary Faults.' The succession consists in the main of a replica of that in North Staffordshire, but it is doubtful if the district came within reach of the Carboniferous waters until a considerable portion, if not the whole, of the Lower Coalmeasures of North Staffordshire had been deposited. The Carboniferous Limestone, Pendleside Series and Millstone Grits are certainly absent, the Coal-measures being deposited on an irregular floor of Silurian rocks visible at the surface in the Dudley, Walsall and Sedgley areas, but also encountered underground between West Bromwich and Oldbury, where they constitute the so-called 'Silurian bank.'

Lower or True Coal-measures.[1]—In composition the strata (500 to 1,050 feet thick) resemble the chief coal-bearing rocks of North Staffordshire, consisting of grey and white sandstones, shales, clays, ironstones and seams of coal. The most remarkable of the seams known as the 'Ten Yard' or 'Thick Coal,' underlies Smethwick, Dudley, Walsall and Bilston, and was formerly quarried in the open near Tipton. It is not an undivided stratum of coal, but is made up of thirteen or fourteen distinct layers separated from each other by thin partings of shaly material or 'bat.' South of Halesowen it thins out and becomes mixed with shaly matter ; but what is more remarkable when traced northward the component seams gradually separate until at Essington and Pelsall the Thick Coal is represented by fourteen seams lying in a mass of shales and sandstones between 250 and 300 feet in thickness—an excellent example of the unequal rate of sedimentation under which the Coal-measures were deposited. The Thick Coal has been proved to extend beyond the visible limits of the coalfield, having been recently encountered beneath the Red Rocks to the west at Himley, while it is being worked under the same formation to the east in the Sandwell Park and Hamstead Collieries. Again, to the north of the coalfield, pits have been sunk through the 'Pebble Beds' of Cannock Chase, and a new coalfield developed in this direction.

The scenery of the South Staffordshire Coalfield is aptly described under the name 'Black Country.' The original surface features over wide areas are not only entirely obliterated by refuse heaps and grimy manufacturing towns and villages, but over all there rests, day and night, a canopy of black smoke.

In past years a large quantity of local ironstone was raised, but at the present day the greater bulk of the ore for use in the iron furnaces comes from Northamptonshire, the Potteries and elsewhere ; but it was the presence of iron ores, in conjunction with large quantities of cheaply

---

[1] The title assigned to the Coal-measures of South Staffordshire by Prof. Lapworth. Vide *A Sketch of the Geology of the Birmingham District*, Geologists' Association (1898).

got coal, which has made Birmingham and Wolverhampton the great hardware manufacturing centres of the world.

The Dudley Coalfield has been regarded as the typical area for the Middle Coal-measure flora of Great Britain. The genus *Sphenopteris* in this sub-division attains its maximum development. Stumps of the gigantic lycopod, *Lepidodendron*, have been met with in such profusion in the workings of the Parkfield Colliery as to form a veritable fossil forest. As in North Staffordshire the commonest mollusc is *Carbonicola* (*Anthracosia*). In addition to remains of fishes the coalfield has also yielded specimens of *Arachnida* and insects, types rare or unknown in North Staffordshire. All these fossils, excepting the Fishes, indicate the close proximity, if not the absolute presence, of land ; but below the Thick Coal, fossils—such as *Lingula*, *Productus*, *Discina* and *Pterinopecten*—show a temporary incursion of the sea ; though these marine episodes do not appear to have been of such frequent recurrence as in the north.

Upper Coal Measures.—The gradual infilling of the basin and final change in the character of the sediments, accompanied by the gradual passing away of the fauna, is as clearly illustrated in the southern part of the county as it is in the Potteries. In the districts of Corngreaves and Oldhill the ordinary grey Coal-measures graduate upwards into a considerable thickness (over 300 feet) of red clays (*Red Coal-measure Clays* of Jukes) indistinguishable from the Etruria Marls of the northern coalfield. Moreover they contain similar thin bands of ashy green grits known as ' *Espley Rocks.*' As the area is not far distant from the Cambrian and Pre-Cambrian ridges of the Lickey Hills, these green grits, as might be expected, contain angular fragments of the Lickey rocks. Occasionally the grits are so coarse as to form a true breccia, interesting as foreshadowing the breccia conditions so prevalent in the succeeding ' Permian ' rocks of South Staffordshire. The red clays afford some of the material for the famous South Staffordshire blue bricks, and large quarries have been opened round Oldhill.

The brick clays pass up near Halesowen (just beyond the county limits) into grey sandstones and marls (*Halesowen Sandstone Group*), about 400 feet thick, containing an occasional thin seam of coal and a well marked band of *Spirorbis* limestone near the summit. These in turn are surmounted, quite conformably, by red sandstones and marls, generally included in the ' Permian ' formation, but identical with the Keele type of North Staffordshire.

The sequence of the Upper Coal-measures of North Staffordshire is thus at once seen to be repeated around the southern margins of the South Staffordshire Coalfield, and the connection of the two fields— either absolutely, or at least as regards the similarity in the sequence of events—proved beyond dispute. The same sequence too has been detected in the deep sinkings and borings outside the exposed coalfields, where the green ' *Espley Rocks* ' at once afford the miner a clue to his position in the Coal-measure sequence.

Origin of Coal.—As the county abounds in this mineral a few words may be said regarding the prevalent opinions as to its mode of formation. The one most in vogue regards each seam as representing an ancient bed of vegetation, and the usually accompanying underclay or fireclay as the soil on which it grew. Another opinion considers that some at least of the coals are made up of floated vegetable matter, tranquilly deposited in still water at a time when other sedimentation was at a standstill. Under either view there cannot be any doubt that each seam indicates a pause of more or less duration and of frequent recurrence throughout the Coal-measure period.[1]

PERMIAN SYSTEM

The red sandstones and marls succeeding the Halesowen Sandstone group have been regarded as belonging to a special type of 'Permian' developed only on the west side of the Pennine Chain, but recent borings in Nottinghamshire have clearly shown the same type to be present on the east side of the Pennines. The limitation of the Permian system therefore needs revision, but it would be superfluous to discuss this question here. The red strata overlying the grey Halesowen Sandstone group are succeeded conformably by another set of red sandstones and marls with lenticular bands of calcareous conglomerates, which in turn are overlain by the so-called 'Trappoid Breccia' of the Clent Hills (on the northern boundary of Worcestershire). These rocks have been classed as Middle Permian.[2] Very much the same succession occurs round Enville, but above the 'Trappoid Breccia' a set of red marls with an intercalated band of breccia conformably follows, and has been regarded as forming an Upper Permian sub-division.

Whether these distinct groups of rocks are the equivalent of the continental Permian system or not, it is beyond dispute that in this country they are intimately related to the Coal-measures, but separated from the Triassic system by one of the greatest unconformities known in British geology. On the other hand the Magnesian Limestone Series of the eastern counties—considered to be the equivalent of the Permian Zechstein of Germany—is removed from the highest Coal-measures by a strong unconformity, but is hardly separable from the Triassic deposits.

The breccia bands which characterize the South Staffordshire 'Permian Rocks' retain a general lithological facies throughout the district. Set in a sandy or marly paste, angular fragments or blocks of volcanic rocks, mingled with others of fossiliferous, Carboniferous, Silurian and Cambrian sandstones and limestones, show the varied source of their derivation. Their origin has therefore led to much con-

---

[1] For a recent discussion on this interesting subject see *Report of the British Association* (1901), Bradford.

[2] Quite recently a band of *Spirorbis* limestone has been discovered in the so-called Middle Permian at Frankley Lodge farm in the Clent area by T. C. Cantrill (*Summary of Progress of the Geological Survey for* 1901), pp. 63, 64.

GEOLOGY

troversy, of which there are two opposing views. Some geologists, following the brilliant researches of Ramsay,[1] claim a glacial origin for this heterogeneous collection of rock fragments. Others[2] maintain them to be scree material swept down by sub-aerial torrents from a pre-Triassic hilly region situated in the south.

TRIASSIC SYSTEM

To whatever origin the 'Permian' breccias of Clent and Enville be attributed, the next group—the unconformable Triassic rocks—affords a typical example of deposits laid down under continental conditions, as was long ago pointed out by Ramsay and Godwin-Austen. The change from the river-borne muds and silts of the Carboniferous period is not only vividly contrasted in the loosely compacted red sandstones and conglomerates of the Trias, but the vast interval of time intervening between the close of the one set of events and the opening of another is forcibly demonstrated by the newer formation reposing horizontally or at gentle angles on the denuded and intensely plicated carboniferous strata. This is recognized by geologists ending the Palæozoic era with the Carboniferous or Permian systems, and starting an altogether fresh time epoch (Mesozoic) with the red rocks of the Trias.

At its commencement in the Bunter period the Triassic continent—an elevated Carboniferous sea floor—presented a very irregular rocky surface fashioned out of a plane of marine denudation during upheavals succeeding the Carboniferous period, and carved out by long subsequent denudation. This rugged surface of pre-Triassic hill and dale and possibly mountainous country became gradually levelled by dry weathering, torrential rains and wind, while the material derived from these sources was swept into and slowly accumulated in the hollows. In the succeeding Keuper stage the broader depressions were further filled with sediments deposited in a great lake subjected to such intense evaporation as to result in the deposition of thick beds of rock-salt and gypsum. Finally, at the close of the Keuper period the area became depressed, by gentle sinking movements, beneath the waters of the Rhætic and Jurassic seas.

The Triassic system is built up of sandstones and marls of an almost universal red colour due to a thin film of oxide of iron coating each particle. Traced across the district from west to east the individual members show a rapid decrease in thickness : collectively, on the west side of the South Staffordshire Coalfield the thickness amounts to 3,500 feet, which has dwindled to about 1,200 feet on the east side of this coalfield, but there is reason to believe that in the centre of the basin to the north of Stafford the westerly amount is reached or even exceeded. Owing to the general slight inclination of the strata the outcrops are especially broad ; they are narrowest round the Carboniferous tracts in the north

[1] 'On the Occurrence of Angular, Subangular, Polished and Striated Fragments and Boulders in the Permian Breccia of Shropshire, Worcestershire, etc.,' *Quart. Journ. Geol. Soc.* xi. 185 (1855).
[2] 'On the Permian Conglomerates of the Lower Severn Basin,' by W. Wickham King, *Quart. Journ. Geol. Soc.* lv. 97–128 (1899).

and south, from off which they dip to all points of the compass, and are broadest in the great central syncline occupied by the Keuper Marls.

BUNTER PERIOD

Lower Red and Mottled Sandstone.—If the sub-aerial origin of the Bunter, as is now generally accepted, be correct, we might expect to find a varied distribution of the sediments ; especially would this be the case with the wind-borne deposits, to which some geologists consider a large portion of the Lower Mottled Sandstone may be directly or indirectly attributed. To the west of Wolverhampton, where this subdivision appears at its best, it reaches a thickness of 300 feet ; it is only met with locally in North Staffordshire, and is altogether absent on the east side of the South Staffordshire Coalfield.

In the Wolverhampton area the strata consist of sandstones of the most varied hues, ranging from yellow through brown to bright vermilion. Here also the remarkable false-bedding or ' oblique lamination,' characteristic of the sub-division, is admirably exhibited in a road cutting near the entrance to the lower town. Whether this be due to currents of water or wind the general roundness of the sand particles must be attributed to wind action, for no other agency is considered to be capable of rounding small sand grains, while it is one of the characteristic features of the desert sands of to-day.[1]

Owing to their soft nature the rocks are generally denuded into broad valleys, but in the interesting escarpment of Kinver Edge the top beds have been hardened by a calcareous cement, and overhang a deep valley excavated in the underlying softer portion. The ease with which the stone can be quarried has been taken advantage of by the inhabitants of Enville and Kinver, the neighbourhood of these villages showing numerous rock houses, of which those cut out of the sandstone of Holy Austin Rock are the best known.

Bunter Pebble Beds.—The strata of this sub-division are well developed in the north and south, where they hem in the Carboniferous formations against which they abut, sometimes with a faulted junction, but more frequently unconformably superimposed. They consist essentially of coarse false-bedded sandstones, through which pebbles of vein quartz and other rocks are widely scattered or are massed together with little or no intervening matrix, forming beds of shingle sometimes over 50 feet thick. At their outcrop the sandstones and conglomerates are usually incoherent, but in wells and borings the matrix is often highly calcareous, when the rock is intensely hard and much dreaded by well-sinkers. In the shingle beds the pebbles are of all sizes up to or slightly exceeding that of a man's head. The majority are quartzites— white, brown, yellow or liver-coloured ; others consist of well rounded fragments of Mountain Limestone, chert, grits of various Palæozoic

---

[1] For our knowledge of desert conditions the student is referred to *Das gesetz der Wüstenbildung,* by Professor Walther (Berlin, 1900).

formations, and an occasional fragment of granite or volcanic grit.[1] Speaking generally the massed gravels are more abundant in the north than in the south, and more persistent towards the base of the sub-division than near its summit. They are largely quarried for road metal and gravel in Trentham Park, Cannock Chase, south of Cheadle, Longton, and in many localities bordering the South Staffordshire Coalfield.

To the west of the South Staffordshire Coalfield the sub-division is situated with apparent perfect conformity between the Lower and Upper Mottled Sandstone, but elsewhere in the county rests with a great discordance on the various members of the Carboniferous rocks or on 'Permian.' This unconformity can nowhere be better illustrated than by the outliers at Endon and around Leek, where the nearly horizontal pebbly Bunter sandstones rest on highly inclined or sharply folded Lower Carboniferous rocks.

In its course along the western margin of the South Staffordshire Coalfield the outcrop is indicated by conspicuous ridges, such as Abbots Castle Hill, near Trysull, and Kinver Edge. Along the eastern side of the coalfield the outcrop extends in a well marked ridge from near Birmingham northward to Aldridge. The greatest expanse however constitutes the open undulating heather-clad moorland of Cannock Chase on which the characteristic weathering into deep coombes with intermediate rounded lobes is admirably illustrated. The same character is clearly portrayed round the North Staffordshire Coalfield, where the sub-formation gives rise to the picturesque woodlands of Maer, Swynnerton Park, Trentham Park, Burnt Wood and Bishops Wood. Perhaps the most interesting outcrop occurs in the Churnet valley between Cheddleton and Leek, where a small patch about seven miles long has been preserved in a deep pre-Triassic hollow excavated in the Lower Carboniferous rocks which on all sides surround and overlook the much newer formation.

The mode and place of origin of the sandstones and shingle beds have given rise to much controversy among geologists. They have been regarded as the products of powerful oceanic currents; another opinion holds them to be of sub-aerial origin, brought together by large rivers liable to heavy floods, or else by tumultuous torrents the effect of cloudbursts. Some geologists consider the pebbles to be derived from the breaking up of the conglomerates of the Old Red Sandstone; others again would derive them from Palæozoic rocks of different ages in rapid course of destruction by the ordinary agents of denudation acting during the Bunter period. Again, the views as to the source of origin are widely divergent: some geologists maintain that the pebbles were derived from the older formations in the north of England and Scotland; others look to their source from an old rocky ridge extending between the southwest of England and western France; while others think it not improbable that much of the material might have been obtained from the older

[1] W. Molyneux, 'On the Gravel Beds of Trentham Park,' *Trans. North Staff. Nat. Field Club* (1886); *Geol. Mag.* iv. 173 (1867).

formations known to exist in the Midlands beneath the Trias. Divergent as these views appear, they probably all contain an element of truth, for not from one but from many areas should the pebbles be derived if they were laid down under continental conditions.[1]

The strata are almost wholly unfossiliferous. In other parts of England the presence of Labyrinthodonts has been detected, but then only rarely, and consisting chiefly of footprints. The spongy nature of the sandstone and shingle beds renders the sub-division an almost unlimited reservoir of underground water, admirably suited for drinking purposes. The pebble beds are thus the source from which the chief towns of Staffordshire obtain their water supply. The strong springs, issuing from the rocks along lines of faults and major joints, or at their junction with the less pervious Carboniferous strata, help in no small degree to keep the streams and rivers from running dry during the summer months. The springs at Wall Grange pouring out over 2,000,000 gallons daily, supplied to the Potteries, are a case in point ; the Tern river also issues from the spring-fed lake at Maer Hall as a stream of no inconsiderable size. In other respects the Pebble Beds, beyond yielding road-metal for second class roads, possess little commercial importance.

Upper Mottled Sandstone.—This sub-division of vermilion-coloured non-pebbly sandstone, closely resembling the lower sub-division, follows conformably and runs parallel with the outcrop of the Pebble Beds to the west of the southern coalfield, but is hardly separable from them and not always present in North Staffordshire. One of the best sections in the Midlands is opened out in the road cutting at Tettenhall to the west of Wolverhampton. Flanked by the Pebble Beds and overlain by the hard Keuper basement beds the Upper Mottled Sandstone usually occupies low lying tracts overlooked by the inferior and superior sub-divisions of the Trias. Some of the most beautiful country lanes have been cut deep into these soft red sandstones, whose bright red colours so strikingly contrast with the delicate greens of lichen, moss and fern which cling to their damp crumbling surfaces.

The soft incoherent nature of the stone renders it a favourite source of building sand, while the more loamy varieties yield good foundry and moulding sand, and are extensively quarried at Baldwins Gate near Maer for the Crewe Engineering Works.

KEUPER PERIOD

Keuper Basement Beds and Waterstones.—During the whole of the Bunter period the elevatory forces were going on or were only temporarily stationary : in the succeeding Keuper period the successive overlaps of the individual members point to a cessation of any upward movements, while towards its close the Triassic continent began to slowly sink until it became finally submerged beneath the seas which were to hold sway during the whole of Mesozoic times.

[1] T. G. Bonney, *Geol. Mag.* Dec. 11, vii. 404 (1880), ibid. Dec. 4, ii. 75 (1895) ; W. J. Harrison, *Proc. Birm. Phil. Soc.* vol. iii. (1881–3).

GEOLOGY

The Keuper Basement Beds, or, as they are sometimes called, Lower Keuper Sandstones, are typically developed in the western portion of the county where they conformably surmount the Upper Mottled Sandstone. Owing to the general presence of a hard conglomerate or occasionally a breccia at the base they overlook the inferior sub-division in the form of well-marked scarps particularly well exhibited to the west of Wolverhampton between Tettenhall and Shifnall and in the ridges west of Eccleshall. But it is at Alton where denudation has most successfully picked out these harder strata and fashioned a combination of escarpment, rocky cliff and deep ravine unrivalled by any other Triassic area.

In the eastern part of South Staffordshire and generally in North Staffordshire the basal conglomerate and breccia are absent and the Keuper Waterstones rest with apparent conformity or apparent discordance on the ' Pebble Beds.' In most places the basement beds are succeeded by even bedded red and white sandstones with interstratified layers of red and grey marl. Toward the summit the marl partings become more numerous and thicker with a consequent thinning of the intercalated sandstones, and so gradually pass into the Waterstones, so called from the thin sandstones possessing a fancied resemblance to watered silk and not to their affording a good water-bearing stratum as is sometimes stated.

The red and white sandstones overlying the basement beds yield an excellent building stone extensively quarried around Wolverhampton, Rugeley and south of Cheadle. At Hollington and Stanton the stone is of exceptional quality, yielding large blocks sent to many parts of the kingdom. It has been, and still remains, a favourite stone for ecclesiastical architecture, country mansions and the larger buildings of many of the midland cities. Alton Towers is built of a freestone of Lower Keuper age obtained close at hand.

The Lower Keuper Sandstones and building stones yield a few fossils of which remains of plants, poorly preserved, are not infrequent, but the most interesting are the rare remains of the gigantic Amphibian belonging to the sub-order *Labyrinthodontia*.

The impressions of the hand-like feet—chirosaurus (*Cheirotherium*)—of this animal have been met with on the surface of slabs of sandstones in many quarries, notably at Hollington, but the finest remains, consisting of a nearly complete skull, 9 inches long and 6 inches wide, were obtained in the quarries at Stanton.[1]

Throughout the Lower Keuper, but also occasionally in the Bunter, the cementing material frequently consists of barium sulphate standing out in relief on the weathered surfaces as star-like forms or else leached out and redeposited as small veins filling joints. Copper-ore, consisting of the blue and green carbonates, is occasionally present and has been worked at Bearstone.

Keuper Marls.—Nearly the whole of the central and low-lying portions of the county are occupied by this sub-division. Made up

[1] John Ward, 'On the Occurrence of Labyrinthodont Remains in the Keuper Sandstone of Stanton,' *Trans. North Staff. Field Club* (1900).

essentially of soft red marls of nearly uniform composition, and lying at a gentle angle across the great syncline of central Staffordshire, the scenery of the Keuper Marl country lacks interest. Low scarps and ridges, where the strata consist of thin bands of brown and white flags (skerries) occasionally break the monotony, but except towards the base these features are impersistent. In the past the Keuper Marl country was largely covered with woods, of which Needwood Forest and Chartley Park remain as relics.

The marls are of great thickness, possibly as much as 2,000 feet to the north-east of Stafford. That they were laid down under water, in a large lake subjected to intense evaporation, the beds of rocksalt and gypsum afford the most conclusive evidence. As the basin became filled up the marls gradually extended over the underlying sub-divisions, and finally in the north overlapped them all until they invaded the bays and hollows of the Carboniferous rocks which here formed the margins of the basin.

The red marl forms an excellent soil and was formerly dug for ‘ top-dressing,’ the small pits excavated for this purpose or for drinking troughs lying scattered in countless numbers all over its outcrop. The celebrated alabaster quarries of Fauld near Tutbury lie in the Keuper Marl. Alabaster is here obtained in large slabs, and was used extensively for the ornamental work of Croxden Abbey and Lichfield Cathedral. Two hundred years ago, and long before it was quarried near Tettenhall, the Burton workers in alabaster had attained a considerable status. Brine wells have been sunk into the marls to the north of Stafford and at Shirleywich.

RHÆTIC PERIOD

The gradual passing away of the Triassic continental period is revealed in the interesting outliers of the Rhætic formation in Needwood Forest and Bagots Park to the west of Burton-on-Trent. The sections are very meagre, the best being the exposure at Marchington Cliff where the red Keuper Marls pass up imperceptibly into bluish white conchoidal marls and impure limestones containing *Axinus cloacinus* and overlain by a few feet of the characteristic black Rhætic shales.

With the Rhætic Beds the geological history of the county as recorded in the solid rock formations terminates. We know that the Rhætic deposits mark the commencement of a great regional depression during which Britain and western Europe lay submerged for a vast interval of time beneath the ocean, but of which no relics have been detected in Staffordshire. To the east the Jurassic and Cretaceous systems follow each other in consecutive order ; to the west, at Audlem, it is known that at least the Jurassic seas extended, but from Staffordshire its sediments have been swept away. Of the early stages of the Tertiary period, so well exhibited in the south-eastern counties, Staffordshire again presents a blank, so that volume after volume of the geological record has been

OROGRAPHICAL MAP

J.G.Bartholomew.

REFERENCE NOTE

above 1750 feet	
1500 to 1750 feet	
1250 to 1500 feet	
1000 to 1250 feet	
800 to 1000 feet	
600 to 800 feet	
400 to 600 feet	
200 to 400 feet	
100 to 200 feet	
below 100 feet	

County Boundary shown thus

SCALE 4 MILES TO AN INCH

THE VICTORIA HISTORY OF THE COUNTIES OF ENGLAND

The Edinburgh Geographical Institute.

destroyed and we pass abruptly from the deserts of the Trias to the arctic conditions of the Pleistocene period.

Before describing this wonderful contrast of events we must however retrace our steps and briefly consider the igneous rocks breaking through the formations previously described.

IGNEOUS AND VOLCANIC ROCKS

The stratified deposits are in many places but a thin skin overlying a reservoir of molten material ever ready to burst forth and intrude itself along lines of weakness. Evidences of such weak spots are to be met with again and again among the formations whose history we have been tracing, yet it was only rarely that the underlying molten matter found egress from its subterranean reservoir.

The earliest record is afforded by the limestone quarry on Congleton Edge (p. 8), where it becomes evident that during the closing scenes of the Carboniferous Limestone epoch a volcano was close at hand vomiting forth ashes and dust which fell into the surrounding seas and possibly sending forth a submarine lava stream.

The famous basalts or trap rocks intruded into the Coal-measures of South Staffordshire present the next example. These cover no inconsiderable area at Rowley Regis, Barrow Hill, Pouk Hill, and again round Wednesfield. Each occurs as a ' sill ' whose intrusive character is shown by the coal-seams being charred where they came in contact with the molten mass or by the baking of the black Coal-measure shales at their junction with the basalt above and below. The largest sill forms the Rowley Regis mass, through which the tunnel between Rowley Regis Station and Old Hill passes. The lava was here injected into the space of an arched up mass of Coal-measure strata forming what is known as a 'laccolite,' of which the cover has been removed by denudation. During the process of cooling, a beautiful columnar structure, excellently preserved in Turner's Pit, was set up.[1] Huge spheroids of basalt are frequently enclosed between the joints which transversely divide the columns at fairly regular intervals. The Rowley Rag is largely used for road metal.

Some uncertainty exists as to the age of the intrusions owing to the want of conclusive field evidence. Professor Watts[2] comments on the fresh appearance of the constituent minerals and the many features they possess in common with the well known Tertiary dykes of the north of Ireland and Scotland, and also on the fact that the Rowley mass partakes in the fractures affecting the coalfield, some of which, such as the Great Boundary Faults, traverse Jurassic rocks. None of the South Staffordshire intrusions pierce rocks later than high Coal-measures, but an interesting dyke met with in North Staffordshire traverses the marls of the Keuper period. This is a very narrow basaltic dyke, never more

[1] T. G. Bonney, *Quart. Journ. Geol. Soc.* xxxii. 151 (1876).
[2] W. W. Watts, *Geologists' Association*, p. 399 (1898), op. cit., in which references to the literature on the igneous rocks are also given.

than a few feet across, which has been traced from near Keele to a little north of Chebsey.[1] In its course it cuts across and alters rocks of Upper Coal-measure, Bunter and Keuper ages. The mineral constituents are exceedingly fresh, and in many respects the rock closely resembles the South Staffordshire intrusions.

PLEISTOCENE AND RECENT

GLACIAL DEPOSITS

The third great epoch of which the county presents a complete and most interesting record is that of the Pleistocene or Quaternary Period. There is abundant evidence to show that at this late geological time two great ice sheets were formed by the piling up of snow and ice over the North Sea and the Irish Sea and converged until their margins touched in Staffordshire somewhere in the region of Burton-on-Trent ; at the same period local glaciers descended from the Derbyshire and Welsh hills, spreading out their débris at their feet and mingling it with that carried inland by the two great ice sheets coming up from the sea.

Compared with the events recorded in the latest of the solid geological formations—the Rhætic—dealt with in this article, this refrigeration, which extended over the whole of northern Europe, happened but yesterday, its close according to some calculations not being further removed from the present day than 10,000 years. At its commencement the configuration of the land was much as it is to-day ; all that it accomplished was a little rounding off of surface inequalities by the rasping power of the ice and the filling up of pre-existing hollows or alteration of previous surface drainage by the accumulation of detritus or by barriers of ice.

To understand the significance of the phenomena met with in Staffordshire it is essential to bear in mind that the Welsh, Cumbrian, Scotch and Pennine hills were as high at the commencement of the period as they are to-day, and that the chief valleys and plains of central England were in the main blocked out. This being recognized, the course which the ice sheets took will be easily comprehended. The one from the Irish Sea invaded the Cheshire and Shropshire plains, to be there joined by the more local ice flows from the Welsh hills ; the one from the North Sea spread over the eastern counties and pushed its way up the Trent valley, to be joined near Derby by the glaciers sent off from the Derbyshire hills. Such are the broad general outlines of the period. The existence of these moving masses of ice is plainly demonstrated by the character of the foreign material or train of boulders left scattered over the country, and by the ice grooves on the solid rocks radiating outwards from the elevated regions or pointing in the direction of the paths taken by the Irish Sea and North Sea ice.

The three largest glaciers have been named : (1) The *Arenig Glacier*,

[1] J. Kirkby, 'On the Trap Dykes in the Hanchurch Hills,' *Trans. North Staff. Field Club*, vol. xxviii. (1894).

GEOLOGY

(2) the *Irish Sea Glacier*, (3) the *North Sea Glacier*, while the one from the Derbyshire hills may be termed (4) the *Pennine Glacier*. Their history has not been completely made out, and the order in which they invaded the district is uncertain, but the local glaciers had probably reached a considerable size before the foreign ice penetrated into the heart of the country.

We will now briefly describe the phenomena presented by the different ice masses, mentioning neighbouring areas where necessary for a complete comprehension of the subject :—

Arenig Glacier.—Descending from the Arenig Hills (2,817 feet) this glacier passed down the Vale of Llangollen and then debouched on to the Shropshire plain, where it threw down the masses of morainic material at Ruabon and Ellesmere. It would be natural to suppose that it would then have passed northward down the Dee valley with over-flows to the south along the Severn valley. The northern path however was blocked with ice coming from the Irish Sea and the southern course barred with ice from Plinlimmon. It was therefore compelled to assume a south-easterly course, impinging upon Staffordshire, round Wolverhamp-ton and the ground to the south, where occasional boulders of Welsh rocks, but mixed with others brought by the Irish Sea ice, are met with. Around the southern margins of the South Staffordshire Coal-field boulders from Wales become common, but the greatest number and the best sections in the drift lie beyond the county border. The Rowley Hills lie in the direct path of the Arenig glacier. Mr. Jerome Harrison[1] finds no foreign drift on their summit, but on the contrary a train of basalt boulders has been traced from them for some distance to the south and east. On the rock being bared in quarrying operations, clearly striated rock surfaces, with the striæ pointing N.W. to S.E., have been laid bare, and the general contour of the hills Mr. Harrison regards as that of a great *roche moutonnée*.

Carried along by the great moving mass of the Irish sea ice—which also probably helped to push the Arenig glacier up the south-western flanks of the South Staffordshire Coalfield—the glacier from Wales may have impinged on the northern coalfield, as along its western margin some boulders are met with which correspond very well with the rhyolitic lavas of Arenig.

Irish Sea Glacier.—This was the dominant and all-powerful mass of ice of which the presence can be traced over the greater part of the county. Its great thickness and power was derived from the glaciers of the south of Scotland, Ireland and the Lake district, which during glacial times descended into the Irish Sea basin, and uniting there with the glaciers resulting from the accumulated snowfall became ultimately piled up until the ice overrode the summit of Snaefell (2,024 feet) in the Isle of Man. Advancing southward it met with the resistance of the Welsh hills, and consequently split into one lobe which passed down St. George's Channel,

---

[1] 'Glacial Geology of the Birmingham District,' op. cit.

and into another which swept across the Cheshire plain and finally invaded Staffordshire. Exactly where this great ice-sheet terminated has not been made out, but it may be roughly taken to have come to rest along a line joining Burton, Lichfield, Wolverhampton and Enville; for north of this line the country is strewn with boulders and glacial detritus; while to the south the relics are scanty and difficult to separate from the material spread out by the streams issuing from the foot of the ice. As the western ice approached the northern borders of the county it encountered the bold front of the North Staffordshire hills, which are only breached near Kidsgrove and to the east of Congleton. The ice however was of sufficient weight and thickness to override the Pottery Coalfield, and further north, in the direction of main movement, even reached an altitude of 1,300 feet to the east of Macclesfield. The gaps near Congleton however presented an easy overflow, and consequently we find an ice lobe penetrated down the Trent valley system, scattering its sands, clays and boulders in irregular mounds between Biddulph and Stoke-upon-Trent. To the south-east however the high ground around Cheadle almost completely arrested the further eastward course of the western ice, and consequently we meet with none or very little of its detritus between Uttoxeter and Cheadle; on the contrary the influence of the local Pennine glacier becomes apparent.

The greatest accumulation of boulders is found on the western flanks of the North Staffordshire Coalfield and between Wolverhampton and Enville in South Staffordshire. As might be expected, they comprise a heterogeneous collection of Scotch and Lake district rocks, mingled with an occasional boulder from Wales, where the ice-sheet came into contact with the Arenig glacier. The commonest Lake district rocks are boulders of the red granite of Eskdale, granophyres from Buttermere, basalts with large crystals of augite, streaky garnetiferous lavas, amygdaloidal basalts and rhyolites. Rocks from Scotland are represented by blocks of hornblende-bearing granites and the tonalites of Galloway. The iceborne fragments are of all sizes, from mere pebbles up to blocks over 12 feet in length. Many of the larger boulders have been removed by man from their original resting-places and set up along the roadsides or at the corners of the streets in towns and villages, or in public parks, as at Wolverhampton and Longton; while in the western villages the streets are sometimes cobbled with the smaller stones. The boulders however represent but a small amount of the transported material. There are besides thick masses of 'Boulder Clay,' in which stones large and small lie scattered at all angles—constituting in places a true ground moraine—among which lenticular beds and sheets of sand are intercalated. The colour of the clay varies according to the nature of the ground swept over by the ice: it is brown or red when it lies on or has previously crossed an outcrop of Triassic rocks; it is a deep dirty blue colour over tracts of Carboniferous rocks or in contiguous areas in advance of the ice-sheet, when it contains fragments of the Lower Carboniferous rocks, pieces of coal and even in one case portions of a coal seam, disrupted and carried onward by the ice. The clays are in many places used for bricks. The intercalated sands occur in masses sometimes exceeding a hundred feet in thickness, and are generally clean red, yellow, or buff sands, sometimes free of pebbles, but more often containing lenticles of gravel. They have been a favourite source for local water supplies, and the sites of many of the villages—such as Betley, Wrinehill and Madeley—were no doubt originally selected for this reason. It was originally thought, and the opinion is still sometimes upheld, that the clays and sands maintain a definite relationship. Thus there is considered to be an old stiff clay full of scratched stones (*Till or Lower Boulder Clay*) on which the sands and gravels (*Middle Glacial Sands*) rest. The latter have been taken by some glacialists to indicate an amelioration of climate and depression, followed by a re-elevation and second refrigeration represented by an overlying sheet of clay (*Upper Boulder Clay*). In the Trent basin Mr. Deeley[1] introduces further sub-divisions, each of which he regards as indicative of different stages of glaciation. Though this threefold sub-division can be frequently observed, it is commonly acknowledged that the presence of the three members at any one spot is accidental, while one or even two are as often absent as present.

Both sands and clays, but more frequently the coarser bands of sand and lenticles of gravel, contain fragments of recent marine shells of types met with in the Irish Sea and in more northern waters. An entire specimen is the exception, the merest fragments being generally met with. Faint glacial striæ can sometimes be observed on the larger fragments. The commonest shells and fragments are cockle (*Cardium edule*), *Mytilus edulis*, *Turritella terebra*, *Tellina balthica*, *Cyprina*, *Mya*. They are to be found in fair abundance round Wolverhampton, Madeley (Staffs), from Woore to Alsager, and near Biddulph, in pits opened in the clays and sands.

North Sea Glacier.—While the Irish Sea basin was filling up with ice, the North Sea, fed with glaciers from Scandinavia, was likewise being piled thick with ice which reached the English coast a little north of Flamborough Head. Sweeping inland it crossed the Trent at Gainsborough, and thence pushed its way up the Trent valley to Derby and Burton-on-Trent. Its influence on Staffordshire is scarcely appreciable, though it exercised a strong hold on Leicestershire. Passing as it did over the Jurassic and Cretaceous deposits of the eastern counties, its débris, gathered from these rocks, is at once distinguishable from the fragments of Palæozoic rocks brought into the county by the Irish Sea glacier. Flints, Chalk and fragments of the Lias and Oolites, mingled with an occasional Scandinavian gneiss or igneous rock, at once betray the presence of the North Sea ice. Only its fringe however reached Staffordshire, and scattered its far distant collected rocks around Burton-on-Trent, Abbots Bromley and possibly even as far west as Uttoxeter, though here the flinty gravel may in part be attributed to material washed out of the eastern ice.

[1] 'The Pleistocene Succession in the Trent Basin,' *Quart. Journ. Geol. Soc.* xlii. 437 (1886).

Pennine Glacier. — The Pennine hills evidently nourished their glaciers at the time the Welsh hills were swathed in ice. Their lobes of ice descended down the main valleys—the Dove and Derwent —carrying with them the rocks of the Derbyshire hills, and spreading them out on the rising ground south of Uttoxeter, Tutbury and Derby.

Clear as to its origin, and of comparatively recent geological date, the Pleistocene period plainly shows its influence on the pre-existing physiographical outlines of the county. Remove the drift deposits on the north-western borders of the county, and a hollow, occasionally sinking below sea-level, would extend where now there is a plain from 200–300 feet above sea-level. Before the ice dropped its detritus in the Trent valley, between Bucknall and Stockton Brook, it can be clearly shown that the Trent flowed at the foot of the high bank of Carboniferous rocks descending from Wetley Moor, and that it is less in volume by that now carried off by the Stockton Brook, which feeds the Churnet, but in pre-glacial times flowed into the Trent. It is probable also that greater changes in drainage took place in the Dove valley system, but this comparatively modern line of research has not been worked out for this valley.

RIVER DRIFT AND CAVE EARTH

Between the final passing away of the ice-sheets and the earliest records of the human period in Staffordshire a long time elapses, during which the rivers were gradually assuming their present channels and rate of flow. The history of these lesser changes of river shrinkage and alteration of channel, accompanied by a slow modification of the fauna and flora, has not been sufficiently studied throughout the county, and the results obtained have depended largely upon chance excavations, so that our knowledge is necessarily imperfect.

The older river deposits consist of terraces of gravel, sand and loam frequently met with at levels high above the present streams, though in some cases glacial gravels may have been mistaken for former river deposits and vice versa.

On the west banks of the Trent, at Burton, old river gravels have been met with at Stretton 100 feet above the present water-level of the Trent. At a lower level, from 18 to 36 feet above the Trent, another platform of gravel extends between Stretton and Horninglow.

Further down in the valley the town of Burton is situated on an old river gravel from 8 to 10 feet above the present water-level. The material composing it consists of well washed sand and gravel, from 20 to 30 feet thick. High Street, Burton, and the older parts of the town are located on this terrace, the gravels and sands of which for many years alone yielded the water used in the celebrated breweries. Bones, jaws and teeth of *Sus scrofa*, *Bos taurus* var. *longifrons*, horse and those of the dog and wolf have been obtained at times from these deposits.

From the older river gravels of the Trent at Trentham Dr. Plot

GEOLOGY

mentions the unearthing of the tusk of elephant ; Dr. Garner[1] also records remains of elephant and rhinoceros, associated with the bones of red deer and roebuck, from the 'diluvial' gravels of the same neighbourhood. In altering the course of the Fowlea brook a fine skull of the wild bull (*Bos taurus* var. *primigenius*) with the horn cores complete was found near Etruria station.[2] Remains of *Bos taurus* var. *longifrons* and *Bos urus* have also been met with at Stone.[3]

It might be expected that, regarding their frequent occurrence in Derbyshire where recent discoveries show that the caves have probably existed from Pliocene times,[4] the remains of animals would be plentifully met with in fissures and caverns of the Carboniferous Limestone country of Staffordshire. This however is not the case, but from a fissure in the limestone at Bank End quarry, Waterhouses, in the valley of the Hamps, a large number of remains of *Elephas primigenius* (mammoth) have been extracted from a red loamy clay mixed with fragments of limestone and rolled boulders of grit.[5]

The rivers continued to suffer shrinkage down to the historical period and further modified their channels. This is best exhibited around Burton,[6] in the Trent valley, where a narrow fringe of alluvium borders the river. This, as well as the higher, more elevated terraces, has been liable to floods, of which the record will be dealt with by the historian.

The solid framework of the county has now been traced from the earliest rock-written record to the time when the landscape assumed its familiar outline. Everywhere physical feature has been found dependent on geological structure : the diversified moorland of the north, the two great coalfields, the enveloping lowlands, have all been traced to the composition of the rocks and their structure. The history of the past contained in the rocks is everywhere incomplete, and may be faithfully summed up in the words of Charles Darwin in speaking of the geological record as a whole : 'For my part, I look at the geological record as a history of the world imperfectly kept, and written in a changing dialect—only here and there a short chapter has been preserved ; and of each page only here and there a few lines.'

1 *Natural History of the County of Stafford*, p. 202 (1686).
2 *Trans. North Staff. Field Club*, vol. for 1878.
3 Ibid. xxx. 110.
4 W. Boyd Dawkins, *Quart. Journ. Geol. Soc.* vol. xlix. (1903).
5 W. Brockbank, *Proc. Lit. and Phill. Soc. Manchester* (1862–4) ; J. Aitken, *Trans. Manchester Geol. Soc.* vol. xii. (1870–3).
6 W. Molyneux, *Burton-on-Trent ; its History, its Waters, etc.* (1868).

PALAEONTOLOGY

WITH the exception of a very few obtained from the superficial deposits, the vertebrate fossils of Staffordshire seem to be restricted to the horizons of the Trias and the Coal Measures. Although the Coal Measure vertebrates are by far the more numerous, those from the Trias are, as a whole, much the more interesting, on account of the rarity, at least in this country, of the types to which they belong. An exception in this respect must, however, be made in the case of the shark-remains from the Coal Measures belonging to the genus *Edestus*, of which they are the only known British representatives.

Of mammalian remains from the Pleistocene formations of the county a list has been drawn up by Mr. John Ward of Longton, and published in the *Transactions of the North Staffordshire Field Club* for 1902.[1] The earliest record dates back to 1688, when Robert Plot, in his *Natural History of Staffordshire*, relates that a jaw and a tooth of a young elephant—doubtless the mammoth (*Elephas primigenius*)—were found in a marl-pit near Trentham. Probably it is these specimens which are referred to on page 258 of Owen's *British Fossil Mammals and Birds*, as having come under the observation of Dean Buckland. Be this as it may, Robert Garner, in his *Natural History of the County of Stafford* (1844), refers to the occurrence at Trentham and other places in the county, both in diluvial gravel, and also in the clay at the bottom of certain caves, of the bones of the red deer (*Cervus elaphus*), roe-buck (*Capreolus capreolus*), rhinoceros, elephant, and hyaena. The rhinoceros was doubtless the woolly Siberian *Rhinoceros antiquitatis*, while the elephant was probably the mammoth, and the hyaena the large cave race (*Hyaena crocuta spelaea*) of the existing South African spotted species.

Parkinson, in his *Organic Remains*, figured a mammoth's molar from Staffordshire, which figure is reproduced on page 239 of Owen's work already cited ; and in 1864 Mr. J. Plant[2] exhibited before the Manchester Geological Society a series of the teeth and bones of the mammoth, the woolly rhinoceros, and the Pleistocene race of the hippopotamus (*Hippopotamus amphibius major*) which had been found in the county.

---

[1] Vol. xxxvi, 90.   [2] *Trans. Manchester Geol. Soc.* v, 42.

A HISTORY OF STAFFORDSHIRE

In 1864 Mr. Brockbank[3] recorded from a fissure in the Carboniferous Limestone at Bank End Quarry, Waterhouses, on the bank of the River Hamps, numerous remains of the mammoth, and it has been subsequently stated[4] that the collection obtained by Plant came from this spot.

Mr. Ward records the extinct wild ox, or aurochs (*Bos taurus primigenius*), from a bed near Etruria station, where a fine skull was found in 1877, and also a mammoth-tusk from Fenton. The aurochs and the domesticated Celtic shorthorn (the so-called *Bos longifrons*) are also recorded from Stone.

The first evidence of vertebrate life recorded from the Keuper, or Upper Division of the Trias (New Red Sandstone), was in the form of casts of footsteps. These have been observed in quarries at Hollington and Alton[5] in North Staffordshire, in the building-stones of the Lower Keuper ; while others have been recorded from South Staffordshire along the outcrop of the harder beds of the Keuper a few miles north-west of Wolverhampton.[6] Yet others have been described from Stanton, two and a half miles from Burton-on-Trent, and also from Coven, near Brewood, in the southern division of the county.[7] These latter have been provisionally assigned to the rhynchocephalian reptile *Rhynchosaurus*, a forerunner of the living New Zealand tuatera (*Sphenodon*), of which remains are recorded from the Keuper of Grinshill in Shropshire. Of those from the first-named localities some, at any rate, are, however, referable to *Chirosaurus* (or *Chirotherium*), creatures definitely known only by footprints of this type, but which have been generally regarded as large primeval salamanders, or labyrinthodont amphibians.

This view is to some extent supported by the discovery in the Staffordshire Keuper of the skull of an undoubted labyrinthodont of considerable size, although not perhaps sufficiently large to have made footsteps of the biggest size known. This skull, which exhibits chiefly a cast of the inside of the upper surface, was discovered in a quarry at Stanton, about three miles from Norbury, in the building-stone of the Keuper. It was first described and figured by the late Mr. John Ward in the *Transactions of the North Staffordshire Field Club* for 1900,[8] where it is referred to the genus *Dasyceps*, typically from the Permian of Kenilworth ; but it has been again described and figured by Dr. A. Smith Woodward in the *Proceedings of the Zoological Society of London* for 1904,[9] under the name of *Capitosaurus stantonensis*. The genus to which the Stanton labyrinthodont is now referred occurs typically in the Keuper of Würtemberg.

Some of the Keuper footprints may, on the other hand, have belonged to rhynchocephalian reptiles, of the occurrence of which in this formation decisive evidence has been recently obtained. This evidence

---

[3] *Proc. Manchester Lit. and Phil. Soc.* (1864), 46.   [4] Aitkin, *Trans. Manchester Geol. Soc.* xii, 25.
[5] H. C. Beasley, *Proc. Liverpool Geol. Soc.*
[6] J. Lomas, *Rep. Brit. Assoc.* for 1903, p. 5 ; and Beeby Thompson, *Geol. Mag.* (4), ix, (1902).
[7] Lydekker, *Cat. Foss. Rept. Brit. Mus.* iv, 219.
[8] Vol. xxxiv, 108, pls. iv, v.   [9] Vol. ii, 171, pls. xi, xii.

takes the form of a slab of Keuper Sandstone obtained by Mr. J. N. B. Masefield from the Hollington quarries, displaying in great perfection the impression of the peculiar system of abdominal ribs characteristic of these reptiles. The specimen has been described and figured by Dr. Smith Woodward,[10] and referred to the genus *Hyperodapedon*, an ally of *Rhynchosaurus*, of which other remains are known from the Keuper of Warwick and Devonshire.

Passing on to the vertebrate fauna of the Coal Measures of the county, we have first to refer to the occurrence in this formation of remains of primeval salamanders, some of which belong to true labyrinthodonts, while others are referable to allied sections of the group now collectively known as Stegocephalia. These are recorded by Mr. John Ward in two papers, the first of which was contributed to the *Transactions of the N. Staffordshire Institute of Mining Engineers* for 1890,[11] and the second to the *Transactions of the N. Staffordshire Field Club* for 1900.[12]

First in the list comes the fully-armoured species described by Professor Huxley on the evidence of a Yorkshire specimen under the name of *Pholiderpeton scutiferum*, of which genus it is the type. The species was recorded from the Coal Measures of Fenton by Mr. Ward in 1875.[13] Many years ago (1844) Mr. Garner in his *Natural History of the County of Stafford* figured, as that of some kind of unknown fish, a tooth from Skelton Colliery, which now turns out to belong to the labyrinthodont known as *Loxomma allmanni*. This large species, of which a practically entire and uncrushed skull is known, is characterized by the large size and diamond-shape of the sockets of the eyes and by the lancet-like teeth ; and a fine series of its remains has been discovered in the county. They occur, for instance, in the shale overlying the Cockshead Ironstone at Adderley Green ; in shale above the Knowles and Chalky Mine Ironstones at Fenton and Longton ; in the Brown Mine Ironstone at Silverdale ; and in the Gubbin Ironstone at Skelton. Of the still larger Coal Measure labyrinthodont described by Huxley as *Anthracosaurus russelli*, a number of well-preserved, although fragmentary, remains have been obtained from the Rag Mine Ironstone at Fenton and the Ash Ironstone at Longton.

By far the most interesting of the Staffordshire stegocephalians is, however, *Ceraterpeton galvani*, a member of the group Microsauria, measuring about ten inches in total length, and typically from Jarrow Colliery, Kilkenny. A single skeleton has been obtained from the shale overlying the Ash Ironstone at Longton Hall Colliery, Longton, which has been described by Dr. C. W. Andrews.[14] At one time it was incorrectly identified with the allied genus *Urocordylus*. The genus *Ceraterpeton* takes its name from the long horn-like projections arising from the hind border of the skull.

In addition to the forms above-mentioned, remains of other stegocephalians are known from the Coal Measures of the county, some of

---

[10] *Trans. N. Staff. Field Club*, xxxix, 115, pl. iii (1905).   [11] Vol. x.   [12] Vol. xxxiv, 101.
[13] *Trans. N. Staff. Field Club* (1875), p. 249.   [14] *Geol. Mag.* (4), ii, 83 (1895).

which are provisionally assigned by Mr. Ward to the species known as *Pteroplax cornuta*, typically from the Northumberland Coal-field.

Of the fishes of the Coal Measures of the county, by far the most interesting is a species of shark of the genus *Edestus*, the only British representative of its kind at present known. For many years certain remarkable bodies, somewhat resembling a large watch-spring armed on the convex side with teeth, have been known from the Carboniferous and Permian rocks of various countries : the most nearly complete coming from Russia. There has, however, been much uncertainty as to their true nature. At first they were supposed to be the fin-spines of fishes ; but the aforesaid Russian specimens clearly showed that they belong to the front of the jaws of sharks, and that they are true teeth, which are mounted upon their supporting bases in such a manner as to form a spiral. Hence the name of spiral-sawed sharks for the group to which they pertained. For a long time this group was known only from North America, Australia, Japan, and Russia ; the type genus being *Edestus*. Mr. E. T. Newton, in the *Quarterly Journal of the Geological Society*,[15] has, however, described part of the 'saw' of one of these remarkable sharks from a marine band in the Coal Measures of Nettlebank, North Staffordshire, giving the name of *Edestus triserratus* to the species it represents.

Of the primitive group of shark-like fishes known as Ichthyotomi, and characterized, among other features, by the exceedingly imperfect calcification of the spinal column and the long-jointed axis of the pectoral fins, there are several Staffordshire representatives, belonging to the family *Pleuracanthidae*. Of these, the species *Pleuracanthus laevissimus* is typified by a fin-spine from Staffordshire, and is known to occur in the Coal Measures of the southern half of the county and at Longton. The second species, *P. cylindricus*, which occurs both at Longton and Fenton, and is also known by the spines, does not appear to have been originally named from Staffordshire specimens. The genus *Diplodus* takes its name from having been founded on peculiar two-pronged teeth, which may really belong to *Pleuracanthus*. The species *D. gibbosus* was established on the evidence of teeth of this type from the Coal Measures of Silverdale, in South Staffordshire, but it also occurs at Longton.

Most of the other Staffordshire shark-like fishes (Elasmobranchii) belong to the existing group Selachii, although chiefly to extinct families. In the family *Petalodontidae*, characterized by the teeth being so much reflexed and thickened that in some cases they almost assume a crushing type, we have in the first place remains of the two common Carboniferous species *Janassa linguaeformis* and *J. clavata* from the Coal Measures of the county. To the same family belong the species *Ctenoptychius apicalis*, from Silverdale, Longton, Fenton, and Harecastle, and *Callopristodus pectinatus*, from Fenton, neither of which is, however, typically from the county. On the other hand, *Helodus simplex* and *Pleuroplax rankinei*, belong to another family, the *Cochliodontiae*, a specialized ancestral type of the

[15] Vol. lx, 1 (1904).

modern Port Jackson sharks (*Cestraciontidae*), characterized by the fusion of their crushing teeth into spirally twisted oblique plates. The first-named species, which is the sole representative of its genus, appears to have been founded on the evidence of teeth from Staffordshire, where it occurs at Longton, Fenton, and Silverdale, but the second seems to be typically from Northumberland. The existing *Cestraciontidae* have a Staffordshire representative in the form of *Sphenacanthus hybodoides*, a member of a widely spread extinct genus with several species. Within the county it occurs at Longton and also near Dudley.

The other Staffordshire elasmobranch fish is *Acanthodes wardi*, which takes its specific title from the late Mr. John Ward, of Longton, who did such good work in collecting and describing the fossil vertebrates of the county. It is a member of the Palaeozoic group Acanthodii, charac-terized among other features, by the persistent notochord, and the pres-ence of prominent dermal appendages to the gill-arches, which during life probably carried flaps of skin ; from this character the members of the group have been called fringe-gilled sharks. *Acanthodes* includes several other species, but *A. wardi* occurs typically in the Deep-Mine Ironstone of Longton, although it is also known from the Scottish Coal-fields. A species of the allied genus *Acanthodopsis* from the Woodhouse Coal of the Cheadle Coalfield has been described by Dr. R. H. Traquair in the *Annals and Magazine of Natural History* for 1894 [16] as *A. microdon*, on the evidence of a specimen now in the British Museum.

In addition to the foregoing, certain fin or dorsal spines of sharks or chimaeroids have been recorded from the Coal Measures of the county belonging to so-called genera of which the precise systematic position cannot at present be determined. Such is *Gyracanthus formosus*, widely distributed in the British Coalfields, and occurring in the county at Fenton. Another type is *Euctenius unilateralis*, originally described from a Lanarkshire specimen. Greater interest attaches to two masses of rock discovered by Mr. John Ward in the Middle Coal Measures of North Staffordshire containing numerous species of the doubtful type long known as *Listracanthus*. These have been described by Dr. Smith Woodward,[17] and are made the type of a new species, *Listracanthus wardi*. From these specimens it appears evident that the *Listracanthus* spines are strangely modified dermal tubercles occurring in considerable numbers on part at least of the head and body of the fish to which they pertain. They are identical with at least some of the structures from the Coal Measures of Indiana, U.S.A., described as *Petrodus*.

With *Ctenodus cristatus* and *Ct. murchisoni* we come to two well-known representatives of the typical genus of the Carboniferous family *Ctenodontidae*, which belongs to the sub-class of Dipnoi, or lung-fishes, and takes its name from the somewhat comb-like structure of the fine ridges on the large and flattened palatal teeth. The first species is recorded from Hanley and Tunstall, and the second from the Bassey Mine Ironstone of the Middle Coal Measures.

[16] Ser. 6, xiv, 372 (1894).   [17] *Geol. Mag.* (4), x, 486 (1903).

The ganoids, or enamel-scaled fishes, of the Staffordshire Coal Measures include a considerable number of species belonging to the primitive fringe-finned group (Crossopterygii), now represented by the bichir and the reed-fish (*Polypteridae*) of the rivers of tropical Africa. In the Palaeozoic family *Rhizodontidae*, characterized by the foldings of the walls of the base of the teeth in a manner recalling that of the labyrinthodonts, we have, in the first place, two species of the genus *Strepsodus* from Longton, namely *S. sauroides* and *S. sulcidens*, the former being widely distributed in the British Coalfields, while the latter is known elsewhere from Midlothian and Northumberland. The second Staffordshire member of the family is the widely distributed *Rhizodopsis sauroides*, of which remains are recorded from Fenton. The allied family *Osteolepididae*, in which the walls of the teeth are less folded while the scales are rhomboidal (instead of cycloidal) and more fully enamelled, is represented by four species, *Megalichthys hibberti*, *M. coccolepis*, *M. intermedius*, and *M. pygmaeus*, of which the first is very widely distributed, while neither of the others is peculiar to, or typically from, the county. Finally, in the family *Coelacanthidae*, characterized by the cycloidal scales and (in the fossil state) the hollow spines of the vertebrae, we have the species *Caelacanthus elegans*, which although typically from the Coalfields of Ohio, is also common in those of England.

Passing on to the fan-finned group (Actinopterygii), we have among the section Chondrostei, or sturgeon-like fishes, numerous representatives of the extinct families *Palaeoniscidae* and *Platysomatidae*. Both these, it may be observed, are fully scaled types, the former characterized by the elongated, and the latter by the deep contour of the body. In the first-named of these a fish from the Deep-Mine Ironstone Shale of Longton, at first described under the name of *Microconodus molyneuxi*, has been provisionally included in the genus *Gonatodus*, although its real systematic position is still uncertain. To the same family belongs *Cycloptychius carbonarius*, typified by a fish from the aforesaid bed at Longton, collected by Mr. Ward, and the type of the genus. The allied *Rhadinichthys* is represented by the four species, *R. wardi*, *R. monensis*, *R. macrodon*, and *R. planti*, of which the first and third are peculiar to the county. Of the genus *Elonichthys*, which is more nearly allied to the typical Permian *Palaeoniscus*, no less than five species have been recorded from the Carboniferous of the county, although some of these are still imperfectly known. They are *E. semistriatus*, from the Knowles Ironstone Shale of Fenton, *E. aitkeni*, from the Lower Coal Measures and Millstone Grit of North Staffordshire, *E. egertoni*, from Silverdale, Fenton, Longton, and Hanley, *E. microlepidotus*, from Longton, and *E. oblongus*, from Fenton. All but the second were described from Staffordshire specimens, and the last two are known only from the county. Another species peculiar to the county is *Eurylepis anglica*, described in 1894 by Dr. R. H. Traquair [18] on the evidence of a specimen from the Ash Shale of Longton.

[18] *Ann. Mag. Nat. Hist.* (6), xiv, 372 (1894).

PALAEONTOLOGY

In the family *Platysomatidae* the two recognized representatives of the genus *Mesolepis*, namely *M. wardi* and *M. scalaris*, were described from Staffordshire specimens, the first alone being known elsewhere, and then but doubtfully. *Mesolepis*, it may be mentioned, is characterized by the very deeply fusiform contour of the trunk, which is angulated at the back-fin, as is also the head. Finally the type genus *Platysomus*, in which the body is fully rhomboidal, is represented by *P. parvulus*, a species named on the evidence of specimens from the Knowles Ironstone Shale of Fenton. *Chirodus granulatus* is another member of the family of which remains have been obtained from the Staffordshire Carboniferous.

Towards the close of his career the late Mr. John Ward, who did so much for the palaeontology of the country, contributed (in conjunction with Mr. J. T. Stobbs) to the *Transactions of the North Staffordshire Field Club* [19] a paper on a newly discovered fish-bed in the Cheadle Coalfield, with notes on the distribution of fossil fishes in that district. The remains occur in a bed overlying the Cobble Coal, and are referable to *Acanthodes wardi*, *Gyracanthus fumosus*, *Lepracanthus colei*, *Pleuracanthus cylindricus*, *Pleuroplax rankinei*, *Helodus simplex*, *Sphenacanthus hybodoides*, *Ctenoptychius apicalis*, *Megalichthys hibberti*, *M. coccolepis* (?), *Strepsodus sauroides*, *Elonichthys semistriatus*, *E. aitkini*, *Platysomus parvulus*, and *Coelacanthus elegans*. All are well-known species, but a few, like *Lepracanthus colei*, are unknown elsewhere in the county.

[19] Vol. xi, 87 (1905-6).

BOTANICAL DISTRICTS

LIST OF BOTANICAL DISTRICTS
Based on the River Basins

I. *Weaver*
II. *Dove*
III. *Trent*
IV. *Sow*
V. *Severn*

SCALE 4 MILES TO AN INCH

THE VICTORIA HISTORY OF THE COUNTIES OF ENGLAND

BOTANY

GENERAL PHYSICAL CHARACTER OF THE COUNTY WITH RELATION TO THE FLORA

STAFFORDSHIRE is rhomboidal in shape and somewhat irregular in outline ; its surface is richly undulating and greatly diversified. The long range of hills extending from the Cheviots in Scotland southward enters Staffordshire at the extreme north, and forms a range of mountain-like hills having a south-west direction from above Flash to below Bosley, and rising from 600 to over 1,700 feet above sea level. On the north-west side of the county this elevated ridge is continued past Cloud Hill and over Congleton Edge and Mow Cop, and the elevation in many places is over 1,000 feet above the sea. The prevailing geological character of the rocks are those of the Coal Measures and Millstone Grit, and the prevailing vegetation is that peculiar to the mountain moorland, such as the black crowberry (*Empetrum nigrum*), the whortleberry (*Vaccinium Vitis-Idæa*), ling (*Calluna Vulgaris*), heath (*Erica cinerea*), bilberry (*Vaccinium Myrtillus*), an abundant growth of bracken (*Pteris aquilina*), thin grass, grey lichens and dark masses of hair moss (*Polytrichum commune*). A narrow belt of mixed woodland, Forest Banks and Back Forest clothe a portion of the summit above Swithamley. Here is found the cow wheat (*Melampyrum pratense*), moss crop (*Scirpus cæspitosus*) and the hawkweed (*Hieracium umbellatum*). The intervening valleys have a somewhat impervious subsoil, and are watered by frequent springs, which render them swampy, hence many of the bog-loving species are abundant, as sheep's rot (*Hydrocotyle vulgaris*), sundew (*Drosera rotundifolia*), the arrow grass (*Triglochin palustre*) and the pearl wort (*Sagina nodosa*). A ridge of high land, over which the high road from Leek to Buxton is carried, rising from 500 feet at Leek to about 1,400 feet at Axe Edge, forms the partings of the Dane and several of the important rivers of the county—the Dove, Manyfold, Churnet and Hamps. The country they water is wild flat lands, grass lands, moors and some little arable land, with small woodlands and several round topped hills, attaining in places an elevation of 1,200 to 1,300 feet above the sea. These hills are covered with short herbage, beautifully green in the early season, but soon scorched in the hotter months of summer. The limestone rock is abundantly exposed on their sides, and many of the more rare lime-loving species have here their home, such as wild pansy (*Viola lutea*), the rock rose (*Helianthemum vulgare*), the Jacob's ladder (*Polemonium cæruleum*), *Corydalis claviculata* and the rare little *Hutchinsia petræa*.

The country around is broken by deep valleys, dales or gullies, watered by rivers and rivulets, in which are found the trailing stems of the water milfoil (*Myriophyllum spicatum*) or streaming stems of water ranunculus (*Ranunculus pseudo-fluitans*), and on the marshy moorlands the golden saxifrage (*Chrysosplenium alternifolium*), the marsh violet (*Viola palustris*) and the beautiful grass of Parnassus (*Parnassia palustris*). In the beautiful Dove dale the limestone rocks have been rent by the geological convulsions of nature, and present their naked faces or escarpments in the form of perpendicular rocks rising high above the level of the stream, attaining an elevation of over 1,000 feet above sea level, to which many fanciful names have been given. These rocks, abounding in fissures, are the homes of many of the rarest plants of the district, as the hairy violet (*Viola hirta*), the barberry (*Berberis vulgaris*), the wall whitlow grass (*Draba muralis*), the rare bitter cress (*Cardamine impatiens*), the kidney vetch (*Anthyllis Vulneraria*) and the dwarf furze (*Ulex nanus*). In the valleys of the Hamps and Manyfold are similar mountain limestone rocks, fantastic in appearance, one of the more notable being Beeston Tor. Here is found the wild pansy (*Viola lutea*), the white beam (*Pyrus Aria*) and the mossy saxifrage (*Saxifraga hypnoides*), and on Ecton Hill the vernal sandwort (*Arenaria verna*). South of this are the fine limestone eminences, the Weaver Hills, rising to some 1,150 feet above the sea, clothed with rich grass in spring, but very bare in the hotter months, and with abundant exposed rocky surfaces, affording a home for many of the limestone loving species, such as the rock rose (*Helianthemum vulgare*), the dropwort (*Spiræa Filipendula*), the sandwort (*Arenaria tenuifolia*), the autumn gentian (*Gentiana Amarella*), the field gentian (*G. campestris*) and the long-stalked crane's bill (*Geranium columbinum*). In the southern portion of the county, south-west of Rugeley, the country though richly undulating rarely rises to greater altitudes than from 600 to 800 feet above sea level. Here are a series of round topped hills, a portion of the extensive Cannock Chase. These are usually clothed with thin grass, abundant bracken (*Pteris aquilina*), and grey with a rich clothing of ling (*Calluna vulgaris*), heath (*Erica cinerea* and *E. tetralix*), with dark green bushes of crowberry (*Empetrum nigrum*), the whortleberry (*Vaccinium Vitis-Idæa*), and here and there gay with the golden flowers of the broom (*Cytisus scoparius*), but with furze and bramble really rare ; very well wooded in parts with oak, elm and pine, and with a rich undergrowth of bilberry and bracken and often bluebells (*Scilla nutans*). In the valleys between the hills are swampy grass lands, watered by small rapid streams and rich in marsh plants, as the forget-me-not (*Myosotis palustris*), and here also the bog asphodel (*Narthecium ossifragum*), the grass of Parnassus (*Parnassia palustris*), the marsh violet (*Viola palustris*) and the trailing stems of the cranberry are abundant. South-west of this are the limestone hills of Dudley Castle and Sedgley Beacon. These are slight elevations, but appear more elevated by contrast with the low level of most of the country around. Dudley Castle is 730 feet above the sea, and its ruins were formerly the home of *Cheiranthus Cheiri*, and in the grounds is the toothwort (*Lathræa Squamaria*) and the deadly nightshade (*Atropa Bella-donna*). Sedgley Beacon is about 716 feet above the sea, the limestone quarries there being the home of the rare woolly thistle (*Carduus hetero-phyllus*), the hawkweed (*Picris hieracioides*), the mignonette (*Reseda lutea*), the gromwell (*Lithospermum officinale*) and the rare soft rose (*Rosa mollis*). The igneous rocks of Rowley Regis (820 ft.) do not harbour any special plants.

In several places in the county salt springs exist, and at Shirley Wich, Ingestre and Salt are the seat of extensive salt works. In these localities maritime plants have been found and sometimes in abundance ; these are lingerers possibly of a former rich maritime flora. Among the more notable are the sea aster (*Aster Tripolium*), the sea milkwort (*Glaux maritima*), the stork's-bill (*Erodium maritimum*), the sea sandwort (*Spergu-laria maritima*) and the celery *Apium graveolens*. Near these localities is Kingston Pool near Stafford, formerly an extensive sheet of water yielding many salt loving plants, as *Erodium maritimum*, sea sedge (*Scirpus maritimus*) and the sea dock (*Rumex maritimus*) ; and at Branstone near Burton-on-Trent salt springs also exist, and here are found *R. maritimus* and the celery *Apium graveolens*.

Marshes and bogs have in former times been extensive in many of the districts, more especially in the north and north-west, where even in comparatively recent times extensive moorlands existed ; but drainage, reclamation and the growth of centres of industry have greatly lessened their area. The remains of what have been extensive bogs or mosses are still found near Biddulph and Congleton Edge, where are the rare marsh hawkweed (*Crepis paludosa*), the golden saxifrage (*Chrysosplenium oppositi-folium*), sheep's penny rot (*Hydrocotyle vulgaris*) and the pondweed *Pota-mogeton rufescens*.

About Betley and Madeley much of the moorland is still marsh and bog, as at Craddock's Moss, formerly very extensive and the home of many rare bog plants, as the bladderwort (*Utricularia minor*), the bogbell (*Andromeda Polifolia*), grass of Parnassus (*Parnassia palustris*), the rare water soldier (*Stratiotes aloides*), the sundew (*Drosera longifolia*) and the small reed mace (*Typha angustifolia*) ; and a most notable marshy bog still exists near the ancient Chartley Castle, Chartley Moss. Here until lately the surroundings remained in their primitive condition, and many of the rarest paludal plants were to be found, such as the marsh St. John's wort (*Hypericum elodes*), the cranberry (*Vaccinium oxy-coccus*), the bog pimpernel (*Anagalis tenella*), the bogbell (*Andromeda Polifolia*), the fen sedge (*Cladium Mariscus*), the royal fern (*Osmunda regalis*) ; and in the adjoining woods, the rare shield ferns, *Nephrodium cristatum*, *N. Thelypteris* and *N. Oreopteris*. In the southern part of the county was an extensive morass, Norton Bog, now a great mining centre ; but here still linger noticeable bog plants, as the black schœnus (*Schœnus nigricans*), the butter wort (*Pinguicula vulgaris*), the marsh violet (*Viola palustris*), the marsh crowfoot (*Ranunculus Lenormandi*) and the marsh bedstraw (*Galium uliginosum*) ; and a small marsh near Penkridge has yielded one of our rarest marsh plants, *Elatine Hydropiper*.

There are no natural lakes in Staffordshire, but many of the pools are natural and some of them extensive and like lakes in character. The large lake at Rudyard is purely artificial and has been formed by damming up a deep valley. Swampy places are on its margins, where are found the mud wort (*Limosella aquatica*), the marsh cinquefoil (*Comarum palustre*), the money wort (*Lysimachia vulgaris*), and on the bank the trailing stems of *Corydalis claviculata*. On the north-west borders at Betley and Balterly are large pools where are found several water-loving plants as the white water lily (*Nymphæa alba*), the sweet flag (*Acorus Calamus*) and the frog bit (*Hydrocharis Morsus-Ranæ*), and in the valley of the Sow is the natural pool, Copmere Pool, very picturesque, clothed with a fringe of tall rushes and bulrushes, and in its waters a too abundant growth of *Anacharis* ; here are also *Ranunculus circinatus*, the pond weed *Potamogeton filiforme*, and all the British duck weeds (*Lemna trisulca, L. gibba, L. polyrhizza* and *L. minor*). Near this is the large pool of Maer, in which is an abundant growth of sweet flag (*Acorus Calamus*), and on its banks the trailing St. John's wort (*Hypericum humifusum*). In the park at Trentham is a fine lake-like pool formed by the river Trent. This is beautifully reed grown and fringed with the flowering rush (*Butomus umbellatus*), the arrow-head (*Sagittaria sagittifolia*), the rare bur reed (*Sparganium neglectum*), wood sedge (*Scirpus sylvaticus*), wood rush (*Luzula sylvatica*), and the rare pillwort (*Pilularia pilulifera*). But the finest natural sheet of water in the county is the large one, perfectly oval in form, called Aqualate Mere, which is one mile long and half a mile broad ; the margins are marshy and yield much floral wealth ; here are found the water violet (*Hottonia palustris*), the brook weed (*Samolus Valerandi*), the reed grasses *Calamagrostis Epigejos* and *C. lanceolatus*, and on the banks the wild liquorice (*Astragalus glycyphyllos*), the spindle tree (*Euonymus europæus*), the bog myrtle (*Myrica gale*), and the narrow-leaved reed mace (*Typha angustifolia*) ; near here is Forton Pool, where are the pondweeds *Potamogeton heterophyllus* and *P. pectinatus*. In the south-west of the county is Perton Pool ; here are the mare's tail (*Hippurus vulgaris*), and the rare water milfoil (*Myriophyllum verticillatum*), and on the confines of Birmingham is Harborn reservoir, where are *Ranunculus circinatus* and the rare mousetail (*Myosurus minimus*). The woodlands of Staffordshire are extensive, forming indeed one-twentieth of the whole area ; those of the southern portion of the county are usually destitute of any special wild flora, though often beautiful in the summer by the abundance of wild hyacinth (*Scilla nutans*), but in the north the woodlands are extensive and are the homes of some of our rarer native plants. The woods near Belmont in the valley of the Churnet possess craggy ravines watered by rapid streams, their banks clothed with a rich abundance of wild vegetation, and here are found the globe flower (*Trollius europæus*), the bear's foot (*Helleborus fœtidus*), the everlasting pea (*Lathyrus Nissolia*) and the London pride (*Saxifraga umbrosa*) ; and in the rich woods about Frog Hall and Oakamore are water-worn ravines yielding a wealth of rare plants, as the mountain nightshade (*Circæa alpina*), the mountain polypody (*Polypodium Dryopteris*), the winter green (*Pyrola rotundifolia*), the mountain valerian (*Valeriana pyrenaica*), sweet Cicely (*Myrrhis odorata*), the bladder fern (*Cystopteris fragilis*) and *Veronica Buxbaumia*; and on the rocks near Alton Castle the deadly nightshade (*Atropa Belladonna*). On the north-west side of the county are the extensive woodlands about Whitmore, where are the smaller skullcap (*Scutellaria minor*), abundance of woodruff (*Asperula odorata*) and the rare bramble *Rubus suberectus*. South of this is Bishop's Wood; here are found the columbine (*Aquilegia vulgaris*), the stork's bill (*Erodium moschatum*), the bog bean (*Menyanthes trifoliata*), the sundew (*Drosera rotundifolia*) and the shield ferns *Nephrodium filix-mas* and *N. spinulosum*. Near High Offley are the woods around Norbury, rich in rare brambles such as *Rubus Lejeuni, R. hirtus* and *R. Bellardi,* and near the large pool the sedges *Carex stricta* and *C. teretiuscula* and the rare water dropwort *Œnanthe Phellandrium*. In the south-west of the county in the valley of the small river Smestow are extensive woodlands around Himley and Bagginton; here are found the elecampane (*Inula Helenium*), the rare white mullein (*Verbascum Lychnites*), the mignonette (*Reseda lutea*), herb Paris (*Paris quadrifolia*), the lily of the valley (*Convallaria majalis*) and the rare *Lonicera Xylosteum*; on the south-eastern side of the county are extensive elevated woodlands, the remains of the great forest of Needwood, where are still found lingerers of a former rich sylvan flora, as the needle furze (*Genista anglica*), the small-leaved lime (*Tilia parvifolia*), frog orchis (*Habernaria viridis*), mezerion (*Daphne Mezereon*), Jacob's ladder (*Polemonium cæruleum*), the borage (*Borago officinale*) and the burnet saxifrage (*Pimpinella major*).

A comparison may be made here between the flora of Staffordshire and that of the surrounding counties. Staffordshire has 94 plants not found in Worcestershire, 70 not recorded from Warwickshire, 118 not recorded from Leicestershire, 168 not recorded from Derbyshire, 121 not recorded from Cheshire, and 106 not recorded from Shropshire. Worcestershire has 65 not recorded from Staffordshire, Warwickshire 65, Leicestershire 50, Derbyshire 26, Cheshire 85, and Shropshire 38. The total flora of Staffordshire is 948 species, including flowering plants, ferns, horsetails and charas. The total flora of Great Britain is 1,958 species; hence it will be seen that Staffordshire yields less than half the British species.

From its central position it naturally possesses a large percentage of the common or British type, namely 515 out of 532 for the whole kingdom; of the southern or English type 295 out of 409, one-eighth of the western type, one-sixth of the eastern type, and about one-eighth of the northern type.

The botanical districts are based on the river basins. These are: 1, the Weaver; 2, the Dove; 3, the Trent; 4, the Sow; 5, the Severn. With the exception of the Dane all the rivers of Staffordshire rise within the limits of the county, and nearly all have their whole course in the county and are tributary to the Trent. By an Act of Parliament, 1897, the small peninsula-like prolongation of Staffordshire in which Upper Arley is situated has been added to Worcestershire, so that the Severn proper flows through no portion of the county, but drains a portion of the west and south-west by streams tributary to the Severn.

1. The Weaver

The Weaver is a Cheshire river tributary to the Mersey, and is fed by the waters of several streams draining the north and north-west of Staffordshire. The most important is the Dane. This river enters Staffordshire at Three Shires Head north-east of Flash, and is a rapid mountain stream forming the boundary between Staffordshire and Cheshire from near Flash to below Bosley; here it passes into Cheshire, and after a long and varying course joins the Weaver near Northwick. It drains by numerous small tributaries a considerable portion of north Staffordshire, such as the country around Flash, Quarnford, the Roaches, Gradbach Hills, Swithamley, Rushton Marsh, and by an important stream rising on the east side of Mow Cop and Bradley Green, Gillow Heath and Biddulph. A portion of the county south-west of Biddulph is drained by small streams tributary to the Wheelock, which enters the Dane near Middlewick, and by Checkley Brook which joins the Weaver near Nantwich. These minor streams drain the country around Kidsgrove, Audley, Betley, Wrinehill, Madeley and the northern portion of Whitmore, a district rich in some of the rarer plants, among which are :—

Ranunculus fluitans	Andromeda polifolia	Utricularia vulgaris
Nymphæa alba	Vaccinium Vitis-Idæa	— minor
Empetrum nigrum	— Oxycoccus	Potamogeton rufescens
Cotyledon Umbilicus	Cynoglossum officinale	Osmunda regalis
Crepis paludosa		

2. The Dove

The Dove rises in a natural spring on Axe Edge at an elevation of 1,684 feet above sea level and enters the county near Patch Edge, and flows south-east through a narrow valley to Longnor, where it receives a small feeder from the west rising on the high ground near Quarnford. After flowing 4 miles through another narrow valley it passes near Hartington. From here its course is a little more south through Pike Pool in Berresford Dale and 2 miles further through the weird narrow dale, the entrance to which it appears to have carved out of the solid rock. From this it flows between the craggy hills of Mill Dale, and below the beautiful Alstonfield church to the wild and romantic Dove Dale. Dove Dale is nearly 3 miles long and is entered by a pathway between of lofty rocks and cliffs, surmounted by isolated crags called tors. The rocks are grand in aspect and covered with vegetation, trees and shrubs and smaller plants, many of them the rarest elements of the county flora, too frequently growing in inaccessible places. Here the Dove murmurs along over miniature falls and weirs, and amid boulders covered with rare cryptogamic wealth, with floating masses of *Ranunculus pseudo-fluitans* and the local float-grass *Glyceria fluitans*, and passing under Dove Bridge enters a broad fertile valley, and near Ilam is joined by its important affluent the Manyfold. The Manyfold is formed by streams rising in the moorlands near Flash and near Croft Bottom, and flows south-east by Wiltshaw Hill and east through part of Longnor, then south through Ludbourne and Brund to Hulme End. Here the limestone hills divert its course south-west by Ecton Hill, near where it is fed by Blake brook and Warslow brook, draining a large extent of country around Warslow; thence flowing through the beautiful Wetton valley, past Ossum's Hill and Thor's Cave to Beeston Tor, its bed unites with that of the Hamps. Near Wetton the river disappears for several miles, passing through an underground channel and emerging at Ilam. The Hamps rises on the wild moors south-west of the Manyfold and has a course of 5 miles south through Keywall Green to Onecote; it then flows eastward through Ford, then west through Winkshill; here the high limestone hills divert its course easterly by Crowtrees and Waterhouses to Stoneyrock, where its course becomes northward through a beautiful rocky valley of about 3 miles to the union of its bed with that of the Manyfold at Beeston Tor. This river near here disappears for several miles and emerges at Ilam, where it unites with the Manyfold, and the united stream joins the Dove near Thorpe. The Dove now continues its southward course near Okeover, Mayfield and Rocester, near where it is joined by the Churnet. The Churnet rises on the moorlands near Stoke Gutter and has a westerly course of about 4 miles to Tettesworth Reservoir, where it receives waters from Leek Frith and takes a southerly course through Tettesworth Reservoir, then westerly past Leek and near Rudyard, receiving waters from Wolf Low and Fair Edge, and here turns southward past Longsdon and then flows south and south-west through Cheddleton, Kingsley, Oakamore and Alton to its confluence with the Dove below Rocester. The beautiful Churnet valley from Cheddleton to beyond Alton is formed by high rocks and rocky woods, with deep rocky ravines whose steep banks are clothed with trees, shrubs and rare wild flowers and mosses. Emerging from the hills the Churnet flows through a wide expanse of flat lands and enters the Dove below Rocester. Still flowing south past Uttoxeter the Dove receives two small feeders, Tean brook and Stoneyford brook, draining the country around Cheadle, Leigh and Uttoxeter ; the Dove now flows south-east past Marchington, Draycote and Tutbury, and enters the Trent near Newton Solney. The total length of the Dove is 45 miles ; it has a fall of 1,550 feet from its source to its mouth, and drains nearly 400 square miles of country. The following are some of its rarer plants :—

Helleborus fœtidus	Anthyllis vulneraria	Polemonium ceruleum
Fumaria Vaillantii	Lathyrus Nissolia	Veronica polita
Arabis hirsuta	Prunus Padus	Salvia Verbenaca
Cardamine impatiens	Rubus gratus	Daphne Mezereon
Draba muralis	— Leyanus	Carex pallescens
Helianthemum vulgare	— serpens	Avena pratensis
Viola hirta	— saxatilis	Melica nutans
Silene nutans	Rosa involuta	Polypodium calcareum
Stellaria nemorum	Saxifraga umbrosa	Botrychium Lunaria
Geranium pusillum	Doronicum Pardialianches	Lycopodium clavatum
— columbinum		

3. THE TRENT

The Trent rises in the north-west of the county between Biddulph and Mow Cop at about 700 feet above sea level. The stream almost immediately passes into Knypersley Pools, where several streams unite, with the surplus water proceeding from Biddulph Moor. The Trent now flows on 3 miles to Norton, below which a considerable tributary comes in called Fowlea, which rises near the Trent source, and flows through a parallel valley. The united stream flows about 3 miles to Stoke-upon-Trent, passing the town of Hanley and a long line of thickly-populated country, which it leaves to the west. Beyond Stoke it flows 2 miles further to Hanford, where it receives the Lyme from the north, a brook about 5 miles long flowing near Newcastle. A short distance from this it enters Trentham Park, where it forms a lake of about 80 acres. After leaving Trentham it flows near Barlaston, being fed by waters from the high lands about Hilderstone, and passing west of Stone it flows south-east near Sandon, Salt and Weston-on-Trent, being joined by Amerton brook and Gayton brook on its left bank and waters from Ingestre and Tixall on its right bank, and at Great Heywood is joined on its right bank by its important tributary the Sow. From its confluence with the Sow it still flows south-east through Rugeley, receiving on its right bank the Sherbrook, which waters a rich botanical valley on Cannock Chase, and flowing through Armitage its course becomes more easterly by Pipe Ridware, where it is joined by the river Blythe. The Blythe rises north-east of Chartley Park and flows south-east towards Leigh and through Gradwich and Grindley under Blithe Bridge, near Blithford Hall and through Blithford and Sandborough to its confluence with the Trent near Kings Bromley, being fed by waters from Chartley, Bagot Wood, Rake End and Kingston. The Trent now flows west near Wichnor Park, and above Alrewas to its confluence with the Tame near Croxall. The Tame rises north of Pelsall in the south of Cannock Chase, collecting waters from the Silurian Hills about Dudley and also from the country east of Wolverhampton and from the western ridge of Hamstead Hill and Walsall. These numerous feeders join the Tame near West Bromwich, and the Tame flowing through Perry Barr enters Warwickshire at Witton. Flowing through Castle Bromwich, Curdworth and Fazely it re-enters Staffordshire at Tamworth, receiving here an important tributary, Black brook, which drains a large extent of country about Chesterfield, Stonnall, Weeford and Hints, and passing through Drayton Park unites with the Tame near Fazeley. The Tame then flows through Elford to its confluence with the Trent near Croxall.

The Trent now makes a sharp turn to the north and takes the direction of the Tame at the confluence. After a further flow of 6 miles it reaches Burton-on-Trent, and 2 miles lower receives the Dove. The area drained by the Trent is about 800 square miles, and in a distance of about 50 miles the bed of the river has fallen from 700 feet above sea to 180 feet, most part of this fall of 520 feet occurring in the first 11 miles, between the source and the confluence with Fowlea brook, where the bed of the stream is not more than 370 feet above sea. The mean fall of the first 5 miles of the Trent is at the rate of nearly 50 feet to the mile, and of the next five of 18 feet. After this the fall nowhere exceeds 8 feet to a mile. The following are some of the more noteworthy species :—

Myosurus minimus	Rosa rubiginosa	Habenaria conopsea
Ranunculus Lingua	Sedum Telephium	Galanthus nivalis
Cheiranthus Cheiri	Drosera intermedia	Fritillaria Meleagris
Lepidium ruderale	Carum segetum	Acorus Calamus
Dianthus Armeria	Sambucus Ebulus	Triglochin maritimum
Hypericum elodes	Carduus eriophorus	Scirpus pauciflorus
Radiola Millegrana	Lactuca virosa	Agrostis fulvus
Genista anglica	Campanula hederacea	Polypodium Dryopteris
Trifolium striatum	Andromedia polifolia	Lycopodium Selago
Rubus suberectus	Linaria repens	Nitella flexilis
— micans	Scutellaria minor	— opaca
Rosa mollis	Orchis pyramidalis	

4. THE SOW

The Sow rises about 1 mile south-west of Hookham in a spring called Sowhead, 617 feet above sea, and flows south by Bishop's Wood and New Inn Bank ; here its course turns eastward above Bishop's Offley and through Copmere and north of Eccleshall, where it receives a stream coming from the north near Foxley ; still flowing south-east to Worston Mill it is joined by a considerable stream, Meece brook, from the north-west. The Meece originates from three small streams south-west of Keel Park ; these unite near Whitmore, passing through the large pool in Whitmore Park and running parallel with the railway for several miles, flowing through Mill Mease and Norton Bridge, receiving tributaries on either side and draining a wide area east and west. The Sow now flows through Great Bridgeford and Stafford, being fed by waters from Seighford and on the east from Marstone. Below Stafford the Penk enters its right bank from the south-west. The Penk rises north-west of Wolverhampton, and is joined by Billbrook near Codsall, and flows north through Brewood and Penkridge, bringing waters from Teddesley, Acton Trussell and Radford, north of which village it enters the Sow, draining a wide extent of country around Gnosall and Blymhill and the west portion of Cannock Chase. The Sow continues to flow south-east to its union with the Trent at Great Heywood, at an elevation of 238 feet above the sea.

The Sow has a course of 20 miles, draining about 150,130 acres; it flows through a comparatively flat country and has a fall of about 380 feet. The following are some of the more noticeable plants :—

Ranunculus hirsutus	Rubus Boreanus	Glaux maritima
Sisymbrium Sophia	— crineger	Limosella aquatica
Lepidium hirtum	— Bloxamianus	Orobanche major
Cerastium quaternellum	Rosa coriifolia	Quercus sessiliflora
Geranium lucidum	Myriophyllum verticillatum	Sparganium minimum
Erodium moschatum	Œnanthe Phellandrium	Sagittaria sagittifolia
Elatine Hydropiper	Anthemis nobilis	Calamagrostis lanceolata
Euonymus europæus	Specularia hybrida	Pilularia globulifera
Onobrychis sativa	Pyrola rotundifolia	Chara fragilis

5. THE SEVERN

The Severn drains a large portion of the west and south-west of Staffordshire by small streams, which are the tributaries of larger streams flowing in Shropshire ; that portion of the county south-west of Wolverhampton is watered by the two small rivers, the Smestow and Stour.

The river Tern is a brook-like stream, forming the boundary between Shropshire and Staffordshire for many miles, that is from Willoughby Wells to a point south-east of Market

BOTANY

Drayton, and is fed by streams from Maer and west of Fair Oak. The Meese, a tributary to the Tern, receives Lanco brook, draining Offley Marsh, High Offley and the surrounding country, and has feeders from Norbury and Oulton ; and Dawford brook, draining Weston under Lizard and part of Blymhill, and flowing through Aqualate Mere, enters the Meese near Forton. Farther south the county is watered by the Stour and its affluents. The Stour enters the county east of Cradley, forming the county boundary for several miles, and drains a thickly populated district, yielding little of interest except the ever present coltsfoot, and passing through Stourbridge and Prestwood is joined by the small river Smestow at Stourton. The Smestow with its affluents is far reaching, receiving waters from Patingham, Wolverhampton, the west side of Dudley, Himley, Trysull and Enville, and at Stourton joins the Stour. The Stour here takes the course of the Smestow, and flowing through Kinver and part of Worcestershire joins the Severn at Stourport.

The following are some of the more rare plants of this district :—

Ranunculus parviflorus	Hypericum Androsæmum	Utricularia neglecta
Aquilegia vulgaris	Erodium maritimum	Myrica Gale
Diplotaxis tenuifolia	Lathyrus Aphaca	Habenaria albida
Senebiera didyma	Rubus curvidens	Sparganium minimum
Reseda lutea	— Babingtonii	Potamogeton trichodes
Viola canina	Potentilla procumbens	Carex teretiuscula
Silene anglica	Rosa scabriuscula	Festuca elatior
Cerastium semidecandrum	Ribes rubrum	Asplenium Ceterach
— arvense	Caucalis nodosa	Chara hispida
Vicia lathyroides	Hippopithys multiflora	

SUMMARY OF ORDERS, NUMBER OF GENERA AND OF SPECIES IN EACH ORDER, Etc.

	Number of Genera	Number of Species	Excluded Species		Number of Genera	Number of Species	Excluded Species
CLASS I				Div. II. *Calycifloræ*			
DICOTYLYDONES OR EXOGENÆ				22. Celastrineæ . .	1	1	—
				23. Rhamneæ . . .	1	2	—
				24. Sapindaceæ . . .	1	1	1
Div. I. *Thalamifloræ*				25. Leguminosæ . .	15	40	6
1. Ranunculaceæ . .	10	30	2	26. Rosaceæ . . .	12	92	2
2. Berberideæ . . .	1	1	1	27. Saxifrageæ . . .	4	10	1
3. Nymphæaceæ . .	2	2	—	28. Crassulaceæ . .	2	5	2
4. Papaveraceæ . .	2	4	1	29. Droseraceæ. . .	1	2	—
5. Fumariaceæ . .	2	5	2	30. Halorageæ . . .	3	7	—
6. Cruciferæ . . .	19	42	7	31. Lythraceæ . . .	2	3	—
7. Resedaceæ . . .	1	2	—	32. Onagrarieæ . .	2	11	1
8. Cistineæ . . .	1	1	—	33. Cucubitaceæ . .	1	1	—
9. Violaceæ . . .	1	8	—	34. Umbelliferæ . .	23	31	5
10. Polygaleæ . . .	1	2	—	35. Araliaceæ . . .	1	1	—
12. Caryophylleæ . .	12	37	2	36. Cornaceæ . . .	1	1	—
13. Portulaceæ . . .	1	1	2				
14. Elatineæ . . .	1	1	—	Div. III. *Corollifloræ*			
15. Hypericineæ . .	1	8	—	37. Caprifoliaceæ . .	4	5	1
16. Malvaceæ . . .	1	3	1	38. Rubiaceæ . . .	3	11	—
17. Tiliaceæ . . .	1	1	1	39. Valerianeæ. . .	2	6	2
18. Lineæ	2	4	1	40. Dipsaceæ . . .	2	5	—
19. Geraniaceæ . .	4	13	1	41. Compositæ . . .	40	81	5
20. Ilicineæ	1	1	—	42. Campanulaceæ .	4	8	—
21. Empetraceæ . .	1	1	—	43. Ericaceæ . . .	5	11	1

	Number of Genera	Number of Species	Excluded Species		Number of Genera	Number of Species	Excluded Species
44. Monotropeæ	I	I	—	**CLASS II**			
46. Primulaceæ	7	12	—	MONOCOTYLEDONS			
47. Oleaceæ	2	2	—	Div. I. *Petaloideæ*			
48. Apocynaceæ	I	I	I	75. Hydrocharideæ	2	2	I
49. Gentianeæ	4	5	—	76. Orchideæ	8	18	—
50. Polemoniaceæ	I	I	—	77. Irideæ	I	I	2
51. Boragineæ	6	14	3	78. Amaryllideæ	2	2	2
52. Convolvulaceæ	2	3	I	79. Dioscoreæ	I	I	—
53. Solanaceæ	3	4	I	80. Liliaceæ	9	12	—
54. Plantagineæ	2	5	—	81. Junceæ	2	15	—
55. Scrophularineæ	13	34	2	83. Typhaceæ	2	7	—
56. Orobancheæ	I	2	—	84. Aroideæ	2	2	—
57. Lentibularineæ	2	4	—	85. Lemnaceæ	I	4	—
58. Verbenaceæ	I	I	—	86. Alismaceæ	3	4	—
59. Labiatæ	15	34	5	87. Naiadaceæ	3	19	—
Div. IV. *Monochlamydeæ*				**Div. II. *Glumaceæ***			
60. Illecebraceæ	2	2	—	88. Cyperaceæ	7	51	—
61. Chenopodiaceæ	2	9	—	89. Gramineæ	32	67	3
62. Polygonaceæ	2	20	I	**CLASS III**			
64. Thymelæaceæ	I	2	—	ACOTYLEDONS OR CRYPTOGAMIA			
66. Loranthaceæ	I	I	—				
68. Euphorbiaceæ	3	7	I	**Div. I. *Vasculares***			
69. Urticaceæ	3	6	—	90. Filices	12	27	—
70. Myricaceæ	I	I	—	91. Equisetaceæ	I	6	—
71. Cupuliferæ	6	8	—	92. Lycopodiaceæ	I	3	—
72. Salicineæ	2	21	—	94. Marsileaceæ	I	I	—
73. Ceratophylleæ	I	I	—	**Div. II. *Cellulares***			
Div. V. *Gymnospermæ*				95. Characeæ	2	6	—
74. Coniferæ	3	3	—				

SUMMARY OF THE GEOGRAPHICAL DISTRIBUTION OF SPECIES AND VARIETIES[1]

RANUNCULACEÆ

Clematis Vitalba, L.   3–5
Thalictrum flavum, L.   3–5
Anemone nemorosa, L.   1–5
[Adonis autumnalis], L.   3
Myosurus minimus, L.   3, 5
Ranunculus circinatus, Sibth.   2–5
— fluitans, Lam.   1–5
   b. Bachii, Wirtg.   2, 3, 5
— pseudo-fluitans, Bab.   2, 3, 5
— trichophyllus, Chaix.   4, 5
— Drouettii, Godr.   3–5
   b. Godronii, Gren.   4
— heterophyllus, Web.   2
— peltatus, Schrank.   2–4
   b. truncatus, Hiern.   3, 4
   c. floribundus, Bab.   1–5
   d. penicillatus, Hiern.   2
— Lenormandi, F. Schultz.   1–5
— hederaceus, L.   1–5

Ranunculus sceleratus, L.   1–5
— Flammula, L.   1–5
   b. pseudo-reptans, Syme.   2
— Lingua, L.   3–5
— auricomus, L.   2–5
— acris, L.   1–5
— repens, L.   1–5
— bulbosus, L.   1–5
— hirsutus, Curtis.   3–5
— parviflorus, L.   2–5
— arvensis, L.   2–5
— Ficaria, L.   1–5
Caltha palustris, L.   1–5
   b. Guerangerii, Bor.   3
Trollius europæus, L.   2
Helleborus viridis, L.   2, 3
— fœtidus, L.   2
Aquilegia vulgaris, L.   3–5
[Delphinium Ajacis], Reichb.   3
Aconitum Napellus, L.   2, 3

[1] The numbers refer to the botanical districts.

BOTANY

51

Sagina apetala, L.   2–4
— ciliata, Fries.   3, 5
— procumbens, L.   1–5
— subulata, Presl.   2, 3
— nodosa, E. Mey.   2–5
Spergula arvensis a. vulgaris, Boenn.   1–5
        b. sativa, Boenn.   3, 5
Spergularia rubra, Pers.   1–5
— salina, Presl.   3

PORTULACEÆ

Montia fontana, L., a. repens, Pers.   1–5
        b. rivularis, Gmel.   3–5
[Claytonia perfoliata], Donn.   3
[— Sibirica], L.   3

ELATINEÆ

Elatine Hydropiper, L.   4

HYPERICINEÆ

Hypericum Androsæmum, L.   3–5
— perforatum, L.   1–5
        b. angustifolium, Bab.   5
— quadrangulum, L.   3–5
— tetrapterum, Fries.   3–5
— humifusum, L.   2–5
— pulchrum, L.   1–5
— hirsutum, L.   2–5
— montanum, L.   3
— elodes, Huds.   3, 5

MALVACEÆ

Malva moschata, L.   2–5
— sylvestris, L.   2–5
— rotundifolia, L.   3–5
[— alcea.]   3

TILIACEÆ

[Tilia vulgaris], Hayne.   1–5
— parvifolia, Ehrh.   3, 4

LINEÆ

Radiola linoides, Gmel.   3, 5
Linum catharticum, L.   1–5
— perenne, L.   3, 4
— angustifolium, L.   3
[— usitatissimum], L.   1–5

GERANIACEÆ

Geranium sylvaticum, L.   3
— pratense, L.   2–5
— perenne, Huds.   2, 5
[— Pheum.], L.   5
— molle, L.   1–5
— pusillum, L.   3–5
— columbinum, L.   2, 3, 5
— dissectum, L.   1–5
— Robertianum, L.   1–5
— lucidum, L.   2–4
Erodium cicutarium, L'Herit.   2–5
— moschatum, L'Herit.   4, 5
— maritimum, L'Herit.   3, 5
Oxalis Acetosella, L.   2–5
        forma subpurpurascens, DC.   1
[Impatiens parviflora], DC.   5

ILICINEÆ

Ilex Aquifolium, L.   1–5

EMPETRACEÆ

Empetrum nigrum, L.   1–3

CELESTRINEÆ

Euonymus europæus, L.   1–5

RHAMNEÆ

Rhamnus catharticus, L.   1–5
— Frangula, L.   1–5

SAPINDACEÆ

Acer campestre, L.   2–5
[— Pseudo-platanus], L.   1–5

LEGUMINOSÆ

Genista tinctoria, L.   2–5
— anglica, L.   2, 3, 5
Ulex europæus, L.   1–5
— nanus, Forst.   5
— Gallii, Planch.   2–5
Cytisus scoparius, Link.   1–5
Ononis spinosa, L.   2–4
— repens, L.   2, 3, 5
[Medicago sativa], L.   2, 3, 5
— lupulina, L.   1–5
— denticulata, Willd.   5
Melilotus altissima, Thuil.   2–4
— alba, Desr.   3–5
[— officinalis], Desr.   3, 4
[— parviflora], Lam.   5
Trifolium pratense, L.   1–5
— arvense, L.   2–5
[— incarnatum], L.   1, 2
— medium, Huds.   1–5
— striatum, L.   3, 4
— repens, L.   1–5
[— hybridum], L.   2, 3
— procumbens, L.   1–5
— dubium, Sibth.   1–5
— filiforme, L.   3, 5
Anthyllis Vulneraria, L.   2
Lotus corniculatus, L.   1–5
— tenuis, Waldst and Kit.   2, 4, 5
— uliginosus, Schk.   1–5
Astragalus glycyphyllos, L.   3–5
Ornithopus perpusillus, L.   2–5
Hippocrepis comosa, L.   2
Onobrychis sativa, Lamk.   4
Vicia tetrasperma, Mœnch.   2–4
— hirsuta, Koch.   1–5
— Cracca, L.   1–5
— sylvatica, L.   2, 3, 5
— sepium, L.   1–5
[— sativa], L.   2–4
— angustifolia, Roth.   1–5
        b. Bobartii, Forst.   3–5
— lathyroides, L.   4, 5
Lathyrus Aphaca, L.   5
— Nissolia, L.   2–4
— pratensis, L.   1–5
— sylvestris, L.   3
— macrorrhizus, Wimm.   2–5
        b. tenuifolius (Roth.).   2, 5

ROSACEÆ

Prunus communis, Huds.   1–5
— insititia, L.   3, 5

BOTANY

Prunus Avium, L.   2–5
— Cerasus, L.   4
— Padus, L.   2–5
Spiræa Ulmaria, L.   1–5
— Filipendula, L.   2, 3
[— salicifolia], L.   3
Rubus idæus, L.   1–5
— fissus, Lindl.   2, 3
— suberectus, Anders.   3, 5
— plicatus, W. & N.   1–3
— nitidus, W. & N.   3
— carpinifolius, W. & N.   1–4
— incurvatus, Bab.   3, 5
— Lindleianus, Lees.   1–5
— erythrinus, Genev.   3–5
— rhamnifolius, W. & N.   2–5
    b. Bakeri, F. A. Lees.   3–5
— nemoralis, P. J. Muell.   3
    b. glabratus, Bab.   3–5
— pulcherrimus, Neum.   1–5
— Lindebergii, P. J. Muell.   1–3, 5
— villicaulis, Kœhl.   2, 3, 5
    b. Selmeri, Lindeb.   1, 3–5
    c. insularis, F. Aresch.   3
    d. calvatus, Blox.   1–5
— gratus, Focke.   2
— argentatus, P. J. Muell.   3
    b. robustus, P. J. Muell.   3
— rusticanus, Merc.   1–5
— pubescens, Weihe.   2, 3
    b. subinermis, Rogers.   5
— thyrsoideus, Wimm.   5
— macrophyllus, W. & N.   3–5
    b. Schlectendalii, Weihe.   3
    d. amplificatus, Lees.   2–5
— Sprengelii, Weihe.   2–4
— micans, Gren. & Godr.   3
— hirtifolius, Muell & Wirt.   1, 3
— pyramidalis, Kalt.   1–5
— leucostachys, Schliech.   1–5
— Boræanus, Genev.   3–5
— curvidens, A. Ley.   3, 5
— mucronatus, Blox.   2–5
— Gelertii b. criniger, Linton.   2–5
— anglosaxonicus, Gelert.   2–5
    b. raduloides, Rogers.   1
— infestus, Weihe.   3–5
— Leyanus, Rogers.   2–4
— radula, Weihe.   1–5
    b. anglicanus, Rogers.   3–5
— podophyllus, P. J. Muell.   1–3
— echinatus, Lindl.   2–5
— oigoclados, Muell & Lefv.   3
    b. Newbouldii, Bab.   3–5
    c. Bloxamianus, Coleman.   4
— Babingtonii, Bell Salt.   3, 5
— Lejeunii b. ericetorum, Lefv.   5
— Bloxamii, Lees.   2–5
— scaber, W. & N.   2–5
— fuscus, W. & N.   3
    b. nutans, Rogers.   3
— pallidus, W. & N.   2, 5
— foliosus, W. & N.   4, 5
— rosaceus, W. & N.   2, 4, 5
    b. hystrix, W. & N.   1–5
    c. sylvestris, P. J. M.   3, 5

Rubus rosaceus, W. & N.
    e. infecundus, Rogers.   2–5
— adornatus, P. J. Muell.   3, 5
— Kœhleri, W. & N.   2, 3, 5
    c. dasyphyllus, Rogers.   1–5
— fusco-ater, Weihe.   3, 5
— Bellardi, W. & N.   2, 5
    b. dentatus, Bab.   4, 5
— serpens, Weihe.   2
— hirtus, W. & N.   5
    b. rotundifolius.   4, 5
    c. Kaltenbachii, Metsch.   3
— tereticaulis b. minutiflorus.   5
— dumetorum, W. & N.   3–5
    var diversifolius, Lindl.   2–5
    var. tuberculatus, Bab.   3–5
    var. concinnus, Warren.   2–5
    var. fasciculatus, P.J.M.   2–5
— corylifolius var. sublustris, Sm.   2–5
    var. cyclophyllus, Linden.   3
— Balfourianus, Blox.   2–5
— cæsius, L.   1–3, 5
    + tenuis, Bell Salt.   2, 3, 5
— saxatilis, L.   2
Geum urbanum, L.   1–5
— rivale, L.   2–5
    + intermedium, Ehrh.   4
Fragaria vesca, L.   1–5
Potentilla Comarum, Nestl.   2–5
— Tormentilla, Scop.   1–5
— procumbens, Sibth.   1, 5
    + mixta, Nalte.   3, 5
— reptans, L.   1–5
— anserina, L.   1–5
— Fragariastrum, Ehrh.   1–5
— argentea, L.   3, 5
Alchemilla arvensis, Lamk.   1–5
— vulgaris, L.   1–5
Agrimonia Eupatoria, L.   1–5
— odorata, Mill.   4
Poterium Sanguisorba, L.   2–4
[— muricata], Spach.   3
— officinale, Hook fil.   2–5
Rosa spinosissima, L.   2
— Sabini, Woods.   2
— rubiginosa, L.   2–5
— micrantha, Smith.   2, 4
— tomentosa, Smith.   2–5
    b. subglobosa, Smith.   1–4
    d. scabriuscula, Smith.   2–5
— canina a. lutetiana, Leman.   1–5
    c. sphærica, Gren.   2
    d. senticosa, Ach.   2
    e. dumalis, Bech.   1–5
    f. vinacea, Baker.   2
    g. urbica, Leman.   1–4
    h. frondosa, Steven.   1, 3
    i. arvatica, Baker.   2, 3
    j. dumetorum, Thuill.   1, 4
    k. obtusifolium, Desv.   3
    n. tomentilla, Leman.   3–5
    p. verticillacantha, Merat.   1–5
    q. collina, Jacq.   3
    s. cæsia, Smith.   3, 4
    v. glauca, Vill.   1–5
    w. subcristata, Baker.   2–5

Rosa canina
    x. coriifolia, Fr. 1–5
    y. Watsoni, Baker. 2, 3
    z. Borreri, Woods. 4
— arvensis, Huds. 1–5
Pyrus communis, L. 3, 4
— Malus *a*. acerba, DC. 1–5
    b. mitis, Wallr. 1, 2, 5
— torminalis, Ehrh. 2–5
— Aria, Ehrh. 1, 2
    b. rupicola, Syme. 2
    c. scandica, Syme. 5
— Aucuparia, Ehrh. 1–5
Cratægus Oxyacantha, L. 2, 3, 5
    var. laciniata, Wallr. 2
    var. monogyna, Jacq. 1–5

SAXIFRAGEÆ

Saxifraga umbrosa, L. 2
— tridactylites, L. 2–5
— granulata, L. 1–5
— hypnoides, L. 2
Chrysosplenium alternifolium, L. 2–4
— oppositifolium, L. 1–5
Parnassia palustris, L. 2–5
[Ribes Grossularia], L. 2–5
— alpinum, L. 2, 3
— rubrum, L. 4, 5
— nigrum, L. 3, 4

CRASSULACEÆ

Cotyledon Umbillicus, L. 1, 2
Sedum Telephium, L. 2–4
— album, L. 3
— acre, L. 2–4
[— reflexum], L. 1–4
[Sempervivum tectorum], L. 3

DROSERACEÆ

Drosera rotundifolia, L. 1, 3–5
— intermedia, Hayne. 2, 3, 5

HALORAGEÆ

Hippuris vulgaris, L. 4, 5
Myriophyllum verticillatum, L. 4, 5
— alterniflorum, DC. 3–5
— spicatum, L. 2, 3, 5
Callitriche platycarpa, Kuetz. 1–5
— hamulata, Kuetz. 2, 3
— obtusangula, Leg. 3

LYTHRARIEÆ

Lythrum Salicaria, L. 2–5
— hyssopifolia (?), L. 3
Peplis Portula, L. 2, 3

ONAGRARIEÆ

Epilobium angustifolium, L. 2–5
— hirsutum, L. 1–5
— parviflorum, Schreb. 1–5
— montanum, L. 1–5
— roseum, Schreb. 2, 3
    f. roseum obscurum. 3
— obscurum, Schreb. 2, 3
— tetragonum, L. 3, 5
— palustre, L. 3–5
[Œnothera biennis], L. 3

Circæa lutetiana, L. 2–5
— intermedia, L. C. 2
— alpina, L. 1, 2

CUCUBITACEÆ

Bryonia dioica, L. 3–5

UMBELLIFERÆ

Hydrocotyle vulgaris, L. 1–5
Sanicula europæa, L. 2–5
Conium maculatum, L. 1–5
[Smyrnium Olusatrum], L. 3
Apium graveolens, L. 2, 3
— nodiflorum, Reichb. 1–5
    b. repens, Hook fil. 3, 4
— inundatum, Reichb. 2, 3, 5
Cicuta virosa, L. 3, 4
[Carum Petroselinum], B. & H. 2
— segetum, B. & H. 2, 3
[— Carui], L. 3, 5
Sison Amomum, L. 4
Sium angustifolium, L. 2–5
Ægopodium Podagraria, L. 1–5
Pimpinella Saxifraga, L. 2–5
— magna, Huds. 2–5
Conopodium denudatum, Koch. 1–5
Myrrhis odorata, Scop. 1–4
Chærophyllum temulum, L. 1–5
Scandix Pecten-Veneris, L. 1–5
Anthriscus vulgaris, Pers. 3, 4
— sylvestris, Hoffm. 1–5
Œnanthe fistulosa, L. 2–5
— crocata, L. 3, 5
— Phellandrium, Lam. 2, 4, 5
Æthusa Cynapium, L. 1–5
Silaus pratensis, Bess. 2–5
Angelica sylvestris, L. 1–5
[Archangelica officinalis], Hoff. 3
[Peucedanum Ostruthium], Koch. 2, 3
— sativum, Benth. 2–5
Heracleum Sphondylium, L. 1–5
Daucus Carota, L. 1–5
Caucalis Anthriscus, Huds. 1–5
— arvensis, Huds. 2–5
— nodosa, Scop. 2, 5

ARALIACEÆ

Hedera Helix, L. 1–5

CORNACEÆ

Cornus sanguinea, L. 2–5

CAPRIFOLIACEÆ

Viburnum Opulus, L. 1–5
Sambucus Ebulus, L. 2, 3
— nigra, L. 1–5
Adoxa Moschatellina, L. 1–5
Lonicera Periclymenum, L. 1–5
[— xylosteum], L. 3, 5

RUBIACEÆ

Galium verum, L. 1–5
— cruciata, Scop. 1–5
— palustre, L. 1–5
    b. elongatum, Presl. 2, 5
    c. Witheringii, Sm. 3, 5
— uliginosum, L. 5
— saxatile, L. 1–5

Galium sylvestre, Poll. **2**
— Mollugo, L. **2**, 3, 5
— erectum, Huds. 3
— Aparine, L. 1–5
Asperula odorata, L. 2–5
Sherardia arvensis, L. 1–5

VALERIANEÆ

Valeriana dioica, L. 1–5
— Mikani, Syme. **2**
— sambucifolia, Willd. 2–5
[— pyrenaica], L. **2**
[Centranthus ruber], DC. **2**
Valerianella olitoria, Poll. 2–4
— dentata, Poll. 2–4
    b. mixta, Dufr. 2, 3
— eriocarpa, Desv. 2, 3

DIPSACEÆ

Dipsacus sylvestris, L. 2–5
— pilosus, L. 2–5
Scabiosa succisa, L. 3, 5
— Columbaria, L. **2**
— arvensis, L. 1–5

COMPOSITÆ

Eupatorium cannabinum, L. 1–5
Aster Tripolium, L. 3, 4
Erigeron acre, L. 2, 3, 5
[— canadense], L. 3
Bellis perennis, L. 1–5
Solidago Virgaurea, L. 2, 3, 5
Inula Conyza, DC. 5
— Helenium, L. 1, 5
Pulicaria dysenterica, Gært. 1–5
Gnaphalium sylvaticum, L. 3, 5
— uliginosum, L. 1–5
Antennaria dioica, Br. **2**
[— margaritacea], Br. **2**
Filago germanica, L. 1–5
— minima, Fr. 2, 3, 5
Bidens cernua, L. 2–5
    b. radiata, Sond. 4
— tripartita, L. 2, 3, 5
Anthemis arvensis, L. 2–5
— Cotula, L. 1–5
— nobilis, L. 3–5
Achillea Ptarmica, L. 3–5
— Millefolium, L. 1–5
Matricaria Chamomilla, L. 2–5
— inodora, L. 1–5
Chrysanthemum segetum, L. 1, 3
— Leucanthemum, L. 1–5
[— Parthenium], Pers. 2, 3, 5
Tanacetum vulgare, L. 2–5
Artemisia vulgaris, L. 1–5
    b. coarctata (Forcell). 3–5
— Absinthium, L. 4, 5
Petasites vulgaris, Desf. 1–5
[— alba], Gært. **2**
Tussilago Farfara, L. 1–5
Doronicum Pardalianches, L. **2**
Senecio vulgaris, L. 1–5
— sylvaticus, L. 2–5
— Jacobæa, L. 1–5
— erucifolius, L. 1–5

Senecio aquaticus, Huds. 1–5
[— saracenicus], L. 3
Arctium majus, Schk. 3, 5
— nemorosum, Lej. 2–5
— minus, Schk. 1–5
— intermedium, Lange. 3, 5
Carlina vulgaris, L. 2–5
Centauria nigra, L. 1–5
— Scabiosa, L. 2–5
— Cyanus, L. 1–4
Serratula tinctoria, L. 2, 3, 5
Carduus nutans, L. 2–5
— crispus, L. 2–5
Cnicus lanceolatus, Willd. 1–5
— eriophorus, Roth. 3, 5
— arvensis, Hoffm. 1–5
— palustris, Willd. 1–5
— pratensis, Willd. 2–5
— heterophyllus, Willd. **2**
Onopordon Acanthium, L. 5
[Sylybum Marianum], Gært. 2, 3
Cichorium Intybus, L. 3, 4
Lapsana communis, L. 1–5
Picris hieracioides, L. 2, 3, 5
Crepis virens, L. 1–5
— paludosa, Mœnch. 1, 2, 4
Hieracium Pilosella, L. 1–5
— anglicum, Fries. **2**
— murorum, L. 2, 5
— sylvaticum, Sm. 1, 3–5
— maculatum, Sm. 4
— sciaphilum, Uechtr. 1.
— tridentatum, Fr. 3, 5
— umbellatum, L. 1, 3, 5
— boreale, Fr. 1–5
Hypochæris glabra, L. 3
— radicata, L. 1–5
Leontodon hirtus, L. 2, 3, 5
— hispidus, L. 1–5
— autumnalis, L. 1–5
Taraxacum officinale, Web. 1–5
    b. erythrospermum (Andrz.). 2, 3, 5
    c. palustre (DC.). 2, 3, 5
    d. udum (Jord.). 3
Lactuca virosa, L. 2, 3
— muralis, Fresen. 1–5
Sonchus oleraceus, L. 1–5
— asper, Hoffm. 1–5
— arvensis, L. 1–5
— palustris, L. 4 (?)
Tragopogon pratense, L. 2–5
    b. minus (Mill.). 1–5
[— porrifolium], L. 2, 3, 5

CAMPANULACEÆ

Jasione montana, L. 1–5
Wahlenbergia hederacea, Reich. 3
Campanula rotundifolia, L. 1–5
    b. lancifolia (Mert. & Kit.). 3
— Rapunculus, L. 3, 5
— patula, L. 3, 5
— latifolia, L. 2–4
    b. flore-alba (Auct.). 3
[— Rapunculoides], L. 3
— Trachelium, L. 2, 3, 5
Specularia hybrida, DC. 4, 5

Ericaceæ

Vaccinium Myrtillus, L.   2, 4, 5
— intermedia (Ruthe).   3, 4
— Vitis-Idæa, L.   1–5
— occycoccus, L.   1–5
Andromeda polifolia, L.   1, 3, 4
Erica Tetralix, L.   1–5
— cinerea, L.   1–5
Calluna vulgaris, Salisb.   1–5
    b. incana (Auct.).   3, 4
Pyrola minor, Sw.   2
— media, Sw.   5
— rotundifolia, (?) L.   2–4

Monotropeæ

Hypopithys monotropa, Crantz.   5

Primulaceæ

Primula vulgaris, Huds.   1–5
    b. caulescens (Auct.).   2, 3, 5
— veris, L.   1–5
Lysimachia vulgaris, L.   2, 3, 5
— nemorum, L.   2–5
— Nummularia, L.   2–5
Glaux maritima, L.   3, 4
Centunculus minimus, L.   3
Anagalis arvensis, L.   1–5
— cerulea, Schreb.   3
— tenella, L.   3–5
Hottonia palustris, L.   3, 5
Samolus Valerandi, L.   5

Oleaceæ

Ligustrum vulgare, L.   2–4
Fraxinus excelsior, L.   1–5

Apocynaceæ

Vinca minor, L.   1–5
[— major], L.   3, 5

Gentianeæ

Chlora perfoliata, L.   2–5
Erythræa Centaurium, Pers.   1–5
Gentiana Amarella, L.   2, 5
— campestris, L.   3
Menyanthes trifoliata, L.   1–5

Polemoniaceæ

Polemonium ceruleum, L.   2, 3, 5

Boragineæ

Echium vulgare, L.   3–5
[Borago officinalis], L.   2, 3
Symphytum officinale, L.
    b. patens (Sibth.).   1
— tuberosum, L.   2, 3
Anchusa arvensis, Bieb.   3–5
[— sempervirens], L.   3
Lithospermum officinale, L.   2, 3, 5
— arvense, L.   2–5
[Pulmonaria officinalis], L.   3
Myosotis palustris, Relh.   3–5
    b. strigulosa (Mert. & Koch).   1, 2
— repens, G. Don.   1–4
— cæspitosa, Schultz.   2–5
— sylvatica, Hoffm.   2–4
— arvensis, Lam.   1–5
    b. umbrosa (Bab.).   2–5
— collina, Hoffm.   2, 3, 5

Myosotis versicolor, Reich.   1–3
Cynoglossum officinale, L.   1–3, 5

Convolvulaceæ

Convolvulus arvensis, L.   1–5
— sepium, L.   1–5
Cuscuta europæa, L.   3
[— Trifolii], Bab.   3

Solanaceæ

Hyoscyamus niger, L.   2–4
Solanum Dulcamara, L.   1–5
— nigrum, L.   3, 5
Atropa Belladonna, L.   2–5
[Datura Stramonium], L.   3

Plantagineæ

Plantago major, L.   1–5
    b. intermedia, Gilib.   3
— media, L.   2–5
— lanceolata, L.   1–5
    b. Timbali, Jord.   3
— Coronopus, L.   2, 3, 5
Littorella lacustris, L.   2–4

Scrophularineæ

Verbascum Thapsus, L.   2–5
— Lychnites, L.   5
— nigrum, L.   3, 5
— Blattaria, L.   3, 5
[Linaria Cymbalaria], Mill.   1–5
— vulgaris, Mill.   1–5
— repens, Mill.   3
— minor, Desf.   3, 5
Antirrhinum Orontium, L.   3
[— majus], L.   3
Scrophularia nodosa, L.   1–5
— aquatica, L.   1–5
— umbrosa, Dum.   5 (?)
[Mimulus luteus], L.   2, 3
Limosella aquatica, L.   2–5
Digitalis purpurea, L.   2–5
Veronica agrestis, L.   1–5
— polita, Fr.   2, 3
— Buxbaumii, Ten.   2–5
— hederæfolia, L.   1–5
— arvensis, L.   1–5
— serpyllifolia, L.   1–5
— officinalis, L.   1–5
— Chamædrys, L.   1–5
— montana, L.   2–5
— scutellata, L.   2–5
— Beccabunga, L.   1–5
— Anagallis, L.   3–5
Bartsia Odontites a. verna, Reich.   3–5
    b. serotina, Reich.   2, 3, 5
Euphrasia officinalis, L.   1–5
Rhinanthus Crista-galli, L.   1–5
— major, Ehrh.   2, 4
Pedicularis palustris, L.   2–5
— sylvatica, L.   1–3, 5
Melampyrum pratense, L.   3–5
Lathræa squamaria, L.   2, 3, 5

Orobancheæ

Orobanche major, L.   1, 2, 4, 5
— elatior, Sutt.   2

BOTANY

Salix triandra. 3, 4
— amygdalina, L. 4
— Hoffmanniana, Sm. 3, 4
— undulata, Ehrh. 3, 5
— pentandra, L. 1–4
— fragilis, L. 2–5
    b. brittanica, F. B. White. 1, 5
— alba, L. 1–5
    b. cærulea, Sm. 3
    c. vitellina, L. 1, 3
— Caprea, L. 1–5
— cinerea, L. 1–5
— aurita, L. 1–5
— repens, L. 2, 5
— laurina, Sm. 5
— viminalis, L. 1–5
— Smithiana, Willd. 1–5
— purpurea, L. 1–3
— rubra, Huds. 4
— Lambertiana, Sm. 5

CERATOPHYLLEÆ

Ceratophyllum demersum, L. 3–5

CONIFERÆ

Pinus sylvestris, L. 1–3
Juniperus communis, L. 1
Taxus baccata, L. 2–4

HYDROCHARIDEÆ

Hydrocharis Morsus-Ranæ, L. 1, 5
Stratiotes aloides, L. 1
[Elodea canadensis], Michx. 1–5

ORCHIDEÆ

Neottia Nidus-avis, L. 2, 4
Listera ovata, Br. 2–5
Spiranthes autumnalis, Rich. 5
Epipactis latifolia, Sw. 2–5
— palustris, Sw. 1, 3, 4
Cephalanthera ensifolia, Rich. 4
Orchis mascula, L. 1–3
— latifolia, L. 2–5
— maculata, L. 1–5
— Morio, L. 2, 3, 5
— ustulata, L. 5
— pyramidalis, L. 2, 3
Ophrys apifera, Huds. 3, 5
Habenaria conopsea, Benth. 2, 3, 5
— viridis, Br. 1–5
— albida, Br. 5
— bifolia, Br. 2, 3, 5
— chlorantha, Bab. 1–3

IRIDEÆ

[Crocus vernus], All. 3
[— nudiflorus], Sm. 2, 3
Iris pseud-acorus, L. 1, 3–5

AMARYLLIDEÆ

Narcissus Pseudo-narcissus, L. 1–5
[— biflorus], Curt. 3
[— poeticus], L. 3
Galanthus nivalis, L. 2–4

DIOSCOREÆ

Tamus communis, L. 1–5

LILIACEÆ

Convallaria majalis, L. 2, 3
Polygonatum multiflorum, All. 2, 3
Allium vineale, L. 2
— oleraceum, L. 2, 3
— ursinum, L. 1–5
Scilla autumnalis, L. 3
— nutans, Sm. 1–5
Fritillaria Meleagris, L. 2, 3, 5
Tulipa sylvestris, L. 3
Colchicum autumnale, L. 3, 5
Narthecium ossifragum, Huds. 2, 3, 5
Paris quadrifolia, L. 2–5

JUNCACEÆ

Juncus effusus, L. 1–5
— conglomeratus, L. 1–5
— glaucus, Ehrh. 1–5
— squarrosus, L. 1, 3, 4
— compressus, Jacq. 3, 4
— Gerardi, Loisel. 3
— obtusiflorus, Ehrh. 3
— acutiflorus, Ehrh. 1–5
— supinus, L. Mœnch. 1–5
— lamprocarpus, Ehrh. 1–5
— bufonius, L. 1–5
Luzula maxima, DC. 1–5
— vernalis, DC. 1–5
— campestris, Willd. 1–5
— erecta, Desv. 2, 3
    b. congesta, Koch. 1, 5

TYPHACEÆ

Sparganium ramosum, Huds. 1–5
— simplex, Huds. 1–5
— neglectum, Beeby. 1–5
— affine, Sch. 4, 5
— minimum, Fries. 3, 5
Typha latifolia, L. 1–5
— angustifolia, L. 1–5

AROIDEÆ

Arum maculatum, L. 1–5
Acorus Calamus, L. 1, 3, 4

LEMNACEÆ

Lemna minor, L. 1–5
— trisulca, L. 2–5
— gibba, L. 3–5
— polyrrhiza, L. 3–5

ALISMACEÆ

Alisma Plantago, L. 1–5
    b. lanceolatum, With. 3–5
— ranunculoides, L. 3–5
Sagittaria sagittifolia, L. 2–5
Butomus umbellatus, L. 3–5

NAIADACEÆ

Triglochin palustre, L. 2–5
— maritimum, L. 3
Potamogeton natans, L. 1, 3–5
— polygonifolius, Power. 2–4
— rufescens, Schrad. 1, 3, 5
— heterophyllus, Schreb. 3
— lucens, L. 1–5
— prælongus, Wulf. 3, 4

Potamogeton perfoliatus, L. 3–5
— crispus, L. 1–5
— densus, L. 2
— zosterifolius, Schum. 3, 4
— obtusifolius, Mert. & Koch. 3
— pusillus, L. 2–5
— Friesii, Rupr. 3
— trichodes, Cham. 5
— pectinatus, L. 1–5
— flabellatus, Bab. 3–5
Zannichellia palustris, L. 3–5

CYPERACEÆ

Eleocharis acicularis, Sm. 3
— palustris, Sm. 1–5
— multicaulis, Sm. 3, 4
Scirpus lacustris, L. 1–5
— Tabernæmontani, Gmel. 3, 5
— maritimus, L. 3, 4
— sylvaticus, L. 2, 3, 5
— setaceus, L. 1–5
— fluitans, L. 1, 3, 5
— cæspitosus, L. 1, 3
— pauciflorus, Lightf. 3
Eriophorum vaginatum, L. 1–4
— angustifolium, Roth. 1–4
Rhynchospora alba, Vahl. 1, 3
Schœnus nigricans, L. 3, 5
Cladium Mariscus, Br. 3, 4
Carex dioica, L. 3, 4
— pulicaris, L. 3, 5
— disticha, Huds. 3–5
— paniculata, L. 1–5
— teretiuscula, Good. 5
— muricata, L. 3–5
— divulsa, Good. 2, 3
— vulpina, L. 1–5
— echinata, Murr. 1–5
— remota, L. 1–5
— leporina, L. 1–5
— canescens, L. 2–5
— acuta, L. 3–5
— stricta, Good. 3, 5
— Goodenovii, Gay. 1–5
— limosa, Schreb. 4 (?), 5 (?)
— glauca, Schreb. 1–5
— pallescens, L. 1, 3, 5
— panicea, L. 1–5
— pendula, Huds. 1–4
— præcox, Jacq. 1, 3, 4
— pilulifera, L. 1–5
— hirta, L. 1–5
— flava, L. 1–5
   b. lepidocarpa, Tausch. 3, 4
— distans, L. 4, 5
— fulva, Good. 1, 4
— binervis, Sm. 1–5
— lævigata, Sm. 3
— sylvatica, Huds. 2, 3, 5
— strigosa, Huds. 2, 3, 5
— vesicaria, L. 1–5
— ampullacea, Good. 1–5
— Pseudo-cyperus, L. 1–5
— paludosa, Good. 2–5
— riparia, Curt. 2–5

GRAMINEÆ

Setaria viridis, Beauv. 3
[Phalaris canariensis], L. 3, 5
— arundinacea, L. 1–5
Anthoxanthum odoratum, L. 1–5
[— Puelii], Lecoq. 3–5
Alopecurus agrestis, L. 3, 4
— pratensis, L. 1–5
— geniculatus, L. 1–5
— fulvus, Sm. 3
Milium effusum, L. 2–5
Phleum pratense, L. 1–5
Agrostis canina, L. 2–5
— vulgaris, With. 1–5
   b. pumila, L. 3
— nigra, With. 3–5
— alba, L. 2–5
   b. stolonifera, L. 5
Calamagrostis Epigejos, Roth. 3–5
— lanceolata, Roth. 3–5
Aira caryophyllea, L. 1, 3–5
— præcox, L. 1, 3–5
Deschampsia flexuosa, Trin. 1–5
— cæspitosa, Beauv. 1–5
Holcus lanatus, L. 1–5
— mollis, L. 2–5
Trisetum flavescens, Beauv. 1–5
Avena fatua, L. 3
[— strigosa], Schreb. 3
— pratensis. 2, 3
— pubescens, Huds. 1–5
Arrhenatherum avenaceum, Beauv. 1–5
Triodia decumbens, Beauv. 1–5
Phragmites communis, Trin. 1, 3–5
Cynosurus cristatus, L. 1–5
Kochleria cristata, Pers. 2
Molinia cærulea, Mœnch. 1–4
Catabrosa aquatica, Beauv. 2–5
Melica nutans, L. 2
— uniflora, Retz. 1–5
Dactylis glomerata, L. 1–5
Briza media, L. 2–5
Poa annua, L. 1–5
— pratensis, L. 1–5
   b. subcerulea, Sm. 3, 4
— compressa, L. 3
— trivialis, L. 1–5
— nemoralis, L. 1–4
Glyceria aquatica, Sm. 1–5
— fluitans, Br. 1–5
   b. plicata, Fr. 2–4
   c. pedicellata, Towns. 2, 3, 5
Festuca elatior, L. 3, 5
— pratensis, Huds. 3
— gigantea, Vill. 1–5
— sylvatica, Vill. 5 (?)
— ovina, L. 2–5
— duriuscula, L. 3
— rubra, L. 1, 3
— myuros, L. 5
— sciuroides, Roth. 1–5
— rigida, Kth. 2, 3
Bromus asper, Murr. 1–5
— sterilis, L. 1–5
— mollis, L. 1–5

Bromus racemosus, L. 2, 3
— secalinus, L. 3
— commutatus, Schreb. 2, 3, 5
Brachypodium sylvaticum, R. & S. 1–5
— pinnatum, Beauv. 3
Lolium perenne, L. 1–5
    b. italicum, Br. 3
Agropyrum caninum, Beauv. 3–5
— repens, Beauv. 1–5
Nardus stricta, L. 1–5
Hordeum pratense, Huds. 2–4
— murinum, L. 1–4

FILICES

Hymenophyllum unilaterale, Willd. 1
Pteris aquilina, L. 1–5
Lomaria Spicant, Desv. 1, 3–5
Asplenium Ruta-muraria, L. 2–5
— Trichomanes, L. 1–4
— viride, Huds. 2
— Adiantum-nigrum, L. 1, 2
— filix-fœmina, Bernh. 1–5
    b. rhæticum, Roth. 2–5
— Ceterach, L. 2, 5
Scolopendrium vulgare, Sm. 3, 4
Cystopteris fragilis, Bernh. 2, 3
Aspidium aculeatum, Sw. 2–5
— lobatum, Sw. 2–4
— angulare, Willd. 2, 4, 5
Nephrodium Filix-mas. 1–5
    b. affinis, Fisch. 2–4
    c. Borreri, Newm. 2, 3, 5
— cristata, Rich. 3, 4
    b. uliginosum, Newnm.
— spinulosum, Desv. 2–5
— dilatatum, Desv. 2–5

Nephrodium Thelypteris, Desv. 3, 5
— Oreopteris, Desv. 2, 3, 5
Polypodium vulgare, L. 1–5
— Phegopteris, L. 3
— Dryopteris, L. 2, 3, 5
— Robertianum, Hoffm. 2
Osmunda regalis, L. 1, 3, 5
Ophioglossum vulgatum, L. 2–5
Botrychium Lunaria, Sw. 1–3, 5

EQUISETACEÆ

Equisetum arvense, L.
— maximum, Lam. 2, 3, 5
— sylvaticum, L. 2–4
— palustre, L. 1–5
    b. nudum, Newm. 3, 4
— limosum, L. 2–4
    b. fluviatile, L. 2–4
— variegatum, Schliech. 2, 3, 5

LYCOPODIACEÆ

Lycopodium clavatum. 1–4
— inundatum. 2, 3, 5
— Selago, L. 1, 3, 5

MARSILEACEÆ

Pilularia globulifera, L. 1, 4, 5

CHARACEÆ

Chara fragilis, Desv. 3–5
    d. Hedwigii, Kuetz. 3
— hispida, L. 1, 3, 5
— vulgaris, L. 2, 3, 5
Nitella translucens, Agard. 3, 4
— flexilis, Agard. 3, 5
— opaca, Agard. 3

THE MOSSES (*Musci*)

Although a considerable area of Staffordshire is thickly populated and has the contaminated neighbourhood of busy centres of industry, there are still large stretches of undulating moorland, usually watered by streams liable to flooding, with marshy and boggy surroundings favourable to a rich growth of mosses and their moisture loving allies the hepatics. Such is Sherbrook Valley, and there are many similar valleys north of Cannock where are found many of the rarer sphagnums, such as *Sphagnum viride.* Again west of Cannock are the remains of what were formerly extensive bog lands, such as Norton bog, where is the rare *S. tenellum,* and near Uttoxeter, in the deep and treacherous Chartley bog, are many of the sphagnums and other moisture loving species, such as the rare *Polytrichum strictum.* The woodlands of the county, though extensive, are usually dry and rarely the homes of any but the more common species; but some of the woodlands around Gnosall and Norbury yield rarer mosses, such as the hair moss *Polytrichum gracile, Bryum uliginosum* and *Fontinalis squamosa* and other rare species; and the rich woodlands of the south-west have yielded some of our rarest species, such as *Fumaria ericetorum, Pterygophyllum lucens* and the rare *Heterocladium fallax*, first recorded from that locality as a British moss. But the most fertile localities for our rarer mosses are the water-splashed rocks of the limestone districts, as in the Dove dale; here the ever present humidity renders the moss flora rich and varied; on rocks in the stream are *Eurhynchium crassinervium*, *Brachythecium illecebrum*, and on the limestone rocks the rare *Amblestegium confervoides*, its first British locality, and great masses of *Weissia rupestris*, *Hypnum rugosum*, and now and again *Trichostomum mutabile*. The calcareous rocks too of the Manyfold valley yield many lime lovers of interest, such as *Weissia verticillata* and *Trichostomum crispulum*, and on the grit and limestone walls of Alton *Encalypta streptocarpa* is abundant, and the only fruiting example of *Aulocomnion androgynum* found in Britain was from these stone fences. In some of the limestone valleys of the Manyfold and Churnet are hollow cave-like openings worn out by water action in the ages past, and in these is seen, though rarely, the phosphorescent luminosity of the pretty little cavern moss *Schistostega osmundacea* and some of the more delicate forms of *Webera*. The total moss flora of Staffordshire is larger than that of any of the surrounding counties so far as these are known, but as there are no properly representative lists published of some of them comparisons would be valueless. The total moss flora of Staffordshire is 285 species and 83 varieties, a total of 368 for the county.

To show in a slight measure the distribution of the mosses enumerated, the county has been divided into the three districts drained by the rivers: (1) the Weaver; (2) the Trent, including the Dove and the Sow; and (3) the Severn; and the numbers given in the list following refer to these districts.

Sphagnum cymbifolium, Ehrh.   1–3
   β. squarrosulum, N. & H.   2
— papillosum, Ldb.   2, 3
   β. confertum, Ldb.   2
   γ. stenophyllum, Ldb.   2
— molle, Sull.   2
   γ. tenerum, Braith.   2
— tenellum, Ehrh.   2
— subsecundum, Nees.   1–3
   β. contortum, Schp.   1–3
   δ. obesum, Schp.   2
   ε. viride, Boul.   1–3
— squarrosum, Pers.   2
— acutifolium, Ehrh.   2
   β. rubellum, Russ.   2
   μ. patulum, Schp.   2
   ν. lætevirens, Braith.   2
— Girgensohnii, Russ.   2
— fimbriatum, Wils.   2
— intermedium, Hoffm.   2
   β. riparium, Ldb.   2
   γ. pulchrum, Ldb.   2
— cuspidatum, Ehrh.   1, 2
   β. falcatum, Russ.   2
Tetraphis pellucida, Hedw.   1–3
Catharinea undulata, W. & N.   1–3
   γ. Haussknechtii, Dixon.   3
Oligotrichum incurvum, 1, 2

Polytrichum nanum, Neck.   2, 3
   β. longisetum, Ldb.   2
— aloides, Hedw.   2, 3
— urnigerum, Linn.   1, 2
— piliferum, Schreb.   1–3
— juniperinum, Willd.   2, 3
— strictum, Banks.   2
— gracile, Dicks.   2
— formosum, Hedw.   2, 3
— commune, Linn.   1–3
   β. perigoniale, B. & S.   2
   γ. minus, Weis.   2
Buxbaumia aphylla, Linn.   2
Diphyscium foliosum, Mohr.   2
Archidium alternifolium, Schp.   2
Pleuridium axillare, Ldb.   2
— subulatum, Rab.   2, 3
— alternifolium, Rab.   2
Ditrichum homomallum, Hpe.   2, 3
— flexicaule, Hpe.   1, 2
   β. densum, Braith.   2
Seligeria pusilla, B. & S.   2
Ceratodon purpureus, Brid.   1–3
   β. paludosa, Bagnall.   2
— conicus, Ldb.   1
Rhabdoweissia fugax, B. & S.   2
Cynodontium Bruntoni, B. & S.   3
Dichodontium pellucidum, Schp.   1–3

Dichodontium pellucidum, Schp.
 β. fagimontanum, Schp. 2
— flavescens, Ldb. 1, 2
Dicranella heteromalla, Schp. 1–3
 γ. interrupta, B. & S. 2
 δ. sericea, Schp. 2, 3
— cerviculata, Schp. 2
 β. pusilla, Schp. 2
— crispa, Schp. 2
— rufescens, Schp. 2, 3
— varia, Schp. 2, 3
 γ. tenella, Schp. 3
— Schreberi, Schp. 2
 β. elata, Schp. 2, 3
— squarrosa, Schp. 1, 2
Dicranoweissia cirrata, Ldb. 1–3
— crispula, Ldb. 1, 2
Campylopus flexuosus, Brid. 1, 2
 γ. paradoxus, Husn. 2
— pyriformis, Brid. 1–3
— fragilis, B. & S. 1, 2
Dicranodontium longirostrum, B. & S. 2
Dicranum Bonjeani, De Not. 1–3
 δ. rugifolium, Bosw. 2
— scoparium, Hedw. 1–3
 β. paludosum, Schp. 2
 γ. orthophyllum, Brid. 2
— majus, Turn. 2, 3
— fuscescens, Turn. 2, 3
 γ. congestum, Husn. 1
— strictum, Scliech. 2
— flagellare, Hedw. 2
— montanum, Hedw. 2, 3
Leucobryum glaucum, Schp. 1, 2
Fissedens exilis, Hedw. 2
— viridulus, Wahl. 2, 3
 β. Lylei, Wils. 2
— exiguus, Sull. 2
— pusillus, Wils. 3
— incurvus, Starke. 2
— tamarindifolius, Wils. 2, 3
— bryoides, Hedw. 1–3
— crassipes, Wils. 3
— adiantoides, Hedw. 2, 3
— decipiens, De Not. 2, 3
— taxifolius, Hedw. 1–3
Grimmia apocarpa, Hedw. 1–3
 β. rivularis, W. & M. 1–3
 γ. gracilis, W. & M. 3
 δ. pumila, Schp. 1, 2
— pulvinata, Sm. 1–3
 β. obtusa, Hüb. 1, 2
— trichophylla, Grev. 1, 2
— ovata, Schwgr. 2
Rhacomitrium aciculare, Brid. 1–3
 β. denticulatum, B. & S. 1
— fasciculare, Brid. 1, 2
— heterostichum, Brid. 1, 2
 β. alopecurum, Hüb. 1, 2
— lanuginosum, Brid. 1, 2
— canescens, Brid. 1, 2
 β. ericoides, B. & S. 2
Ptychomitrium polyphyllum, Für. 2, 3
Hedwigia ciliata, Ehrh. 1
Acaulon muticum, C.M. 2

Phascum cuspidatum, Schreb. 2, 3
 β. piliferum, H. & T. 2
 γ. Schreberianum, Brid. 2
 δ. curvisetum, N. & H. 2
Pottia bryoides, Mitt. 2
— truncatula, Lind. 1–3
— intermedia, Für. 2, 3
— minutula, Für. 2, 3
— lanceolata, C.M. 2
Tortula rigida, Schrad. 2
— ambigua, Angst. 2, 3
— aloides, De Not. 2
— cuneifolia, Roth. 3
— marginata, Spr. 2, 3
— muralis, Hedw. 1–3
 β. rupestris, Wils. 2, 3
 γ. æstiva, Brid. 2
— subulata, Hedw. 1–3
— mutica, Ldb. 2, 3
— lævipila, Schw. 3
— intermedia, Berk. 1, 2
— ruralis, Ehrh. 1–3
Barbula lurida, Ldb. 2
— rubella, Mitt. 1–3
 β. dentata, Braith. 2
 γ. ruberrima, Braith. 2
— tophacea, Mitt. 1–3
— fallax, Hedw. 1–3
 β. brevifolia, Schultz. 2
— recurvifolia, Schp. 1, 2
— spadicea, Mitt. 1, 2
— rigidula, Mitt. 2
— cylindrica, Schp. 2, 3
— vinealis, Brid. 2, 3
— sinuosa, Braith. 2
— Hornschuchiana, Schultz. 2, 3
— revoluta, Brid. 1–3
— convoluta, Hedw. 2
 β. Sardoa, B. & S. 2
— unguiculata, Hedw. 1–3
 β. cuspidata, Braith. 2, 3
 δ. obtusifolia, Shultz. 2
Leptodontium flexifolium, Hampe. 1, 2
Weissia crispa, Mitt. 2
— microstoma, C.M. 2, 3
— tortilis, C.M. 2
— viridula, Hedw. 1–3
 γ gymnostomoides, B. & S. 2
— mucronata, B. & S. 2
— tenui, C.M. 2
— rupestris, C.M. 2
 β. ramosissima, C.M. 2
— verticillata, Brid. 2
Trichostomum crispulum, Bruch. 2
— mutabile, Bruch. 2
 γ. cophocarpum, Schp. 2
— tenuirostre, Ldb. 2
— nitidum, Schp. 2
— tortuosum, Dixon. 2
Cinclidotus Brebissoni, Husn. 3
— fontinaloides, P. B. 2, 3
Encalypta vulgaris, Hedw. 2, 3
 β. pilifera, Funck. 2
 γ. obtusifolia, Funck. 2, 3
— streptocarpa, Hedw. 1–3
Anæctangium compactum, Schwg. 2

Zygodon viridissimus, R. Br.   2, 3
 β. rupestris, Ldb.   2
— Stirtoni, Schp.   2
Ulota crispa, Brid.   2
Orthotrichum anomalum, Hedw.   2
 β. saxatile, Milde.   2
— cupulatum, Hoffm.   2
 β. nudum, Braith.   2
— leiocarpum, B. & S.   3
— affine, Schrad.   2, 3
— rivulare, Turn.   2, 3
— Sprucei, Mont.   3
— stramineum, Hornsch.   2
— diaphanum, Schrad.   2, 3
Schistostega osmundacea, Mohr.   2
Splachnum ampullaceum, Linn.   2
Ephemerum serratum, Hampe.   2
Physcomitrella patens, B. & S.   2
Physcomitrium sphæricum, Brid.   2
— pyriforme, Brid.   1–3
Funaria fascicularis, Schp.   3
— ericetorum, Dixon.   3
— calcarea, Wahl.   3
— hygrometrica, Sibth.   1–3
 β. calvescens, B. & S.   3
Aulacomnium palustre, Schwg.   1–3
— androgynum, Schwg.   1–3
Bartramia pomiformis, Hedw.   2, 3
 β. crispa, B. & S.   2
— Œderi, Sw.   2
Philonotis fontana, Brid.   1–3
 δ. pumila, Dixon.   2
— cæspitosa, Wils.   1, 2
— calcarea, Schp.   2
Breutelia arcuata, Schp.   2
Orthodontium gracile, Schw.   2
Leptobryum pyriforme, Wils.   2
Webera elongata, Schw.   2
— cruda, Schw.   2
— nutans, Hedw.   1–3
 β. longiseta, B. & S.   2
— annotina, Schw.   2
— carnea, Schp.   2, 3
— albicans, Schp.   2, 3
Bryum pendulum, Schp.   2, 3
— lacustre, Brid.   1, 2
— inclinatum, Bland.   1, 2
— uliginosum, B. & S.   2
— pallens, Sw.   2, 3
— turbinatum, Schw.   2
— bimum, Schreb.   2
— pseudo-triquetrum, Schw.   2
— affine, Ldb.   2
— intermedium, Brid.   2
— cæspiticium, Linn.   1–3
— capillare, Linn.   1–3
 γ. macrocarpum, Hübn.   2, 3
 ε. flaccidum, B. & S.   2, 3
— erythrocarpum, Schw.   2
— atropurpureum, W. & M.   2, 3
 β. gracilentum, Tayl.   2
— murale, Wils.   2
— argenteum, Linn.   1–3
 β. majus, B. & S.   2
 γ. lanatum, B. & S.   3
— roseum, Schreb.   2

Mnium cuspidatum, Hedw.   2
— affine, Bland.   2
— rostratum, Schrad.   2, 3
— undulatum, Linn.   1–3
— hornum, Linn.   1–3
— serratum, Schrad.   2
— stellare, Reich.   2, 3
— punctatum, Linn.   2, 3
 β. elatum, Schp.   2
— subglobosum, B. & S.   2, 3
Fontinalis antipyretica, Linn.   1–3
 γ. gracilis, Schp.   1–3
— dolosa, Card.   2
— squamosa, Linn.   2, 3
Cryphæa heteromalla, Mohr.   3
Neckera crispa, Hedw.   1–3
 β. falcata, Boul.   2
— complanata, Hübn.   2, 3
Homalia trichomanoides, Brid.   2, 3
Pterygophyllum lucens, Brid.   3
Leucodon sciuroides, Schw.   2, 3
Antitrichia curtipendula, Brid.   1
Porotrichum alopecurum, Mitt.   2, 3
Leskea polycarpa, Ehrh.   1–3
 β. paludosa, Schp.   2, 3
Anomoden viticulosum, H. & T.   2
Heterocladium heteropterum, B. & S.   3
 β. fallax, Milde.   3
Thuidium tamariscinum, B. & S.   1–3
— recognitum, Lindb.   2
Climacium dendroides, W. & N.   2
Isothecium myurum, Brid.   2, 3
 β. robustum, B. & S.   2
Pleuropus sericeus, Dixon.   1–3
Camptothecium lutescens, B. & S.   2
Brachythecium glareosum, B. &. S.   2, 3
— albicans, B. & S.   2, 3
— salebrosum, B. & S.   3
 β. palustre, Schp.   2, 3
— rutabulum, B. & S.   1–3
 β. robustum, Schp.   2, 3
 γ. longisetum, B. & S.   2
— rivulare, B. & S.   1–3
 δ. chrysophyllum, Bagnall.   2
— velutinum, B. & S.   1–3
— populeum, B. & S.   2, 3
— plumosum, B. & S.   1–3
 β. homomallum, B. & S.   1
— cæspitosum, Dixon.   2, 3
— illecebrum, De Not.   2
— purum, Dixon.   1–3
Hyocomium flagellare, B. & S.   2
Eurhynchium piliferum, B. & S.   2, 3
— crassinervum, B. & S.   2
— prælongum, B. & S.   1–3
 β. Stokesii, L. Cat.   2, 3
— Swartzii, Hobk.   2, 3
— pumilum, Schp.   2, 3
— Teesdalei, Schp.   3
— tenellum, Milde.   2, 3
— myosuroides, Schp.   1–3
— striatum, B. & S.   2, 3
— rusciforme, Milde.   1–3
 β. prolixum, Brid.   2
 γ. atlanticum, Brid.   1
— murale, Milde.   1–3

Eurhynchium murale, Milde.
　γ. julaceum, Schp.　1–3
— confertum, Milde.　1–3
— megapolitana, Bland.　3
Plagiothecium depressum, Dixon.　3
— Borrerianum, Spruce.　2, 3
— denticulatum, B. & S.　1–3
　β. aptychus, L. Cat.　2, 3
　ε. laxum.　3
— sylvaticum, B. & S.　1–3
— undulatum, B. & S.　1–3
Amblestegium confervoides, B. & S.　2
— serpens, B. & S.　1–3
　β. majus, Brid.　3
— varium, Ldb.　2
— irriguum, B. & S.　2
— fluviatile, B. & S.　2
— filicinum, De Not.　1–3
Hypnum riparium, Linn.　1–3
　β. longifolium, Schp.　2, 3
　γ. splendens, De Not.　3
— polygamum, Schp.　2, 3
　β. stagnatum.　3
— stellatum, Schreb.　2
　β. protensum, B. & S.　2
— chrysophyllum, Brid.　2, 3
　β. erectum, Bagnall.　2
— Sommerfeltii, Myr.　2
— aduncum, Hedw.　2, 3
　β. Knieffii, Schp.　2, 3
— fluitans, Linn.　1–3
　β. submersum, Schpr.　2
— exannulatum, Gümb.　2

Hypnum uncinatum, Hedw.　1, 2
— vernicosum, Ldb.　2
— revolvens, Sw.　1–3
　β. Cossonii, Ren.　1, 2
— commutatum, Hedw.　2, 3
— fulcatum, Brid.　2
　β. gracilescens, Schp.　2
— cupressiforme, Linn.　1–3
　β. resupinatum, Schp.　1–3
　γ. filiforme, Brid.　2, 3
　δ. minus, Wils.　2
　ζ. ericetorum, B. & S.　2, 3
　η. tectorum, Brid.　2, 3
　θ. elatum, B. & S.　2, 3
— Patientiæ, Ldb.　2, 3
— molluscum, Hedw.　1–3
　γ. fastigiatum, Bosw.　1, 3
— palustre, Linn.　1–3
　β. hamulosum, B. & S.　2, 3
　γ. subsphæricarpon, B. & S.　2
— ochraceum, Turn.　1, 2
— stramineum, Dicks.　1, 2
— cordifolium, Hedw.　2, 3
— giganteum, Schp.　2
— cuspidatum, Linn.　1–3
— Schreberi, Willd.　1–3
Hylocomium splendens, B. & S.　1–3
— loreum, B. & S.　2, 3
— squarrosum, B. & S.　1–3
　β. calvescens, Hobk.　2, 3
— triquetrum, B. & S.　1–3
— rugosum, De Not.　2

THE LIVERWORTS (*Hepaticæ*)

The following list of the liverworts of Staffordshire is incomplete, for this interesting group of plants has been only studied incidentally. The natural features of the county are such as promise a much richer record ; the wide moorlands of the northern portion of the county will probably yield many species not recorded below, and the valleys of the Dove, the Manyfold and the Churnet have been only partially examined; these districts alone if fully explored should very materially increase the record.

The total number here recorded is only 82 species and varieties, being little more than one-third of those recorded for Great Britain. The more rare of these are *Lejeunia Mackaii*, *Kantia arguta*, *Scapania curta*, *Cephalozia lunulæfolia*, *Jungermania cordifolia* and *Fossombronia cristata*. So little has been done in the study of this group of plants in the neighbouring counties as to render any attempt at a comparison of little real value.

Frullania Tamarisci, L.　1–3
— dilatata, L.　1–3
Lejeunea Mackaii, Hook.　2
— serpyllifolia, Dicks.　2, 3
Radula complanata, L.　1–3
Porella lævigata, Schrad.　2
— platyphylla, L.　2, 3

Blepharozia ciliaris, L.　2
Trichocolea tomentella, Ehrh.　2, 3
Blepharostoma trichophyllum, Dill.　3
Lepidozia reptans, L.　2, 3
— setacea, Web.　2
Bazzania trilobata, L.　2
Kantia trichomanis, L.　2, 3

Kantia arguta, Mart. 2
Cephalozia lunulæfolia, Dum. 2
— bicuspidata, L. 1–3
— Lammersiana, Hüben. 2
— connivens, Dicks. 2
— Sphagni, Dicks. 2
— divaricata, Sm. 2, 3
  var. byssacea, Roth. 2
— stellulifera, Tayl. 2
Scapania resupinata, Dill. ; L. 2
— æquiloba, Schw. 2
— aspera, Mull. & Bern. 2
— nemorosa, L. 2, 3
— undulata, L. 2, 3
— irrigua, Nees. 2
— curta, Mart. 2
— umbrosa, Schrad. 2
Diplophyllum albicans, L. 1–3
Lophocolea bidentata, L. 1–3
— cuspidata, Limpr. 2
— heterophylla, Schrad. 1–3
Chiloscyphus polyanthos, L. 1–3
  b. rivularis, Nees. 2
Mylia Taylori, Hook. 2
— anomala, Hook.
Plagiochila asplenioides, L. 2, 3
  c. minor, Carr. 3
Jungermania cordifolia, Hook. 2
— pumila, With. 3
— riparia, Tayl. 3
— inflata, Huds. 2, 3
— turbinata, Raddi. 3
— sphærocarpa, Hook. 2
— exsecta, Schmid. 2

Jungermania Flœrkii, Web. & Mohr. 2
— barbata, Schmid. 2
— Lyoni, Tayl. 2
— incisa, Schrad. 2
— capitata, Hook. 2
— bicrenata, Schmid. 2
— porphyroleuca, Nees. 2
— ventricosa, Dicks. 2, 3
— crenulata, Sm. 2
— gracillima, Sm. 3
Eucalyx hyalina, Lyell. 2
Nardia scalaris, Schrad. 2, 3
  b. major, Carr. 2
Saccogyna viticulosa, Mich. 3
Fossombronia cæspitiformis, De Not. 2
— pusilla, L. 2, 3
— cristata, Lindb. 2
Blasia pusilla, L. 2, 3
Pellia epiphylla, L. 2, 3
— calycina, Tayl. 3
Aneura multifidia, L. 2
— sinuata, Dicks. 2, 3
— pinguis, L. 2, 3
Metzgeria pubescens, Schrank. 2
— furcata, L. 2, 3
Marchantia polymorpha, L. 2, 3
Conocephalus conicus, L. 2, 3
Reboulia hemispherica, L. 2
Lunularia cruciata, L. 2, 3
Targionia hypophylla, L. 2
Riccia glauca, L. 2, 3
— glaucescens, Carr. 2
Anthoceros punctatus, L. 2, 3

THE LICHENS (*Lichenes*)

The lichens are a large tribe of cryptogams intermediate between the algæ and the fungi, approaching the algæ through the gelatinous forms of the Collemacei and the fungi through the Ascomycetes, but they differ from the fungi in not deriving nourishment from the matrix on which they grow but from the atmosphere, in their slow growth, their perennial existence, and in the presence in their structure of the green algæ-like bodies, the gonidia. The researches of Schwendener have shown that the lichens are true fungi, parasitical on unicellular algæ, the gonidia, which exist immediately beneath the cortical layer, being algæ forms allied to Nostoc, Chroolepus or Palmella. The lichens are found throughout the county in one or other form from the low-lying heathlands of the south to the highest points of the north, but are abundant in the normal condition only where the atmospheric conditions are good and wholesome. Over a large portion of the colliery districts and the more smoky surroundings of the Potteries they do not fully develop, but exist in an abnormal state, forming dust-like or filamentous patches, usually greyish white or yellow, on walls, trees or rocks, and in this state will exist for an indefinite time, increasing as do the algæ by the division of their cells ; this condition was known to the older botanists by the pseudo-generic names of *Lepraria*, *Variolaria*, etc. But in the more open districts, as on the high lands about Swithamly, Flash and Quanford the gritstone and limestone rocks are rich in such species as *Placodium murorum, Coniocype furfuraceum, Cladina pungens, Platysma triste* and *Alectoria jubata*. In the Wetton valley and the beautiful valley of the Dove the rocks of mountain limestone form a congenial home for some of the rarer species, as *Umbillicaria polyphila, Platysma glauca*, bright yellow patches of *Lecidia geographica, Sphærophoron coralloides, Squamaria crassa, Lecanora parella* and *Solorina saccata*; over a great portion of the county the more conspicuous tree-loving species are singularly absent, and only rarely are the tree trunks beautified with the conspicuous fronds of *Ramalina fraxinea, R. fastigiata* or *Usnea barbata*.

In the rich woodland districts around Whitmore and Trentham the trees are clothed with grey patches of *Parmelia pulverulenta, P. physodes* and *P. stellaris* ; the old palings of some of the damp woods are coated with *Lecanora candelaria, Usnea hirta, Parmelia olivacea* and *P. parietina* ; and the wild moorlands about Cannock and Norton, notwithstanding the proximity of large colliery workings, are still a home for many of the heath-loving species, as *Cladonia pyxidata, C. cornucopioides, C. digitata, C. rangiferina* and *Cladina sylvatica*. The sandstone rocks of the country around Stone yield their special species, as *Lecanora squamulosa, Placodium callopismum* and *Verrucaria rupestris*, and on the smooth bark of the holly the lime and crab are the singular forms of *Graphis scripta, G. elegans, Arthonia astroidea, A. lurida, Opegrapha vulgata* and *O. atra*.

The following list is an incomplete record of the Staffordshire lichens compiled in part from Garner's *Natural History of the County of Stafford* and the writer's personal observations.

Family I. COLLEMACEI
Collema melænum, Ach.
— crispum, Huds.
— cristatum, Hoffm.
— flaccidum, Ach.
— multipartitum, Sm.
— nigrescens, Huds.
Leptogium lacerum, Ach.
    var. pulvinatum (Hoff.)
— fragrans, Sm.
— tremelloides, L.
— turgidum, Ach.
— Schraderi, Bernh.
    Family II. LICHENACEI
Sphinctrina turbinata, Pers.
— anglica, Nyl.
Calcium trichiale, Ach.
    var. ferrugineum (Borr.)
— hyperellum, Ach.
— trachelinum, Ach.
— quercinum, Pers.
— curtum, Borr.
Coniocybe furfuracea, Ach.
Trachylia tigillaris, Fr.
— tympanella, Fr.
Sphærophoron coralloides, Pers.

Sphærophoron fragile, Pers.
Bæomyces rufus, DC.
— icmadophilus, Ehrh.
Cladonia pungens, Flk.
— cervicornis, Schær.
— delicata, Flk.
    var. subsquamosa (Nyl.)
— alcicornis, Flk.
— pyxidata, Fr.
    var. fimbriata (Hoffm.)
— gracilis, Hoffm.
— furcata, Hoffm.
— squamosa, Hoffm.
— cornucopioides, Fr.
— deformis, Hoffm.
    var. macilenta (Hoffm.)
    var. polydactyla (Flk.)
Cladina sylvatica, Hoffm.
— rangiferina, Hoffm.
— uncialis, Hoffm.
Stereocaulon paschale, Ach.
— denudatum, Flk.
Usnea barbata, L.
    var. florida (L.)
    var. hirta (L.)
    var. plicata (L.)

BOTANY

Alectoria jubata, L.
— lanata, L.
Evernia furfuracea, Mann.
— prunastri, L.
Ramalina calicaris, Hoffm.
— farinacea, L.
— fraxinea, L.
— fastigiata, Pers.
— evernioides, Nyl.
Cetraria aculeata, Fr.
Platysma triste, Web.
— diffusum, Web.
— glaucum, L.
Nephromium lusitanicum, Schær.
Peltigera canina, L.
— rufescens, Hoffm.
— spuria, Ach.
— horizontalis, L.
Solorina saccata, L.
Stictina scrobiculata, Scop.
Sticta pulmonaria, Ach.
Ricasolia amplissima, Scop.
Parmelia caperata, L.
— olivacea, L.
— physodes, L.
— ambigua, Wulf.
— perlata, L.
— pertusa, Schrank.
— tiliacea, Ach.
— Borreri, Turn.
— fuliginosa, Dub.
— perforata, Wulf.
— conspersa, Ehrh.
— acetabulum, Neck.
— saxatilis, L.
    var. omphalodes (L.)
Physcia flavicans, Sw.
— parietina, L.
    var. lychnea (Ach.)
    var. polycarpa (Ehrh.)
— ciliaris, L.
— pulverulenta, Schreb.
    f. pityrea (Ach.)
— obscura, Ehrh.
— stellaris, L.
    var. tenella (Scop.)
    var. cæsia (Hoffm.)
Umbilicaria pustulata, Hoffm.
— polyphylla, L.
    f. congregata (T. & B.)
— flocculosa, Wulf.
— erosa, Ach.
— polyrhiza, L.
Psoroma hypnorum, Vahl.
Pannaria pezizoides, Web.
— nigra, Huds.
Amphiloma lanuginosum, Ach.
Squamaria crassa, Huds.
— saxicola, Poll.
Placodium murorum, Hoffm.

Placodium callopisum, Ach.
— citrinum, Ach.
— candicans, Dicks.
Lecanora vitellina, Ach.
— candelaria, Ach.
— glaucocarpa f. pruinosa (Ach.)
— squamulosa, Schrad.
— fuscata, Schrad.
— tartarea, L.
— varia, Ehrh.
— atra, Huds.
— sulphurea, Hoffm.
— symmicta, Ach.
— lutescens, DC.
— subfusca, L.
— galactina, Ach.
— calcarea, L.
    f. Hoffmanni (Ach.)
— Dicksonii, Ach.
— badia, Ach.
— parella, L.
    f. pallescens (L.)
— rupestris, Scop.
    f. calva (Dicks.)
— glaucoma, Hoffm.
— albella, Pers.
— aurantiaca, Lightf.
— ochracea, Schær.
— ferruginea, Huds.
— cerina, Ehrh.
— arenaria, Pers.
— sophodes, Ach.
    f. exigua (Ach.)
— hæmatomma, Ehrh.
— ventosa, L.
Pertusaria dealbata, Ach.
— communis, DC.
    f. rupestris (DC.)
— fallax, Pers.
— globulifera, Turn.
— leioplaca, Ach.
Phlyctis agelæa, Ach.
— argena, Ach.
Thelotrema lepadinum, Ach.
Urceolaria scruposa, L.
Lecidea ostreata, Hoffm.
— fuliginosa, Tayl.
— dispansa, Nyl.
— lucida, Ach.
— flexuosa, Fries
    f. æruginosa (Borr.)
— decolorans, Flk.
— vernalis, L.
— atrofusca, Hepp.
— dubia, Borr.
— quernea, Dicks.
— viridescens, Schrad.
— sanguinaria, L.
— parasema, Ach.
    var. elæochroma (Ach.)

Lecidea uliginosa, Schrad.
— coarctata, Sm.
— rivulosa, Ach.
— contigua, Fr.
  f. leprosa (Leight.)
  f. flavicunda (Ach.)
— calcivora, Ehrh.
— canescens, Dicks.
— myriocarpa, DC.
— alocizoides, Leight.
— chalybeia, Borr.
— grossa, Pers.
— cæruleonigricans, **Light.**
— denigrata, Fr.
— tricolor, With.
— Ehrhartiana, Ach.
— diluta, Pers.
— Caradocensis, Leight.
— incompta, Borr.
— alboatra, Hoffm.
  f. epipolia (Ach.)
— aromatica, Sm.
— carneo-lutea, Turn.
— umbrina, Ach.
— pachycarpa, Dur.
— milliaria, Fr.
— sabuletorum, Flk.
— premnea, Ach.
— carneola, Ach.
— endoleuca, Nyl.
— rubella, Ehrh.
— geographica, L.
— petræa, Wulf.
— concentrica, Dav.
— cupularis, Ehrh.
— trucigena, Ach.
— Parmeliarum, Smrf.
— parasitica, Flk.

Opegrapha herpetica, Ach.
  f. rubella (Pers.)
  f. rufescens (Pers.)
— atra, Pers.
— Turneri, Leight.
— varia, Pers.
  f. notha (Ach.)
  f. diaphora (Ach.)
— vulgata, Ach.
— Leightonii, Crombie
— lyncea, Sm.
Stigmatidium crassum, Dub.
Arthonia lurida, Ach.
— astroidea, Ach.
— Swartziana, Ach.
— pruinosa, Ach.
Graphis elegans, Sm.
— scripta, Ach.
    var. serpentina (Ach.)
    var. pulverulenta (Ach.)
— inusta, Ach.
— sophistica, Nyl.
Endocarpon miniatum, L.
— hepaticum, Ach.
Verrucaria epigea, Ach.
— Dufourei, DC.
— nigrescens, Pers.
— glaucina, Ach.
— viridula, Schrad.
— rupestris, Schrad.
— conoidea, Fries
— gemmata, Ach.
— epidermidis, Ach.
— biformis, Borr.
— chlorotica, Ach.
  f. trachona (Tay.)
— nitida, Weig.

THE FRESHWATER ALGÆ (*Algæ*)

The freshwater algæ are universally distributed and are to be found in every situation where moisture exists, amid the most deleterious surroundings or where the atmospheric conditions are good and healthful ; ' on damp walls and palings, on soil heaps, damp earth, pathways, roadsides ; on wet rocks, stones in streams, in every ditch and watercourse ; in canals, ponds, and attached to the various aquatic plants therein, in puddles, and the hoof holes of cattle in boggy places,' etc. The green dust-like growth on tree trunks, palings and old walls is one of the lower forms of algæ, *Pleurococcus vulgaris* ; in nearly every ditch one or other species of *Vaucheria* may be found ; old canals are frequently covered with the yellowish green masses of *Enteromorpha intestinalis*, and many of the old clay holes in the coal districts are rich in species of *Nostoc* and *Conferva*. The bogs, pools and watercourses of the Cannock district yield many of the more rare and beautiful species, as *Chætophora elegans*, *C. endivæfolia*, or the elegant fronds of *Drapardnaldia plumosa*, the tufts of sphagnum rich gatherings of *Desmids*. The hoof holes formed in the marshy heathland are usually rich in *Micrasterias*, *Euastrum* and *Straurastrum*, and in some of the clear pools the beautiful *Volvox globata* may be found in abundance. On wet rocks in the Dove dale *Glæocystis botryoides*, *Nostoc pruniforme* and *Chroolepus aureus* have been found, and in the Dove and other rapid streams of that district the gelatinous masses of *Batrachospermum moniliforme* and *B. atrum* are sometimes abundant.

The following list of freshwater algæ has been compiled partly from Garner's *Natural History of Staffordshire*, from the *Proceedings of the Birmingham Natural History Society* and from the writer's observations.

Ord. I. *COCCOPHYCEÆ*
I. PALMELLACEÆ

Pleurococcus vulgaris, Menegh
Gleocystis botryoides, Kütz
Palmella hyalina, Bréb.
Porphyridium cruentum, Nag.
Botrydina vulgaris, Bréb.
Tetraspora bullosa, Ag.
— lubrica, Ag.
Botryococcus Braunii, Kütz
Apiocystis Brauniana, Näg.

II. PROTOCOCCACEÆ

Protococcos viridis, Cohn
Scenedesmus quadricaudatus, Bréb.
Pediastrum angulosum, Ehr.
— Boryanum, Turp.

III. VOLVOCINEÆ

Chlamydococcus pluvialis, A. Braun
Volvox globator, L.
Pandorinum morum, Ehr.
Gonium pectorale, Müll.

Ord. II. *ZYGOPHYCEÆ*
IV. DESMIDIEÆ

Desmidium Swartzii, Kütz
Closterium lunula, Müll.
— Dianæ, Ehr.
— juncidum, Ralfs.
— rostratum, Ehr.
Penium digitus (Ehr.), Ralfs.
Tetmemorus Brebissonii, Ralfs.
Micrasterias rotata, Ralfs.
— denticulata, Bréb.
— truncata, Corda
— papillifera, Bréb.
Euastrum verrucosum, Ehr.
— oblongum, Ehr.
— didelta, Turp.
— insigne, Hass.
— elegans, Ehr.
Cosmarium pyramidatum, Bréb.

Cosmarium Meneghinii, Ralfs.
— undulatum, Cor.
— Brebissonii, Meneg.
— botrytis, Bory.
— biretum, Bréb.
Xanthidium cristatum, Ralfs.
Arthrodesmus incus, Bréb.
Straurastrum dejectum, Ralfs.
— polymorphum, Bréb.
— orbiculare, Ralfs.
— punctulatum, Bréb.
— hirsutum

V. ZYGNEMACEÆ

Zygnema cruciata, Vauch.
Spirogyra nitida, Dillwyn
— condensata, Vauch.
— flavescens (Hass.), Cleve.
— longata, Vauch.
— porticalis v. quinina, Ag.
Zygogonium ericetorum v. terrestris, De Bary
Mesocarpus scalaris, Hass.

Ord. III. *SIPHOPHYCEÆ*
VI. BOTRYDIACEÆ

Botrydium granulatum, L.

VII. VAUCHERIACEÆ

Vaucheria Dillwynii, Ag.
— terrestris, Lyngb.
— sessilis, Vauch.
— geminata, Vauch.

Ord. IV. *NEMATOPHYCEÆ*
VIII. ULVACEÆ

Prasiola crispa, Kütz
Enteromorpha intestinalis, Link.

IX. CONFERVACEÆ

Conferva bombycina, Ag.
Cladophora crispata, Roth.
— glomerata, L. (Dillw.)

X. ŒDOGONIACEÆ

Bulbochæte setigera, Ag.

XI. ULOTRICHEÆ

Schizogonium murale, Kütz

XII. CHROOLEPIDEÆ

Chroolepus aureus (L.), Kütz

XIII. CHÆTOPHORACEÆ

Stigeoclonium nanum (Dillw.), Kütz
Draparnaldia glomerata, Ag.
— plumosa (Vauch.), Ag.
Chætophora pisiformis, Ag.
— tuberculosa, Ag.
— elegans, Ag.
— ændivæfolia, Ag.

CLASS II. PHYCOCHROMOPHYCEÆ
Ord. II. *NEMATOGENEÆ*
XV. NOSTOCEÆ

Nostoc muscorum, Ag.

Nostoc commune, Vauch.
— cæruleum, Lyng.
— verrucosum, Vauch.

XVI. LYNGBYÆ

Oscillaria tenuis, Ag.
— limosa, Ag.
— nigra, Vauch.
Lyngbia ochracea, Thur.

XVIII. CALOTRICHEÆ

Gloiotrichia natans, Thur.

XX. BATRACHOSPERMEÆ

Batrachospermum moniliforme, Roth.
— atrum, Harv.
— vagum, Harv.

XXII. LEMANEACEÆ

Lemanea fluviatilis, Ag.

THE FUNGI

The following list of the fungi of Staffordshire is in no way a complete one; the county has not been exhaustively examined from a botanical point of view. Many of the districts, such as the extensive woodlands about Trentham, Swinnerton and Maer, have yielded a rich fungus flora, among others *Polyporus hispidus*, *P. abietinus*, *P. frondosa*, *P. annosus*, the esculent *Boletus edulis* and *Fistulina hepatica*, and in some of these woods *Boletus subtomentosus* and *B. flavus* are abundant, and in places where the soil has been burnt and on the dried twigs abundance of the singular *Hydnum membranaceum* has been seen. The esculent *Cantharellus cibarius* is sometimes abundant in the woods, on the heathy lands the beautiful *C. aurantiacus*, and in boggy places near Betley *C. lobatus*. In many of these woodlands the beautiful but fetid *Phallus impudicus* is frequent, and in those of Swinnerton the rarer and less fetid *Cyanophallus caninus* has been found. In the district around Blymhill many rare species have been recorded in the long past, as *Cortinarius violaceus*, *C. gentilis*, *Lactarius torminosus* and the edible *L. deliciosus*, and frequently throughout the county the fairy ring fungus (*Marasmius oreades*), is abundant. In the limestone districts of the Wetton valley some of the rarer species of *Peziza* are found, the common morel (*Morchella esculenta*), *Helvella crispa*, *Thelephora canina* and *Boletus asper*; but to localize even a tithe of the more interesting species would occupy too much space; all at present known to the writer are recorded below.

The nomenclature is that of Fries' *Hymenomycete Europœa*, and Berkley's *Outlines of British Fungology*; the authorities quoted are Garner's *Natural History of Staffordshire*, *The Reports and Transactions of the North Staffordshire and Archæological Society* and the writer.

BOTANY

Family. I. HYMENOMYCETES

Genus I. AGARICUS, L.

Sub-genus I. AMANITA, Fr.

Agaricus phalloides, F.
     var. vernus (Bull.)
— mappa, Fr.
— muscarius, L.
— pantherinus, DC.
— rubescens, Pers.
— nitidus, Fr.
— asper, Fr.
— vaginatus, Bull.
— strangulatus, Fr.

Sub-genus II. LEPIOTA, Fr.

Agaricus procerus, Scop.
— rachodes, Vitt.
— clypeolarius, Bull.
— carcharius, Pers.
— granulosus, Batsch.
— amianthinus, Scop.

Sub-genus III. ARMILLARIA, Fr.

Agaricus melleus, Vahl.

Sub-genus IV. TRICHOLOMA, Fr.

Agaricus sejunctus, Sow.
— albo-brunneus, Pers.
— rutilans, Schæff.
— luridus, Schæff.
— columbetta, Fr.
— scalpturatus, Fr.
— imbricatus, Fr.
— vaccinus, Pers.
— terreus, Schæff.
— saponaceus, Fr.
— cuneifolius, Fr.
— virgatus, Fr.
— borealis, Fr.
— personatus, Fr.
— nudus, Bull.
— grammopodius, Bull.
— melaleucus, Pers.
— brevipes, Bull.

Sub-genus V. CLITOCYBE, Fr.

Agaricus nebularis, Batsch.
— clavipes, Pers.
— odorus, Bull.
— phyllophilus, Fr.
— pithyophilus, Fr.
— candicans, Pers.
— dealbatus, Sow.
— gallinaceus, Scop.
— giganteus, Fr.
— infundibuliformis, Schæff.
— geotropus, Bull.
— inversus, Scop.

Agaricus tuba, Fr.
— cyathiformis, Fr.
— brumalis, Fr.
— metachrous, Fr.
— ditopus, Fr.
— fragrans, Sow.
— laccatus, Scop.
     var. amethystinus, Bolt.

Sub-genus VI. COLLYBIA, Fr.

Agaricus radicatus, Relhan.
— platyphyllus, Fr.
— maculatus, A. & S.
— fusipes, Bull.
— butyraceus, Bull.
— velutipes, Curt.
— vertirugis, Cooke
— confluens, Pers.
— conigenus, Pers.
— cirrhatus, Schum.
— tuberosus, Bull.
— collinus, Scop.
— dryophilus, Bull.
— rancidus, Fr.

Sub-genus VII. MYCENA, Fr.

Agaricus purus, Pers.
— pseudo-purus, Cooke
— flavo-albus, Fr.
— galericulatus, Scop.
     var. calopus, Fr.
— polygrammus, Bull.
— ammoniacus, Fr.
— metatus, Fr.
— tenuis, Bolt.
— filopes, Bull.
— amictus, Fr.
— vitilis, Fr.
— acicula, Schæff.
— sanguinolentus, A. & S.
— galopus, Pers.
— leucogalus, Cooke
— epipterygius, Scop.
— tenerrimus, Berk.
— electicus, Buckn.
— corticola, Schum.

Sub-genus VIII. OMPHALIA, Fr.

Agaricus sphagnicola, Berk.
— hepaticus, Batsch.
— umbelliferus, Linn.
— stellatus, Fr.
— fibula, Bull.

Sub-genus IX. PLEUROTUS, Fr.

Agaricus corticatus, Fr.
— dryinus, Pers.
— ulmarius, Bull.
— fimbriatus, Bolt.

71

Agaricus ostreatus, Jacq.
— salignus, Fr.
— acerosus, Fr.
— applicatus, Batsch.
— chioneus, Pers.

Sub-genus X.   VOLVARIA, Fr.

Agaricus speciosus, Fr.
— parvulus, Weinm.

Sub-genus XI.   PLUTEUS, Fr.

Agaricus cervinus, Schæff.
— nanus, Pers.
— chrysophæus, Schæff.
— phlebophorus, Dittm.

Sub-genus XII.   ENTOLOMA, Fr.

Agaricus sinuatus, Fr.
— prunuloides, Fr.
— jubatus, Fr.
— sericellus, Fr.
— clypeatus, Linn.
— rhodopolius, Fr.
— sericeus, Bull.
— nidorosus, Fr.

Sub-genus XIII.   CLITOPILUS, Fr.

Agaricus prunulus, Scop.
— cancrinus, Fr.

Sub-genus XIV.   LEPTONIA, Fr.

Agaricus lampropus, Fr.
— euchrous, Pers.
— chalybæus, Pers.
— incanus, Fr.

Sub-genus XV.   NOLANEA, Fr.

Agaricus pascuus, Pers.
— pisciodorus, Ces.

Sub-genus XVI.   CLAUDOPUS, Fr.

Agaricus variabilis, Pers.

Sub-genus XVII.   PHOLIOTA, Fr.

Agaricus durus, Bolt.
— radicosus, Bull.
— heteroclitus, Fr.
— aurivellus, Batsch.
— squarrosus, Müll.
— spectabilis, Fr.
— adiposus, Fr.
— mutabilis, Schæff.

Sub-genus XVIII.   INOCYBE, Fr.

Agaricus lanuginosus, Bull.
— scaber, Müll.
— flocculosus, Berk.
— rimosus, Bull.
— asterosporus, Quel.
— eutheles, B. & Br.

Agaricus geophyllus, Sow.

Sub-genus XIX.   HEBELOMA, Fr.

Agaricus fastibilis, Fr.
— testaceus, Batsch.
— versipellis, Fr.
— mesophæus, Fr.
— sinapizans, Fr.
— crustuliniformis, Bull.

Sub-genus XX.   FLAMMULA, Fr.

Agaricus lentus, Pers.
— flavidus, Schæff.
— inopus, Fr.
— sapineus, Fr.

Sub-genus XXI.   NAUCORIA, Fr.

Agaricus melinoides, Fr.
— striæpes, Cooke
— sideroides, Bull.
— pediades, Fr.
— semiorbicularis, Bull.
— conspersus, Pers.
— escharoides, Fr.

Sub-genus XXII.   GALERA, Fr.

Agaricus lateritius, Fr.
— tener, Schæff.
— hypnorum, Batsch.
— mycenopsis (Fr.)

Sub-genus XXIII.   TUBARIA, Fr.

Agaricus furfuraceus, Pers.

Sub-genus XXIV.   CREPIDOTUS, Fr.

Agaricus alveolus, Lasch.
— mollis, Schæff.

Sub-genus XXV.   PSALLIOTA, Fr.

Agaricus arvensis, Schæff.
— campestris, Linn.

Sub-genus XXVI.   STROPHARIA, Fr.

Agaricus æruginosa, Curt.
— albo-cyaneus, Desm.
— squamosus, Fr.
— stercorarius, Fr.
— semiglobatus, Batsch.

Sub-genus XXVII.   HYPHOLOMA, Fr.

Agaricus sublateritius, Fr.
— fascicularis, Huds.
— lacrymabundus, Fr.
— velutinus, Fr.
— Candolleanus, Fr.
— appendiculatus, Bull.
— hydrophilus, Bull.

Sub-genus XXVIII. Psilosybe, Fr.

Agaricus ericæus, Pers.
— udus, Pers.
— semilanceatus, Fr.
— spadiceus, Fr.
— fœnisecii, Pers.

Sub-genus XXIX. Psathyra, Pers.

Agaricus mastiger, B & Br.
— corrugis, Pers.
— spadiceogriseus, Schæff.
— pennatus, Fr.

Sub-genus XXX. Panæolus, Fr.

Agaricus separatus, Linn.
— leucophanes, B. & Br.
— fimiputris, Bull.
— retirugis, Fr.
— campanulatus, Linn.
— papilionaceus, Fr.
— acuminatus, Fr.

Sub-genus XXXI. Psathyrella, Fr.

Agaricus gracilis, Fr.
— pronus, Fr.
— atomatus, Fr.
— disseminatus, Fr.

Genus III. COPRINUS, Fr.

Coprinus comatus, Fr.
— ovatus, Fr.
— atramentarius, Fr.
— fimetarius, Fr.
    var. cinereus (Schæff.)
— tomentosus, Fr.
— niveus, Fr.
— micaceus, Fr.
— deliquescens, Fr.
— congregatus, Fr.
— domesticus, Fr.
— lagopus, Fr.
— ephemerus, Fr.
— plicatilis, Curt.

Genus IV. BOLBITIUS, Fr.

Bolbitius titubans, Fr.
— fragilis, Fr.

Genus V. CORTINARIUS, Fr.

(Phlegmacium) varius, Fr.
— anfractus, Fr.
— multiformis, Fr.
— purpurascens, Fr.
(Myxacium) collinitus, Fr.
— elatior, Fr.
— delibutus, Fr.
(Inoloma) violaceus, Fr.
— pholideus, Fr.
(Dermocybe) ochroleucus, Schæff.
— decumbens, Pers.

(Dermocybe) tabularis, Fr.
— caninus, Fr.
— anomalus, Fr.
— sanguineus, Fr.
— cinnamomeus, Fr.
(Telamonia) bulbosus, Sow.
— torvus, Fr.
— hinnuleus, Fr.
— gentilis, Fr.
— brunneus, Fr.
— rigidus, Scop.
(Hydrocybe) castaneus, Bull.
— leucopus, Bull.
— decipiens, Pers.

Genus VI. GOMPHIDIUS, Fr.

Gomphidius glutinosus, Fr.
— viscidus, Fr.
— gracilis, B. & Br.

Genus VII. PAXILLUS, Fr.

Paxillus involutus, Fr.

Genus VIII. HYGROPHORUS, Fr.

(Limacium) eburneus, Fr.
— hypothejus, Fr.
(Camarophyllus) pratensis, Fr.
— virgineus, Fr.
(Hygrocybye) lætus, Pers.
— ceraceus, Wulf.
— coccineus, Schæff.
— miniatus, Fr.
— puniceus, Fr.
— conicus, Fr.
— chlorophanus, Fr.
— psittacinus, Schæff.
— unguinosus, Fr.

Genus IX. LACTARIUS, Fr.

(Piperites) torminosus, Fr.
— cilicioides, Fr.
— turpis, Fr.
— controversus, Fr.
— insulsus, Fr.
— utilis, Weinm.
— blennius, Fr.
— hysginus, Fr.
— uvidus, Fr.
— pyrogalus, Bull.
— pergamenus, Fr.
— vellereus, Fr.
(Dapetes) deliciosus, Lim.
(Russulares) pallidus, Pers.
— quietus, Fr.
— rufus, Scop.
— glyciosmus, Fr.
— serifluus, De Cand.
— subdulcis, Bull.
— mitissimus, Fr.
— camphoratus, Bull.

Genus X. RUSSULA, Pers.

Russula nigricans, Fr.
— adusta, Fr.
— furcata, Fr.
— depallens, Fr.
— drimeia, Cooke
— virescens, Schæff.
— rubra, Fr.
— vesca, Fr.
— cyanoxantha, Fr.
— consobrina, Fr.
    var. sororia (Fr.)
— fœtens, Fr.
— fellea, Fr.
— emetica, Fr.
— ochroleuca, Fr.
— citrina, Gillet
— fragilis, Fr.
    var. violacea (Quillet)
— decolorans, Fr.
— aurata, Fr.
— alutacea, Fr.
— lutea, Fr.

Genus XI. CANTHARELLUS, Adans.

Cantharellus cibarius, Fr.
— aurantiacus, Fr.
— lobatus, Fr.

Genus XII. NYCTALUS, Fr.

Nyctalis parasitica, Fr.

Genus XIII. MARASMIUS, Fr.

Marasmius urens, Fr.
— peronatus, Fr.
— oreades, Fr.
— fusco-purpureus, Pers.
— rotula, Fr.
— androsaceus, Fr.
— epiphyllus, Fr.

Genus XIV. LENTINUS, Fr.

Lentinus tigrinus, Fr.
— cochleatus, Fr.

Genus XV. PANUS

Panus torulosus, Fr.
— stypticus, Fr.

Genus XVII. LENZITES, Fr.

Lenzites betulinus, Fr.
— sæpiaria, Fr.

Ord. II. *POLYPOREI*

Genus XVIII. BOLETUS, Dill.

Boletus luteus, Linn.
— elegans, Schum.
— flavus, With.
— granulatus, Linn.
— bovinus, Linn.

Boletus badius, Fr.
— piperatus, Bull.
— striæpes, Secr.
— chrysenteron, Fr.
— subtomentosus, Linn.
— parasiticus, Bull.
— pachypus, Fr.
— edulis, Bull.
— impolitus, Fr.
— luridus, Schæff.
— laricinus, Berk.
— scaber, Fr.
— castaneus, Bull.

Genus XIX. FISTULINA, Bull.

Fistulina hepatica, Fr.

Genus XX. POLYPORUS, Fr.

Polyporus leptocephalus, Fr.
— rufescens, Fr.
— perennis, Fr.
— squamosus, Fr.
— varius, Fr.
— frondosus, Fr.
— intybaceus, Fr.
— cristatus, Fr.
— giganteus, Fr.
— sulphureus, Fr.
— nidulans, Fr.
— fumosus, Fr.
— hispidus, Fr.
— dryadeus, Fr.
—— betulinus, Fr.
— fomentarius, Fr.
— igniarius, Fr.
— conchatus, Fr.
— ulmarius, Fr.
— annosus, Fr.
— radiatus, Fr.
— versicolor, Fr.
— abietinus, Fr.
— sanguinolentus, Fr.

Genus XXI. TRAMETES, Fr.

Trametes gibbosa, Fr.
— serpens, Fr.

Genus XXII. DÆDALEA, Fr

Dædalea quercina, Pers.
— unicolor, Fr.

Genus XXIII. MERULIUS, Fr.

Merulius corium, Fr.
— lachrymans, Fr.

Ord. III. *HYDNEI*

Genus XXV. HYDNUM, Linn.

Hydnum repandum, Linn.
— auriscalpium, Linn.
— ferruginosum, Fr.

Hydnum udum, Fr.
— niveum, Pers.
— farinaceum, Pers.

Genus XXX. PHLEBIA, Fr.

Phlebia merismoides, Fr.

Genus XXXI. GRANDINIA, Fr.

Grandinia granulosa, Fr.

Ord. IV. *THELEPHOREI*

Genus XXXIV. CRATERELLUS, Fr.

Craterellus cornucopioides, Fr.

Genus XXXV. THELEPHORA, Ehrh.

Thelephora laciniata, Pers.

Genus XXXVI. STEREUM, Fr.

Stereum purpureum, Fr.
— hirsutum, Fr.
— spadiceum, Fr.
— sanguinolentum, Fr.

Genus XXXVII. HYMENOCHÆTE, Lév.

Hymenochæte rubiginosa, Lév.
— corrugata, Berk.

Genus XXXVIII. AURICULARIA, Bull.

Auricularia mesenterica, Fr.

Genus XXXIX. CORTICIUM, Fr.

Corticium evolvens, Fr.
— giganteum, Fr.
— læve, Fr.
— sanguineum, Fr.
— quercinum, Fr.
— cinereum, Fr.
— incarnatum, Fr.
— nudum, Fr.
— aridum, Fr.
— sambuci, Fr.

Genus XL. CYPHELLA, Fr.

Cyphella capula, Fr.

Ord. V. *CLAVARIEI*

Genus XLI. CLAVARIA, Linn.

Clavaria fastigiata, Linn.
— coralloides, Linn.
— cinerea, Bull.
— cristata, Pers.
— rugosa, Bull.
— flaccida, Fr.
— stricta, Pers.

Clavaria inequalis, Fl. Dan.
— vermicularis, Scop.
— fragilis, Holmsk.
— pistillaris, Linn.

Genus XLII. CALOCERA, Fr.

Calocera viscosa, Fr.
— cornea, Fr.

Genus XLIV. PISTILLARIA, Fr.

Pistillaria quisquiliaris, Fr.

Ord. VI. *TREMELLINI*

Genus XLV. TREMELLA, Fr.

Tremella foliacea, Pers.
— mesenterica, Retz.
— albida, Huds.

Genus XLVI. EXIDIA, Fr.

Exidia glandulosa, Fr.

Genus XLVII. HIRNEOLA, Fr.

Hirneola Auricula-Judæ, Berk.

Genus XLIX. DACRYMYCES, Nees

Dacrymyces stillatus, Nees

Family II. GASTEROMYCETES

Ord. VIII. *PHALLOIDEI*

Genus LIX. PHALLUS, Linn.

Phallus impudicus, Linn.

Genus LX. CYNOPHALLUS, Fr.

Cynophallus caninus, Fr.

Ord. IX. *TRICHOGASTRES*

Genus LXIV. GEASTER, Mich.

Geaster fornicatus, Fr.
— fimbriatus, Fr.

Genus LXV. BOVISTA, Dill.

Bovista nigrescens, Pers.
— plumbea, Pers.

Genus LXVI. LYCOPERDON, Tourn.

Lycoperdon giganteum, Batsch.
— cælatum, Fr.
— gemmatum, Fr.
— pyriforme, Schæff.

Genus LXVII. SCLERODERMA, Pers.

Scleroderma vulgare, Fr.
— verrucosum, Pers.
— Geaster, Fr.

ADDENDA

Since the above has been printed the following species have been recorded for the county :—

PLANTAGINEAE

Plantago major, L. 1–5
— media, L. 2–4
— lanceolata, L. 1–5
— coronopus, L. 2–4
Littorella juncea, Berg. 2, 3

EMPETRACEAE

Empetrum nigrum, L. 1–3

ZOOLOGY
MOLLUSCS

With the exception of the limestone patches in the extreme north and south of the county, the soil of Staffordshire is not favourable to molluscan life, consequently the greater number of the land shells are recorded from those calcareous districts. The larger Helices cannot be called abundant in any part of the county, and are most numerous along roadsides and in gardens, suggesting their comparatively late incursion into the area. The aquatic species on the other hand are abundant, and some forms such as *Dreissensia* appear to be extending their range.

Altogether ninety-three species have been recorded for the county, exclusive of the following, due mostly to errors of identification, viz. *Pupa secale*, *Clausilia biplicata*, *Succinea oblonga*, *Amphipeplea glutinosa*, *Planorbis lineatus*, *Vivipara contecta* and *Pisidium nitidum*, as well as *Helicella virgata* and *H. cantiana*; the two last are however represented by colonies introduced, the former at Wren's Nest in 1887 and the latter at Sedgley in 1886.

An introduction from abroad of some note is *Physa heterostropha*, Say, an American species that has recently been taken in a millpond fed by the Tame at Wood Green, Wednesbury.

The whole assemblage is of the average British facies, with the interesting addition of *Acanthinula lamellata*, which till lately was thought to attain its southernmost present day range in this county, though formerly it lived quite down in the south of England; recently however it has been ascertained that it occurs close to Reading.

The principal records are those of Robert Garner,[1] Edwin Brown,[2] J. R. B. Masefield[3] and G. Sherriff Tye.[4]

A. GASTROPODA

I. PULMONATA

a. STYLOMMATOPHORA

Testacella haliotidea, Drap. Hanchurch near Trentham

Limax maximus, Linn.
— *flavus*, Linn. Cheadle; Stone; Stafford
— *arborum*, Bouch.-Chant.
Agriolimax agrestis (Linn.)
— *lævis* (Müll.)

---

[1] *Natural History of the County of Stafford* (1844).
[2] In Sir O. Moseley's *Natural History of Tutbury* (1863).
[3] 'The Land and Freshwater Mollusca of North Staffordshire,' *Trans. North Staffs Field Club*, vol. xxxvi. (1902).
[4] 'Mollusca of Birmingham and neighbourhood, *Journ. Conch.* (1874), i. 57, 68.

Amalia sowerbii (Fér.)   Garden of the Old Hall, Stone.   ? Introduced

— *gagates* (Drap.)   Two specimens near Stafford.   ? Introduced

Vitrina pellucida (Müll.)

Vitrea crystallina (Müll.)

— *alliaria* (Miller)

— *glabra* (Brit. Auct.)   Stafford ; Heighley Castle ; Consall near Cheadle ; Longdon

— *cellaria* (Müll.)

— *nitidula* (Drap.)

— *pura* (Ald.)   Stafford ; Cheadle ; Wren's Nest ; Stone

— *radiatula* (Ald.)   Stafford ; Cheadle ; Stone ; Wren's Nest

— *excavata* (Bean)   Maer ; Basford, near Leek ; Oakamoor ; Stafford

— *nitida* (Müll.)

— *fulva* (Müll.)

Arion ater (Linn.)   Common ; a white variety has been taken at Trentham

— *hortensis,* Fér.

— *circumscriptus,* John.   Cheadle ; Stafford ; Harborne

— *intermedius,* Norm.

— *subfuscus* (Drap.)   Cheadle ; Stafford ; Brewood ; near Birmingham

Punctum pygmæum (Drap.)   Cheadle ; Stafford ; Stone

Pyramidula rupestris (Drap.)

— *rotundata* (Müll.)

Helicella itala (Linn.)   Dovedale ; Grindon ; Wren's Nest ; Walsall ; Sedgley

— *caperata* (Mont.)

Hygromia fusca (Mont.)   Rare, Weaver Hills and Cotton Dale, Oakamoor ; Wren's Nest ; Harborne

— *hispida* (Linn.)

— *rufescens* (Penn.)   Very local

Acanthinula aculeata (Müll.)

— *lamellata* (Jeff.)   Cotton Dale, Oakamoor, under beech leaves ; Stafford (one dead specimen)

Vallonia pulchella (Müll.)

Helicigona lapicida (Linn.)

— *arbustorum* (Linn.)

Helix aspersa, Müll.   Rare and local ; said not to occur further north than Barlaston

— *nemoralis,* Linn.

— *hortensis,* Müll.

Buliminus obscurus (Müll.)

Cochlicopa lubrica (Müll.)

Azeca tridens (Pult.)   Ilam ; Weaver Hills ; Clent, Wolverhampton ; Sedgley ; Himley ; near Harborne

Cæcilianella acicula (Müll.)   Grindon ; Dovedale ; Sedgley ; Wren's Nest

Pupa cylindracea (Da C.)

— *muscorum* (Linn.)   Grindon ; Stone

Sphyradium edentulum (Drap.)   Cheadle ; Leek ; Stafford

Vertigo substriata (Jeff.)   Leek (one specimen)

— *pygmæa* (Drap.)   Grindon ; Weaver Hills ; Sedgley ; Dovedale

Balea perversa (Linn.)   Rare and local in the north

Clausilia laminata (Mont.)

— *bidentata* (Ström.)

Succinea putris (Linn.)

— *elegans,* Risso.   Stafford ; Stone ; Dovedale

b. BASOMMATOPHORA

Carychium minimum, Müll.

Ancylus fluviatilis, Müll.

Velletia lacustris (Linn.)

Limnæa auricularia (Linn.)

— *pereger* (Müll.)

— *palustris* (Müll.)

— *truncatula* (Müll.)

— *stagnalis* (Linn.)

— *glabra* (Müll.)   Local in limestone district of the north ; canal at Stoke ; ponds near Cheadle

Planorbis corneus (Linn.)

— *albus,* Müll.

— *nautileus* (Linn.)   Maer ; Coppenhall ; Tixall ; Stafford ; River Penk

— *carinatus,* Müll.

— *marginatus,* Drap.

— *vortex* (Linn.)

— *spirorbis,* Müll.   Stafford ; Stone ; Froghall ; Lithfield

— *contortus* (Linn.)   Stone ; Stafford

— *fontanus* (Lightf.)   Stafford ; Oakamoor ; Harborne

Physa fontinalis (Linn.)

— *hypnorum* (Linn.)   Stafford ; near Weston ; Burton-on-Trent ; Oldbury ; Wolverhampton

II. PROSOBRANCHIATA

Paludestrina jenkinsi (Smith)   Canal at Dudley ; canal at Lichfield ; Willenhall

Bithynia tentaculata (Linn.)

— *leachii* (Shepp.)

Vivipara vivipara (Linn.)

Valvata piscinalis (Müll.)

— *cristata,* Müll.   Stafford

Neritina fluviatilis (Linn.)   Canal at Colwich ; Stone ; Kings Bromley ; Lichfield ; Milford

MOLLUSCS

B. PELECYPODA

Dreissensia polymorpha (Pall.) Canals as far north as Stoke-on-Trent. Specimens have been found containing pearls (*North Staff. Field Club Report*, xxxiv. 65)

Unio pictorum (Linn.)

— *tumidus*, Retz.

Anodonta cygnæa (Linn.)

Sphærium rivicola (Leach)

— *corneum* (Linn.)

Sphærium ovale (Fér.) Canals: Stoke-on-Trent; Froghall; Stone; Dudley Port

— *lacustre* (Müll.)

Pisidium amnicum (Müll.)

— *pusillum* (Gmel.)

— *fontinale* (Drap.) Common (the form *P. henslowianum* occurs at Lichfield)

— *milium* (Held.) Froghall; Milford; Coppenhall

INSECTS

ORTHOPTERA

(Earwigs, Cockroaches, Grasshoppers, and Crickets)

Very little recent work appears to have been done in this order. R. Garner, in his *Natural History of the County of Stafford* (1844), mentions nine species, and the late Edwin Brown, in his 'Fauna of Burton-on-Trent' (*Natural History of Tutbury*, p. 163), gives a list of fourteen species from the Burton district. *Anisolabis maritima* appears to have been introduced in bundles of returned cask staves into a Burton brewery. Those species marked † have been determined by Mr. W. J. Lucas.

R.G. = R. Garner.   E.B. = Edwin Brown.   F.J. = Rev. F. C. R. Jourdain.

FORFICULARIA

Anisolabis maritima, Bonelli. Several living specimens occurred in a brewery at *Burton* 'some years ago' (E.B.) [1863]

Labia minor, L. (R.G.) ; frequent, *Burton* (E.B.)

Forficula auricularia, L. General

BLATTODEA

Blatta orientalis, L.

Periplaneta americana, L. First recorded from *Burton* by E.B. in 1842 (R.G.) ; now resident there

ACRIDIODEA

Stenobothrus viridulus, L. Common *Burton* district (E.B.) ; † common on slopes near *Ramshorn Woods, Ellastone* (F.J.)

— parallelus, Zett.† Also common near *Ramshorn Woods, Ellastone* (F.J.)

Gomphocerus maculatus, Thnb. (biguttatus, Charp.). Said to have been taken near *Burton* (E.B.) ;† among the screes on *Bunster, Dovedale* (F.J.)

ACRIDIODEA (*continued*)

Pachytylus migratorius, L. 'Has been captured . . . many times in this district' (E.B.) ; one at *Burton* in 1842 ; another in 1846, also at *Stoke-on-Trent* in 1857 (R.G.)

— cinerascens, Fb. One taken near *Burton* (E.B.)

Schistocerca peregrina, Oliv. Visited the south-eastern counties in some numbers in 1869, spreading into *Derbyshire, Staffordshire*, &c. No later records

GRYLLODEA

[Gryllus campestris. 'Rare, but caught in *N. Staffs.*' (R.G.) Requires confirmation]

— domesticus, L.

[Gryllotalpa gryllotalpa, L. 'Taken in gardens about *Birmingham*' (R.G.). Not confirmed by subsequent observers. One was, however, found in 1898 in a stove-house at *Meaford Hall*, near *Stone*, and a second was discovered while unloading a truck of 'oxide' at *Longton* on 14 September, 1906, both probably imported accidentally (*Zool.* 1906, p. 437)]

NEUROPTERA

(Psocids, Stone Flies, Dragon Flies, Lace-wings, etc.)

The Neuroptera of Staffordshire have been but little studied. Mr. E. Brown (*Natural History of Tutbury*, pp. 171–4) mentions ten species of Odonata, but gives very scanty information regarding the rest of the order. Upwards of thirty years ago Mr. Brown's collection was critically examined by Mr. R. McLachlan, F.R.S., and the Rev. A. E. Eaton. As will be seen from the following list, our knowledge of the Perlidae, Ephemeridae, and Hydroptilidae of Staffordshire is practically confined to what has been recorded by the Rev. A. E. Eaton, who paid special attention to those families in the Dove Valley in the neighbourhood of Ashburne.

R.G. = R. Garner.   E.B. = E. Brown.   A.E.E. = A. E. Eaton.
McL. = R. McLachlan.   G.P. = G. Pullen.   R.C.B. = R. C. Bradley.
W.H.B. = W. Harcourt Bath.   A.D.I. = A. D. Imms.
F.J. = Rev. F. C. R. Jourdain.   *Ent.* = *Entomologist.*

INSECTS

PSEUDO-NEUROPTERA

(*Psocids, Stone Flies, and May Flies*)

PSOCIDAE

Atropos divinatoria, Müll. 'In great numbers in our houses' (E.B.)

Lachesilla fatidica, Westw. Not nearly so plentiful (E.B.)

PERLIDAE

Dictyopteryx microcephala, Pictet (bicaudata, Steph.). The *Dove* (coll. E.B.)

Perla marginata, Panz. The *Dove*, near *Mapleton* (A.E.E.) ; *Dovedale* (G.P.)

— cephalotes, Curt. The *Dove*, *Mapleton*, plentiful (A.E.E.)

Chloroperla grammatica, Poda (virescens, Pict.). Not uncommon near the *Dove* (E.B.) ; *Mapleton* (A.E.E.)

Isopteryx tripunctata, Scop. Generally distributed in the *Dove Valley*

Taeniopteryx nebulosa, L. Occurs in March on a bridge over the *Trent* (coll. E.B. ; A.E.E.)

Leuctra geniculata, Steph. The slower parts of the *Dove*, near *Mapleton*, common (A.E.E.)

Nemoura variegata, Oliv. ? Morton. *Burton* district (E.B.) ; common near *Ashburne* (A.E.E.)

EPHEMERIDAE

Ephemera vulgata, L. Common on the *Trent* near *Burton* (coll. E.B.)

— danica, Müll. The mayfly of the *Dove* (A.E.E.)

EPHEMERIDAE (*continued*)

Leptophlebia submarginata, Steph. (helvipes, Steph.; geerii, Pict.). *Dovedale* (A.E.E.)

— cincta, Retz. Trout streams in the lower parts of the county (A.E.E.)

Ephemerella ignita, Poda. The *Dove* and smaller streams (A.E.E.)

— Caenis dimidiata, Steph. On the *Trent* (A.E.E.)

— rivulorum, Eaton. The *Dove*, near *Mayfield*. Abundant in June (A.E.E.)

— halterata, Fb. *Trent* and lower parts of the *Dove Valley* (A.E.E.)

Baëtis scambus, Eaton. The *Dove*, near *Hanging Bridge* and *Norbury* (A.E.E.)

— vernus, Curt. Streams and brooks, common (A.E.E.)

— rhodani, Pict. The *Dove*, &c. (A.E.E.)

— pumilus, Burmeister. Brooks and trout-streams (A.E.E.)

Centroptilum luteolum, Müll. Common (A.E.E.)

— pennulatum, Eaton. The *Manifold*, *Ilam* (A.E.E.)

Rhithrogena semicolorata, Curt. Swift parts of the *Dove*, near *Mayfield*, &c. (A.E.E.)

Heptagenia sulphurea, Müll. *Mapleton* (A.E.E.)

Ecdyurus venosus, Fb. The *Dove*, near *Thorpe* (A.E.E.)

— insignis, Eaton. Near *Mapleton :* needs confirmation (A.E.E.)

ODONATA

(*Dragon Flies*)

ANISOPTERIDES

LIBELLULIDAE

Leucorrhina dubia, Lind. *Cannock Chase* (R.C.B. in *Ent.* 1895, p. 282)

Sympetrum striolatum, Charp. Probably the species recorded by E. Brown from *Branston* as L. flaveola, L.

— scoticum, Don. *Whitmore Moss* (R.G.)

Libellula depressa, L. Common (R.G.) ; frequent in *Burton* district (E.B.) ; occasional in *Dove Valley* (F.J.) ; once *Alstonfield* (W. H. Purchas)

— quadrimaculata, L. The *Trent*, near *Burton* (F.J.)

Cordulia aenea, L. Moist woods (R.G.) ? ; *Staffordshire* (W.H.B. in *Handbook*)

AESCHNIDAE

Cordulegaster annulatus, Latr. *Birmingham* district (A.D.I.)

Aeschna juncea, L. *Sutton Park* (R.C.B.) ; *Dove Valley*, 1903–7 (F.J.)

— cyanea, Müll. Very common, *Burton* (E.B.) ; *Sutton Park* (R.C.B.) ; a ♀, *Stone*, 1904 (E. D. Bostock)

ANISOPTERIDES (*continued*)

AESCHNIDAE (*continued*)

Aeschna grandis, L. Common (R.G.); very common, *Burton* (E.B.) ; *Dove Valley* (F.J.) ; *Sutton Park* (R.C.B.) ; *Birmingham* district (A.D.I.)

ZYGOPTERIDES

AGRIONIDAE

Calopteryx virgo, L. Common (R.G.) ; near *Bretby Mill* (E.B.)

— splendens, Harr. Common on the *Trent* (E.B.) ; *Cannock Chase* (W. J. Lucas)

Erythromma naias, Hansem. *Cannock Chase* (R.C.B.) ; *Sutton Park* (R.C.B.)

Pyrrhosoma nymphula, Sulz. (minium, Harr.). Common near the *Trent* (E.B.) ; *Birmingham* district, abundant (A.D.I.) ; *Mayfield* and *Dove Valley* (F.J.)

Ischnura elegans, L'nd. Common near the *Trent* (E.B. ; F.J.)

Agrion puella, L. Common (R.G.) ; common near the *Trent* (E.B.) ; *Birmingham* district, common (A.D.I.)

Enallagma cyathigerum, Charp. *Cannock Chase* (R.C.B.) ; *Sutton Coldfield* (A.D.I.)

PLANIPENNIA

(Snake Flies, Lacewing Flies, and Scorpion Flies)

SIALIDAE

Sialis lutaria, L.   Common on the banks of ponds and rivers ; banks of *Dove* and *Trent* (E.B.)
— fuliginosa, Pict.   Near *Mapleton* (A.E.E.)

HEMEROBIIDAE

Osmylus fulvicephalus, Scop. (chrysops, auct.). Near *Mapleton* (A.E.E.)
Sisyra fuscata, Fb.   Common (A.E.E.)
Micromus variegatus, Fb.   Common (A.E.E.)
Hemerobius [the Staffordshire species have not been worked out]

CONIOPTERYGIDAE

Coniopteryx tineiformis, Curt.   Common (A.E.E.)

CHRYSOPIDAE

Chrysopa vittata, Wesm.   'Common in our woods,' *Burton* district (E.B.)
— perla, L.   'Also common in woods,' *Burton* district (E.B.)

PANORPIDAE

Panorpa communis, L.   Common (R.G.) ; very common, *Burton* district (E.B.)

TRICHOPTERA

(Caddis Flies)

The few species of Staffordshire Caddis flies here mentioned are mostly recorded from this county in the monographs of Robert McLachlan, F.R.S., published in 1865 and from 1874 to 1884, and in the pages of the *Entomologists' Monthly Magazine*.

E. M. M. = *Entom. Monthly Magazine*.
A. E. E. = A. E. Eaton.

McL. = R. McLachlan.
J. C. = Joseph Chappell.

INA QUIPALPIA

PHRYGANEIDAE

Neuronia clathrata, Kol. First recorded from Britain by J. Chappell in the *E.M.M.*, 1868, § i, vol. iv, p. 204, as taken in *Bishop's Wood*

LIMNOPHILIDAE

Limnophilus vittatus, Fab.   *Burnt* and *Bishop's Woods* (J. C. in *E.M.M.*, 1868, § 1, vol. v, p. 48)
— auricula, Curt.   *Burnt* and *Bishop's Woods* (J. C. ibid.)
— luridus, Curt.   In a greenhouse at *Willoughbridge* (J. C. ibid.)
— fuscicornis, Ramb. (fumigatus, Hag.).   *Burton-on-Trent* (McL.)
Stenophylax alpestris, Kol.   Recorded for the first time in Great Britain by R. McLachlan in the *E.M.M.*, 1868, § 1, vol. iv, p. 205, as taken in *Burnt Woods* by J. Chappell. (In Dale's mus.)
Metanaea (Halesus) flavipennis, Pict. (guttatipennis, McL.).   Probably taken by Edwin Brown near *Burton-on-Trent* (McL.)

INAEQUIPALPIA (*continued*)

SERICOSTOMATIDAE

Lasiocephala (Mormonia) basalis, Kol.   *Dovedale* (A. E. E.)

AEQUIPALPIA

LEPTOCERIDAE

Leptocerus alboguttatus, Hag. (bimaculatus, Steph.).   *Burton-on-Trent* (McL.)
— annulicornis, Steph.   *Burton-on-Trent* (McL.)
Triaenodes commutatus, McL.   *Dovedale* (McL.)
— conspersa, Ramb.   *Dovedale* (B. Cooke in Dale's mus.)

RHYACOPHILIDAE

Glossoma boltoni, Curt.   Near *Ashburne* (A. E. E.)

HYDROPTILIDAE

Hydroptila (Phrixocoma, Eaton) sparsa, Curt.   *Burton-on-Trent*, abundant (A. E. E.)
— forcipata, Eaton.   *Oakamoor* and the *R. Dove*, near *Norbury* and *Ashburne* (A. E. E.)
— occulta, Eaton.   The *R. Dove*, near *Mapleton* (A. E. E.)
— femoralis, Eaton (longispina, McL., 1884).   The *R. Dove*, near *Mapleton* (A.E.E.)

HYMENOPTERA

(Ants, Wasps, Bees, Sawflies, &c.)

The following list has been compiled from various sources which may be summarized as follows :—

The earliest county list is that of R. Garner (*History of the County of Stafford*, 1844), a brief list of some nineteen species of no particular value. In 1863 was published Edwin Brown's 'Fauna of Burton' (*Natural History of Tutbury*), which contains lists of sixty-eight species of Phytophagous and eighty-one Aculeate Hymenoptera. The Entomophaga are scarcely more than noticed in passing, but five species of Chrysididae are mentioned. As Mr. Brown's collections have been dispersed and the specimens are not available for examination, the synonymy presents many difficulties and a good deal of uncertainty is attached to the identification of several species. The area included is also somewhat vaguely defined, embracing parts of Derbyshire and Leicestershire, and only in a few cases is the exact locality given.

ACULEATA

Of late years Mr. E. D. Bostock has contributed a list of nineteen species taken near Stone in 1888 to the *Report of the N. Staffs. Field Club* for 1889, p. 17, and a brief list of twelve species from near Tittensor by the Rev. F. A. Walker appeared in the same publication in 1896 (p. 63). Mr. J. R. B. Masefield took thirty-four species of Aculeata near Cheadle in 1896, which were determined by Mr. E. Saunders (*Report N.S.F.C.*, 1897, p. 59), and has since supplemented this list by several fresh records. Mr. A. H. Martineau has also furnished me with a list of twenty-seven species which he has taken at Colwich and has kindly contributed some notes on the Heterogyna. Most of these records are incorporated in a paper by the writer in the *Report of the N. Staffs. Field Club* for 1902–3, pp. 81–7, in which 113 species are recorded.

From the above it will be seen that the only recent work is that which has been done in the Aculeata ; with the exception of a few notes by Mr. Brett on the gall-makers, the Phytophaga have been unworked for forty years past, and the Entomophaga have up to the present received no attention whatever.

The following abbreviations have been used :—

> R. G. = R. Garner (*Nat. Hist. of the County of Stafford*)
> E. B. = E. Brown (Burton)
> F. D. M. = the Rev. F. D. Morice
> J. R. B. M. = J. R. B. Masefield (Cheadle)
> E. D. B. = E. D. Bostock (Tixall)
> A. H. M. = A. H. Martineau (Colwich)
> R. C. B. = R. C. Bradley (Cannock Chase)
> F. A. W. = the Rev. F. A. Walker (Tittensor)
> C. B. = Cyril Brett (Alton)
> F. J. = the Rev. F. C. R. Jourdain (Mayfield, &c.)

An asterisk (*) prefixed to the name of any species signifies that specimens have been determined by Mr. E. Saunders. Where Burton is given as the locality, without authority, the record is taken from Mr. E. Brown's list.

HYMENOPTERA ACULEATA

(*Ants, Wasps, and Bees*)

HETEROGYNA

FORMICIDAE

Formica rufa, L. Common in most large woods
— fusca, Latr. Very common generally, in banks and hedgerows
Lasius fuliginosus, Latr. *Outwood Hills* (E. B.) ; not common, generally nests in decayed stumps, &c. (A. H. M.)
— umbratus, Nyl. *Colwich*, but not common as a rule ; near roots of decayed stumps (A. H. M.)
— flavus, De G. Very common on eastern slope of *Outwood Hills* (E. B.) ; generally common in fields where soil is light (A. H. M.)
— niger, L. Common, *Burton ;* very common, often in gardens (A. H. M.)

MYRMICIDAE

Myrmecina latreillii, Curt. *Cannock* (*Ent.* 1901, p. 232) ; *Colwich* in dead tree stumps, not common (A. H. M.)

HETEROGYNA (*continued*)

MYRMICIDAE (*continued*)

Leptothorax acervorum, Fb. Rare, usually found under bark in old stumps, *Colwich* (A. H. M.)
Myrmica rubra, L. Common, nesting in ground (A. H. M.) ; race scabrinodis, Nyl. Near *Burton.*
[Crematogaster scutellaris, Oliv. Recorded by Dr. Mason from a fernery at *Burton* ; probably imported with cork (*E.M.M.*, xxv, 330 ; *Ent.* 1889, p. 191.)]

FOSSORES

SAPYGIDAE

Sapyga quinquepunctata, Fb. *Burton*
— clavicornis, L. *Burton*, not common ('one in P. B. Mason's collection, without data, E. Saunders'). Mr. A. H. Martineau informs me that Dr. Mason has also taken this species on several occasions at *Burton* since the publication of Saunders' monograph

FOSSORES (*continued*)

POMPILIDAE

Pompilus viaticus, L. (fuscus, Sm.). *Burton*
— gibbus, Fb. The *Oaks marlpit*, near *Burton; Colwich*, common (A. H. M.)
*— pectinipes, V. de L. *Cheadle* (J. R. B. M.)
Salius exaltatus, Fb. *Burton*
*— pusillus, Schiöd. *Cheadle* (J. R. B. M.)

SPHEGIDAE

Tachytes pectinipes, L. One taken at *Cannock* (*Ent.* 1899, p. 46) ; *Colwich*, common (A.H.M.)
Trypoxylon figulus, L. *Burton; Colwich*, in wood posts, common (A. H. M.)
— clavicerum, St. F. *Colwich*, in wood posts, rare (A. H. M.)
— attenuatum, Sm. *Colwich*, in wood posts, rare (A. H. M.)
Ammophila sabulosa, L. *Cannock* (R. C B., *Ent.* 1894, p. 77)
Pemphredon shuckardi, Moraw. (Cemonus unicolor, Smith *pars*). *Burton.*
Diodontus minutus, Fb. *Burton*
— tristis, V. de L. *Burton*
Psen pallipes, Pz. *Burton*
*Gorytes mystaceus, L. *Cheadle* (J. R. B. M.) ; *Colwich*, common (A. H. M.)
*Mellinus arvensis, L. *Shobnall*, &c. (E. B.) ; *Cheadle* (J. R. B. M.)
Oxybelus uniglumis, L. *Colwich*, common (A. H. M.)
*Crabro palmipes, L. *Cheadle* (J. R. B. M.) ; *Colwich*, common (A. H. M.)
*— elongatulus, V. de L. *Cheadle* (J. R. B. M.)

FOSSORES (*continued*)

SPHEGIDAE (*continued*)

*Crabro dimidiatus, Fb. *Cheadle* (J. R. B. M.)
*— cephalotes, Pz. *Cheadle* (J. R. B. M.)
— cribrarius, L. *Shobnall*, &c. (E. B.)
— chrysostoma, St. F. (xylurgus, Shuck). *Burton*
— peltarius, Schr. (patellatus, Pz.). *Burton*

DIPLOPTERA

VESPIDAE

Vespa crabro, L. Not rare, *Whitmore* (R. G.) ; rare in *Burton* district ; *Mayfield*, a nest Sept. 1902 (F. J.)
*— vulgaris, L. Common everywhere
*— germanica, Fb. Also very common
— rufa, L. *Dovedale*, not uncommon (E. B.) ; *Colwich*, common (A. H. M.)
*— sylvestris, Scop. *Burton*, scarce ; *Cheadle* (J. R. B. M.) ; *Tittensor* (F. A. W.) ; *Dove Valley* (F. J.)
*— norvegica, Fb. *Burton*, not uncommon ; ♀ *Cheadle*, 1903 (J. R. B. M.) ; *Dove Valley* (F.J.)

EUMENIDAE

Odynerus spinipes, L. *Burton*
*— parietum, L. Common : *Burton; Mayfield* and *Dove* valley (F. J.)
*— pictus, Curt. *Eccleshall* (F. D. M.) ; *Cheadle* (J. R. B. M.) ; *Colwich*, common (A. H. M.)
*— trimarginatus, Zett. *Cheadle* (J. R. B. M.) · *Mayfield* and *Dove Valley* (F. J.)
* — parietinus, L. *Cheadle* (J. R. B. M.)

ANTHOPHILA

OBTUSILINGUES

COLLETIDAE

Colletes succinctus, L. *Cannock* (F. D. M.)
— daviesanus, Smith. *Burton* ; one ♂, *Colwich* (A. H. M.)
*— cunicularius, L. *Cheadle* (J. R. B. M.)
Prosopis communis, Nyl. *Burton*

ACUTILINGUES

ANDRENIDAE

Sphecodes gibbus, L. *Shobnall marlpit* (E. B.) ; *Stone* (E. D. B.)
— subquadratus, Smith. *Stone* (E. D. B.)
— pilifrons, Thoms. (prob. rufescens, Sm.). *Burton* ?
— affinis, V. Hag. *Colwich*, common (A. H. M.)
*Halictus rubicundus, Chr. General : *Burton; Stone* (E. D. B.) ; *Mayfield* (F. J.) ; *Cheadle* (J. R. B. M.) ; *Colwich*, common (A. H. M.)
— quadrinotatus, Kirb. *Burton*
— cylindricus, Fb. *Burton*
— albipes, Kirb. *Burton*
— longulus, Smith. *Burton* (?)
*— nitidiusculus, Kirb. *Cheadle* (J. R. B. M.) ; *Stone* (E. D. B.)
— tumulorum, L. *Colwich*, common (A. H. M.)

ACUTILINGUES (*continued*)

ANDRENIDAE (*continued*)

Halictus smeathmanellus, Kirb. *Cheadle* (J.R.B.M.)
— morio, Fb. *Burton*
*Andrena albicans, Kirb. *Burton* ; *Cheadle* (J. R. B. M.) ; *Stone* (E. D. B.)
*— rosae, Pz. *Cheadle* (J. R. B. M.) var. trimmerana, Kirb. *Stone* (E. D. B.)
— nitida, Fourc. *Burton; Trentham Park*, very common (F. A. W.)
— cineraria, L. *Burton; Store* (E. D. B.) ; *Trentham Park*, very local (F. A. W.)
*— fulva, Schr. *Burton; Cheadle*, large colonies (J. R. B. M.) ; *Stone* (E. D. B.) ; *Trentham Park*, not very common (F. A. W.)
*— nigroaenea, Kirb. *Cheadle* (J. R. B. M.) ; *Trentham Park*, very common (F. A. W.)
*— angustior, Kirb. *Cheadle* (J. R. B. M.) ; *Colwich*, rare (A. H. M.)
*— helvola, L. *Cheadle* (J. R. B. M.) ; *Stone* (E. D. B.)
* — fucata, Smith. *Cheadle* (J. R. B..M.) ; *Colwich*, rare (A. H. M.)
— fuscipes, Kirb. Several on heather, *Cannock Chase* (F. D. M.)
— fulvicrus, Kirb. *Burton*

ACUTILINGUES (continued)

ANDRENIDAE (continued)

Andrena cingulata, Fb. *Cheadle* (J. R. B. M.)
*— albicrus, Kirb. *Burton ; Cheadle* (J. R. B. M.); *Stone* (E. D. B.) ; *Colwich*, common (A. H. M.)
— minutula, Kirb. *Colwich*, common (A. H. M.)
*— nana, Kirb. ♀, *Cheadle*, 1903 (J. R. B. M.)
— wilkella, Kirb. *Colwich*, common (A. H. M.)
*— similis, Smith. *Colwich*, common (A. H. M.)
Nomada succincta, Pz. *Shobnall*, &c. (E. B.)
*— alternata, Kirb. *Cheadle* (J. R. B. M.) ; *Stone* (E. D. B.) ; *Trentham Park*, plentiful (F. A. W.)
— lathburiana, Kirb. *Stone*, rare (E. D. B.) ; *Colwich*, rare (A. H. M.)
— ruficornis, L. *Cannock* (R. C. B., *Ent.* 1895, p. 283) ; *Stone* (E. D. B.) ; *Colwich*, common (A. H. M.)
*— bifida, Thoms. *Cheadle* (J. R. B. M.) ; *Colwich* (C. J. W., *Ent.* 1896, p. 222) ; *Stone*, rare (E. D. B.)
— lateralis, Pz. *Trentham Park*, near *Tittensor*, one or two only (F. A. W.)
— ochrostoma, Kirb. *Burton* ; *Cannock* (R. C. B. *Ent.* 1895, p. 283) ; *Colwich*, common (A. H. M.)
— ferruginata, Kirb. (germanica, Smith). *Burton*
— fabriciana, L. *Burton* ; *Stone* (E. D. B.) ; *Colwich*, common (A. H. M.)
— flavoguttata, Kirb. *Burton* ; *Cannock* (R. C. B. *Ent.* 1895, p. 283)

APIDAE

Chelostoma florisomne, L. *Burton* ; *Colwich*, common (A. H. M.)
Coelioxys elongata, St. F. (simplex, Nyl.). *Burton*

ACUTILINGUES (continued)

APIDAE (continued)

*Megachile willughbiella, Kirb. *Burton* ; *Cheadle* (J. R. B. M.) ; *Mayfield* (F. J.)
*— centuncularis, L. *Maer* and *Whitmore* (R. G.); *Burton* ; *Cheadle* (J. R. B. M.)
*Osmia rufa, L. *Burton* ; *Cheadle* (J. R. B. M.) ; *Stone* (E. D. B.)
— bicolor, Schr. *Burton*
Anthidium manicatum, L. *Burton*
Eucera longicornis, L. *Scalpcliff Hill* near *Burton* (E. B.)
Melecta armata, Pz. *Burton*
Anthophora pilipes, Fb. (acervorum, Smith). *Burton* ; *Stone* (E. D. B.)
*Psithyrus vestalis, Fourc. *Burton* ; *Cheadle* (J. R. B. M.) ; *Dove Valley* (F. J.)
*— campestris, Pz. *Burton* ; *Cheadle* (J. R. B. M.)
— quadricolor, St. F. (barbutellus, Smith). *Burton*
*Bombus venustus, Smith (senilis, Fb.). *Burton* ; *Cheadle* (J. R. B. M.)
*— agrorum, Fb. *Burton* ; *Cheadle* (J. R. B. M) ; *Trentham Park* (F. A. W.) ; *Mayfield* (F. J.), &c.
*— hortorum, L. *Burton* ; *Cheadle* (J. R. B. M.). var. harrisellus, Kirb. *Cheadle* (J.R.B.M.)
*— latreillellus, Kirb. *Burton* ; *Cheadle* (J.R.B.M.)
— sylvarum, L. *Burton*
— derhamellus, Kirb. *Burton*
*— lapidarius, L. Common, *Burton* ; *Cheadle* (J. R. B. M.) ; *Stone* (E. D. B.) ; one, at *Tittensor* (F. A. W.) ; *Dove Valley* (F. J.)
— lapponicus, Fb. One ♀ *Cannock* (F. D. M.)
*— pratorum, L. *Burton* ; *Cheadle* (J. R. B. M.); *Stone* (E. D. B.) ; *Mayfield* (F. J.), &c.
— terrestris, L. Very common. Var. virginalis. One ♀, *Cheadle*, 1903 (J. R. B. M.)
Apis mellifica, L. Occasionally reverts to wild state. Nests in woodpeckers' holes, *Cannock Chase* (F. J.) Var. ligustica, introduced

PHYTOPHAGA

(Saw Flies and Gall Flies)

TENTHREDINIDAE

TENTHREDINA

Tenthredo livida, L. *Burton*
— solitaria, Scop. *Burton*
— rufiventris, Pz. *Burton*
— punctulata, Klug. *Burton*
— viridis, L. *Burton*
— gibbosa, Fall. (aucupariae, Klug.), *Burton*
Tenthredopsis nigricollis, St. F. *Burton*
— scutellaris, Fb. *Burton*
— nassata, L. (melanorrhaea, Gmel.), *Burton*
Pachyprotasis rapae, L. *Burton*
Macrophya blanda, Fb. *Burton*
— neglecta, Klug. *Burton*
— albicincta, Schr. *Burton*
— punctum album, L. (punctum, Fb.). *Burton*
Allantus scrophulariae, L. *Burton*
— tricinctus, Fb. (vespiformis, L.). *Burton*
— marginellus, Fb. (viennensis, Pz.). *Burton*

TENTHREDINIDAE (continued)

TENTHREDINA (continued)

Allantus arcuatus, Forst. *Burton*
— macula, Fourc. (zonata, Pz.), *Burton* ; *Dovedale*, W. E. Ryles
Dolerus gonagra, Fb. *Burton*
— chappelli, Cam. 'One taken by Mr. J. Chappell in *Staffordshire*' (Cameron, *Mon. Phyt. Hymenoptera*, i, 166)
— haematodis, Schr. *Burton*
— coracinus, Klug. *Burton*
— niger, L. *Burton*
Strongylogaster cingulatus, Fb. *Burton*
— delicatulus, Fall (eborinus, Klug.). *Burton*
Selandria serva, Fb. *Burton*
— stramineipes, Klug. *Burton*
Taxonus glabratus, Fall (rufipes, St. F). *Burton*
Eriocampa limacina, Retz. *Burton* ; *Dove Valley*, (F. J.)

A HISTORY OF STAFFORDSHIRE

TENTHREDINIDAE (*continued*)

TENTHREDINA (*continued*)

Eriocampa rosae, Harris. Occasionally in south (F. J.)

Blennocampa albipes, Gmel. *Burton*
— bipunctata, Klug. *Burton*
— fuscipennis, Fall. (luteiventris, Klug.) *Burton*
— fuliginosa, Schr. *Burton*
— pusilla, Klug. *Burton*

Athalia spinarum, Fb. The 'nigger' or turnip fly. *Burton*, &c.
— rosae, L. *Burton*

NEMATINA

Dineura stilata, Klug. (bicolor, Steph.) *Burton*

Cladius pectinicornis, Fourc. (difformis, Pz.) *Burton*, common
— viminalis, Fall (grandis, St. F.), *Burton*
— eradiatus, Htg. (morio, St. F.). *Burton*, common

Nematus appendiculatus, Htg. (pallipes, St. F.), *Burton*
— lucidus, Pz. *Burton*
— haemorrhoidalis, Cam. *Burton*
— miliaris, Pz. *Burton*
— myosotidis, Fb. *Burton*
— croceus, Fall (dorsalis, St. F.). *Burton*
— salicis, L. (capreae, Fb.). *Burton*
— ribesii, Scop. (trimaculatus, St. F.), R. G. ; *Burton ; Dove Valley* (F. J.), &c.
— salicis-cinereae, Retz. On Salix alba at *Alton*, August, 03 (C.B.)
— gallicola, Westw., on Salix fragilis, L. *Alton* (C.B.) ; *R. Trent* (F.J.)

CIMBICINA

Cimbex lutea, L. (femorata, L.). Near *Burton*, on alder and birch, rare

Trichiosoma lucorum, L. Common in early spring, *Burton ; Dove Valley* (F. J.)

HYLOTOMINA

Hylotoma rosae, L. *Burton*, infests rose trees
— cyaneocrocea, Forst. *Burton*

PAMPHILINA

Pamphilus sylvaticus, L. *Burton*

TENTHREDINIDAE (*continued*)

CEPHIDAE

Cephus phthisiacus, Fb. (pallipes, Klug.). *Burton*
— tabidus, Fb. *Burton*
— pygmaeus, L. *Burton*

SIRICIDAE

Sirex gigas, L. Females occur occasionally, *Ilam* (R.G.) ; *Dove Valley* ; *Uttoxeter* (F. J.) ; *Hanley* (W. Bladen) ; *Stone*, fairly common ; *Cheadle* (J. R. B. M.) ; *Heleigh Castle Wood* (T. W. Daltry)
— juvencus, L. Large numbers found in a dead spruce-fir, in all stages of development, in August, 1850 (Sir O. Mosley, *Zool.* 1850, p. 2960). 'Produced some years ago in great numbers from a diseased spruce fir at *Rolleston*' (E. B.) [1863] ; one taken near *Stone* (W. Wells Bladen)
— melanocerus, Thoms. (noctilio, Fb.). ♂ taken at *Cheadle* in 1897 (J. R. B. M., *N.S.F.C. Report*, 1898, p. 64). (Regarded by Cameron as probably not a distinct species.)

CYNIPIDAE

Rhodites eglanteriae, Htg. On Rosa canina, L., at *Alton* (C. B.)
— rosae, L. Generally distributed
— forma-tuberculata. *Great Gate* (C. B.)

Aulax heiracii, Bouché. On H. umbellatum (R. G.)

Xestophanes brevitarsis, Thoms. On Potentilla silvestris, Neck. *Alton* (C. B.)

Andricus fecundatrix, Htg. On Quercus robur, L. *Alton* (C.B.)

Cynips kollari, Htg. Already established in the district round *Burton* in 1863 ; now common on Q. robur, L. everywhere

Biorhiza terminalis, Fb. Also common on Q. robur, L. everywhere

Dryophanta folii, Htg. (scutellaris, Adler) ? *Alton* (C. B.)

Neuroterus numismatis, Oliv. Common
— lenticularis, Oliv. Common on Q. robur, L. *Alton* (C. B.)

HYMENOPTERA ENTOMOPHAGA

(*Chrysids, Ichneumons, &c.*)

CHRYSIDIDAE

Cleptes pallipes, St. F. (semiaurata, L.). *Burton*
Elampus (Hedychrum) auratus, L. *Burton*
Chrysis cyanea, L. *Burton*
— viridula, L. *Burton*
— ignita, L. *Burton ; Mayfield*, and *Dove Valley*, not uncommon (F. J.)

ICHNEUMONIDAE

[Still remain unworked. R. C. Bradley (*Ent.* 1896, p. 222) records a pair of Banchus pictus, Fb. from *Colwich*, and specimens of

ICHNEUMONIDAE (*continued*)

Pimpla turionellae, L. and Ichneumon extensorius, L. were identified by Mr. C. Morley among some insects taken at *Cheadle* in 1903]

BRACONIDAE

[Also unworked up to the present. Edwin Brown mentions Microgaster glomeratus as 'very common,' and also records Evania appendigaster as parasitic on the cockroach in the *Burton* district]

INSECTS

COLEOPTERA

(*Beetles*)

The materials from which the subsequent list has been compiled are mainly as follows :—
(1) R. Garner's *Natural History of the County of Stafford*, 1844, with a supplement dated 1860, containing a list of 171 species in all ; most of these are species of ubiquitous occurrence, and the identifications in some cases are almost certainly wrong. Garner had the assistance of Messrs. Pinder and J. B. Davis in drawing up his list of Coleoptera, and says (p. 241) that to Mr. Davis he is indebted to a considerable extent for the list. (2) A list in *Fauna of the Neighbourhood of Burton on Trent* by Edwin Brown (J. Van Voorst), 1863. This contains 623 species, mostly collected in Staffordshire, but a few are from Derbyshire only, the district round Burton embracing portions of both counties. (3) A list of 'Coleoptera collected in the Neighbourhood of Burton,' by H. W. Bates, in the *Zoologist* for 1848, p. 1997, noting 77 species. (4) A list of 491 species by Mr. L. H. Jahn in the *Report of the N. Staffs. Field Club*, 1904–5, pp. 73–90, and a supplementary list of 93 species, *t.c.*, 1906–7, p. 81–5. Nearly all Mr. Jahn's material has been through my hands. It includes several purely northern forms introduced in timber for the pits, but as several of these seem to be establishing themselves in the Hanley neighbourhood, it is better to include them.

I have been able to supplement these lists considerably from scattered records in Fowler's *British Coleoptera* and in the *Entomologist's Monthly Magazine*, as well as from a small list of captures at Cheadle by Mr. Johnston. It is hoped that the county list thus compiled, though very imperfect, especially in the Staphylinidae and Curculionidae, will act as a useful basis and stimulus for further collecting. Where no authority for the record is given, it is to be understood that it stands on the authority of Mr. Brown (Burton), Canon Fowler, or myself (Cannock Chase and Needwood Forest) ; Mr. Jahn (Hanley and Swynnerton) or Mr. Johnston (Cheadle). Otherwise the author's name is invariably given. Species whose occurrence in the county seems, for various reasons, to need confirmation, are inclosed in square brackets [ ]. Absence of locality points to general distribution, inferred at present rather than ascertained.

CICINDELIDAE

Cicindela campestris, L.

CARABIDAE

Cychrus rostratus, L.
Carabus granulatus, L.
— monilis, F.
— catenulatus, Scop.
— nemoralis, Müll.
— violaceus, L.
— nitens, L.   *Cannock Chase* (Brown) ; *Wetley Moor* (Jahn)
Notiophilus biguttatus, F.
— aquaticus, L.
Leistus spinibarbis, F.
— fulvibarbis, Dej.
— ferrugineus, L.
— rufescens, F.
Nebria brevicollis, F.
— gyllenhali, Sch.   *Cheadle*
— livida,   F.   *Cannock Chase* (Garneys and Harris)
Elaphrus riparius, L.
— cupreus, Duft.
Loricera pilicornis, F.
Clivina fossor, L.
— collaris, Hbst. *Hanley ; Burton*, occasional
Dyschirius aeneus, Dej.   *Burton* and *Cannock Chase* (Fowler)

CARABIDAE (*cont.*)

Miscodera arctica, Payk.   *Cannock Chase* ; cf. **Ent.** 1898, p. 271
Broscus cephalotes, L.   *Swynnerton*
Badister bipustulatus, F.
Licinus depressus, Payk.   *Dovedale* (Brown and Jahn)
Chlaenius vestitus, Payk.   *Cannock Chase*
— nigricornis,   F.   *Doveside* (Brown)
Oodes helopioides, F.   *Burton*
Acupalpus meridianus, L.   *Henhurst* (Brown)
Bradycellus cognatus, Gyll.
— verbasci, Duft.
— harpalinus, Dej.
Harpalus rupicola, St.   *Burton* (Fowler)
— ruficornis, F.
— aeneus, F.
— latus, L.
Anisodactylus binotatus, F.   *Burton*
Stomis pumicatus, Panz.   *Burton ; Cheadle ; Hanley*
Platyderus   ruficollis,   Marsh.   *Lichfield* and *Burton* (Fowler)
Pterostichus cupreus, L.

CARABIDAE (*cont.*)

Pterostichus versicolor, St.
— madidus, F.
— lepidus, F.   *Cannock Chase* in some number, *vide* also *Ent.* 1895, p. 236
— niger, Sch.
— vulgaris, L.
— nigrita, F.
-— gracilis, Dej.   *Burton* (Fowler)
— strenuus, Panz.
— diligens, St.
— picimanus, Duft.   *Cannock Chase*
— vernalis, Gyll.   *Burton*
— striola, F.
Amara apricaria, Payk.
— consularis,   Duft.   *Cannock Chase*
— aulica, Panz.
— patricia, Duft.   *Cannock Chase*
— bifrons,   Gyll.   *Manifold Valley* (Jahn)
— ovata, F.   *Cheadle*
— similata,   Gyll.   *Burton ; Cheadle*
— acuminata, Payk.   *Burton*
— tibialis, Payk.
— lunicollis,   Sch.   *Burton ; Cannock Chase*
— spreta, Dej.   *Cannock Chase*

CARABIDAE (cont.)

Amara familiaris, Duft.
— anthobia, Villa. *Hanley*
— trivialis, Gyll.
— communis, Panz.
— plebeia, Gyll
Calathus cisteloides, Panz.
— fuscus, F. *Stone* and *Dovedale* (Jahn)
— melanocephalus, L.
— piceus, Marsh. *Trentham* (Jahn)
Taphria nivalis, Panz. *Burton*, rare
Pristonychus terricola, Hbst.
Sphodrus leucophthalmus, L. *Burton*
Anchomenus angusticollis, F.
— dorsalis, Müll.
— albipes, F.
— marginatus, L.
— sexpunctatus, L. One specimen in *Dovedale* (Jahn)
— parumpunctatus, F.
— viduus, Panz., and var. moestus, Duft. *Hanley*, *Burton*
— fuliginosus, Panz.
— gracilis, Gyll. *Hanley*
— piceus, L. *Hanley*, *Burton*
— thoreyi, Dej. *Burton* (Fowler)
— puellus, Dej. *Burton* (Fowler)
Olisthopus rotundatus, Payk.
Bembidium rufescens, Guér.
— quinquestriatum, Gyll. *Burton* (Fowler) ; *Churnet Valley* (Jahn)
— obtusum, St.
— guttula, F.
— mannerheimi, Sahl. *Hanley*
— biguttatum, F.
— articulatum, Panz. *Burton*
— lampros, Hbst.
— nigricorne, Gyll. *Cannock Chase* (Blatch)
— atrocaeruleum, Steph. *Burton* (Bates)
— tibiale, Duft. *Burton* (Fowler)
— decorum, Panz. *Burton* (Bates)
— monticola, St. *Burton*
— quadriguttatum, F.
— quadrimaculatum, Gyll.
— femoratum, St.
— bruxellense, Wesm. *Cannock Chase*
— littorale, Ol.
— fluviatile, Dej. *Burton*
— punctulatum, Drap. *Burton*
— bipunctatum, L. *Cannock Chase*
— flammulatum, Clairv. By the *Trent* and *Dove* (Garneys and Gorham)

CARABIDAE (cont.)

Bembidium obliquum, St. Near *Burton*. one specimen (Fowler)
Tachypus flavipes, L.
Trechus discus, F. Rare by the *Trent* and *Dove* (Garneys)
— rubens, F. *Cannock Chase ; Hanley*
— minutus, F.
— secalis, Payk. *Burton*
Patrobus excavatus, Payk.
— assimilis, Ch. *Cannock Chase*
Cymindis vaporariorum, L. *Cannock Chase* (Smith in *Ent.* 1895, p. 236, and Blatch, l.c. 1890, p. 208)
Lebia chlorocephala, Hoff. *Burton*, occasional ; *Dovedale* (Jahn)
Demetrias atricapillus, L.
Dromius linearis, Ol.
— agilis, F. *Burton* common, *Trentham* (Jahn)
— quadrimaculatus, L.
— quadrinotatus, Panz.
— melanocephalus, Dej.
Metabletus foveola, Gyll.
— truncatellus, L. *Cannock Chase*

HALIPLIDAE

Brychius elevatus, Panz. *R. Dove* (Jahn)
Haliplus obliquus, Er.
— mucronatus, Steph. *Burton*, very rare (Garneys)
— flavicollis, St. *Burton* (Bates)
— variegatus, St.
— ruficollis, De G.
— fluviatilis, Aubé. *Newcastle under Lyme* (Jahn)
— lineatocollis, Marsh.

PELOBIIDAE

Pelobius tardus, Hbst. Two at *Stone* (Jahn)

DYTISCIDAE

Noterus clavicornis, De G. *Burton*
— sparsus, Marsh. *Newcastle under Lyme* (Jahn)
Laccophilus interruptus, Panz.
— obscurus, Panz.
Hyphydrus ovatus, L.
Coelambus versicolor, Sch.
— inaequalis, F.
— parallelogrammus, Ahr. *Burton*
Deronectes depressus, F.
— assimilis, Payk. One at *Burton* (Bates)
Hydroporus pictus, F.

DYTISCIDAE (cont.)

Hydroporus dorsalis, F. *Newcastle under Lyme* (Jahn)
— rivalis, Gyll. *Burton*, not scarce in *River Dove* (Jahn)
— lineatus, F.
— palustris, L.
— erythrocephalus, L.
— pubescens, Gyll.
— planus, F.
— melanarius, St. *Cannock Chase*, a specimen intermediate between type and var. monticola Sharp
— marginatus, Duft. *Cannock Chase* (Blatch)
Agabus guttatus, Payk. *Newcastle under Lyme* (Jahn), *Cheadle*
— paludosus, F. *Burton*
— nebulosus, Först.
— sturmi, Gyll.
— chalconotus, Panz.
— bipustulatus, L.
Platambus maculatus, L.
Ilybius fuliginosus, F.
— fenestratus, F. *Burton* (Bates)
— ater, De G.
— obscurus, Marsh. *Burton*
Rhantus exoletus, Först. Recorded by Garner
— bistriatus, Berg. *Burton* (Fowler)
Colymbetes fuscus, L.
Dytiscus marginalis, L.
— punctulatus, F.
Acilius sulcatus, L.

GYRINIDAE

Gyrinus natator, Scop.
— elongatus, Aubé. *Cannock Chase*
Orectochilus villosus, Müll. *Burton*

HYDROPHILIDAE

Hydrobius fuscipes, L.
Philhydrus nigricans, Z. *Newcastle under Lyme* (Jahn), *Swynnerton*
— minutus, F. *Burton*
— coarctatus, Gred. *Hanley*
Anacaena globulus, Payk.
— limbata, F.
Helochares lividus, Först.
Laccobius minutus, L. *Needwood Forest*
— nigriceps, Thoms.
Berosus luridus, L. *Burton*
Limnebius truncatellus, Th.
Chaetarthria seminulum, Herbst. *Cannock Chase*
Helophorus rugosus, Ol.

INSECTS

Helophorus aquaticus, L. and var. aequalis, Th. *Cheadle*
— aeneipennis, Thoms.
— mulsanti, Rye. *Cheadle*
— brevipalpis, Bedel
Hydrochus elongatus, Schall. *Hanley*, common
Henicocerus exsculptus, Germ. *Burton* (Bates); *Stone* (Jahn)
Hydraena pulchella, Germ. *River Dove*, near *Burton* (Fowler)
— palustris, Er. *Cheadle*
Sphaeridium scarabaeoïdes, F.
— bipustulatum, F. and var. marginatum, F.
Cercyon haemorrhoidalis, Herbst.
— obsoletus, Gyll. *Hanley*; *Burton* (Fowler)
— flavipes, F.
— lateralis, Marsh.
— melanocephalus, L.
— unipunctatus, L.
— quisquilius, L.
— pygmaeus, Ill. *Burton*
Megasternum boletophagum, Marsh.
Cryptopleurum atomarium, Muls.

STAPHYLINIDAE

Aleochara fuscipes, F.
— lanuginosa, Gr.
— moerens, Gyll. *Burton* (Fowler)
Oxypoda spectabilis, Märk. *Hanley*
— alternans, Grav.
— nigrina, Wat. *Needwood Forest*
Ischnoglossa prolixa, Grav. *Burton* (Fowler)
— corticina, Er. *Needwood Forest*
Ocyusa incrassata, Kr. *Needwood Forest*
Phloeopora reptans, Grav.
— corticalis, Grav. *Cannock Chase; Needwood Forest*
Ocalea castanea, Er. *Hanley*
Calodera aethiops, Grav. *Needwood Forest*
Astilbus canaliculatus, F.
Homalota gyllenhali, Thoms. *Needwood Forest*
— hygrotopora, Kr. *Cannock Chase*
— silvicola, Fuss. *Cannock Chase*
— graminicola, Gyll.
— aequata, Er. *Needwood Forest*
— linearis, Gr. *Cannock Chase*
— pilicornis, Thoms. *Needwood Forest*
— immersa, Er. *Cannock Chase; Needwood Forest*
— trinotata, Kr.

Homalota xanthopus, Thoms. *Needwood Forest*
— diversa, Sharp. *Cannock Chase* (Blatch in *Ent.* 1890, p. 208)
— sodalis, Er. *Needwood Forest*
— nigra, Kr.
— cinnamoptera, Thoms. *Needwood Forest*
— marcida, Er. *Hanley*
— pygmaea, Gr. *Cannock Chase*
Tachyusa atra, Gr. *Cannock Chase*
Autalia impressa, Ol.
Encephalus complicans, Westw. *Needwood Forest*
Gyrophaena affinis, Man. *Cannock Chase*
— pulchella, Heer. *Hanchurch*
— nana, Payk. *Cannock Chase*
— laevipennis, Kr. *Hanchurch* (Jahn)
Agaricochara laevicollis, Kr. *Cannock Chase*
Placusa pumilio, Gr. *Cannock Chase*
Bolitochara lucida, Gr. *Hanley*
Hygronoma dimidiata, Gr. *Hanley*
Gymnusa brevicollis, Payk. *Cannock Chase*
— variegata, Kies. *Cannock Chase*
Hypocyptus longicornis, Payk.
— laeviusculus, Man. *Cannock Chase*
Conosoma pubescens, Gr.
Tachyporus obtusus, L.
— chrysomelinus, L.
— humerosus, Er.
— hypnorum, F.
— brunneus, F.
Cilea silphoides, L.
Tachinus humeralis, Gr.
— rufipes, L. A ferruginous var. near *Burton* (Fowler)
— subterraneus, L.
— marginellus, F.
Megacronus cingulatus, Man. *Cannock Chase*
— analis, F. *Cheadle; Cannock Chase*
— inclinans, Gr. *Hanchurch*
Bolitobius lunulatus, L.
— trinotatus, Gr.
— pygmaeus, F.
Mycetoporus lucidus, Er.
— lepidus, Gr. *Hanchurch* (Jahn)
— splendidus, Gr.
Heterothops dissimilis, Gr.
Quedius ventralis, Kr. *Rudyard* (Jahn)
— mesomelinus, Marsh. *Stone* (Jahn)

Quedius fulgidus, F. *Burton*
— cruentus, Ol. *Swynnerton*
— xanthopus, Er. *Burton*
— impressus, Panz. (cinctus, Payk.)
— fuliginosus, Gr.
— tristis, Gr.
— molochinus, Gr.
— nigriceps, Kr. *Burton*
— umbrinus, Er. *Hanley*
— scintillans, Gr. *Needwood Forest*
— rufipes, Gr.
— attenuatus, Gyll. *Burton*
— semiaeneus, Steph. *Cannock Chase; Needwood Forest*
Creophilus maxillosus, L.
Leistotrophus nebulosus, F.
— murinus, L. *Burton*
Staphylinus pubescens, De G. *Burton*
— stercorarius, Ol. *Burton; Dovedale* (Jahn)
— latebricola, Gr. *Burton*
— erythropterus, L.
— caesareus, Ceder
Ocypus olens, Müll.
— similis, F. *Burton*
— brunnipes, F. *Dovedale* (Jahn)
— cupreus, Rossi
— morio, Gr.
— compressus, Marsh. *Burton*
Philonthus splendens, F.
— intermedius, Boisd.
— laminatus, Cr.
— aeneus, Rossi
— proximus, Kr. *Cannock Chase*
— decorus, Gr.
— politus, F.
— varius, Gyll.
— marginatus, F.
— fimetarius, Gr.
— ebeninus, Gr. *Hanley*
— sanguinolentus, Gr. *Burton; Hanley*
— cruentatus, Gm.
— varians, Payk
— nigrita, Nord. *Cannock Chase*
— fulvipes, F. *Burton* (Fowler)
— puella, Nord. *Needwood Forest; Dovedale*
Cafius xantholoma, Gr. *Burton; Cannock Chase* (Jahn)
Xantholinus glabratus, Gr.
— punctulatus, Gr.
— tricolor, F. *Cheadle*
— linearis, Ol.
— longiventris, Heer
Nudobius lentus, Gr. *Hanley* No doubt introduced
Baptolinus alternans, Gr.
Othius fulvipennis, F.
— myrmecophilus, Kies.
Lathrobium elongatum, L.

STAPHYLINIDAE (*cont.*)

Lathrobium fulvipenne, Gr.
— brunnipes, F.
-- rufipenne, Gyll. *Cannock Chase* (Blatch)
— longulum, Gr. *Burton*
— multipunctum, Gr. *Burton*
Cryptobium glaberrimum, Hbst. *Cannock Chase*
Stilicus orbiculatus, Er. *Burton ; Needwood Forest*
— affinis, Er.
Medon obsoletus, Nord. *Burton* (Harris)
Lithocharis ochracea, Gr. *Burton*
Sunius angustatus, Payk.
Paederus littoralis, Gr.
— riparius, L. *Burton*
Evaesthetus ruficapillus, Lac. *Needwood Forest*
Dianous coerulescens, Gyll. *Dovedale* (Fowler)
Stenus biguttatus, L. Banks of *Dove* near *Burton* (Fowler)
— bipunctatus, Er. Banks of *Dove* near *Burton* (Fowler)
— guttula, Müll. Banks of *Dove* near *Burton* (Fowler)
— juno, F.
— guynemeri, Duv. *Cannock Chase* (Blatch in *Ent.* 1890, p. 208)
— speculator, Er.
— brunnipes, Steph.
— impressus, Germ.
— carbonarius, Gyll. *Burton* (Fowler)
— pallipes, Gr. *Needwood Forest*
— flavipes, Gr. *Needwood Forest*
— pubescens, Steph.
— binotatus, Lj. *Cannock Chase*
— cicindeloides, Gr.
— similis, Hbst.
Bledius opacus, Block. *Burton* (Fowler); *Hanchurch* (Jahn)
Platystethus arenarius, Fourc.
Oxytelus rugosus, Gr.
— fulvipes, Er. *Needwood* (Gorham, Harris, and others)
— laqueatus, Marsh
— inustus, Gr. *Cannock Chase*
— sculpturatus, Gr.
— tetracarinatus, Block
Trogophloeus rivularis, Mots. *Cannock Chase*
— corticinus, Gr. *Cannock Chase*
— pusillus, Gr. *Burton* (Fowler)
Lesteva longelytrata, Goeze
Olophrum piceum, Gyll.
Lathrimaeum unicolor, Steph.
Deliphrum tectum, Payk. *Hanley*
Coryphium angusticolle, Steph. *Needwood Forest*
Homalium rivulare, Payk.

STAPHYLINIDAE (*cont.*)

Homalium oxyacanthae, Grav.
— excavatum, Steph. *Burton*
— rufipes, Fourc.
— deplanatum, Gyll. *Cannock Chase*
Anthobium minutum, F.
— ophthalmicum, Payk.
— torquatum, Marsh.
Proteinus brachypterus, F.
Megarthrus depressus, Lac.
Prognatha quadricornis, Lac. *Needwood Forest*

LEPTINIDAE

Leptinus testaceus, Müll. *Needwood Forest*, in large numbers, in a humble-bee's nest (Gorham)

SILPHIDAE

Agathidium nigripenne, Kug. *Needwood Forest; Trentham* (Jahn)
— atrum, Payk. *Cannock Chase; Needwood Forest*
— seminulum, L. *Cannock Chase*
— varians, Beck. *Needwood Forest*
— globosum, Muls. *Cannock Chase*
— rotundatum, Gyll. *Cannock Chase*
— nigrinum, St. *Needwood Forest; Trentham* (Jahn)
Amphicyllis globus, F. *Burton*
Liodes humeralis, Kug.
— orbicularis, Hbst. *Cannock Chase*
Anisotoma calcarata, Er. *Swynnerton; Cannock Chase*
— punctulata, Gyll. *Burton* (Harris)
— cinnamomea, Panz. *Cheadle*
Necrophorus humator, Goeze
— mortuorum, F.
— ruspator, Er. *Hanley*
— vespillo, L.
— vestigator, Hers. *Burton; Hanley* (Garner)
Necrodes littoralis, L. *Trentham* (Jahn), *Throwley* and *Tittensor* (Garner) ; *Burton*
Silpha nigrita, Cr. *Burton*
— obscura, L. *Burton*, also recorded by Garner
-- quadripunctata, L. *Burton* (Fowler) ; *Swynnerton*
— opaca, L. *Cannock Chase*
— thoracica, L.
— rugosa, L.
— sinuata, F.
— laevigata, F. *Cannock Chase; Burton*

SILPHIDAE (*cont.*)

Silpha atrata, L.
var. brunnea, Hbst. Recorded by Garner
Choleva angustata, F. *Burton*
— cisteloides, Panz. *Cheadle; Hanley*
— coracina, Kell. *Needwood Forest; Trentham* (Jahn)
— grandicollis, Er.
— nigrita, Er. *Cannock Chase*
— tristis, Pz.
— kirbyi, Spence. *Cannock Chase*
— chrysomeloides, Panz.
— fumata, Spence
Catops sericeus, F.

SCYDMAENIDAE

Neuraphes sparshalli, Den. *Burton* (Fowler)
Scydmaenus collaris, Müll.
— exilis, Er. *Cannock Chase, Hanchurch* (Jahn)

PSELAPHIDAE

Pselaphus heisei, Hbst. *Henhurst* (Brown) ; *R. Dove* (Bates)
Tychus niger, Payk.
Bythinus puncticollis, Den. *Burton*, common (Fowler)
— curtisii, Den. *Henhurst* (Brown)
Bryaxis fossulata, Reich. *Henhurst* (Brown)
— haematica, Reich. *Henhurst* (Brown) ; *R. Dove* (Bates)
— impressa, Panz.
Batrisus venustus, Reich. *Bagot's Park* (Gorham)
Bibloporus bicolor, Den. *Cannock Chase*
Euplectus punctatus, Muls. *Cannock Chase*
— karsteni, Reich. *Cannock Chase*
— nanus, Reich. *Cannock Chase*
— piceus, Mots. *Cannock Chase*

TRICHOPTERYGIDAE

Pteryx suturalis, Heer. *Hanchurch* (Jahn)
Ptinella denticollis, Fairm. *Needwood Forest* (Blatch); *Hanley*
— aptera, Guér. *Cannock Chase*
— angustula, Gill. *Cannock Chase*
Trichopteryx thoracica, Walt. *Burton ; Needwood Forest*
Nossidium pilosellum, Marsh. *Needwood Forest* (Gorham)
Ptenidium evanescens, Marsh *Needwood Forest* (Gorham).

PHALACRIDAE

Phalacrus corruscus, Payk.
Stilbus testaceus, Panz.

INSECTS

COCCINELLIDAE

Subcoccinella 24-punctata, L. *Burton ; Dovedale* (Jahn)
Hippodamia variegata, Goeze. *Burton*
Anisosticta 19-punctata, L. *Cannock Chase* (Jahn)
Adalia obliterata, L.
— bipunctata, L.
Mysia oblongoguttata, L. *Swynnerton ; Cannock Chase* (Brown) ; *Cheadle*
Anatis ocellata, L.
Coccinella 10-punctata, L.
— hieroglyphica, L. *Cannock Chase*
— 11-punctata, L.
— 5-punctata, L. *Burton*
— 7-punctata, L.
Halyzia 14-guttata, L.
— 18-guttata, L.
— conglobata, L. *Swynnerton*
— 22-punctata, L.
Micraspis 16-punctata, L. *Burton*
Hyperaspis reppensis, Hbst. *Staffordshire* (Fowler)
Scymnus nigrinus, Kug. *Cannock Chase*
— capitatus, F. *Cannock Chase ; Hanley*
Chilocorus similis, Rossi. *Burton*
— bipustulatus, L. *Cannock Chase ; Burton*
Exochomus quadripustulatus, L. *Cannock Chase ; Burton*
Rhizobius litura, F.
Coccidula rufa, Hbst.

ENDOMYCHIDAE

Mycetaea hirta, Marsh. *Hanley*

EROTYLIDAE

Dacne humeralis, F. *Needwood Forest*
— rufifrons, F. *Burton ; Hanchurch* (Jahn)
Triplax russica, L. *Needwood Forest ; Cannock Chase*
— aenea, Schall. *Needwood Forest; Byrkley Park* (Brown)
Cyrtotriplax bipustulata, F. *Hanchurch* (Jahn)

COLYDIIDAE

Cerylon histeroides, F.
— ferrugineum, Steph. *Cannock Chase ; Trentham* (Jahn)
— fagi, Bris. One at *Hanchurch*

HISTERIDAE

Hister unicolor, L.
— cadaverinus, Hoff. *Hanley*
— succicola, Thoms. *Cannock Chase*
— purpurascens, Hbst. *Burton*

HISTERIDAE (*cont.*)

Hister carbonarius, Ill.
— bimaculatus, L.
Gnathoncus nannetensis, Marsh. *Cannock Chase*
Saprinus nitidulus, Payk.
— aeneus, F.
Onthophilus striatus, F.

MICROPEPLIDAE

Micropeplus margaritae, Duv.

NITIDULIDAE

Brachypterus pubescens, Er.
Cercus rufilabris, Latr.
Epuraea aestiva, L.
— deleta, Er. *Hanley*
— obsoleta, F.
— pusilla, Er.
— angustula, Er. *Stone* (Jahn)
Nitidula bipustulata, L.
Soronia punctatissima, Ill. *Burton*
— grisea, L.
Omosita colon, L.
— discoidea, F.
Pocadius ferrugineus, F. *Burton*
Meligethes rufipes, Gyll.
— aeneus, F.
— viridescens, F.
— difficilis, Heer. *Staffordshire* (Fowler)
Cychramus luteus, F. *Burton*
Ips quadriguttata, F. *Needwood Forest ; Hanchurch* (Jahn)
— quadripunctata, Hbst. *Needwood Forest ; Hanchurch* (Jahn)
Rhizophagus parallelocollis, Er. *Cannock Chase*
— ferrugineus, Pk.
— nitidulus, F. *Cannock Chase ; Needwood Forest*
— dispar, Gyll
— bipustulatus, F.

TROGOSITIDAE

Nemosoma elongatum, L. Introduced in Welsh timber
Thymalus limbatus, F. *Dovedale* (Jahn) ; *Cannock Chase*

LATHRIDIIDAE

Lathridius lardarius, De G.
Coninomus nodifer, Westw.
[— constrictus, Humm. Recorded doubtfully by Fowler from *Burton*]
Enicmus minutus, L.
— fungicola, Thoms. *Cannock Chase*, in numbers
— brevicornis, Mannh. *Cannock Chase*, under birch bark (Blatch)
Cartodere filum, Aubé. *Burton*, in a herbarium (Fowler)
Corticaria pubescens, Gyll. *Hanley*

LATHRIDIIDAE (*cont.*)

Melanophthalma gibbosa, Hbst.
— fuscula, Humm.
Pediacus dermestoides, F. *Stone* (Jahn)

CUCUJIDAE

Silvanus unidentatus, Ol.

BYTURIDAE

Byturus tomentosus, F.

CRYPTOPHAGIDAE

Antherophagus nigricornis, F. *Hanchurch* (Jahn)
— pallens, Gyll. *Cannock Chase*
Cryptophagus lycoperdi, Hbst.
— scanicus, L.
— dentatus, Hbst.
Micrambe vini, Panz.
Atomaria barani, Bris. *Hanley*
— fuscipes, Gyll. *Cannock Chase*
— nigripennis, Payk. *Burton* (Harris)
— fuscata, Sch.
— pusilla, Payk.
— basalis, Er. *Burton* (Fowler)
— mesomelas, Hbst. *Burton* (Bates)
— ruficornis, Marsh.

SCAPHIDIIDAE

Scaphidium quadrimaculatum, Ol. *Cannock Chase*
Scaphisoma boleti, Panz. *Needwood Forest ; Hanley*

MYCETOPHAGIDAE

Typhaea fumata, L.
Triphyllus suturalis, F.
— punctatus, F. *Burton ; Swynnerton*
Litargus bifasciatus, F. *Swynnerton and Meaford* (Jahn)
Mycetophagus quadripustulatus, L.
— piceus, F.
— atomarius, F. *Burton*

DERMESTIDAE

Dermestes vulpinus, F. *Wolstanton* (Jahn)
— murinus, L. *Knightley Park* (Brown) ; *Hanley*
— lardarius, L.
Attagenus pellio, L.
Megatoma undata, Er. *Burton ; Cannock Chase*
Anthrenus musaeorum, L. *Burton*
— claviger, Er. *Meaford* (Jahn)

BYRRHIDAE

Byrrhus pilula, L.
— fasciatus, F.
— dorsalis, F.
Simplocaria semistriata, F. *Cannock Chase*

PARNIDAE

Elmis aeneus, Müll.
— volkmari, Panz. *Burton* (Fowler)
Potaminus substriatus, Müll. *R. Dove* near *Burton* (Fowler)
Parnus auriculatus, Panz.
— prolifericornis, F.

LUCANIDAE

Dorcus parallelopipedus, L. *Brereton* (R.G.) ; *Burton*, one at *Trentham* (Jahn)
Sinodendron cylindricum, L.

SCARABAEIDAE

Copris lunaris, L. *Whitmore* (Chappell)
Onthophagus ovatus, L. *Scalpcliff Hill* (Brown) ; *Burton* (Bates), also recorded by Garner
— coenobita, Hbst. *Needwood Forest*
Aphodius erraticus, L. *Burton*
— subterraneus, L.
— fossor, L.
— haemorrhoidalis, L.
— foetens, F.
— fimetarius, L.
— scybalarius, F.
— ater, De G.
— granarius, L.
— sordidus, F. *Burton*
— rufescens, F. *Burton*
— pusillus, Hbst.
— merdarius, F.
— inquinatus, F. *Hanley*
— sticticus, Panz. *Burton* (Bates)
— punctatosulcatus, St.
— prodromus, Br.
— contaminatus, Hbst.
— obliteratus, Panz. *Needwood Forest*
Aphodius luridus, F. *Burton*
var. nigripes, F. *Burton* (Bates)
— rufipes, L.
— depressus, Kug.
Aegialia arenaria, F. *Hanley*
Geotrupes typhoeus, L. Abundant on *Swynnerton* and *Whitmore Heaths* (Pinder *fide* Garner)
— stercorarius, L.
— spiniger, Marsh.
— mutator, Marsh. *Needwood Forest ; Dovedale* (Brown)
— vernalis, L. Recorded by Garner
— sylvaticus, Panz. *Hanley*, common

SCARABAEIDAE (*cont.*)

Trox sabulosus, L. *Burton ; Cannock Chase*, *vide* also *Ent.* 1896, p. 200
Hoplia philanthus, Fuss. *Hanley*
Serica brunnea, L.
Melolontha vulgaris, F.
Rhizotrogus solstitialis, L. One at *Stone* (Jahn)
Phyllopertha horticola, L.
Cetonia aurata, L. *North Staffs.* (Garner)

BUPRESTIDAE

Agrilus viridis, L. *Burton* (Bates)

THROSCIDAE

Throscus dermestoides, L. *Hanley ; Cannock Chase*

ELATERIDAE

Lacon murinus, L.
Cryptohypnus quadripustulatus, F. *Burton ; Dovedale* (Jahn)
— riparius, F.
Elater pomorum, Hbst. *Cannock Chase*
— balteatus, L.. *Cannock Chase ; Hanley*
— nigrinus, Payk. *Burnt Wood* (Chappell) ; *Trentham* (Jahn)
Melanotus rufipes, Hbst.
Athous niger, L.
— haemorrhoidalis, F.
— vittatus, F. *Burton ; Cannock Chase*
— longicollis, Ol. *Burton*
Limonius minutus, L. *Burton*
Sericosomus brunneus, L. *Cannock Chase ; Burnt Wood* (Fowler)
Adrastus limbatus, F.
Agriotes sputator, L.
— obscurus, L.
— lineatus, L.
— sobrinus, Kies.
— pallidulus, Ill.
Dolopius marginatus, L.
Corymbites pectinicornis, L. *Burton ; Trentham* (Jahn)
— cupreus, F.
var. aeruginosus, F.
— tessellatus, F. *Burton*
— quercus, Gyll
var. ochropterus, Steph. *Cheadle ; Cannock Chase*
— holosericeus, F. *Burton*
— aeneus, L. *Burton ; Cannock Chase*
Campylus linearis, L.

DASCILLIDAE

Dascillus cervinus, L. *Burton ; Dovedale* (Jahn)
Helodes marginata, F.
— minuta, L.
Microcara livida, F.
Cyphon coarctatus, Payk
— nitidulus, Th.
— variabilis, Th.
— pallidulus, Boh. *Cannock Chase*

LAMPYRIDAE

Lampyris noctiluca, L. Widely distributed

TELEPHORIDAE

Podabrus alpinus, Payk. *Cannock Chase ; Weel* and *Stone* (Jahn)
Ancistronycha abdominalis, F. *Dovedale* (Jahn)
Telephorus fuscus, L. (*fide* Garner)
— rusticus, Fall
— lividus, L.
var. dispar, F. *Cheadle*
— pellucidus, F.
— nigricans, Mül.
var. discoideus, Steph *Cheadle*
— lituratus, Fall.
— bicolor, F.
— haemorrhoidalis, F. *Trentham* (Jahn), *Burton*
— flavilabris, Fall.
— thoracicus, Ol. *Burton*
Rhagonycha unicolor, Curt. *Cannock Chase*
— fulva, Scop.
— testacea, L.
— limbata, Thoms.
— pallida, F.
Malthinus punctatus, Fourc.
— fasciatus, Ol. *Burton*
— frontalis, Marsh. *Cannock Chase*
Malthodes marginatus, Latr.
— guttifer, Kies. *Cannock Chase* (Blatch)
— minimus, L.

MELYRIDAE

Malachius aeneus, L. *Burton*
— bipustulatus, L.
— viridis, F. *Trentham Park* (Garner)
Axinotarsus ruficollis, Ol. *Burton* (Bates)
Anthocomus fasciatus, L. *Hanley*
Dasytes aerosus, Kies. *Burton*
Haplocnemus impressus, Marsh. *Cannock Chase*

INSECTS

CLERIDAE

Thanasimus formicarius, L. *Hanley*

Necrobia ruficollis, F. *Burton*

Corynetes coeruleus, De G. *Burton*

LIMEXYLONIDAE

Hylecoetus dermestoides, L. *Cannock Chase*

PTINIDAE

Ptinus fur, L.

— lichenum, Marsh. *Burton*

Niptus hololeucus, Fald. *Vide Mason in E.M.M. 1893, p. 238*

— crenatus, F. *Burton; Staffs. (Garner)*

Hedobia imperialis, L. *Burton; Needwood Forest; Hanley*

ANOBIIDAE

Dryophilus pusillus, Gyll.

Priobium castaneum, F.

Anobium domesticum, Fourc.

— paniceum, L. *Burton*

Xestobium tessellatum, F. *Burton; Needwood Forest*

Ptilinus pectinicornis, L. *Burton; Swynnerton*

Ernobius mollis, L. *Burton*

Xyletinus ater, Panz. *Burton (Bates)*

BOSTRICHIDAE

Bostrichus capucinus, L. *Burton* (E. Brown in coll. Power)

SPHINDIDAE

Sphindus dubius, Gyll. *Cannock Chase*

CISSIDAE

Cis boleti, Scop.

— villosulus, Marsh. *Needwood Forest*

— hispidus, Payk. *Cannock Chase*

— bidentatus, Ol. *Cannock Chase*

— pygmaeus, Marsh. *Burton*

— fuscatus, Mell. *Cannock Chase*

Ennearthron cornutum, Gyll. *Cannock Chase*

Octotemnus glabriculus, Gyll.

PRIONIDAE

Prionus coriarius, L. Old trees in Staffs. (Garner), *Cannock Chase* in 1890 and 1892 (Masefield), one at *Trentham* (Jahn)

CERAMBYCIDAE

Aromia moschata, L. *Burton*

Callidium violaceum, L. *North Staffs.* (Garner)

Clytus arietis, L.

— mysticus, L. *Burton*

Gracilia minuta, F. *Burton*

Rhagium inquisitor, F. *Trentham* (Garner)

— bifasciatum, F. *Scalpcliff Hill*, Brown; *Swynnerton*, common (Garner)

— indagator, Gyll. *Swynnerton.* This northern species is very rare in England

Toxotus meridianus, Panz. *Burton; Barlaston* (Jahn)

Pachyta cerambyciformis, Schr. On wild Angelica (Garner)

Leptura livida, F. *Burnt Wood* (Fowler)

Strangalia quadrifasciata, L. One at *Swynnerton*

— armata, Hbst.

— melanura, L. *Burnt Wood* (Fowler)

Grammoptera tabacicolor, De G. *Oakamoor* (Garner); *Hanchurch* (Jahn)

— ruficornis, F.

[— praeusta, F. *Oakamoor* (Garner)]

LAMIIDAE

Acanthocinus aedilis, L. One in the *Trent* meadows below *Hanley*, four at *Hanley* and *Stoke* (Jahn)

Pogonochaerus fasciculatus, De G. *Hanley*

— bidentatus, Th.

— dentatus, Fourc. *Swynnerton*

Leiopus nebulosus, L. *Cannock Chase; Trentham* (Jahn)

Monochammus sutor, L. *Burton;* introduced in timber

Agapanthia lineatocollis, Don. *Cannock Chase* (Jahn)

Saperda populnea, L.

Tetrops praeusta, L. *Burton*

Stenostola ferrea, Schr. *Henhurst* (Brown)

BRUCHIDAE

Bruchus rufimanus, Boh. *Cheadle*

EUPODA

Donacia crassipes, F. *Burton* (Fowler); *Trent* side (Brown)

— versicolorea, Brahm. *Burton; Trentham* (Jahn)

— sparganii, Ahr. *Burton*

— limbata, Panz. *Burton*

EUPODA (cont.)

Donacia bicolora, Zsch. *Cannock Chase; Burnt Wood* (Fowler)

— simplex, F. *Trent* side (Brown); *Hanley*, common

— semicuprea, Panz. *Hanley*

— clavipes, F. *Burton* (Fowler)

— sericea, L. *Burton*, very common, *Trentham* (Jahn)

— discolor, Panz. *Cannock Chase*

— affinis, Kunze. *Trent* side (Brown)

[Haemonia curtisi, Lac. *Trent* side and *Burton*, probably should be succeeding species]

— appendiculata, Panz. *Burton* (Rev. C. F. Thornewill)

Zeugophora subspinosa, F. *Burton; Hanley*

Lema cyanella, L.

— lichenis, Voet.

— melanopa, L.

Crioceris asparagi, L. *Burton; Hanley*

CAMPTOSOMATA

Clythra quadripunctata, L. *Burnt Wood* (Fowler); two in *Churnet Valley* (Jahn)

Cryptocephalus coryli, L. *Cannock Chase* on birch (Blatch)

— bipunctatus, L. var. lineola, F. *Chartley Moss* and *Burnt Wood* (Fowler); *Dovedale* (Jahn)

— aureolus, Suffr. *Dovedale* on Hieracium (Fowler and Jahn)

— punctiger, Payk. *Cannock Chase*

— parvulus, Müll. *Chartley Moss* and *Burnt Wood* (Fowler)

— decemmaculatus, L. *Chartley Moss* (Harris and Garneys) var. bothnicus, L. *Chartley Moss* (Harris and Garneys)

— fulvus, Goeze. *Hanley*

— pusillus, F. *Burton*

— labiatus, L.

CYCLICA

Timarcha tenebricosa, F.

— violaceonigra, De G.

Chrysomela staphylea, L.

— polita, L.

— orichalcia, Müll. *Burton; Hanley*

— varians, Sch.

— goettingensis, L. Near *Burton* (Fowler)

— graminis, L. *Burton*

CYCLICA (cont.)

Chrysomela menthrasti, Suff. *Burton* (Fowler); *Cheadle*; common on mint in gardens at *Wolverhampton* (Jahn)
— fastuosa, Scop. *Burton*; *Cheadle*; *Swynnerton*
— didymata, Scr. *Henhurst* (Brown); *Burton*
— hyperici, Forst. *Henhurst* (Brown); *Dovedale* (Jahn)
Melasoma aeneum, L. *Dovedale* (Brown); *Burnt Wood* (Fowler); *Cannock Chase*
— populi, L. *Cannock Chase*; only at *Swynnerton* (Jahn); recorded by Garner
— longicolle, Suffr. *Dovedale*, not uncommon (Jahn); recorded by Garner
Phytodecta rufipes, De G. *Burnt Wood* (Fowler); *Burton* (Bates)
— olivacea, Forst. *Burton*
— pallida, L. *Burton* (Bates); *Cheadle*
Gastroidea viridula, De G. *Burton*; *Cheadle*
— polygoni, L.
Phaedon tumidulus, Germ.
— armoraciae, L. *Burton*; *Hanley*
— cochleariae, F.
Phyllodecta vulgatissima, L.
— vitellinae, L.
Hydrothassa aucta, F.
— marginella, L.
Prasocuris junci, Br.
— phellandrii, L.
Phyllobrotica 4-maculata, L. *Swynnerton*; *Trentham* (Jahn)
Luperus rufipes, Scop.
— flavipes, L. *Cheadle*
Lochmaea capreae, L.
— suturalis, Thoms. *Cheadle*; *Hanley*
— crataegi, Forst.
Galerucella viburni, Payk. *Burton* (Bates)
— nymphaeae, L. *Cannock Chase*
— sagittariae, Gyll. *Burton*
— tenella, L. *Burton*
Adimonia tanaceti, L. *Burton Cannock Chase*; *Burnt Wood* (Fowler)
Sermyla halensis, L.

HALTICIDAE

Longitarsus luridus, Scop.
— suturellus, Duft.
— atricillus, L.
— melanocephalus, All.

HALTICIDAE (cont.)

Longitarsus nasturtii, F. Near *Burton* (Fowler)
— lycopi, Foudr. *Hanley*
— membranaceus, Foudr. *Hanley*
— flavicornis, Steph. *Hanley*
— pusillus, Gyll.
— reichei, All. *Needwood Forest* (Gorham)
— jacobaeae, Wat.
— gracilis, Kuts.
— laevis, Duft. *Hanley*
— pellucidus, Foudr. *Hanley*
Haltica oleracea, L.
— ericeti, All.
Phyllotreta nigripes, F. *Needwood Forest* (Gorham)
— punctulata, Marsh. *Needwood Forest*
— atra, Pk. *Cannock Chase*
— cruciferae, Goeze
— vittula, Redt.
— undulata, Kuts.
— nemorum, L. Very destructive in 1843 (Garner)
— exclamationis, Th. *Cannock Chase*
Aphthona nonstriata, Goeze
— venustula, Kuts. *Needwood Forest*
— virescens, Foudr. *Dovedale* (Jahn)
Sphaeroderma testaceum, F.
— cardui, Gyll. Recorded by Garner
Mniophila muscorum, Koch. *Hanley*
Mantura chrysanthemi, Koch. *Trentham* (Garner)
Crepidodera transversa, Marsh.
— ferruginea, Scop.
— rufipes, L.
— helxines, L. *Rolleston*, &c. (Brown)
— nitidula, L. *Hanley*; recorded by Garner
— aurata, Marsh.
Hippuriphila modeeri, L.
Chaetocnema hortensis, Fourc.
Plectroscelis concinna, Marsh.
Psylliodes chalcomera, Ill.
— chrysocephala, L. *Hanley*
— napi, Koch.
— affinis, Payk. *Hanley*

CRYPTOSTOMATA

Cassida vibex, F. *Dovedale* (Jahn)
— flaveola, Th. *Burton*, *Hanley*
— equestris, F. *Burton*
— viridis, F.
— hemisphaerica, Hbst. Near *Burton* (Harris)

TENEBRIONIDAE

Blaps mortisaga, L. *Burton*. Garner's records of *Shelton* and *Madeley Mill* probably refer to B. mucronata
— mucronata, Latr. One at *Hanley*
Crypticus quisquilius, L. *Hanley*
Scaphidema metallicum, F. *Lichfield* (Fowler); *Byrkley Park* (Brown)
Tenebrio molitor, L.
Gnathocerus cornutus, F. *Hanley*
Tribolium ferrugineum, F. *Burton* (Fowler)
— confusum, Duv. *Burton* (Fowler)
Hypophloeus linearis, F. *Trentham* (Jahn)
Helops striatus, Fourc.

LAGRIIDAE

Lagria hirta, L.
Cistela murina, L

MELANDRYIDAE

Tetratoma fungorum, F. *Cannock Chase*
Orchesia micans, Panz. *Burton*, *Cannock Chase*. (Ellis in *Ent.* 1898, p. 271)
Hallomenus humeralis, Panz.
Conopalpus testaceus, Ol.

PYTHIDAE

Pytho depressus, L. *Hanley*, in imported timber
Salpingus castaneus, Panz. *Cannock Chase*
— aeratus, Muls. *Hanley*
Lissodema quadripustulata, Marsh. *Burton*
Rhinosimus ruficollis, L.
— planirostris, F.

OEDEMERIDAE

Oedemera nobilis, Scop.
Nacerdes melanura, Schm. *Burton*, probably introduced with timber

PYROCHROIDAE

Pyrochroa serraticornis, Scop.

MORDELLIDAE

Anaspis frontalis, L.
— pulicaria, Costa. *Needwood Forest*
— geoffroyi, Müll.
— ruficollis, F.
— maculata, Fourc.

ANTHICIDAE

Anthicus floralis, L.
— antherinus, L

Meloidae

Meloe proscarabaeus, L.
— violaceus, Marsh. *Bagnall* (Garner) ; *Burton*

Platyrrhinidae

Brachytarsus fasciatus, Först. *Burton ; Cannock Chase*
— varius, F. *Burton ; Stableford* (Jahn)

Curculionidae

Apoderus coryli, L. *Burton*
Attelabus curculionoides, L. *Burnt Wood* (Fowler) ; *Cheadle ; Burton ; Swynnerton*
Rhinomacer attelaboides, F. *Swynnerton*, not common
Rhynchites aequatus, L. *Burton*
— cupreus, L. *Cheadle ; Swynnerton*
— aeneovirens, Marsh. *Burnt Wood* (Fowler) ; *Burton*
— coeruleus, De G. *Burton*
— minutus, Hbst.
— interpunctatus, Steph. *Burton*
— nanus, Payk. *Hanley*
— uncinatus, Thoms. *Cannock Chase*
— sericeus, Hbst. *Burton* (Bates)
— pubescens, F. *Burton;* a few at *Swynnerton*
Deporaus megacephalus, Germ.
— betulae, L.
Apion pomonae, F.
— craccae, L. *Burton*
— ulicis, Först.
— malvae, F. *Burton*
— haematodes, Kirby
— miniatum, Germ. *Burton*
— rufirostre, F. *Burton*
— varipes, Germ.
— apricans, Hbst. *Burton*
— assimile, Kirby
— trifolii, L.
— dichroum, Bed.
— nigritarse, Kirby
— aeneum, F.
— carduorum, Kirby
— pisi, F.
— striatum, Kirby
— ervi, Kirby
— vorax, Hbst. *Burton; Cheadle*
— meliloti, Kirby. *Burton*
— scutellare, Kirby
— loti, Kirby
— seniculum, Kirby
— violaceum, Kirby
— hydrolapathi, Kirby
— humile, Germ.
Otiorrhynchus tenebricosus, Hbst. *Burton ;* also recorded by Garner

Curculionidae (*cont.*)

Otiorrhynchus picipes, F. Here belong Garner's O. notatus and O. septentrionis
— sulcatus, F.
— rugifrons, Gyll.
— ovatus, L.
— muscorum, Bris. *Hanley ;* banks of *R. Dove,* near *Burton* (Fowler)
Trachyphloeus squamulatus, Ol. *Cannock Chase ; Burton*
Caenopsis fissirostris, Walt. *Cannock Chase* and *Hednesford* (Blatch)
— waltoni, Boh. *Cannock Chase*
Strophosomus coryli, F.
— capitatus, De G.
— retusus, Marsh.
— lateralis, Payk.
Exomias araneiformis, Sch.
Omias mollinus, Boh. *Burton*
Brachysomus echinatus, Bonsd. *Burton ; Swynnerton*
Sciaphilus muricatus, F.
Tropiphorus tomentosus, Marsh. *Burton*
Liophloeus nubilus, F. *Burton*
Polydrusus micans, F. *Burton* (Bates) ; recorded also by Garner
— tereticollis, De G.
— pterygomalis, Boh.
— cervinus, L.
Phyllobius oblongus, L.
— calcaratus, F. Recorded by Garner
— urticae, De G.
— pyri, L.
— argentatus, L.
— maculicornis, Germ.
— pomonae, Ol.
— viridiaeris, Laich.
— viridicollis, F. *Dovedale* (Fowler) ; *Cheadle ; Swynnerton*
Philopedon geminatus, F. *Burton*
Atactogenus exaratus, Marsh. *Burton* (Bates)
Barynotus obscurus, F.
— schönherri, Zett. *Hanley*
— elevatus, Marsh. *Burton*
Alophus triguttatus, F.
Sitones cambricus, Steph. *Burton* (Bates)
— regensteinensis, Hbst.
— tibialis, Hbst.
[— crinitus, Hbst. Recorded as well as S. griseus, F. by Garner, but both require confirmation ; cf. Fowler on these two species]
— hispidulus, F.
— humeralis, Steph. *Burton*
— flavescens, Marsh.

Curculionidae (*cont.*)

Sitones puncticollis, Steph. Recorded by Garner
— suturalis, Steph.
— lineatus, L.
— sulcifrons, Th.
Hypera punctata, F.
— rumicis, L.
— suspiciosa, Hbst.
— polygoni, L.
— variabilis, Hbst.
— plantaginis, De G.
— trilineata, Marsh. *Burton ; Churnet Valley* (Jahn)
— nigrirostris, F.
Cleonus sulcirostris, L. *Burton*
— nebulosus, L. *Burton*
Liosoma ovatulum, Clair.
Liparus coronatus, Goeze. *Burton ;* also recorded by Garner
Curculio abietis, L.
Pissodes pini, L. *Hanley,* in introduced timber
— notatus, F. *Hanley*
Orchestes quercus, L.
— alni, L.
— ilicis, F. *Burton* (Bates)
— fagi, L.
— rusci, Hbst. *Hanley*
— avellanae, Don. *Burton*
— salicis, L. *Henhurst* (Brown); *Hanley*
Rhamphus flavicornis, Clair.
Grypidius equiseti, F. *Needwood Forest ; Cannock Chase*
Erirrhinus bimaculatus, F. *Knightley Park* (Brown)
— acridulus, L.
[— aethiops, F. *Burton* (Bates and Brown) ; recorded also by Garner, but in view of its rarity requires confirmation. Fowler does not give these records]
Thryogenes nereis, Payk. *Needwood Forest*
Dorytomus vorax, F. *Hanley,* common
— tortrix, L. *Burton* (Bates) ; *Henhurst* (Brown)
— pectoralis, Panz. *Burton* (Bates) ; *Needwood Forest ; Swynnerton*
— validirostris, Gyll. *Needwood Forest* (Gorham); *Henhurst* (Brown)
— maculatus, Marsh.
var. costirostris, Gyll. *Henhurst* (Brown)
Tanysphyrus lemnae, F.
Bagous alismatis, Marsh.
[— frit, Hbst. *Burton*]
— tempestivus, Marsh. *Burton*
Anoplus plantaris, Naez.

CURCULIONIDAE (*cont.*)

Elleschus bipunctatus, L. *Burton* (Bates); *Henhurst*(Brown); *Burnt Wood* (Fowler)
Tychius meliloti, Steph. *Burton*
— tomentosus, Hbst. *Burton*
Miccotrogus picirostris, F.
Mecinus pyraster, Hbst.
Anthonomus ulmi, De G.
— pedicularius, L.
— pomorum, L. *Burton*
— rubi, Hbst.
Cionus scrophulariae, L.
— blattariae, F.
— pulchellus, Hbst.
Cryptorrhynchus lapathi, L. *Burton ; Cannock Chase*
Acalles roboris, Curt. *Cannock Chase*
— ptinoides, Marsh. *Burton ; Cannock Chase*
Coeliodes rubicundus, Hbst.
— quercus, F.
— quadrimaculatus, L.
Poophagus sisymbrii, F.
Ceuthorrhynchus assimilis, Payk.
— erysimi, F. Recorded by Garner ; one at *Swynnerton* (Jahn)
— contractus, Marsh.
— quadridens, Panz.

CURCULIONIDAE (*cont.*)

Ceuthorrhynchus pollinarius, Först.
— litura, F.
— trimaculatus, F. *Dovedale* (Jahn)
Ceuthorrhynchidius floralis, Payk.
— pyrrhorhynchus, Marsh.
— troglodytes, F.
Amalus haemorrhous, Hbst. *Cheadle*
Rhinoncus pericarpius, L.
— perpendicularis, Reich.
Litodactylus leucogaster, Marsh. *Burton* (Bates)
Limnobaris T-album, L. *Hanley*
Baris picicornis, Marsh. *Knightley* (Brown)
Balaninus venosus, Gr. *Sandon* (Jahn)
— nucum, L.
— villosus, F. *Burnt Wood* (Fowler)
— pyrrhoceras, Marsh.
— salicivorus, Payk.
Calandra granaria, L.
— oryzae, L.
Magdalis carbonaria, L. *Burton* (Bates and Brown)
— armigera, Fourc. *Hanley ; Burton*

CURCULIONIDAE (*cont.*)

Magdalis cerasi, L. *Cannock Chase; Sandon* (Jahn)
— pruni, L.

SCOLYTIDAE

Scolytus destructor, Ol.
Hylastes ater, Pk.
— palliatus, Gyll
Hylesinus crenatus, F. *Burton ;* very common and destructive about *Madeley* (Blandford) ; *Meaford* (Jahn)
— fraxini, Panz.
— vittatus, F. *Burton ; Needwood Forest ; Trentham* (Fowler)
Myelophilus piniperda, L.
Pityophthorus pubescens, Marsh. *Burton* (Fowler)
Dryocaetes autographus, Ratz. *Hanley,* probably in imported timber
— villosus, F.
Tomicus typographus, L. *Hanley*
— acuminatus, Gyll. *Hanley*
— laricis, F. *Hanley*
Pityogenes chalcographus, L. *Hanley*
— bidentatus, Hbst.
Trypodendron domesticum, L.

The following species have from time to time occurred at Hanley in imported timber :—*Ernobius nigrinus*, St. ; *Anthaxia quadripunctata*, L. ; *Semanotus undatus*, L. ; *Callidium coriaceum*, Pk. ; *Curculio piceus*, de G. ; *Crypturgus pusillus*, Gyll. The last-named seems to be establishing itself locally.

LEPIDOPTERA

(*Butterflies and Moths*)

Staffordshire cannot be said to be rich in Rhopalocera (Butterflies) as only forty-two or rather more than half of the British species have been met with in the county, and these with the exception of the commoner 'Whites,' *E. cardamines*, *V. urticae*, and *atalanta* and perhaps *E. ianira*, cannot be considered as abundant or even fairly common. The rarer species are uncertain both in appearance and in numbers, and generally very local in distribution. Two species (*L. sinapis* and *A. paphia*) are only represented in the county records by a single occurrence each, although other records may have been overlooked. The county is, however, of great interest to entomologists as it was formerly a home of the now extinct large Copper Butterfly (*Polyommatus dispar*, Haw.) if the following account of its occurrence in Staffordshire is authentic. The late Richard Weaver, in *The Entomologist's Weekly Intelligencer* for 1856, p. 18 (quoted in *The Field* in December, 1893), states :—'A few days ago a gentleman brought and showed me a male and female of that species, namely *Polyommatus dispar*, Haw. (the large Copper Butterfly), which he had captured last year in Staffordshire. This is a new locality to me and I suppose is to most entomologists.'

The species of Heterocera (moths) found in the county are on the other hand numerous, and many of the species are themselves frequently met with in great numbers, and their larvae are at times most destructive to trees and crops. The county of Stafford being situated nearly in the centre of England, and the northern portion of it being at an altitude running to considerably over 1,000 ft. above sea level, may be considered as somewhere about the dividing line between the northern and southern species of British Lepidoptera, and thus we find many species of both northern and southern insects in our lists.

INSECTS

The county is an attractive one from the fact that two of our rarest British moths (*Lasciocampa ilicifolia*, L. and *Notodonta bicolor*, Hb.) were first captured within its bounds. The first authentic British record of *L. ilicifolia* was of a specimen taken by Atkinson on Cannock Chase on 17 May, 1851, although Stephens had previously described this moth as British in 1828, and it is figured by Humphreys and Westwood, but at that time no British specimen was known. Atkinson's insect was exhibited at a meeting of the Entomological Society in London on 2 June, 1851, by Mr. Smith. Since then other specimens have been taken on Cannock Chase by Partridge, Weaver and the Brothers Bonney, and on the 17 May, 1896, an anniversary of the date of the capture of the first insect of this species, Dr. Freer took the last recorded example of this moth from that locality. Larvae have since been met with in the same locality. *N. bicolor*, Hb., the other rare British insect before mentioned, was taken in the Burnt Woods in Staffordshire on several occasions in 1861 and following years. The only other reputed British locality for this insect is Killarney, in Ireland. The actual number of species of the various families recorded as having been met with in Staffordshire is as follows :—

	British List	Staffordshire List
Rhopalocera	65	42
Heterocera		
Sphinges	39	23
Bombyces	111	69
Noctuae	324	182
Geometrae	280	178
Pyralides	78	34
Pterophori	37	11
Crambi	83	27
Tortrices	343	144
Tineae	720	238
	2,080	948

The principal authorities on the Macro-Lepidoptera of Staffordshire are Garner's *Natural History of the County of Stafford*, published in 1840 ; Sir O. Mosley's *Natural History of Tutbury*, published in 1863, which contains a list of the Lepidoptera of the Burton district by the well-known entomologist, Mr. Edwin Brown ; *Contributions to the Fauna and Flora of Repton*, by Mr. W. Garneys and others (ed. 2, 1881) ; the *Annual Reports of the North Staffordshire Field Club* (1866 to 1906) ; a paper on 'the Lepidoptera of Burton-on-Trent and neighbourhood,' which first appeared in the *Entomologist* for 1885, and was afterwards reprinted with additions in the *Transactions of the Burton-on-Trent Natural History Society* for 1889 ; besides various notes and papers which have appeared in the *Entomologist*, the *Midland Naturalist*, and other Natural History magazines and works on Entomology. In the following list the records of Macro-Lepidoptera are taken from the reports of the *North Staffordshire Field Club* unless otherwise stated.

Much less attention has been given to the Micro-Lepidoptera. Mr. Brown's list comprised some 280 species of Tortrices and Tineae ; Mr. C. G. Barrett collected sixty species, chiefly at Cannock, in June 1886 (*Report N.S.F.C.* 1887, p. 13), and in 1880 the Rev. T. W. Daltry contributed his first notes on the subject to the same publication. In 1891 (*Report*, p. 17) seventy-nine species had been recorded by him, and subsequently a few more have been added. In 1892 Messrs. J. T. Harris and P. B. Mason published a list of the Crambi, Tortrices, and Tineae of the Burton district (*Transactions Burton-on-Trent Natural History Society*, ii, p. 1), while in the *Report of the North Staffordshire Field Club* for 1899, p. 60, Mr. E. D. Bostock recorded 17 species, many of which were new to the county list. The present list also contains a number of records by Messrs. W. G. Blatch and R. C. Bradley, for which I am indebted to Mr. C. J. Wainwright, and Dr. R. Freer has contributed a list of 131 species taken by himself in the Rugeley district and the adjoining part of Cannock Chase.

E. B = E. Brown.　　C. G. B. = C. G. Barrett.　　T. W. D = Rev. T. W. Daltry.
B. L. = Burton Society, List of Macro-Lepidoptera (1885–9).
B. S. = J. T. Harris and Dr. Mason (1892).　　E. D. B. = E. D. Bostock.
C. J. W. = C. J. Wainwright.　　R. C. B. = R. C. Bradley.
W. G. B. = W. G. Blatch.　　R. F. = Dr. R. Freer.

RHOPALOCERA

PIERIDAE

Pieris brassicae, L.   General
— rapae, L.   Plentiful throughout the county
— napi, L.   In gardens and meadows, but not so plentiful as the two last species
Euchloë cardamines, L.   Very general in the spring and frequents lilac bloom
Leucophasia sinapis, L.   Only recorded as having occurred once at *Swynnerton* by Mr. Alfred Smith
Colias edusa, Fb.   Rare, but has been observed in most parts of the county.   The var. helice, Hb. has been taken once near *Stafford*
Gonopteryx rhamni, L.   Rare.   *Madeley, Craddock's Moss, Dovedale, Cheadle, Oakamoor, Hamps Valley, Mayfield*

NYMPHALIDAE

Argynnis selene, Schiff.   *Burnt Woods, Bagot's Park, Dovedale, Chartley* (B. L.)
— euphrosyne, L.   Common in *Burnt Woods* in some seasons
— aglaia, L.   Fairly plentiful on *Cannock Chase*, one dark var. formerly *Dovedale*
— adippe, L.   *Trentham* in June, 1901, and *Downs Banks*, near *Stone*, 1893 ; formerly *Dovedale* (late Rev. H. Harpur Crewe)
— paphia, L.   One in *Swynnerton Old Park*, 1890
Melitaea aurinia, Rott.   *Craddock's Moss*, but very uncertain in appearance ; one at *Burton* (B. L.)
— athalia, Rott.   *Burnt Woods* (J. B. Hodgkinson), abundant in one locality in *South Staffordshire* (J. Hardy, *vide Newman's British Butterflies*, 48)
Vanessa C-album, L.   A few noted most years, but far from common.   *Madeley, Cheadle, Oakamoor, Cannock Chase, Leek, Tixall, Stone*
— polychloros, L.   One pupa at *Madeley*.   An imago, *Alstonfield*, 1875 ; *Dovedale, Fradswell Heath*, near *Stone*, 1902 ; *Burton, Needwood Forest* (B. L.)
— urticae, L.   Very common everywhere, and often emerges from hibernation on sunny days in winter
— io, L.   Very general in September and hibernated specimens in early spring
— antiopa, L.   Very rare, but has been taken at *Badenhall* near *Eccleshall, Swynnerton, Swythamley, Madeley*, and has been observed at *Alstonfield* by Rev. W. H. Purchas in 1880. A noticeable immigration of this insect into North Staffordshire took place in 1872. One was seen near *Warslow* on 28 August, and another in the same district about the same time.   Miss Malleson observed one near *Hulme End* the same morning, and Miss Purchas took a specimen (probably the same individual) on the following afternoon.   Another was taken near *Longnor* on

NYMPHALIDAE (*cont.*)

2 September, and two not far from *Leek* on 3 September.   Mr. Hugo H. Crewe saw one near *Warslow* on 5 September, and two more were taken on the moors shortly after
Vanessa atalanta, L.   Some years very abundant and general throughout the county
— cardui, L.   Very uncertain, but plentiful some years

SATYRIDAE

Pararge megaera, L.   Occasional, but nowhere common ; *Forest Banks, Needwood* (B. L.). Not met with in the north of the county
Satyrus semele, L.   *Bunster Hill, Dovedale* (B. L.)
Epinephele ianira, L.   Common generally, but local
— tithonus, L.   Not common.   *Cannock Chase, Madeley, Burton* (B. L.)
— hyperanthes, L.   Local.   *Burnt Woods, Madeley, Needwood Forest* (B. L.)
Coenonympha typhon, Rott. Very local. *Chartley, Chorlton Moss*, and all the specimens appear to be of the var. rothliebi, Stgr.   Staffordshire appears to be about the southern limit of this insect
— pamphilus, L.   Very common on heaths

LYCAENIDAE

Thecla W-album, Knoch.   One taken near *Moddershall* in 1899 ; *Burton, Knightley Park*, (B. L.), *Market Drayton*, 1902 (E. D. B.)
— quercus, L.   *Swynnerton*, plentiful
— rubi, L.   Common, but local.   *Cannock Chase, Cheadle, Maer, Stone, Dovedale ;* formerly plentiful (B. L.)
Polyommatus phloeas, L.   Common generally in late summer and autumn
Lycaena aegon, Schiff.   Very rare at *Wolverhampton* (F. O. Morris, *vide Newman's British Butterflies*, p. 121)
— astrarche, Bgstr.   Some years abundant in *Dovedale*
— icarus, Rott.   Fairly common, but not in great abundance
— argiolus, L.   *Maer, Needwood Forest, Burnt Woods, Rugeley, Whitmore, Parson's Brake*
— minima, Fues.   Rare, *Dovedale*

HESPERIIDAE

Syrichthus malvae, L.   Very rare.   *Burnt Woods*
Nisoniades tages, L.   *Leycett* on coal-pit lows, near *Market Drayton; Dovedale* (B. L.)
Hesperia thaumas, Hufn.   Local on railway banks at *Madeley ; Burton*, not uncommon (B. L.)
— sylvanus, Esp.   Local, *Burnt Woods, Maer ; Bagot's Park*, common ; *Chartley ; Burton*, not uncommon (B. L.)
— comma, L.   *Chartley* (B. L.)

INSECTS

HETEROCERA

SPHINGES

SPHINGIDAE

Acherontia atropos, L. Very general. No less than 200 larvae of this species were brought to one entomologist in this county in 1900

Sphinx convolvuli, L. Occurs occasionally, *Madeley*, *Stone*, several years ; *Stoke* and *Hanley*, 1903 ; *Rugeley*, 1904 ; *Burton* (B. L.)

— ligustri, L. The larva is said to have been taken near *Stoke on Trent ;* not infrequent at *Burton* (B. L.)

Deilephila gallii, Schiff. One taken at *Handsworth*, 1888 (C. J. Wainwright)

— livornica, Esp. Taken twice at *Wolstanton* in 1897 and 1900. One at *Mayfield* on 18 May, 1904

Choerocampa [1] celerio, L. One at *Rugeley*, 1853 (R. W. Hawkins). One taken at *Burton* in October, 1880 (B. L.)

— porcellus, L. Not uncommon at valerian and rhododendron flowers, *Stone*, *Stafford*, *Cheadle ; Oakedge*, *Rugeley* (B. L.)

— elpenor, L. General in larval stage

Smerinthus ocellatus, L. General in the middle and south of the county in orchards

— populi, L. Common throughout the county

— tiliae, L. Very rare. Larvae said to have been taken at *Trentham*, and one imago near *Market Drayton*. Two larvae *Rugeley*, 1902

Macroglossa stellatarum, L. Very general most years, appearing in spring, and again in early autumn

— bombyliformis, Och. *Craddock's Moss*

SESIIDAE

Trochilium apiformis, Clerck. Rare, *Stoke-on-Trent*, *Cheadle*, *Warslow*

— crabroniformis, Lewin. General

Sesia sphegiformis, Fb. Plentiful in *Burnt Woods* some years, *Craddocks Moss*

— tipuliformis, Clerck. General in gardens where currants are grown

— culiciformis, L. Plentiful some years in *Burnt Woods*, *Cannock Chase*, E. D. B.

ZYGAENIDAE

Ino statices, L. Rare and local, *Madeley ; Dovedale* (B. L.)

— geryon, Hb. Rare, Staffordshire side of *Dovedale*

Zygaena trifolii, Esp. Rare and local *Cannock Chase*

— lonicerae, Esp. Canal bank *Cheswardine*, rare

— filipendulae, L. Rare, railway cutting near *Madeley*, *Cannock Chase*, *Grindon ; Burton*, *Dovedale* (B. L.)

[1] Choerocampa nerii, L. One at *Burton*, 1888 (B. L.) One at *Hanley*, Sept. 1896.

BOMBYCES

NYCTEOLIDAE

Sarothripus undulanus, Hb. One at *Swynnerton*

Hylophila prasinana, L. Not uncommon in woods, *Madeley*, *Leek ; Burton* (B. L.)

— bicolorana, Fues. One pupa at *Stone* in 1905, which duly hatched out (E. D. B.)

NOLIDAE

Nola cucullatella, L. Not generally common, *Madeley*, *Rugeley;* common at *Burton* (B. L.)

— confusalis, H.-S. *Bishop's* and *Burnt Woods ; Burton* (B. L.)

LITHOSIIDAE

Nudaria mundana, L. General, *Madeley*, *Chorlton Moss*, *Weaver Hills*, *Dovedale*, *Leek ;* scarce, *Burton* (B. L.)

Lithosia mezomella, L. *Burnt Woods*, *Swynnerton*, *Cannock Chase*, *Chartley*

— lurideola, Zinck. Common, *Burton* (B. L.)

EUCHELIIDAE

Deiopeia pulchella, L. Once taken in a meadow near *Walton's Wood*, *Madeley*, 25 June, 1892

Euchelia iacobaeae, L. *Pell Wall* near *Market Drayton*, and larvae on *Cannock Chase ;* in a garden at *Burton* once (B. L.)

CHELONIIDAE

Nemeophila russula, L. (♂ sannio, L.). Not uncommon on most mosses

— plantaginis, L. Local, but occurs in many districts

Arctia caia, L. Common in south of county, but gets rarer further north, and doubtful if it occurs at all in extreme north of the county

Spilosoma fuliginosa, L. Not common, *Chorlton Moss*, *Stone*, *Cannock Chase*, *Gun* near *Leek ; Chartley*, *Dovedale* (B. L.)

— mendica, Clerck. Near *Marchington* (E. B.)

— lubricipeda, Esp. ⎫ Very common everywhere
— menthrastri, Esp. ⎭

— urticae, Esp. Larvae found once near *Burton* (E. B.)

HEPIALIDAE

Hepialus humuli, L. Common in meadows, the silvery white wings of the male being very conspicuous at dusk when hovering over grass

— sylvanus, L. General

— velleda, Hb. General on heaths and commons, but Staffordshire is about the southern limit where this insect is found commonly

— lupulinus, L. ⎫ Very common
— hectus, L. ⎭

99

BOMBYCES (*continued*)

COSSIDAE

Cossus ligniperda, Fb. Not common, larvae in ash and willow trees

Zeuzera pyrina, L. Rare, *Yoxall* (E. B.), *Burton, Rolleston* (B. L.) ; *Stafford, Hanley, Cheadle ; Handsworth* (C. J. W.), *Stone,* E. D. B.

COCHLIOPODIDAE

Heterogenea limacodes, Hufn. Two specimens taken at *Hanley,* 15 July, 1903

LIPARIDAE

Porthesia chrysorrhoea, L. Several at *Rugeley* in 1892–3 ; at electric light at *Stoke Station,* 1905

— similis, Fues. Common throughout the county

Leucoma salicis, L. *Burton* (B. L.)

Dasychira pudibunda, L. Not uncommon in south, but not recorded in north of the county

Orgyia gonostigma, Fb. One larva at *Rugeley* (B. L.)

— antiqua, L. General, and some years abundant as far north as *Cheadle* and *Leek*

BOMBYCIDAE

Trichiura crataegi, L. Rare, two taken at gas lamps at *Stone ;* larva, *Market Drayton; Burton* (B. L.)

Poecilocampa populi, L. Not uncommon coming to light, *Swynnerton, Stone, Tixall, Rugeley, Cheadle ; Needwood* (B. L.)

Eriogaster lanestris, L. Nests of larvae, *Market Drayton ; Needwood Forest,* common *Burton* (B. L.)

Bombyx rubi, L. Common on heaths, *Madeley, Leek ; Cannock Chase ; Dovedale* (B. L.)

— quercus, L. Common some years about *Stone* and other places, but generally of the variety callunae, Palmer

Odonestis potatoria, L. Common throughout the southern half of the county

Lasiocampa quercifolia, L. Larvae taken near *Rugeley* (B. L.)

— ilicifolia, L. Taken several times on *Cannock Chase,* which is one of the very few localities where this moth occurs in England. (For particulars see p. 97)

ENDROMIDAE

Endromis versicolor, L. Used to be taken in the *Burnt Woods*

SATURNIIDAE

Saturnia pavonia, L. Common on heaths all through the county. Males assemble from long distances to a virgin female

BOMBYCES (*continued*)

DREPANULIDAE

Drepana lacertinaria, L. Fairly common on birch trees

— falcataria, L. Not uncommon

— binaria, Hufn. *Burnt Woods,* 1902

Cilix glaucata, Scop. Common some years. *Stone, Cheadle, Rugeley, Market Drayton ; Burton* (B. L.)

DICRANURIDAE

Dicranura bicuspis, Bork. Not common. *Chorlton Moss ; Cannock Chase, Rolleston* (B. L.)

— furcula, L. Occasional, *Burnt Woods, Madeley; Burton* (E. B.)

— bifida, Hb. Occasional, *Stoke-on-Trent, Stone, Burnt Woods, Cannock Chase ; Burton* (B. L.)

— vinula, L. Very common throughout the county

NOTODONTIDAE

Pterostoma palpina, L. *Chorlton, Stone, Burnt Woods, Cannock Chase ; Burton* (B.L.)

Lophopteryx camelina, L. Common

— carmelita, Esp. *Rugeley* (B. L.)

Notodonta bicolor, Hb. Eight specimens of this rare moth were taken in the *Burnt Woods* by Messrs. I. Smith, Chappell, and Charlton (see *Zoologist,* 1861, p. 7682 ; also Newman's *British Moths,* p. 228). The following is an account of the capture of the first specimen of this insect in Staffordshire, taken from the *Zoologist,* 1861, p. 7682 : 'At the ordinary monthly meeting of the Manchester Entomological Society held on 3 July, Mr. John Smith, an artisan collector resident here, exhibited a specimen of Notodonta bicolor captured by himself at *Burnt Woods,* Staffordshire, in the latter part of June last. The specimen, a fine male, though a little rubbed through being boxed out of the net, excited much interest at the meeting as being the first of the species known to have occurred in Great Britain, J. Hardy, pro Sec.'

— dictaea, L. Not uncommon. *Whitmore, Stoke-on-Trent, Cannock Chase, Cheadle, Burnt Woods ; Burton* (B. L.)

— dictaeoides, Esp. Not uncommon, *Bishop's Woods, Cannock Chase, Leek*

— dromedarius, L. The larvae frequently taken *Madeley, Swynnerton, Burnt Woods, Cheadle, Consall ; Cannock Chase* (B. L.)

— ziczac, L. Larvae not uncommon on willow and sallow ; *Madeley, Cheadle, Bishop's* and *Burnt Woods*

— trepida, Esp. Rare *Swynnerton, Burnt Woods*

— chaonia, Hb. One at *Swynnerton*

— trimacula, Esp. *Burnt Woods, Swynnerton, Cannock Chase*

PYGAERIDAE

Phalera bucephala, L. Very common, the larvae frequently stripping branches of trees of all their leaves.

Pygaera curtula, L. *Burton* (E. B.)

INSECTS

BOMBYCES (continued)

CYMATOPHORIDAE

Thyatira derasa, L.   Not common *Madeley*, *Burnt Woods*, *Dovedale*, *Leek* ; *Burton* (B. L.)
— batis, L.   General, but not plentiful; *Cheadle*, *Madeley*, *Rugeley*, *Leek*, *Burnt Woods* ; *Burton* (B. L.)
Cymatophora duplaris, L.   Not uncommon, *Cannock Chase*, *Madeley*, *Burnt Woods*, *Cheadle* ; *Henhurst* near *Burton* (E. B.)
Asphalia diluta, Fb.   Rare, *Burnt Woods* ; *Henhurst* near *Burton* (E. B.)
— flavicornis, L.   Common, *Swynnerton*, *Cannock Chase*, *Cheadle* ; *Burton* once (B. L.)
— ridens, Fb.   Rare, *Swynnerton*, *Trentham*

NOCTUAE

BRYOPHILIDAE

Bryophila perla, Fb.   Common on walls, the larvae feeding on lichens

BOMBYCOIDAE

Demas coryli, L.   Rare, larvae on birch and oak at *Swynnerton* and *Dimmingsdale* near *Cheadle*; *Dovedale* (B. L.)
Acronycta tridens, Schiff.   Fairly common at *Burton* (B. L.), *Rugeley*
— psi, L.   Common throughout the county
— leporina, L.   General, but not common, *Leek*, *Chorlton*, *Cheadle*, *Barlaston*, *Burnt Woods*, *Cannock Chase*, *Chartley* ; *Burton* (B. L.)
— megacephala, Fb.   Not common, *Bishop's* and *Burnt Woods*, *Cannock Chase*
— alni, L.   General, and reported from n.ost parts of the county
— rumicis, L.   Common, and variety ' salicis' not uncommon
— menyanthidis, View.   Rare, *Craddock's Moss*, *Chorlton*, *Warslow*, *Chartley*, *Leek*
Diloba caeruleocephala, L.   Common throughout the middle and south of the county

LEUCANIIDAE

Leucania conigera, Fb.   *Rugeley* ; *Burton* (B. L.)
— lithargyria, Esp.   Common
— comma, L.   *Burnt Woods*, *Rugeley* ; *Henhurst* and *Burton* (B. L.)
— impura, Hb. ⎱
— pallens, L. ⎰ Common
Coenobia rufa, Haw.   *Henhurst* near *Burton* (E. B.)
Tapinostola fulva, Hb.   Fairly common, *Chorlton*, *Madeley*, *Betton*, *Cheadle*, *Cannock Chase* ; *Bagot's Park*, *Burton* (B. L.)
Nonagria arundinis, Fb.   Larvae common in bulrushes
— lutosa, Hb.   One at light *Stone* ; at light *Burton* (B.L.)

APAMEIDAE

Gortyna ochracea, Hb.   Fairly common
Hydroecia nictitans, Bork.   Not common, *Whitmore*, *Cheadle*, *Burnt Woods*, *Cannock Chase* ; *Henhurst*, *Burton*, *Rugeley* (B. L.)

NOCTUAE (continued)

APAMEIDAE (continued)

Hydroecia petasitis, Dbl.   One at *Froghall* near *Cheadle*, and larvae in stems of Petasitis vulgaris
— micacea, Esp.   Occasional, *Swynnerton*, *Madeley*, *Oakamoor*, *Rugeley* ; *Burton* (B. L.)
Axylia putris, L.   Fairly common
Xylophasia rurea, Fb.   Common with the var. combusta, Dup.
— lithoxylea, Fb.   Common
— monoglypha, Hufn.   Very abundant everywhere with its melanic var.
— hepatica, L.   Not common, *Madeley* ; *Henhurst*, *Burton* (B. L.)
— scolopacina, Esp.   Local.   *Cheadle* ; *Leek* ; *Knightley Park* ; *Shobnall* (B. L.) ; *Burnt Woods*, E. D. B.
Dipterygia scabriuscula, L.   Rare.   *Swynnerton* ; *Madeley* ; *Burnt Woods*
Aporophyla australis, Bdv.   One at light at *Stoke-on-Trent*
Neuria reticulata, Vill.   *Swynnerton* ; *Burnt Woods* ; *Henhurst*, nr. *Burton* (E. B.)
Neuronia popularis, Fb.   General.   *Madeley* ; *Cheadle* ; *Rugeley* ; *Market Drayton* ; *Burton* (B. L.)
Charaeas graminis, L.   Common
Cerigo matura, Hufn.   *Rugeley* occasionally at light ; one at *Branston*, Sept. 1905 ; *Knightley* (E. B.)
Luperina testacea, Hb.   Common
— cespitis, Fb.   General
Mamestra sordida, Bork.   *Market Drayton* ; *Burton*, at sugar (B. L.)
— brassicae, L.   Very abundant, and the larvae very destructive to plants of the cabbage tribe
— persicariae, L.   Local.   *Burton* (B. L.) ; *Madeley* ; *Rugeley* ; *Handsworth* (C. J. W.)
Apamea basilinea, Fb.   Common, and larvae destructive
— gemina, Hb.   Not uncommon, and the var. remissa, Tr. occasionally
— unanimis, Tr.   Not common.   *Clayton* ; *Madeley* ; *Rugeley* ; *Burton* (B. L.)
— leucostigma, Hb.   Occasional.   *Cannock Chase*, *Tixall*
— didyma, Esp.   Common
Miana strigilis, Clerck.   Abundant and very variable, the black form being very common
— fasciuncula, Haw.   Fairly common.   *Madeley* ; *Cheadle* ; *Rugeley* ; *Burnt Woods* ; *Burton* (B. L.)
— literosa, Haw.   Occasional.   *Madeley* ; *Burnt Woods* ; *Rugeley*
— bicoloria, Vill.   Rare.   *Chorlton Moss* ; *Rugeley*
— arcuosa, Haw.   Not uncommon.   *Madeley* ; *Dovedale* ; *Cheadle* ; *Rugeley* ; *Henhurst* ; *Burton* (E. B.)
Celaena haworthii, Curt.   Rare.   *Dane Valley*

CARADRINIDAE

Grammesia trigrammica, Hufn.   Not common.   *Dovedale* ; *Swynnerton* ; *Burton* (B. L.)
Stilbia anomala, Haw.   Not uncommon in *Cannock Chase*

NOCTUAE (*continued*)

CARADRINIDAE (*continued*)

Caradrina morpheus, Hufn.   Common
— alsines, Brahm.   Local ; very plentiful some years at *Rugeley*
— taraxaci, Hb.   *Rugeley ; Madeley ; Market Drayton*
— quadripunctata, Fb.   Very common
Rusina tenebrosa, Hb.   Common in woods, coming to sugar

NOCTUIDAE

Agrotis suffusa, Hb.   Rare.   *Madeley ; Burnt Woods ; Rugeley ; Burton* (B. L.)
— saucia, Hb.   Rare.   *Swynnerton ; Chorlton Moss ; Clayton ; Burnt Woods ; Rugeley ; Burton* (B. L.)
— segetum, Schiff.   Very common, and larvae destructive to farm crops
— exclamationis, L.   Very abundant
— corticea, Hb.   Rare.   *Swynnerton*
— nigricans, L.   Local ; *Rugeley ;* common some years
— tritici, L.   Not common.   *Market Drayton ; Rugeley*
— aquilina, Hb.   *The Lawns, Burton* (E. B.)
— strigula, Thnb.   Common some years.   *Swynnerton ; Burnt Woods ; Chartley Moss ; Cannock Chase*
— obscura, Brahm.   One *Burnt Woods ; Burton,* rare (E. B.)
— simulans, Hufn.   Reported from Staffordshire (see Newman's *British Moths,* p. 336)
Noctua glareosa, Esp.   Common some years, *Madeley ; Cheadle ; Burnt Woods ; Cannock Chase ; Rugeley*
— augur, Fb.   Common throughout the county
— plecta, L.   } General
— C-nigrum, L.   }
— triangulum, Hufn.   *Madeley ; Burnt Woods ; Rugeley ; Henhurst,* nr. *Burton* (B. L.)
— brunnea, Fb.   Common
— festiva, Hb.   Very abundant
— dahlii, Hb.   Fairly common, but uncertain.   *Cheadle ; Burnt Woods,* very abundant Aug., 1905 ; *Cannock Chase*
— rubi, View.   General
— umbrosa, Hb.   } Common
— baia, Fb.   }
— castanea, Esp.   Often plentiful on heaths ; *Swynnerton ; Burnt Woods.*   Very variable in colouration.   A striking yellow variety (var. xanthe) has been taken by Mr. Woodforde in the *Burnt Woods* several years in August, and is not known to occur elsewhere (see *Rep. North Staffs. Field Club* 1900–1, p. 64, for a paper and coloured plate of this interesting variety)
— xanthographa, Fb.   Common generally with many red and dark varieties
Triphaena ianthina, Esp.   Fairly common.   *Madeley ; Craddock's Moss ; Cheadle ; Stone ; Rugeley ; Henhurst ; Burton* (B. L.)

NOCTUAE (*continued*)

NOCTUIDAE (*continued*)

Triphaena fimbria, L.   Uncertain in appearance, but common some years.   *Swynnerton ; Stone ; Cheadle ; Burnt Woods,* in all its varieties.   *Rugeley ; Henhurst ; Burton* (B. L.)
— interjecta, Hb.   Rare.   *Rugeley ; Burton* (B. L.)
— comes, Hb.   Common some years
— pronuba, L.   Very abundant everywhere.   A hermaphrodite variety was taken by Mr. E. W. H. Blagg and Mr. F. C. Woodforde in *Dovedale* in 1893 with left forewing, var. inuba, and right forewing mottled as in the type

AMPHIPYRIDAE

Amphipyra pyramidea, L.   Rare.   *Swynnerton ; Burton* (B. L.)
— tragopogonis, L.   Very common
Mania typica, L.   Very common
— maura, L.   Common

ORTHOSIIDAE

Panolis piniperda, Panz.   Common at sallow bloom and in pine woods
Pachnobia rubricosa, Fb.   Common at sallow bloom
Taeniocampa gothica, L.   } Very common
— incerta, Hufn.   }
— opima, Hb.   Two specimens taken at *Cannock Chase* by Mr. Burnett
— populeti, Fb.   Not common.   *Madeley ; Leek ; Cheadle ; Burnt Woods ; Henhurst,* nr. *Burton* (B. L.)
— stabilis, View.   Very abundant
— gracilis, Fb.   Rare.   *Madeley ; Rugeley ; Burton ; Branston* (B. L.).   Not reported in the north of the county
— miniosa, Fb.   Rare.   *Swynnerton ; Burnt Woods*
— munda, Esp.   Not common.   *Madeley ; Burnt Woods*
— pulverulenta, Esp.   Common at sallows in south of the county, rare in the north
Orthosia suspecta, Hb.   Common locally and variable in colour
— upsilon, Bork.   Not common.   *Chorlton,* larva ; *Cheadle ;* larvae common, *Burton* (B. L.)
— lota, Clerck   } Common
— macilenta, Hb.   }
Anchocelis rufina, L.   Common some years
— pistacina, Fb.   Not uncommon.   *Burnt Woods ; Market Drayton ; Rugeley ; Burton* (B. L.)
— litura, L.   Common
Cerastis vaccinii, L.   }
— spadicea, Hb.   } Very common
Scopelosoma satellitia, L.   }
Xanthia citrago, L.   Not uncommon.   *Cheadle ; Rugeley ; Market Drayton*
— fulvago, L.   Common, var. flavescens, Esp.   *Madeley*
— flavago, Fb.   Common some years.   *Rugeley ; Cheadle ; Burnt Woods ; Burton* (B. L.)
— gilvago, Esp.   Not common.   *Burnt Woods ; Rugeley ; Oakamoor ; Burton* (E. B.)
— circellaris, Hufn.   Common

NOCTUAE (*continued*)

ORTHOSIIDAE (*continued*)

Cirrhoedia xerampelina, Hb. Common some years. *Madeley ; Stone ; Tixall ; Cheadle ; Leek,* nr. *Mow Cop ; Dovedale ; Burton* (B. L.)

COSMIIDAE

Tethea subtusa, Och. Larvae, *Stoke-on-Trent ; Madeley ; Henhurst,* nr. *Burton* (E. B.) ; *Handsworth* (C. J. W.)
— retusa, L. Larvae on sallow, *Wrinehill*
Cosmia paleacea, Esp. Very local and not common. *Cannock Chase*
Calymnia traperina, L. Common
— diffinis, L. *Burton* (E. B.)
— affinis, L. Rare. *Burnt Woods ; Burton* (B. L.)

HADENIDAE

Dianthoecia nana, Rott. Rare. *Market Drayton*
— capsincola, Hb. Common
— cucubali, Fues. Not common. *Madeley ; Rugeley ; Burton,* common (B. L.)
— carpophaga, Bork. Rare. *Rugeley ; Shobnall ; Burton* (B. L.)
Hecatera serena, Fb. Not common. *Swynnerton ; Leek ; Rugeley*
Polia chi, L. Generally common, especially in the north of the county
Dasypolia templi, Thnb. One at *Cheadle ; Warslow* (Hugo H. Crewe) ; *Cauldon,* nr. *Cheadle,* 1906
Cleoceris viminalis, Fb. *Rudyard ; Madeley ; Chartley ; Leek ; Rugeley ; Burnt Woods ; Henhurst,* nr. *Burton* (B. L.)
Miselia oxyacanthae, L. Very common, and var. capucina frequent
Agriopis aprilina, L. ⎫
Euplexia lucipara, L. ⎬ Common
Phlogophora meticulosa, L. ⎭
Aplecta prasina, Fb. Fairly common. *Swynnerton ; Madeley ; Burnt Woods ; Cheadle ; Dovedale*
— occulta, L. One taken in *Bagot's Park* (C. A. E. Rodgers, *Ent.* 1895, p. 284)
— nebulosa, Hufm. Common in woods
— tincta, Brahm. Common at sugar. *Burnt Woods ; Cannock Chase*
Hadena adusta, Esp. Not common. *Burnt Woods ; Cannock Chase ; Henhurst ; Burton* (B. L.)
— protea, Bork. Fairly common. *Cheadle ; Leek ; Cannock Chase ; Burton* (B. L.)
— glauca, Hb. Not uncommon. *Swynnerton ; Cannock Chase ; Burnt Woods ; Leek*
— dentina, Esp. Not common. *Madeley ; Burnt Woods ; Rugeley ;* common *Burton* (B. L.)
— trifolii, Rott. Larvae occasionally *Rugeley.* This county is probably the northern limit for this species ; common *Burton* (B. L.)
— dissimilis, Knoch. Not common, *Whitmore ; Market Drayton ; Madeley ;* scarce at *Rugeley ; Henhurst ;* and *Burton* (B. L.)
— oleracea, L. Common everywhere

NOCTUAE (*continued*)

HADENIDAE (*continued*)

Hadena pisi, L. Common some seasons, and larvae on broom and sallow
— thalassina, Rott. Common
— contigua, Vill. Fairly common on *Cannock Chase*
— genistae, Bork. Rare. *Burnt Woods*

XYLINIDAE

Xylocampa areola, Esp. General
Calocampa vetusta, Hb. Rare. *Swynnerton ; Burnt Woods ; Henhurst ;* and *Burton* (B. L.)
— exoleta, L. General. *Burnt Woods ; Cheadle ; Henhurst,* nr. *Burton* (B. L.)
— solidaginis, Hb. Common where the bilberry grows. *Swythamley ; Leek ; Cannock Chase ; Burnt Woods*
Asteroscopus sphinx, Hufn. At lamps on *Burton Bridge* (E. B.)
Cucullia verbasci, L. Larvae taken at *Madeley,* and at *Grindon,* June, 1905, in considerable numbers
— chamomillae, Schiff. Not common *Madeley ; Market Drayton ; Handsworth* (C. J. W.)
— umbratica, L. Common. *Cheadle ; Stone ; Market Drayton ; Rugeley ; Burton* (B. L.)

GONOPTERIDAE

Gonoptera libatrix, L. Common everywhere

PLUSIIDAE

Habrostola tripartita, Hufn. Local. *Cheadle ; Rugeley ; Market Drayton ; Burton* (B. L.)
— triplasia, L. Fairly common. *Cheadle ; Rugeley ; Market Drayton ; Burton* (B. L.) ; *Handsworth*
Plusia chrysitis, L. Common
— festucae, L. Local. *Madeley ; Betton Moss ; Leek ; Cheadle ; Rugeley ; Burton* (B. L.) ; common *Trent Valley,* nr. *Lichfield*
— iota, L. ⎫
— pulchrina, Haw. ⎬ Common
— gamma, L. ⎭
— interrogationis, L. Rare. *Maer ; Cannock Chase ; Leek*

HELIOTHIDAE

Anarta myrtilli, L. Common on heather throughout the county
Heliaca tenebrata, Scop. Not common. *Swynnerton ; Madeley ; Rugeley ;* common some years, *Burton*

POAPHILIDAE.

Phytometra viridaria, Clerck. *Craddock's Moss ; Cannock Chase*

EUCLIDIIDAE

Euclidia mi, Clerck. Rare. *Craddock's Moss ; Dovedale ; The Lawns, Burton ;* and *Chartley* (B. L.)
— glyphica, L. Rare. *Madeley*

NOCTUAE (*continued*)

CATOCALIDAE

Catocala fraxini, L. Once at *Burton*, 2 Oct. 1852 (E. B.)

AVENTIIDAE

Aventia flexula, Schiff. *Chartley Moss*

HERMINIIDAE

Zanclognatha grisealis. Hb. Not uncommon. *Rugeley; Walton's Wood; Madeley; Burnt Woods; Henhurst*, nr. *Burton* (B. L.); *Handsworth* (C. J. W.)
— tarsipennalis, Tr. One at *Tixall*, and one at *Market Drayton*
Pechypogon barbalis, Clerck. *Burnt Woods*

NOCTUAE (*continued*)

HERMINIIDAE (*continued*)

Bomolocha pontis, Thnb. Common but local. *Swynnerton Heath; Burnt Woods; Maer; Cheadle*
Hypena proboscidalis, L. Common everywhere on nettles
Hypenodes costaestrigalis, St. *Burnt Woods*, very abundant, Aug. 1905 (E. D. B.)

BREPHIDES

Brephos parthenias, L. Plentiful in March around birch trees. *Swynnerton; Cheadle; Burnt Woods; Chartley; Cannock Chase*

GEOMETRAE

UROPTERYGIDAE

Uropteryx sambucaria, L. Common throughout the county

ENNOMIDAE

Epione apiciaria, Schiff. Not common. *Madeley; Bagot's Park; Cheadle; Handsworth; Rugeley; Henhurst;* and *Burton* (E. B.)
Rumia luteolata, L. Common
Venilia macularia, L. Rare and local. *Dovedale; Dydon Wood* (B.L.)
Angerona prunaria, L. Local. *Swynnerton; Burnt Woods*
Metrocampa margaritaria, L. General. *Stone; Cheadle; Cannock Chase; Swynnerton; Burton* (B.L.)
Ellopia prosapiaria, L. Common in all pine woods
Eurymene dolobraria, L. Rare. *Swynnerton; Burnt Woods; Madeley; Henhurst* nr. *Burton* (E. B.)
Pericallia syringaria, L. Occasional. *Madeley; Stone; Ellastone; Burnt Woods; Rolleston;* and *Burton* (B.L.); *Handsworth* (C. J. W.)
Selenia bilunaria, Esp. } General in the southern
— lunaria, Schiff. } half of the county
Odontopera bidentata, Clerck. Common
Crocallis elinguaria, L. Very generally distributed
Eugonia almaria, L. *Chorlton Moss; Burnt Woods; Cannock Chase; Oakedge;* and *Burton* (B. L.)
— fuscantaria, Haw. One at *Madeley; Stone*, at light; *Stoke-on-Trent*, at electric light; *Burton* (E. B.)
— erosaria, Bork. *Swynnerton; Burnt Woods; Madeley; Burton*, rare (E. B.)
— quercinaria, Hufn. Fairly common. *Burnt Woods; Burton* (B. L.)
Himera pennaria, L. Common

AMPHIDASYDAE

Phigalia pedaria, Fb. Plentifully distributed
Nyssia hispidaria, Fb. Rare. *Bishop's Woods*, in March
Biston hirtaria, Clerck. *Rugeley* (B.L.); *Stone, Trentham*

AMPHIDASYDAE (*continued*)

Amphidasys strataria, Hufn. General, but not common. *Trentham, Madeley, Stone, Cheadle, Rugeley; Cannock Chase* and *Burton* (B. L.); *Handsworth* (C. J. W.)
— betularia, L. Fairly common and the variety doubledayaria, Mill. more common than the type of recent years

BOARMIIDAE

Hemerophila abruptaria, Thnb. Rare. *Madeley, Market Drayton; Burton* (B. L.); *Handsworth* (C. J. W.)
Cleora lichenaria, Hufn. *Henhurst* nr. *Burton* (B. L.)
Boarmia repandata, L. Very common and variable in markings and colour, and given to melanism
— gemmaria, Brahm. Common everywhere
Tephrosia crepuscularia, Hb. } Common
— biundularia, Bork. }
— punctularia, Hb. Common on *Cannock Chase*

GEOMETRIDAE

Geometra papilionaria, L. Not uncommon. *Chorlton Moss, Cannock Chase, Burnt Woods, Cheadle; Oakedge, Burton* (B. L.)
Phorodesma pustulata, Hufn. Once taken at *Swynnerton;* once *Shobnall* (B. L.); at electric light, *Hanley*, July, 1905
Iodis lactearia, L. *Rugeley; Burton*, common (B. L.)
Hemithea strigata, Müll. *Market Drayton; Henhurst* nr. *Burton* (B. L.)

EPHYRIDAE

Zonosoma porata, Fb. Not common. *Swynnerton, Burnt Woods*
— punctaria, L. *Burnt Woods; Cannock Chase* (B. L.)
— pendularia, Clerck. Numerous some years in *Burnt Woods*

ACIDALIIDAE

Asthena luteata, Schiff. Local. *Burnt Woods* and *Cannock Chase; Oakedge* (B. L.)
— candidata, Schiff. Fairly common

INSECTS

GEOMETRAE (*continued*)

ACIDALIIDAE (*continued*)

Asthena sylvata, Hb. Not common. *Bishop's Woods, Madeley, Dovedale, Rushton*; *Henhurst* nr. *Cannock Chase* (B. L.)
— blomeri, Curt. Very local and rare, *Stone, Dovedale, Shobnall, Hoar Cross*, and *Needwood* (B. L.)
Euvisteria obliterata, Hufn. *Burnt Woods* and *Cannock Chase*; *Oakedge*, common (B. L.)
Venusia cambrica, Curt. Common in woods around *Cheadle* and *Leek*, which is probably the southern limit of this insect
Acidalia dimidiata, Hufn.
— bisetata, Hufn. } Fairly common
— virgularia, Hb.
— subsericeata, Haw. Local, *Dovedale*
— immutata, L. *Chartley*
— remutaria, Hb. Common
— fumata, St. *Swynnerton, Maer* nr. *Cheadle, Dovedale*; *Chartley* (B. L.)
— imitaria, Hb. Scarce. *Madeley, Market Drayton, Rugeley*; *Burton* (B. L.)
— aversata, L. Common generally
— inornata, Haw. *Swynnerton, Burnt Woods, Cannock Chase*
— emarginata, L. Rare. *Madeley*; *Burton* (B. L.)
Timandra amataria, L. Rare and local. *Stoke-on-Trent, Rugeley*; *Tatenhill* and *Henhurst* nr. *Burton* (B. L.)

CABERIDAE

Cabera pusaria, L. Common
— rotundaria, Haw. Very rare, *Heleigh Castle* nr. *Madeley*
— exanthemata, L. Very general
Bapta temerata, Hb. *Henhurst* nr. *Burton* (E. B.)

MACARIIDAE

Macaria notata, L. Local, *Swynnerton, Burnt Woods*, very abundant some years
— liturata, Clerck. *Swynnerton, Maer, Cheadle, Cannock Chase*
Halia vauaria, L. Very common

FIDONIIDAE

Panagra petraria, Hb. Common on heaths
Numeria pulveraria, L. Occasional and local, *Burnt Woods*; *Henhurst* nr. *Burton* (E. B.)
Scodiona belgiaria, Hb. Rare, one at *Whitmore, Cannock Chase*, nr. *Cheadle, Leek*
Ematurga atomaria, L.
Bupalus piniaria, L. } Abundant
Aspilates strigillaria, Hb.

ZERENIDAE

Abroxas grossulariata, L. Very common in gardens
— sylvata, Scop. General and abundant in many valleys in the north of the county.
Ligdia adustata, Schiff. Very rare, one at *Madeley*
Lomaspilis marginata, L. Common locally

GEOMETRAE (*continued*)

HYBERNIIDAE

Hybernia rupicapraria, Hb.
— leucophearia, Schiff.
— aurantiaria, Esp. } Common throughout the county
— marginaria, Bork.
— defoliaria, L.
Anisopteryx aescularia, Schiff. General

LARENTIIDAE

Cheimatobia brumata, L. } Abundant
— boreata, Hb.
Oporabia dilutata, Bork. Common
— filigrammaria, H. S. Rare. *Gun* nr. *Leek*
Larentia didymata, L. Very common
— multistrigaria, Haw. Fairly common. *Madeley, Cheadle, Burnt Woods, Cannock Chase*
— caesiata, Lang. On heaths, *Cheadle* and *Leek*, not further south; *Dovedale* (B. L.)
— flavicinctata, Hb. Rare, *Dovedale*
— salicata, Hb. Moors nr. *Leek*
— olivata, Bork. Rare, one in *Dovedale*, 1886
— viridaria, Fb. Common in woods
Emmelesia affinitata, St. Common, but local
— alchemillata, L. Not uncommon, *Whitmore, Stone, Stoke-on-Trent, Rugeley*; *Burton* (B. L.)
— albulata, Schiff. Common where food plant (Rhinanthus crista-galli) grows
— decolorata, Hb. Local, *Madeley, Cheadle, Rugeley*; *Handsworth* (C. J. W.)
— taeniata, St. *Dovedale* (B. L.)
Eupithecia venosata, Fb. *Ashley, Rugeley*; *Shobnall* (B. L.)
— linariata, Fb. *Market Drayton*
— pulchellata, St. Common
— oblongata, Thnb. *Rugeley*; *Burton* (B. L.), *Madeley*, 1902
— succenturiata, L. *Rugeley*
— subfulvata, Haw. *Madeley, Rugeley, Stone*
— plumbeolata, Haw. *Swynnerton, Bishop's* and *Burnt Woods, Cannock Chase*
— isogrammaria, H. S. One at *Burton* (B. L.)
— pygmaeata, Hb. *Chorlton Moss, Burnt Woods*
— satyrata, Hb. *Cannock Chase, Burnt Woods*
— castigata, Hb. Common
— trisignaria, H. S. *Market Drayton*
— fraxinata, Crewe. *Madeley, Rugeley*; *Burton* (B. L.); *Handsworth* (C. J. W.)
— valerianata, Hb. nr. *Madeley*, 1907 (F. C. Woodforde)
— indigata, Hb. Common in pine woods
— nanata, Hb. Common on heaths, *Cannock Chase, Chartley, Burnt Woods*
— subnotata, Hb. } Common
— vulgata, Haw.
— albipunctata, Haw. *Rugeley*, occasionally var. angelicata, Bar. *Madeley*
— absinthiata, Clerck. Common where food plant grows
— minutata, Gn. *Madeley, Burnt Woods, Rugeley*
— assimilata, Gn. Common on food plant
— tenuiata, Hb. *Swynnerton, Madeley, Bagot's Park*
— lariciata, Frr. Common in larch woods
— abbreviata, St. Not uncommon, *Swynnerton, Cheadle, Burnt Woods*; *Burton* (B. L.)

GEOMETRAE (*continued*)

LARENTIIDAE (*continued*)

Eupithecia exiguata, Hb.   Common
— sobrinata, Hb. Local, *Madeley ;* *Burton* (B. L.)
— pumilata, Hb.   Not common
— rectangulata, L.   General, *Madeley, Cheadle, Rugeley ; Handsworth* (C. J. W.) ;*Burton* (B. L.)
— debiliata, Hb. Common nr. *Cheadle* and where bilberry grows
Lobophora halterata, Hufn.   *Burnt Woods ; Henhurst* nr. *Burton* (B. L.)
— viretata, Hb.   *Burnt Woods ; Bishop's Woods, Parson's Brake* (B. L.)
— carpinata, Bork.   *Swynnerton ; Burnt Woods ; Henhurst, Hopwas Wood* (B. L.)
Thera variata, Schiff.   } Common in pine woods,
— firmata, Hb.   } general
Hysipetes ruberata, Frr.   *Chorlton Moss, Cheadle, Rugeley, Warslow*
— trifasciata, Bork.   Local, *Burnt Woods, Cannock Chase ; Newborough, Oakedge, Burton* (B. L.)
— sordidata, Fb.   Common throughout the county, and very variable in colour and markings
Melanthia bicolorata, Hufn.   *Knightley* and *Oakedge Park* (B. L.) ; *Chorlton, Cannock Chase*
— ocellata, L.   General
— albicillata, L.   Not uncommon
Melanippe hastata, L.   Fairly common some years, *Craddock's Moss, Bishop's* and *Burnt Woods, Hanchurch, Rugeley*
— tristata, L.   Not common, *Chartley, Leek ;* common, *Rugeley* (B. L.)
— procellata, Fb.   Very rare, two at *Trentham* in two successive years
— rivata, Hb.   Rare, *Burnt Woods*
— sociata, Bork.   } Very common
— montanata, Bork.   }
— galiata, Hb.   Local and rare, *Dovedale, Cheadle*
— fluctuata, L.   Common
Anticlea badiata, Hb.   Not uncommon
— nigrofasciaria, Göze.   Fairly common
Coremia munitata, Hb.   Very rare, one *Trentham*
— designata, Hufn.   }
— ferrugata, Clerck.   } Common
— unidentaria, Haw.   }
Camptogramma bilineata, L. }
— fluviata, Hb.   One at gas light, *Trent Vale*
Phibalapteryx vittata, Bork.   *Stoke-on-Trent, Market Drayton ; Burton* (B. L.)
Triphosa dubitata, L.   Not common, *Madeley.* In limestone caves, *Grindon* and *Dovedale ; Burnt Woods* at sallow, *Rugeley ; Burton* district (B. L.)
Eucosmia certata, Hb.   *Market Drayton, Rugeley ; Burton* (B.L.)
— undulata, L.   *Swynnerton, Maer, Cheadle, Bishop's* and *Burnt Woods ; Cannock Chase* (B. L.)
Scotosia rhamnata, Schiff.   Rare, *Dovedale*
Cidaria siderata, Hufn.   One near *Market Drayton*
— miata, L.   *Dovedale* (B. L.)
— corylata, Thnb.   Common in woods
— truncata, Hufn.   Common in pine woods
— immanata, Haw.   Very common

GEOMETRAE (*continued*)

LARENTIIDAE (*continued*)

Cidaria suffumata, Hb.   General, *Chorlton Moss, Bishop's* and *Burnt Woods ; Stone, Leek ; Burton* (B. L.)
  var. piceata, St.   *Stone, Trentham, Tixall* (E. D. B.)
— silaceata, Hb.   Not common, *Madeley, Dovedale ; Henhurst* and *Knightley Park ; Burton* (B. L.)
— prunata, L.   *Bishop's Woods, Cheadle, Rugeley, Market Drayton ; Burton, Colwich* (B. L.)
— testata, L.   }
— populata, L.   } Common
— fulvata, Forst.   }
— dotata, L.   Fairly common
— associata, Bork.   Common
Pelurga comitata, L.   *Market Drayton ; Burton, Shobnall* (B.L.)

EUBOLIIDAE

Eubolia cervinata, Schiff.   Local, *Madeley, Market Drayton ; Burton* (B. L.)
— limitata, Scop.   Common
— plumbaria, Fb.   Common on heaths
— bipunctaria, Schiff.   Common on the limestone in the north of the county
Carsia paludata, Thnb.   Rare, *Chartley ;* sparingly in *Dovedale* (B. L.)
Anaitis plagiata, L.   Fairly common on the limestone in the north of the county ; *Cannock Chase*
Chesias spartiata, Fues.   *Chorlton, Pipe Gate, Stone ; Burton* (E. B.) ; *Handsworth* (C. J. W.)
— rufata, Fb.   Rare, *Chorlton, Market Drayton ;* one at light, *Burton* (B. L.)

SIONIDAE

Tanagra atrata, L.   Common, especially in dales in the north of the county

PYRALIDES

PYRALIDIIDAE

Aglossa pinguinalis, L.   General, *Madeley, Rugeley, Burton,* &c.
Pyralis glaucinalis, L.   *Burnt Woods, Burton* (B. L.)
— farinalis, L.   Common throughout the county
Scoparia ambigualis, Tr.   Common
— cembrae, Haw.   Fairly common, *Cannock Chase*
— dubitalis, Hb.   Common, *Dovedale, Cannock Chase*
— murana, Curt.   *Burton, Cannock* (B. L.)
[— ingratella, Zell.   ? *Parson's Brake* (B. L.)]
— mercurella, L.   *Burton* (E. B.)
— ulmella, Dale.   Wood near *Uttoxeter* (B. L.) ; *Cannock Chase*
— crataegella, Hb.   *Rugeley*
— truncicolella,Sta.   Common in woods.
Nomophila noctuella, Schiff.   *Madeley, Burton* (B. L.)
Pyrausta aurata, Scop.   *Dovedale*
— purpurales, L.   Not common, *Craddock's Moss, Dovedale, Cannock Chase, Knightley Park* (E. B.)

INSECTS

PYRALIDES (continued)

PYRALIDIIDAE (continued)

Herbula cespitalis, Schiff. *Weaver Hills, Dovedale*
Ennychia cingulata, L. *Dovedale*

BOTYDAE

Eurrhypara urticata, L. Common on Nettles.
Scopula lutealis, Hb. ⎫
— olivalis, Schiff. ⎬ Common
— prunalis, Schiff. ⎭
— ferrugalis, Hb. *Burnt Woods*
Botys pandalis, Hb. *Tixall*
— ruralis, Schiff. One at *Little Madeley, Rugeley,* common, *Burton* district (B. L.)
— fuscalis, Schiff. Common in meadows
Ebulea crocealis Hb. *Grafton's Wood, Madeley, Cannock Chase*
— sambucalis, Schiff. Common on elder
Spilodes verticalis, L. *Stone,* (E. D. B.)
Pionea forficalis, L. Common

HYDROCAMPIDAE

Cataclysta lemnata, L. Common on duckweed
Paraponyx stratiotata, L. *Madeley* ; *Burton* (B. L.)
Hydrocampa nymphaeata, L. Common
— stagnata, Don. *Madeley* ; *Burton,* common (B. L.)

ACENTROPODIDAE

Acentropus niveus, Oliv. Common on the *Trent, Burton* (B. L.)

PTEROPHORI

CHRYSOCORIDIDAE

Chrysocorus festaliella, Hb. *Henhurst* near *Burton* (E. B.)

PTEROPHORIDAE

Platyptilia gonodactyla, Schiff. Near *Burton* (B. L.)
Amblyptilia acanthodactyla, Hb. *Burton, Cannock Chase*
Oxyptilus teucrii, Greening. *Cannock Chase*
Mimaeseoptilus plagiodactylus, Sta. *Tixall*
— pterodactylus, L. *Tixall; Burton* (B. L.)
Aedematophorus lithodactylus, Tr. Near *Burton* (B. L.)
Pterophorus monodactylus, L. Common *Burton* (B. L.)
Aciptilia tetradactyla, L. *Burton* (E. B.)
— pentadactyla, L. Common *Burton* (B. L.); *Mayfield,* very common (F. J.)

ALUCITIDAE

Alucita hexadactyla, L. Common *Burton* (B. L.); *Dove Valley,* occasional (F. J.) ; *Alstonfield* (W. H. Purchas)

CRAMBI

CHILIDAE

Schoenobius forficellus, Thnb. *Burton* (B. S.)
— mucronellus, Schiff. Rare, one at *Madeley;* one at *Rugeley; Shobnall Canal* (B. S.)
— gigantellus, Schiff. *Burton* (B. S.)

CRAMBI (continued)

CRAMBIDAE

Crambus falsellus, Schiff. *Rugeley ; Burton* (B. S.)
— pratellus, L. Common in grassfields
— pascuellus, L. Common
— uliginosellus, Zell. *Tixall,* rare
— margaritellus, Hb. Common on mosses, *Chorlton, Cannock Chase*
— pinellus, L. One in *Burnt Woods;* common *Cannock Chase*
— perlellus, Scop. Two at *Swynnerton, Rugeley; Burton* (B. S.)
— warringtonellus, Zell. *Chorlton, Craddock's Moss*
— tristellus, Fb. Common
— inquinatellus, Schiff. *Rugeley; Sinai Park* (B. S.)
— culmellus, L. ⎫
— hortuellus, Hb. ⎬ Abundant

PHYCIDAE

Ephestia elutella, Hb. *Burton* (B. S.)
— ficella, St. *Madeley*
Cryptoblabes bistriga, Haw. *Hopwas*
Plodia interpunctella, Hb. *Madeley*
Phycis betulae, Göze. *Swynnerton*
— fusca, Haw. Common on heaths, *Cannock Chase, Swynnerton*
Nephopteryx spissicella, Fb. *Swynnerton*
Pempelia, palumbella, Fb. *Cannock Chase, Swynnerton*
Rhodophaea advenella, Zinck. *Rugeley*
— consociella, Hb. Common, *Swynnerton*

GALLERIDAE

Aphormia sociella, L. *Market Drayton*
Achroea grisella, Fb. *Madeley ; Burton* (B. S.)

TORTRICES

TORTRICIDAE

Tortrix podana, Scop. *Burton,* common (E. B., B. S.) ; *N. Staffs.* (T. W. D.) ; very common, *Rugeley* (R. F.)
— xylosteana, L. *Burton* (E. B., B. S.) ; *N. Staffs.* (T. D. W.) ; *Rugeley* (R. F.)
— sorbiana, Hb. *The Oaks,* &c. (E. B.) ; *Burton* (B. S.) ; *N. Staffs.* (T. W. D.) ; common, *Rugeley* (R. F.)
— rosana, L. *Burton,* common (E. B., B. S.) ; *N. Staffs.* (T. W. D.) ; very common, *Rugeley,* (R. F.)
— cinnamomeana, Tr. *Maer Woods* plentiful (T. W. D.)
— heparana, Schiff. *N. Staffs.* (T. W. D.) ; very common, *Rugeley* (R. F.)
— ribeana, Hb. *Burton,* common (E. B., B. S.); *N. Staffs.* (T. W. D.) ; very common, *Rugeley* (R. F.)
— corylana, Fb. *Henhurst* (E. B.) ; *Burton* (B. S.) ; *Swynnerton Old Park* (T. W. D.) ; common, *Rugeley* (R. F.)
— unifasciana, Dup. *Burton,* common (E. B.. B. S.) ; very common, *Rugeley* (R. F.)

TORTRICIDAE (*continued*)

Tortrix costana, Fb. *Henhurst* (E. B.) ; very common, *Rugeley* (R. F.)
— viburnana, Fb. *Burton*, rare (E. B.) ; *Cannock Chase* (C.G.B.); *Rugeley*, common (R.F.)
— palleana, Fb. *Burton*, rare (E. B., B. S.)
    var. icterana, Fröl. *N. Staffs* (T.W.D.)
— viridana, L. Everywhere very common (E. D. B.) ; *Burton* (E. B., B. S.) ; *N. Staffs.* (T. W. D.) ; *Dydon Wood* (F. J.) ; *Rugeley*, (R. F.)
— ministrana, L. *Cannock Chase* (C. G. B., R. F.); *N. Staffs.* (T. W. D.)
    var. ferrugana, Hb. *Burton* (B. S.)
— forsterana, Fb. *Burton*, common (E. B., B. S.); *N. Staffs.* (T. W. D.) ; *Rugeley*, very common (R. F.)
Amphisa gerningana, Schiff. *Chorlton Moss* (T. W. D.)
— prodromana, Hb. *Chorlton Moss* (T. W. D.)
Oenectra pilleriana, Schiff. *Rugeley* (R. F.)
Leptogramma literana, L. *Burton*, rare (E. B.) ; *Madeley* and *Swynnerton* (T. W. D.)
Peronea sponsana, Fb. *Drakelow* (E. B.) ; *Rugeley* (R. F.)
— rufana, Schiff. *Burton*, common (E. B., B. S.)
— mixtana, Hb. *Maer Woods* in heather (T. W. D.)
— schalleriana, L. *Burton*, common (E. B., B. S.)
— variegana, Schiff. *Burton* (E. B., B. S.) ; *N. Staffs.* (T. W. D.) ; very common, *Rugeley* (R. F.)
— ferrugana, Tr. *Burton* (E. B., B. S.) ; *N. Staffs.* (T. W. D.) ; *Rugeley* (R. F.)
— aspersana, Hb. *N. Staffs.* (T. W. D.)
Rhacodia caudana, Fb. *Henhurst*, common (E. B.) ; *Burton* (B. S.)
Teras contaminana, Hb. *Burton*, common (E. B., B. S.) ; *N. Staffs.* (T. W. D.) ; very common, *Rugeley* (R. F.)
Dictyopteryx loeflingiana, L. *Henhurst* (E. B.) ; *Burton* (B. S.) ; *N. Staffs.* (T. W. D.)
— holmiana, L. *Henhurst* (E. B.) ; *Burton* (B.S.); *N. Staffs.* (T. W. D.) ; common, *Rugeley* (R. F.)
— bergmanniana, L. *Burton*, common (E. B., B. S.) ; *N. Staffs.* (T. W. D.) ; common, *Rugeley* (R. F.)
— forskaleana, L. *Burton*, common (E. B., B. S.); *N. Staffs.* (T. W. D.) ; very common, *Rugeley* (R. F.)
Argyrotoxa conwayana, Fb. *Burton*, common (E. B., B. S.) ; *Stafford* (C. G. B.) ; *N. Staffs.* (T. W. D.) ; common *Rugeley* (R. F.)
Ptycholoma lecheana, L. *Cannock Chase* (C. G. B., R. C. B.) ; *Hopwas Wood* (W. G. B.) ; *N. Staffs.* (T. W. D.) ; *Rugeley* (R. F.)

PENTHINIDAE

Penthina corticana, Hb. *N. Staffs.* (T. W. D.) ; very common, *Rugeley* (R. F)
— betulaetana, Haw. *Burton* (E. B., B. S.) ; *Cannock* (C. J. W.) ; *Sutton* (R. C. B.) ; *Rugeley*, very common (R. F.)

PENTHINIDAE (*continued*)

Penthina sororculana, Zett. *Cannock* (W. G. B.); *N. Staffs.* (T. W. D.) ; common, *Rugeley*, (R. F.)
— pruniana, Hb. *Burton* (E. B., B. S.) ; *N. Staffs.* (T. W. D.)
— ochroleucana, Hb. *Tixall* (E. D. B) ; common, *Rugeley* (R. F.)
— variegana, Hb. *Burton* (E. B., B. S.) ; very common, *Rugeley* (R. F.)
— sauciana, Hb. Plentiful *Maer Woods*, &c. (T. W. D.) ; *Cannock* (C. J. W.) ; *Sutton* (W. G. B.)
— marginana, Haw. *Burton*, rare (E. B.)
— fuligana, Hb. *Burton*, rare (E. B.)

SPILONOTIDAE

Hedya ocellana, Fb. *Burton*, common (E. B., B. S.) ; very common, *Rugeley* (R. F.)
— neglectana, Dup. *Burton*, common (E. B.)
Spilonota trimaculana, Haw. *Burton*, common (E. B.) ; *Tixall* (E. D. B.) ; very common, *Rugeley* (R. F.)
— rosaecolona, Dbl. *Burton*, common (E. B., B. S.) ; very common, *Rugeley* (R. F.)
— roborana, Tr. *Burton*, common (E. B., B. S.); *N. Staffs.* (T. W. D.)
Pardia tripunctana, Fb. *Burton*, common (E. B.) ; *N. Staffs.* (T. W. D.) ; very common, *Rugeley* (R. F.)

SERICORIDAE

Aspis udmanniana, L. *Henhurst* (E. B., B. S.) ; *Burton* (B. S.) ; *N. Staffs.* (T. W. D.) ; common *Rugeley* (R. F.)
Sideria achatana, Fb. *N. Staffs.* (T. W. D.)
Sericoris bifasciana, Haw. (decrepitana). One beaten from Scotch fir, *Cannock Chase* (W. S. Atkinson)
— rivulana, Scop. *Burton* (F. B.) ; *Cannock Chase* (W. G. B.)
— urticana, Hb. *N. Staffs.* (T. W. D.)
— lacunana, Dup. *Burton*, very common (E. B., B. S.) ; *Cannock Chase* (C. G. B.) ; *N. Staffs.* (T. W. D.)
Mixodia schulziana, Fb. *Craddock's Moss, Chartley Moss* (R. C. B.)
Roxana arcuana, Clerck. *Cannock Chase*, abundant in June (W. S. Atkinson) ; *N. Staffs.* (T. W. D.)
Orthotaenia antiquana, Hb. *Rugeley* (R. F.)
— striana, Schiff. *Burton*, rare (E. B., B. S.); *N. Staffs.* (T. W. D.)

SCIAPHILIDAE

Phtheochroa rugosana, Hb. *Burton* (E. B., B. S.); one at *Handsworth* (C. J. W.)
Cnephasia musculana, Hb. *Burton* (E. B., B. S.); *Cannock Chase* (C. G. B., W. G. B.) ; *N. Staffs.* (T. W. D.) ; common *Rugeley* (R. F.)
Sciaphila nubilana, Hb. *Burton*, common (E. B.); common, *Rugeley* (R. F.)
— subjectana, Gn. *Burton*, common (E. B., B. S.); *N. Staffs.* (T. W. D.)

INSECTS

SCIAPHILIDAE (*continued*)

Sciaphila virgaureana, Tr. *Burton*, common (E. B., B. S.); *N. Staffs.* (T. W. D.); common, *Rugeley* (R. F.)

— pascuana, Hb. *Tixall* (E. D. B.); *Rugeley* (R. F.)

— chrysantheana, Dup. *Rugeley* (R. F.)

— hybridana, Hb. *Burton*, common (E. B., B. S.); *Stafford* (C. G. B.); *N. Staffs.* (T. W. D.); common, *Rugeley* (R. F.)

Sphaleroptera ictericana, Haw. *N. Staffs.* (T. W. D.)

Capua favillaceana, Hb. *Cannock Chase* (G. C. B.); *N. Staffs.* (T. W. D.); *Rugeley* (R. F.)

Clepsis rusticana, Tr. *Cannock Chase* (C. G. B.)

GRAPHOLITHIDAE

Bactra lanceolana, Hb. *Cannock Chase* (C. G. B); *N. Staffs.* (T. W. D.); very common, *Rugeley* (R. F.)

Phoxopteryx myrtillana, Tr. *Cannock Chase* and *Rugeley*, abundant (R.F., C. G. B., W.G.B); *Maer, Craddock's Moss*, plentiful on bilberry (T. W. D.)

— lundana Fb. *Burton*, common (E. B., B. S.); *Stafford* (C. G. B.); on trefoil (T. W. D.)

— diminutana, Haw. *Burton* (E. B.)

— mitterpacheriana, Schiff. *Burton*, common (E. B., B. S.); *N. Staffs.* (T. W. D.)

— lactana, Fl. *N. Staffs.* (T. W. D.)

Grapholitha ramella, L. *Burton* (E. B.); *Hopwas Wood* (W. G. B.); common, *Rugeley* (R. F.)

— nisella, Clerck. *Burton* (E. B., B. S.)

— subocellana, Don. *Burton* (E. B., B. S.)

— trimaculana, Don. *Burton*, common (E. B., B. S.)

— penkleriana, Fisch. *Burton* (E. B.); *Cannock* (R. C. B.); *N. Staffs.* (T. W. D.)

— naevana, Hb. *N. Staffs.* (T. W. D.); *Rugeley* (R. F.)

— geminana, St. Plentiful in pine and fir woods *N. Staffs.* (T. W. D.)

Phloeodes tetraquetrana, Haw. *Burton* (E. B., B. S.); *Cannock Chase* (C. G. B., W. G. B.); *Rugeley* (R. F.); *N. Staffs.* (T. W. D.)

Hypermecia angustana, Hb. *Henhurst* (E. B.); *N. Staffs.* (T. W. D.)

Batodes angustiorana, Haw. *Burton*, common (E. B., B. S.); *N. Staffs.* (T. W. D.); *Rugeley* (R. F.)

Paedisca bilunana, Haw. *Cannock Chase* (C. G. B.); *Rugeley*, very common (R. F.); *Hopwas Wood* (W. G. B.)

— ratzeburghiana, Sax. *The Oaks, Burton* (E. B., B. S.)

— corticana, Hb. *Henhurst* (E. B., B. S.); *Hopwas Woods* (W. G. B.); *N. Staffs.* (T. W. D.); *Rugeley* (R. F.)

— occultana, Dougl. *N. Staffs.* (T. W. D.); *Rugeley* (R. F.)

— solandriana, L. *Henhurst* (E. B., B. S.); *Madeley*, on birch (T. W. D.); *Cannock Chase* (W. G. B.); *Rugeley*, very common (R. F.)

GRAPHOLITHIDAE (*continued*)

Ephippiphora similana, Hb. *N. Staffs.* (T. W. D.)

— cirsiana, Zell. *N. Staffs.* (T. W. D.)

— pflugiana, Haw. *Burton* (E. B., B. S.); *N. Staffs.* (T. W. D.); *Cannock Chase* (C. G. B.); *Rugeley* (R. F.)

— brunnichiana, Fröl. *Burton* (E. B., B. S.); *Rugeley* (R. F)

[— foenella, L. *Cannock Chase* ? (C. G. B., fide B. S.); probably for pflugiana, Haw.]

— nigricostana, Haw. *Burton* (E. B., B. S.)

— trigeminana, St. *Rugeley* (R. F.)

— tetragonana, St. *Burton* (E. B.)

Semasia ianthinana, Dup. *Burton* (E. B., B. S.); *Rugeley* (R. F.)

— rufillana, Wilk. *Burton* (E. B.)

— woeberiana, Schiff. *Burton* (E. B., B. S.)

Coccyx argyrana, Hb. *Burton* (E. B.); *Cannock Chase* (C. G. B.): *Needwood* (B. S.); *Sutton* (R. C. B.); *Hopwas* (W. G. B.); *N. Staffs.* (T. W. D.) &c.

— taedella, Clerck. *Burton*, &c., common, (E. B., B. S.); *Milford* (C. G. B.); *Maer Woods*, abundant on spruce (T. W. D.)

— nanana, Tr. *Burton* (E. B., B. S.)

Heusimine fimbriana, Haw. *Swynnerton Old Park* (T. W. D.); *Sutton Park* (W. G. B.)

Retinia buoliana, Schiff. *Burton* (B. S.)

— pinivorana, Zell. Beaten from Scotch fir (T. W. D.); *Rugeley* (R. F.)

Carpocapsa pomonella, L. *Burton* (E. B.)

Endopisa nigricana, St. *Burton* (E. B.)

Stigmonota coniferana, (Rlz.). *The Oaks, Burton* (E. B.)

— perlepidana, Haw. *Burton* (E. B.)

— nitidana, Fb. *Burton* (E. B.)

— regiana, Zell. *Madeley*, on sycamore (T. W. D.)

— roseticolana, Zell. *Burton* (E. B.)

Dicrorhampha sequana, Hb. *Burton* (B. S.)

— petiverella, L. *Burton* (E. B., B. S.)

— plumbana, Scop. *Burton* (B. S.)

— saturnana, Gn. *Burton* ? (E. B.); *Rugeley* (R. F.)

— plumbagana, Tr. *Burton* (E. B.)

— acuminata, Zell. *Tixall* (E. D. B.)

— tanaceti, St. *Rugeley*, very common locally (R. F.)

Catoptria ulicetana, Haw. *Burton* (E. B., B. S.); on gorse (T. W. D.); *Cannock Chase* (W. G. B.); *Rugeley*, very common (R. F.)

— hypericana, Hb. *Burton* (E. B., B. S.)

— cana, Haw. *The Oaks* (B. S.)

— scopoliana, Haw. *The Oaks* (E. B.)

— expallidana, Haw. *The Oaks* (E. B.)

— citrana, Hb. *Rugeley* (R. F.)

Trycheris aurana, Fb. *Burton* (E. B.)

PYRALOIDIDAE

Symaethis oxyacanthella, L. *Burton*, very common (E. B., B. S.); very common *Rugeley* (R. F.)

TORTRICES (*continued*)

CONCHYLIDAE

Eupoecilia nana, Haw. *The Oaks, Burton* (E.B.), abundant *Cannock Chase* (C. G. B.) ; very common *Rugeley* (R. F.)
— dubitana, Hb. *Rugeley* (R. F.)
— hybridella, Hb. *The Oaks, Burton* (E. B.) ; on heaths (T. W. D.)
— angustana, Hb. *The Oaks, Burton* (E. B.) ; abundant on all heaths (T. W.D.); *Cannock* (R. C. B.) ; *Rugeley* (R. F.)
— roseana, Haw. *The Oaks, Burton* (E. B.) ; *Shobnall marlpit* (B. S.)
Xanthosetia zoegana, L. *Burton, Sinai Park* (B. S.), *N. Staffs.* (T. W. D.) ; common *Rugeley* (R.F.)
— hamana, L. *The Oaks,* &c. (E. B.), *Burton* (B.S.), *N. Staffs.* (T.W.D.), *Rugeley* (R. F.)
Chrosis alcella, Schutz. *N. Staffs.* (T. W. D.)
Argyrolepia hartmanniana, Clerck. *Craddock's Moss* (T. W. D.)
— zephyrana, Fr. *Henhurst* (E. B.) ?
— badiana, Hb. *The Oaks, Burton* (E.B.) ; *N. Staffs.* (T. W. D.)
— cnicana, Dbl. *The Oaks, Burton* (E. B.) ; *Colwich* (C. G. B.);? *Cannock* (C. G. B. fide B. S.)
Conchylis straminea, Haw. *Madeley* on thistles (T. W. D.); *Rugeley* (R. F.)

APHELIIDAE.

Aphelia osseana, Scop. *Burton* (B.S.) ; *N. Staffs.* (T. W. D.) ; *Rugeley* (R. F.)
Tortricodes hyemana, Hb. *Henhurst,* &c., (E. B., B.S.) ; *Sutton Park,* common (C. J.W.) ; *N. Staffs.* (T. W. D.)

TINEAE

EPIGRAPHIIDAE

Lemnatophila phryganella, Hb. Common *Rugeley* (R. F.)
Diurnea fagella, Fb. *Burton,* common (E. B.) ; very common, *Rugeley* (R. F.) ; probably common everywhere (E. D. B.)
Semioscopus avellanella, Hb. *Hopwas Wood* (W. G. B.); *Rugeley* (R. F.)
Epigraphia steinkellneriana, Schiff. *Henhurst* (E. B.); *Rugeley* (R. F.)

PSYCHIDAE

Talaeporia pseudo-bombycella, Hb. *Cannock Chase* (C.G.B., W.G.B.); common *Rugeley* (R.F.)
Fumea intermediella, Brd. *Cannock Chase* (C. G. B., R. F.) ; common *Rugeley* (R. F.)
Solenobia inconspicuella, Sta. *Hopwas Wood* (E. B.); *Rugeley* (R. F.)

TINEIDAE

Diplodoma marginepunctella, St. *Cannock Chase* (C. G. B.)
Scardia corticella, Curt. *Rugeley* (R. F.)
— granella, L. *Burton* (B. S.)

TINEAE (*continued*)

TINEIDAE (*continued*)

Scardia cloacella, Haw. *Burton* (E. B., B. S.) ; *Cannock Chase* (C. G. B.) ; very common *Rugeley* (R. F.)
— arcella, Fb. *Henhurst* (E. B.)
Blabophanes rusticella, Hb. *Burton* (E. B., B. S.); *Cannock Chase* (C. G. B.) ; very common *Rugeley* (R. F.)
Tinea fulvimitrella, Sodof. *Burton* (E. B., B. S.) ; *Cannock Chase* (C. G. B., W. G. B) ; *Rugeley* (R. F.)
— tapetzella, L. *Burton* common (E. B., B. S.) ; common *Rugeley* (R. F.)
— misella, Zell. *Tatenhill* (E. B.); *Rugeley* (R. F.)
— pellionella, L. *Burton* (B. S.)
— fuscipunctella, Haw. *Tatenhill* and *Burton* (E. B., B. S.) ; *Rugeley* (R. F.)
— pallescentella, Sta. *Burton* (B. S.)
— lapella, Hb. *Burton* (E. B.) ; *Rugeley* (R. F.)
— merdella, Zell. *Burton* (B. S.)
— semifulvella, Haw. *Henhurst* (E. B.) ; *Burton* (B. S.) ; *Tixall* (E. D. B.) ; *Rugeley* (R. F.)
Tineola biselliella, Hm¹. *Tixall* (E. D. B.)
Lampronia luzella, Hb. *Burton* (E. B.)
— praelatella, Schiff. *Sinai Park* (E. B.)
— rubiella, Bjerk. *Tixall* (E. D. B.)
Incurvaria muscalella, Fb. *Henhurst,* &c. (E. B.) ; *Cannock Chase* (C. G. B.) ; *Hopwas Wood* (W. G. B.) ; *Rugeley* (R. F.)
— pectinea, Haw. *Hopwas Wood* (R. C. B.); *Rugeley* (R. F.)
— capitella, Clerck. *Tixall* (E. D. B.)
Micropteryx calthella, L. *Henhurst* (E.B.) ; *Burton* (B.S.) ; *Stafford* (C. G. B.)
— seppella, Fb. *Henhurst* (E. B.)
— aureatella, Scop. *Burton* (E. B.) ; *Cannock Chase* (C. G. B.)
— thunbergella, Fb. *Henhurst* (E. B.)
— fastuosella, Zell. *Burton* (B. S.)
— semipurpurella, St. *Rugeley* (R. F.)
— subpurpurella, Haw. *Henhurst* (E. B.); *Burton* (B. S.) ; *Hopwas Wood* (W. G. B.)
Nemophora swammerdammella, L. *Burton* (E. B.); *Cannock Chase* (C. G. B.) ; *Rugeley* (R. F.)
— schwarziella, Zell. *Burton* (E. B.); *Cannock Chase* (C. G. B.)
— metaxella, Hb. *Burton* (E. B.)

ADELIDAE

Adela rufimitrel'a, Scop. *Needwood,* common (B. S.)
— croesella, Scop. *Cannock Chase* (C. G. B.)
— degeerella, L. *Cannock Chase* (C. G. B.) ; *Rugeley,* common (R. F.)
— viridella, L. *Cannock Chase* (C. G. B.) ; *Rugeley,* common (R. F.)

HYPONOMEUTIDAE

Swammerdammia combinella, Hb. *Henhurst* (E. B.); *Rugeley* (R. F.)
— caesiella, Hb. *Henhurst,* &c. (E. B.)
— oxyacanthella, Dup. *Burton* (B. S.)
— pyrella, Vill. *Burton* (E. B.) ; *Rugeley* (R. F.)
— spiniella, Hb. *Burton* (B. S.)

INSECTS

HYPONOMEUTIDAE (*continued*)

Hyponomeuta padellus, L. *Burton*, common (E. B., B. S.) ; *Rugeley*, very common (R. F.)
— cagnagellus, Hb. *Burton* (E. B.) ? ; *Rugeley*, very common (R. F.)
— evonymellus, L. Near *Uttoxeter* (E. B.)
Prays curtisellus, Don. *Henhurst* (E. B.) ; common in *Handsworth*, both type and black form (C. J. W.) ; *Rugeley*, common (R. F.)

PLUTELLIDAE

Plutella cruciferarum, Zell. *Burton*, common (E. B.) ; *Cannock Chase* (C. G. B.) ; *Rugeley*, very common (R. F.)
— porrectella, L. *Burton*, rare (B. S.)
Cerostoma vittella, L. *Henhurst* (E. B.)
— radiatella, Don. *Henhurst*, common (E. B.)
— costella, Fb. *Henhurst*, common (E. B.)
Harpipteryx nemorella, L. *Henhurst*, scarce (E. B.)
— xylostella, L. *Henhurst*, common (E. B.) ; *Tixall* (E. D. B.)

GELECHIIDAE

Orthotelia sparganella, Thnb. *Burton* (B. S.)
Phibalocera quercana, Fb. *Burton* (? B. S.) ; *Cannock Chase* (E. D. B.) ; *Rugeley*, very common (R. F.)
— Depressaria costosa, Haw. *Burton* (E. B.) ; *Rugeley* (R. F.)
— flavella, Hb. *Burton* (E. B.)
— assimilella, Tr. *Rugeley* (R. F.)
— arenella, Schiff. *Henhurst*, common (E. B.)
— propinquella, Tr. *Henhurst*, common (E. B.) ; *Rugeley* (R. F.)
– alstroemeriana Clerck. *Henhurst* (E. B.)
— purpurea, Haw. *Henhurst* (E.B.)
-- liturella, Hb. *The Oaks, Burton* (E. B.)
— angelicella, Hb. *Henhurst* (E. B.)
— ocellana, Fb. *Henhurst* (E. B., B. S.)
— applana, Fb. *Burton*, common (E. B.); *Rugeley* (R. F.)
— ciliella, Sta. *Henhurst*, plentiful (E. B.)
— heracleana, De G. *Burton* (E. B.) ; *Rugeley*, common (R. F.)
[Gelechia malvella, Hb. *Burton* (E. B. *fide* B. S.)]
— velocella, Fisch. *Cannock Chase* (C. G. B.)
— ericetella, Hb. *Cannock Chase*, swarming (C. G. B.); *Rugeley*, very common (R.F.)
— sororculella, Hb. *Burton* (E. B.)
— longicornis, Curt. *Cannock Chase*, common (C. G. B.); *Rugeley* (R. F.)
— diffinis, Haw. *Cannock Chase* (C. G. B.)
— rhombella, Schiff. *Rugeley* (R. F.)
Brachmia mouffetella, Schiff. *Burton* (E. B.)
Bryotropha terrella, Hb. *Burton*, common (E. B.); *Cannock Chase* (C. G. B.) ; *Rugeley* (R. F.)
— politella, Dougl. *Cannock Chase* (C. G. B.)
— senectella, Zell. *Burton* (E. B., B. S.)
— affinis, Dougl. *Burton* (E. B.)
— domestica, Haw. *Burton* (E. B.)
Lita artemisiella, Tr. *Burton* (E. B.)
— viscariella, Logan. *Stapenhill* (B. S.)

GELECHIIDAE (*continued*)

Lita maculea, Haw. *Burton* (E. B.)
— tricolorella, Haw. *Tatenhill*, common (B. S.)
— fraternella, Dougl. *Burton* (E. B.)
— maculiferella, Dougl. *Burton.*
— hübneri, Haw. *Burton* (E. B.); *Hopwas Wood* (J. Sang)
— atriplicella, Fisch. *Burton* (E. B.)
Teleia proximella, Hb. *Cannock Chase* (C. G. B.); *Rugeley*, very common (R. F.)
— notatella, Hb. *Burton* (E. B.)
— vulgella, Hb. *Burton* (E. B.)
— luculella, Hb. *Cannock Chase* (C. G. B.) ; *Hopwas Wood* (C. J. W.) ; *Sutton Park* (W. G. B.)
— fugitivella, Zell. *Burton* (E. B.)
— triparella, Zell. *Rugeley* (R. F.)
Ptocheuusa subocellea, St. *Burton* (E. B.)
Ergatis ericinella, Dup. *Tixall* (E. D. B.)
Doryphora lucidella, St. *Burton* (E. B.)
Monochroa tenebrella, Hb. *Burton* (E. B.)
Lamprotes atrella, Haw. *Burton* (E. B.)
Anacampsis ligulella, Zell. *Burton* (E. B.)
— anthyllidella, Hb. *Burton* (E. B.)
Brachycrossata cinerella, Clerck. *Burton* (E. B.)
Ceratophora rufescens, Haw. *Burton* (E. B.)
Chelaria hübnerella, Don. *Henhurst*, &c. (E. B.) ; *Rugeley* (R. F.)
Anarsia spartiella, Schr. Railway cuttings (B. S.)
Hypsilophus marginellus, Fb. *Burton* (E. B.)
Pleurota bicostella, Clerck. *Cannock Chase*, common (C. G. B.) ; *Chartley Moss* (R. C. B.) ; *Rugeley*, very common (R. F.)
Harpella geoffrella, L. *Burton* (E. B., B. S.) ; *Rugeley* (R. F.)
Dasycera sulphurella, Fb. *Burton*, common (E. B.); *Cannock Chase* (C. G. B. *fide* B. L.); *Stafford*, everywhere (C. G. B.) ; *Rugeley*, common (R. F.)
Oecophora minutella, L. *Henhurst* (E. B.) ; *Rugeley* (R. F.)
— fulviguttella, Zell. *Henhurst* (E. B.) ; *Hopwas Wood* (W. G. B.)
— stipella, L. *Cannock Chase* (C. G. B.); *Rugeley* (R. F.)
— fuscencens, Haw. *Burton* (E. B.)
— pseudopretella, Sta. *Burton* (E. B., B. S.) ; *Tixall* (E. D. B.) ; *Rugeley*, very common (R. F.)
Endrosis fenestrella, Scop. *Tixall* (E. D. B.) ; *Rugeley*, very common (R. F.)

GLYPHIPTERYGIDAE

Glyphipteryx fuscoviridella, Haw. *Burton* (E. B.); *Cannock Chase* (C. G. B.) ; *Rugeley*, (R. F.)
— equitella, Scop. *Burton* (E. B.)
— fischeriella, Zell. *Burton* (E. B., B. S.) ; *Stafford* (C. G. B.)
Heliozele sericiella, Haw. *Henhurst* (E. B.)

ARGYRESTHIIDAE

Argyresthia ephippella, Fb. *Stapenhill*, &c (B. S.)
— nitidella, Fb. *Henhurst*, &c., common (E. B.); *Cannock Chase* (B. S., C. G. B.)

ARGYRESTHIIDAE (*continued*)

Argyresthia spiniella, Zell. *Burton* (F. B.); *Rugeley* (R. F.)
— albistria, Haw. *Henhurst*, &c. common (E. B.); *Tutbury Road, Burton* (B. S.)
— semifusca, Haw. *Henhurst* (E. B.) ; *Rugeley* (R. F.)
— glaucinella, Zell. *Bradgate Park* (B. S.)
— retinella, Zell. *Burton* (E. B.)
— dilectella, Zell. *Stapenhill* (B. S.)
— curvella, L. *The Oaks*, &c., *Burton* (E. B.) ; *Rugeley*, very common (R. F.)
— pygmaeella, Hb. *Henhurst*, &c. (E. B.) ; *Chartley* (R. C. B.)
— goedartella, L. *Henhurst*, &c. (E. B.) ; *Rugeley* (R. F.)
— brochella, Hb. *Henhurst*, &c. (E. B.) ; *Tixall* (E. D. B.)
Zelleria insignipennella, Sta. *Henhurst* (E. B.); *Shobnall, Burton* (B. S.)

GRACILARIIDAE

Gracilaria alchimiella, Scop. *Henhurst*, &c. (E. B.)
— stigmatella, Fb. *Henhurst* (E. B.) ; *Rugeley* (R. F.)
— hemidactylella, Fb. *Henhurst* (E. B.)
— elongella, L. *Burton* (E. B., B. S.) ; *Cannock Chase* (C. G. B., R. C. B.) ; *Rugeley* (R. F.)
— syringella, Fb. *Burton* (E. B.)
— auroguttella, St. *Henhurst* (E. B.)
Coriscium culculipennellum, Hb. *Henhurst* (E. B.)
Ornix anglicella, St. *Burton* (E. B.) ; *Cannock Chase* (C.G.B.) ; *Rugeley* (R. F.)
— betulae, Sta. *Cannock Chase* (C. G. B.) and (W. G. B.)
— torquilella, Sta. *Burton* (E. B.)
— guttea, Haw. *Rugeley* (R. F.)

COLEOPHORIDAE

Coleophora paripennella, Zell. *Burton*, &c. (B. S.)
— murinipennella, Fisch. *Burton* (E. B.) ?
— caespititiella, Zell. *Burton* (E. B., B. S.) ; *Cannock Chase* (C. G. B.)
— laripennella, Zett. *Henhurst* (E. B.) ; *Burton* (B. S.)
— argentula, Zell. *Burton* (E. B.)
— albitarsella, Zell. *Burton* (B. S.)
— nigricella, St. *Burton* (E. B.) ; *Cannock Chase* (C. G. B.); *Rugeley* (R. F.)
— fuscedinella, Zell. *Burton* (E. B.) ; *Rugeley* (R. F.)
— gryphipennella, Bonché. *Burton* (B. S.)
— siccifolia, Sta. *Tutbury Road, Burton* (B. S.) ; *Tixall* (E .D. B.)
— viminetella, Heyd. *Burton* (E. B.)
— badiipennella, Fisch. *Burton* (E. B., B. S.)

ELACHISTIDAE

Batrachedra praeangusta, Haw. *Burton* (B. S.)
Chauliodus illigerellus, Hb. *Burton* (E. B.)

ELACHISTIDAE (*continued*)

Laverna propinquella, Sta. *Burton* (E. B.) ?
— epilobiella, Schr. *Burton* (E. B.)
— decorella, St. *Burton* (E. B.)
— vinolentella, H. S. *Burton* (B. S.)
— atra, Haw. *Burton* (E. B.); *Rugeley* (R. F.)
Chrysoclysta schrankella, Hb. *Cannock Chase* (C. J. W.) ; *Sutton* (R. C. B.)
— aurifrontella, Hb. *Burton* (E. B., B. S.)
Asychna terminella, Dale. *Rosliston Road, Burton* (B. S.)
Stephensia brunnichella, L. *The Oaks, Burton* (E. B.)
Elachista albifrontella, Hb. *The Oaks, Burton* (E. B.) ; *Burton* (B. S.)
— atricomella, Sta. *Burton* (E. B.)
— luticomella, Zell. *The Oaks, Burton* (E. B.) ; *Henhurst* (B. S.) ; *Rugeley* (R. F.)
— monticola, Wk. *Drakelow Mill* (B. S.)
— nigrella, Hb. *Burton* (E. B.) ?
— subnigrella, Dougl. (B. S.)
— humilis, Zell. *Burton* (E. B.) ?
— perplexella, Sta. *Burton* (B. S.)
— obscurella, Sta. *Burton* (E. B., B. S.) ; *Cannock Chase* (C. G. B.)
— zonariella, Tgstr. *Burton* (E. B.)
— megerlella, Zell. *Burton* (E. B., B. S.)
— cerussella, Hb. *Burton* (E. B., B. S.)
— paludum, Frey. *Drakelow Mill* (B. S.)
— biatomella, Sta. *Tixall* (E. D. B.)
— rufocinerea, Haw. *Burton*, very common (E. B., B.S) ; *Rugeley* (R.F.)
— argentella, Clerck. *The Oaks, Burton* (E. B.) ; *Cannock Chase* (C. G. B.). ; *Rugeley* (R. F.)
Tischeria complanella, Hb. *Burton* (E. B., B. S.); *Cannock Chase* (C. G. B.) ; *Hopwas Wood* (W. G. B.)
— marginea, Haw. *Burton* (E. B.)

LITHOCOLLETIDAE

Lithocolletis roboris, Zell. *Cannock Chase* (C.G.B.)
— pomifoliella, Zell. *Burton* (E. B., B. S.)
— coryli, Nicelli. *Burton* (B. S.)
— spinicolella, Kol. *Rolleston Road, Burton* (B. S.)
— faginella, Mann. *Burton* (E. B., B. S.)
— salicicolella, Sircom. *Burton* (E. B.)
— ulmifoliella, Hb. *Burton* (E. B., B. S) ; *Cannock Chase* (C. G. B.)
— spinolella, Dup. *Burton* (E. B.)
— quercifoliella, Fisch. *Burton* (E. B., B. S.) ; *Cannock Chase* (C. G. B.)
— messaniella, Zell. *Burton* (E. B.)
— corylifoliella, Haw. *Burton* (E. B., B. S.)
— viminiella, Sircom. *Burton* (E. B., B. S.)
— alnifoliella, Hb. *Burton* (E. B., B. S.)
— heegeriella, Zell. *Burton* (E. B.)
— cramerella, Fb. *Burton* (E. B., B. S.) ; *Cannock Chase* (C. G. B.)
— sylvella, Haw. *Burton* (E. B.)
— nicellii, Zell. *Burton*, common (B. S.)
— tristrigella, Haw. *Burton* (E. B.)
— trifasciella, Haw. *Burton* (E. B.)

INSECTS

Lyonetiidae

Lyonetia clerckella, L. *Henhurst* (E. B.) ; *Burton* (B. S.)

Cemiostoma spartifoliella, Hb. *Burton* (E. B.)
— laburnella, Heyd. *Burton*, common (B. S.)
— scitella, Zell. *Burton* (E. B., B. S.)
Bucculatrix ulmella, Mann. *Burton* (E. B.)
— crataegi, Zell. *Burton* (E. B.)
— boyerella, Dup. *Burton* (E. B.)
— thoracella, Thnb. *Burton* (E. B.)

Nepticulidae

Nepticula ruficapitella, Haw. *Burton* (E. B., B. S.)
— anomalella, Göze. *Burton* (B. S.)
— pygmaeella, Haw. *Burton* (B. S.)
— oxyacanthella, Sta. *Burton* (B. S.) ; *Tixall* (E. D. B.)

Nepticulidae (*continued*)

Nepticula intimella, Zell. *Burton* (E. B., B. S.)
— sub-bimaculella, Haw. *Burton* (B.S.)
— trimaculella, Haw. *Burton* (B. S.)
— floslactella, Haw. *Burton* (E. B., B. S.)
— myrtillella, Edl. *Cannock Chase* (C. G. B.)
— microtheriella, Wing. *Burton* (B. S.)
— ignobilella, Sta. *Burton* (E. B., B. S.)
— argentipedella, Zell. *Burton* (E. B., B. S.)
— plagicolella, Sta. *Henhurst* (B. S.)
— tityrella, Dougl. *Branston* (B. S.)
— malella, Sta. *Burton* (B. S.)
— angulifasciella, Sta. *Burton* (E. B., B. S.)
— gratiosella, Sta. *Burton* (E. B., B. S.)
— marginicolella, Sta. *Burton* (B. S.)
— aurella, Fb. *Burton* (E. B., B. S.)
— splendidissimella, H. S. *Burton* (B. S.)

DIPTERA

Flies

The following list can only be regarded as a first instalment towards the compilation of a county list, for the number of species therein recorded only amounts to a little over 300, while some 3,000 species of Diptera are known to exist in Great Britain. It is founded on the late Mr. Edwin Brown's list of the Diptera of the Burton-on-Trent district, published in the *Natural History of Tutbury* in 1863 (pp. 210–23). Several species as to the identification of which some doubt exists or which are not now recognized as British, have been omitted. An asterisk (*) prefixed to the name of any species denotes that local specimens are to be found in the British Museum collection of British Diptera. Some notes on the gall-making Cecidomyidae, by Mr. Cyril Brett, as observed in the Alton district, have appeared in the *Reports and Transactions of the North Staffs. Field Club*, 1902–3 (pp. 92–3) and 1905–6, (pp. 75–6).

Where Burton is given as a locality without further particulars it must be understood that the statement is made on the authority of Mr. E. Brown's list.

Species marked (†) have been kindly determined by the Rev. A. Thornley, and those marked (¶) by Mr. E. E. Austen.

The following abbreviations have been used :—

R. G. = R. Garner, *Nat. History of the County of Stafford* (1840)
E. B. = Edwin Brown, 'Fauna of Burton-on-Trent' in *Nat. Hist. of Tutbury* (1863)
R. C. B. = R. C. Bradley (Cannock Chase)
C. J. W. = C. J. Wainwright (Handsworth)
C. B. = Cyril Brett (Alton)
F. J. = Rev. F. C. R. Jourdain (Dove Valley)
G. H. V. = G. H. Verrall (Dovedale and Colwich)
Br. Fl. = G. H. Verrall, *British Flies*, vol. viii.
E. M. M. = *The Entomologists' Monthly Magazine*
Ent. = *The Entomologist*

ORTHORRHAPHA

NEMATOCERA

Pulicidae

Pulex irritans, L.
— canis, Curt. On dogs
Trichopsylla sciurorum, Bouché. On squirrels (E. B.)
— gallinae, Schrk. In fowl houses, general

NEMATOCERA (*continued*)

Pulicidae (*continued*)

Trichopsylla hirundinis, Curt. On the house martin (E. B.)
Ctenopsyllus musculi, Dugés. On the rat (E. B.)

NEMATOCERA (*continued*)

CECIDOMYIDAE

Cecidomyia betulae, Winn. *Alton*, galls on Betula verrucosa, Erhrh. Sept. 1902 ; *Coombe Woods*, 22 July, 1905 (C. B.)
— bursaria, Bremi. Common, galls on Nepeta glechoma, Benth. (C. B.)
— crataegi, Winn. Common, galls on Crataegus oxyacantha, L. (C. B.)
— galii, Lw. Between *Alton* and *Denstone*, galls on Galium verum, 25 July, 1904 ; *Three Lowes*, 14 Aug., 1905 (C. B.)
— lathyri, Frfld. *Cotton*, 31 July, 1905 (C. B.)
— marginem-torquens, Bremi. Galls on Salix viminalis, L. (C. B.)
— persicariae, L. *Bradley*, galls on Polygonum amphibium, L., 25 Sept., 1902 ; *Alton*, July, 1905 (C. B.)
— pteridis, Müll. Common, galls on Pteris aquilina, L., Aug., 1903; *Belmont*, 22 July, 1905 (C. B.)
— ranunculi, Bremi. *Three Lowes*, 22 Aug., 1905 (C. B.)
— rosarum, Hardy. Common, 1903, on Rosa canina, L. (C. B.)
— taxi, Inch. *Bradley*, galls on Taxus baccata, L., Sept., 1903 (C. B.)
— tiliae, Schrk. *Alton*, galls on Tilia grandifolia, Ehrh. 22 July, 1903 ; *Rudyard*, 25 July, 1905 (C. B.)
— ulmariae, Bremi. *Alton* district, common, galls on Spiraea ulmaria, L., July, 1903 and 1905 (C. B.)
— urticae, Perris. *Alton* district, galls on Urtica dioica, L., Aug., 1903 (C. B.)
— veronicae, Vallot. *Burton* (E. B.) ; common, galls on Veronica chamaedrys, L. (C. B)
Diplosis botularia,Winn. *Alton*, galls on Fraxinus excelsior, L., Aug., 1903 (C. B.)
— loti, Deg. *Alton*, 5 Aug., 1905 (C. B.)
— tritici, Kirb. In wheat ears (E. B.)
Hormomyia annulipes,Hart. (piligera, Lw.). Common, galls on Fagus silvatica, L.; *Rudyard*, 25 July, 1905 (C. B.)
— capreae, Winn. On Salix caprea, L. *Alton*, Aug., 1903 (C. B.)
— fagi, Hart. *Dimmingsdale*, galls on F. silvatica, L., Sept., 1902 ; *Rudyard*, 25 July, 1905 (C. B.)
— millefolii, Lw. *Three Lowes*, 11 Aug., 1905 (C. B.)

MYCETOPHILIDAE

Sciara thomae, L. *Cannock* (R. C. B. *Ent.* 1891, p. 78)
*Mycetophila lineola, Mg. *Colwich* (G. H. V.)
*Rhymosia fasciata, Mg. *Colwich* (G. H. V.)
— fenestralis, Mg. Common
Exechia fungorum, De G. *Burton*
Allodia crassicornis, Stan. *Burton*
Phronia crassipes, Winn. *Colwich*, common (G. H. V. in *E. M. M.* xxx, 78)
— dubia, Dzied. *Colwich* (G. H.V. in *E. M. M.* xxx, 79)

NEMATOCERA (*continued*)

MYCETOPHILIDAE (*continued*)

*Boletina trivittata, Mg. *Colwich* (G. H. V.)
[Lasiosoma maura, Wlk. *Burton*]
Sciophila fasciata, Ztt. *Burton*
Platyura fasciata, Ltr. *Burton*
Macrocera lutea, Mg. *Burton*
*— centralis, Mg. *Dovedale* (G. H. V.)
*Bolitophila cinerea, Mg. *Colwich* (G. H. V.)

BIBIONIDAE

Scatopse notata, L. Common about manure heaps
— pulicaria, Lw. *Colwich* (G. H. V. in *E. M. M.* xxx, 79)
Bibio pomonae, F. 'Frequent' (R. G.)
— marci, L. Common
— leucopterus, Mg. *Burton*
— ferruginatus, Gmel. *Burton*
— laniger, Mg. *Burton*
— clavipes, Mg. *Burton*

SIMULIDAE

Simulium reptans, L. Common
— nanum, Ztt. *Colwich* (G. H. V. in *E. M. M.* xxx, 79)

CHIRONOMIDAE

Chironomus plumosus, L. *Burton*
— prasinus, Mg. *Burton*
— tentans, F. *Burton*
*— pedellus, De G. Common, *Burton* ; also *Dovedale* (G. H. V.)
— viridis, Mcq. Very common, *Burton*
*— viridulus, L. *Colwich* (G. H. V.)
*— nigrimanus, Staeg. *Colwich* (G. H. V.)
*— pictulus, Mg. *Dovedale* (G. H. V.)
*— albimanus, Mg. *Dovedale* (G. H. V.)
*— nubilus, Mg. *Dovedale* (G. H. V.)
*Cricotopus tremulus, L. *Dovedale* (G. H. V.)
*Orthocladius variabilis, Staeg. *Dovedale* (G. H. V.)
*Diamesa obscurimanus, Mg. *Colwich* (G. H. V.)
Tanypus varius, F. *Burton*
— nebulosus, Mg. *Burton*
*— punctatus, F. *Colwich* (G. H. V.)
— ornatus, Mg. *Colwich* (G. H. V. in *E. M. M.* xxx, 79)
*— trifascipennis, Ztt. *Dovedale* (G. H. V.) and *Colwich*, abundant (G. H. V. in *E. M. M.* xxx, 79)
[— zonatus, F. *Burton*]
Ceratopogon pulicaris, L. *Burton*, very common
— nitidus, Mcq. *Burton*, very common
*— femoratus, Mg. *Colwich* (G. H. V.)

PSYCHODIDAE

Pericoma nubila, Mg. *Burton*
Psychoda phalaenoides, L. *Burton*, common

CULICIDAE

Corethra plumicornis, F. *Burton*
Culex annulatus, Schrk. Very common
— nemorosus, Mg. Very common
— pipiens, L. (ciliaris, L.). Very common

INSECTS

NEMATOCERA (*continued*)

PTYCHOPTERIDAE

*Ptychoptera paludosa, Mg. *Dovedale* (G. H. V.)

LIMNOBIDAE

Limnobia nubeculosa, Mg.   *Burton*
— tripunctata, F.   *Burton*
Dicranomyia modesta, Mg.   *Burton*
*Rhiphidia maculata, Mg.   *Burton ; Colwich*
   (G. H. V.)
*Molophilus propinquus, Egg.   *Dovedale*
   (G. H. V.)
Rhypholophus lineatus, Mg.   *Burton*
*Lipsothrix errans, Wlk.   *Dovedale* (G H. V.) ;
   also *Cannock* (R. C. B. in *E. M. M.*
   xxxii, 53)
Ephelia submarmorata,Verr. *Colwich* (G. H. V.);
   also *Cannock* (R. C. B. ibid.)
— marmorata, Mg.   *Cannock* (R. C. B. ibid.)
*Dactylolabis frauenfeldi, Egg.   *Dovedale*
   (G. H. V.)
Trichocera hiemalis, De G.   Very common
Pedicia rivosa, L.   (R. G.)
Cylindrotoma distinctissima, Mg.   *Cannock*
   (R. C. B. in *E. M. M.* xxxii, 53)

TIPULIDAE

Dolichopeza sylvicola, Curt.   *Cannock* (R. C. B.
   ibid.)
Pachyrrhina crocata, L.   *Burton ; Cannock*
   (R. C. B. ibid.)
— maculosa, Mg   *Cannock* (R. C. B. ibid)
— quadrifaria, Mg.   *Burton*
— annulicornis, Mg.   *Burton ; Cannock* (R.C.B.
   ibid.)
*Tipula varipennis, Mg.   *Dovedale* (G. H. V.) ;
   Cannock (R. C. B. ibid.)
— lunata, L.   *Cannock* (R. C. B. ibid.)
— gigantea, Schrk.   Common, *Burton ; Dove
   Valley* (F. J.) ; *Cheadle* (J. Masefield) ;
   Cannock (R. C. B. ibid.)
— lutescens, F.   Very common
— oleracea, L.   Very common

BRACHYCERA

STRATIOMYIDAE

Oxycera pulchella, Mg. (rara, Wlk.).   *Burton*
Chrysonotus bipunctatus, Scop.   *Burton*
Sargus flavipes, Mg.   *Burton*
— cuprarius, L.   *Burton*

BRACHYCERA (*continued*)

STRATIOMYIDAE (*continued*)

Chloromyia formosa, Scop.   *Burton*
Microchrysa polita, L   *Burton*
Beris clavipes, L.   *Burton*

TABANIDAE

Haematopota pluvialis, L.   Common
Therioplectes tropicus, Mg.   *Burton*
Tabanus bovinus, L.   *Cannock Chase* (E. B.)
Chrysops caecutiens, L.   Common (R. G.)

LEPTIDAE

Leptis scolopacea, L.   *Burton ; Dove Valley*, &c.
Chrysopilus aureus, Mg.   *Burton*
Atherix ibis, F.   *Burton*

ASILIDAE

Dioctria oelandica, L.   *Burton*
— rufipes, De G.   *Burton*
Asilus crabroniformis, L.   *Burton,* rare

BOMBYLIDAE

[Anthrax hottentotta, L. (?)   *Burton*]
Bombylius, sp. (?)   *Burton*

THEREVIDAE

Thereva annulata, F.   *Burton*

EMPIDAE

*Rhamphomyia nigripes, F. *Dovedale* (G. H. V.)
— sulcata, Fln.   *Burton*
Empis tessellata, F.   *Burton*
— livida, L.   *Burton*
*— bilineata, Lw.   *Dovedale* (G. H. V.)
— chioptera, Fln.   *Burton*
Hilara cilipes, Mg.   *Burton*
*— maura, F.   *Dovedale* (G. H. V.)
*— fuscipes, F.   *Colwich* (G. H. V.)
*Tachydromia agilis, Mg.   *Dovedale* (G. H. V.)

DOLICHOPODIDAE

Poecilobothrus nobilitatus, L.   *Burton*
*Porphyrops praerosa, Lw.   *Dovedale* (G. H. V.)

LONCHOPTERIDAE

Lonchoptera punctum, Mg.   *Burton*
— trestes, Mg.   *Burton*

CYCLORRHAPHA

PROBOSCIDEA

SYRPHIDAE

Paragus tibialis, Fln. (obscurus, Mg.).   *Burton*
Pipizella flavitarsis, Mg.   *Burton*
Pipiza noctiluca, L.   *Burton*
— bimaculata, Mg. (guttata, Mg.).   *Burton*
Cnemodon vitripennis, Mg.   *Burton*

PROBOSCIDEA (*continued*)

SYRPHIDAE (*continued*)

Liogaster metallina, F. (discicornis, Mg.).
   Burton
Chrysogaster splendens, Mg.   *Burton*
[— hirtella, Lw. (? viduata, Fln.).   *Burton*]
— solstitialis, Fln. (fumipennis, Steph.).   *Burton*

A HISTORY OF STAFFORDSHIRE

PROBOSCIDEA *(continued)*

SYRPHIDAE *(continued)*

Chilosia scutellata, Fln.   *Burton*
— pulchripes, Lw.   *Dovedale (Br. Fl.)*
— variabilis, Pz.   *Burton*
[— illustrata, Harr. (? oestracea, L.).   *Burton*]
— grossa, Fln.   *Burton*
¶Platychirus manicatus, Mg.   *Burton ; Dove Valley* (F. J.)
— clypeatus, Mg.   *Burton*
Pyrophaena granditarsa, Först.   *Burton*
— rosarum, F.   *Burton*
Melanostoma mellinum, L.   *Burton*
— scalare, F.   *Burton*
Leucozona lucorum, L.   *Burton ; Dove Valley* (F. J.)
Ischyrosyrphus glaucius, L.   *Burton*
— laterarius, Müll.   *Burton*
†Catabomba pyrastri, L.   *Burton ; Mayfield* and *Dove Valley* (F. J.)
Syrphus albostriatus, Fln.   *Burton*
— torvus, O.-S. (topiarius, Mg.).   *Burton*
†¶— ribesii, L.   *Burton ; Dove Valley*, common (F. J.)
— vitripennis, Mg.   *Burton*
— corollae, F.   *Burton*
— bifasciatus, F.   *Burton*
†— balteatus, De G.   *Burton ; Mayfield* and *Dove Valley* (F. J.)
— auricollis, Mg.   *Burton*
— umbellatarum F.   *Burton ; Colwich* (C. J. W.)
— compositarum, Verr.   *Colwich* (C. J. W.)
— arcticus, Ztt.   *Colwich* (C. J. W.)
Xanthogramma ornatum, Mg.   *Burton*
— citrofasciatum, De G.   *Burton*
Baccha obscuripennis, Mg.   *Burton*
— elongata, F.   *Burton*
†Sphegina clunipes, Fln.   One in *Dove Valley*, 6 Sept., 1902 (F. J.)
Ascia podagrica, F.   *Burton*
Brachyopa bicolor, Fln.   *Burton*
Rhingia rostrata, L.   *Burton*
†— campestris, Mg.   *Mayfield* and *Dove Valley* (F. J.)
Volucella bombylans, L.   *Burton*
¶— pellucens, L.   *Henhurst* (E. B.) ; *Dove Valley* (F. J.), &c.
Eristalis sepulchralis, L.   *Burton*
†— tenax, L.   Common
¶†— intricarius, L.   *Burton ; Dove Valley* (F. J.)
¶†— arbustorum, L.   *Burton ; Dove Valley* (F. J.)
¶— nemorum, L.   *Burton ; Dove Valley* (F. J.)
¶†— pertinax, Scop.   *Dove Valley* (F. J.)
— horticola, De G.   *Burton*
Myiatropa florea, L.   *Burton*
Helophilus trivittatus, F.   *Cannock* (R. C. B. *Ent.* 1890, p. 352)
†— pendulus, L.   *Burton ; Mayfield* and *Dove Valley* (F. J.)
— lineatus, F.   *Burton*
Criorrhina asilica, Fln.   *Burton*
Xylota segnis, L.   *Burton*
— lenta, Mg.   *Burton*
— sylvarum, L.   *Burton*

PROBOSCIDEA *(continued)*

SYRPHIDAE *(continued)*

Xylota nemorum, F.   *Colwich* (C. J. W.) ; *Cannock*, one (R. C. B. in *E.M.M.* xxxii, p. 52)
¶Syritta pipiens, L.   *Burton ; Dove Valley*, common (F. J.)
Eumerus strigatus, Fln.   *Burton*
Chrysochlamys cuprea, Scop.   *Burton*
Calliprobola speciosa, Rossi.   *Burton ?*
*Sericomyia borealis, Fln.   *Burton ;* also *Cannock* (F. D. Morice)
— lappona, L.   *Burton*
Chrysotoxum arcuatum, L.   *Burton*
— bicinctum, L.   *Burton*

CONOPIDAE

Conops quadrifusciata, De G.   *Burton*
†— flavipes, L.   *Mayfield* and *Dove Valley* (F. J.)
Oncomyia atra, F.   *Burton*
Sicus ferrugineus, L.   *Burton*

OESTRIDAE

Gastrophilus equi, F.   Common
Hypoderma bovis, De G.   Common, doing considerable damage to the hides of oxen
Oestrus ovis, L.   Very common in some years

TACHINIDAE

†Olivieria lateralis, F.   *Burton ; Mayfield* and *Dove Valley* (F. J.)
Micropalpus vulpinus, Fln.   *Burton*
Echinomyia fera, L.   *Burton*
Fabricia ferox, L.   *Burton*
†Sarcophaga carnaria, L.   Generally distributed †var. similis, Meade.   *Dove Valley* (F. J.)
— melanura, Mg.   *Burton*
Dexiosoma caninum, F.   *Burton*
Prosena sybarita, F.   *Burton*

MUSCIDAE

Stomoxys calcitrans, L.   *Burton ;* scarce in *Dove Valley* (F. J.)
Pollenia vespillo, F.   *Burton*
— rudis, F.   *Burton*
Graphomyia maculata, Scop.   *Burton*
Musca domestica, L.   Everywhere
— corvina, F.   *Burton*
Cyrtoneura stabulans, Fln.   *Burton*
Morellia hortorum, Fln.   *Burton*
Mesembrina meridiana, L.   Frequently seen on the trunks of trees in many places (R. G.); *Burton*
Pyrellia lasiophthalma, Mcq.   *Burton*
Calliphora vomitoria, L.   Everywhere
Euphoria cornicina, F.   *Burton*
†Lucilia caesar, L.   Common
[— illustris, Mg.   ? *Burton*]

INSECTS

ANTHOMYIDAE

Polietes lardaria, F. *Burton*
Hyetodesia jncana, W. *Burton*
— signata, Mg. *Burton*
— erratica, Fln. *Burton*
Mydaea angelicae, Scop. *Burton*
Mydea pagana, F. *Burton*
— impuncta, Fln. *Burton*
Hydrophoria conica, W. *Burton*
*Hylemyia virginea, Mg. *Colwich* (G. H. V.)
— praepotens, W. *Burton*
Anthomyia pluvialis, L. *Burton*
— radicum, L. *Burton*, &c.
*Chortophila cinerella, Fln. *Dovedale* (G. H. V.)
— sepia, Mg. *Burton*.
Phorbia cepetorum, Meade. *Burton*, &c.
Pegomyia betae, Curt. Common in some years
Homalomyia canicularis, L. *Burton*
Caricea tigrina, F. *Burton*

CORDYLURIDAE

Scatophaga lutaria, F. *Burton*
— stercoraria, L. Everywhere

HELOMYZIDAE

Helomyza flava, Mg. *Burton*
Blepharoptera serrata, L. *Burton*

SCIOMYZIDAE

Dryomyza flaveola, F. *Burton*
Neottiophilum praeustum, Mg. *Burton*
Sciomyza obtusa, Fln. *Burton*
— cinerella, Fln. *Burton*
— albocostata, Fln. *Burton*
Tetanocera ferruginea, Fln. *Burton*
*— robusta, Lw. *Cannock* (R. C. B.)
Limnia marginata, F. *Burton*
— rufifrons, F. *Burton*
Elgiva cucularia, L. *Burton*

PSILIDAE

Psila fimetaria, L. *Burton*
— pallida, Fln. *Burton*

MICROPEZIDAE

Calobata trivialis, Lw. *Dovedale* (G. H. V. in
E.M.M. xxx, p. 145)

ORTALIDAE

Pteropaectria afflicta, Mg. *Burton*
Anacampta urticae, L. *Burton*
Platystoma seminationis, F. *Burton*
Seoptera vibrans, L. *Burton*

TRYPETIDAE

Acidia heraclei, L. *Burton ; Handsworth*, common (C. J. W.)
Spilographia zoë, Mg. *Handsworth* (C. J. W.)
— artemisiae, F. *Burton*
Rhagoletis cerasi, L. *Burton*
Trypeta cornuta, F. *Burton*
— serratulae, L. *Burton*

TRYPETIDAE (*continued*)

Urophora solstitialis, L. *Burton ; Denstone,*
28 July and Aug., 1905, *Alton*, Aug.,
1905 (C. B.)
Carphotricha guttularis, Mg. *Burton*
Tephrites parietina, L. *Burton*
— leontodontis, De G. *Burton*
Urellia stellata, Fuessl. *Burton*

LONCHAEIDAE

Lonchaea vaginalis, Fln. *Burton*
Palloptera saltuum, L. *Burton*
— ustulata, Fln. *Burton*
— umbellatarum, F. *Burton*
— arcuata, Fln. *Burton*

SAPROMYZIDAE

Lauxania cylindricornis, F. *Burton*
— aenea, Fln. *Burton*

OPOMYZIDAE

Balioptera combinata, L. *Burton*
Opomyza florum, F. *Burton*

SEPSIDAE

Nemopoda tarsalis, Wlk. *Burton*

PIOPHILIDAE

Piophila casei, L. Larvae in cheese

EPHYDRIDAE

Notiphila cinerea, Fln. *Burton*
Psilopa leucostoma, Mg. *Burton*
Ephydra riparia, Fln. *Burton*

CHLOROPIDAE

Meromyza variegata, Mg. *Burton*
Chlorops cinctipes, Mg. *Burton*

PHYTOMYZIDAE

Napomyza lateralis, Fln. *Burton*

BORBORIDAE

Borborus nitidus, Mg. *Burton*
— equinus, Fln. *Burton*
Sphaerocera subsultans, F. *Burton*
Limosina sylvatica, Mg. *Burton*
— ochripes, Mg. *Burton*
— fungicola, Hal. *Burton*

PHORIDAE

Phora rufipes, Mg. *Burton*

EPROBOSCIDEA

HIPPOBOSCIDAE

Ornithomyia avicularia, L. On owls, &c., at
Burton
Stenopteryx hirundinis, L. On martins and
swallows (E. B., F. J.)
Melophagus ovinus, L. Common on sheep
everywhere

HEMIPTERA HETEROPTERA

(Bugs)

GYMNOCERATA

PENTATOMIDAE

Asopus punctatus, L. *Cannock Chase* (Blatch)
Acanthosoma haemorrhoidale, L. *Cannock Chase*
(Blatch)

LYGAEIDAE

Gastrodes abietis, L. *Burton* (J. T. Harris)

TINGIDAE

Monanthia costata, Fieb. *Cannock Chase* (Blatch)
— humuli, Fb. *Sutton Park* (Blatch)

HEBRIDAE

Hebrus ruficeps, Thoms. *Cannock Chase* (Blatch)

HYDROMETRIDAE

Mesovelia furcata, Muls. and Rey. One from the
R. Trent, near *Burton* (E.B.) ; see *E. M. M.*
iv, 5 (1867)
Hydrometra stagnorum, L. Common.
Velia currens, Fb. On the *R. Trent* (E. B.)
Gerris paludum, Fb. Very abundant

SALDIDAE

Salda orthochila, Fieb. *Cannock Chase* (Blatch)
— cocksii, Curt. *Cannock Chase* (Blatch)
— cincta, H. Sch. *Cannock Chase* (Blatch)

CIMICIDAE

Cimex lectularius, L.
Piezostethus cursitans, Fall. *Needwood Forest*
(Blatch)

GYMNOCERATA *(continued)*

CAPSIDAE

Lopus gothicus, L. *Cannock Chase* (Blatch)
— flavomarginatus, Don. 'On nettles' (R. G.)
Calocoris sex-guttatus, Fl. Common near *Barlaston* (J. W. Ellis)
— alpestris, Mey. *Burton* (E. B.)
Atractotomus mali, Mey. *Cannock Chase* (Blatch)

CRYPTOCERATA

NAUCORIDAE

Naucoris cimicoides, L. Common in brooks
(R. G.) ; in railway cuttings at *Wetmore*
(E. B.)

NEPIDAE

Nepa cinerea, L. Common. Canals at *Stoke-on-Trent* (R. G.), &c. ; *Burton* (E. B.) ; *Dove Valley* (F. J.)

NOTONECTIDAE

Notonecta glauca, L. Very common. *Fenton Pool*
(R. G.), &c.
    var. furcata and maculata (E. B.)

CORIXIDAE

Corixa geoffroyi, Leach. Not uncommon, *Burton*
district (E.B.)
— atomaria, Illig. (affinis, Leach). Common (E.B.)
— coleoptrata, Fl. *Burton* (W. W. F.)
Sigara minutissima, L. *Burton* (W. W. F.); not uncommon in the *R. Trent* near *Burton* (E.B.)

HEMIPTERA HOMOPTERA

CICADINA

ISSIDAE

Issus coleoptratus, Geoff. Near *Burton*, not common (E. B.) ; *Dovedale* (B. Cooke)

CIXIIDAE

Cixius pilosus, Ol., or nervosus, L. (?cynosbatis,
Fb. of E. B.). Common in woods, *Burton*
district (E. B.)

DELPHACIDE

['Several species are abundant' (E. B.)]
[Stiroma borealis, J. Sahl. In mus. P. B. Mason of
Burton, but without locality]

CICADINA *(continued)*

CERCOPIDAE

?Triecphora vulnerata, Illig. ?
Philaenus spumarius, L. Very common

LEDRIDAE

Ledra aurita, L. *Burton* district, in woods, rare
(E. B.)

ACOCEPHALIDAE

Acocephalus nervosus, Schr. ?

PSYLLINA

PSYLLIDAE

Psylla. [Many species, E. B.]

INSECTS

APHIDES, &c.

The late Sir O. Mosley contributed some articles on Aphides to the early volumes of the *Gardeners' Chronicle*, and Mr. E. Brown gives some observations in his account of the fauna of the Burton district (*Natural History of Tutbury*, &c., p. 167). Mr. C. Brett has also recorded a few species from the Alton district (*Report North Staffs. Field Club*, 1905–6, p. 75–6).

Sir O. Mosley = O.M.   E. Brown = E.B.   C. Brett = C.B.   Rev. F. C. R. Jourdain = F. J.

APHIDIDAE

Siphonophora pisi, Kalt. (lathyri) (O. M.)
— avellanae, Schr. (coryli) (O. M.)
Phorodon humuli, Schr.   On Humulus lupulus (E. B., F. J.)
Myzus ribis, L.   *Alton*, July, 1905 (C. B.)
Rhopalosiphum ribis, L.   On Ribes nigrum, *Dove Valley*, common (F. J.) ; *Uttoxeter*, August, 1904 (C. B.)
Siphocoryne xylostei, Schrank.   On Lonicera periclymenum, *Alton*, August, 1903 (C. B.)
Aphis brassicae L.   On Brassica oleracea, common (F. J.)
— crataegi, Kalt.   On Crataegus oxyacantha, *Dove Valley* (F. J.); *Alton*, July, 1904 (C. B.)
— malvae, Walk. (O. M.)
— mali, Fb.   On Pyrus malus, *Dove Valley* (F. J.)
— atriplicis, L.   On Atriplex patula, *Alton*, July, 1903 ; *Denstone*, July, 1905 (C. B.)
— rumicis, L.   On Hedera helix, &c. (F. J.)
— amygdali, Fonsc.   'On Peach and Plum trees' (E. B.)
— pyri, Fonsc.   On Pyrus malus, *Alton*, 21 July, 1904 (C. B.)
Callipterus coryli, Götze.   On Corylus avellana, &c. (O. M.)
Dryobius roboris, L. (O. M.)

APHIDIDAE (*continued*)

Schizoneura lanigera, Hausm.   'Eriosoma mali' (O. M.) ; 'American Blight,' *Dove Valley* (F. J.)
— ulmi, L.   On Ulmus montana, *Alton*, August, 1903 (C. B.)
Tetraneura ulmi, De Geer.   On U. campestris, *Roston*, August, 1903 (C. B.)
Chermes abietis, L.   On spruce fir (E. B.) ; *Alton*, on Abies excelsa, August, 1903 (C. B.)
— laricis, Htg.   On larch (E. B.)

COCCIDAE

Aspidiotus, sp. (Scale Insects).   Common on greenhouse plants
Lecanium persicae, Burm.   'On plum and apricot trees, *Burton*' (E. B.)
Dorthesia cataphracta, Shaw.   *Henhurst* (E. B.)

ALEYRODIDAE

Alleyrodes proletella, Wlk.   Frequently found flying in lanes (E.B.)
— fragariae, Wlk.   On strawberry (E. B.)
— phillyreae, Hal.   Common on Phillyrea (E. B.)
Dactylopius, sp. (Mealy bug).   On vines in greenhouses (F. J.)

ARACHNIDA

Spiders, etc.

Very few species of spiders, eighty-two in all, have been collected in the county of Staffordshire, and the greater number of these were taken in the neighbourhood of Handsworth by Mr. F. P. Smith, while the rest were taken by myself near Cannock.

ARANEÆ

ARACHNOMORPHÆ

DYSDERIDÆ

Spiders with six eyes and two pairs of stigmatic openings, situated close together on the genital rima ; the anterior pair communicating with lung books, the posterior with tracheal tubes. Tarsal claws, two in *Dysdera*, three in *Harpactes* and *Segestria*.

1. *Dysdera cambridgii*, Thorell.
   Cannock.

   Not uncommon under stones and bark of trees, where it lurks within a tubular retreat. The spider is easily recognizable by its elongate form, orange legs, dark mahogany carapace and pale clay-yellow abdomen. The palpal bulb of the male has no cross-piece at the apex. The spider is also known as *D. erythryna*, Blackwall.

2. *Dysdera crocota*, C. L. Koch.
   Handsworth (F.P.S.).

   Larger than the last species, with a deep orange-pink carapace, orange legs, and abdomen with a delicate rosy-pink flush. The palpal bulb of the male has a cross-piece at the apex. This spider is also known as *D. rubicunda*, Blackwall.

3. *Segestria senoculata* (Linnæus).
   Handsworth (F.P.S.).

   Not common ; under bark of trees, in the crevices of loose stone walls and amongst detached rocks. Recognizable by its linear form and the black diamond-shaped blotches on the dorsal surface of the abdomen.

4. *Oonops pulcher*, Templeton.
   Handsworth (F.P.S.).

   Rare ; a very small linear brick-red spider.

DRASSIDÆ

Spiders with eight eyes, situated in two transverse rows. The tracheal openings lie just in front of the spinners. The tarsal claws are two in number, the anterior pair of spinners are set wide apart at the base, and the maxillæ are more or less impressed across the middle.

5. *Drassodes lapidosus* (Walckenaer).
   Cannock.

   Very common under stones. Also known as *Drassus lapidicolens*.

CLUBIONIDÆ

Spiders with eight eyes, situated in two transverse rows. The tracheal openings lie immediately in front of the spinners. The tarsal claws are two in number, but the anterior pair of spinners are set close together at the base ; the maxillæ are convex and not impressed across the middle.

6. *Clubiona pallidula* (Clerck).
   Handsworth (F.P.S.).

7. *Clubiona terrestris*, Westring.
   Handsworth (F.P.S.).

8. *Clubiona compta*, C. L. Koch.
   Handsworth (F.P.S.).

9. *Clubiona corticalis*, Walckenaer.
   Handsworth (F.P.S.).

10. *Clubiona trivialis*, L. Koch.
    Cannock.

ANYPHÆNIDÆ

The spiders of this family resemble those of the *Clubionidæ* in most respects, except that the tracheal stigmatic openings beneath the abdomen are situated about midway between the

SPIDERS

genital rima and the spinners, and not, as in the last family, immediately in front of the spinners.   One species only is indigenous to Great Britain and is very common amongst the foliage of trees in May and June.

11. *Anyphæna accentuata* (Walckenaer).   Handsworth (F.P.S.).

THOMISIDÆ

Spiders with eight eyes, situated in two transverse rows, two tarsal claws and anterior spinners close together at their base.   Maxillæ not impressed.   The crab-like shape and side-long movements of these spiders are their chief characteristics, enabling them to be easily distinguished from the more elongate *Drassidæ* and *Clubionidæ*.

12. *Philodromus aureolus* (Clerck).
Handsworth (F.P.S.).

13. *Tibellus oblongus* (Walckenaer).
Handsworth (F.P.S.).

14. *Xysticus cristatus* (Clerck).
Handsworth (F.P.S.).

15. *Oxyptila praticola* (C. L. Koch).
Handsworth (F.P.S.).

ATTIDÆ

The spiders of this family may be recognized in a general way by their mode of progression, consisting of a series of leaps.   More particularly they may be known by the square shape of the cephalic region and the fact that the eyes are arranged in three rows of 4, 2, 2, the centrals of the anterior row being much the largest.   Otherwise the spiders are simply specialized Clubionids with two tarsal claws and other minor characters possessed in common with other members of this family.

16. *Salticus scenicus* (Clerck).
Handsworth (F.P.S.) ; Cannock.

17. *Ergane falcata* (Clerck).
Handsworth (F.P.S.).
Known also as *Salticus coronatus*, Blackwall.

PISAURIDÆ

Spiders with eight eyes in three rows of 4, 2, 2 ; the small anterior eyes being sometimes in a straight line, sometimes recurved and sometimes procurved.   Those of the other two rows are situated in the form of a rectangle of various proportions and are much larger than the eyes of the anterior row.   The tarsal claws are three in number.   *Pisaura* runs freely over the herbage, carrying its egg-sac beneath the sternum ; while *Dolomedes* is a dweller in marshes and swamps.

18. *Pisaura mirabilis* (Clerck).
Cannock.

Known also as *Dolomedes*, or *Ocyale*, *mirabilis*.

LYCOSIDÆ

The members of this family are to be found running freely over the ground, and carrying the egg-sac attached to the spinners.   Many of the larger species make a short burrow in the soil and there keep guard over the egg-sac.   Eyes and tarsal claws as in the *Pisauridæ*, with slight differences.

19. *Lycosa ruricola* (De Geer).
Handsworth (F.P.S.).
Known also as *L. campestris*, Blackwall.

20. *Lycosa terricola*, Thorell.
Handsworth (F.P.S.).
Known also as *L. agretica*, Blackwall.

21. *Lycosa pulverulenta* (Clerck).
Cannock ; Handsworth (F.P.S.).
Known also as *L. rapax*, Blackwall, and *Tarentula pulverulenta*.

22. *Pardosa lugubris* (Walckenaer).
Cannock.

23. *Pardosa pullata* (Clerck).
Cannock.
Known also as *Lycosa obscura*, Blackwall.

24. *Pardosa prativaga* (C. L. Koch).
Handsworth (F.P.S.).
This species is given in Mr. Campbell's list as *Lycosa riparia*, C. L. Koch.

25. *Pardosa amentata* (Clerck).
Handsworth (F.P.S.).

AGELENIDÆ

Spiders with eight eyes, situated in two straight or more or less curved transverse rows. Tarsal claws, three. The species of this family spin a large sheet-like web, and construct a tubular retreat at the back of it, which leads to some crevice amongst the rocks or in the herbage, or in the chinks in the walls of outhouses and barns, wherever the various species may happen to be found. The habits of *Argyroneta*, the water spider, are however quite different. The posterior pair of spinners is much longer than the others in the more typical genera of this family.

26. *Agelena labyrinthica* (Clerck).
Handsworth (F.P.S.).

27. *Tegenaria derhami* (Scopoli).
Handsworth (F.P.S.).
A very common species everywhere.

28. *Tegenaria silvestris*, L. Koch.
Handsworth (F.P.S.).

29. *Cœlotes atropos* (Walckenaer).
Handsworth (F.P.S.).

ARGIOPIDÆ

The spiders included in this family have eight eyes, situated in two rows, the lateral eyes of both rows being usually adjacent, if not in actual contact, while the central eyes form a quadrangle. The tarsal claws are three, often with other supernumerary claws. The web is either an orbicular snare, as in the case of the 'common garden spider,' or consists of a sheet of webbing, beneath which the spider hangs and captures its prey as it falls upon the sheet. This immense family includes those usually separated under the names *Epeiridæ* and *Linyphiidæ*.

30. *Nesticus cellulanus* (Clerck).
Cannock.
Known also as *Linyphia crypticolens*, Blackwall.

31. *Meta segmentata* (Clerck).
Handsworth (F.P.S.).
Very abundant. Known also as *Epeira inclinata*, Blackwall.

32. *Meta merianæ* (Scopoli).
Handsworth (F.P.S.).
Not uncommon. Known also as *Epeira antriada*, Blackwall, and a striking variety as *E. celata*, Blackwall.

33. *Cyclosa conica* (Pallas).
Handsworth (F.P.S.).
A few specimens only have been taken. Known also as *Epeira conica*, Blackwall.

34. *Zilla* x - *notata* (Clerck).
Handsworth (F.P.S.).
Very common. Known also as *Epeira similis*, Blackwall.

35. *Zilla atrica*, C. L. Koch.
Handsworth (F.P.S.).
Almost as common as the above. Known also as *Epeira callophylla*, Blackwall.

36. *Araneus diadematus* (Clerck).
Handsworth (F.P.S.) ; Cannock.

37. *Araneus gibbosus* (Walckenaer).
Handsworth (F.P.S.).

38. *Pachygnatha clerckii*, Sundevall.
Handsworth (F.P.S.).

39. *Pachygnatha degeerii*, Sundevall.
Handsworth (F.P.S.).

40. *Pachygnatha listeri*, Sundevall.
Handsworth (F.P.S.).
Much rarer than the other two species above.

41. *Linyphia triangularis* (Clerck).
Handsworth (F.P.S.).

42. *Linyphia clathrata*, Sundevall.
Handsworth (F.P.S.).

43. *Drapetisca socialis* (Sundevall).
Handsworth (F.P.S.).

44. *Stemonyphantes lineatus* (Linnæus).
Handsworth (F.P.S.).

45. *Labulla thoracica* (Wider).
Handsworth (F.P.S.).

46. *Bolyphantes luteolus* (Blackwall).
Handsworth (F.P.S.).

47. *Tapinopa longideus* (Wider).
Handsworth (F.P.S.).

48. *Lepthyphantes minutus* (Blackwall).
Handsworth (F.P.S.).

49. *Lepthyphantes leprosus* (Ohlert).
Cannock.

50. *Lepthyphantes nebulosus* (Sundevall).
Cannock.

51. *Lepthyphantes ericeus* (Blackwall).
Cannock.

52. *Lepthyphantes tenuis* (Blackwall).
Handsworth (F.P.S.).

SPIDERS

53. *Lepthyphantes blackwallii*, Kulczynski.
   Handsworth (F.P.S.).

54. *Bathyphantes dorsalis* (Wider).
   Handsworth (F.P.S.).

55. *Bathyphantes gracilis* (Blackwall).
   Handsworth (F.P.S.).

56. *Bathyphantes concolor* (Wider).
   Handsworth (F.P.S.).

57. *Centromerus sylvaticus* (Blackwall).
   Handsworth (F.P.S.).

58. *Macrargus rufus* (Wider).
   Cannock.

59. *Centromerus simplex* (F. P.-Cambridge).
   Cannock, Brewery cellar.

60. *Microneta viaria* (Blackwall).
   Cannock.

61. *Microneta fuscipalpis* (C. L. Koch).
   Handsworth (F.P.S.).

62. *Pedanostethus lividus* (Blackwall).
   Handsworth (F.P.S.).

63. *Kulczynskiellum fuscum* (Blackwall).
   Handsworth (F.P.S.).

64. *Gonatium rubens* (Blackwall).
   Handsworth (F.P.S.).

65. *Dicyphus cornutus* (Blackwall).
   Handsworth (F.P.S.).

66. *Dicymbium nigrum* (Blackwall).
   Handsworth (F.P.S.).

67. *Erigone dentipalpis* (Wider).
   Handsworth (F.P.S.).

68. *Tiso vagans* (Blackwall).
   Handsworth (F.P.S.).

69. *Lophomma punctatum* (Blackwall).
   Handsworth (F.P.S.).

70. *Plæsiocrærus fuscipes* (Blackwall).
   Handsworth (F.P.S.).

71. *Entelecara acuminata* (Wider).
   Handsworth (F.P.S.).

72. *Arrecerus acuminatus* (Blackwall).
   Handsworth (F.P.S.) ; Cannock.

THERIDIIDÆ

The members of this family have eight eyes, situated very much like those of the *Argiopidæ* ; but the mandibles are usually weak, the maxillæ are inclined over the labium, and the posterior legs have a comb of stiff curved spines beneath the tarsi. The web consists of a tangle of crossing lines, and the spider often constructs a tent-like retreat wherein the egg-sac is hung up. The tarsal claws are three in number.

73. *Theridion pictum* (Walckenaer).
   Handsworth (F.P.S.).

74. *Theridion sisyphium* (Clerck).
   Cannock.
   Known also as *T. nervosum*, Blackwall.

75. *Theridion denticulatum* (Walckenaer).
   Cannock.

76. *Theridion varians*, Hahn.
   Cannock.

77. *Theridion ovatum* (Clerck).
   Handsworth (F.P.S.).

78. *Pholcomma gibbum* (Westring).
   Handsworth (F.P.S.).

79. *Crustulina guttata* (Wider).
   Handsworth (F.P.S.).

MIMETIDÆ

Spiders of this family are similar in general respects to the *Theridiidæ*, having eight eyes and three tarsal claws. The species of *Ero* construct a small brown pear-shaped or *cylindrical* egg-cocoon suspended on a fine silken stalk.

80. *Ero furcata* (Villers). Handsworth (F.P.S.).
   This spider is known also as *E. thoracica* and *Theridion variegatum*, Blackwall.

DICTYNIDÆ

The spiders belonging to this family possess three tarsal claws, and the eyes, eight in number, situated in two transverse rows, the laterals being in contact. The cribellum (or extra pair of spinning organs) and the calamistrum (a row of curving bristles on the protarsi of the fourth pair of legs) are present in all members of the family. They construct a tubular retreat with an outer sheet of webbing, which is covered with a flocculent silk made with the calamistrum from threads furnished by the cribellum.

81. *Amaurobius fenestralis* (Stroem).
   Handsworth (F.P.S.).
   Not so common as *similis*. Known also as *Ciniflo atrox*, Blackwall.

82. *Amaurobius similis* (Blackwall).
   Handsworth (F.P.S.).
   Common. Known also under the name *Ciniflo*.

ACARINA

Mites

The following list is compiled from the records contributed by Mr. Cyril Brett to the *Reports of the N. Staff. Field Club* for 1902–3 (pp. 92–3), and 1905–6 (pp. 75–6).

ERIOPHYINAE

Eriophyes aucupariae, Conn. On Pyrus aucuparia Gaert., Alton, Aug. 1903 ; Rudyard, 25 July, 1905 ; Manifold Valley, Aug. 1905

— *axillaris*, auct. On Alnus glutinosa, Medic., Alton, 12 Sept. 1902 ; Consall, Rudyard, July, 1905

— *brevitarsus*, Nal. On Alnus glutinosa, Medic., Alton, 11 Sept. 1902

— *goniothorax*, Nal. On Crataegus oxyacantha, L., Alton, Aug. 1903 ; Belmont, July, 1905

— *laevis*, Nal. On Alnus glutinosa, Medic., Alton, 12 Sept. 1902

— *macrochelus*, Nal. On Acer campestre, L., Denstone, Aug. 1903

— *macrorhynchus*, Nal. On Acer campestre, L., Denstone, Aug. 1903 ; near Prestwood, 20 Aug. 1905

— *rudis*, Canest. On Betula verrucosa, Erhr., common, Alton, Sept. 1902

ERIOPHYINAE—*continued*

Eriophyes thomasi. On Thymus serpyllum, L., Ramshorn, July, 1903

— *similis*, Nal. On Prunus spinosa, L., Alton, 21 July, 1904 ; Denstone, 11 Aug. 1905

— *tetanothrix laevis*, Nal. On Salix caprea, L., Alton, Aug. 1903

PHYLLOCOPTINAE

Phyllocoptes acericola, Nal. On Acer pseudo-platanus, L., Dimmingsdale, 24 Sept. 1902

— *arianus*, Nal. On leaves of Pyrus aria, Erhr., Belmont Woods, 22 July, 1905

— *fraxini*, Nal. On Fraxinus excelsior, L., Alton, Aug. 1903 ; Belmont, 22 July ; Rudyard, 25 July ; near Foxt, 31 July, 1905

CRUSTACEANS

In maritime counties this branch of our fauna forces itself upon the attention of the most unobservant. In many inland districts, on the other hand, the keenest students of natural history have suffered it to lie in absolute neglect. Staffordshire, therefore, is rather exceptionally fortunate in having been long exempt from this indifference. The earlier notices, it is true, have their scientific interest suffused with an antiquarian glamour. At many points also they attest the presence of crustaceans in the bogs and streams of the county by implication rather than by express mention of any particular genera and species. Amongst these remote authorities *The Natural History of Staffordshire*, by Robert Plot, LL.D., Keeper of the Ashmolean Museum and professor of chemistry in the University of Oxford, has the first claim on our consideration. For a predominantly aquatic group of animals we must welcome Plot's quaint conclusion in dealing with the hydrography of the shire :—

> All which summ'd up together, we find at the foot of the account, that it is water'd with no less than 24 *Rivers* of name, though a *Mediterranean* county ; besides the endless number of *anonymous Rindles* and small brooks that must needs attend them ; a number perhaps that very few *Countries* of the like extent can be found to surpass, if any that equals it.[1]

It is, in fact, in anonymous rindles and small pools that some species of Entomostraca are most surely obtained. For direct record, however, of any crustacean, Plot must be consulted in a part of his work which, with our modern views of classification, would be thought very unlikely to supply it. The heading 'Of Brutes' to the chapter in question is more concise than discriminating. 'Under the title of *Brutes*,' he says, 'I comprehend (as in Oxfordshire) all *Animals* whatever that have *sense* and *locomotion*, except the *rational*, whether they are the inhabitants of the *Air*, *Water*, or *Earth*, such as *Birds*, *Insects*, *Fishes*, *Reptiles*, and *Quadrupeds*.'[2] A long period indeed elapsed before either popular or scientific opinion effectively disentangled crustacea from the insects and fishes of this miscellaneous host. After a discussion of the burbot or birdbolt, sometimes called the nonsuch because of its rarity, and provisionally identified with *Mustela fluviatilis*, Plot remarks :—

> But though I heard only of this single fish that I think undescribed (for that there are a sort of *Crevices* in the stream that passes by *Overend* and *Longdon*, that will not boile *red*, is only accidental, as was shown before in Oxfordshire) yet I was informed of divers very unusual observations, concerning *scaled*, as well as *smooth* fish.[3]

The crevices mentioned in the queer parenthesis are obviously the common river crayfish, properly called *Potamobius pallipes* (Lereboullet). In his next section Plot says :—

> There are other fish, too, both of the scaled and shell'd kinds, that will live and breed in places very uncommon to their species, thus *Gudgeons* and *Crevices* live well and breed in the *pooles* at Bentley and thrive to a just magnitude, but then these ponds are always fedd with *Springs*.

In the distinction between scaled fishes on the one hand and smooth or shelled fishes on the other, there seems to be a glimmering of suspicion that, though the crevice with its polished coat was just as much a fish as the barbel and the carp, it was still a fish with a difference. That the Entomostraca parasitic on carp and other freshwater fishes did not attract Plot's attention is a definite loss, as we are left without any of the unusual observations upon them which he might otherwise have reported. He discusses at much length the brine-pits of Staffordshire, but takes no notice of the so-called brine-worm, *Artemia salina* (Linn.), once so abundant at Lymington,

[1] Op. cit. chap. 2, § 21, p. 43 (1686). [2] Ibid. chap. 7, p. 228.
[3] Ibid. § 29, p. 241.

in Hampshire. It may reasonably be inferred from Plot's silence on the subject that this interesting phyllopod did not occur in Staffordshire.

An interval of more than a hundred years brings us to the publication of another important work, *The History and Antiquities of Staffordshire*, by the Rev. Stebbing Shaw, B.D., F.A.S., and fellow of Queens' College, Cambridge. Although this intervening period includes the birth and death of Linnaeus, and great strides in carcinology, due to such men as Pallas, J. C. Fabricius, and Herbst, it cannot be said that Mr. Shaw's work betrays any acquaintance with the progress made in this branch of science. Only a single passage from his two folio volumes, other than quotations from Plot, has any direct bearing on our subject. In the account of Mavesyn Ridware (proper), when describing the fishery within Armitage and Handsacre, he explains that there the River Trent is not navigable, adding,

> and perhaps within the boundaries of this fishery there is an unusual number of deeps and shallows, so necessary to the different tribes with which it is plentifully stored. The best sorts are pike, perch, greyling, eel, gudgeon, and crawfish in plenty ; more rare are trout and burbot ; of tench 3 or 4 in a year ; carp very rare ; and within memory a brace or two of salmon ; but these were white and out of season. Of the coarse sorts, barbel and chub may be seen in large shoals.[4]

The crayfish, it will be observed, is here still counted as a fish. To this day apparently the spelling and pronunciation of the name varies without rule in different parts of England between crayfish and crawfish. As a matter of convenience the latter should be restricted to the marine *Palinurus*, sometimes called the spiny lobster, leaving the term crayfish to the river species. Shaw's work contains a long catalogue of plants by Samuel Dickenson, LL.B., rector of Blymhill, Staffordshire, ending with '*Utricularia vulgaris*—hooded water-milfoile. Bogs. In a bog near Blymhill.'[5] Just as the names of fishes are an indirect testimony to the occurrence of various Entomostraca known to be commonly parasitic upon them, so the names of various water-plants in Mr. Dickenson's list are a guarantee that a large assemblage of Cladocera and Copepoda, which almost invariably accompany these plants, will not be found wanting to the waters of the county.

From the life of the celebrated entomologist and palaeographer, John Obadiah Westwood, it appears that he was born in Sheffield in 1805, and at first educated there, but afterwards at a school in Lichfield, whither the family had removed.[6] Professor Westwood, as is well known, made his mark in carcinology as well as in other departments of learning, and in this respect it is interesting to trace his connexion with this county. In the *British Cyclopaedia of Natural History*, by Charles Partington, Westwood wrote sundry articles on Crustacea, one of which contains the following passages :—' Cray fish. A crustaceous animal, belonging to the order *Decapoda* and section *Macroura*, and forming the genus *Potamobius* of Leach, although Desmarets and others unite it with the lobster in the genus *Astacus*.' Further on he says :—

> They are caught by sinking a net, or spiny faggots, in the middle of which a piece of putrid meat is placed. We well remember the delight with which in our schoolboy days we would escape from the trammels of Bonnycastle and Virgil, and go groping, with our shirt sleeves tucked up, in the holes in brooks where the crayfish were met with, and can therefore speak from experience of the sharpness of the bite they can inflict with their claws.[7]

As Bonnycastle and Virgil must have been concerned with his later schooldays, it is fair to conclude that the youthful Westwood was nipped by the chelipeds of Staffordshire crayfish. His determination of the generic name should not be overlooked.

A few years later *The Natural History of the County of Stafford*, by Robert Garner, F.L.S., considerably enlarges our outlook. Under the heading 'Crustacea,' Mr. Garner supplies the following information :—

> The animals composing the *Crustacea* are very beautiful ; most of them inhabit salt water, many, however, fresh, and of these some are interesting.
> *Argulus foliaceus.*—Very common on the stickleback ; most of which little fish, in our canals, we have noticed to be affected with this parasite. The *Argulus* is very curious, and adheres to the fish by two round suckers, generally about the head, or to the side ; when detached it swims beautifully.

---

[4] Op. cit. (1798), vol. i, pp. 188, 189.
[6] *Dict. Nat. Biog.*, Art. ' Westwood.'
[5] Ibid. pp. 97–115.
[7] Op. cit. (1836), vol. ii, p. 187.

CRUSTACEANS

Astacus communis.—Crawfish. Abundant in clear streams. This will live long out of water, but a short time if placed in water from a pond or well.

Gammarus Pulex.—Fresh-water shrimp. Common : this is by no means a test of the purity of water, as has been said ; I find it in muddy brooks, as well as in fountains.

Asellus vulgaris.—Common with the preceding.

Cyclops vulgaris.—This and the following are very minute, and both may be seen in water from most streams or ponds.

Daphnia Pulex.[8]

The following are terrestrial :—

Oniscus Asellus.—Common ; congregated under stones, &c.

Porcellio scaber.—Abundant in decayed wood ; Swinnerton Park.

Armadillo vulgaris.—Under stones, &c. Cheshire cavern.[9]

By the designation *Astacus communis* the river crayfish is evidently intended. The intimation that it will live longer out of water than in water from a pond or well is probably based on the amphibious habits of this animal. Those who try to domesticate it, often no doubt with the kindest intentions, plunge it into a bowl or other aquarium so plentifully supplied with water that the creature is soon practically drowned. Since it is not adapted for climbing steep and slippery walls of glass or earthenware, the depth of liquid in its prison should be only between one and two inches, to give it the same chance which it has in its native haunts of changing from aquatic to aerial surroundings. Other comments on Mr. Garner's records may be reserved till after the introduction of a still later and fuller authority covering much the same ground, but with additional knowledge and more regard for scientific classification. The work in question is *The Natural History of Tutbury*, by Sir Oswald Mosley, bart., D.C.L., F.L.S., together with the Fauna and Flora of the district surrounding Tutbury and Burton-on-Trent, by Edward Brown, with an appendix. This local fauna contains the following notices :—

Sub-class Crustacea :—

Order Podophthalma. Tribe Decapoda Macroura.

Family Astacidea.—*Astacus fluviatilis* (Fabr.). The Common Crayfish. This diminutive freshwater lobster is found abundantly in the Dove, in which stream it is easily captured by means of basket traps baited with bullock's liver. It is valued as an ornamental garnish for dishes, as well as for its own edible properties. It is found occasionally in the Wimshill Brook, a small stream that runs into the Trent, but I have never known it to be taken from that river itself.

Order Edriophthalma. Tribe Amphipoda.

Family Gammaridae. — *Gammarus pulex* (Fabr.). The Freshwater Shrimp. Very abundant in the Trent. It is an interesting species to keep in an aquarium, owing to its lively and eccentric movements.

Tribe Isopoda.

Family Asellidae.—*Asellus vulgaris* (Latr.). The Freshwater Asellus. Exceedingly numerous in the Trent, where it abounds together with the last-mentioned species, more especially in the beds of *Anacharis alsinastrum*. It is probably to be found in all the running streams of the district.[10] *Oniscus asellus* (Linn.). The Wood Louse. Very common underneath stones and rotten wood. A large light-coloured form, occurring underneath stones at Dovedale, is probably a distinct species.

Family Porcellionidae.—*Porcellio scaber* (Latr.). The Scabrous Wood Louse ; *Sclater* or *Slater*. Common in similar situations with the last. *Armadillo vulgaris* (Latr.). The Lesser Pill Millepede. Common amongst moss and underneath stones.

Order Poecilopoda.

Family Argulidae.—*Argulus foliaceus* (Jurine). The Fish Louse. Found sometimes parasitic upon freshwater fishes in ponds. *Daphnia pulex* (Latr.). The Water Flea. Common in stagnant and slowly-running water. *Daphnia vetula* (Straus). The Blunt-headed Water Flea. Common in similar situations with the last. The bivalve shells of some species of *Daphnia* occur in the peat bed at Burton-on-Trent.

Family Lynceidae.—Several undetermined species of the genera *Eurycercus* and *Chydorus* are common in stagnant water.

Family Cypridae.—Species of the genera *Cypris* and *Candona* are abundant in ditches. The minute shell-cases of these little animals are very[11] indestructible in their nature. A species of *Cypris* or *Cythere* occurs in a fossil state abundantly in the shales beneath the Woodfield seam of coal at Newhall and Swadlincote.

---

[8] Op. cit. (1844), p. 329.

[9] Ibid. p. 330.

[10] Ibid. (1863), p. 130.

[11] Ibid. p. 131.

Family Cyclopidae.—*Cyclops quadricornis* (Müll.). The Four-horned Cyclops or Lesser Water Flea. This species swarms in water that is at all stagnant. I have known it to make its appearance in an elevated roof water-cistern a very few months after the cistern had been made. The eggs must, apparently, have been conveyed to the roof either by rain or wind.

Order Rotifera.

This order, which consists of interesting microscopic forms of life, has generally been classed with the Infusoria : but the organization of the Rotifera shows clearly they naturally belong to the Crustacea, and that they follow the Entomostraca in a lineal series. The species of this order are not numerous in the district, but *Rotifer vulgaris* (Ehr.), the Common Wheel Animalcule, is very abundant in the dirt that accumulates in spouts and in roof-gutters, and it is a most pleasing object for the microscope.[12]

So full and intelligent an account of the Crustacea is quite exceptional in the faunistic catalogues of inland districts at the date when the above report by Mr. Edward Brown was published. That it should now in some points be open to criticism is in no way a reproach, but the natural consequence of such progress as science has happily been making in the interval. Thus, to begin with, the systematic position of the rotifers, as at present accepted, while ranking them far above infusorians, by no means gives them admission into the class with which we are here dealing. There is a vast group or phylum of animals to which Sir E. Ray Lankester has applied the term Appendiculata, because their more or less segmented bodies are capable of bearing on each body-segment a pair of hollow lateral appendages or parapodia moved by intrinsic muscles and penetrated by blood-spaces. The phylum is divided into three sub-phyla, respectively called Rotifera, Chaetopoda, Arthropoda. Seeing that the Chaetopods or true worms are interposed between the first of these groups and the Arthropoda, with jointed legs, to which the crustaceans and other important classes belong, the relationship between a rotifer and a shrimp is evidently very remote. In the general history of animals this relationship is not to be disregarded, but it will not justify the inclusion of creatures so very distinct in one and the same class.

The genera and species mentioned by Mr. Garner and Mr. Brown are not very numerous, compared with the whole number which will beyond doubt be eventually found within the waters of Staffordshire. But few as they are, they fortunately spread themselves over most of the chief sections of the class likely to be represented in the district. Any one, therefore, who made himself acquainted with these examples alone would lay the foundation for a very complete mastery of the whole subject. He would have to do, however, only with two of the sub-classes, the Malacostraca and Entomostraca, and in the former he would make no intimacy with the stalk-eyed, ten-footed, short-tailed, true crabs, the Brachyura. This highly organized group might be inclined, after Dr. Plot's example, to lump together almost all other crustaceans as being in comparison with their own intelligent selves mere brutes. In the tropics they have indeed some worthy competitors among the Macrura anomala. But none of the specially gifted land crustaceans have been attracted to our uncertain climate. In the central parts of England the highest representative of the class is the podophthalmous, macruran decapod, already often mentioned, *Potamobius pallipes*. This is included with the lobster in the tribe Astacidea, but belongs to a separate family, the Potamobiidae. As being podophthalmous the river crayfish shares with an endless variety of crabs, lobsters, prawns, and shrimps, the peculiarity of having its eyes on movable stalks or peduncles. The theory is that the organs of vision have been developed on the pair of appendages pertaining to the first body-segment, although in almost all cases the segment itself has become immovably fused with the segment behind it. Also in common with the animals classified in popular speech under the four names above given, the crayfish is a decapod. Its ten feet are distributed in pairs to the body-segments numbered from the tenth to the fourteenth. The Malacostracan body is composed of twenty-one segments, each of them, with doubtful exception of the last, being endowed actually or potentially with a pair of appendages. More or fewer of these are called feet, according as they show more or less plainly an analogy with the legs and arms of vertebrate animals. From crabs the crayfish is separated by being macrurous or long-tailed. Yet in both the tail or pleon consists of the last seven body-segments, from the fifteenth to the twenty-first. But somehow, apart from the question of length or shortness, an additional distinction has arisen, that, while in the genuine Macrura the last segment but one always carries a pair of appendages, this pair is always wanting in the genuine Brachyura.

The drop in dignity is rather abrupt from the only stalk-eyed decapod which our inland counties possess to the Edriophthalma tetradecapoda, or sessile-eyed, fourteen-footed Malacos-

[12] Op. cit. (1863), p. 132.

tracans. The latter are so insignificant in size compared with the crayfish, and differ from it so much in general appearance as well as in some obvious details of structure, that an uninstructed observer would be little likely to suspect their near relationship. To *Gammarus pulex* (de Geer), so widely distributed and so abundant in our brooks and ponds, both Garner and Brown give the vernacular name of freshwater shrimp. Adam White, on the other hand, in his *Popular History of British Crustacea*, calls it the 'freshwater screw.'[13] In his general survey he had other uses for the term 'shrimp,' which precluded his applying it to any sessile-eyed species. The shrimp or shrimps of commerce, some of which can live in fresh water, are Macrura decapoda like the crayfish. But *G. pulex*, besides having no ocular peduncles, has seven pairs of leg-like appendages, beginning with the eighth instead of the tenth body-segment. Nevertheless these striking differences do not outweigh its other shrimp-like affinities. The eyes, it is true, being seated in the head, give no direct evidence of the initial segment, but the second and third segments in front of the mouth are attested by the two pairs of antennae, a true crustacean characteristic, while at and behind the mouth we find in true malacostracan sequence the mandibles, two pairs of maxillae, and one pair of maxillipeds. The difference which then presents itself is far less schismatical than might at first be supposed. In the higher groups the eighth and ninth pairs of appendages are definitely organs of the mouth, known as second and third maxillipeds. These pairs in the lower groups are concerned more in grasping the food than in mincing it up. They are called gnathopods, a name which cannot well be distinguished by interpretation from maxillipeds, the implication being in each case that the appendages in question are either legs that have made themselves useful as jaws or jaws that have made themselves useful as legs. In the family Gammaridae, of which *G. pulex* is an excellent representative, the nearly related genera *Niphargus* and *Crangonyx* contain species which from their habitat have received the common designation of well-shrimps. It remains to be seen whether the wells of Staffordshire will, like those of some neighbouring counties, yield any of these exceptionally interesting and rather rarely-seen forms.

Like the Amphipoda just described the Isopoda are sessile-eyed. They have, too, the same disposition of the mouth-organs, followed by the legs in seven pairs. In both orders alike the cephalothoracic shield or carapace is only produced to cover the maxillipeds, not as in the Brachyura and Macrura extended to the fourteenth segment of the body. A rather startling difference, however, sets the two orders somewhat widely apart. For, whereas the breathing organs of the Amphipoda are, like those of the crayfish, all in front of the pleon, all those of the genuine Isopoda are within it. To counterbalance such separative distinctions among the malacostracan orders, it may be noticed as a unifying character that all along the line the sexual openings of the female belong to the twelfth body-segment, and those of the male to the fourteenth. Of freshwater isopods our Mediterranean counties, as Plot calls them, have only one species, the proper name of which is, not *Asellus vulgaris* (Latreille), but *Asellus aquaticus* (Linn.). It has as much or as little right as *Gammarus pulex* to be called the freshwater shrimp. To call it, as Brown does, the freshwater *Asellus*, is not much to the purpose, because in this genus, established by Geoffroy in 1762, all the species belong exclusively to fresh water. It may also be thought superfluous to have the typical species named *aquaticus*, since none of the species are other than aquatic. But the explanation is found when we look a little further back into its scientific history. Linnaeus regarded it as belonging to the old comprehensive genus *Oniscus*, which at one time included all the terrestrial isopods, so that a species found constantly in water and nowhere else could naturally be distinguished as a water-dwelling *Oniscus*. Again, among the land-dwelling species *Oniscus asellus*, Linn., was the most familiar, so that Geoffroy, when separating the aquatic species from its sub-aërial companions, may have thought it well to preserve a memory of the old connexion by taking *Asellus* as the name of his new genus. The differences between the two species which are thus partially namesakes are now recognized as very considerable, with the result that *Asellus aquaticus* is allotted to a family Asellidae in the tribe Asellota, while *Oniscus asellus* stands in a family Oniscidae in the tribe Oniscidea. Concerning the large light-coloured form to which Mr. Brown alludes as possibly deserving to be specifically distinguished from the last-named species, the caution may be expressed that in some of our common land isopods variations of colour appear without affecting their other characteristics. This is eminently true of the next species, *Porcellio scaber*, Latreille. It belongs to the same family as the *Oniscus*, is nearly its equal in size, and perhaps fully its equal in abundance. It is rather narrower in shape and

---

[13] Op. cit. (1857), p. 184.

has a rougher surface. The flagellum or slender lash-like part of its second antennae is divided into only two joints instead of three, and the first two pairs of pleopods, appendages of the first and second pleon-segments, are furnished with pseudo-tracheae, aids to aërial respiration which are wanting in *Oniscus*. The third species of this tribe in Mr. Brown's catalogue should be called *Armadillidium vulgare* (Latreille). It belongs to a separate family, Armadillidiidae. Its antennae and pleopods have the characters above mentioned as pertaining to *P. scaber*, but among marks distinguishing it from that species are the globular form into which the body can be composed, and the structure of the uropods or last pair of appendages, which have the outer branch laminar instead of cylindrical. The vernacular names, wood louse, scabrous wood louse or slater, and lesser pill millepede are of old standing and will not perhaps easily be dislodged, but they conceal the true position of these animals in the system of nature. By calling them woodland shrimps or garden shrimps we at least run a happy risk of bringing home to the unscientific understanding the fact that they are true crustaceans. The last of the three might better be called in English the pill shrimp than the pill millepede. It is properly distinguished by Mr. Brown from *Glomeris marginata*, Olivier, the greater pill millepede,[14] which really is not a crustacean, but a species of the family Glomeridae, in the order Diplopoda, among the myriapods. *Armadillidium vulgare*, with its modest supply of fourteen legs, has no claim to be noted as either a lesser or a greater member of that many-footed company.

The sub-class Entomostraca, divided into three great sections, Branchiopoda, Ostracoda, Copepoda, does not display that arithmetical unity of body segmentation observable in the Malacostraca. On the contrary, the segments are sometimes many more than twenty-one, and sometimes are left almost entirely to the imagination. The family Argulidae, which Mr. Brown assigns to the Poecilopoda, as to an order of equal rank with the Entomostraca, is now generally grouped with the latter. Its peculiarities, however, still leave its exact status uncertain. Some authorities place it among the Branchiopoda, others among the Copepoda. In the former section it has to be distinguished from the Phyllopoda and Cladocera as an order Branchiura, or as a sub-order, if the Branchiopoda are themselves regarded as an order. The genus *Argulus*, O. F. Müller, has the strange character that its second maxillae are metamorphosed into sucker-disks, by which it can attach itself firmly to a fish, and also march freely over the surface of its victim by holding on with one sucker and moving the other alternately. These disks are a striking example of the adaptability with which crustacean appendages lend themselves to varying circumstances. The adhesive apparatus in the Argulidae, however, is not always or entirely dependent on the method of suction, but is always partially and sometimes wholly contrived by hook and by crook. In any case the adhesion is intended to subserve another kind of suction, effected by the siphon or mouth-tube, in the structure of which the lips, mandibles, and first maxillae take part. An unpaired venomous sting may or may not be present. *Argulus foliaceus* (Linn.), sometimes called the carp-louse, is a very indiscriminate feeder, attaching itself not only to carp and sticklebacks, but to several other freshwater fishes, and even to tadpoles. It is a powerful swimmer. If it is to be classed with the parasitic Copepoda, it markedly differs from that group in general in that the females do not carry their eggs about with them after extrusion, but deposit them on some extraneous substance.

Records of Phyllopoda are for the moment wanting in this county. The Cladocera have received more attention. For though Mr. Brown's examples are for the most part very vague, a welcome contribution to this branch of our subject was supplied in 1895 in the *Synopsis of the British Cladocera*[15] by Mr. T. V. Hodgson, a gentleman since distinguished as biologist to the National Antarctic Expedition on the 'Discovery.' In the same year was published the first part of a classical work on this group, entitled *Révision des Cladocères*, by Jules Richard.[16] M. Richard defines the Cladocera as

> small free Entomostraca, with distinct head, the rest of the body usually compressed from side to side, and enclosed in a two-valved carapace ; the antennae of the second pair two-branched, each branch carrying setae, and composed of only two to four joints ; the mandibles altogether devoid of palps ; the pairs of feet four to six in number, of which usually the majority or all are foliaceous, lobate ; the eye single.[17]

[14] *Nat. Hist. Tutbury*, p. 137.
[15] *Journ. Birmingham Nat. Hist. and Phil. Soc.* 101.
[16] *Ann. Sci. Nat. Zool.* (ser. 7), vol. xviii, p. 279, continued in (ser. 8) vol. ii, p. 187 (1896).
[17] *Op. cit.* 304.

CRUSTACEANS

Unlike most crustaceans, the Cladocera swim by means of the branching second antennae, to which the name of the group refers. Another comparatively uncommon feature, uncommon at least as affecting adult life, is the extreme transparency of the test or carapace which covers without concealing the details of the organism. There are two sections of the group, each divided into two subsections, but as it happens all the species as yet definitely recorded from this county belong to one and the same subsection. In the section Calyptomera, the feet and body of the animal are well covered by the carapace. In the subsection Anomopoda, instead of six pairs of feet all alike foliaceous, branchial, and non-prehensile, there are five or six pairs, of which the two anterior are more or less prehensile, not branchial and foliaceous, and differing from the hinder pairs. This sub-section includes the majority of the Cladocera in general, and among them that which is most widely known, *Daphnia pulex* (de Geer). The familiarity which breeds contempt allows men to speak and write of this innocent crustacean as 'the water flea.' That either Mr. Garner or Mr. Brown observed the true *D. pulex* in this county, it is impossible to guarantee. Within the genus *Daphne* or *Daphnia* there are many species and varieties which only experts laboriously distinguish. That the family Daphniidae is here really represented may be trusted from the mention of *Daphnia vetula* (Straus) as the blunt-headed water flea. But this species dates back further than Straus to O. F. Müller, and at a later date became the type of Schödler's genus *Simocephalus*, so named because the head is obtuse at the top instead of keeled, as in *Daphnia*. The new generic name, however, was preoccupied, and has recently been changed by Dr. Norman to *Simosa*. Two other members of the same family have been found by Mr. Hodgson in Staffordshire, namely, *Scapholeberis mucronata* (O.F.M.) at Kingswood, and *Moina rectirostris* (Jurine) in a horsepond near Harborne.[18] The last genus is distinguished from the other three by not having a distinct rostrum, and by having the first antennae of the female long and freely mobile. In *Daphnia* the dorsal and ventral margins of the valves are drawn gradually together to end in a long or short process, which may be ventral or inclining to dorsal, but which leaves nothing that can be clearly distinguished as a hind margin. In *Scapholeberis*, on the other hand, the straight or nearly straight ventral margins are produced into processes, the bases of which are connected with the dorsal edge by a clear stretch of hind margin. In *Simosa* the hind margin is large and rounded off at each extremity. Mr. Hodgson reports *Ilyocryptus sordidus* (Liévin) from Kingswood. This mud-loving species belongs to the family Macrotrichidae, in which long and mobile first antennae are the rule, instead of the exception as in the case of *Moina* among the Daphniidae. The species with which we are here concerned is said to lead an unromantic existence, having given up the natural use of its second antennae as swimming organs, to employ them only for crawling over the mud or burrowing in it, usually in a considerable depth of water. Under the family Lynceidae Mr. Brown reports that several undetermined species of the genera *Eurycercus* and *Chydorus* are common in stagnant water. The statement is partially redeemed from indefiniteness by the circumstance that the former genus is, so far as known, represented in England only by a single species, *Eurycercus lamellatus* (O.F.M.). *Chydorus*, it is true, has some four or five species recorded from the British Isles, but of these *C. sphaericus* (O.F.M.) is considered to be the commonest and most widely distributed of all the Cladocera, so that its occurrence here may be regarded as certain. *Alonella nanus* (Baird) was taken by Mr. Hodgson at Kingswood. For the family containing these three species the name Chydoridae should be adopted in place of Lynceidae, since the genus *Lynceus* has been shown to have its systematic place elsewhere.[19] *A. nanus* is said to be the smallest Entomostracan known at present.[20] It may well be called the dwarf, since the female is only just over and the male is just under one hundredth of an inch in length. *Chydorus sphaericus*, however, in the male sex is never much longer. But its female is sometimes twice as long, and this in turn is surpassed in sevenfold degree by the female of *Eurycercus lamellatus*. That species, therefore, exhibits a veritable giant measuring nearly a sixth of an inch from head to tail, and matching this length by a similarly unusual depth between the dorsal and ventral margins.

Concerning the Ostracoda or box-entomostracans—which, unlike the Cladocera, have no distinct head, but are shut up in their two valves like little molluscs—authorities for this county supply no definite information. That species of the genera *Cypris*, Müller, and *Candona*, Baird, both belonging to the family Cyprididae, 'are abundant in ditches,' is a statement that would no doubt be applicable to all our counties.

[18] *Synopsis*, p. 111.
[19] *The Zool.* (1902), p. 101.
[20] *Journ. Quekett Microsc. Club* (ser. 2), vol. viii, p. 444 (1903).

Similarly, with regard to the Copepoda or oar-footed Entomostraca, the notice that *Cyclops quadricornis*, Müller, of the family Cyclopidae, occurs in stagnant water, is not very instructive. It is uncertain which of several species may be intended by the name *quadricornis*, and the use of it without any explanatory details implies a rather superficial acquaintance with Copepoda in general.

In 1895 Mr. D. J. Scourfield made a guarded suggestion that the little-known ento-mostracan fauna of Wales might eventually show some essential differences from that of the south-east of England, which has been investigated with much assiduity.[21] Should this prove to be so it will be interesting to learn where the line of cleavage or fusion between the discrepant faunas should be drawn, and whether the rarities or distinctive species of east and west may chance to have a common gathering place in the waters of Staffordshire.

[21] *Journ. Quekett Microsc. Club* (ser. 2), vol. vi, 137.

FISHES

In compiling the following list recently introduced species, such as the American brook trout (*Salmo fontinalis*, Mitch.), the rainbow trout (*S. irideus*, Günther), etc., have not been mentioned, the indigenous and long-resident species only being included. I must here acknowledge my indebtedness to the lists of the late Robert Garner and Edwin Brown, the names of these authorities being mentioned whenever their observations have been quoted. A paper on ' North Staffordshire Freshwater Fish,' by Mr. John R. B. Masefield, M.A., in the *Annual Report and Transactions of the North Staffordshire Naturalists' Field Club and Archæological Society*, vol. xxviii., is especially useful from containing lists of localities which show the distribution of the several species in the district of which he treats.

TELEOSTEANS

ACANTHOPTERYGII

1. Perch. *Perca fluviatilis*, Linn.

Common throughout the county. Perch have been taken in the Trent up to 4½ lb. in weight.

2. Ruffe or Daddy Ruffe. *Acerina cernua*, Linn.

Common in rivers and canals.

3. Bullhead or Miller's Thumb. *Cottus gobio*, Linn.

Plentiful in streams and in rivers where gravel and stones are found.

ANACANTHINI

4. Burbot or Burbolt. *Lota vulgaris*, Cuv. *Locally*, Eel Pout.

This curious and interesting fish is occasionally taken in the Trent and its larger tributaries up to 4 lb. in weight. It has long been known as a Staffordshire fish, having been very quaintly described and figured by Plot in his *Natural History of Staffordshire* (1686). Plot's figure is a reduced copy of a picture drawn for Colonel Comberford of a specimen ' taken in the Tame, near Faseley Bridge, by Goodyer Holt, a Free Mason, as he was repairing it, August 11th, 1654.' Plot recorded three other instances of the occurrence of the burbot in Staffordshire.

HEMIBRANCHII

5. Three - spined Stickleback. *Gastrosteus aculeatus*, Linn.

This little fish is common in rivers, streams and ponds throughout the county, and the forms, originally described as distinct species and now considered only varieties, known as the rough-tailed (*G. trachurus*, Cuv.), half-armed (*G. semiarmatus*, Cuv.) and smooth-tailed sticklebacks (*G. leuirus*, Cuv.), are all found in the Trent and its tributaries. The brilliant colours assumed by the males during the breeding season, their pugnacity and especially their nest-building, have rendered these little fish famous, but the nest, according to my own observations, is often a very flimsy affair, being at times merely a little heap of Conferva or other weed through which the body of the male has made a tunnel and which he jealously guards. The best example however of a stickleback's nest which I have ever seen I found in a pond in the neighbouring county of Leicester. This was a well-built, roughly cylindrical structure of roots and small twigs, so well placed together that the whole did not collapse when taken from the water. In this case the materials of the nest were not glued or cemented together in any way, and I have never been able to see the male engaged in strengthening the walls of his house by means of the sticky mucus he is said to exude for this purpose.[1] The particular nest just described resembled very greatly a diminutive copy of the play-bowers of the Australian bower-birds, but unlike them was well roofed in above.

The large short-spined stickleback (*G. brachycentrus*, Cuv.), regarded by Günther as a separate species and by White and others as a variety only of *G. aculeatus*, has been recorded from Stow Pool near Lichfield by Thompson in his *Natural History of Ireland*. In July, 1836, Thompson obtained from Stow Pool the largest example of this fish which had come under his notice, and gives this place as the only English habitat known to him. Up to the present I have not met with this fish myself in Staffordshire, but have taken it in company with the common stickleback in Leicestershire and have kept it in aquaria. Unfortunately all my specimens proved to be females, and as they were unprovided with nests the ova were devoured by the other sticklebacks as soon as deposited. There is little doubt but for the solicitude bestowed on the developing eggs and young fry by the male fish the voracity of the stickleback would long ago have led to its own annihilation.

Amongst the many names by which the common stickleback is known locally are robin—applied to the male in his breeding dress, jack-sharp and jack-bannock.

6. Ten-spined Stickleback. *Gastrosteus pungitius*, Linn.

Generally distributed, but not so abundant as the common stickleback. This is more slender in form than the last-named and less brilliantly coloured, being olive green on the back and white on the sides and belly. The fins and frequently the whole body are suffused with a yellowish tinge. The underside is generally marked with little black spots, which in the male predominate to such a degree that it is not inaptly called the 'tinker' by boys.

HAPLOMI

7. Pike or Jack. *Esox lucius*, Linn.

Common and of large size. Several of 20 lb. weight have been taken near Burton, and fish of 30 lb. and over have been recorded from the Trent.

OSTARIOPHYSI

8. Carp. *Cyprinus carpio*, Linn.

In the large pools and ponds of the county

and in the Trent carp of 15 (Plot) and even of 19½ lb. have been recorded (Garner).

9. Crucian Carp. *Cyprinus carassius*, Linn.

Naturalized in ponds in the county, as are also its varieties, the gold carp (*C. auratus*, Linn.) and the Prussian carp (*C. gibelio*, Bloch).

10. Barbel. *Barbus vulgaris*, Fleming.

Common in the Trent and the lower part of the Dove, and attaining a large size. There are several noted haunts of the barbel near Burton, and when the water is clear the fish may be seen rooting like swine in the mud of the deep holes.

11. Gudgeon. *Gobio fluviatilis*, Fleming.

12. Roach. *Leuciscus rutilus*, Linn.

In rivers and meres : very common. In Aqualate Mere the hybrid between this fish and the bream (*Abramis brama*, Linn.), known as the Pomeranian bream (*A. buggenhagii*, Bloch) exists, and an interesting account of its capture there is given by the Rev. W. Houghton in his *British Freshwater Fishes*.

13. Chub. *Leuciscus cephalus*, Linn.

14. Dace. *Leuciscus dobula*, Linn.
    Day—*Leuciscus vulgaris*.

15. Rudd or Red-eye. *Leuciscus erythrophthalmus*, Linn.

16. Minnow. *Leuciscus phoxinus*, Linn.

Locally called 'pink,' from the bright tints it assumes in the breeding season.

17. Tench. *Tinca vulgaris*, Cuv.
    In pools and meres.

18. Bream. *Abramis brama*, Linn.

In rivers and meres. Up to 7 lb. in weight (Garner).

19. White Bream or Bream Flat. *Abramis blicca*, Bloch.

This fish is included in the Staffordshire lists on the authority of the late Mr. Edwin Brown, who wrote : 'Bailey, the angler of Nottingham, says this fish is mixed up with the preceding in the Trent.'

20. Bleak. *Alburnus lucidus*, Heck. et Kner.

21. Loach. *Nemachilus barbatulus*, Linn.

22. Spined Loach. *Cobitis tœnia*, Linn.

This fish, generally considered somewhat rare, is common in the Trent, but is frequently confused with small individuals of the last species. The presence of the small

[1] Günther, quoting Coste, in *Introduction to the Study of Fishes* (1880), p. 506.

bifid spine beneath the eye will at once distinguish the spined loach from the common or 'stone' loach.

MALACOPTERYGII

23. Salmon. *Salmo salar*, Linn.

Passes up the Trent on its way from the sea to spawn, but at Newton Solney, where the Dove joins the main river, the salmon almost invariably enter the smaller stream. At Dove Cliff, two miles above this point, is a well known salmon leap provided with a ladder, where on favourable occasions the keeper of the mill told me he had seen as many as twenty salmon ascend in an hour. Some individuals, especially when the river is in flood, pass onwards up the Trent and have even forced their way into ditches, where when the water has fallen they have met an ignominious death.

24. Trout. *Salmo trutta*, Linn.

According to the latest authorities the sea trout (*S. trutta, S. cambricus*) and the brown river trout (*S. fario*) are regarded as merely local races of one species.

It is perhaps unnecessary to say that the brown trout is common in Staffordshire, and that from the days of Izaac Walton at least the Dove has been famous for its large and well flavoured fish.

The Rev. F. C. R. Jourdain has called my attention to the following records of what must have been the largest trout ever taken in Staffordshire :—

From the *Zoologist* for 1848, p. 2342 : 'Capture of an enormous trout at Drayton Manor.—A trout weighing upwards of 21 lb. and measuring 41½ inches in length was taken on the 4th of November [1848], in a small tributary of the Trent, on the property of Sir Robert Peel, at Drayton Manor. It was transmitted to London by Sir Robert, and a faithful portrait of the fish has been painted for the honourable baronet by Mr. Waterhouse Hawkins.—Edward Newman.'

Again, in the *Zoologist* for 1896, p. 360, the following extract from the *Angler's Journal* of 20 December, 1884, is quoted, and seems to indicate the same fish as that referred to by E. Newman, although the weights given are not identical : 'The largest English trout on record is believed to be that from Drayton Park, which weighed 22½ lb., the skeleton of which was presented to the College of Surgeons.'

25. Grayling. *Thymallus vexillifer*, Linn.

Common in many of our rivers, especially the Dove and the Blythe.

APODES

26. Common Eel. *Anguilla vulgaris*, Turt.

Both varieties of the common eel—the sharp-nosed (*A. acutirostris*, Yarrell) and the broad-nosed eel or grig (*A. latirostris*, Yarrell) are common in Staffordshire. Adult eels begin to descend the Trent towards the sea, with us, in July. They breed in the sea, and from the larval form, the *Leptocephalus brevirostris*, Kaup., is developed the young eel or elver which ascends the rivers in numbers during spring and early summer.

GANOIDS

27. Sturgeon. *Acipenser sturio*, Linn.

The late Mr. Edwin Brown, writing in 1863, says : 'Instances are on record of this, the so-called royal, fish having in olden times made its way up the Trent as high as this district [Burton], but no such occurrence has been known of late years.'

CYCLOSTOMES

28. Sea Lamprey. *Petromyzon marinus*, Linn.

Rarely ascends from the sea as far as Staffordshire. Brown mentions an instance of one, 2½ feet in length, taken in the Dove in June, 1863.

29. Lampern or River Lamprey. *Petromyzon fluviatilis*, Linn.

Not uncommon.

30. Mud Lamprey or Pride. *Petromyzon branchialis*, Linn.

REPTILES
AND BATRACHIANS

Staffordshire is not rich either in the number of species of its reptiles, as compared with more southern counties, or in the individual abundance of such forms which do occur within the county boundaries. Thus Staffordshire possesses two lizards—the common lizard and the blindworm, and two snakes—the harmless grass snake and the viper. Neither the sand lizard (*Lacerta agilis*, Linn.) nor the smooth snake (*Coronella austriaca*, Laur.) are found in Staffordshire, although both have been reported, on one occasion each, as met with by individuals quite incapable of identifying these species at a glance, and no specimen of either has hitherto been obtained in Staffordshire.

Staffordshire can claim one species of frog, one toad and three newts in her list of batrachians. In the neighbouring county of Chester however the second British species of toad is met with—the pretty active natterjack toad (*Bufo calamita*, Laur.), and from thence many years ago specimens were introduced into Staffordshire by the late Mr. Edwin Brown, and turned out by Sir Oswald Mosley in his grounds at Rolleston. This colony still survived ten years after its introduction, so that it is just possible that descendants may still exist and be claimed as indigenous by some observer ignorant of their history. In a somewhat similar manner I was myself the means of unintentionally introducing the natterjack into Leicestershire, having presented a series of living specimens of various ages to the Leicester Museum, which I had collected in Lancashire. Some of these were turned out in the museum grounds by the curator, Mr. Montagu Browne, F.G.S., F.Z.S., as recorded in his *Vertebrate Animals of Leicestershire and Rutland*, p. 182. It is scarcely probable that in this case any would long survive.

It may be well to mention perhaps that the natterjack toad may readily be recognized by the yellow line down the middle of the back and by its active movements. It can also withstand heat far better than the common toad.

REPTILES

LACERTILIA

1. Common, Scaly, or Viviparous Lizard.
   Lacerta vivipara, Jacquin.

   Not uncommon in the wilder, heathy parts of the county, especially in the north and on Cannock Chase. In Staffordshire however it never appears in such numbers as it does in the Charnwood Forest district of Leicestershire, where I have more frequently met with it than in any other part of the midlands known to me.

2. Blind-worm or Slow-worm. *Anguis fragilis*, Linn.

Not uncommon in similar situations to those affected by the common lizard. The blind-worm varies greatly in colour according to age. The young, for some time after birth, are nearly white above and black below. Half-grown individuals are sometimes copper coloured, whilst mature specimens, especially females, become dark grey and so thick as to be mistaken for vipers at a casual glance by unsophisticated persons. Although usually the most gentle of reptiles and possessing only the startling habit of suddenly breaking off the tail when seized, such aged individuals will occasionally, though rarely, strike at the hand in a very snake-like manner.

OPHIDIA

3. Common Ringed or Grass Snake. *Tropidonotus natrix*, Linn.

Ray—*Natrix torquata*.

Generally distributed, but becoming more rare every year, although it holds its own against the advance of cultivation far better than does the viper or even the blind-worm.

4. Viper or Adder. *Vipera berus*, Linn.

Occurs at Chartley Park, Cannock Chase and other places in the county, but is decreasing in numbers as its haunts become drained and the land cultivated. It was formerly abundant at Chartley, where Sir Oswald Mosley records that in a single day's shooting he has 'disturbed several of them; and their venomous bite has sometimes proved fatal to valuable pointers, which stand at them as if they had the scent of game' (*Natural History of Tutbury*, p. 60).

Although the viper varies a great deal individually both in ground colour and markings, this is largely a matter of sex; bright, light-coloured specimens with a black, well defined zig-zag dorsal line being males, whilst the shorter, thinner-tailed females are brown or reddish with the markings more indistinct.

BATRACHIANS

ECAUDATA

1. Common Frog. *Rana temporaria*, Linn.
Common and generally distributed.

2. Common Toad. *Bufo vulgaris*, Laur.
Fairly abundant.

CAUDATA

3. Great Crested or Warty Newt. *Molge cristata*, Laur.

Common in ponds and ditches.

4. Smooth Newt. *Molge vulgaris*, Linn.

Abundant in similar situations to the last. This species possesses the power of restoring its damaged members, and is sometimes met with having additional toes on either the fore or the hind feet. Mr. James Yates, M.R.C.S., of Cambridge, for many years resident in Staffordshire, writes me under date 4 February, 1901, that he has frequently seen newts in cellars from which they could not set out in search of ponds, and in such places he has 'seen their eggs connected together like a string of pearls.' This is also the case, according to my own experience, when the ova are deposited in water containing no aquatic plants. Ordinarily, as is well known, the female newt carefully encloses each egg in the coil of a leaf which forms a hollow cylinder around it, and whilst it protects the egg allows free access of water to the developing embryo.

5. Palmated Newt. *Molge palmata*, Sch.

Mr. J. R. B. Masefield, M.A., informs me that he has a note of the occurrence of this interesting species of newt in the south of the county, but in Staffordshire it would seem to be local, as I have been unable to meet with it in mid-Staffordshire, and Mr. Masefield himself has failed to obtain it in the Cheadle district.

The palmated newt, especially when immature, is doubtless frequently confused with the smooth newt, from which however it can always be distinguished by its unspotted throat, and the male in the breeding season by his webbed feet and the curious mucro or thread at the end of his tail.

BIRDS

As Staffordshire is an exclusively inland county, and occupies an area comprising some of the highest land in the centre of England, with bleak moorlands rising to an altitude of upwards of 1,500 feet above sea level it contains no large rivers, but at the same time it is the birthplace of the Trent and the Dove, and numerous smaller streams which become tributaries of the Severn and the Mersey. These smaller streams have in many cases during past centuries gradually formed deep gorges and well sheltered and wooded valleys much frequented by many of the warblers and other small birds, and forming also the home of the dipper (*Cinclus aquaticus*) and the ring-ouzel (*Turdus torquatus*). The large meres of Aqualate and Copmere and lakes and reservoirs at Trentham, Hanchurch, Rudyard, Madeley, Chillington and elsewhere find a home for the grebes and are frequented in winter time by many species of wild-fowl. In the south-east of the county we have the extensive and barren heather covered tract known as Cannock Chase, where the red grouse (*Lagopus scoticus*) and the black grouse (*Tetrao tetrix*), owing to careful protection, once more abound, after having at one time almost reached the verge of extinction. The physiographical features of the county before referred to attract several species of wild birds in the breeding season which do not nest in many counties in England, such as the curlew (*Numenius arquata*), the ring-ouzel (*Turdus torquatus*), the grey wagtail (*Motacilla melanope*), and the dipper (*Cinclus aquaticus*). Staffordshire also borders closely upon, if it does not actually lie within, the range of one of the great flight lines of many of our British migratory birds, namely that from the mouth of the Humber and the north-east coast across England to the Bristol Channel. 'By this flight line,' says Whitlock (*Birds of Derbyshire*, pp. 16, 17), 'travel in autumn the whimbrel, curlew, greenshank, green sandpiper, wood sandpiper, little stint, longtailed duck, common scoter, Manx shearwater, gulls, terns, lapwings, golden and ringed plovers, hooded crows, fieldfares, redwings, sky-larks, chaffinches and mistle-thrushes, with occasional visits of the grey plover and bar-tailed godwit.' The return migration of these birds takes place by the same route to a great extent, and these birds meet our spring migrants coming by the same route, and thus Whitlock goes on to say 'we have two opposing streams of birds on the move at the same time.' Referring to this same flight line Dr. McAldowie[1] says :—

I believe this migratory route to be of great ornithological importance not only to Staffordshire but to the country generally. It brings many fine birds to our county

[1] 'Birds of Staffordshire' in *Report North Staffordshire Field Club,* 1893, pp. 15-17.

... I believe it is an ancient route and in pleistocene times was a great migratory highway and that it has been gradually abandoned by the majority of migrants since the formation of the present coast line ... Staffordshire appears to be the natural boundary between the habitats of northern and southern species of birds in Great Britain, for example it forms the northern boundary of the Nightingale, the Nuthatch, the Reed Warbler and perhaps of the Hobby, and on the other hand to limit on the south the haunts of the Red Grouse and the Sandpiper ... A hill route migration in which the Dotterel and the Rough-legged Buzzard are prominent species also affects our county.

The list of Staffordshire birds though somewhat deficient in aquatic species otherwise compares favourably with those of adjoining counties. At the time of publication of the *Birds of Staffordshire* (1893) no fewer than 234 species were included in the county list, of which 66 were then considered as residents, 30 as summer migrants, 18 as winter migrants and 120 as occasional visitors and stragglers. A revision of this list shows that considerable alterations must be made in order to gain a correct idea of our county avifauna. Three new species may be added since 1893, namely white-tailed eagle, shore-lark and flamingo. On the other hand the records of the following species must be considered as too doubtful to be retained in the list : black redstart (mistaken identification of eggs), pine-grosbeak and great black woodpecker ; and the following species were included in error, not having been recorded within the limits of our county : Bewick's swan, long-tailed duck, purple sandpiper, black-tailed godwit ; while the following species must be regarded as escapes and are not included in the British list : Virginian colin, Canada goose, Egyptian goose, summer duck.

In the case of the following species the evidence is at present insufficient to admit them into our list : Aquatic warbler, Dartford warbler, firecrest, mealy redpoll, crested-lark, bean-goose, little crake, eared grebe, little stint, grey plover.

The evidence is also somewhat unsatisfactory with regard to two species mentioned below, but they are retained in the list : blue-headed wagtail and marsh-harrier.

The revised total, including the 3 new species and exclusive of the 21 which have been removed from the list, now amounts to 216 Of these 94 breed regularly in the county and 9 others have been known to nest, while there is some reason to suppose that the hobby, shoveler and spotted-crake may nest occasionally, and the hen-harrier, honey buzzard, kite, raven, bittern and bearded-tit undoubtedly bred formerly in the county.

The following species regularly nest in the county :—

1. Mistle-Thrush	10. Lesser Whitethroat	19. Grasshopper-Warbler
2. Song-Thrush	11. Blackcap	20. Hedge-Sparrow
3. Blackbird	12. Garden-Warbler	21. Dipper
4. Ring-Ouzel	13. Goldcrest	22. Long-tailed Tit
5. Wheatear	14. Chiffchaff	23. Great Tit
6. Whinchat	15. Willow-Warbler	24. Coal-Tit
7. Redstart	16. Wood-Warbler	25. Marsh-Tit
8. Redbreast	17. Reed-Warbler	26. Blue Tit
9. Whitethroat	18. Sedge-Warbler	27. Nuthatch

28. Wren	51. Reed-Bunting	72. Mute Swan
29. Tree-Creeper	52. Starling	73. Mallard
30. Pied Wagtail	53. Jay	74. Teal
31. Grey Wagtail	54. Magpie	75. Tufted-Duck
32. Yellow Wagtail	55. Jackdaw	76. Wood-Pigeon
33. Tree-Pipit	56. Carrion-Crow	77. Stock-Dove
34. Meadow-Pipit	57. Rook	78. Turtle-Dove
35. Red-backed Shrike	58. Sky-Lark	79. Black Grouse
36. Spotted Flycatcher	59. Swift	80. Red Grouse
37. Swallow	60. Nightjar	81. Pheasant
38. House-Martin	61. Green Woodpecker	82. Partridge
39. Sand-Martin	62. Great Spotted Wood-	83. Red-legged Partridge
40. Greenfinch	pecker	84. Land-Rail
41. Hawfinch	63. Lesser Spotted Wood-	85. Water-Rail
42. Goldfinch	pecker	86. Moorhen
43. House-Sparrow	64. Kingfisher	87. Coot
44. Tree-Sparrow	65. Cuckoo	88. Lapwing
45. Chaffinch	66. Barn-Owl	89. Woodcock
46. Linnet	67. Long-eared Owl	90. Common Snipe
47. Lesser Redpoll	68. Tawny Owl	91. Common Sandpiper
48. Bullfinch	69. Sparrow-Hawk	92. Curlew
49. Corn-Bunting	70. Kestrel	93. Great Crested Grebe
50. Yellow Hammer	71. Heron	94. Little Grebe

The following occasionally nest in the county :—

95. Stonechat	98. Crossbill	101. Merlin
96. Nightingale	99. Wood-Lark	102. Quail
97. Twite	100. Wryneck	103. Redshank

The birds of prey are well represented, and several species might once again become general if not destroyed owing to the supposed exigencies of game preservation and its accompanying cruel pole-trap, while on the other hand game preservation and the consequently quiet and carefully guarded woods have during recent years conduced to the nesting of the woodcock (*Scolopax rusticula*) in increasing numbers and of the tufted-duck (*Fuligula cristata*), many pairs of which now breed in the south-west of the county.

The greater interest recently taken in wild bird life has directed public attention to our fast diminishing avifauna, with the result that the County Council orders made in pursuance of the Wild Bird Protection Acts are without doubt beginning to bear fruit, and it is possible that some species of wild birds such as the great crested grebe (*Podicipes cristatus*), the kingfisher (*Alcedo ispida*) and the white owl (*Strix flammea*) now fast decreasing in numbers in the county, may yet be saved. As education advances and the game preserver and gamekeeper become conversant with the life history and food of the hobby (*Falco subbuteo*), the merlin (*Falco æsalon*), the nightjar (*Caprimulgus europæus*) and the woodpeckers, it is to be hoped they may stay their hand when on the trigger of deadly firearms, and also abolish the cruel pole-trap which even proves fatal sometimes to the very birds which it is supposed to protect.

The bibliography of Staffordshire birds, or list of books containing references thereto, commences with the year 1676 and is as follows :—

1676.—*Ornithologia* (London), Francis Willoughby.
1678.—English translation of same (London), John Ray.
1686.—*Natural History of Staffordshire* (Oxford), Dr. Robert Plot, LL.D.
1798.—*History and Antiquities of Staffordshire* (London), Stebbing Shaw, containing sketch of Zoology of Staffordshire by John H. Dickenson.
1836.—*British Song Birds* (London), Neville Wood.
1836.—*The Ornithologist's Text Book* (London), Neville Wood.
1844.—*Natural History of the County of Stafford*, Robert Garner, with supplement, 1860.
1863.—*The Natural History of Tutbury* (London), Sir Oswald Mosley, D.C.L., including the Fauna of Burton-on-Trent, Edwin Brown.
1865 to 1903.—Papers and Notes in *Reports of the North Staffordshire Field Club*, by Dr. McAldowie, Ernest W. H. Blagg, M.B.O.U., John R. B. Masefield, M.A., W. Wells Bladen and others.
1878.—*Scientific Rambles around Macclesfield*, J. D. Sainter.
1879.—'Birds and their Habits,' pt. 1, *Midland Naturalist* (London and Birmingham), H. G. Tomlinson.
1880.—'Birds and their habits,' pt. 2, *Burton-on-Trent Natural History Society Report*.
1881.—'Our Summer Migrants,' *Midland Naturalist*.
1892.—*Birds of Derbyshire* (London and Derby), F. B. Whitlock.
1893.—*Birds of Staffordshire* (Stoke-on-Trent), A. M. McAldowie, M.D., F.R.S.Ed.

To the Rev. F. C. R. Jourdain our thanks are especially due for his invaluable assistance and for many notes and additions to the following list of Staffordshire birds.

1. Mistle-Thrush. *Turdus viscivorus*, Linn.
   Locally, Shrite, Stormcock (Garner), Thricecock.

A common resident, nesting in woods, copses and orchards, and migrating south in severe weather.

2. Song-Thrush. *Turdus musicus*, Linn.
   Locally, Throstle.

Common and partly migratory in winter. Pied varieties have occurred at Thickbroom in 1842 and Swythamley in 1859 (*Birds of Staffordshire*, p. 36).

3. Redwing. *Turdus iliacus*, Linn.

A winter visitor in flocks to our meadows, arriving in October and roosting in sheltered woods or thick shrubberies, where they are frequently followed and preyed upon by the sparrow-hawk.

4. Fieldfare. *Turdus pilaris*, Linn.

A winter visitor in flocks, feeding upon holly berries, hips and haws, and occasionally remaining till May. A somewhat shyer bird than the redwing. Mr. E. Brown ('Fauna of Burton-on-Trent,' p. 94 in Sir O. Mosley's *Nat. Hist. of Tutbury*) asserts that a nest was obtained by Mr. Allen at Longcroft a few years ago.

5. Blackbird. *Turdus merula*, Linn.

Very common. Many migrate south in severe weather. Albino, pied and cream or buff varieties are not uncommon.

6. Ring-Ouzel. *Turdus torquatus*, Linn.

A regular summer visitant to the high moorland districts in the north of the county, where it nests regularly, assembling in flocks prior to migration in autumn. The berries of the mountain ash (*Pyrus aucuparia*) are a favourite food of this bird.

7. Wheatear. *Saxicola œnanthe* (Linn.)

A summer visitor to our heaths and moorlands, even frequenting disused colliery mounds, but has diminished in numbers of late years.

8. Whinchat. *Pratincola rubetra* (Linn.)
   Locally, Utic.

A common summer visitant to heaths and meadows.

9. Stonechat. *Pratincola rubicola* (Linn.)

Formerly a common resident, but now only occasionally seen and its nest rarely found.

10. Redstart. *Ruticilla phœnicurus* (Linn.)
    Locally, Firetail.

A summer migrant, generally distributed,

and nesting in walls and holes of trees. It is a shy bird and its soft alarm note is frequently heard when the bird itself is not seen. Mr. E. W. H. Blagg has taken eggs with distinct fine red spots.

[Black Redstart. *Ruticilla titys* (Scopoli)

The *Zoologist* for 1852 (p. 3503) contains an account of the discovery of a nest supposed to belong to this species, which is also referred to by Hewitson in the third edition of his *Eggs of British Birds* (p. 106). The birds, however, do not appear to have been identified at the nest, and the description of the situation in which the nest was found points pretty conclusively to the next species, which is known occasionally to lay white eggs.]

11. Redbreast. *Erithacus rubecula* (Linn.)

Common and partially migratory in very severe weather. A pied variety was observed by Mr. E. W. H. Blagg at Forsbrook near Cheadle in 1892 (*Birds of Staffordshire*, p. 43)

12. Nightingale. *Daulias luscinia* (Linn.)

A rare summer visitor. Mr. E. Brown (*Fauna of Burton*, p. 96) records it as extraordinarily abundant near Burton about 1853, but rare subsequently. Further notes of its appearances will be found in the *Birds of Staffordshire* (p. 43) and the *Reports of the North Staffordshire Field Club* for 1880, 1893 and 1896.

13. Whitethroat. *Sylvia cinerea* (Bechstein)
     Locally, Peggy Whitethroat.

A very common summer migrant, arriving in May.

14. Lesser Whitethroat. *Sylvia curruca* (Linn.)

A summer migrant, but rarer than the last named species.

15. Blackcap. *Sylvia atricapilla* (Linn.)

A fairly common summer visitor, with a sweet little song.

16. Garden-Warbler. *Sylvia hortensis* (Bechstein)

A summer visitant and generally distributed.

[Dartford Warbler. *Sylvia undata* (Boddaert)

This species is said to have been observed on Cannock Chase, but no specimen appears to have been obtained, and without further evidence its occurrence so far from its usual habitat can hardly be considered as proved (*Birds of Staffordshire*, p. 47).]

17. Goldcrest. *Regulus cristatus*, K. L. Koch.

A resident and to be found in small family parties in winter.

[Firecrest. *Regulus ignicapillus* (C. L. Brehm)

Noted by Garner as 'occasional,' and included in Sainter's list, but no satisfactory identification of this bird has been recorded in the county.]

18. Chiffchaff. *Phylloscopus rufus* (Bechstein)

The earliest of our summer migrants, arriving in March and common in most districts.

19. Willow-Warbler. *Phylloscopus trochilus* (Linn.)
     Locally, Peep.

A common summer visitant throughout the county.

20. Wood-Warbler. *Phylloscopus sibilatrix* (Bechstein)

A summer migrant, arriving later than the willow-warbler. It is generally distributed in fair numbers in the valleys of the county.

21. Reed-Warbler. *Acrocephalus streperus* (Vieillot)
     Locally, Reed Sparrow (E. Brown).

A local summer migrant to the Trent, the lower part of the Dove and the larger meres of the county, such as Aqualate, Copmere, etc. It is much less common now than formerly on the Trent and Dove.

22. Sedge-Warbler. *Acrocephalus phragmitis* (Bechstein)

A common summer visitor to marshy districts.

[Aquatic Warbler. *Acrocephalus aquaticus* (J. F. Gmelin)

A nest and eggs supposed to belong to this species have been taken at Copmere, but no specimens of the bird have been secured and the resemblance of the eggs of the aquatic warbler to those of the preceding species renders identification very doubtful (*Birds of Staffordshire*, p. 50).]

23. Grasshopper-Warbler. *Locustella nævia* (Boddaert)

A summer migrant, local in its distribution and far from common. It has been recorded as nesting near Cheadle (1888), Trentham, Stone and Burton-on-Trent (see *Reports of the North Staffs Field Club*).

24. Hedge - Sparrow.   *Accentor modularis* (Linn.)

A common resident throughout the county. It has a cheerful song, and is one of our most useful and harmless birds.

25. Dipper.   *Cinclus aquaticus*, Bechstein.

A fairly common resident on most of the streams in the north of the county, nesting regularly under bridges and against rocks. A few nests are placed under banks and in hollows of tree stumps. It is also found occasionally in other parts of the county as far south as Stone, where it breeds, and Madeley, and it has been recorded in winter from Handsworth (12 Jan. 1882).

26. Reedling or Bearded Tit.   *Panurus biarmicus* (Linn.)

The only record of this species is that of Garner, who says, ' Rare, but has occurred at Aqualate Mere and on the Dove : Mr. Emery ' (p. 280). Mr. Francis Boughey of Aqualate, writing on 9 December 1888, says : ' I have still got two eggs that were taken out of a nest here in my possession ; they were taken out of a gorse bush about half a mile from the house ; the remainder of the nest of eggs were left to hatch which I believe they did and the old birds were seen often. I understand also that one specimen of the bearded tit was shot afterwards here.'

27. Long-tailed Tit.   *Acredula caudata*, Linn. *Locally*, Bottle Tit.

Generally resident throughout the county, occurring in small flocks or family parties during the winter.

28. Great Tit.   *Parus major*, Linn. *Locally*, Sawyer, Ox-eye, Blackcap. Resident and common.

29. Coal-Tit.   *Parus ater*, Linn.

Resident and generally distributed, but not so common as the great or blue tit.

30. Marsh-Tit.   *Parus palustris*, Linn.

Resident, but local and scarcer than the preceding species.

31. Blue Tit.   *Parus cœruleus*, Linn. *Locally*, Tomtit. Resident and common.

32. Nuthatch.   *Sitta cæsia*, Wolf.

Local and scarce. A few pairs however breed with us, and nests have been recorded at Eccleshall in 1884, and at Sandon and Barlaston in 1897 (*Report North Staffs Field Club*, 1898). Sir O. Mosley (*Nat. Hist. of Tutbury*, p. 48) relates how on 16 August, 1846, at least a hundred of these birds visited the gardens at Rolleston, many remaining till the following November. Mr. Meynell reported it at Farley near Cheadle in 1889 (*Report North Staffs Field Club*, 1890, p. 22).

33. Wren.   *Troglodytes parvulus*, K. L. Koch.

Resident and common. In winter a number of these little birds frequently roost together in holes or old nests apparently for warmth (cf. *Nat. Hist. of Tutbury*, p. 48, and *Report North Staffs Field Club*, 1896, p. 49).

34. Tree-Creeper.   *Certhia familiaris*, Linn.

Resident, breeding not uncommonly in the wooded districts, but rarer in the north of the county.

35. Pied Wagtail.   *Motacilla lugubris*, Temminck.

A partial migrant, many moving south in severe weather, although they may be seen during every month in the year. A common foster parent of the cuckoo and one of our most useful birds, being exclusively an insect feeder.

36. White Wagtail.   *Motacilla alba*, Linn.

Mr. E. Brown (*Fauna of Burton*, p. 98) describes this bird as mostly occurring in autumn in the Burton district, and Messrs. E. A. Brown and H. G. Tomlinson have also noticed it on the Trent, but there is no definite record of its appearance in any other part of the county. Possibly it has been overlooked on account of its general resemblance to the last species.

37. Grey Wagtail.   *Motacilla melanope*, Pallas.

A resident or partial migrant, breeding annually by the Dove and other streams in the northern parts of the county, but scarce on the Trent, where however it is well known as a winter visitor. Normally the grey wagtail does not breed in the counties south-east of Staffordshire, although it has been known to do so exceptionally.

38. Blue-headed Yellow Wagtail.   *Motacilla flava*, Linn.

The evidence with regard to the occurrence of this species is not very satisfactory. Garner states that it occurs at Betley and it is also mentioned in Mr. Sainter's list.

39. Yellow Wagtail.   *Motacilla raii* (Bonaparte)

A common summer migrant, arriving about the beginning of April, but Mr. H. G.

Tomlinson has occasionally seen one in March at Burton (*Birds of Derbyshire*, p. 66).

40. Tree-Pipit. *Anthus trivialis* (Linn.)
Locally, Titlark, Bank Lark.

A common spring visitor, generally distributed throughout the county, except on the moors, where it is replaced by the meadow pipit. It is very conspicuous in spring on account of its habit of ascending from its perch on the top of a tree and returning again to its post with outstretched wings, singing all the way.

41. Meadow-Pipit. *Anthus pratensis* (Linn.)

Common on the uplands and moors, and partially migratory in its habits, moving south in severe weather. Many cuckoos are reared in nests of this species in north Staffordshire.

42. Richard's Pipit. *Anthus richardi* (Vieillot)

Garner in his Appendix (p. 34) mentions one example, which was obtained near Stone and was in Mr. Hatton's collection (Garner MS.) Mr. R. W. Chase has an adult male which was taken near Handsworth on 21 October 1887 (*Birds of Staffordshire*, p. 59).

43. Golden Oriole. *Oriolus galbula*, Linn.

A rare visitor which has occurred twice. One was shot near Barton-under-Needwood about 1869 (*Birds of Staffordshire*, p. 59), and another was killed by a boy near Burton-on-Trent on 19 April 1871 (*Birds of Derbyshire*, p. 69).

44. Great Grey Shrike. *Lanius excubitor*, Linn.

Another rare visitor, usually occurring in the autumn and winter months. Garner (p. 274) says it has been obtained at Needwood, Bramshall, etc., and in his MS. notes mentions a later occurrence at Stone, where it was shot by Mr. Hatton (*Birds of Staffordshire*, p. 60). Sir O. Mosley (*Nat. Hist. of Tutbury*, p. 37) mentions two : one shot at Burton Bridge on 2 December 1844, and the other killed by a stone on 4 April 1845 between Dunstall and Burton (*Zool.* p. 1209). In the *North Staffs Field Club Report* for 1886 two are recorded as having been killed near Alton in the spring of the previous year. Somewhere about this time one was shot at Mayfield and passed through the hands of Poole, the Ashbourne bird-stuffer. The latest occurrence is that of one at Grindon in 1898 (*Report North Staffs Field Club*, 1899).

45. Red-backed Shrike. *Lanius collurio*, Linn.

A regular summer migrant to the south, but rare in the north of the county. Nests are mentioned in the *Birds of Staffordshire* (p. 60) at Clayton, King's Bromley (1891), near Stoke and Alton (1892). A pair generally breed near the entrance to Dovedale.

46. Waxwing. *Ampelis garrulus*, Linn.

A rare winter visitor. Garner includes it in his list on the authority of Dr. Hewgill and Mr. Brown. Sir O. Mosley (*Nat. Hist. of Tutbury*, p. 43) says that it visits the banks of the Trent at irregular periods during the winter months, and that many were observed in the Burton district in 1827, 1835 and 1850. Writing later in the *Zoologist* (1868) he states that on Sunday, 31 May, a young bird was caught by his brother near a *Pinus douglasii* in his grounds. When placed on an iron railing the two old birds immediately came to it and were distinctly identified, the red marks on the wing-tips being clearly seen. Although the whole family were noticed by several people for upwards of a week afterwards none were captured. A nest was subsequently found on a branch of the Douglas pine about 60 ft. from the ground, and ' consisted of wool intermixed with fibres of grass and bits of the same fir.' In January 1893 one was killed by a boy at Oulton near Stone while feeding on the fruit of the wild rose.

47. Pied Flycatcher. *Muscicapa atricapilla*, Linn.

A rare summer visitor, recorded by Garner from Bagot's Park and Trentham (1843). Mr. E. Brown (*Fauna of Burton*, p. 94) says it has ' been killed at Bagot's Park and at Stretton, near Burton-on-Trent.' Mr. W. Wells Bladen found a nest at Sandon on 7 May 1880 which he took to be that of this bird, but the date is unusually early and the situation unlikely. In 1883 Mr. E. W. H. Blagg obtained a male near Cheadle, and Mr. H. Meynell observed one at Alton on 2 May 1889, while Dr. McAldowie saw one at Northwood near Trentham in June 1892. Mr. H. G. Tomlinson saw a cock bird in May 1898 near Tutbury, and Mr. Forshaw two at Uttoxeter the same year, and another was seen by the writer at Cheadle 28 April 1902 (*Reports North Staffs Field Club*).

48. Spotted Flycatcher. *Muscicapa grisola*, Linn.

An abundant and familiar summer migrant, arriving in May and frequenting garden railings and bare branches in orchards, from which it takes short flights in search of prey, returning to the same spot after the capture of each fly or other insect. Very soon after its arrival this bird proceeds to build its nest in creepers or shrubs trained against walls, or on beams or even door-hinges, seeming to prefer the vicinity of human dwellings.

49. Swallow. *Hirundo rustica*, Linn.

A common summer migrant, arriving according to F. B. Whitlock by the Trent valley migration route. Several instances of white or cream-coloured varieties are recorded in the *Birds of Staffordshire*, p. 64. In 1887 many were killed by a sudden fall of temperature in May (*Report North Staffs Field Club*), and the same thing appears to have taken place on 31 May 1855 (*Nat. Hist. of Tutbury*, p. 50).

50. House-Martin. *Chelidon urbica* (Linn.)

A common summer migrant, but decreasing in numbers owing chiefly to the persecution to which they are subjected by the house sparrow, which destroys both eggs and young, evicting the rightful owners from their nests. The latest date recorded for the stay of this species with us is 7 November 1891, on which date three were seen at Cheadle (*Birds of Staffordshire*, p. 65).

51. Sand-Martin. *Cotile riparia* (Linn.)
Locally, Bank Swallow.

A common summer visitor, but rather local, varying in numbers according to the accommodation afforded by gravel and sandpits, river banks and railway cuttings for nesting purposes.

52. Greenfinch. *Ligurinus chloris* (Linn.)
Locally, Green Linnet.

Resident and abundant throughout the county, flocking in winter, and frequenting fields and stackyards.

53. Hawfinch. *Coccothraustes vulgaris*, Pallas.

Although formerly regarded as a rare winter visitor, the hawfinch has established itself of recent years as a breeding species and now nests regularly in woods and orchards in many parts of the county. Mr. E. Brown (*Fauna of Burton*, p. 100) seems to have been the first to suspect that it bred with us (1863). At the present time it may be said to be abundant in the Cheadle and Stone districts, and breeds in fair numbers round Eccleshall and Abbots Bromley. In the autumn small flocks frequent gardens and feed on peas, cherries, yew, hawthorn and holly berries.

54. Goldfinch. *Carduelis elegans*, Stephens.
Locally, Seven-coloured Linnet, Red Linnet.

A partial migrant formerly abundant but becoming rarer every year. It still breeds in a few localities and is not uncommon in the damson orchards of the Dove valley. Flocks appear occasionally in the north of the county during the winter. The seeds of thistles form the principal food of this bird, and its wholesale capture is a serious injury to farmers.

55. Siskin. *Carduelis spinus* (Linn.)

A local winter visitor appearing in flocks which feed on the seeds of the alder (*Alnus glutinosa*). Large numbers were observed in Consall Woods, October 1885, and near Trentham, January 1893 (*Birds of Staffordshire*, p. 67). During hard weather they have been observed feeding on the seeds of spent hops from breweries in the town of Stone. A regular winter visitant at Willoughbridge (*Report North Staffs Field Club*, 1894, p. 55).

56. House-Sparrow. *Passer domesticus* (Linn.)

Abundant and resident. Albino and pied varieties have frequently been met with (*Birds of Staffordshire*, p. 70).

57. Tree-Sparrow. *Passer montanus* (Linn.)

A resident in fair numbers, but local and frequently overlooked from its general resemblance to the last species. Mr. W. W. Bladen noticed a colony at Stafford Castle in 1879, and Mr. E. W. H. Blagg observed a large flock at Rocester, but as a rule it is found in small colonies.

58. Chaffinch. *Fringilla cœlebs*, Linn.
Locally, Piedfinch, Piedy, Redfinch, Spink or Pink.

A very abundant species, resident and assembling in large flocks in winter.

59. Brambling. *Fringilla montifringilla*, Linn.

A winter visitant arriving in flocks and feeding on beech mast. In severe weather it frequents stack yards in company with other birds.

60. Linnet. *Linota cannabina* (Linn.)
Locally, Brown Linnet.

A common resident, especially on downs and heaths.

[Mealy Redpoll. *Linota linaria* (Linn.)
Included in Mr. Sainter's list without any particulars. Further evidence is necessary before it can be admitted to our list.]

61. Lesser Redpoll. *Linota rufescens* (Vieillot)

Resident and fairly common in some districts, nesting regularly near Cheadle, Sandon and in the Dove valley.

62. Twite. *Linota flavirostris* (Linn.)

Resident and not uncommon in the moorlands in the north of the county. It is a northern species, and Staffordshire forms part of the southern limit of its breeding range.

63. Bullfinch. *Pyrrhula europæa*, Vieillot.

A very generally distributed resident. It is common in the woods of north Staffordshire during the winter months.

[**Pine-Grosbeak.** *Pyrrhula enucleator* (Linn.)

Garner's work (p. 279) contains the following reference to this species : ' Needwood. Bred in an orchard, north Staffordshire, 1842.' Probably the hawfinch was mistaken for the present species.]

64. Crossbill. *Loxia curvirostra*, Linn.

An uncertain visitor occurring in flocks during the winter months. As it is a very early breeder possibly some of the birds which have been observed in the spring may have bred in the county. Garner records the crossbill as 'seen near Burton, Uttoxeter, etc.,' and E. Brown says it occurred plentifully in the fir plantations near Burton about 1838 (*Fauna of Burton*, p. 100). It has also been reported from Barhill (near Madeley) and near Burton in 1879, and regularly for some years at Swynnerton (*Birds of Staffordshire*, p. 74). A bird in the red plumage from the Blurton collection of Staffordshire birds is now in the Derby Museum. Both old and young birds have been observed in woods near Cheadle (*Report North Staffs Field Club*, 1896).

65. Corn-Bunting. *Emberiza miliaria*, Linn.

Local in the north of the county but not uncommon in the south and south-east, where it breeds. It also occurs in the west of the county at Willoughbridge (*Report North Staffs Field Club*, 1894, p. 55).

66. Yellow Hammer. *Emberiza citrinella*, Linn.

Locally, Goldfinch.

Very common throughout the county, singing all through the summer from the highest twigs of hedgerows and feeding in winter in farmyards with other birds.

67. Cirl Bunting. *Emberiza cirlus*, Linn.

A nest with four eggs is said to have been found at Eccleshall on 24 May 1883 (*Birds of Staffordshire*, p. 75). It is also said on Mr. E. A. Brown's authority to have been recorded from near Burton.

68. Reed - Bunting. *Emberiza schœniclus*, Linn.

Locally, Reed-Sparrow.

Fairly common in the neighbourhood of water, especially where reeds are found.

69. Snow - Bunting. *Plectrophenix nivalis* (Linn.)

A rare winter straggler. There are two specimens in the Rolleston Hall museum, one of which was killed by a labourer with a stone on Rolleston meadows in October 1847 (*Nat. Hist. of Tutbury*, p. 44). Garner records it as seen at Burton, Whitmore Heath and Swynnerton, and in 1871 he says it has been shot at Cloud Hill. Mr. R. W. Chase states that one was found at Beech Lanes, Harborne, on 9 February 1888 (*Birds of Staffordshire*, p. 76). Dr. McAldowie reports one shot on 22 January 1895 at Cliffe Ville close to Stoke-on-Trent while feeding in company with larks (*Report North Staffs Field Club*, 1895, p. 88).

70. Starling. *Sturnus vulgaris*, Linn.

Abundant everywhere, often seen in immense flocks during the autumn and winter. Three white birds and one cream-coloured are recorded in the *Birds of Staffordshire* (p. 76).

71. Rose-coloured Starling. *Pastor roseus* (Linn.)

One was seen near Rushton Spencer in 1875 (*Birds of Staffordshire*, p. 77).

72. Jay. *Garrulus glandarius* (Linn.)

Still fairly numerous in wooded districts although persistently trapped and shot by keepers.

73. Magpie. *Pica rustica* (Scopoli)

Locally, Chatterpie.

Not very numerous, but one or two pairs are nearly always to be seen on the moorlands and near common lands. In winter flocks of twenty to thirty are sometimes seen in the north of the county, and Mr. R. H. Read once counted as many as ninety in one plantation (*Report North Staffs Field Club*, 1894, p. 50). Instances of the eviction of magpies from their nests by kestrels, and also apparently by jackdaws, have been noted in the *Reports of the North Staffs Field Club*.

74. Jackdaw. *Corvus monedula*, Linn.

A common resident everywhere, often nesting in large colonies in holes of trees where there is much old timber as at Okeover, as well as in chimneys and church towers in many towns and villages. At Moddershall near Stone a colony exists which usually build domed nests in high trees (*Reports North Staffs Field Club*, 1898 and 1901). A hatch of five chocolate-coloured jackdaws appeared at Woodhead near Cheadle in 1900.

75. Raven. *Corvus corax*, Linn.

Formerly a not uncommon resident breeding amongst other places at Dovedale, Ramsor, Cheadle and Dimminsdale as late as 1844, and Copmere near Eccleshall (*Report North Staffs Field Club*, 1879, p. 61). Plot in his County History has the following curious note: 'The worthy Mr. Chetwynd in his park at Ingestre observed young ravens to go to bough on New Year's day which therefore must be hatch't in the winter near Christmas, as some also were in Ashmer's Park near Wolverhampton, an. 1665, by a Raven that constantly built there for many years.' Needwood Forest was also a well known haunt of this bird. At Swythamley where they formerly bred one was shot in 1850. In 1881 one visited Hardiwick Wood near Stone, and in the spring of 1883 one was seen in the early morning on Stoke-on-Trent church tower (*Birds of Staffordshire*, p. 80). In 1894 two were reported from Cheadle (*Report North Staffs Field Club*, 1895, p. 47), and in 1898 another was seen at the entrance to Dovedale.

76. Carrion-Crow. *Corvus corone*, Linn.

Getting rarer every year through persecution by game preservers, but still breeds in a good many places and is common in Dovedale and the Ilam valley.

77. Hooded Crow. *Corvus cornix*, Linn.

A casual visitor on migration, recorded from Needwood, Uttoxeter, in 1841 (Garner), Swythamley (1853), on the Trent near Burton in January 1884, near Cheadle in 1886 (*Birds of Staffordshire*, p. 79), and one in Hose Wood, Draycot-in-the-Moors, in November, 1895 (*Report North Staffs Field Club*, 1897, p. 51).

78. Rook. *Corvus frugilegus*, Linn.

Very abundant, rookeries being numerous all over the county. In winter immense numbers of rooks congregate together and roost in some sheltered wood, scattering during the day for many miles around in order to feed and returning to the same roost every night. The average date for the first eggs in the north of the county is about 16 March, for about that time the hens first begin to stay all night at their nests. Pied varieties are not uncommon and albinos have been observed. In 1893 Dr. McAldowie estimated the number of rooks in Staffordshire at over 60,000, but at the present time this number is probably below the mark.

79. Sky-Lark. *Alauda arvensis*, Linn.

A common resident even close to populous towns, but much persecuted by bird catchers and diminishing in numbers prior to the publication of the Wild Bird Protection Orders.

80. Wood-Lark. *Alauda arborea*, Linn.

Local and rare, but may have been overlooked. In Mr. Neville Wood's time it was plentiful in the Dove valley, from which it has now completely disappeared. A nest was found at Eccleshall in 1883 (*Birds of Staffordshire*, p. 81), and Mr. E. A. Brown says it has occurred near Burton. Mr. James Yates records it at Sugnal (*Report North Staffs Field Club*, 1879, p. 62).

[Crested Lark. *Alauda cristata*, Linn.
Included in Sainter's list, but can scarcely be given a place in our local fauna without further evidence.]

81. Shore Lark. *Otocorys alpestris* (Linn.)

One occurrence only of this rare lark has been noted, a specimen having been shot at Enville near Dudley on 17 December 1879 (*Report North Staffs Field Club*, 1900, p. 53).

82. Swift. *Cypselus apus* (Linn.)
Locally, Squealer.

A summer migrant arriving in May, but nowhere abundant. Dr. McAldowie is of opinion that this species must have been less plentiful two centuries ago on the strength of the following passage from Plot's *History of Staffordshire* : 'Of unusual small birds here are also several . . . such as the *Hirundo apus* or *black martin* here called the *martlet*, which I believe is the *bird* intended by that name in *Heraldry* and not the *Hirundo agrestis sive rustica Plinii*, it having so very *long* wings and so *short* legs and *small* feet that it cannot easily rise from the ground unless it be very plain and free from grass ; wherefore it either always flies or sits on the top of *Churches Towers* or else hangs on other *ancient buildings* by its sharp claws, from which it falls and so takes its flight ; of these I saw at Shareshill near Hilton and Beaudesert.'

83. Nightjar. *Caprimulgus europæus*, Linn.
Locally, Fern Owl, Goatsucker.

A common summer migrant to our heaths and ferny commons. It is a most valuable bird, feeding exclusively on insects, many of which are injurious to the agriculturist.

84. Wryneck. *Iÿnx torquilla*, Linn.

A rare summer migrant which has been recorded several times as nesting in the county at Rolleston and Sandon.

85. Green Woodpecker. *Gecinus viridis* (Linn.)

A resident, generally distributed in wooded districts and on the heaths of central and southern Staffordshire ; common on Cannock Chase and around Ashley.

86. Great Spotted Woodpecker. *Dendrocopus major* (Linn.)

Resident, and not uncommon, especially in woods in the north-west and west of the county and on Cannock Chase.

87. Lesser Spotted Woodpecker. *Dendrocopus minor* (Linn.)

A local resident and has been recorded from Burton, Uttoxeter and Barlaston and found nesting at Sandon, Maer, Bishop's Woods, Dimminsdale near Cheadle and Ramsor. Probably the shyness of this little bird is the cause of its supposed scarcity.

[Great Black Woodpecker. *Picus martius*, Linn.

Garner says of this species, 'We may add *Picus martius* on Mr. Brown's authority.' Probably the statement was based on a misunderstanding, for Mr. Brown when compiling his list of the birds of the Burton district omits all mention of this bird (1863).]

88. Kingfisher. *Alcedo ispida*, Linn.

Resident and formerly fairly common on all our streams and lakes, but now scarce except in the Dove valley below Dovedale, where a considerable increase in numbers has taken place during the last few years owing to the protection extended by several riparian owners. A few pairs still breed on backwaters of the Trent in the Burton district and on streams near Stone.

89. Roller. *Coracias garrulus*, Linn.

Included by Mr. Sainter in his list of birds recently met with near Macclesfield (1878). Mr. E. Brown (*Fauna of Burton*, p. 102) states that one has 'been seen near Berkeley.'

90. Hoopoe. *Upupa epops*, Linn.

A rare visitor on migration recorded by Garner from Abbots Bromley, Barton and Tutbury. 'One was winged a few years back at Whitmore and afterwards kept in a cage.' Sir O. Mosley (*Nat. Hist. of Tutbury*, p. 48) saw one on the Dove while fishing near Rolleston. One was reported from near Loxley in the summer of 1885 by Mr. Wilkins, and Mr. R. W. Chase records one in 1893 from Quinton near Birmingham (*Birds of Staffordshire*, p. 86).

91. Cuckoo. *Cuculus canorus*, Linn.

A common summer migrant arriving in April and especially plentiful in the moorland districts. The young cuckoo somewhat resembles a kestrel in the colour and marking of the plumage, hence a foolish saying that the young cuckoo eventually turns into a hawk ! Among the rarer foster parents recorded from Staffordshire may be mentioned the thrush and the pheasant (Sandon Wood, 1879) (*Report North Staffs Field Club*, 1896, p. 24).

92. White or Barn-Owl. *Strix flammea*, Linn.

A resident, most valuable to the farmer and once common, but has unfortunately become rarer of recent years owing in a great measure to the use of the pole-trap. Still breeds where protected.

93. Long-eared Owl. *Asio otus* (Linn.)

Resident, and found in most thick fir woods where not killed by gamekeepers.

94. Short-eared Owl. *Asio accipitrinus* (Pallas)

A rare autumn and winter migrant. Garner describes it as 'frequent,' and Mr. E. Brown (*Fauna of Burton*, p. 92) says that many are killed in the Burton district at the beginning of winter by sportsmen. Sir O. Mosley shot one near Tutbury in October 1840 (*Nat. Hist. of Tutbury*, p. 37), and mentions others killed in the neighbourhood soon afterwards. To other parts of the county it is a rare occasional visitor but has been recorded from Swythamley, Eccleshall and near Alton in 1883 (*Birds of Staffs*, p. 88).

95. Tawny Owl. *Syrnium aluco* (Linn.)
Locally, Brown Owl.

A not uncommon resident, breeding usually in hollow trees, but also occasionally in deserted nests. May frequently be heard hooting at night.

96. Snowy Owl. *Nyctea scandiaca* (Linn.)

The only reference to the occurrence of this species in the county is a rather vague notice by Mr. A. O. Worthington in *Contributions to the Flora and Fauna of Repton*, p. 77. 'Sir John Crewe records one killed near Burton-on-Trent.'

97. Marsh-Harrier. *Circus æruginosus* (Linn.)

Garner says, 'Not very rare,' but no further

particulars are given, and without stronger evidence the record cannot be considered as satisfactory.

98. Hen-Harrier. *Circus cyaneus* (Linn.)

Formerly common and bred in the county, but now a rare occasional visitor. It is noticed without remark by Dickenson in 1798. Garner describes it as occasional. In 1852 one was shot at Swythamley, where it has bred. Mr. Sainter includes it in his list of breeding birds. At Burton it has once been recorded (E. A. Brown). Near Stone it has been seen on the wing (*Birds of Staffordshire*, p. 90). One was shot on Cannock Chase in 1899, and another in 1900, both in Lord Lichfield's collection at Shugborough. This bird is observed on Cannock Chase most years but unfortunately shot or trapped, or would probably remain to breed (*Report North Staffs Field Club*, 1903).

99. Common Buzzard. *Buteo vulgaris*, Leach.

Now a rare visitor to the north of the county but eighty or ninety years ago it was a common resident in the wooded districts, such as Needwood Forest (*Nat. Hist. of Tutbury*, p. 33). One was killed at Horninglow in 1860 (*Fauna of Burton*, p. 92), and others have been reported from Oakamoor in March 1886, and also in 1893, May Bank in 1879, and Endon in 1894 (*Reports North Staffs Field Club*). Mr. Sainter mentions one shot on the Roaches near Leek about 1872 (*Sci. Rambles round Macclesfield*).

100. Rough-legged Buzzard. *Buteo lagopus* (J. F. Gmelin)

Occasionally visits the moorlands of north Staffordshire on migration and has several times been observed in the south of the county. Garner mentions one shot near Leek and another from Needwood. This latter bird is probably the male in the Rolleston Hall museum which was shot at Rangemoor in 1840. Another was seen at Rolleston for several days in January 1846, but was not shot (*Nat. Hist. of Tutbury*, p. 34). One shot on Cannock Chase in January 1895 is now in the collection at Shugborough (*Report North Staffs Field Club*, 1903).

101. Golden Eagle. *Aquila chrysaëtus* (Linn.)

Some doubt rests upon the reported occurrences of this species, as probably the writers were not in every case competent to distinguish between this species and the immature sea eagle. Plot in 1686 writes, 'Witness the eagle in Beaudesert Hall killed in the Park.' Eagles have been observed too in the forest of

Needwood. Garner in 1844 says it has been seen at Needwood 'in late years' and that one was shot on Lichfield Cathedral in the reign of Charles I. About 1873 Mr. H. Evans and Lord Waterpark had a good view of one in Brakenhurst Cover perched in a tree about 60 yards away.

102. White-tailed Eagle. *Haliaëtus albicilla* (Linn.)

The two eagles mentioned by Dickenson in 1798 as seen on Cannock Chase a few years before, and one of which was shot by Sir Edward Littleton's gamekeeper, have been proved to be of this species ('Notes on Birds' by W. E. Beckwith in *Trans. Shropshire Arch. Soc.* 1887).

103. Goshawk. *Astur palumbarius* (Linn.)

One was shot at Swythamley in 1853. Another, a male bird, was killed at Rolleston in 1877 and is now in the Rolleston museum.

104. Sparrow-Hawk. *Accipiter nisus* (Linn.)

One of the few hawks which still nest regularly in the county and is not uncommon except where exterminated by gamekeepers. Several instances have been recorded within the county where this bird has been killed outright or stunned by flying against plate-glass windows when in pursuit of small birds.

105. Kite. *Milvus ictinus* (Savigny)

Although at one time a common bird the kite has long been a rare visitor to the county. Garner speaks of it as 'occasional,' and says it has been trapped in Needwood Forest. Mr. E. Brown (*Fauna of Burton*, p. 92) mentions one seen near Branstone in 1855, and Mr. Rising's collection contained a pair of Staffordshire killed birds, while Mr. R. W. Chase has one shot at Ornslow many years ago in his collection. The latest occurrence was in 1877— one seen at Swynnerton (*Birds of Staffordshire*, p. 93). Dovedale is supposed to have been a former breeding place of this bird.

106. Honey-Buzzard. *Pernis apivorus* (Linn.)

Garner records one shot at Trentham in 1844, and in August 1885 (in error this date is given as October 1884) a second was shot at Swynnerton (*Reports North Staffs Field Club*, 1885). J. E. Harting states that the nest has been found in Stafford (Buchanan) in his handbook. In the *Zoologist*, 1888 (p. 394) one is recorded as having been shot at Beaudesert on 27 July 1888, and another at Little Aston near Birmingham on 16 June 1891 (*Zool.* 1897, p. 271). One shot at The Wergs, near Wolverhampton, 19 June 1903.

107. Greenland Falcon. *Falco candicans* (J. F. Gmelin)

The only record is that of Garner, who states that it has been 'shot in Beaudesert Park' (p. 271).

108. Peregrine Falcon. *Falco peregrinus*, Tunstall.

The Rolleston Hall collection contains an adult female shot at Beaudesert, probably the bird referred to by Garner as having been killed there in 1841. An adult cock shot near Codsall in 1897 is now in the possession of Mr. Heathley of Stoke-on-Trent.

109. Hobby. *Falco subbuteo*, Linn.

A scarce summer visitor, but has been observed several times. Garner's MS notes contain a reference to one shot in Needwood Forest in 1847. In 1883 Dr. McAldowie saw a hobby take a swallow on the wing at Hanford near Stoke (*Birds of Staffordshire*, p. 95), and in the Rolleston Hall museum is a specimen which was shot in June 1890. Judging from the date this bird may have been breeding in the neighbourhood. Mr. R. H. Read shot a hobby at Lee Head near Maer in the summer of 1881 (*Report North Staffs Field Club*, 1894, p. 48).

110. Merlin. *Falco æsalon*, Tunstall.

A few pairs still breed on the moorlands in the north of the county, and stragglers are occasionally observed in other parts. Garner records merlins from Needwood Forest, Tean and Burton, and the Rolleston museum contains one shot on 15 October 1853 in the churchyard (*Nat. Hist. of Tutbury*, p. 34). Sir O. Mosley in the same work describes it as 'not infrequently seen,' and in the Derby Museum is a skin from the Blurton collection. One was shot in 1891 at Swythamley, where it breeds, and a nest with eggs was found 'some years ago' at Newcastle-under-Lyme (*Birds of Staffordshire*, p. 95).

111. Kestrel. *Falco tinnunculus*, Linn.

Fairly common and a partial migrant. Not so plentiful as formerly but still nests regularly. A most useful bird in helping to keep down mice and voles.

112. Osprey. *Pandion haliaëtus* (Linn.)

An occasional visitant. Garner mentions specimens shot at Stafford and Burton 'a few years back,' and Sir O. Mosley observed one at Rolleston in 1841 (*Nat. Hist. of Tutbury*, p. 33). In the summer of 1860 Mr. Brown saw one near Burton which was afterwards shot lower down the Trent (*Fauna of Burton*, p. 227). Mr. R. W. Chase has an immature female in his collection shot near Lichfield 26 September 1881, and another was seen for a week at Copmere in October 1882 (*Birds of Staffordshire*, p. 96). In January 1893 one was shot at Sneyd Green near Burslem (*Report North Staffs Field Club*, 1894, p. 42).

113. Cormorant. *Phalacrocorax carbo* (Linn.)

A straggler to Aqualate on several occasions and has also been observed in the Trent valley. Dickenson in 1798 notes it as 'frequently seen in winter about Aqualate mere.' Sir O. Mosley says one was seen on the Trent and Dove about 20 years previously to 1863, and that he saw one fishing in the Dove 'between 30 and 40 years ago' (*Nat. Hist. of Tutbury*, p. 57). Mr. E. Brown records another killed at Burton in 1838 (*Fauna of Burton*, p. 110), and one was killed during the winter of 1885 at the same place (*Naturalist's World*). There is also a specimen at Swythamley shot in 1872 (*Birds of Staffordshire*, p. 97).

114. Shag or Green Cormorant. *Phalacrocorax graculus* (Linn.)

One shot at Burton weir by Mr. Charles Hanson 'some years ago' (1893) (*Birds of Derbyshire*, p. 152). Three were seen at the same place in September 1902 (*Report North Staffs Field Club*, 1903).

115. Gannet or Solan Goose. *Sula bassana* (Linn.)

According to Garner, 'Occasional on the Trent and Dove ; Aqualate.' Sir O. Mosley (*Nat. Hist. of Tutbury*, p. 57) mentions one killed at Yoxall on 8 November 1853, and in the same work Mr. Brown says it has twice been killed within a few miles of Tutbury (p. 110), but probably one of these cases refers to the Yoxall bird. One shot near Grindon, 1899. On 4 August 1900 two were seen at Clifton flying down the Dove valley (*Report North Staffs Field Club*, 1901).

116. Common Heron. *Ardea cinerea*, Linn. *Locally*, Yarn (Dickenson), Heronshaw (Plot), obs.

A resident in fair numbers. Dr. Plot writing in 1686 says, 'and of unusual birds frequenting the water here are also divers kinds, some of them cloven footed and piscivorous though they build their nests on the tops of trees ; as the Ardea cinerea, or common heron or heronshaw whereof I saw divers sitting on the tops of the highest trees in Norbury Park.' Garner in his supplement (1860) mentions nests at Swythamley, Trentham and Betley, but none of these ever became established heronries. In 1893, when the *Birds of Staffordshire* was published, three heronries were mentioned at Aqualate, where there were only about six nests in 1892 but none in 1893, although as many as forty or fifty have been built in some years in Bagots Park, where there were nineteen nests on young oak trees in 1893, and at Patshull where there were about ten nests, and the birds are strictly preserved by Lord Dartmouth. In 1901 there were only two or three nests at Aqualate. The Aqualate and Bagots Park heronries are of ancient origin, but that of Patshull is more recent. A curious point in reference to the Aqualate birds is that every year one or more pairs nested among the reeds at the side of the mere. Some large pellets picked up at Bagots Park were composed of the hair of voles, rats and mice. Isolated pairs have been also known to breed in Dovedale and the Ilam valley.

117. Purple Heron. *Ardea purpurea*, Linn.

One was shot at Wetmore on 1 July 1856 (E. Brown, *Fauna of Burton*, p. 105). Some additional particulars are given in the *Birds of Derbyshire*, p. 154, on the authority of Mr. C. Hanson, who states that it was killed as it sat in a pollard willow on the banks of the Trent on the Derbyshire side, as he thinks.

118. Squacco Heron. *Ardea ralloides*, Scopoli.

Recorded as having occurred in the county, a male having been shot on the banks of the Dove near Coton on 17 May 1874 (*Birds of Staffordshire*, p. 101 ; see also *Science Gossip*, 1875, p. 4).

119. Little Bittern. *Ardetta minuta* (Linn.)

A rare straggler. Garner mentions one from the Dove or Trent (Mr. Emery), and Mr. E. Brown (*Fauna of Burton*, p. 228) states that one was killed at King's Bromley about 1838. One is reported to have been shot near Hanley, May 1901, but further details are needed.

120. Bittern. *Botaurus stellaris* (Linn.)

Formerly plentiful, nesting in the county. Sir O. Mosley states that when a boy he frequently heard in the evening the ' boom' of the bittern, which then frequented the osier beds on the banks of the Trent and Dove (*Nat. Hist. of Tutbury*, p. 53). A few still visit us as winter migrants, but most of them are unfortunately shot. Stuffed specimens obtained in the district are to be found in many cottages round Eccleshall. In the *Birds of Staffordshire* (p. 101) definite records of some twelve occurrences are given.

121. White Stork. *Ciconia alba*, Bechstein.

Garner says vaguely that it has occurred several times on the Dove (p. 284). Sir O. Mosley gives some details : one was shot by Mr. Emery some years since and another is said to have been obtained near Abbots Bromley (*Nat. Hist. of Tutbury*, pp. 54, 105).

122. Glossy Ibis. *Plegadis falcinellus* (Linn.)

One was shot on the Trent at Fradley in 1840 (*Nat. Hist. of Tutbury*, pp. 54, 105). Another was shot 'many years ago' at Walton-on-Trent (*Birds of Derbyshire*, p. 159).

123. Spoonbill. *Platalea leucorodia*, Linn.

One shot by Mr. D. Hopkins in Rolleston Park on 14 June 1872, is now in the Rolleston Hall museum.

124. Flamingo. *Phœnicopterus roseus*, Pallas.

Early in September 1881 an adult flamingo was seen for a week or so on the estate of the late Sir John H. Crewe in the northern part of Staffordshire, but having crossed the river Manifold to another property it was captured and taken to the owner of the land, by whom it was kept alive for a few days and then killed (H. Saunders, *Manual*, ed. 2, 1899, p. 395, and Yarrell's *British Birds*, ed. 4, iv. 245).

125. Grey Lag-Goose. *Anser cinereus*, Meyer.

A rare winter visitor, formerly frequently seen passing over the county on migration. Sir O. Mosley and Mr. E. Brown agree that it was plentiful 'fifty years ago' (i.e. about 1813), but it is doubtful whether any of the geese that still visit the Trent valley belong to this species. Mr. E. A. Brown has examined one killed at Burton and another was shot at Swythamley in 1869 (*Birds of Staffordshire*, p. 103).

126. White-fronted Goose. *Anser albifrons* (Scopoli)

This species is included in Garner's list but no details are given. It is however known to visit the Trent valley (*Birds of Derbyshire*, p. 160). One was shot near Wolverhampton 12 January 1901 by Mr. Harold Twentyman (*Report North Staffs Field Club*, 1903).

[Bean Goose. *Anser segetum* (J. F. Gmelin) Included in Sainter's list ; a very doubtful record.]

127. Pink-footed Goose. *Anser brachyrhynchus*, Baillon.

Probably this is the species most frequently seen in the Trent valley, but specimens are seldom killed. One killed at Winshill in 1856 (*Fauna of Burton*, p. 107), and others have since been killed in the neighbourhood of Burton-on-Trent.

128. Barnacle-Goose. *Bernicla leucopsis* (Bechstein)

Occasionally shot near Tutbury; one associated with some Canada geese at Rolleston in December 1859 (*Nat. Hist. of Tutbury*, p. 55).

129. Brent Goose. *Bernicla brenta* (Pallas)

Included in Garner's list. One seen in the flesh in March 1893 said to have been shot in Staffordshire (*Birds of Staffordshire*, p. 104). One shot at Rocester about 25 January 1903 (*Report North Staffs Field Club*, 1903).

[Canada Goose. *Bernicla canadensis* (Linn.)
An introduced species, flocks of which often pass up and down the Dove valley.]

[Egyptian Goose. *Chenalopex ægyptiaca*, Linn.
Has several times been shot on the Trent; probably escaped birds.]

130. Whooper Swan. *Cygnus musicus*, Bechstein.
Locally, Whistling Swan (Mosley), Elk or Wild Swan (Brown).

Has frequently been observed in the Trent valley in small flocks. One was shot at Swythamley in 1875 (*Birds of Staffordshire*, p. 106).

[Bewick's Swan. *Cygnus bewicki*, Yarrell.
The bird of this species mentioned in the *Birds of Staffordshire*, p. 106, was killed in Derbyshire.]

131. Mute Swan. *Cygnus olor* (J. F. Gmelin)

In a semi-domesticated condition on our larger rivers and on lakes.

132. Common Sheld-Duck. *Tadorna cornuta* (S. G. Gmelin)

This beautiful duck has been shot several times in the county. The birds recorded by Mr. E. A. Brown as breeding near Burton-on-Trent were probably captives (*Birds of Staffordshire*, p. 106).

133. Mallard or Wild Duck. *Anas boscas*, Linn.

Resident and fairly plentiful where preserved on large meres. It is also numerous in the Dove valley between Rocester and Dovedale. Our resident birds are frequently joined by flocks of migrants in winter.

134. Gadwall. *Anas strepera*, Linn.

A very rare visitor. One obtained on the Tame at Comberford near Lichfield 22 December 1873 (*Birds of Staffordshire*, p. 108).

135. Shoveler. *Spatula clypeata* (Linn.)

A rare winter visitor. Mr. E. Brown (*Fauna of Burton*, p. 108) says that many have been killed on the Trent but it is now rarely seen there. A drake was shot at Rolleston on 3 April 1866, and two others at Woore in September 1896. Mr. Harting states that the nest has been found in the county (*Handbook of Brit. Birds*, ed. 1, p. 62).

136. Pintail. *Dafila acuta* (Linn.)

A winter visitor of which several occurrences have been recorded. Not uncommon in the Tutbury and Burton districts (*Nat. Hist. of Tutbury*, pp. 56, 108). A young drake shot at Barlaston in November 1885, four at Leigh in 1895, one at Bloxwich in February 1898, and a drake at Hilderstone Hall on 4 February 1901 (*Report North Staffs Field Club*, 1901).

137. Teal. *Nettion crecca* (Linn.)

Breeds very sparingly in Staffordshire (*Birds of Staffordshire*, p. 108). In winter and spring small flocks visit the middle and south of the county. Frequents the scattered pits at Lea Head singly or in pairs most winters (*Report North Staffs Field Club*, 1894, p. 58.

[Summer Duck. *Aix sponsa* (Linn.)
One killed on the Trent near Drakelow a few years previous to 1863 (E. Brown, *Fauna of Burton*, p. 228). Probably an escaped bird.]

138. Garganey. *Querquedula circia* (Linn.)

Sir O. Mosley and Mr. E. Brown both state that this duck has occasionally but very rarely been killed on the Trent (*Nat. Hist. of Tutbury*, pp. 56, 108). No recent occurrences.

139. Wigeon. *Mareca penelope* (Linn.)

A winter visitor frequently occurring in large flocks during severe weather on Aqualate, Trentham, Rudyard and other large lakes as well as on the Trent.

140. Pochard. *Fuligula ferina* (Linn.)

A winter visitant, not uncommon on the Trent in hard winters such as 1890-1.

141. Tufted Duck. *Fuligula cristata* (Leach)

By means of careful preservation this duck

has now become resident and has nested regularly since 1880 at Weston Park on the borders of Stafford and Shropshire. About twenty pairs were breeding here in 1900 (H. E. Forrest, *Zool.* 1900, p. 506). It also breeds at Patshull and is occasionally met with in other parts of the county, at Cheadle in 1886 and not infrequently on the Trent, Willoughbridge in 1892, Aston 1879 (*Reports North Staffs Field Club*, 1894, p. 58).

142. Scaup-Duck. *Fuligula marila* (Linn.)

A winter visitor not uncommon on the Trent during the frost of 1890–1. Lord Lewisham observed several near Wolverhampton in November 1887 (*Reports North Staffs Field Club*, 1888).

143. Goldeneye. *Clangula glaucion* (Linn.)

An occasional winter visitor. Frequently seen near Rolleston, and a female killed on 22 November 1847 (*Nat. Hist. of Tutbury*, p. 56), one near Burton in 1881 (E. A. Brown), one near Cheadle in the winter of 1888–9, two at Madeley in 1893, and one at Great Gnosall, 6 January 1901 (*Report North Staffs Field Club*).

[Long-tailed Duck. *Harelda glacialis* (Linn.)

Included in the birds of Staffordshire, but the specimen referred to was killed at Twyford in Derbyshire (*Nat. Hist. of Tutbury*, pp. 56, 109).]

144. Common Scoter. *Œdemia nigra* (Linn.)

A marine species which has frequently visited the Rolleston district. One remained on the pools at Rolleston in January and February 1854 (*Nat. Hist. of Tutbury*, p. 56).

145. Velvet Scoter. *Œdemia fusca* (Linn.)

Dickenson in 1798 mentions one shot at Batchacre, and Garner (p. 287) gives also Aqualate and Burton-on-Trent, 1841, as localities for this species.

146. Goosander. *Mergus merganser*, Linn.
Locally, Sowgouder (Dickenson), Greenheaded Goosander (Garner), obs.

An occasional winter visitant. Dickenson in 1798 records it from Aqualate; Sir O. Mosley mentions two, a male shot on the Dove and female killed at Burton in January 1854 (*Nat. Hist. of Tutbury*, p. 56). A female was shot at Swythamley in 1880 and another at Leigh on 11 January 1901; the latter was accompanied by a second bird (*Report North Staffs Field Club*, 1901). Mr. R. H. Read has observed this bird at Sidway near Willoughbridge several times (*Report North Staffs*

Field Club, 1894, p. 58). Three of these birds, a male and two females, were shot on the Sow at Shugborough a few years ago out of a flock and are now in Lord Lichfield's collection (*Report North Staffs Field Club*, 1903).

147. Red-breasted Merganser. *Mergus serrator*, Linn.

Has occasionally been shot in the Trent valley and is given in Garner's list, but without particulars (p. 288). One seen at Sidway near Willoughbridge in the winter of 1880 by Mr. R. H. Read (*Report North Staffs Field Club*, 1894, p. 58).

148. Smew. *Mergus albellus*, Linn.
Locally, Whiteheaded Goosander (Garner), obs.

Sir O. Mosley records two killed at Sudbury on the Dove 'some years ago,' and a male and female shot at Fradley in 1855 (*Nat. Hist. of Tutbury*, p. 56). Mr. E. A. Brown also speaks of several records from near Burton.

149. Ring-Dove or Wood-Pigeon. *Columba palumbus*, Linn.

Resident and very generally distributed. In winter its numbers are increased by migratory flocks which feed upon acorns in woods during severe weather.

150. Stock Dove. *Columba ænas*, Linn.

Not so common as the last species and more local. Nests in hollow trees or thick ivy and in winter associates with wood-pigeons.

151. Turtle-Dove. *Turtur communis*, Selby.

A summer migrant which has extended its range of late years and is common in the middle and south of the county but rare in the north. First observed breeding at Cheadle in 1887 and now nests there regularly, also at Oakamoor in 1901.

152. Pallas's Sand-Grouse. *Syrrhaptes paradoxus* (Pallas)

The two great immigrations of this central Asian species took place in 1863 and 1888. In the first-named year the two first British examples were shot in Northumberland on 21 May, and on the following day three more were killed out of a flock of about twenty near Eccleshall in Staffordshire by a man who was returning home at dusk when the birds flew over his head. In 1888 a female was shot at Rough Hill, Wolverhampton, on 23 May, and in September a male at Ipstones, a moorland village five miles north of Cheadle (*Birds of Staffordshire*, p. 113).

153. Black Grouse. *Tetrao tetrix*, Linn.

Still breeds annually in the moorland districts near Cheadle and Leek, on the Weaver Hills, on Cannock Chase, in the Bishops' Wood near Eccleshall and at Chartley.

154. Red Grouse. *Lagopus scoticus* (Latham)
Locally, Garcock or Red Game (Plot), (obs)

Resident and plentiful on the moors in the north of the county and also on Cannock Chase. In severe winters they have been seen at Rolleston (1859), Burton-on-Trent (1860–1) and Cheadle (1885–6). In the Swythamley collection is a slate coloured variety shot in 1862 (*Birds of Staffordshire*, p. 118).

155. Pheasant. *Phasianus colchicus* (Linn.)

Abundant where preserved. Owing to crossing and interchange of eggs varieties of plumage are very common, and in some districts it is quite the exception to meet with the normal plumage of the old English bird.

156. Partridge. *Perdix cinerea*, Latham.

Not so common as formerly when there was more arable land. In September 1900, five specimens of a dark chestnut or erythristic variety were shot at Pyrehill near Stone, which correspond with the *Perdix montana* of Brisson (*Report North Staffs Field Club*, 1901). Two others of the same variety were shot near Pyrehill in October 1901. Mr. J. Whitaker has a very pale bird from Staffordshire, formerly in the collection of the late Mr. F. Bond. Four others of the rufous variety, but three of them much splashed with creamy white, were shot on Lord Lichfield's Staffordshire estates and are in the Shugborough collection.

157. Red-legged Partridge. *Caccabis rufa* (Linn.)

Garner mentions this species as introduced at Teddesley, etc. It is still rare, but has been recorded from Great Barr (1881), Woore (1894) and Stone (1900), while nests have been found at King's Bromley (1886) and Caverswall (1896) (*Reports North Staffs Field Club*). In 1901 this bird was reported by sportsmen from several districts in the county and seems to be on the increase.

158. Quail. *Coturnix communis*, Bonnaterre.

An occasional summer migrant. Sir O. Mosley mentions one killed at Rolleston on 15 December, 1856 (*Nat. Hist. of Tutbury*, p. 52). Near Burton it has occurred several times and nests have been recorded from

King's Bromley in 1887 and 1892 and near Stoke sewage works in 1893. Two brace were shot at Gnosall in September 1885, and it has also occurred several times near Eccleshall (*Reports North Staffs Field Club*, 1888, p. 21, and 1894, p. 41).

[Virginian Colin. *Ortyx virginianus* (Linn.)

An introduced species mentioned in Mr. Sainter's list.]

159. Land-Rail or Corn-Crake. *Crex pratensis*, Bechstein.

A common summer migrant, arriving in April and leaving in September, but a few young birds occasionally stay later.

160. Spotted Crake. *Porzana maruetta* (Leach)

Occurs not infrequently in the lower part of the Trent valley but is a rare visitor to other parts of the county (*Nat. Hist. of Tutbury*, p. 55). The Garner MS. mentions Burslem and Stone ; others have been recorded from Fauld (1841), Handsworth (3 Nov. 1890) and Morredge (1891). Lea Head near Maer, 1881 (*Report North Staffs Field Club*, 1894, p. 52).

[Little Crake. *Porzana parva* (Scopoli)
In Sainter's addenda (p. 147) but without any details.]

161. Water-Rail. *Rallus aquaticus*, Linn.

Not uncommon, but seldom seen. Said to have nested at Swythamley and certainly does so in the Dove valley. Usually met with by sportsmen in hard winters.

162. Moor-hen. *Gallinula chloropus* (Linn.)

Common on all our rivers, lakes and pools, and semi-domesticated, feeding on lawns at Trentham, Draycot-in-the-Moors Rectory, Milwich Hall and other places.

163. Coot. *Fulica atra*, Linn.

Frequent on large pools and meres but not so common as the moor-hen.

164. Little Bustard. *Otis tetrax*, Linn.

One specimen shot at Birchfield 'many years ago' is now in the collection at Aston Hall. Another was killed by a keeper about 1899 at Warslow and is now in the Calke Abbey collection.

165. Dotterel. *Eudromias morinellus* (Linn.)

A rare spring and autumn visitor on migration. 'Its line of migration appears to be through Staffordshire by Cannock Chase and the hilly district in the south of the county' (*Birds of Staffordshire*, p. 124). Ten were shot on Cannock Chase on 15 May 1875, two at Perry Barr in 1882, and one at Great Barr on 4 September 1887, and lastly one was shot by a keeper on the Weaver Hills in October 1895 (*Report North Staffs Field Club*, 1901).

166. Ringed Plover. *Ægialitis hiaticula* (Linn.)

Has occurred several times on the Trent but is a very rare visitor to other parts of the county. Recorded by Garner from the Churnet and Cheddleton and at Madeley (1889).

167. Golden Plover. *Charadrius pluvialis*, Linn.

Flocks occasionally visit us during the winter and early spring months. Garner records it from Uttoxeter and Stoke meadows (1843). Sir O. Mosley says considerable flocks are found occasionally in the meadows near Tutbury after winter floods (*Nat. Hist. of Tutbury*, p. 52). Large numbers were seen at Draycot in 1884; one shot at Great Barr 2 January 1885; recorded from Cheadle in 1886; flocks at Cauldon, Endon and Draycot in hard weather, 1890–1, and a flock of about forty at Cheadle in March 1892 (*Reports North Staffs Field Club*).

[Grey Plover. *Squatarola helvetica* (Linn.)

Included in Garner's appendix (1860) without details. In his MS. notes Mr. Hilton is given as his informant.]

168. Lapwing. *Vanellus vulgaris*, Bechstein.

A common resident but partially migrant in severe weather. Diminishing in numbers owing to the persistent taking of the eggs for sale, thus depriving the farmer of one of his most useful friends.

169. Turnstone. *Strepsilas interpres* (Linn.)

Mr. E. A. Brown states that this bird has occurred near Burton-on-Trent (*Birds of Staffordshire*, p. 125).

170. Oyster-Catcher. *Hæmatopus ostralegus*, Linn.

A rare visitor. Garner and Sir O. Mosley say that it has occurred on the Trent, and the latter writer states that one was shot on the Dove on 10 September 1841 (*Nat. Hist. of Tutbury*, p. 53). In November 1883, two were seen at Wootton-under-Weaver, one of which was killed by a keeper and is now in his possession. One was picked up exhausted

at Seabridge near Newcastle on 15 October 1902 (*Report North Staffs Field Club*, 1903).

171. Avocet. *Recurvirostra avocetta*, Linn.

Professor Newton (*Dictionary of Birds*, p. 24) says: 'Plot mentions it so as to lead one to suppose that in his time (1686) it bred in Staffordshire. The actual words are, "Of whole footed waterfowl the Avocetta Italorum or Recurvirostra, is also found here as well as in the Eastern parts of Norfolk and Suffolk, there having been of them killed at the black lakes near Aqualet, eight of them being seen first in the morning and but six at night when they shot.'" It will be seen from the latter part of the passage that the evidence is not very conclusive. One was shot on the Dove near Scropton 'recently' (Garner).

172. Grey Phalarope. *Phalaropus fulicarius* (Linn.)

A rare visitor. Garner and the authors of the *Natural History of Tutbury* record it from near Uttoxeter and other localities in the district, and Mr. E. A. Brown says it has occurred near Burton. Others have been killed at Harborne (Oct. 1885), Handsworth (16 Oct. 1891) and Rowley Regis (20 Oct. 1891) (*Birds of Staffordshire*, p. 126). An adult female was shot on 4 October 1893, at Willenhall (*Zool.* 1894, p. 112).

173. Red-necked Phalarope. *Phalaropus hyperboreus* (Linn.)

One specimen shot at Handsworth on 24 August 1887 (*Birds of Staffordshire*, p. 126).

174. Woodcock. *Scolopax rusticula*, Linn.

A regular winter visitant, a fair number remaining to breed in the larger woods. In Garner's time it was noted as having bred at Betley, and more recently it has been recorded as breeding from Whitmore, Beaudesert, Needwood Forest, Marchington, Bishops' Wood near Cheadle, Ellastone, Stanton and Ilam. Varieties of a light drab colour from Swythamley (1847) and cream colour (1871) are on record (*Birds of Staffordshire*, p. 127).

175. Great Snipe. *Gallinago major* (J. F. Gmelin)

Garner marks this species as 'occasional,' and Mr. E. Brown (*Fauna of Burton*, p. 106) says two or three specimens have occurred in the district.

176. Common Snipe. *Gallinago cœlestis* (Frenzel)

Fairly common, nesting regularly in the north of the county. Sometimes met with in turnip fields in autumn.

177. Jack Snipe. *Gallinago gallinula* (Linn.)

A winter visitor. The earliest record of its arrival is 28 August 1884, when one was shot near Cheadle (*Birds of Staffordshire*, p. 127). A curious variety is recorded from Endon with dirty white streaks in place of buff (*Report North Staffs Field Club*, 1901).

178. Dunlin. *Tringa alpina*, Linn.

Occasionally met with in autumn and winter in the Trent valley and probably on migration in other parts. One at Madeley on 28 March 1892 (*Birds of Staffordshire*, p. 128).

[Little Stint. *Tringa minuta*, Leisler.
Mentioned in Garner's list on Dr. Hewgill's authority without details.]

[Purple Sandpiper. *Tringa striata*, Linn.
The birds of this species recorded in the *Birds of Staffordshire* (p. 128) were not killed at Burton-on-Trent but on the Burton sewage farm which is near Egginton in Derbyshire.]

179. Knot. *Tringa canutus*, Linn.

Three shot near Burton on 5 October 1891 (*Birds of Derbyshire*, p. 209), where they have occasionally been killed in former years. One was killed at Tittensor in December 1892 (*Birds of Staffordshire*, p. 128; *Report North Staffs Field Club*, 1893, p. 55).

180. Sanderling. *Calidris arenaria* (Linn.)

Three shot at Walton-on-Trent about 1878 (*Birds of Derbyshire*, p. 210).

181. Ruff. *Machetes pugnax* (Linn.)

Two birds in immature plumage were shot near Burton in the summer of 1857 (*Fauna of Burton*, p. 106).

182. Common Sandpiper. *Totanus hypoleucus* (Linn.)

A summer migrant breeding regularly on streams in the north of the county. In 1891 a pair hatched off their young in the vicarage garden at Madeley (*Birds of Staffordshire*, p. 129).

183. Green Sandpiper. *Totanus ochropus* (Linn.)

An occasional visitor. Garner records one from Betley, and Mosley and Brown note it as frequently occurring. Several seen at Alton in 1884–5 and one killed. The Rolleston Hall museum contains a specimen shot in January 1894, on the estate.

184. Redshank. *Totanus calidris* (Linn.)
Locally, Whistling Plover.

Formerly only an occasional visitor, but within the last thirty years has established itself as a breeding species in the valleys of the Trent and lower Dove. A good many pairs now nest annually in the meadows by these rivers (*Report North Staffs Field Club*, 1903).

185. Spotted Redshank. *Totanus fuscus* (Linn.)

Mr. Edwin Brown possessed one specimen which was killed on the Dove (*Fauna of Burton*, p. 106).

186. Greenshank. *Totanus canescens* (J. F. Gmelin)

Recorded in the *Birds of Staffordshire* (p. 130) as having been sometimes seen near Burton-on-Trent and shot near Brereton Lodge.

187. Bar-tailed Godwit. *Limosa lapponica* (Linn.)

A rare straggler. Two were shot near Burton 'many years ago' and identified by Mr. C. Hanson (*Birds of Derbyshire*, p. 215). Sir O. Mosley and Mr. Brown state that it has occurred several times on the Trent.

[Black-tailed Godwit. *Limosa belgica* (J. F. Gmelin)
The entry with regard to this species in the *Birds of Staffordshire* is erroneous; no mention of it occurs in the *Natural History of Tutbury*.]

188. Common Curlew. *Numenius arquata* (Linn.)

A few pairs of these birds still breed on the moors in the north of the county and on Cannock Chase and Chartley under careful preservation. Several times recorded in other parts of the county (*Report North Staffs Field Club*).

189. Whimbrel. *Numenius phæopus* (Linn.)

A rare visitor. F. B. Whitlock says that a few pass up and down the Trent valley on migration to and from the north. Two whimbrels which were accompanied by a curlew at the time were shot at Swinscoe on 30 April, 1899 (*Report North Staffs Field Club*, 1901; see also 1894, pp. 53–4).

190. Black Tern. *Hydrochelidon nigra* (Linn.)

A rare straggler during the summer months. One shot near Patshull House, Wolverhampton, about 1876 and another seen for some days in August 1886, on the same piece of water (*Field*). One killed at Madeley Pool in 1889 (*Reports North Staffs Field Club*) and another shot at Rolleston 10 May 1894 is now in the museum.

191. Roseate Tern. *Sterna dougalli*, Montagu.

A rare straggler noted in Garner's, Sir O. Mosley's and E. Brown's lists but without details. No recent occurrences.

192. Common Tern. *Sterna fluviatilis*, Naumann.

An occasional visitor especially to the Trent and Dove valleys. One shot at Swythamley in 1862, and a flock visited Madeley Pool in 1889 (*Birds of Staffordshire*, p. 132). On the Trent it is not uncommon, and large numbers were seen in May 1842 (*Nat. Hist. of Tutbury*, p. 57).

193. Arctic Tern. *Sterna macrura*, Naumann.

Another occasional visitor. 'Great numbers of this species visited North and South Staffordshire in May, 1842' (R. Garner, p. 289). One taken near Hanley in September 1888 (*Report North Staffs Field Club*, 1889, p. 24).

194. Little Tern. *Sterna minuta*, Linn.

One was killed at Drakelow on 17 September, 1855 (*Nat. Hist. of Tutbury*, p. 57), and another shot on the Trent near Burton (*Birds of Derbyshire*, p. 220), and one at Tean near Cheadle 5 August 1895, and one at Pipe Gate in August 1902 (*Reports North Staffs Field Club*).

195. Sooty Tern. *Sterna fuliginosa*, J. F. Gmelin.

A single specimen of this tropical species was killed near Tutbury in 1852 and is now in the collection at Drakelow near Burton-on-Trent. This was the first record of the appearance of this bird in England, though two other instances have since been noted (*Nat. Hist. of Tutbury*, pp. 57, 102).

196. Little Gull. *Larus minutus*, Pallas.

Has been shot on the Trent in several places near Burton (McAldowie, p. 138).

197. Black-headed Gull. *Larus ridibundus*, Linn.

The most common of all the gulls seen in the county, and this species once bred regularly at Norbury near Eccleshall. Dr. McAldowie says: 'The writings of Willoughby, Ray and Plot have made this gullery the most famous in the history of ornithology. No work on Staffordshire would be complete without a record of the writings relating to this interesting breeding place.' Ray visited the colony in 1662 and says: 'We diverted out of our way to see the *Puits* which we judged to be

a sort of *Lari* in a meer at Norbury, belonging to Colonel Skrimshaw. They build together in an islet in the middle of a pool (*Itin.* pp. 216–7).

Willoughby's description states: 'Of this kind also are those birds which yearly build and breed at Norbury in Staffordshire in an island in the middle of a great pool. . . . When the young are almost come to their full growth those entrusted by the Lord of the soil drive them from off the island through the pool into nets set on the banks to take them. When they have taken them they feed them with the entrails of beasts, and when they are fat sell them for four pence or five pence apiece. They take yearly about a thousand two hundred young ones.'

Plot says: 'But the strangest whole footed water fowl that frequents this county is the Larus cinereus Ornithologi, the Larus Anereus tertius Aldrovandi and the Cepphus of Gesner and Turner: in some counties called the black cap, in others the sea or mire-crow, here the pewit, which being of the migratory kind come annually to certain pools in the estate of the right worshipful Sir Charles Skrymsher, Knight, to build and breed.' He then proceeds to describe in detail the arrival and nesting of these birds as well as the method of capture and disposal of the young, which realized an annual profit of from £50 to £60 at the rate of 5s. per dozen, 'they being accounted a good dish at the most plentiful tables.'

Here they continued to breed for nearly a hundred years after occasionally shifting their ground until 1794, since which time scarcely a bird has bred in the county.

198. Common Gull. *Larus canus*, Linn.

An occasional visitor, generally in small flocks after stormy weather on migration. Sir O. Mosley records the visit of a flock of over 100 to the pool at Rolleston (*Nat. Hist. of Tutbury*, p. 57). Two were shot at Whiston near Cheadle in September 1888 (*Report North Staffs Field Club*, 1890, p. 22).

199. Herring-Gull. *Larus argentatus*, J. F. Gmelin.

Parties are occasionally seen passing over the county, generally going north in early spring. They have been observed in the Trent and Dove valleys and also at Hanford, while one was shot at Swythamley in 1875.

200. Lesser Black-backed Gull. *Larus fuscus*, Linn.

A rather infrequent visitor to the Trent valley, usually in immature plumage. An old bird was shot at Handsworth on 29 April 1886, and an immature one at Cheadle in July 1899.

201. Great Black-backed Gull. *Larus marinus*, Linn.

An occasional visitor to the Trent valley. One recorded from near Stafford in 1899 (*Report North Staffs Field Club*, 1900).

202. Kittiwake. *Rissa tridactyla* (Linn.)

An occasional visitor, common in the Trent valley. Several were observed near Tunstall in January 1891 ; also recorded from Cheadle and Uttoxeter (*Reports North Staffs Field Club*, 1892, p. 57, and 1896, p. 48), and from Madeley in 1889.

203. Pomatorhine Skua. *Stercorarius pomatorhinus* (Temminck)

There is a rather doubtful reference to this species in the *Natural History of Tutbury* (p. 58), but Mr. R. W. Chase has recorded one as shot at Oldbury in October 1879 (*Birds of Staffordshire*, p. 138).

204. Arctic or Richardson's Skua. *Stercorarius crepidatus* (J. F. Gmelin)

Two immature birds killed near Rolleston (*Nat. Hist. of Tutbury*, pp. 58, 111).

205. Long-tailed or Buffon's Skua. *Stercorarius parasiticus* (Linn.)

Under the name of Arctic skua Sir O. Mosley doubtfully refers to this species as killed near Burton, but Mr. Brown makes no mention of it in his list. There is however in the Derby Museum a Staffordshire specimen which formed part of the Blurton collection when dispersed in 1883, and an immature bird was shot on the Lichfield racecourse on 7 October 1874 (*Birds of Staffordshire*, p. 139).

206. Guillemot. *Uria troile* (Linn.)

One recorded by Garner near Stoke-on-Trent in 1841 during a severe frost (p. 289).

207. Little Auk. *Mergulus alle* (Linn.)

Several were shot on the Trent after a storm about 1843 (*Nat. Hist. of Tutbury*, pp. 57, 109). One was picked up exhausted between Walsall and Birmingham about 1870 (*Birds of Staffordshire*, p. 144), and another in a similar state at Wheaton Aston near Stafford in January 1901 (*Report North Staffs Field Club*, 1902).

208. Great Northern Diver. *Colymbus glacialis*, Linn.

This fine bird has occurred several times in winter within the county at Aqualate (Garner) on the Tame near Comberford, the Dove near Uttoxeter and several times on the Trent (Sir O. Mosley) and near Macclesfield (Sainter). More recent occurrences are at Rolleston, a female shot on 29 November, 1869, and another about the same time at Wombourne near Wolverhampton, while a third was killed at Tipton on 8 January 1877.

209. Red-throated Diver. *Colymbus septentrionalis*, Linn.

An occasional straggler. Garner records it from Rocester and near Uttoxeter. One was shot at Swythamley in 1880 and in 1871 one was taken alive near Tean (*Report North Staffs Field Club*, 1886). An immature bird was also killed on the Dove below Okeover in the winter of 1895.

210. Great Crested Grebe. *Podicipes cristatus* (Linn.)

Dr. McAldowie says truly : 'This fine bird is the greatest ornithological ornament of our county.' It breeds in some numbers at Aqualate and usually at Copmere and occasionally on other pieces of water such as Trentham Lake, Beech Pool, Knypersley (1892), etc. (*Birds of Staffordshire*, p. 142).

211. Red-necked Grebe. *Podicipes griseigena* (Boddaert)

Included in Garner's list without any particulars. One shot at Burton, April 1849 (J. C. Garth, *Zoologist*, 1850, p. 2706). One obtained at Burton, 20 November 1898 (*Report North Staffs Field Club*, 1903).

212. Slavonian Grebe. *Podicipes auritus* (Linn.)

This species is figured by Plot in his *History of Staffordshire* (tab. 22, fig. 1), and a description is given of a specimen killed at Comberford which had apparently assumed the full breeding plumage. Garner includes it in his list, and in December 1893, one was obtained at Brewood reservoir (*Report North Staffs Field Club*, 1901).

[Eared Grebe. *Podicipes nigricollis* (C. L. Brehm)

Included in Garner's list without data.]

213. Little Grebe or Dabchick. *Podicipes fluviatilis* (Tunstall)

Locally, Dipper, Doucker (obs.)

A resident on our larger rivers and pools, and a summer visitor to small sheets of water, but not so plentiful as in former years.

214. Storm-Petrel. *Procellaria pelagica*, Linn.

Occasionally storm-driven into the county. One was shot about 1885 at Buckmere by Dr. Baddeley, and two have been caught, one near Handsworth in October 1888, and the other between Smethwick and Birmingham on 4 November 1863 (*Birds of Staffordshire*, p. 139).

215. Leach's Fork-tailed Petrel. *Oceanodroma leucorrhoa* (Vieillot).

Another occasional straggler. Sir O. Mosley states that both this and the preceding species have been several times picked up exhausted on the banks of the Trent (*Nat. Hist. of Tutbury*, p. 58). One was found dead at Barton-under-Needwood in March 1890, and another in a similar state was picked up in the grounds of Wootton Lodge on 11 November 1899 (not 1900 as there stated) (*Report North Staffs Field Club*, 1901), and Mr. Fitzherbert Brockholes reports another picked up in a turnip field at Swynnerton on 18 November, 1901.

216. Manx Shearwater. *Puffinus anglorum* (Temminck)

Has occurred several times in the county. One recorded from Weston in 1882, another from Kingsley on 9 September 1887, a third near Stone in September 1891, and a fourth at Lower Gornal near Dudley, 9 September 1891 (*Report North Staffs Field Club* and *Birds of Staffordshire*, p. 140). On 3 September 1892, one was caught in an exhausted state in Burton, and another is said to have been taken previously in the same district (*Birds of Derbyshire*, p. 232).

ADDENDA

The following records have been received since the above list was written :—

12. Nightingale. *Daulias luscinia* (Linn.)

A recent occurrence of this species in the county is noted in *Rep. N. Staffs. Field Club* for 1905.

16A. Dartford Warbler. *Sylvia undata* (Boddaert)

This species can now be included in the county list, as it is proved to have nested on Cannock Chase in 1870 (*Zool.* November, 1903, p. 423, and *Rep. N. Staffs. Field Club*, 1906, p. 46).

57. Tree Sparrow. *Passer montanus* (Linn.)

In 1905 and subsequent years this species has greatly increased in numbers, and nests regularly at Cheadle in boxes put up for tits.

84. Wryneck. *Iÿnx torquilla*, Linn.

Mr. Walter Marchant observed one of these birds near Weston under Lizard on 20 April, 1907.

95A. Little Owl. *Athene noctua* (Scopoli)

A bird of this species was shot in October, 1906, in the county near Newport, Shrops. Probably it had strayed from one of the counties where many of this species have been turned out in recent years, and nest regularly.

98. Hen Harrier. *Circus cyaneus* (Linn.)

One was shot at Enville in December, 1879, and is now in Lord Bradford's collection (*Rep. N. Staffs. Field Club*, 1905).

101. Golden Eagle. *Aquila chrysaëtus* (Linn.)

Mr. Francis Monckton, of Stretton Hall, states that a pair of eagles visited Somerford, near Brewood, in 1856 or 1857, and one was shot. He believes it to have been of this species.

102. White-tailed Eagle. *Haliaëtus albicilla* (Linn.)

A young female was trapped on Cannock Chase on 4 December, 1905, and is now in Lord Lichfield's collection at Shugborough.

116. Common Heron. *Ardea cinerea*, Linn.

A new heronry, with about nine nests, was found in a large wood near Cheadle in 1904, and a few pairs have nested every year since (*Rep. N. Staffs. Field Club*, 1904).

126. White-fronted Goose. *Anser albifrons* (Scopoli)

One shot near Stafford, and another at Stretton, near Stafford (*Rep. N. Staffs. Field Club*, 1906, p. 47).

130. Whooper Swan. *Cygnus musicus*, Bechstein

Nine of these swans visited Gailey Pools on 13 March, 1891 (*Rep. N. Staffs. Field Club*, 1906, p. 50).

130A. Bewick's Swan. *Cygnus bewicki*, Yarrell

The Rev. F. C. R. Jourdain saw a herd of forty flying down the Dove Valley near Mayfield on 27 February, 1904 (*Rep. N. Staffs. Field Club*, 1904).

132. Common Sheld Duck. *Tadorna cornuta* (S. G. Gmelin)

A flock of these birds was observed on Gailey Pools on 30 December, 1904, and one was shot at Cheadle 2 January, 1906 (*Rep. N. Staffs. Field Club*, 1906, pp. 48, 52).

135. Shoveler. *Spatula clypeata* (Linn.)

Visits Gailey Pools most years.

140. Pochard. *Fuligula ferina* (Linn.)

Breeds at Gailey Pools.

142. Scaup-Duck. *Fuligula marila* (Linn.)

This duck also visits Gailey Pools in winter.

143A. Long-tailed Duck. *Harelda glacialis* (Linn.)

One was shot at Weston by Lord Newport on 6 November, 1871 (*Rep. N. Staffs. Field Club*, 1905).

144. Common Scoter. *Oedemia nigra* (Linn.)

Small flocks were seen on Gailey Pools in August, 1887, October, 1890, and November, 1891–2 (*Rep. N. Staffs. Field Club*, 1906, pp. 42–52).

148. Smew. *Mergus albellus*, Linn.

An annual winter visitor to Gailey Pools.

160. Spotted Crake. *Porzana maruetta* (Leach)

One was shot at Gnosall in August, 1904, and being a young bird may have been bred in the county.

166. Ringed Plover. *Aegialitis hiaticula* (Linn.)

Two at Gailey Pools 24 September, 1896 (*Rep. N. Staffs. Field Club*, 1906, p. 51).

172. Grey Phalarope. *Phalaropus fulicarius* (Linn.)

One shot near Anslow in November, 1904 (*Rep. N. Staffs. Field Club*, 1905).

175. Great Snipe. *Gallinago major* (J. F. Gmelin)

One was shot at Stafford some years ago, and is now in the collection of Mr. Conway Morgan, of Stafford.

182A. Wood Sandpiper. *Totanus glareola* (J. F. Gmelin)

One was shot at Barr, near Birmingham, on 26 August, 1858 (*Zool.* 1858, p. 6266).

186. Greenshank. *Totanus canescens* (J. F. Gmelin)

Three were seen at Gailey Pools on 10 August, 1896 (*Rep. N. Staffs. Field Club*, 1906, p. 51).

190. Black Tern. *Hydrochelidon nigra* (Linn.)

Forty visited Gailey Pools in August, 1887, and stayed several days (*Rep. N. Staffs. Field Club*, 1906, p. 49).

192. Common Tern. *Sterna fluviatilis*, Naumann

Occurred at Gailey Pools in 1896.

206. Guillemot. *Uria troile* (Linn.)

One was shot on Gailey Pools 20 April, 1889, and another at the same place in June, 1901 (*Rep. N. Staffs. Field Club*, 1906, pp. 49, 52).

208. Great Northern Diver. *Colymbus glacialis*, Linn.

One shot at Gailey Pools 4 January, 1898, and another seen there 4 January, 1899 (*Rep. N. Staffs. Field Club*, p. 51).

208A. Black-throated Diver. *Colymbus arcticus*, Linn.

One was shot at Gailey Pools, near Penkridge, 11 December, 1896 (*Rep. N. Staffs. Field Club*, 1906, p. 51).

216. Manx Shearwater. *Puffinus anglorum* (Temminck)

In June, 1904, one at Gailey Pools, and one at King's Bromley, 7 September, 1905 (*Rep. N. Staffs. Field Club*, 1906, p. 47, 50).

217. Fulmar. *Fulmarus glacialis* (Linn.)

A specimen of this bird was captured in a field at Perry Barr in January, 1863 (*Zool.* 1863, p. 8448).

MAMMALS

Thirty-six species of mammals may be included in the fauna of Staffordshire as still, or very recently, living more or less in a state of nature within the borders of the county.

Of the Cheiroptera or bats 7 species are recorded, the rarest being Natterer's bat (*Myotis nattereri*) of which one instance only is known. The whiskered bat (*M. mystacinus*) has of late years proved to be more abundant in the county than was formerly thought to be the case, especially in the north. In other districts it may possibly be confounded sometimes with a black variety of the pipistrelle.

All five British species of Insectivora are represented in Staffordshire, the hedgehog, mole and common shrew abundantly, whilst the pigmy shrew and water shrew are more local in their distribution.

The genuine wild cat and the wolf have, of course, long been extinct in the county, although the latter continued abundant even in the reign of Edward II. The fox, the weasel and the stoat still abound, but the pine marten became extinct about fifty years ago, and the last polecat seems to have been killed about 1884. The badger, on the other hand, is still far from rare in the wilder parts of Staffordshire, and, thanks to the humane preservation that is afforded it at the hands of a small but, we are glad to note, increasing number of landowners, may probably long remain so. The outlook for the otter is not so bright, but it still occurs in most of our rivers, particularly in the Dove, where as I learn from the Rev. F. C. R. Jourdain, protection is afforded it ' by a few riparian owners, particularly Capt. H. E. Clowes of Norbury, and Mr. A. C. Duncombe of Culwich.' On the upper waters of the Dove otters are shot down relentlessly, and Mr. Jourdain considers that ' probably most of the otters that are seen on the Dove and Trent are wanderers from the protected length.'

The rodents are well represented—perhaps too much so, the brown rat especially being, sixty years ago, quite a scourge in the valley of the Trent. This happily is no longer the case, but it is still far too abundant and in some districts is almost as amphibious as the water vole. The black rat appears to have been early exterminated, as John Horatio Dickenson in his ' Sketch of the Zoology of Staffordshire ' in Shaw's *History* says that it had become extinct in his time (1798). The mountain or ' Scotch ' hare has been recently introduced into the moorland districts of the county, but Staffordshire has long been noted for the large size and weight of its indigenous ' brown ' hares.

MAMMALS

Turning now to the ungulates or hoofed mammals, passing reference must be made to the famous herd of wild white cattle at Chartley. These grand animals which numbered 29 head in March, 1901, by April, 1903, were reduced to less than a dozen through tuberculous disease. A fine young bull and three heifers have been separated from the remainder of the herd in the hopes that they may thus escape contagion. Should they unfortunately fail to do so there is every probability that this historic herd may speedily become extinct.

Of our three species of deer the red deer is now entirely a park animal, although formerly common enough in the county, and even so late as 1853 one was at large in Swythamly Woods, and in 1870 one was killed there (vide *North Staffs Field Club Report*, 1894, p. 39). The wild fallow deer which in Dickenson's time, 1798, were estimated at more than 3,000, are now represented by a few scattered individuals wandering amongst the oaks and hollies in the Needwood Forest estates and on Cannock Chase ; but many are kept in semi-domestication in the deer parks of the county.

The beautiful little roe deer owes its inclusion in our list to the discovery of its cast antlers in Needwood Forest by Sir Oswald Mosley, where it undoubtedly lived when the wild boar whetted his curved tusks on the trunks of the oaks, and possibly long after he was exterminated.

CHEIROPTERA

1. Lesser Horseshoe Bat. *Rhinolophus hipposiderus*, Bechstein.

This species is included by the late Mr. Edwin Brown in his *Fauna of Burton-on-Trent*, although his specimens came from Derbyshire, where it is not uncommon. The lesser horseshoe bat does not seem to have occurred in Staffordshire of late years, but I am still in hopes that further research in the limestone district of north Stafford will result in its discovery as a resident in the county.

2. Long-eared Bat. *Plecotus auritus*, Linn.

Generally distributed throughout the county. It may be seen on the wing from March till November, and is extremely active in turning and wheeling in the air, as well as in rising from the ground.

3. Great Bat. *Pipistrella noctula*, Schreber.
    Bell—*Scotophilus noctula*.
    White—*Vespertilio altivolans*.

This grand bat—justly named by Mr. Trevor-Battye in honour of the great naturalist who first described it as a British species, White's bat — is generally distributed in Staffordshire, and may be observed in flight from May till August or early September. It is often seen abroad in the day and then flies very high in the air, but I have frequently

seen it skimming the meadows near Burton-on-Trent late in the evening at an elevation of 6 feet or less. At Trentham Park Mr. Collins obtained thirty specimens from a hollow ash in which they were hibernating.[1] These were exhibited alive at the Annual Meeting of the North Staffordshire Field Club held at Stoke on Thursday, 19 March, 1891, Mr. Collins subsequently took ten specimens out of a hollow Scotch fir in the same locality.[2] In captivity, for a bat, this species evinces considerable intelligence. One that I kept for several weeks became remarkably tame, readily recognized my voice and distinguished it from that of any other person. When called it hurried towards me with a peculiar movement of its long fore-arms as if it were mounted on stilts, and having reached me climbed about my person with every evidence of satisfaction.

4. Pipistrelle. *Pipistrellus pipistrellus*, Schreber.
    Bell—*Scotophilus pipistrellus*.

Common and generally distributed. Owing to its partiality for house-roofs and churches this is our most familiar bat. Its winter sleep

[1] *North Staffordshire Naturalists' Field Club Report*, 1891, p. 65.
[2] Ibid. 1894, p. 38.

is very slight and when the weather becomes mild this bat awakes and ventures out to prey upon the few insects which are then abroad. In different years I have seen it in flight during each month from January to December. Mr. John R. B. Masefield has recorded the receipt, in June 1893, of sixty-one pipistrelles from one of the lodges in Trentham Park[1]—a very large colony for this species.

5. Natterer's Bat. *Myotis nattereri*, Leisler.
   Bell—*Vespertilio nattereri.*

Rare. One example only recorded. Of this specimen the late Mr. Edwin Brown wrote : 'Captured in the roof of Stapenhill House some years ago, and is now in the Burton Museum.' This was in 1863, and Burton does not now possess a museum. It would be interesting to learn if this specimen is still in existence, but up to the present I have been unable to trace it.

6. Daubenton's Bat. *Myotis daubentoni*, Leisler.
   Bell—*Vespertilio daubentonii.*

Not common. Has occurred near Uttoxeter (C. Oldham) and at Stafford (L. E. Adams). In June, 1899, I saw two bats playing over the water of the Trent at Drakelow Deeps, which from their manner of touching the water, doubtless when taking gnats from the surface, and their silence whilst on the wing, I imagine to have been of this species. On the following evening I saw the same or similar bats on the Derbyshire side of the river—which here forms the boundary between the two counties, at the point where the Leicester line bridge crosses the Trent. It is probable that when more attention has been directed to the habits of our local bats, Daubenton's bat will prove to be much less uncommon than is at present supposed to be the case.

7. Whiskered Bat. *Myotis mystacinus*, Leisler.
   Bell—*Vespertilio mystacinus.*

First recorded for the county by Garner in his *Natural History of the County of Stafford* (1844), and again by Sir Oswald Mosley in the *Natural History of Tutbury* (1863), apparently from the same specimen captured near Burton. This bat was for many years considered to be one of our rarest species. Of late however many examples have been captured especially in the north of the county, and in the Cheadle district Mr. Masefield considers it the commonest bat. This is however by no means the case near Burton and south of the Trent, where, according to my experience, a small almost black variety of the pipistrelle is by far the most abundant species.

INSECTIVORA

8. Hedgehog. *Erinaceus europæus*, Linn.

Generally distributed and fairly common, though much persecuted by gamekeepers because of its depredations on the eggs and young of game birds. Rewards were formerly given in Staffordshire for killing hedgehogs.

9. Mole. *Talpa europæa*, Linn.
   Common.

10. Common Shrew. *Sorex araneus*, Linn.
    Locally, Nurserow.

Common everywhere in fields and hedgerows.

11. Pigmy Shrew. *Sorex minutus*, Linn.
    Bell—*Sorex pygmæus.*

Far less common than the preceding. The first local specimen was found dead near Consall on 17 September, 1885, by Mr. E. W. H. Blagg, and since then the remains of others have been found by Mr. L. E. Adams in the pellets disgorged by owls at Penkridge and near Stafford (reported by Mr. Masefield in *N.S.F.C. Reports*, 1886, 1897).

12. Water Shrew. *Neomys fodiens*, Pallas.
    Bell—*Crossopus fodiens.*

Widely distributed in the county and not uncommon. I have myself observed it at various places in the Trent and in the Dove, and on one occasion an individual was captured in the canal at Branston by a terrier belonging to me and killed before there was time for interference. This animal sometimes wanders far from any water. Thus on 18 August, 1899, I found an adult male specimen lying dead on the roadside between Rolleston and Horninglow, and on the same road the dead bodies of four common shrews.

The oared shrew, which was formerly considered to be a distinct species, but is now known to be merely an aged form of the water shrew, is stated by Garner to have been taken several times at Great Fenton and other places in the county.

---

[1] *North Staffordshire Naturalists' Field Club Report*, 1894, p. 38.

MAMMALS

CARNIVORA

13. Fox. *Canis vulpes*, Linn.
Bell—*Vulpes vulgaris*.
Common and generally distributed.

14. Pine Marten. *Mustela martes*, Linn.
Bell—*Martes abietum*.

Extinct within the memory of men still living, and formerly fairly distributed in suitable localities, especially in the northern half of the county. Garner says that it has occurred in woods in Dilhorne, Consall, in Needwood Forest and in the limestone district. It seems probable that the headquarters of this species in Staffordshire were the woodlands of the north and east, and that it was never so abundant south of the Trent. Dickenson writing about 1798, although well acquainted with the badger, otter and polecat, which he calls fitchet, does not mention the pine marten, so that it seems possible that even in his day the 'sweet mart' was very rare even if at all known in the centre of the county—with which portion he was evidently most familiar.

15. Polecat or Fitchet. *Putorius putorius,* Linn.
Bell—*Mustela putorius*.

Nearly if not quite extinct although formerly occurring in most parts of the county. Dickenson knew it well under the name of 'fitchet,' by which it is still commonly referred to in Staffordshire, and records that he has known 'a fitchet when confined and unable to escape, attack a large greyhound.' In 1863 Sir Oswald Mosley wrote that it was still found near Tutbury, 'although becoming more scarce every year,' and at the same time Mr. Edwin Brown reported it as 'occasionally haunting detached out-houses' near Burton-on-Trent. It appears to have maintained a precarious footing in the west of the county until about 1884, when, as I am informed by Mr. James Yates, M.R.C.S., one was killed at Swinnerton. On asking Mr. Yates for further particulars, he very kindly wrote me as follows, under date 29 January, 1901 : 'I am sorry I am not able to give you a very satisfactory account of the polecat which was killed at Swinnerton about 1884. I was told of the fact by a gamekeeper who lived between Trentham and Swinnerton, but I had not the opportunity of seeing the animal myself. When I was a boy the "fitchet" was fairly common at Horsley—a farm a few miles from Eccleshall—I have frequently seen them caught in a rat-trap which was covered with fine moss and half-surrounded by a fence made of sticks. The bait was usually a hen's egg.'

16. Stoat. *Mustela erminea*, Linn.
Common. In the winter specimens in the white or 'ermine' dress are sometimes obtained.

17. Weasel. *Putorius nivalis*, Linn.
Bell—*Mustela vulgaris*.
Common, and more frequently seen near farms and out-houses than the last named.

18. Badger. *Meles meles*, Linn.
Bell—*Meles taxus*.

Notwithstanding the persecution to which the badger has been so long subjected, this animal is still far more abundant in Staffordshire than is usually supposed. Its chief haunts are in the high banks and wild parklands of the Needwood Forest district, and in the north and west. The nocturnal habits of the badger doubtless tend to its preservation, but occasionally it ventures from its burrow long before sundown, and has several times been seen and captured in broad daylight. Where it has long been undisturbed its burrows are extremely extensive and might almost be described as cavernous. Very heavy badgers are sometimes captured. One, weighing 34¼ lb. was taken alive in 1894 in the Burnt Woods near Ashley, and the event was reported at the time in the *Field* newspaper.

It is to be hoped that landowners will do all they can to discourage the destruction of this very interesting mammal.

19. Otter. *Lutra lutra*, Linn.
Bell—*Lutra vulgaris*.

Although much rarer than the badger in Staffordshire, instances of the otter being seen, and too often killed, in the county are recorded nearly every year. Sometimes cubs are killed —showing that the otter still breeds within the county boundaries. It occurs chiefly in the Trent, in the Dove and in other smaller tributaries, and also enters Staffordshire from the Severn which crosses the south-western extremity of the county near Arley. Otters have on several occasions come down the Trent to Burton, and on 23 April, 1884, they were seen from Burton Bridge, and, as I learn from Mr. J. E. Nowers, one was shot about this time within the borough boundaries. I heard of another example being seen near the weir in November, 1899, and chased by two ardent, if amateur, sportsmen with a terrier and a dachshund—I need hardly say unsuccessfully.

According to Sir Oswald Mosley, otters were formerly hunted in his district but never with much success, and the sport has been discontinued for many years.

In Plot's time the otter must have been common in Staffordshire, for at Ingestre the worthy doctor was regaled with a dish of 'potted' otter, 'so well ordered by the cook,' he remarked, 'that it required a very nice palate to distinguish it from venison.'

RODENTIA

20. Squirrel. *Sciurus leucourus*, Kerr.

Bell—*Sciurus vulgaris*.

Generally distributed in plantations and woods.

21. Dormouse. *Muscardinus avellanarius*, Linn.

Bell—*Myoxus avellanarius*.

Not rare in the wooded portions of the county, but owing to its retiring habits seems to be much less common than is really the case. Mr. James Yates writes me that he has seen the dormouse amongst hazels at Oakamoor, and at Keele he knew of a farmer who had taken several from a nest. These dormice were examined by Mr. Yates as well as the nest—originally built by a wren—which they had adopted as their home.

22. Harvest Mouse. *Mus minutus*, Pallas.

Occurs in cornfields and in rough marshy places. Mr. Yates, in the letter referred to above, writes as follows concerning this species : 'I have found the nest of the harvest mouse in many places—at Keele, Horsley, Alton, etc., but I have never seen the nest fixed on corn-stalks. It has always been in very coarse grass or sedges ; in particular in tussocks of *Carex paniculata*. The nest is woven into a dense mass and it is very difficult indeed to find the entrance.' To this I may add that the entrance—always I believe in the side—is frequently carefully closed by the mice, and although I have seen the nest built amongst corn, it is also sometimes affixed to brambles and even thistles as well as to the plants mentioned above by Mr. Yates. The notion that this species is confined to corn-fields is quite erroneous.

23. Wood Mouse or Long-tailed Field Mouse. *Mus sylvaticus*, Linn.

Common in fields and gardens.

24. House Mouse. *Mus musculus*, Linn.

25. Black Rat. *Mus rattus*, Linn.

The black rat was probably very early driven out of Staffordshire by the brown rat and totally exterminated, for Dickenson says that it had become extinct in his time (1798),

and as the earliest possible date of the arrival of the brown rat in this county is 1728, the latter must soon have entered upon a warfare of extermination against the creature it found in possession.

26. Brown Rat. *Mus decumanus*, Pallas.

Far too abundant, and in the valley of the Trent almost as amphibious as the water vole taking up its residence in the river banks, and feeding indiscriminately on dead fish, frogs and farmer's produce. Brown says that previous to 1852 the 'numbers that were found in the drains in our meadows were perfectly frightful,' but that the great floods which prevailed at Burton in that year considerably thinned their ranks, and they have never occurred in such numbers since.

27. Field Vole. *Microtus agrestis*, Linn.

Bell—*Arvicola agrestis*.

Abundant.

28. Bank Vole. *Evotomys glareolus*, Schreber.

Bell—*Arvicola glareolus*.

Apparently much less common than the last-named species, but has probably been confused with it in many parts of the county. It has been reported from the northern district, and I have myself also found it at Tutbury and Horninglow in the east of the county.

29. Water Vole. *Microtus amphibius*, Linn.

Bell—*Arvicola amphibius*.

Common, and generally distributed.

30. Common Hare. *Lepus europæus*, Pallas.

Bell—*Lepus timidus*.

Common, and frequently attaining to a large size and heavy weight.

31. Mountain Hare. *Lepus timidus*, Linn.

Bell—*Lepus variabilis*.

Introduced in the county. Mr. Masefield in the *North Staffordshire Naturalist's Field Club Report*, 1895, xxix. 46, says : 'Sportsmen have reported to me last season that several mountain hares (*Lepus variabilis*) have been killed around Cheadle—some of these I find were turned out in the spring of last year, but Mr. Bill of Farley tells me that there have generally been a few in the moorland district of our county.' Of course no one will suppose that the mountain or 'Scotch' hare is indigenous in Staffordshire.

32. Rabbit. *Lepus cuniculus*, Linn.

Plentiful.

UNGULATA

33. Chartley White Cattle. *Bos taurus*, Linn.

No account of the mammals of Staffordshire could be considered complete without reference to the famous herd of white cattle so long preserved in a half-wild condition at Chartley Park by the Earls Ferrers. These magnificent animals are white, with the ears, hoofs, and generally the muzzle, black. Black spots and blotches are usually seen on the lower part of the fore-legs and sometimes on the hind-legs also. The horns are white finely tipped with black, are long and sweeping, not short and sharply curved upwards as in the Chillingham and Cadzow herds, and remind one of the fine Old English long-horn cattle and the Highland breed in the bold way in which they stand out from the sides of the head. A remarkable feature is a large tuft of long curly hair which adorns the forehead and reaches as low as the inner corners of the eyes, and especially in old bulls possesses a parting down the centre which gives to the tuft the appearance of a carefully arranged and very beautiful wig. In the cows the horns are thinner than in the bulls and with a more decided upward trend.

As a rule the disposition of these Chartley cattle is mild and timorous, and when approached by strangers the herd slowly retreats. At certain seasons the animals become dangerous, and it is at all times unsafe to approach too closely to the cows when accompanied by their calves, the first signs of a projected attack being stamping with the fore-feet and an angry tossing of the head. When alarmed the members of the herd collect together and at first retreat a short distance. They then suddenly turn and face the object of their resentment, the herd standing in the form of a semicircle. On being further pressed they again retreat and again turn towards their adversary, and if still molested do not hesitate to charge. Few spectators, however rash and curious, will be found to await the latter consummation, and prudently retire to the shelter of some pine-clump or group of birch trees after one or two demonstrations of hostility on the part of the herd. Even young calves but a few days old when met with away from their dams butt with great spirit and fierceness.

Black calves are occasionally born and are invariably destroyed by the keepers, but black and white calves seem to be unknown. The birth of a black calf was anciently considered to foretell disaster to some member of the Ferrers family.

Originally driven into Chartley Park from Needwood Forest by William, Earl of Derby, in the reign of Henry III., these cattle have been carefully preserved pure by his descendants, the Earls Ferrers, and although inbred for over 650 years they still survive. At times however they have been very near extinction, for about twenty years ago they were reduced to 17 head. By 1887 the herd had doubled in numbers, and from 1890 to 1900 averaged about 45 head. Within the last few years the numbers have steadily declined, and in April, 1903, they were reduced to less than a dozen.

34. Red Deer. *Cervus elaphus*, Linn.

The red deer preserved at Chartley, Bagot's Park, and elsewhere in the county are probably the direct descendants of the wild deer which anciently inhabited Needwood Forest, the largest herd being that at Chartley which now numbers 50 head.

35. Fallow Deer. *Cervus dama*, Linn.

Although not indigenous to Staffordshire any more than to other parts of these islands, fallow deer have from very ancient days abounded in the county and great herds wandered at liberty on Needwood Forest, and in smaller numbers on Cannock Chase, down to comparatively recent times. In 1798 Dickenson estimated the number of deer on Needwood Forest at more than 3,000, and remarked that many of them were of the dark brown variety 'introduced from Norway by James I.' Dickenson, like many a writer since his day, was probably in error when he penned the remark quoted above, for Mr. J. E. Harting has shown (*Essays on Sport and Natural History*) that a dark race of fallow deer existed in England as early as 1465.

In a state of semi-domestication fallow deer are kept in the deer-parks at Chartley, Bagots-Bromley, Wooton, Dunstall, etc., whilst a few exist in a state of freedom on Cannock Chase, and one or two stray animals appear from time to time in the woods and plantations at Swilcar Lawn and elsewhere on Needwood Forest.

36. Roe Deer. *Capreolus capreolus*, Linn.
     Bell—*Capreolus caprea.*

Sir Oswald Mosley (*Natural History of Tutbury*, p. 17) says : 'Several horns of the roe-buck have been found on Needwood Forest,' and then goes on to describe the fallow deer found there before the enclosure ; with this exception I can find no recent reference to the occurrence of this little deer in Staffordshire, and it seems certain that for the last hundred years at least the roe deer has been extinct in the county.

NOTE.—I cannot conclude this paper without expressing my indebtedness to the pages of the *Reports and Transactions of the North Staffordshire Field Club* (especially the Reports of the section on Zoology compiled by the chairman, John R. B. Masefield, Esq., M.A.) and to the works of Plot, Dickenson (in Shaw's *Staffordshire*), Garner, Sir Oswald Mosley and Edwin Brown. My thanks are also due for much interesting information to James Yates, Esq., M.R.C.S. ; to J. E. Nowers, Esq. ; and for particulars as to the cattle and deer of Chartley Park to Earl Ferrers' head keeper, Mr. W. Goring.

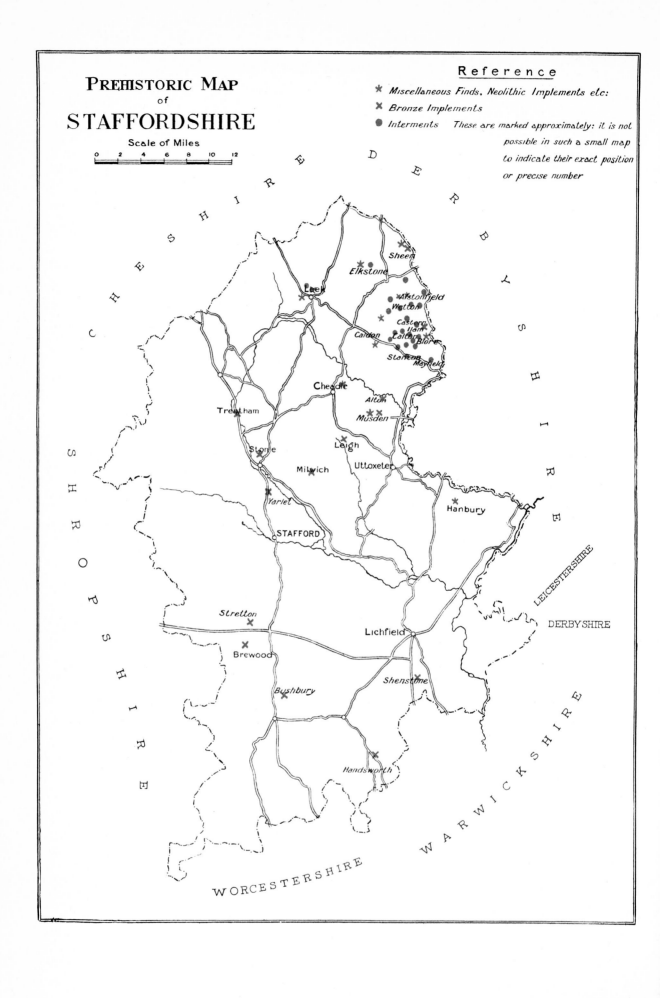

PREHISTORIC MAP
of
STAFFORDSHIRE

Scale of Miles

0 2 4 6 8 10 12

Reference

* Miscellaneous Finds, Neolithic Implements etc:
✗ Bronze Implements
● Interments   These are marked approximately: it is not
possible in such a small map
to indicate their exact position
or precise number

CHESHIRE

DERBYSHIRE

SHROPSHIRE

WORCESTERSHIRE

WARWICKSHIRE

LEICESTERSHIRE

DERBYSHIRE

Sheen
Elkstone
Leek
Alstonfield
Wetton
Castern
Ilam
Caldon
Calton
Blore
Stanton
Mayfield
Cheadle
Alton
Musden
Trentham
Leigh
Stone
Milwich
Uttoxeter
Yarlet
Hanbury
STAFFORD
Stretton
Lichfield
Brewood
Shenstone
Bushbury
Handsworth

EARLY MAN

TRACES of man in very early times, prior to the period of written records, are by no means rare in Staffordshire, and although the actual antiquities are now somewhat scattered, it is an interesting fact that Dr. Robert Plot, in his well-known *Natural History* of the county, was one of the first to record and figure prehistoric implements of bronze and stone. The book was printed in 1686, and contains in the tenth chapter 'Of Antiquities' descriptions and copper-plate engravings of several well-known types of Neolithic and Bronze Age weapons. The fact that Dr. Plot assigns the bronze celts, etc., to a Roman origin excites no wonder when it is remembered that the field of prehistoric archaeology was at that time quite unexplored. One must be grateful, rather, for such an early record of local antiquities.

Of the earliest prehistoric period, the Palaeolithic Age, when man shaped his flint tools merely by chipping and was ignorant of the art of grinding them, Staffordshire affords no evidence.

THE NEOLITHIC AGE

The traces of man's presence in Staffordshire in the Neolithic Age are neither numerous nor important, but, as will presently be shown, they are really of considerable interest as showing the diffusion of what was probably the earliest race to inhabit this part of Britain.

A word or two may here be said as to the conditions of life at this remote period. The Neolithic Age represents a phase of civilization antecedent to the use of metal, yet not devoid of certain accomplishments. For instance, Neolithic man was able to make his tools and weapons of stone and flint not merely by chipping, but also by grinding, whereby regular smooth edges were produced. He was able to till the soil, to construct dwellings and to throw up earthworks as a defence against his enemies. He had also acquired the art of making a rough kind of pottery. Altogether, considering the very early period in which he lived, he had made substantial progress in civilization, and it is practically certain that our inability to recognize his proper place in the scale of human progress arises, not so much from the barbarity of the times, as from the fact that many traces of such a remote period have necessarily perished by decay.

Dwellings, and many of the appliances of Neolithic life, have to a very large extent been swept away, and this gives a special value to the buried sepulchral remains, both in the form of actual human remains and grave furniture, such as pottery, flint implements, and many other objects which were commonly interred with the dead.

The stone implements found in Staffordshire, some of which evidently belong to the Neolithic Age and some to the Bronze Age, present one or two interesting facts which are worthy of consideration. These points consist mainly of the association of the stone objects with other articles rather than individual and actual features, and they tend to illustrate the transition and overlapping of the ages of stone and metal.

Thus, in the Mouse Low barrow, a flint arrow-head (a weapon which it was formerly the custom to regard as Neolithic) was found in a Bronze Age drinking-cup, a circumstance which implies but does not prove contemporaneity, because the arrow-head may have been preserved as a relic from a former age. At Mouse Low, also, two barbed arrow-heads of flint were found in association with bone pins. The same combination of objects was found in Ribden Low barrow.

Thor's Cave, at Wetton, furnished two decidedly curious objects, viz., a carved sandstone vessel and a bronze kettle-like vessel. The objects are probably both later than the Bronze Age, as the handle is of iron. The sandstone vessel belongs to a type found in more abundance in Scotland than England, where they are decidedly rare.

In the details of the contents of Staffordshire barrows given in this article it will be noted, again and again, that flint flakes and implements occur in the sepulchral mounds in intimate association with burnt burials and pottery bearing the characteristics, both in fabric and decoration, of the Bronze Age. The conclusion to which these facts point is that the two races, the Neolithic and the Bronze-using people, intermingled, intermarried, and buried their dead side by side, some individuals retaining the old customs and others adopting the new.

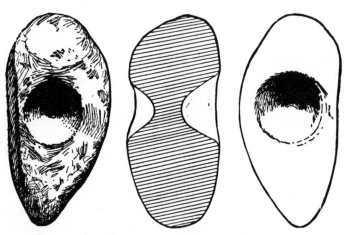

GRANITE AXE-HEAD FOUND AT STONE (12 in. in length)

The bone pins referred to may be either of the Neolithic or the Bronze Age. Their purpose has been the subject of a good deal of speculation amongst antiquaries, some regarding them as instruments for piercing leather or soft materials. When they occur in barrows, however, there seems reason to believe that they served as fastenings for some kind of shroud in the case of unburnt interments, and in the case of burnt burials it is believed that they served to pin together the cloth in which the ashes were placed, after being collected from the funeral pile.[1]

THE BRONZE AGE

The main points of difference between the later age of stone or the Neolithic Age, and the earliest period of metal or the Bronze Age, may be summed up in a few words, although it would be difficult, if not impossible, for us in modern times to realize all that the great transition meant.

[1] Evans, *Stone Imp.* (2nd ed.), 432.

The introduction of metal in the place of stone must have given to the possessors immense advantages in warfare, in the chase, and in the ordinary pursuits of life, and one would naturally be inclined to imagine that a struggle for supremacy would take place between those who possessed the secret of working bronze, and those who did not possess it. If such a conflict occurred it must have been of short duration ; at any rate its effects are not perceptible in the surviving remains, sepulchral deposits indicating that there was a more or less friendly relation between the two races.

The knowledge of working in bronze is believed to have been introduced by a branch of the Celtic family known as Goidels, or Gaels.

One natural effect of the discovery of the properties of such a metal as bronze was to put into the hands of the builders of houses the power of cleaving and shaping large timbers. Houses of the Bronze Age, therefore, in strong contrast with those of the Neolithic circular huts, were built in rectangular plan and with regular gabled roofs.

From what has been already stated it will be gathered that the evidence of the Neolithic Age and the Bronze Age, as far as Staffordshire is concerned, indicates a considerable amount of transition and overlapping. This is more particularly apparent, perhaps, in the case of sepulchral deposits, and it will be convenient at this stage to deal with these remains before describing the isolated finds which are unquestionably referable to the Bronze Age.

SEPULCHRAL MOUNDS OR BARROWS

Some important details of the prehistoric archaeology of Staffordshire are given in Bateman's *Ten Years' Diggings*, a work published in 1861. The facts were obtained by Mr. Samuel Carrington during exploratory excavations in barrows extending over the years 1848 to 1858. The following are the more important of the discoveries.

1. Barrow situated on a hill called Hanging Bank, at Ecton Mine, 20 yds. in diameter, 4 ft. high, and concave in centre like a bowl.—In the middle was found a deposit of calcined human bones accompanied by bones of the water-rat in abundance, and also a large bone pin 5 in. in length, two spear points and two arrow-heads of flint, all of which bore traces of having passed through the fire.

2. Barrow on Arbour Hill, near Throwley Hall, 30 yds. in diameter.— This contained a cist constructed of flat slabs of limestone neatly arranged. In the cist were found burnt human bones and a flint arrow-point. There was a smaller cist adjoining the eastern end of that just described containing burnt bones. Another interment contained two skeletons in close proximity and each buried in a contracted posture. One skeleton, that of a young person, was accompanied by a slender arrow-head of flint. In yet another interment in this barrow was found an iron spike about 3 in. long, which had been inserted into wood.

3. Barrow on the top of Mare Hill, near Throwley Hall.—In this was found a grave cut in the rock, containing two skeletons with a spear-point of calcined flint. A piece of pottery, and a small quantity of lead (which had been accidentally fused from metalliferous gravel present upon the spot where a cremation took place) were found near the grave.

The barrow also contained a cist in which were three interments on different levels. A bronze dagger 3 in. in length was found with the remains of the burnt burial, which occupied a middle position between the lowest interment, which consisted of almost an entire skeleton, and the uppermost, which was the skeleton of a child.

In still another part of the barrow, at a depth of about 2 ft. from the surface, was the skeleton of a child, laid on the left side, with the knees drawn up. An ornamented vase or urn, 5 in. in height, lay close by. In addition to the interments described traces of three or four other burials were noticed. It is obvious that the barrow must have been an important burial-place and that both Stone Age and Bronze Age folk buried their dead within it.

4. A barrow at Deepdale, 17 yds. in diameter and of small elevation, was found to contain a grave in which was a human skeleton, in a crouched posture, accompanied by a well-preserved bronze dagger provided with three rivets by which it had been fastened to a semi-lunar handle.

5. A barrow, called Mouse Low, situated between Deepdale and the village of Grindon, 14 yds. in diameter, and about 2 ft. high, upon being examined was found to contain the skeleton of a large man in contracted posture. Near the head was a peculiarly elegant and well-finished drinking cup, within which there were two implements cut from the ribs of a large animal, a spear head, and two beautiful barbed arrows of white flint. Outside the cup were two more arrows of the same kind.

6. Small barrow, known as Green Low, at Castern.—In this was found the skeleton of a child, with a flint arrow-point, and certain objects of later date, including a Roman fibula of bronze.

7. Musden Low, a barrow situated on Musden Hill, near Calton, originally 27 yds. in diameter, on examination was found to contain a skeleton completely embedded in rats' bones. Close by were found the remains of a burnt interment, the fire employed for which having partially blackened both the skeleton and the rats' bones. Calcined implements of flint, and pieces of urns, ranging apparently from the Celtic to the Romano-British period, were found in the barrow.

8. A tumulus called Thorncliff, situated on Calton Moor, about a mile from the village of Calton, contained the remains of a large skeleton 'accompanied by a neat instrument of flint and a bronze dagger, with three rivets of the usual form.'

9. A second barrow at Musden Hill (see 7) upon being opened was found to contain a human skeleton with the head to the outside of the barrow. Above and around it were fragments of two globular narrow-necked urns, ornamented with a few projections upon the shoulders, which had contained burnt bones. The discoverers were inclined to assign this interment to the Anglo-Saxon period, but it seems just possible that the pottery found was Neolithic.

10. A barrow on Readon Hill, Ramshorn, was opened and found to contain about the centre two extended skeletons. They were accompanied by an iron spear and a narrow iron knife. These may have been Anglo-Saxon interments.

11. A barrow at Dale, near Stanton, on being opened was found to contain two skeletons lying on the original surface of the earth. These presented

evidences of an unusual method of sepulture differing from any other that had previously been noticed. It was clear that the bodies had been intentionally subjected to the action of fire upon the spot where they lay, in such a manner as to preserve the bones in their natural order, entire and unwarped by the heat. The bones, which were of both sexes, were surrounded by charcoal and earth, to which a red colour had been imparted by the operation, themselves exhibiting a curious variety of tints from the same cause. They were accompanied simply by some chips of flint and one piece of primitive pottery.

12. Two contracted and much decayed skeletons inclosed within a rude kind of cist, and accompanied by 'a few mean implements of flint,' were found in a barrow at Stanton.

13. Another cist-burial was discovered in a barrow called Ribden Low, situated between the villages of Cotton and Caldon. There were actually two cist-burials in the mound, and the objects found with the skeletons comprised three barbed arrow-heads of flint, three large flint implements, five bone implements, and two very small pieces of bronze slightly ornamented. The bone implements were of peculiar interest from the fact that some were pointed at each end and perforated through the middle, and had apparently been used as netting tools.

14. A barrow of unusual form near the village or Calton, opened in 1849, was found to contain evidence of repeated interments distributed throughout the area of the mound. The barrow was of the type designated 'Druid Barrows' by Stukeley and Hoare. Charcoal and numerous calcined flint implements were found in association with the human remains.

15. In a barrow situated on an eminence called the Cop, near Calton, was found an interesting example of the careful interment of part of the head of an ox. It also contained (1) a small quadrangular cist, in which were the bones of a young person about twelve years of age ; (2) another small cist constructed of four flat stones ; and (3) still another cist of circular form. Within the small cist (2) was found the right half of the upper jaw of an ox, making the fifth instance of the intentional burial of ox bones, a circumstance which goes far to prove the existence of some peculiar superstition or rite connected with the bones of that animal.

16. In a tumulus situated midway between Throwley and Calton, and composed almost entirely of burnt earth, was found a deposit of large pieces of calcined human bone placed within a circular hole in the natural soil about a foot deep. This hole was of well-defined shape, resulting from contact with a wooden or wicker-work vessel in which the bones were placed when buried. On the bones lay part of a small bronze pin, and a very beautiful miniature 'incense cup' $2\frac{1}{8}$ in. high and $3\frac{1}{2}$ in. in diameter. Among the bones were found two small pointed pieces of flint and a quartz pebble, and close by the deposit were four other small heaps of calcined bone in the form of powder.

17. In a field called Stonesteads, a quarter of a mile from the village cf Waterhouses, was a barrow in which the skeleton of a tall and strongly-built man was found lying on a pavement of thin flat stones raised 6 in. above the natural level of the ground. Near the feet was the tusk of a large boar

rubbed down on the inner surface to about half the natural thickness. Part of an arrow-point and several pieces of cut bone were found near the skeleton.

18. Cist interment at Lumberlow, near Waterhouses.—The cist contained the skeleton of a fully-grown young person, a good spear-head of mottled grey flint, and a highly polished flint implement of uncertain use. Above it were numerous pebbles, the leg-bone of a large dog, and a little charcoal.

19. 'Druid Barrow,' called Farlow, near Caldon.—This contained the skeleton of a young person laid upon the ribs of an ox or other large animal placed transversely to the human bones, at regular intervals side by side. The barrow also contained the skeleton of a young person in a rock grave, accompanied by an ornamented vase 5 in. high, perhaps a 'drinking cup.' Part of a large urn, the upper portion of which was ornamented with cheverons, had been found at an earlier period, and was broken up into fragments in order that each bystander might possess a memento of the discovery.

20. Swinscoe. — An important elliptical or long barrow, called Top Low, measuring 45 ft. long by 21 ft. wide, was found, on examination, to contain evidences of no less than fourteen interments. The barrow is believed to have been originally circular, and to have assumed an elliptical shape in consequence of subsequent additions. The following are brief particulars of the various burials in this barrow, which are also indicated on the accompanying plan :—

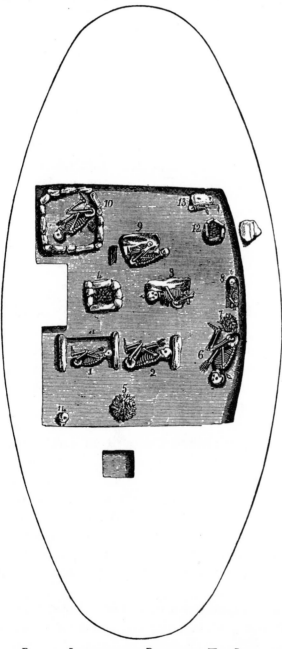

PLAN OF INTERMENTS IN BARROW AT TOP LOW, SWINSCOE

1. Skeleton of a young person in a contracted posture in a shallow grave, cut about six inches deep in the chert rock, having a stone placed on edge at each end. With it were a three-cornered piece of flint and a small bronze clasp which had been riveted to a strap.

2. Skeleton of young adult, with an upright stone at the head, and a round-ended flint near the feet.

3. Skeleton of middle-aged person, accompanied by a neatly chipped spear-head of flint.

4. Skeleton of a young hog inclosed in a roughly constructed cist. A tine from a stag's horn was buried with the hog.

5. Cinerary urn decorated with a cheveron pattern containing calcined bones, portions of bone implements (probably tools for modelling pottery), and part of a fine flint which had been damaged by fire.

6. Skeleton with legs drawn up. Near it was a thin layer of charred wood and two flakes of flint.

7. Deposit of calcined bones.

8. Skeleton accompanied by an arrow-head of white flint, and pieces of ornamented pottery.

9. Two skeletons, one that of an adult, the other that of a child a few months old.

10. Skeleton of an aged man with legs drawn up, accompanied by a handsome drinking cup 7¼ in. high, and a few chippings of flint.

11. This was a somewhat doubtful deposit near one end of the ellipse, consisting mainly of rats' bones, pebbles, and a long triangular flake of calcined flint.

12. Decayed bones including part of a skull were placed within a pentagonal cist, and covered by a broad and thin slab.

13. Skeleton of very young person, placed close to an upright flat stone, and accompanied by a flint chip.

14. Skull, much decayed, accompanied by one piece of burnt flint.

The great importance of this series of interments within one mound is obvious; and not the least remarkable feature is the cist containing the skeleton of a hog. This deposit, it will be noticed, occupies practically the central position in the barrow. It is impossible to resist the impression that this burial must have been closely associated with superstitions or religious beliefs of the ancient people who here buried their dead.

21. Wetton near Hill.—Two skeletons were found in this barrow, one being accompanied by a beautiful little earthen vase, 4½ in. high, with a fluted border and four perforated ears. Pieces of flint and a tine of stag's horn lay near.

22. Ilam.—In a barrow on the top of Hazleton Hill above Inkley Wood, and at the back of Ilam Hall, were found :—

1. A rock grave surrounded by flat stones placed on edge, and divided into two equal compartments by the same means, one containing calcined human bones, two inferior arrow-points of flint and a broken pebble, and the other containing wood ashes and a few pieces of bone.

2. A plain urn of thin pottery inverted over a few burnt bones which lay on a flat stone.

3. Pieces of a coarse urn, black ashes, burnt earth, a fine circular instrument, and numerous pieces of calcined flint, all contained in a depression in the earth.

4. A similar deposit surrounded by large stones containing a few calcined bones, a fine round instrument and chippings of flint, and a piece of lead weighing 3½ oz.

5. There were also found in the barrow four more circular instruments, numerous pebbles, and a piece of iron ore.

23. Gateham.—In a flat barrow near Gateham were found, under a broken urn with cheveron pattern in dotted lines, a few crumbling fragments of calcined bone.

24. Blore.—Barrow in a field called Nettles. On being opened there were found a deposit of calcined bones and a broken urn of red clay containing a small vase or incense cup. The larger vessel had a deep border ornamented with diagonal lines disposed in triangles in alternate directions.

Traces were also found of a later interment consisting of parts of an unburnt skeleton, a small iron ring, and the bottom of a kiln-baked vessel of blue clay turned on the potter's wheel.

25. Stanshope.—In a barrow here four different interments were discovered, viz. :—

1. Two deposits of calcined bones.
2. Calcined bones, two flint implements, and two bone needles.
3. Two skeletons buried in a kind of cist, and
4. A very large and coarse sepulchral urn inverted over a deposit of burnt bones.

The first and second interments had been made in natural clefts of rock.

26. Wetton.—In 1849 a very large cist was found in a barrow at Long Low, near Wetton, the stone-paved floor of which was covered from end to end with remains of human beings, bones of the ox, hog, deer, and dog, also three very finely chipped arrow-heads and many other pieces of calcined flint. The discovery was one of unusual interest and importance, and there was evidence that the remains discovered represented at least thirteen human beings, some being women.

The barrow evidently belonged to a period anterior to the discovery of metal, and may be regarded as a typical Neolithic sepulchral mound.

27. Ecton.—A barrow on Ecton Hill was opened and found to contain a deposit of burnt bones placed in a large urn, with a projecting border ornamented with diagonal lines.

28. Musden.—Fourth barrow. This was found to contain twelve interments.

29. Caldon Hill.—A third barrow opened here contained a broken, slightly ornamented cinerary urn and some burnt bones, beneath which was a small hole in the rock filled with charcoal. One arrow-head and some flint chippings were found in the barrow.

30. In a barrow on Calton Moor were found a cist with double walls of stones set on edge covered over by two larger slabs and inclosing a deposit of calcined bones accompanied by two burnt flint implements.

31. Mayfield Low, Mayfield.—This was a flat barrow, 18 yds. in diameter, containing a stone cist in which an urn was found.

32. Castern.—In a barrow situated between Bitchin Hill and Castern, 18 yds. in diameter, were found (1) the decayed skeleton of a young person, (2) a large skeleton lying on its left side in a contracted posture, at the bottom of an oval grave, (3) quite near the skeleton a highly polished stud of jet with two oblique holes meeting at an angle behind, (4) a small piece of calcined flint, (5) many rats' bones, and (6) the remains of a young person.

33. Grindon.—In the hamlet of Deepdale a barrow was opened containing the skeleton of a young person, some bones of a child, and broken pieces of a drinking cup.

34. Throwley.—Barrow containing large sepulchral urn with the mouth uppermost, in which were found a double-edged axe of basaltic stone, bronze awl, and bone pins, &c.

35. Blore.—Barrow called Lady Low containing deposit of calcined bones, arrow-head of flint, bone pin, and fragments of very thin bronze ;

also a small oval cavity suggestive of a wooden or wicker vessel long since decayed.

36. Throwley.—In a barrow at Throwley Moor, opened by Mr. Carrington in 1849, were found fragments of a large but plain, globular earthen vessel, perforated at the side with two small holes.

37. At Stanshope, a hamlet in the parish of Alstonfield, a barrow at Ram's Croft Field was opened, and in it were discovered several interments and flint implements, bronze dagger, earthern drinking cup, &c., indicative of the Bronze Age.

38. Wetton, Thor's Cave.—An interment of considerable importance was opened here. Near the centre, about a foot below the surface, two curious vessels were found ; one of rather globular form, 4 in. high, carved in sandstone, and ornamented by four grooves round the outside ; the other was a bronze pan or kettle, 4 in. high and 6 in. across, and was furnished with a slender iron bow like a bucket handle. It had been first cast and then hammered, and was found in an inverted position.

In addition to the above barrows, some important sepulchral deposits were found at Warslow, Elkstone, Sheen, and Leek, and fuller details than are here necessary may be found in Bateman's *Ten Years' Diggings*.

This important group of ancient burials in North Staffordshire, large as it is, may really be considered as part of the group in the adjoining county of Derby. The sepulchral pottery and other remains found in the course of the explorations of Mr. Thomas Bateman, his son Mr. William Bateman, F.S.A., and their antiquarian coadjutors, are now preserved as part of the Bateman Collection in the Public Museum, Weston Park, Sheffield.[2] The collection also comprises many antiquities of like character found under similar circumstances in Derbyshire and in the North Riding of Yorkshire.

Compared with the Derbyshire barrows, the Staffordshire interments afford proportionately a larger number of drinking-cups, some examples of which are figured in this article.

These vessels, known as 'drinking-cups,' are of peculiar interest from the fact that they usually occur with unburnt burials, and are sometimes found in association with implements of flint and polished stone. There is reason to believe that they represent the earliest type of pottery made by Bronze Age man in this country. The name 'drinking-cup' has been applied not as an indication of the purpose of this class of pottery, but simply to identify the form. Like 'incense-cup' and 'food-vessel,' it has been adopted as a convenient method of describing Bronze Age urns, &c., without any intention of defining their purpose. Vessels of the drinking-cup type occur throughout England, and particularly in Wiltshire, but they are not found in Ireland.

The methods of ornamentation are ingenious, consisting, as will be noticed in the accompanying plates, of horizontal lines running round the circumference of the vessels, and a series of zig-zags or cheveron-like markings, which appear in some cases to have been impressed in the moist clay by means of an instrument having a series of tooth-like projections. The result is a number of punctured marks, and this is particularly well

---

[2] The writer wishes to record his thanks for the permission of the museum authorities to inspect and photograph the objects found in Staffordshire.

shown on the vessel, 7 in. high, found in a barrow at Stanshope. Here the horizontal lines, as well as the rather roughly executed zigzags, have been produced with the same instrument.

Another interesting 'drinking-cup,' of even larger size, measuring 8¾ in. in height, found in a barrow at Castern, is represented beside the Stanshope specimen. The ornamentation, which is of the same general character, has been executed with far more care.

In the Mouse Low and Top Low examples the body of each urn is covered with a species of lozenge ornament produced by ingenious variations of the cheveron form. The four urns figured on this plate afford what, perhaps, may be taken as a chronological sequence in the appearance and development of the rim. In the Stanshope urn it is entirely wanting; it appears in the Castern cup as a bevel on the upper part sloping inwards; and in the two other specimens we find two stages of the appearance of a raised rib, and the development of breadth of rim.

The four vessels figured in the second plate furnish examples of types quite distinct from the 'drinking-cup' form. The Throwley 'incense-cup' is figured full-size, namely 2¼ in. high. Its ornamentation consists of both horizontal lines and roughly executed cheverons. The lip is well developed and projecting, and the outline has a character which suggests a somewhat late date. Just below the middle ridge of the body there are shown two holes pierced through the clay. Perforations of this kind, but proportionately larger and more numerous, are usually found in 'incense-cups,' and afford one of the reasons why this term was applied to them. This kind of small vessel is always found in association with burnt burials, and their geographical distribution corresponds with that of cinerary urns.

The three other urns figured belong to a type usually called 'food-vessels,' the predominant forms of which will be seen from the illustrations. The three specimens given are arranged, as far as may be, in order according to development, especially with regard to their outline, and the growth of hollows or grooves round the body. The decoration of the Mare Hill urn has obviously been produced by means of a sharp flat instrument, possibly a flake of flint, or a fragment of stone rubbed down for the purpose. The other urns are decorated with less care but in a similar manner. The occurrence of fragments of bone, the remains of a cremation, in the Narrow-dale Hill urn enables us to classify it with the grave furniture of a burnt burial, and it may therefore be regarded as a small cinerary urn made possibly to contain only a portion of the remains of the body.

These interesting pieces of pottery, apart from their antiquity and the information they give as to ancient interments, have a special value from the fact that they represent probably the very earliest efforts in the direction of the artistic decoration of pottery.

Amongst the antiquities of unquestionable Bronze Age character found in the county there are some of very great importance, although the finds cannot be considered remarkable numerically.

One of the more important discoveries was the hoard of bronze weapons found in the year 1824 at Shenstone. It comprised, according to the brief account published in *Archaeologia*,[3] 'two swords, some spear-heads, celts, and

[3] *Arch.* xxi, 548–9.

'Drinking Cup' (7 in. high), Stanshope

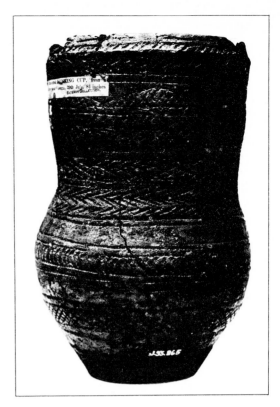

'Drinking Cup' (8¾ in. high), Castern

'Drinking Cup' (8¼ in. high), Mouse Low,
near Deepdale

'Drinking Cup' (7 in. high), Top Low,
near Swinscoe

Plate I : Bronze-Age Pottery found in Sepulchral Barrows

several reliques, all of bronze.' The discovery of 'fragments of human bones, and a piece of decayed wood about the size of two hands,' by labourers employed in digging out sand, suggested to the discoverers that the deposit was of a sepulchral character; indeed, the account communicated to the Society of Antiquaries of London expressly mentions 'a grave cut north and south in the sand-rock.' The explanation, apparently, is that a hoard of bronze objects was hidden during the Bronze Age on Greensborough Hill, a pleasant knoll overlooking an extensive tract of country. On the same natural hill, either before or after this period, a grave was cut into the ground, and some human remains were deposited therein.

Hoards of bronze objects, of which this affords an instance, are among the most valuable of the traces of this remote age which we possess. We may regard them, in certain respects, as of even greater importance than sepulchral deposits, partly from the fact that the contents are of a practically indestructible character, but mainly because they represent the collected valuables belonging to a worker or dealer in bronze. The archaeological value of associated objects of one definite period is, of course, very great, proving the contemporaneity of forms of tools, weapons, &c., in the earliest age of metal.

In addition to the Shenstone hoard there are several individual bronze objects worthy of note. Among them are :—

1. A bronze armilla, made of a flat piece of metal, half an inch in breadth, having on the outside a lozengy pattern engraved, found at Castern, near Wetton.
2. Another armlet (imperfect), made of thick bronze wire, found in a barrow at Wetton.
3. Bronze knife-daggers found at Lett Low, near Warslow; Musden; Lady Low Barrow, near Blore; and Stanshope.
4. Palstaves found at Brewood; Biddulph; Bushbury; and Stretton.
5. Bronze sword with seven rivet-holes found at Alton Castle.
6. A leaf-shaped spear-head found at Yarlet.

THE EARLY IRON AGE

Staffordshire has furnished only a few remains which can be with any certainty referred to this, the last period of prehistoric time. The introduction of iron as a material for making implements and weapons must have given an immense advantage to its possessors, and it marked a very distinct stage in the progress of human civilization. It is possible that the fewness of Early Iron Age discoveries in the county may be accounted for by the perishable nature of the newly-discovered or imported metal, but it is perhaps more particularly due to the comparative shortness of the period between the introduction of iron and the beginning of the historic period which dates from the appearance of the Romans.

Among the discoveries to be recorded is a leaf-shaped iron lance-head [4] found in 1895 at Stone,[5] in association with a flint flake, and bones of *Bos*

[4] Mr. Reginald A. Smith, F.S.A., who has kindly favoured the writer with his opinion on this lance-head, considers that, whilst the form of the blade resembles Anglo-Saxon workmanship, the unsplit socket is sufficient and conclusive evidence that it belongs to the Early Iron Age.
[5] *North Staffs. Nat. Field Club and Arch. Soc. Trans.* xxx, 108–15.

primigenius, *B. longifrons*, horse, red deer, sheep, and goat. These discoveries were made in the course of excavations for a deep-drainage scheme.

Another indication of this early period was found in the Late Celtic ornament on a bronze bowl found in an interment at the Upper House, Barlaston, soon after the year 1850. All the circumstances of the burial point to an Anglo-Saxon date, but the ornament certainly displays Late Celtic tradition.

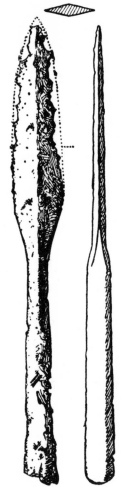

IRON LANCE-HEAD
FOUND AT STONE
($\frac{2}{3}$ Actual Size)

An interment in a barrow called Steep Low, near Alstonfield, which the late Mr. J. Romilly Allen considered to be of the Early Iron Age,[6] was discovered by Mr. Thomas Bateman in 1845. The barrow, a mound about 50 yds. in diameter, and 15 ft. in elevation in the centre, was constructed almost entirely of loose stones, a circumstance which made its exploration at once difficult and dangerous. Previously to the examination by Mr. Bateman the neighbouring villagers, in the course of searching for treasure, had found the skeleton of a—

> Romanized Briton, extended on its back, accompanied by an iron spear-head, a lance-head and knife of the same, placed near the head, and three Roman coins, in third brass, namely, one of Constantine the Great, one of Tetricus, the other illegible from the friction of sand-paper applied by the finder. . . . They also found some pieces of a highly-ornamental drinking-cup, a curious piece of iron ore, and various animal bones.[7]

In addition to these relics there were found (1) a small stud or circular ornament of amber, perforated with a double hole at the back for attachment, and (2) a large plain urn of globular form, with four holes through the upper edge, and containing burnt human bones, two quartz pebbles, and a piece of flint.

Two important gold collars or torques have been found in the county; one at Pattingham in 1700, measuring 2 ft. in length, and weighing 3 lb. 2 oz., and another at Hanbury in 1848, which is now in the royal collections at Windsor Castle.

The writer desires to express his thanks for kind assistance to Mr. Charles Lynam, F.S.A., and Mr. Reginald A. Smith, B.A., F.S.A.

TOPOGRAPHICAL LIST

Arch. Journ. = *Archaeological Journal.*
Arch. = *Archaeologia.*
Evans, *Bronze Imp.* = *Ancient Bronze Implements*, &c. By Sir John Evans.
Evans, *Brit. Coins* = *Ancient British Coins.* By Sir John Evans.
Evans, *Stone Imp.* = *Ancient Stone Implements*, 2nd ed. By Sir John Evans.

ALTON.—Perforated stone axe-hammer, in the possession of Mr. Walker of Alton.
ALTON Castle.—Bronze sword with seven rivet-holes. [*Arch.* xi, 431 ; Evans, *Bronze Imp.* 282.]
BARLASTON.—Bronze bowl with late Celtic ornamentation. [*Arch.* lvi, 44, 45.]

[6] *Celtic Art*, 68.
[7] *Vestiges of the Antiq. of Derb.* 76-7.

'INCENSE CUP' (2¼ in. high), THROWLEY

URN ['FOOD VESSEL'?] (5 in. high), MARE HILL

'FOOD VESSEL' (6 in. high), WETTON HILL

URN CONTAINING BONES (5½ in. high), NARROWDALE HILL
NEAR ALSTONFIELD

PLATE II : BRONZE-AGE POTTERY FOUND IN SEPULCHRAL BARROWS

BERESFORD HALL.—Barbed flint arrow-head. [Plot, *Nat. Hist. of Staffs.* 396.]

Socketed chisel, or celt of bronze. [Plot, *Nat. Hist. of Staffs.* 404.]

BREWOOD.—Palstave, without loops. [Plot, *Nat. Hist. of Staffs.* 403 ; Evans, *Bronze Imp.* 86.]

BUSHBURY.—Palstave, without loops. [Plot, *Nat. Hist. of Staffs.* 403 ; Evans, *Bronze Imp.* 86.]

CALDON.—Neolithic flint celts.

CASTERN.—Piece of sandstone rubbed hollow on one side, found in barrow. Jet button, 1¾ in. in diameter, found in barrow. [Evans, *Stone Imp.* 263, 455.]

Bronze armilla, found in barrow. [Bateman, *Ten Years' Diggings*, 167.]

CHEADLE.—Stone celt found in a peat bog.

ELKSTONE.—Large piece of sandstone, with a small bowl-shaped concavity worked in it (? Neolithic), found in a barrow. [Evans, *Stone Imp.* 253.]

GRUB LOW (situated between Grindon and Waterfall).—Leaf-shaped arrow-head of flint, found with bones in a barrow. [Evans, *Stone Imp.* 377.]

HANBURY.—Fine gold collar made of seven strands of twisted wire uniting in a loop at each termination, found in 1848, and now in the royal collection at Windsor Castle. [*Arch.* xxxix, 175–6.]

HANDSWORTH.—Bronze palstave without loops, described by Plot [*Nat. Hist. of Staffs.* 403] as the 'brass head of the *bolt* of a Catapulta.'

ILAM.—Plain bronze celt, described by Plot [*Nat. Hist. of Staffs.* 403–4] as the 'Head of a Roman *Securis* with which the popae slew their sacrifices.' [Evans, *Bronze Imp.* 42.]

At ILAM MOOR.—Bronze awl found in barrow. [Evans, *Bronze Imp.* 190.]

LADY LOW.—Small bronze blade found in barrow. [*Arch.* xliii, pl. xxxiii, fig. 4.]

Bronze dagger found in barrow. [Evans, *Bronze Imp.* 224.]

LEEK.—Flint arrow-head, with jagged edges and two barbs, found near Leek. [Plot, *Nat. Hist. of Staffs.* 396 ; Evans, *Stone Imp.* 362.]

LEIGH.—Bronze celt, or axe-head found at the foot of a rounded eminence. [*Trans. N. Staffs. Field Club*, xxxix, 141.]

MILWICH.—Stone celt or hatchet, 7 in. long, found in a stream.

MORRIDGE.—Bronze palstave without loop, found in a barrow. [Plot, *Nat. Hist. of Staffs.* 403 ; Evans, *Bronze Imp.* 86.]

MOUSE LOW.—Flint arrow-head (? Neolithic), found in Bronze Age drinking-cup. [Evans, *Stone Imp.* 399 ; Bateman, *Ten Years' Diggings*, 116.]

Bone pins, found with two bashed flint arrow-heads. [Evans, *Stone Imp.* 432].

MUSDEN.—Trimmed flint flake, flat on one face and carefully chipped to a convex shape on the other, found in barrow ; probably a knife of the Bronze Age. [Evans, *Stone Imp.* 330.]

Bronze knife-dagger found in barrow. [Evans, *Bronze Imp.* 240.]

NEEDWOOD FOREST.—Polished flint celt and Bronze Age palstave, with loop (broken), found in 1864, both now in the British Museum.

PATTINGHAM.—Gold torque, found in 1700. [Camden, *Brit.* (ed. Gough, 1789), ii, 380 ; *Arch.* xxxiii, 176.]

RIBDEN LOW.—Flint knife, probably of the Bronze Age, found in barrow ; also barbed flint arrow-heads and bone pins found in barrow. [Evans, *Stone Imp.* 330, 432.]

SAXON LOW.—Fragments of Bronze Age urns, now in the possession of Mr. Charles Lynam, F.S.A.

SHARPCLIFFE, NEAR LEEK.—Perforated boulder or pebble, stone maul, and bronze (or rather nearly pure copper) palstave, with curiously narrow blade.

SHENSTONE.—Hoard of bronze objects, comprising two swords, some spear-heads, celts, and several other relics, found at Greensborough Hill, lying in loose sand. [*Arch.* xxi, 548–9.]

STAFFORDSHIRE, LID LOW.—Fragments of a Bronze Age urn, now in the British Museum.

STONE.—Fine perforated axe-head of granite, 12 in. long, now in the British Museum. [Evans, *Stone Imp.* 202].

Early Iron Age leaf-shaped lance-head. [*N. Staffs. Nat. Field Club Trans.* xxx, 108–15.]

STRETTON.—Bronze palstave with one loop. [*Arch.* v, 113.]

TRENTHAM.—Neolithic celt, now in the possession of Mr. Masefield.

WARSLOW.—Bronze knife-dagger found in Lett Low, a barrow. [Evans, *Bronze Imp.* 225.]

WATERHOUSES.—Socketed and looped bronze celt, now in the British Museum.

WETTON LONG LOW.—Three leaf-shaped arrow-heads and many flakes of flint. [Evans, *Stone Imp.* 377.] Imperfect armlet of thick bronze.

——THOR'S CAVE.—Two curious vessels, one of carved sandstone, and one of cast and hammered bronze, with iron handle, found in barrow. [Evans, *Stone Imp.* 451 ; Evans, *Bronze Imp.* 409 ; Bateman, *Ten Years' Diggings*, 173.]

WEAVER HILLS, between Ramshorn and Blore.—Stone axe, entirely ground, and the sides having an inward curvature. [Plot, *Nat. Hist. of Staffs.* 397.]

YARLET.—Socketed bronze spear-head. [Plot, *Nat. Hist. of Staffs.* 404, pl. xxxiii, fig. 8.]

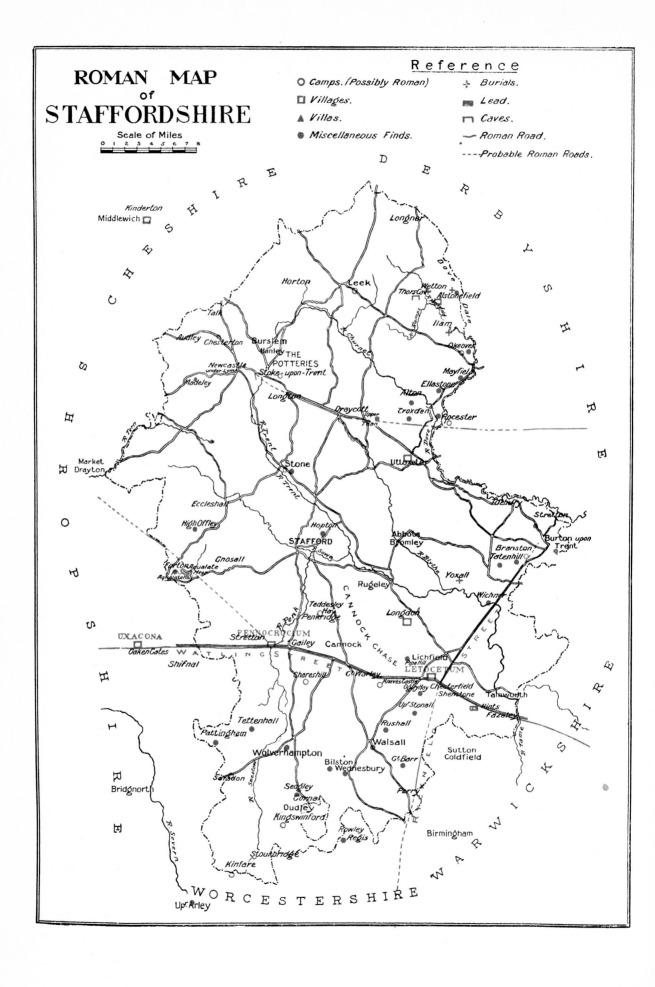

ROMAN MAP
of
STAFFORDSHIRE

Scale of Miles
0 1 2 3 4 5 6 7 8

Reference

○ Camps. (Possibly Roman)   + Burials.
□ Villages.   Lead.
▲ Villas.   ⊓ Caves.
● Miscellaneous Finds.   Roman Road.
                          ---- Probable Roman Roads.

ROMANO-BRITISH STAFFORDSHIRE

DURING the period of the Roman occupation of Britain there were no districts which correspond to our present counties. Neither the boundaries of the British tribes nor those of the Roman administrative areas, as far as we know them, agree exactly with existing county boundaries.[1]   At the time of the Roman invasion the greater part of Staffordshire was most probably inhabited by the Cornavii, a British tribe whose territory, we learn from Ptolemy, writing about A.D. 120, included Deva (Chester), and Viroconium (Wroxeter).[2]

The Roman occupation under the Emperor Claudius began in A.D. 43 ; at first the subjugation of the country was comparatively easy. A strong foot-hold was obtained in Kent and Essex, and then the army was formed into three divisions, the Second Legion going south-west towards Somerset and Devon, the Fourteenth and Twentieth Legions north-west towards Shrewsbury and Chester, and the Ninth Legion north towards Lincoln. Professor Haverfield, in writing of this period, divides Britain into two districts ;[3] the lowlands, comprising the southern, south-western, and eastern districts up to the Humber he describes as civilian ; whilst the uplands, including the northern and western districts, he describes as military. The former, including probably the southern and middle parts of Staffordshire, was occupied by A.D. 47 or 48, and the latter, possibly comprising the northern part of the county, which partakes of the characteristics of Derbyshire, was subjugated about A.D. 48 or shortly afterwards.

There can be little doubt that at the time of the Roman occupation of Britain, Staffordshire was woodland or waste, and thinly populated. For this reason the Romano-British period as regards this district has little history. The county is mostly hilly. In the north it rises in places to 1,500 ft. ; in the middle it is undulating and was formerly forest ; to the south it is again hilly. By the Romans it would have been thought unattractive and inhospitable, and it therefore became to them merely a portion of territory through which roads and waterways passed across Britain. Except in the extreme north of the county few, if any, Roman remains have been found away from the great highways—the roads and the rivers.

[1] Much of the information contained in this article has been taken from Professor Haverfield's contributions on ' Roman Remains ' to the volumes of this series.

[2] Ptolemy, *Geographia* (ed. Firmin Didot, 1883), i, 99.   There is no satisfactory evidence that the Cornavii also inhabited Warwickshire, Worcestershire, and part of Derbyshire, as stated by Camden, Horsley, and Baxter. See as to this point Camden, *Brit.* (ed. Gough) ; Horsley, *Brit. Rom.* 368 ; Baxter, *Glossarium Antiquitatum Brit.* (1709), 73 ; Haverfield, in *V.C.H. Warw.* i, 229.

[3] *V.C.H. Derb.* i, 192.

The iron and coal fields of Staffordshire, which attract so large a population in the present day, were little if at all known during the Roman occupation. Iron ore was possibly smelted in the district during the late Celtic age, in evidence of which some smelted ore has been found in barrows, probably of this date, at Alstonfield and elsewhere,[4] but nothing has hitherto been discovered to indicate that it was worked here in the Romano-British period. The Romans apparently used coal as fuel in this country, but there is no evidence that the Staffordshire coalfields were known to them.

Lead-mining was carried on actively in Derbyshire by the Romans, and there is some evidence that this mineral was worked in the northern part of Staffordshire, which forms a portion of the same beds. At Wetton there appears to have been a Romano-British village where lead ore and the remains of a smelting furnace are said to have been found.[5] This village, being within the lead-mining district, may have been a miners' settlement, and from the objects found in it the inhabitants appear to have been poor and probably of the labouring class. One pig of lead was discovered beside Watling Street, at Hints in the south-east of the county, but from the inscription upon it there is no doubt that it came from the Flintshire mines and had no connexion with the locality in which it was found.[6]

What is now known as potter's clay is not found in Staffordshire, and though there can be little doubt that clays indigenous to the county were used for pottery discovered at Viroconium and on other Roman sites,[7] there is no evidence in favour of its local manufacture on any considerable scale, as at Castor in Northamptonshire, or at Upchurch, and in the New Forest. It has been thought that indications of ancient kilns have been discovered at Burslem, but whether they were Roman is altogether uncertain. Pieces of rough pottery are said to have been found in digging foundations in the neighbourhood, but again there is no certainty as to their Romano-British origin.[8]

We are no better off with regard to the agricultural resources of the middle and south of the county. As yet there have been found none of the villas so frequently discovered in the south of England, which formed the country houses of the wealthy, and the farm-houses of the agricultural class.

The most important of the permanent settlements of the Romano-British period in the county is Letocetum—often, but incorrectly, called Etocetum—now Wall, at the crossing of Watling Street and Rycknield Street. From the remains found this would appear to have been one of the more important 'stations' along Watling Street, and perhaps even a small walled town with buildings of considerable size.

The actual site of Pennocrucium, a station on Watling Street which is placed at Stretton, is not definitely known, and there is nothing apparently above ground to indicate its position. It was probably only a small posting station, such as existed elsewhere along the Roman roads, without masonry walls or earthworks. The name survives in Penk and Penkridge. At Chesterton there is a large camp which may have formed a

[4] Bateman, *Vestiges*, 76, 77, &c.
[5] Bateman, *Ten Years' Diggings*, 194–6 ; Carrington, *Reliq.* v, 201 ; *Intellectual Observer*, vii, 391.
[6] See Hints in Topog. Index.
[7] Wright, *Celt. Rom. Sax.* ; Jewitt, *Ceramic Art in Great Brit.* 32.
[8] Aikins, *Hist. Manchester*, 524–6 ; Ward, *Hist. Stoke-on-Trent*, 24.

station on the conjectured Roman road from Derby, which runs through Stoke-upon-Trent and continues in a north-easterly direction. At Rocester is another Roman site near the same road. Romano-British villages existed at Wetton and Uttoxeter, and a settlement probably adjoined the cemetery discovered at Yoxall. There are some indefinite records of settlements at Madeley and Tettenhall, but they are too vague to enable an opinion to be formed regarding them. Besides these there are numerous camps generally attributed to the Roman period which appear mostly to lie in the valleys of the rivers. Along the western side of the River Dove below Dovedale there are camps at Okeover, Rocester, and Uttoxeter; in the Trent valley, at Stoke-upon-Trent and Stone; in the valley of the Churnet, at Leek; in the valley of the Penk, at Teddesley Hay and Shareshill; in the valley of the Stour, at Kinver and Kingswinford; and in the valley of the Smestow River at Seisdon. These may possibly have been used during the early part of the Roman occupation and afterwards abandoned, or may have been Romano-British villages. But most of them probably are not Roman at all, and in hardly any have Roman objects been found. The spade alone can decide their origin and use.

The limestone region on the border of Derbyshire contains numerous caves of various forms and sizes, which have at different times provided habitations for men or beasts. The best known of these belong to pre-historic ages, but a few of them have been found to contain in the upper and lower strata of their floors traces of habitation dating from the Roman period.[9] The most important of such caves in Staffordshire are ' Thor's Cave,'[10] near Wetton, 'Thirse House' at Alton, and that known locally as 'Old Hannah's Cave' near Redhurst.[11] The explanation usually offered of the cave life of the Romano-British period is that fugitives took refuge in these caves in the fifth or sixth century, when fleeing from the English invaders.[12] But, as Professor Haverfield has pointed out, the evidence of date from the remains found contradicts this theory, as hardly a trace occurs of anything later than the third century. The objects also in the more important caves imply a tolerably long occupation, and a more plausible explanation is that in some hill districts cave life formed a feature of Romano-British civilization. Here, apparently, some of the poorest and wildest of the hill-men lived, probably largely on robbery. Plot mentions that as late as 1680 Thirse House Cave at Alton or Alveton was definitely occupied, and doubtless many parallels could be cited from even later ages.[13]

Sepulchral mounds or barrows exist in great numbers over Staffordshire. Many were scientifically excavated by Mr. Bateman and Mr. Carrington between 1848 and 1858. In these tumuli were found numerous varieties of remains, chiefly Celtic, but including a sufficient number of Roman objects to show that the barrows were occasionally used, or perhaps re-used, for sepulchral purposes during the Roman period.[14]

Only four hoards of coins have been recorded in the county, one at Tatenhill of thirty gold coins dating from B.C. 29 to A.D. 96; one at Rowley

[9] *V.C.H. Derb.* i, 233.
[10] See Wetton in Topog. Index.
[11] *N. Staffs. Field Club,* xxxiii, 105.
[12] Green, *Making of Engl.* 67–68.
[13] Haverfield in *V.C.H. Derb.* i, 242. Besides the caves in Derbyshire and Staffordshire others occur in the limestone hills of Craven in West Yorkshire, also near Arncliffe, Settle, and Giggleswick, and two in Devonshire.
[14] Bateman, *Ten Years' Diggings,* Int. xii, xiii.

Regis, of over a thousand silver coins, covering the 'whole period' of the Roman occupation ; one at Madeley of late copper coins, from A.D. 235 to 340 ; and one at Mayfield, which was dispersed and the coins unidentified. Three gold coins were found at Alton dating from A.D. 70 to A.D. 96. No very definite information can be deduced from these particular finds beyond the fact that the Romans probably occupied this part of the country from an early period.

A reference should perhaps be made to the theory which has been put forward[15] that a line of forts was built between the Dove and the Severn by Ostorius Scapula after the campaign of A.D. 50, which line formed the *Limes Britannicus* of the *Notitia*.[16] This *limes* consisted of a supposed chain of stations with a connecting road, and an occasional raised earthwork or wall for further defence. The most important evidence of the link between the various stations is the Grey Ditch at Bradwell in Derbyshire, considerable traces of a *vallum* on a hill called Gun above Leek in Staffordshire, and of a *vallum* or raised road in the neighbourhood of Ranton Abbey. Leek is identified as the Concangios of the *Notitia*, Stone as Lavatres, Gnosall as Veterum or Veteris, and Shifnal as Braboniacum. Professor Haverfield, however, states that the Grey Ditch is not Roman,[17] and it is plain that Lavatres, Veteris, and Braboniacum probably represent Lavatris, Verteris, and Bravonacis, three stations in the second Iter of Antoninus which lay between Isurium (Aldborough in Yorkshire) and Carlisle, and must have been far removed from Staffordshire. Professor Haverfield has further shown that the whole theory of the Ostorian forts has been founded upon a corrupt text and bad translation of Tacitus. The passage referred to does not relate to a line of forts, but probably to a consolidation of the Roman dominion within the frontiers of the Severn and Trent.[18]

THE ROADS

There are two sources from which evidence of Roman roads can be obtained, namely, archaeological and literary. The first of these is supplied by the actual remains, such as Roman milestones or ancient metalling, and occasionally by the persistent straightness with which a road runs from one Roman site to another. The written evidence is principally obtained from the *Itinerarium Antonini*, a Roman road-book which gives the distances between the 'stations' on the various routes in the empire. The date of this work is uncertain. Only one of the routes mentioned in this itinerary passes through Staffordshire, and that is the well-known Roman road called, since the Saxon period, Watling Street. There are also portions of the Rycknield or Icknield Street, and a road running from Derby possibly to Chester. Besides these there are certain roads which have been suggested as Roman, some of which are probable, but there appears to be insufficient evidence for the others.

1. *Watling Street.*—This road forms a part of the second Iter of the Antonine itineraries. It starts from the Roman port of Richborough in Kent and runs in a north-westerly direction through London and the Midlands to

[15] The Rev. T. Barns in *Antiq.* xxxviii, 337 et seq.
[16] *Notitia Dignitatum* (ed. O. Seeck, 1876).   [17] *V.C.H. Derb.* i, 255.
[18] Tacitus, *Ann.* xii, 31 ; H. Bradley, *Academy*, April, July, 1883 ; *V.C.H. Somers.* i, 217 ; *V.C.H. Northants*, i, 213.

Wroxeter. Its course is definite almost throughout its length, being used at the present day as one of the main highways across England. After leaving Viroconium (Wroxeter) it runs to Uxacona (probably Oakengates in Shropshire), eleven Roman miles; thence to Pennocrucium (which has been identified with Stretton where the road crosses the River Penk), a distance of twelve Roman miles, which corresponds approximately with the actual distance. The next station from Pennocrucium is Letocetum or Etocetum (Wall), according to the itinerary a distance of twelve Roman miles, which, if the identification of Pennocrucium with Stretton is correct, is too short, the actual distance being about thirteen and a quarter English miles or fifteen Roman miles. A little to the east of Wall Watling Street crosses Rycknield Street. From Letocetum the road runs to Manduessedum (Mancetter in Warwickshire), and so on in a south-easterly direction. Throughout its course in Staffordshire Watling Street runs from point to point in straight lines; that is to say from Oakengates to Gailey, 2 miles east of Stretton, it runs almost due east and west. From Gailey it turns slightly southward to Wyrley Common and Knaves Castle, and then again turns almost due east and west to Wall. At this point its course is not quite certain, the existing road called Watling Street from the south-east joins the Rycknield Street about three-quarters of a mile south of Wall, but apparently the Roman road turned in a south-easterly direction a quarter of a mile east of Wall, following the line of an existing footpath, and joined the present road at Lawton Grange, continuing in a straight line to Hints. It there takes another turn in a slightly less southerly direction to the county boundary at Fazeley.[1] On the 25-in. Ordnance map the position of a stone to the south-east of Wall is marked which is supposed to indicate the intersection of Watling Street and Rycknield Street.

2. *Rycknield* or *Icknield Street*.—This road starts from the Fosse at Bourton-on-the-Water in Gloucestershire, running through Alcester and Birmingham, where it enters what is now the county of Stafford. Its course in this county does not exist as a modern road to the south of Kettle House in Perry. From this point it runs for approximately four miles in an almost straight line to the park of Little Aston Hall, and for about two miles of this distance it forms the county boundary. A piece of it, about a quarter of a mile in length, is found slightly to the north at Little Aston, where again it is lost till another small portion of it is apparent at Shenstone in a short straight piece of road about half a mile in length, running from the Waterworks northward towards Chesterfield. Here again it is lost, but it probably crossed Watling Street at the point where the site of a stone before referred to is shown on the Ordnance maps, and thence in a straight line to Knowle Farm, where it changes its direction a little to the east, and continues in a straight line to Branston, where its course is again lost for about two and a half miles. It is, however, found again to the north of Burton-on-Trent, whence it runs in the same straight line to the county boundary, crossing the River Dove at Monks Bridge and keeping a direct course to Derby. At Wichnor Bridges the road was formed on piles over the marshy meadows, and when in 1795 these bridges were destroyed by a flood the road was washed away, leaving the piles exposed.[2] It is of course not wholly certain that these

---

[1] Codrington, *Rom. Roads in Britain*, 75–6 ; Pitt, *Hist. Staffs.* i, 3.
[2] Stebbing Shaw, *Hist. Staffs.* i, 18, 125 ; Pennant, *Journey from Chester to London*, 121–3.

piles date so far back as the Roman period. There is no indication of a station between Wall and Derby, a distance of about twenty-four miles, but not being one of the Antonine routes we have little information in this respect regarding it. At Sutton Coldfield, where it forms the boundary between the counties of Stafford and Warwick, it was in 1752 said to be in its original condition, and was described as

> a very spacious road, not less than sixty feet in breadth, though the surface be in general over-run with heath, and for a short space in the park overspread with oaks of considerable magnitude . . . It is formed by gravel and materials on the spot, high raised in the centre, —the preservation wonderful—owing to its not being a public road.[3]

3. *Road from Derby to Stoke-upon-Trent.*—This road, which has also been called Rycknield Street,[4] apparently follows an almost straight line from Derby past Rocester to Totmonslow near Draycott-in-the-Moors, and then turns slightly northward to Stoke-upon-Trent, from which point its course is lost. An ancient boulder pavement was found at Stoke-upon-Trent in 1903[5] at the junction of the London Road and High Street which probably formed a part of this road.

4. *Probable road from Stretton to the Longford Road.*—There are indications of a Roman road running apparently from Whitchurch in Shropshire to Stretton, identified as Pennocrucium on Watling Street, which would have formed a short cut to Chester. Certain traces of it are found in the long straight piece of road called the Long Ford, running from Bletchley near Market Drayton to Hinstock in Shropshire. It is here lost for nearly two miles, and then forms the county boundary between Shropshire and Staffordshire for about three miles. Its course is again lost, but it probably passed to the north of Aqualate Mere in Forton parish by Rye Mill to a point near to Longnor Hall, where there is a straight road of about three miles in length which joins Watling Street at Stretton.[6]

English antiquaries have often laid down on their maps and in their books a 'Via Devana' running more or less directly from Colchester by Cambridge and Huntingdon to Leicester, and finally to Chester, the Roman fortress of Deva. There is no evidence of the existence of this supposed 'through-route' across Britain, and the name 'Via Devana' is a modern invention. Parts of the route may be accepted as independent roads of really Roman origin,[7] and it has been suggested that this way crossed Staffordshire from Burton-upon-Trent, through Needwood Forest to Uttoxeter, thence to Longton and Chesterton, and so on to Chester. There does not seem, however, to be any evidence of this road in the county.[8]

Other supposed Roman roads are one from Wroxeter to Chesterton, and another from Chester to Chesterton. The existence of these roads has been suggested by reason of the identification of Chesterton with the Antonine station of Mediolanum, mentioned in the second and tenth itineraries. But the exact site of Mediolanum referred to in the second itinerary is quite

---

[3] Stebbing Shaw, *Hist. Staffs.* i, 18. For the name of the road, Rycknield or Icknield Street, see Professor Haverfield's notes in *V.H.C. Warw.* i, 241 ; *V.C.H. Derb.* i, 245–6.
[4] Molyneux, *Journ. Brit. Arch. Assoc.* xxix, 288 ; *V.C.H. Derb.* i, 246.
[5] *North Staffs. Field Club,* xxxviii, 159.
[6] See *V.C.H. Shrops.* i, section on Roman roads, for a further account.
[7] *V.C.H. Northants.* i, 207.
[8] Molyneux, *Journ. Brit. Arch. Assoc.* xxix, 288.

unknown. It is impossible that it can have been situated at Chesterton, as by the course of the itinerary it must have been somewhere to the west in Shropshire. The reason for identifying Mediolanum of the tenth itinerary with Chesterton is that its position agrees approximately with the distance given by Antoninus (nineteen Roman miles) from Condate (Kinderton in Cheshire), the previous station; but it is improbable that there should have been two stations of the same name comparatively near to one another.[9] The remains as yet discovered at Chesterton do not indicate more than the existence of a large rectangular camp of an (as yet) undetermined age, lying on the west side of the road leading from Audley to Newcastle-under-Lyme, here called Newcastle Street, which road may here be part of a Roman highway from Stoke-upon-Trent to Kinderton. The evidence as to its identification with Mediolanum, however, is wholly inconclusive.

INDEX

---

[9] There is probably an error in the distance in this section of the second itinerary (*V.C.H. Shrops.* i, 'Roman Remains'). The Mediolanum of the second iter was on the road from Viroconium (Wroxeter) to Deva (Chester) between Rutunium near Roden in Shropshire and Bovium, probably near to Stretton in Cheshire. Mediolanum was described by Ptolemy as a town of the Ordovices, which would also place it west of Staffordshire. See further Chesterton in Topog. Index.

to be inadequate. The name alone is suggestive of Roman origin. The north *vallum* and fosse still remain, and the east and west defences can be traced [*Journ. Brit. Arch. Assoc.* (New Ser.), ii, 121 et seq.]. The camp forms a parallelogram measuring 365 yds. by 300 yds. (outside measure), and incloses upwards of 20 acres, the ditch being about 20 yds. wide. So far as is known no Roman or other relics have been found on the site. Erdeswick, writing about 1603, mentions remains of masonry which were to be seen in his time in sufficiently good preservation for it to be perceived 'that the walls have been of marvellous thickness' [Erdeswick, *Surv. of Staffs.* (ed. Harwood, 1844), 22]. The site was excavated in 1905, and the only result was the finding of some pieces of flat red sandstone joined with mortar. Mr. Charles Lynam, however, does not seem to have considered that the mortar was Roman [*Journ. Brit. Arch. Assoc.* (Ser. 2), ii, 121 et seq.].

CROXDEN.—Roman remains are reported to have been turned up on a farm about three-quarters of a mile south-east of Croxden Abbey. The supposed Roman road between Hollington and Rocester is not far from this place [*Antiq.* xxviii, 255].

ELLASTONE.—Some gold coins of the Roman period are said to have been found near Wootton Lodge [Stebbing Shaw, *Hist. Staffs.* i, 32].

FORTON.—Plot and Camden record 'some Roman works' at Moreton, not far from this place. The Ordnance map marks a Roman well on the north side of the mere called Aqualate in this parish [Plot, *Nat. Hist. Staffs.* 395 ; Camden, *Brit.* (ed. Gough), ii, 380 ; *Antiq.* xxviii, 255]. At Oulton, about a mile off, some arms were found which it has been suggested were Roman [Pitt, *Hist. Staffs.* i, 275].

GREAT BARR.—On Hardwick Farm, about half a mile from the Icknield Street, was found the boss or umbo of a shield, thought to be Roman. It was made of bronze ornamented with embossed figures, and measured about 2 in. across [Willmore, *Hist. Walsall*, 25].

GREENSFORGE.—(See KINGSWINFORD.)

GOURNAL.—(See SEDGLEY.)

HAWKBACK.—(See UPPER ARELEY.)

HINTS.—In 1771 a pig of lead was discovered on Hints Common, with the following inscription on the bottom, in relief : IMP. VESP. VII. T. IMP. V. COS. (Imperatore Vespasiano septimum. Tito Imperatore quintum, Consulibus). On the side, DECEAN. G. The date would have been about A.D. 76. The letters on the side are thought to refer to the *Deceangi*, a tribe which inhabited the district about the county of Flint, and the pig is, therefore, supposed, with others found in different parts of the country, to have come from that locality. The weight is 150 lb., the length 22½ in., and it was found at a depth of 4 ft. below the surface. It is now in the British Museum [*Gent. Mag.* (1772), p. 558 ; (1773), p. 61 ; Camden, *Brit.* (ed. Gough), ii, 382 ; Hübner, *Corpus Inscrip.* vii, 1205 ; *Arch.* v, 371 ; lvii, 402 ; *Arch. Journ.* xvi, 28 ; Haverfield, *Proc. Soc. Antiq.* (Ser. 2), xv, 187 ; Pitt, *Hist. Staffs.* i, 164 ; Stebbing Shaw, *Hist. Staffs.* i, 331].

HOPTON.—An iron spear-head was found when making a road near Hopton in 1792 which Bateman thought to be Roman [Bateman, op. cit. 10].

ILAM.—In 1845 two barrows known as Bitchenhill Harbour, between Wetton and Ilam, were opened. In one was found the remains of an urn of coarse pottery with a deposit of burnt bones, and a third brass of Constantine the Great (A.D. 291–306) [Bateman, op. cit. 81]. A small barrow called 'Green Low' in the hamlet of Castern was opened in 1860. It was in the same field as a larger one excavated in 1846, which was not thought to contain anything Roman. In 'Green Low' several articles of different periods were found ; a green hone celt, a round-ended flint, a piece of coarse pottery, and a very perfect harp-shaped bronze *fibula*, said to be of a Roman type. These articles appeared to be independent of each other or of any interment. In another cutting the skeleton of a child with a flint arrow point was discovered, and in a third trench another juvenile skeleton. Pieces of stags' horns, animals' teeth, rats' bones, numerous pebbles and flints were also found [Bateman, *Ten Years' Diggings*, 116 ; *Ante*, 'Early Man'].

KINGSWINFORD.—There is said to be a Roman camp, on the level ground called Ashwood Heath, near Greensforge, in the parish of Kingswinford. It is square, easily to be traced, and lies on the south-east side of the road. It measures 206 yds. in length and 160 yds. in width, containing an area of 6¾ acres, and is surrounded by a single ditch [O.S. Staffordshire, 25 in., lxx, 4]. It used to be known as 'Wolverhampton Church Yard.' The road crosses it, and the western side is the most perfect. Coins have been found in the locality. The camp at Chesterton in Shropshire, on the same road, is said to resemble it very closely [*Ante*, 'Ancient Earthworks' ; Camden, *Brit.* (add. by Gough), ii, 380 ; Plot, *Nat. Hist. Staffs.* 406 ; Erdeswick, *Survey of Staffs.* 374 ; Cox, *Mag. Brit.* v, 35, 46 ; Stebbing Shaw, *Hist. Staffs.* ii, 233 ; Pitt, *Hist. Staffs.* i, 5, 193].

KINVER.—On the height known as 'Kinver Edge' half a mile east of the village, are the remains of an encampment of oblong form measuring 300 yds. by 180 yds., with a single ditch [*Post*, 'Anct. Earthworks']. It is supposed to be Roman, but there is no record of Roman remains having been found within it [O.S. Staffordshire, 25 in. lxx, 15]. Near it is a large square stone about 6 ft. in height and 12 ft. in circumference, tapering towards the top, where it is divided into three. It is known as the 'Barton,' 'Boltstone,' or 'Battlestone,' and is generally considered Celtic, like the 'Devil's Bolts' in Yorkshire, or 'Devil's Coits' in Oxfordshire. Mr. Coote suggests, however, that it was an *agrimensura* or terminal stone [Coote, *Romans of Britain*, 98; Stebbing Shaw, *Hist. Staffs.* i, 22, 37, 263; Pitt, *Hist. Staffs.* i, 197; Cox, *Mag. Brit.* v, 33; Camden, *Brit.* (adds. by Gough), ii, 381]. There are no records of coins or other remains discovered in the neighbourhood.

LEEK.—There are traces of an entrenched camp of an oblong shape, with rectangular corners, in the fields to the east of Abbey or Abbey Green Farm, at a little distance from the town [*Antiq.* xxxviii, 337 (1902)]. On the top of a hill called 'Gun,' about 1½ miles from the abbey, is another square entrenchment, said to be Roman, but the identification of both sites is very problematical [*Antiq.* xxxviii, 359; *Staffs. Field Club* (1902-3), xxxviii, 150]. Several relics, thought to be pieces of Roman armour, &c., have been found near the town [Kelly, *Dir.* 224].

LICHFIELD.—A tradition exists that 'Christianfield,' near Stitchbrook, was the supposed scene of the execution of 1,000 martyrs during the persecution of Maximian (A.D. 286), but no evidence can be adduced in support of this legend. At Pipe Hill, between Wall (q.v.) and Lichfield, are the remains of what is called a 'barricade,' said to be of the Roman period [Plot, *Nat. Hist. Staffs.* 398-9]. It is made of the whole trunks of oak trees, fixed at some depth in the ground. The upper part had, of course, vanished, but a great deal of the lower part was found intact, the wood being quite black, uniform in length and shape, the marks of the axe being still visible. From some which had apparently fallen and remained whole under the surface, it was concluded that the height was 12 ft., the largest diameter being from 12 in. to 14 in., and it is said to have been flanked with bastions. Each piece of timber had a cavity 4 in. wide, 3 ft. from the top, cut down its middle. The barricade was traced for 500 yards, not quite straight, so as to include a natural swell or bank of earth. Palisades as defences were, however, used for a considerable time before and after the Roman occupation of Britain, and the structure was possibly of a date later than the Roman occupation. A copper coin of Hadrian (A.D. 120) was found on the site [MS. Min. Soc. Antiq. xxvi, 317 (1794); Erdeswick, *Surv. of Staffs.* (ed. Harwood), 302; Pitt, *Hist. Staffs.* i, 128; Stebbing Shaw, *Hist. Staffs.* i, 19].

LONGDON.—To the north-east of Longdon Church are traces of a fortification thought to be Roman, the east and west sides being still apparent [Plot, *Nat. Hist. Staffs*, 406; Cox, *Mag. Brit.* v, 35; *Antiq.* ii, 272]. The remains consist of several short lengths of slopes, but without discernible boundaries [*Post*, 'Anct. Earthworks'].

MADELEY.—In 1817 two urns, containing a quantity of Roman copper coins, were turned up by the plough on a farm called Little Madeley Parks, about three miles from Chesterton. The urns were destroyed; a horseshoe and a key were found at the same time. The coins identified were as follows :—Maximinus (A.D. 235-238), Diocletian (A.D. 284-305), Constantine (A.D. 306-337), Licinius (A.D. 307-324), Crispus (A.D. 317-326), Constantine P.F. (four reverses) (A.D. 317-337), Constantine Junior (four reverses) (A.D. 337-340) [Pitt, *Hist. Staffs*, i, 447]. During draining operations in a field called 'Cheshire Meadow,' foundations of buildings, carved and moulded stone work, are said to have been discovered; a field adjoining this, called Wall Croft, has a deep fosse and a *vallum*, which may give its name to the croft. In Madeley field is an entrenchment, and in 1871 Roman pottery, corroded pieces of iron, and an iron *fibula* were found there. Near the camp is a hollow, paved with large boulders, and over the field traces of roads and buildings are said to exist below the surface. A little north of the camp, at Overton, a circular leaden case was found, from 16 in. to 18 in. across, 9 in. in depth, which, it is suggested, may have been a sepulchral urn case, but it is doubtful if it was Roman [Redfern, *Hist. Uttoxeter*, 63].

MAYFIELD.—In a field called Dale-close, an urn containing Roman coins was found, and in Church-town-field in Upper Mayfield another urn was discovered [Plot, *Nat. Hist. Staffs.* 404; Cox, *Mag. Brit.* v, 105; Brayley, *Beauties of Engl. and Wales*, xiii, pt. 2, pp. 1006, 1018].

MORETON.—See Forton.

OFFLEY (or HIGH OFFLEY).—It was conjectured by Pitt in his history of Staffordshire that the station called Mediolanum stood here, but there is little evidence in support of such a theory. Traces of a Roman road are thought to have been discovered, and Roman coins in great numbers, tiles, armour, fragments of pottery, &c., have been found on the side of a hill south of the churchyard [Pitt, *Hist. Staffs.* 319]. These remains have either been grossly exaggerated by Pitt or his informants, or they indicate a house or hamlet of some sort.

OGLEY HAY.—There are slight remains of an earthwork here, known as 'Knaves' Castle' [*Post*, 'Anct. Earthworks'; Erdeswick, *Surv. of Staffs.* 302].

OKEOVER.—A square intrenchment, called 'The Halsteads,' about a quarter of a mile south of the church, is considered possibly Roman [Cox, *Mag. Brit.* v, 107; Plot, *Hist. Staffs.* 404].

PATTINGHAM.—Several Roman relics (not described) are said to have been found here at different times [Stebbing Shaw, *Hist. Staffs.* ii, 279; Pitt, *Hist. Staffs.* i, 188; Cox, *Mag. Brit.* v, 43; Camden, *Brit.* (ed. Gough), ii, 380].

PIPE HILL.—See Lichfield and Wall.

ROCESTER.—While making foundations for a cotton mill in 1792 some foundations were discovered, together with a brass spear-head and some copper coins, much corroded and defaced, which were, however, thought to be Roman. Human bones and fragments of pottery were also found [Stebbing Shaw, *Hist. Staffs.* i, 34, note]. In a field near the church is an earthwork about 45 yds. square, with a circular mound in the centre, and the remains of a *vallum* on three sides [*Antiq.* xxviii, 238; Redfern, *Hist. Uttoxeter*, 65]. About three-quarters of a mile north of Rocester is a 'camp' called Barrow Hill, on the side of Dove Cliff. The camp is rectangular, with rounded angles, measuring 147 yds. north and south, 167 yds. east and west, and contains an area of 6¾ acres. The north-west and south-east angles are extant, and the sides can be traced. In 1894 some fragments of Roman pottery and glass were disclosed slightly under the surface [*Post*, 'Anct. Earthworks'; *N. Staffs. Field Club* (1894)]. In a barrow or tumulus to the north of the camp Roman coins and pottery were found in 1872 [O.S. Staffs. xxvi, 6].

ROWLEY REGIS.—In 1794, in pulling down an old stone wall, an urn, described as an 'earthen globe,' was found, containing about 1,200 silver coins. They were all dispersed except 300, which were kept by the Rev. J. Cartwright, and were said to cover the whole period of the Roman occupation [Stebbing Shaw, *Hist. Staffs.* i, 35; Pitt, *Hist. Staffs.* i, 8]. In 1804 a further discovery of coins was made, one said to be a silver *denarius* of Marcus Aurelius (A.D. 161–180) [*Gent. Mag.* 1805, ii, 696].

RUSHALL.—In 1795 some silver and two copper coins, together with two pieces of metal, supposed to be *fibulae*, were found in digging a canal here [Stebbing Shaw, *Hist. Staffs.* i, 35; Pitt, *Hist. Staffs.* i, 148].

SEDGLEY.—At Gournal, in the parish of Sedgley, Roman foundations are supposed to have been discovered in the sixteenth century, and mention is made of 'grindstones' or querns being found in the same place, but there is nothing to show that they were Roman [Erdeswick, *Surv. of Staffs.* (ed. Harwood, 1844), 370].

SEISDON.—On Seisdon Common, near Abbots' or Apwood Castle, is a small square intrenchment with a single ditch, situated on a round promontory. [Camden, *Brit.* (ed. Gough), ii, 381; Pitt. *Hist. Staffs.* i, 187; Stebbing Shaw, *Hist. Staffs.* ii, 210]. Near the common is a large triangular stone called the War Stone, which Mr. Coote suggests is a 'trifinnial' boundary stone [Coote, *Romans of Britain*, 97; Pitt, *Hist. Staffs.* i, 187; Stebbing Shaw, *Hist. Staffs.* ii, 210].

SHARESHILL.—On the north and south sides of this village were vestiges of two encampments, supposed from their square form to have been Roman; remains of one still exist [*Post*, 'Anct. Earthworks'; Pitt, *Hist. Staffs.* i, 259; Brayley, *Beauties of Engl. and Wales*, xiii, 868].

STAPENHILL.—Roman coins were found here in a Saxon cemetery [*V.C.H. Derb.* i, 262].

STONE.—An urn of unglazed red clay was dug up in the corner of Stoke Lane, at the east entrance into Stone. It was of a wide-mouthed or 'bell' shape, diameter 3½ in. at the bottom, 9 in. at the top; height 10 in.; it was ornamented with incised lines in a zigzag pattern, and contained ashes and small pieces of human bones [Pitt, *Hist. Staffs.* i, 6; Stebbing Shaw, *Hist. Staffs.* i, 35]. There is a square entrenchment a mile out of Stone, at Hollywood, in a coppice known as Campfield, and in the meadows near the Hilderstone Brook is another earthwork with a double fosse, the outer one representing a quadrilateral figure of 200 yds. A small bronze Roman coin was dug up here. On the road from Stone to Gnosall was a 'high paved way' near Eccleshall, mentioned by Plot about 1686 [*Antiq.* xxxviii, 361; Plot, *Nat. Hist. Staffs.* 402].

STRETTON (near Brewood).—The site of Pennocrucium, the Roman station of the Antonine *Itinerary* on Watling Street, 12 Roman miles from Uxacona (Oakengates) and 12 from Letocetum (Wall), is generally thought to be here because the distances approximately agree. The name Pennocrucium suggests a connexion with the River Penk which the Watling Street here crosses, and the name of Stretton suggests a Roman site. No Roman coins or other antiquities, however, have been discovered, but no systematic excavations have been attempted. There are two small eminences near the street, called Rowley Hill and Beacon Hill. The larger, Rowley Hill, occupies about five acres, rises from meadows near the river, and is surmounted by a tumulus in which a few Celtic remains have been found [Pitt, *Hist. Staffs.* i, 260; Stebbing Shaw, *Hist. Staffs.* i, 31; Wright, *Celt. Rom. Sax.* 124; Horsley, *Brit. Rom.* 420; MS. Min. Soc. Antiq. i, 203; *Arch.* v, 113; Plot, *Hist. Staffs.* 401].

STRETTON (near Burton-on-Trent).—In the 'Monks' Bridge,' which crosses the river here, certain remains of wooden piles have been found, which, it has been suggested, formed part of a Roman bridge carrying the Rycknield Street across the River Dove [*Trans. Burton-on-Trent Nat. Hist. and Arch. Soc.* iv, 32; cf. Burton-on-Trent].

TATENHILL.—An old road way, a field or two from the east end of the church, is said to be of Roman construction. An ornament, probably a *fibula*, was found in 1819 near the road [*N. Staffs. Field Club*, xxxvii, 153; MS. Min. Antiq. Soc. xxxiv, 188]. In the hamlet of Callingwood, about a mile west of the Rycknield Street, on the border of Needwood Forest, were found in 1793 upwards of thirty gold coins in very good preservation; of Augustus (B.C. 29–A.D. 14), Nero (A.D. 54–68), Galba (A.D. 68–69), Vespasian (A.D. 70–79), Domitian (A.D. 81–96) [Stebbing Shaw, *Hist. Staffs.* i, 18, 35; Pitt, *Hist. Staffs.* i, 8; *Gent. Mag.* (1796), 983; *Reliq.* ii, 209].

TEDDESLEY HAY.—In Teddesley Park is a small square entrenchment, and in the fosse a short sword or dagger of iron, considered Roman, was found in 1780 [Stebbing Shaw, *Hist. Staffs.* ii, 2].

TETTENHALL.—In the hamlet of Wrottesley are the remains of foundations. Dr. Plot, about 1686, stated that he was able to trace the lines of streets, &c. The circuit of the whole was said to be between three and four miles, lying partly in Staffordshire, partly in Shropshire. The foundations have unfortunately been dug up and used for various purposes. Squared stones, metal clamps or hinges, and a bronze dagger have been found at different times. There is, however, no evidence as to the date of these remains, which may have been later than the Roman period. Near the place is the 'Low Hill' field, where many human bones have been discovered [Plot, *Nat. Hist. Staffs.* 394; Stebbing Shaw, *Hist. Staffs.* ii, 194; Cox, *Mag. Brit.* v, 47, 48].

UPPER ARELEY.—A square entrenchment surrounded with double, and on one side treble, ditches is in Areley Wood. Remains indicative of a Roman settlement are said to have existed at Hawkback. Roman coins have been found in the vicinity, some said to be gold, one of Tiberius (A.D. 14–37) [Pitt, *Hist. Staffs.* i, 202; Camden, *Brit.* (ed. Gough), ii, 381; Stebbing Shaw, *Hist. Staffs.* ii, 253]. This parish, originally in Staffordshire, is now included in Worcestershire.

UPPER STONNAL.—On a hill in this parish a camp exists which Plot thought Roman. Spear-heads and other implements have been dug up on the site, but whether they were of Roman date is uncertain [Plot, *Nat. Hist. Staffs.* 396]. Coins are also said to have been found in the neighbourhood [Willmore, *Hist. Walsall*, 25].

UPPER TEAN.—In 1728 two urns of unglazed red clay, holding about six quarts apiece were found in a garden. They were in an inverted position, and under one of them were several fragments of human bones, skulls, &c. [Stebbing Shaw, *Hist. Staffs.* i, 35].

UTTOXETER.—Romano-British pottery and bronze articles have been found here. In 1872 two pieces of pottery were found on Uttoxeter Heath, near the Ashbourne Road. An entrenchment on the south of the town is quadrangular in form and of a fairly large size; the north side is perfect, in a field known as the 'Sandfort' field. The west and south sides are also discernible. Pottery has been found on the site, and an *amphora* near it. In Bradley Street numerous fragments of pottery were found, also a large quantity of grey clay, and one piece of unfinished ware, which led to the conjecture that the articles may have been manufactured on the spot. There were found also a bronze buckle, part of a brass *fibula* enamelled in red, a white hard metal button or ornament, a bronze disc, a piece of lead with a circular edge, the handle of a bronze key, a quern, boars' tusks, pieces of iron, a coin, and fragments of pottery scattered for 70 yds. round. Only one piece of Samian ware was discovered. In all parts of the town potsherds and small coins have been found [Redfern, *Hist. Uttoxeter*, 50-1]. At Stramshall in this parish a field was opened in five different places, and fragments of pottery were discovered at each place, but no Samian ware. An old well near the church, surrounded by pavement a foot below the surface, was supposed to be Roman [*Journ. Brit. Arch. Soc.* xxix, 263]. It was faced from top to bottom with stone; at the bottom was a sandstone flag, with a hollow space chiselled out in the centre about one foot in width. Pottery was found in a bank near it [Redfern, *Hist. Uttoxeter*, 59].

WALL.—Here was undoubtedly the station of Letocetum or Etocetum of the Antonine *Itinerary* and the 'Lectoceto civitas' of Ravennas, the distances laid down in the second *Iter* agreeing approximately with the actual measurements [Haverfield, *V.C.H. Worc.* i, 214; Horsley, *Brit. Rom.* 436; *Journ. Brit. Arch. Assoc.* ii, 15; *Arch.* viii, 95; xi, 92; Pitt, *Hist. Staffs.* i, 4; Wrottesley, in *N. Staffs. Field Club Trans.* (1901–2), xxxvi, 130-1;

Stukeley, *Itin. Cur.* i, 58 ; Camden, *Brit.* (ed. Gough), ii, 385]. The site of the Roman town appears to have been on high ground north of Watling Street, extending from a line running north in a field called Castle Croft on the east to the brook just beyond the village pound on the west ; the northern limit appears to have been to the north of a field called ' the Butts,' and so in a line eastward. This would give an area of about 30 acres. Indications of earth-works may perhaps be traced here and there along these lines. Unlike the usual practice of the Roman period the town does not stand at the actual crossing of the two Roman roads, but is about half a mile from the point where Watling Street crosses Rycknield Street. Unfortunately, we know very little of the Roman town ; from time to time excavations have been made, but no plans having been preserved they have yielded us practically no information.[1] It is conjectured that Letocetum was a walled site, as foundations of a wall about 11 ft. thick, traced for 50 yds., were discovered by the late Colonel Bagnall in 1887 in Castle Croft, which could scarcely have been other than the east wall of the town, but the report on the excavations gives neither the exact site nor direction of the wall [*Journ. Brit. Arch. Assoc.* xlvi, 228]. Probably it was this same wall which was referred to by Stebbing Shaw, writing about 1752, who stated that by the side of the road going northward from Wall to Pipe Hill (probably Wall Lane) the Roman walls were then to be seen extending for 100 yds. made up of ragstone with sloping courses of bonding tiles held together with very strong white mortar. The best portion of the wall was in Stebbing Shaw's time to be seen in the garden of Mr. Thomas Jackson [Stebbing Shaw, *Hist. Staffs.* i, 18, 19, 356]. The only pieces of Roman wall now showing above ground are at the points marked A and B on the accompanying plan, and apparently belonged to some important building. Although a considerable quantity of Roman remains, including some *tesserae* and the base of a column, have been found on the south side of Watling Street, there is great doubt whether the Roman area extended across the road. There is no evidence that the *tesserae* and base were *in situ*, and the other remains discovered indicate rather the site of the cemetery, which undoubtedly extended along Watling Street to the east of Wall [Plot, *Nat. Hist. Staffs.* 401 (1686)].

Probably the greater part of the remains have been found in the field called ' the Butts,' on the west side of the site. Erdeswick, writing in the sixteenth century, speaks of walls being visible here which were afterwards carried away for building purposes. Writers of the eighteenth century mention walls 3 ft. thick, 12 ft. high, running equidistant 12 ft. apart, forming rooms 'like square cellars' [Stukeley, *Itin. Cur.* i, 58 ; Camden, *Brit.* (ed. Gough), ii, 385 ; Erdeswick, *Surv. of Staffs.* (ed. Harwood), 301; Stebbing Shaw, *Hist. Staffs.* i, 18, 19]. Plot, in 1686, mentions that in the field called ' the Butts' he was shown two pavements 'one above another at least 4 ft.,' the uppermost (which lay within 18 in. of the surface) being made for the most part ' of lime and rubble stone ' ; and the lowermost ' of pebbles and gravel knit together with a very hard cement about 4 in. thick laid upon a foundation of Roman brick ; and under them boulder stone of a foot thick or more.' Above the uppermost of these Roman coins were often found, and he was shown three, one of Nero (A.D. 54–68), one of Domitian (A.D. 81–96), and one undecipherable [Plot, *Nat. Hist. Staffs.* 401]. In 1887 some excavations were made by Colonel Bagnall, and in the lower part of ' the Butts,' south of the footpath across the field, several chambers were discovered, each about 6 ft. square with floors of layers of charcoal. A large quantity of roof-tiles and common pottery, some blue-grey, some red and whitish yellow, and some with potters' marks ; tiles with PS on them (now in the Lichfield Museum) and animal bones, quantities of wall-plaster, with stripes of red, brown, and green, many oyster and snail shells, fragments of Bangor slates perforated with holes for nails, many iron nails and some circular earthen pipes about 1½ in. in diameter were also found. Near these chambers, in a hedge, was discovered a large worked stone with a hole in the middle where a hinge might work, and not far off what is thought to have been a road made of common pebbles [*Journ. Brit. Arch. Assoc.* (Ser. i), xlvi, 227–31]. It is said in Lomax's *Guide to Lichfield* that a man employed in draining the land near Wall mentioned that he often found coins and other relics, and once, where the church now is, he found ' a figure of earthenware as big as a man, but a woman's figure—in a strange dress— with a man's cap like a soldier's helmet ; we broke it in pieces to mend the bank of the drain.' The coins were said to be of Tiberius (A.D. 14–37) and others, in gold, silver, and copper. Not far off, but whether within or outside the Roman town is not stated, a farmer

---

[1] These finds are recorded by ' Antiquary ' in a letter to the *Staffs. Advertiser* in 1859 ; by Col. Bagnall in a communication to the *Birmingham and Midland Institute* in 1873, and by Mr. J. T. Irvine in the *Journ. of the Brit. Arch. Assoc.* for 1890. All three accounts appear to be substantially the same, and to note the same discoveries.

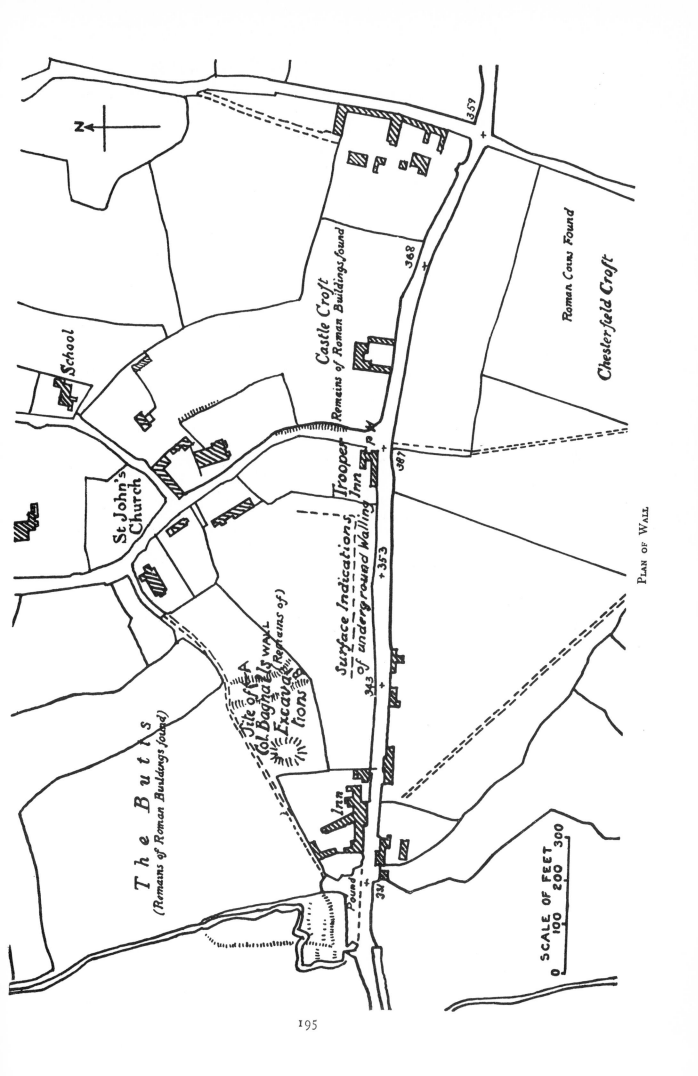

School

St John's
Church

Castle Croft

Remains of Roman Buildings found

Roman Coins Found

Chesterfield Croft

+ 359

+ 368

+ 387

+ 353

+ 343

Trooper Inn

Surface Indications
of underground Walling

Site of
Col. Bagnall's
Excavations
(Remains of)

The Butts
(Remains of Roman Buildings found)

Inn

Pound

PLAN OF WALL

SCALE OF FEET
0   100   200   300

found three earthen vessels full of bones, but broke them to pieces. Higher in 'the Butts,' other walls were found, apparently of a large number of small apartments, together with the same sort of remains as those already described, a small silver ornament and two copper articles, thought to be a buckle and a brooch, and bones of animals. There is a tradition in the neighbourhood that a subterranean passage went from 'the Butts' to Castle Croft, and that it was opened when the road was altered, but it could not be found in 1872, though search was made for it [*Journ. Brit. Arch. Assoc.* (Ser. 1), xlvi, 227–31]. The field called 'Castle Croft' is said to have been surrounded by walls, apparently visible in 1817, and in a garden there pavements, said to be 'of Roman brick,' and great quantities of foundation stones were dug up [Pitt, *Hist. Staffs.* i, 128–9; Cox, *Mag. Brit.* v, 25].

Some excavations were made in 1859 in Castle Croft, when a trench was cut through a wall, apparently to the south-west of the field running parallel to Watling Street, and 'a quadrangular room was opened, though not cleared, with a floor about 3 ft. below the surface composed of hard concrete covered with a coat of plaster. Here was an abundance of ridged tiles of fine red clay.' These tiles were probably flue-tiles, one of them had the letters PS upon it (see *ante*); slates of a greenish colour with nail or peg holes and the nails, pieces of wall plaster covered with stripes of red, green, yellow, brown and white were also found. Animal bones, oyster shells, potsherds, glass, coins supposed to be of Nero (A.D. 54–68) and Constantius (A.D. 291–306) were also discovered and sent to the Lichfield Museum [Letter by 'Antiquary' to the *Staffs. Advertiser*, 18 June, 1859]. This site was apparently again excavated in 1872; a small chamber, the walls of which were 2 ft. thick, was disclosed. No coins were found, but Samian ware and other pottery, large worked stones about 1 ft. square, fragments of roofing-tiles, coloured wall plaster with floral designs, blocks of concrete made of pounded brick and Walsall lime, also pebbles and lime and a great variety of other remains of buildings were discovered. Human and animal bones are said to have been found [*Journ. Brit. Arch. Assoc.* (Ser. 1), xxix, 116]. Many fragments of Samian ware were discovered in Castle Croft, though there were none in 'the Butts.' A few coins, pieces of flint and a very little glass were also found. In the field on the south side of Watling Street called Chesterfield were found remains which have been conjectured, probably on insufficient grounds, to have been lead works. There are no traces of masonry, but at about 4 ft. from the surface a layer of clay was found, about 6 in. thick, and under it, in different places, charcoal and sand; the clay must have been brought to the spot, as there is none in the neighbourhood. Beneath it were quantities of animals' bones, and pieces of iron and iron-cinder. One piece of iron was thought to be a horse-bit, and two were probably door-handles 16 in. in length. Very little pottery was seen, but quantities of lead and copper, some smelted lead, a copper key, a *fibula*, small copper nails, pieces of plate or sheet copper, a few coins and some fragments of glass. A considerable amount of ashes and burnt clay was also found with the metals [*Journ. Brit. Arch. Assoc.* (Ser. 1), xlvi, 227–31]. In Chesterfield Roman coins were found. One of Nero (A.D. 54–68), one of Vespasian (A.D. 70–9), one of Domitian (A.D. 81–96) [O.S. lviii, 6], also the remains of a column, already alluded to, a piece of Samian ware, some *tesserae* from a pavement, &c. A gold Otho (A.D. 69) was dug up in 1690, but exactly where is not known [Plot, *Nat. Hist. Staffs.* 401; Erdeswick, *Surv. of Staffs.* (ed. Harwood), 301; Stebbing Shaw, *Hist. Staffs.* i, 18]. Colonel Bagnall states that he was told upon good authority that in Green Lane, near the point where it branches off from Watling Street, a stone coffin containing human remains was discovered [*Journ. Brit. Arch. Assoc.* (Ser. 1), xlvi, 230]. If the coffin was Roman this is an improbable site, as the Romans did not bury their dead within their towns.

Probably we have here a village or even a small town, but proper excavation alone can tell us its story.

WALSALL.—At Linley, near Walsall, a *fibula* and several coins were found in 1759 [Willmore, *Hist. Walsall*, 25].

WEDNESBURY.—A quantity of Roman coins in good preservation was dug up on Sir H. St. Paul's property in 1817. Among them were said to be coins of Nero (A.D. 54–68), Vespasian (A.D. 70–9), and Trajan (A.D. 98–117) [*Gent. Mag.* (1817), ii, 551; Willmore, *Hist. Walsall*, 25].

WETTON.—Between 1848 and 1852 the fields known as the 'Borough Hole' near Wetton were systematically excavated, and the sites of numerous dwellings, forming probably a Romano-British village, were discovered. This settlement may possibly have been inhabited by the miners who worked at the lead mines in this district during the Romano-British period. Pavements of rough limestone, large blocks of stone, quantities of charcoal, ashes, animal bones, numerous pieces of Roman and British pottery, broken querns, iron utensils, &c. were disinterred. Coins of Gallienus (A.D. 253–68), Tetricus (A.D. 268–73) and Constantine

BRONZE OBJECT FROM WALL

TILE FROM WALL

PIG OF LEAD, FOUND AT HINTS

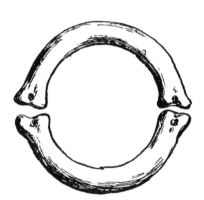

IRON KNIFE,
FOUND AT WETTON

LEAD COLLAR,
FOUND AT WETTON

IRON KNIFE,
FOUND AT WETTON

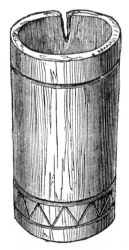

WHETSTONE, FOUND AT WETTON

BONE DRINKING-CUP,
FOUND AT WETTON

HORN OBJECT, FOUND AT WETTON

(A.D. 306–37) were found, some glass and a plain bronze ring *fibula*. In one place a female skeleton with some beads, &c., and in other places human bones and skulls were dug up. Among the two or three *fibulae* found was one in bronze, enamelled with red and yellow lozenges, but most of the articles were of a rough and primitive character [Carrington, *Reliq.* v, 201 ; Bateman, *Ten Years' Diggings*, 193–203 ; *Intellectual Observer*, vii, 391]. The site has evidently been used as a quarry for building materials by the inhabitants of the neighbourhood. The following articles found at Wetton were preserved in Mr. Bateman's collection [*Catalogue Bateman Collection, Lomberdale House*, 1855]. Those marked with an asterisk were afterwards presented to the Sheffield Museum [*Catalogue Bateman Antiquities, Sheffield Museum*, 1899] :—* Part of a reeded handle from a glass vase ; pieces of burnt glass ; lilac and blue glass beads ;* harp-shaped bronze *fibula*, enamelled with a diamond pattern in yellow, red, and green ; * bronze ring *fibula*, 1⅜ in. in diameter ; small slip of bronze, perforated at each end ; bronze pin 1½ in. long, the thicker end representing the foot of an ox ; iron knives, one with stag's horn handle, *fibulae* ; shears, spear-heads, nails, &c. ; two cinerary urns ; fragments of *mortaria* and other vessels ; * small cylindrical vessel, 3¼ in. high, 1¾ in. in diameter, with cheveron pattern, made of one large bone ; two imitations of brass coins of Tetricus ; * two flat sandstone pebbles, worked to a circular shape, 2 in. and 2¾ in. in diameter ;* perforated disc of red earthenware 1¼ in. in diameter ;* whetstones, one of grey sandstone, in Sheffield Museum ; * pieces of red paint ; pieces of stag's horn with marks of tooling. Twenty-three barrows or lows have been investigated in the vicinity since 1845, which showed evidences of occupation from remote times to the Roman period. A 'third brass' of Gallienus (A.D. 253–68) was found in one of them with a skeleton. 'Thor's Cave,' which is in the side of a lofty precipice above the River Manifold, about half a mile from Wetton, was explored in 1864–5, and in it were found Samian and other Roman potsherds, stone querns, a sandstone disk, bone pins and combs, iron knives and arrow-heads, a lead spindle-whorl, a 'second brass' coin of Hadrian (A.D. 117–38), a bronze armlet, pins and two *fibulae*, which may be ascribed to the second or early third century. All these objects were found in the earth forming the floor of the cave, together with many animal bones and signs of cooking and fires. Some human bones were also discovered, but no distinct vestiges of a burial [Pitt, *Hist. Staffs.* i, 240 ; Haverfield in *V.C.H. Derb.* i, 238 ; Carrington in *Reliq.* v, 201–17 ; Brown in *Mid. Scient. Assoc. Papers* (1864–5)]. Professor Haverfield identifies 'Thor's Cave' with Thirst or Thirse House, the name of one of the most extensively explored Romano-British caves in Derbyshire, and also of two other caves in Staffordshire, one at Alton and one near Wetton [*V.C.H. Derb.* i, 233, n. 1].

WICHNOR.—In the park are remains of an intrenchment where several Roman coins have been found [Stebbing Shaw, *Hist. Staffs.* i, 18, 125 ; Pennant, *Journey from Chester to London*, 121–2].

WOLSTANTON.—See CHESTERTON.

WOLVERHAMPTON.—A Roman urn, 9¼ in. deep, 2 ft. in girth in the thickest part, of a coarse texture and pale red clay, was found in 1793 near St. Peter's Church. It lay on its side 9 ft. below the surface, and contained dark earth. The surrounding stratum was sand. Near it were considerable remains of human bones and teeth [Stebbing Shaw, *Hist. Staffs.* i, 35]. A bronze ring was also found here [*Proc. Soc. Antiq.* (Ser. 2) vi, 415].

YOXALL.—In levelling a piece of ground in 1778 nearly forty urns of coarse brown pottery were found, containing ashes and fragments of human bones. Most of the vessels were broken in taking them up, but one is in the Lichfield Museum. The site was probably a Romano-British cemetery near to which there may have been a settlement [Stebbing Shaw, *Hist. Staffs.* i, 35, 331 ; *Gent. Mag.* xliv, 358 ; Camden, *Brit.* (ed. Gough) ii, 393].

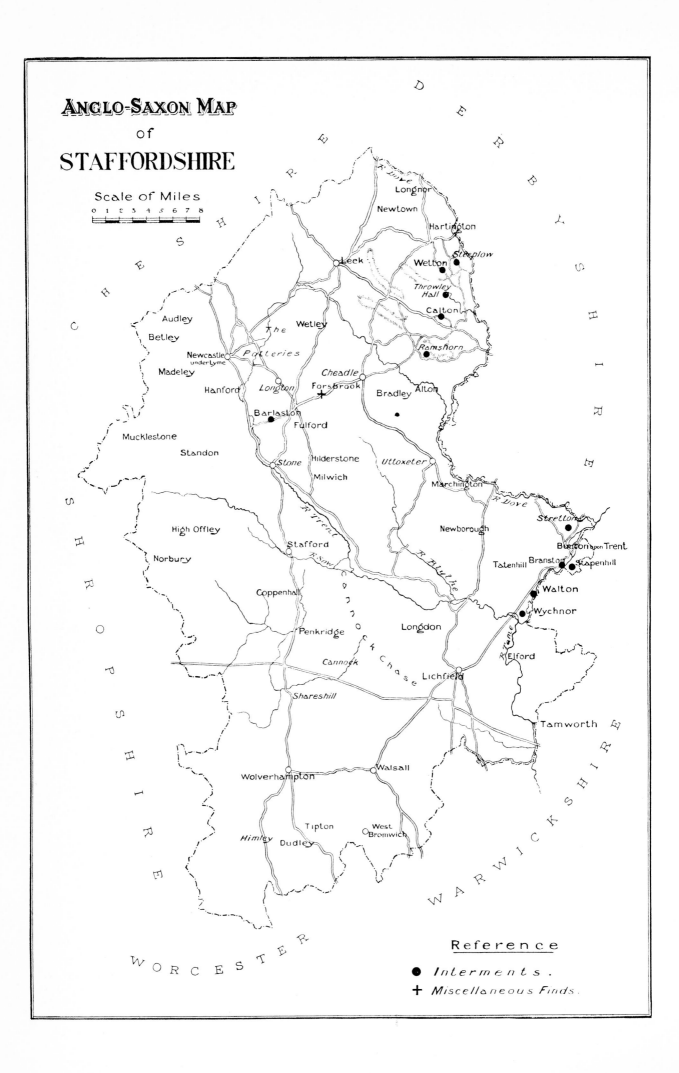

ANGLO-SAXON MAP
of
STAFFORDSHIRE

Scale of Miles
0 1 2 3 4 5 6 7 8

Reference

● *Interments.*
+ *Miscellaneous Finds.*

ANGLO-SAXON
REMAINS

THE districts occupied by the Teutonic invaders of Britain in the sixth century are approximately defined by sepulchral relics recovered from the soil. Such discoveries are, in the nature of things, accidental, and are generally due to workmen, who are seldom at the pains to ensure a complete record of the finds. Much valuable material has been lost in this way, and doubtless many areas at present unproductive only await excavation to fill up gaps in our knowledge of the period ; but it may be taken for granted that where, in spite of all hindrances, much of the kind has been discovered the pagan population was comparatively dense. The converse is not so safe a rule, but negative evidence may be sometimes corroborated by a consideration of the geographical features, as the early Anglo-Saxon settlers were all on the same level of culture, and would have the same preferences in the matter of soil and situation. To such arguments may be added the few indications in history or tradition as to the origins of England, but it must be confessed that for most of the English counties early records are either wanting or open to more than one interpretation, and it is now only in the domain of archaeology that there is any hope of fuller information.

The present county owes its geographical limits to the political arrangements of the later Saxon period, when England had become a kingdom ; but as most of the remains to be considered in this chapter are clearly of the pagan period, the present boundaries must be disregarded in favour of certain archaeological and physical divisions. Further, for the period in question, the coalfields and potteries may be neglected, though during the Roman occupation coal was evidently used for fuel, and the clays of this neighbourhood were used for pottery.[1] A pastoral and agricultural people would naturally settle in the vicinity of rivers, which, indeed, offered one of the easiest roads into the interior before the primeval forests were cleared or the marsh lands drained.

The accompanying map, which aims at locating all the authentic Anglo-Saxon discoveries of the pagan period, makes it clear that the earliest Teutonic settlements fall into two main groups, on the north and east of the present county. Except for the south Staffordshire coalfield, practically all south of Cheadle and Stone is Triassic formation, consisting of the Keuper and Bunter beds, which are peculiarly productive of forest. Such, for instance, is the

---

[1] Hence the name ' Salopian ' applied by Thos. Wright and others to pottery found on the Roman site of Uriconium (Wroxeter), and probably manufactured in the vicinity of Broseley.

geological basis of the vast areas known as Sherwood, Arden, and Charnwood, where no Anglo-Saxon remains are found ; and it is not, therefore, surprising to find that Needwood and Cannock Chase are similarly unproductive. Besides the two coalfields (Cheadle and Potteries) in the north of the county there is an area, mainly east of Leek, consisting of Yoredale and carboniferous limestone rock connected with a much larger area of the same formation in the north-west of Derbyshire. South of High Peak this soil was evidently appreciated by the early Anglo-Saxon inhabitants, who have left numerous traces of their settlements and civilization. South of Ashbourne and Derby is an unproductive area of Triassic formation continuous with central Staffordshire, but Anglo-Saxon cemeteries again appear in the Trent valley at Melbourne and Foremark.[2]

It is with the traces of a further advance up the Trent valley that a survey of post-Roman Staffordshire may best begin ; and the first discovery on entering this county from this side has, indeed, been noticed under Derbyshire, as the site has only recently been added to Staffordshire.

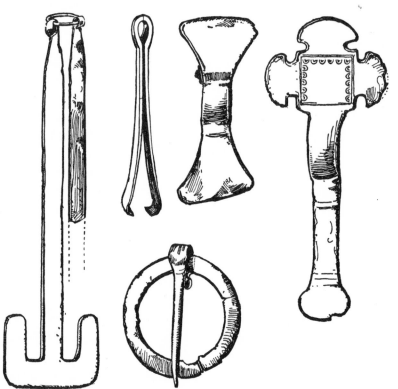

FIG. I.—BRONZE BROOCHES, TWEEZERS, AND CHÂTELAINE, STAPENHILL (¼)

The most important Anglo-Saxon discovery in the county was made in 1881 at Stapenhill, a village just within the boundary of Burton-on-Trent, though on the Derbyshire bank of the river.[3] The site of what proved to be a cemetery is on the crest of a ridge 120 ft. above the level of the Trent and 300 ft. above sea-level. The village lies to the north, the parish church being about half a mile north-north-west; and the burial ground lies between the Stanton and Rosliston roads, but nearer the former. Plans and details of the burials, with several plates of the antiquities discovered, were published in the following year by the Burton-on-Trent Natural History and Archaeological Society, and an excellent description of the excavations undertaken by a committee for the society was furnished by Mr. John Heron.[4] From that account a good deal may be learnt with regard to the first Anglo-Saxon occupation of this part of the county, and the following is a summary, with additional remarks as to similar finds elsewhere.

[2] The distribution is clear from the map of Anglo-Saxon remains in *V.C.H. Derb.* i, 265.
[3] Ibid. i, 266, 273.   [4] *Trans.* vol. i, 156–93, plates i–x, and frontispiece.

ANGLO-SAXON REMAINS

The actual area of the brickfield examined was about 150 ft. by 96 ft., its length being approximately on an east-and-west line. While excavating for brick-earth the workmen came upon two large earthenware urns, and straightway destroyed them in the vain hope of finding treasure. The fragments show their Anglo-Saxon origin, and one, if not both, contained incinerated human remains. Near the spot was found an iron javelin head, 6 in. long, which may safely be attributed to the same era. Two skeletons laid at full length were next discovered, and others were subsequently unearthed, but further investigations were entrusted to the society by the proprietor, and proved most successful. As many as thirty-one skeletons were noticed, in various conditions, and five cases of cremation are recorded, the ashes having been collected and placed in rudely-made cinerary urns of the ordinary type. In nineteen cases the direction of the interment could be determined, the head in five cases being at the west end of the grave, as was customary in early Christian times. Six more were approximately north-west, and four inclined towards south-west, showing that the western position was by far the most usual here; and the variations to the north or south may possibly be due to the interments having been made at different seasons, bearings being no doubt taken at sunrise or sunset for the purpose of orientation. The head in one case, however, was at the east end, another lay east-north-east, and two more south-south-east, so that uniformity was not enforced; and it would in any case be rash to infer that the east-and-west burials were necessarily Christian. Cremation, which appears to have been practised side by side with inhumation on this site, was frankly pagan, and even apart from signs of partial cremation noticed in some cases, the presence of weapons, ornaments, and utensils in several of the graves shows that the Christian rule was not rigidly observed.

FIG. 2.—VASE FOUND AT STAPENHILL ($\frac{1}{2}$)

The richest and most interesting grave was that of a woman of middle age, whose height was 5 ft. 10 in. The bones were in excellent preservation, and the body had been laid on the back with the head towards the west; the right arm was by the side, the left across the chest, and the legs straight. Close to the left side of the head was a vase of dark pottery decorated in the usual manner, with groups of incised lines and a band of stamped star pattern (fig. 2). It measured 5½ in. in height, with a maximum diameter of 5 in., being somewhat smaller than the average cinerary urn. On either shoulder was a brooch of bronze-gilt, with trefoil or cruciform head and punched borders (fig. 1). It belongs to a type fairly common in this country, and related to the 'long' brooch of Scandinavia, though the latter terminates at the foot in a conventional horse's head. The spreading foot of the Stapenhill example points rather to Prussia as the centre of dispersion,[5] but it is clear that the evolution of the brooch was not uniform in

[5] Haakon Schetelig, *Cruciform Brooches of Norway*, 49, 50, 86, 146.

all the Teutonic areas, and this expanding foot seems to be a specially English feature. Round the neck of the skeleton was a string of twenty or more beads, some being annular specimens of dark blue glass, and one (described as glass) was evidently of crystal ; four were of amber, roughly shaped like a spindle-whorl ; one consisted of a pierced garnet disc, and the rest were of opaque glass of various colours. Near the beads were several pieces of tubular bronze, such as have been found elsewhere on necklaces ; and on the chest were fragments of a clasp, apparently of the type sometimes found at the wrist, to fasten a bracelet. An iron buckle at the waist evidently belonged to a leathern girdle, and there were also two key-shaped objects of bronze which are usually called châtelaines or girdle-hangers, and may have been worn as a symbol, just as keys were carried by Roman matrons. A spindle-whorl of Kimmeridge shale completed the list from this burial, which agrees closely with several in the Anglian districts, and may be regarded as typical of the richer class.

It will not be necessary to describe the graves individually, but the next deserves special mention. Of the skeleton, nothing remained but the teeth [6] of a child, but from their position it was clear that the body had been buried unburnt, or possibly after partial cremation, as a small vase near the teeth showed traces of intense heat. In the position of the shoulder was a small gilded bronze brooch of a form most unusual in England, but allied to certain German specimens, and near it lay four beads, including Roman melon-shaped specimens of turquoise glass. The partial burning suggested here finds parallels in the same cemetery and elsewhere in England. Two Stapen-hill burials—one in a triple grave and the other that of a body with the head west-north-west—were surrounded by a ring of charcoal,[7] and in the former case the bones that remained showed evident traces of fire, while in two other graves were lumps of iron that had been subjected to great heat. Though in some cases decayed wood may have been mistaken for charcoal (which is often found in graves), there is positive evidence at Stapenhill of a practice that may well represent a compromise between the pagan and Christian ritual. It is most improbable that the bulk of unburnt burials are those of Christian Anglo-Saxons, but it is fairly certain that no convert was cremated at that period ; and in view of Christian relics in the adjoining county of Derby it is possible that a ceremonial burning of the dead was retained, in deference to pagan traditions, for some time after inhumation had been introduced. The transition may be further illustrated by the unburnt graves at Stapenhill that have not the Christian orientation, but the question cannot be settled without further evidence. The direction of the Stapenhill interments without grave-furniture is by no means uniform ; and weapons were found in others, a spear or lance-head, when present, being on the right of the skull ; and in one case a shield lay on the left arm, the iron boss and handle being preserved, as well as several rivets, that showed the 'war-board' to have been $\frac{3}{4}$ in. thick. The knife, which was commonly carried by both sexes for use at meals, was frequently found in this cemetery, but its position was not constant. A few rude vases of pottery were found either near the

[6] A similar case at Wyaston : *V.C.H. Derb.* i, 269 ; Bateman, *Ten Years' Diggings,* 188.
[7] For examples in Derbyshire see *V.C.H. Derb.* i, 274.

head or shoulder, and were probably placed in the grave to contain food or drink for the dead,[8] though they may also represent the cinerary urns of the pagan period.

One skeleton was found without the skull, and the upper part of another was wanting. This may be due to subsequent disturbance (and there seems to have been much rubbish buried on this site), but such occurrences are not uncommon,[9] and may be due to the fortune of war, stray skulls being included in several graves at Mitcham, Surrey. Nor are flexed skeletons peculiar to this cemetery ; slight contraction of the lower limbs was noticed in five cases ; but such was the general rule in the extensive cemetery at Slea-ford, Lincs., and many casual instances are recorded[10] both in England and across the Channel.

Bronze was comparatively scarce, but besides the objects already mentioned was a ring-brooch from a child's grave, which also contained beads and a coin of Constantine (struck in 327) pierced for use as a pendant. A pair of tweezers was found with another skeleton, the customary knife in this instance being still in its sheath ; one cinerary urn contained an engraved spindle-whorl made of deer-horn, and inside another, with cremated bones, were several beads and part of a thin bronze disc, which was doubtless the base of a brooch of the 'applied' variety, the position of the pin-head and catch being distinguishable on one side. The type is practically confined to England, a late Roman specimen from Sigy, near Neufchâtel (Seine-inférieure),[11] giving some clue to its origin : the principal site is the ceme-tery at Kempston, Beds., but all were there found in association with skeletons.[12] It is noteworthy that the same cemetery produced a trefoil-headed brooch almost identical with that from Stapenhill, and what seems to be the prototype of the equal-armed brooch here illustrated (fig. 1). The latter closely resembles one from Cambridgeshire, but the type is rare in England, and only a few specimens are known abroad. This equal-armed brooch differs widely from that found in southern France, and probably reached England and southern Scandinavia from the neigh-bourhood of Hanover, where elaborate examples of earlier date are comparatively common. And it is remarkable that the fifth-century specimens in England outnumber those of the sixth, which are plain and common-place as that from Stapenhill. The evolution of this type has been briefly indicated by Dr. Bernhard Salin, who illustrates the specimens mentioned above.[12a]

Both at Stapenhill and Kempston were found coins of the Constantine period, pierced for suspension, and tubular 'beads' of bronze. Further, the cinerary urns and accessory vessels are of the same types, and both cemeteries contained cremations as well as inhumations. Partial cremation was also

---

[8] Pottery vessels were included in coffins of the Middle Ages: *Arch.* xxxvii, 417.

[9] White Horse Hill, Berks. (*Crania Britannica*, pt. ii) ; E. Yorkshire (Mortimer, *Thirty Years' Researches*, pp. xxxiii, xxxvi, 321) ; Mitcham, Surrey (*Arch.* lx, 53, 57).

[10] Sleaford, *Arch.* l, 385 ; other instances in E. Yorks. ; Kempston, Beds. ; Marston St. Lawrence, Northants ; Leagrave, Beds. Cf. Cochet, *Normandie Souterraine* (ed. 2), 218.

[11] *Proc. Soc. Antiq. Lond.* (Ser. 1), iv, 237.

[12] *V.C.H. Beds.* i, 180 (figs. 11 and 13 on plate) ; other brooches referred to are fig. 2 on plate, and 'engraved bronze brooch' on p. 179.

[12a] *Die Altgermanische Thierornamentik*, 74, figs. 174, 176, 699, &c.

noticed at Kempston, and the following extract throws some light on the process :—

> A pit was discovered over 7 ft. in length, from 3 to 4 ft. wide, and the same in depth, where a body stretched at full length had been consumed by fire. About 2 ft. from the surface was a large quantity of ashes, and among them were found portions of a human skull, vertebrae and other bones, all charred, but the leg-bones showing less traces of fire than the rest of the skeleton. In the ashes and on the left side of the body was a long iron spear-head with a portion of the wooden shaft left in the socket, and also an iron knife ; while surrounding these remains lay numerous pieces of charred wood, and ends of branches not quite burnt through. It seemed as if the pit had been partially filled with live embers, on which the deceased was laid, and then large branches heaped over.[13]

Animal bones were found in at least four of the Stapenhill graves, and in large quantities elsewhere on the site, especially in a trench 92 ft. long, 5 ft. 9 in. deep at the south end, and 2 ft. 6 in. deep at the north. Plans and sections are given in the original account, but it seems clear that this fosse had nothing to do with the burials, but was dug for the reception of rubbish by the previous Romano-British, or even pre-Roman, inhabitants; and, to judge from the few Anglo-Saxon sherds near the surface of the ditch, the site may have been occupied by Teutonic settlers before it was appropriated for burials. No grave-mounds were observed by the excavators ; and as the plan shows great irregularity, surface indications were perhaps dispensed with altogether, but even on sites where some memorial must have existed to mark the regular lines of interments [14] all trace has disappeared before our time. The discoveries in this cemetery are held to prove that the two rites of burial (cremation and inhumation) were practised by contemporaries, and such seems to be the case on certain other sites ; but the contention would be hard to prove by crucial instances.

Facing Stapenhill, on the other side of the Trent, is another Anglo-Saxon burial ground, of which a few details are recorded by Molyneux.[15] Some gravel pits adjoining the Lichfield Road, close to the Leicester branch of the railway, yielded about 1868 an iron spear-head, 9 in. long and much corroded, also some fragments of brown pottery 'which agrees in appearance rather with the Saxon than the Roman form of manufacture.' The nature of these finds is clear from Stapenhill and other discoveries higher up the valley.

The next site to be noticed is close to the Barton and Walton station, on the south side, and is recorded by Molyneux. A ballast pit was opened by the Midland Railway Company about 1851, and a great number of urns containing human bones were then found about three feet below the surface. Some were described as British and others as Roman or Saxon, but as two iron knives were found with the bones in one specimen, and iron weapons were found in others, their Anglo-Saxon origin is fairly established. The field from which these remains were exhumed consisted of a somewhat circular knoll of gravel that sloped gently down to the banks of the old river-course, and was beyond question the site of an ancient cemetery.[16]

The sepulchral series from Wichnor, now happily preserved by the Natural History Society at Burton, includes some interesting types of the

[13] V.C.H. Beds. i, 177 ; Roach Smith, Collectanea Antiqua, vi, 205.

[14] Mounds existed on Farthing Down (V.C.H. Surr. i, 265), but not in recent times on High Down (V.C.H. Suss. i, 341).

[15] Burton-on-Trent (1869), 22.   [16] Molyneux, Burton-on-Trent, 189 note.

more ordinary objects, but has little artistic importance. The sand-pit, in which several burials were found, is alongside the railway on the east side, close to the junction of Wichnor, about 1½ miles south of the site just mentioned; and details have been kindly supplied by Mr. H. L. Hind, of Burton.

The remains found in 1899[17] were about four feet below the surface of the pit, and more have been found since; but the conditions were unfavourable for determining their association, and all that is now possible is to consider them under various headings as products of a single cemetery. Several warriors were evidently buried here, as six shield-bosses (fig. 6) are preserved, slightly varying in their dimensions, but all of the same general form: the largest diameter of the base rim is 6½ in., with a height of 2¾ in., while the tallest specimen measures 3 in., and is nearly 5 in. across at the base. These bosses are usually very well wrought and are exceptionally durable, testifying to the skill of the Anglo-Saxon armourer, whose praises were sung in verse and whose life was assessed very high in the primitive code of laws. The spear-heads belong to two main types (fig. 3), most on this site being of the willow-leaf form, one specimen measuring 16¼ in., without its point or socket. Three others belong to a common type with waved edges to the blade and a sudden widening at the base. The sockets, where preserved, are as usual split to receive and hold firmly the wooden shaft, and there is one ferrule, 3¼ in. in length, originally fixed to the butt-end. Of the small knife usually found in the graves, only a tang 2¼ in. long remains, the bone or horn handle having perished. The only other iron object is a small oval buckle (fig. 4), but so corroded as to be barely recognizable. It probably belonged to a leather girdle, and the type is commonly found. Unfortunately only one brooch was found, and that is without the foot (or part of the stem below the bow), which is indicated in the illustration (fig. 5). It has a square head-plate with trefoil extensions, and closely resembles the only brooch of the kind found at Stapenhill. To the bronze body was attached an iron pin at the back, but only a rusted

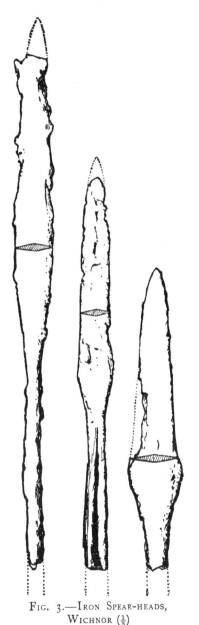

FIG. 3.—IRON SPEAR-HEADS, WICHNOR (⅓)

fragment remains. Remains of the textile which the brooch was used to fasten are often found preserved by rust on the back, but the only trace at Wichnor is on one of the spear-heads. There were besides several staves of a small bronze-mounted bucket, commonly found at the head or feet of the skeleton, but at present of uncertain use and meaning. The present example was about 3¾ in. high, and the groove in which the bottom was inserted is plainly

[17] J. O'Sullivan, *Trans. Burton-on-Trent Nat. Hist. and Arch. Soc.* iv, pt. ii, 80.

visible. Of pottery four well-preserved but very rude hand-made specimens are extant : they are quite devoid of ornament, and of different profile (see fig. 7), the base being more or less rounded as if intended to rest on

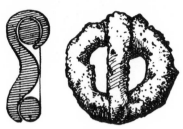

FIG. 4.—IRON BUCKLE, WICHNOR, WITH SECTION (¼)

soft earth, and the paste being soft and fairly smooth, of a brownish colour. The tallest measures 5¾ in., and the smallest 3⅛ in., and they were all evidently used as accessory vessels, not as cinerary urns to contain cremated remains. Mr. J. O'Sullivan states that no bones, weapons, or other antiquities were found with the two urns that were first discovered. All had been buried in holes or trenches, about 3 ft. or 4 ft. deep and about 8 ft. apart. The other objects enumerated above were found subsequently, but not in association with the pottery.

At Burrough Fields Farm,[18] south of Walton, bones and other objects not specified were found many years ago, and the name is suggestive of a cemetery, but no other remains are reported from this part of the Trent Valley, and it is highly· probable that Needwood and Cannock Chase discouraged further advance in this direction, at least along the main stream : the pioneers may at this point have turned south along the Tame and founded Tamworth. Whether the lower valley of the Dove was occupied by these early settlers is not apparent ; but there is one site to be noticed in the angle made by that river with the Trent, and its proximity to the Roman road which here passes into Derbyshire is significant. During excavations for the original branch of the North Staffordshire Railway, through the rising ground on the south or Burton side of Stretton, several cinerary urns of reddish clay containing bones and ashes are reported to have been found and, as usual, broken by the workmen. At the same time a human skeleton, lying at full length with the feet pointing south, is said to have been discovered near the village. Some years previously numerous urns containing ashes and bones, deposited about 3 ft. below the surface, were exhumed from some gravel workings in a field near the house occupied by Mr. Gretton at the Beach. They are described as being made of soft reddish clay, and the mouth of each was closed with a small slab of sandstone. The author refers the pottery to the Britons rather than the Romans, and adds that the skeleton may be later.[19]

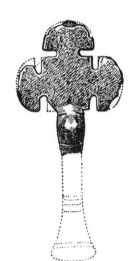

FIG. 5.—BROOCH FOUND AT WICHNOR (⅔)

Except that the pottery was evidently of poor quality and not wheel-made, one might be inclined to regard the cemetery as Roman, especially as it adjoined the Icknield Street ; but the sepulchral pottery of the Anglo-Saxons was a blackish or brownish grey, the larger (cinerary) urns being generally ornamented on the shoulder with incised lines and stamped patterns. No mention is made of such designs, but it is possible that red earth was still attached to the pottery when examined, and the ornamentation, if any, passed unnoticed. It should be remarked, however, that a few specimens found at Stapenhill were ' so highly

---

[18] *Trans. Burton-on-Trent Arch. Soc.* iv, pt. ii, 81.   [19] Wm. Molyneux, *Burton-on-Trent,* 21.

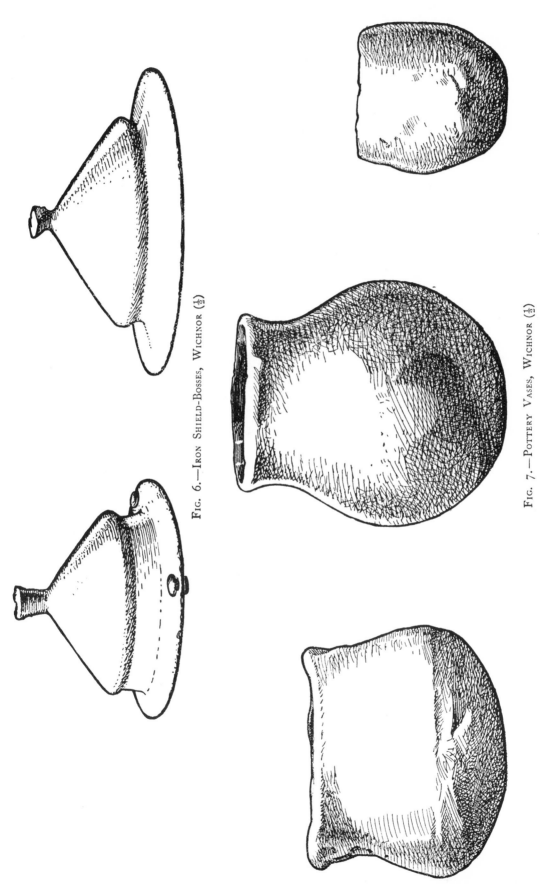

Fig. 6.—Iron Shield-Bosses, Wichnor ($\frac{1}{2}$)

Fig. 7.—Pottery Vases, Wichnor ($\frac{1}{2}$)

burnt as to acquire a reddish-brown tinge, and are extremely hard to the touch.'[20]   There is also some doubt as to the origin of the unburnt burial in the same neighbourhood. The grave-furniture, such as spear-head, knife, and shield, or brooches and beads, may have been overlooked or concealed by the workmen, and the position is by no means unusual at this period both in England (as at Little Wilbraham, Cambs.) and in Normandy.

Obviously distinct from the sites already dealt with are several in the north-east angle of the county that as clearly range with a compact group beyond the Dove in Derbyshire, and the physical similarity of the two areas has been noticed above. At Steep Low, near Alstonfield, there seems clear evidence of secondary Anglo-Saxon burials. The large mound, 150 ft. in diameter and 15 ft. high, was opened in 1845, and found to contain Bronze Age incinerations quite near the surface, but the primary burial was not reached. Before the excavators arrived some villagers had found near the top the body of a 'Romanized Briton,' extended on his back, accompanied by an iron spear-head, and a lance-head and knife of the same material[21] placed near the head, also three Roman coins, one being of Constantine (307-337), and another of Tetricus (268-273). The coins simply show that the burial was not earlier than the fourth century, and Constantinian coins are frequently found in Anglo-Saxon burials, whereas weapons are not found with Romano-British interments, either burnt or unburnt. Further, the present specimens have the split-socket characteristic of early Anglo-Saxon times, and it may be assumed that one warrior, at least, was laid to rest in a shallow grave cut in the mound that had been used for burials about 1,000 years before.

At the Boroughs, Wetton, there seem to have been several Anglo-Saxon inhumations, but the remains[22] are very fragmentary, and the records incomplete. A flat bronze ring with rust at one point may be a ring-brooch with remains of the pin ; and an iron ring belongs to a type common in Anglo-Saxon graves, perhaps attached to the girdle. More determinate are a tanged knife, part of a pair of shears, and part of a whetstone of blue slate, all found with a skeleton here in 1852. There are Roman objects from the same site, and evidence of a Romano-British village near Wetton.[23] An iron spear-head $10\frac{1}{4}$ in. long, and a knife 6 in. long, found with a skeleton in a mound at the Boroughs in 1844, are sufficient evidence of an Anglo-Saxon warrior's burial, either primary or secondary, and render it at least probable that another iron knife, 6 in. long, also belonged to a burial of the period.[24] A knife of this kind seems to have been commonly carried by both sexes for use at meals, and was usually deposited in the grave, as at Barlaston.

Somewhat doubtful is an iron knife,[25] now in fragments, from a barrow at Blore's field, Calton (1849); and a flat iron ring,[26] $1\frac{3}{8}$ in. in diameter, found in a barrow near Blore in the same year is insufficient evidence of a burial, though such rings are frequently found in Anglo-Saxon graves. The presence of such people in the neighbourhood of Throwley is attested by an iron spear-head[27] of ordinary type 9 in. long found near the River Manifold

---

[20] *Trans. Burton Nat. Hist. and Arch. Soc.* i, 185.
[21] *Sheffield Mus. Cat.* 99, 232 (figs.), 235 ; Bateman, *Vestiges,* p. 76.
[22] *Sheffield Mus. Cat.* 195-219.   [23] Bateman, *Ten Years' Diggings,* 194.
[24] *Sheffield Mus. Cat.* 232 (1844), 235 (1857).   [25] Ibid. 220.
[26] Ibid. 239.   [27] Ibid. 232.

in 1858, and a glass bead[28] of ring pattern, 1 in. in diameter, found in a field in 1856. An almost identical bead, of translucent yellow glass with a thread of bright yellow within the ring, is exhibited with it at Sheffield, and came from Kirkham's land, Middleton Moor (by Youlgreave), Derbyshire.

The Anglo-Saxon origin of a find on Readon (Wredon) Hill, one mile north of Ramshorn, is open to question. On 4 September, 1848, a barrow 19 yds. in diameter and 3 ft. high was opened and found to contain two skeletons extended near the centre, with no protection but a few stones in contact with one of the bodies, which was possibly interred later than the other. It was not more than 2 ft. from the surface, while the other lay on the natural level at least 3 ft. from the turf covering the mound. Of the former, the skull, which was that of a young man with a longitudinal index of 76, remained in perfect preservation with some of the hair, and a small pebble was found at the right hand. The lower skeleton was covered with a layer of charcoal, and the skull belonged to a middle-aged man. An iron spear-head lay at least two yards from the upper, and further from the lower burial, and measures 13 in., with part of the shaft still preserved by rust in the socket. With it was a narrow war knife 8 in. long, and their association points to an Anglo-Saxon burial; but they do not seem to have belonged to either of the bodies found. The microscope revealed the fact that the shaft of the spear was of ash, and the surface of the weapon and knife shows traces of

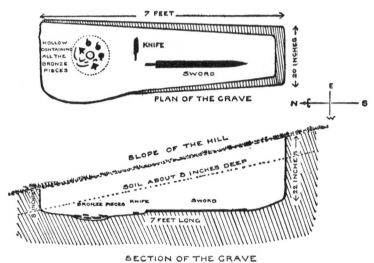

FIG. 8.—GRAVE AT BARLASTON (PLAN AND SECTION)

grass and the larvae of insects with which they had been in contact.[29]

There are reasons for classing with those in the north (the nearest of which is 12 miles distant) an isolated burial in the Trent valley, but nearly 30 miles above Wichnor, and separated by the whole width of Needwood Forest. This remarkable discovery was made in 1850 on the estate of the late Mr. Francis Wedgwood, at Barlaston, some twenty years before it was first published by Llewellyn Jewitt.[30] It has since been included in a paper on bronze bowls with enamel mounts, by the late Mr. Romilly Allen,[31] and an illustrated account was presented to the local society by Mr. Lawrence Wedgwood in 1905.

On a slope of red sandstone a grave (fig. 8) 7 ft. long and 2 ft. wide was found cut into the solid rock when the gravel-pit hill to the east of the house was dug over for the planting of trees. It was evidently an isolated burial, and

---

[28] *Sheffield Mus. Cat.* 227. [29] *Diggings,* 122–3 ; *Sheffield Mus. Cat.* 162 (skull), 235.
[30] *Grave-mounds and their Contents* (1870), 258, figs. 434, 435 ; Lawrence Wedgwood, 'Notes on Celtic Remains found at the Upper House, Barlaston,' *Trans. N. Staffs. Field Club,* xl (1906), 148. [31] *Arch.* lvi, 44.

lay north and south, the greatest depth (15 in. in the rock) being at the south-east corner. About 8 in. of soil covered the rock, and the floor of the grave at the north end was immediately beneath. At that end there was a basin-shaped cavity two or three inches deep in the rock beyond the original position of the skull, though the skeleton had completely disappeared. On the right or western side of the grave, near and parallel to the side, was a long two-edged sword, and to the north-east of the handle was an iron knife characteristic of the Anglo-Saxon period.

Such is the story derived from the published accounts, and the site is now carefully railed in for preservation. A few remarks may be added by way of comment and illustration, but little is as yet known as to the precise significance of the enamelled bowls of this period found in various parts of England. The Barlaston specimen, though sadly injured by time, must have been exceptionally ornate, and is peculiar in having been cast, not wrought like the rest. It is on this account comparatively heavy, and there are marks of the lathe on the base, which seems to have been indented and ornamented on the outside[32] with the enamelled ring (fig. 9). The three discs were attached originally to the outside of the bowl at equal intervals below the rim, which is slightly thickened, and served, with the hooks above the discs, to form loops for suspension by three chains which have as usual perished. The enamelled discs are of the ordinary size and character, mounted in circular frames of bronze; and the ornamentation on them and the ring that fitted into the base is of the late Celtic character. The enamel which fills the ground is of the usual red colour, but is remarkable in another respect. Irregularly set in it are discs of millefiore glass, produced by cutting thin slices off a bundle of glass rods so that the arrangement of the coloured chequers is constant. This inlaying of millefiore in enamel is again seen on similar discs for a bowl found in the north of England, and acquired for the national collection; and the fourth enamelled disc in that find may well have been inserted in a broad ring at the base like that found at Barlaston. The narrow bronze bands ornamented with incised rings were evidently fixed horizontally to the outside of the bowl between the three discs, their centre line being about $\frac{3}{8}$ in. below the rim, as is shown by rivet-holes for repair; but these strips were originally fixed without rivets (perhaps by brazing), and the reason for their slanting ends is not obvious. They are 5½ in. long on the outside curve, whereas the intervals between the disc-frames must have been about 7 in., the circumference being about 27½ in., and each of the disc-frames being just over 2 in. across.

Though an isolated burial the Barlaston discovery falls into line with others made just across the Derbyshire border. Remains of no less than three such bowls[33] have been found in the neighbourhood of Dovedale : at Middleton-by-Youlgreave, Over Haddon, and Benty Grange, the last lying in the grave beside the hair of a warrior, in association with a leather bowl ornamented with applied crosses. At Barlaston the bowl was found just where the head would have lain, and seems to have been in the centre line of the grave, so that perhaps the head rested within it at the time of burial.

---

[32] At Caistor, Lincs. the ring was apparently inside. The form of the base, whether indented or protruding, is often uncertain, but ornament may have been applied on both sides (*Proc. Soc. Antiq.* xxi, 78).
[33] All noticed in *Arch.* lvi, 42, 46 ; *V.C.H. Derb.* i, 271, 269, fig. on left of plate.

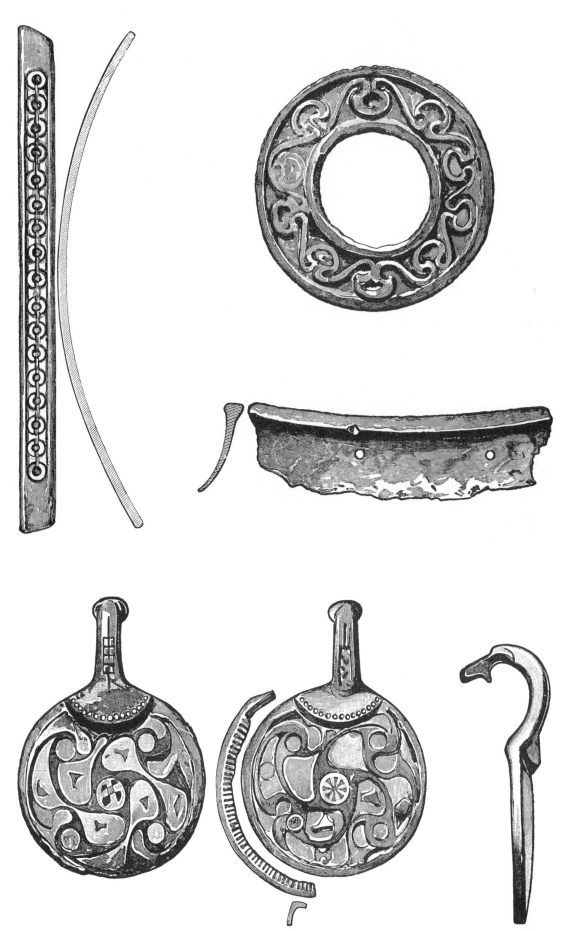

FIG. 9.—REMAINS OF BRONZE BOWL AND ENAMELLED DISCS FOUND AT BARLASTON ($\frac{1}{1}$)

According to the plan the knife would be as usual at the waist, and the sword, as occasionally elsewhere,[34] beside the right leg.

Special interest is attached to the discovery of an Anglo-Saxon jewel at a point between the burials of the north-east and Barlaston. The latter site now appears to be an outpost of the community centred in the Peak district, and in contact with the Celtic population which had not been displaced by the Teutonic advance westward. Jewellery of the period is specially abundant in Derbyshire, and extremely rare in the Trent valley cemeteries already noticed, so that the connexion is practically demonstrated in spite of the absence of details as to the discovery. All that is known is that in levelling a hedge bank at Forsbrook, about half a mile from Blyth Bridge station about 1879, the coin-pendant here illustrated (fig. 10) was found by a labourer and subsequently passed into the British Museum. Its excellent condition suggests that it accompanied an unburnt burial, but nothing further was noticed on the site or in the neighbourhood. The centre of the pendant consists of a gold casting from a coin of the Emperor Valentinian II (375–92), but the reverse is hidden by a plain gold plate at the back, and round the edge are slight mouldings separated by two twisted strands of gold. The front border

FIG. 10. — COIN-PEN-
DANT, FORSBROOK (¾)

is inlaid with garnets relieved by blue glass in the semi-circular cells, the whole being a typical example of Anglo-Saxon *cloisonné* work in gold. Some of the settings are now missing, both from the border and barrel-shaped loop for suspension, but otherwise the pendant is perfect. This style of ornament is particularly common in Kent, where the richest graves belong to the sixth and early seventh centuries, and any erroneous conclusions from the inclosed coin of the Staffordshire specimen may be avoided by reference to other examples in the national collection. Thus a pendant from Bacton, Norfolk, which bears a striking resemblance to it, incloses a coin of the Emperor Mauritius (582–602); and a jewelled cross from Wilton, in the same county, with a coin of Heraclius and Heraclius Constantine (610–41),[34a] must be of about the same date, though of somewhat finer workmanship. That the coins of earlier emperors were utilized in the seventh century is shown by a somewhat plainer pendant, of the same type as that from Forsbrook, containing a coin of Valens (364–78); and one of Valentinian II was again copied for a bracteate found in England, and now in the British Museum. The embossed discs of gold-foil that are known under that name are plentiful in Scandinavia, and exceedingly rare in this country, but two specimens[34b] are preserved from the adjoining county of Warwick; and though the choice of a Valentinian coin for the design was no doubt accidental, everything points to a close agreement in date between the bracteates and coin-pendants set with garnets. Imperial coins had no doubt already become rare curiosities in England when the Anglo-Saxon goldsmith showed his skill upon them.

According to the Ordnance Survey map (6 in. scale, xx, SW.) a Saxon sword and celt were found in 1834 about a quarter mile west of Alton

---

[34] At Sibertswold, Kent; *Inventorium Sepulchrale*, 118, 124. The position varied, but the left side was more usual.   [34a] Both are illustrated in colours in *V.C.H. Norf.* i, 341–2, figs. 2 and 7 on plate.
[34b] *V.C.H. Warw.* i, 263–4, figs. 10, 11, on coloured plate.

Towers, near the road from the station, but the association does not inspire confidence, and need only be mentioned. On the same sheet is marked 'the site of a battle between the West Saxons and Mercians A.D. 716,' at Slain Hollow, just over a quarter mile east of the mansion. The statement appears arbitrary, but it is possible that burials of some kind on the site have given rise to the name, and the tendency formerly was to regard such a discovery as proof of a battle in the neighbourhood.

The foregoing survey of Anglo-Saxon remains in Staffordshire may now be brought into touch with historical records, though these refer mostly to a period subsequent to that treated above. The early history of Mercia is even more obscure than that of the other kingdoms that disputed the hegemony of Britain in the seventh and eighth centuries ; but the date of one important event can be decided within narrow limits. Penda, who came to the throne in 626, was apparently about eighty years of age at his death in 655.[35] He fell at the battle of the Winwaed as the stubborn antagonist of Christianity, and Oswiu the victor came into temporary possession of the great dominion built up by Penda, installing the latter's Christian son Peada as sub-king of the South Mercians in what is now Leicestershire. From that date Mercia officially professed the new faith, and in 673 the seal was set to its conversion by Archbishop Theodore, who consecrated St. Chad the first bishop of Lichfield. The see chosen, about nine miles from the royal seat at Tamworth, shows the political centre of gravity at that time, and marks the revival of Mercia under Penda's son Wulfhere, who acceded to the throne in 659 and reigned for sixteen eventful years. For a century and a half Mercia was the dominant power in England, under a succession of great kings ; but its fortunes as a Christian power will be followed elsewhere, and a few words may now be added as to the part played by those early settlers whose remains are here under discussion.

The name Mercia is generally held to mean the march or border-kingdom ; and though Offa's Dyke shows the position of the frontier against the Welsh or Britons in the latter part of the eighth century, it is certain that two hundred years earlier the natives, who were slowly driven west by the English advance, retained a broad belt of country to the east of that north-and-south line. In this connexion mention must be made of the view that the battle of Fethan-Leag, mentioned in the *Anglo-Saxon Chronicle* under the year 584, was fought at Faddiley in Cheshire, five miles west of Nantwich. This location is supported by the tradition that Pengwyrn (Shrewsbury) was fired and Bassa's churches (perhaps Baschurch) wrecked, both sites being on the road north from Gloucestershire ; but on archaeological grounds the site of the battle should rather be looked for somewhere on the Warwickshire Avon ; there was, in fact, a place called Faehhaleah not far from Stratford.[36]

In any case the West Saxons under Ceawlin at once retreated southward, and it may be assumed that beyond Staffordshire, if not along the western half of the county itself, the Britons were in possession when the Trent and Dove valleys were being colonized by Teutonic strangers. The evident

---

[35] Green has a note on these dates : *Making of Engl.* (1897), i, 97 ; see also Chadwick, *Origin of the Engl. Nation*, 16.

[36] *Trans. Bristol and Glouc. Arch. Soc.* (1896–7), 254 ; *V.C.H. Warw.* i, 252.

connexion between the find at Barlaston and the series from the north-east of the county and the opposite district of Derbyshire has been already noticed ; and we cannot be far wrong in identifying the Dove valley colonists with the Pecsaetan, or dwellers in the Peak, mentioned in the remarkable list of settlements known as the Tribal Hidage, and dating from the first half of the seventh century.[37] These settlers were evidently accustomed to bury their dead in the grave-mounds or barrows of the Bronze period, but the reason may simply be that such mounds are particularly plentiful and conspicuous south of the Peak, and the practice was by no means confined to this area.[38]

The Pecsaetan were evidently included in the Mercian kingdom, but the archaeological material is too meagre to settle the question whether they were akin to the occupants of the Trent valley near Burton. The available evidence points to their isolation, and the frequent discovery of enamels executed in the traditional British style points to their close contact with the native element. Further investigations with regard to the manufacture and distribution of the enamelled bowls may eventually throw some light on this question of intercourse.

In connexion with the English occupation of this district, reference may be made to the varieties of dialect observed within the county borders.[38a] East and west, approximately through Stone, runs the southern limit of the use of a 'suspended' t, or a voiceless th, for the test-word the ; and this peculiarity of pronunciation suggests a somewhat close racial connexion between the inhabitants of the Potteries and those of Cheshire, Derbyshire, and Nottinghamshire, the limit following roughly the line of the Trent below Burton. Minor differences have also been noticed in this group of counties, and in view of what has been said with regard to north Staffordshire and Derbyshire, it is of interest to find that the dialect of Derbyshire south of Buxton is also heard along a strip of north-east Staffordshire parallel to the Dove, and bounded by a line from Buxton to Uttoxeter, thus embracing practically all the early burials apart from those in the neighbourhood of Burton. The latter is connected by dialect with south Staffordshire, north Warwickshire, Leicestershire, and east Shropshire.

It is probable that the original centre of Mercia was the Trent valley near Burton, and the remains support the view that these were the most westerly body of Angles, their kinsmen (the Middle and South Angles) having occupied or obtained control of that part of the Midlands lying between Sherwood on the north and Arden and Rockingham Forest on the south.[39] They would thus be the neighbours of the West Saxons and their early allies the Hwiccas of the Lower Severn ; but as the southern kingdom declined, the Mercians pressed south and became the masters of south-east England in the days of Wulfhere. This digression will help to explain why there is much in the original West Saxon area that resembles the products of Anglian graves in Staffordshire and other parts of Mercia ; whereas objects distinctively West Saxon are not found in the northern Midlands. If there

[37] *Trans. Roy. Hist. Soc.* (New Ser.), xiv, 191.

[38] An example occurred at Oldbury, near Atherstone, Warwickshire (*V.C.H. Warw.* i, 267) ; and many are recorded from Yorkshire.

[38a] These details are taken from A. J. Ellis, *English Dialects, their Sounds and Homes*, 7, 90, 92, 101, and map.

[39] For the limits of Mercia see H. M. Chadwick, *Origin of the Engl. Nation*, 7.

was any racial difference between Angle and Saxon [40] it would naturally be reflected in the archaeological data.

It is more than probable from the map that the Anglian immigrants who ventured farthest west ascended the Trent and its tributaries ; but another means of access to the interior must not be overlooked in tracing their progress. There were in the sixth century at least two Roman military roads available here for crossing vast areas that would otherwise have remained practically impassable. Neither forest nor swamp could deter the Romans, and most of their highways through Staffordshire are still in use to-day. The Watling Street, which enters the county at Fazeley, passes through Wall and westward south of Cannock on its way to Wroxeter and Chester, in long straight stretches ; and from the south the Icknield (or Ryknield) Street [41] crosses it near Wall and then strikes north-east down the Trent valley. This road would not have materially assisted the newcomers, but the Watling Street communicated with the central plain and London ; and, at least in later Anglo-Saxon times, was recognized as a thoroughfare and controlled at the county border by the stronghold at Tamworth erected by Æthelflaed of Mercia in 914. When the West Saxons were pushing northward in the sixth century both roads would have been of strategical importance ; [42] and it may have been originally due to such considerations that the Mercian king frequently resided at Tamworth. [43]

What little is known concerning the pagan or semi-pagan settlers who gained a footing in Staffordshire in post-Roman times is derived from their grave furniture and modes of burial ; and it should be observed that nothing definitely referring to the Christian belief has been recovered from their cemeteries. Neither is there anything that can be referred to the fifth century, when we may suppose the Roman tradition was still strong and the Teutons were struggling to effect an entry on the east. It is therefore to the sixth and early seventh centuries that these remains must be attributed, and some of the graves without arms or ornaments may even be later, for though the priest may have effected this reform, it was not till the middle of the eighth century that the law as to burial of converts in the consecrated churchyard was rigidly enforced. Archaeology suffers by these changes, but the pious then began to found monasteries and secure charters, to build stone churches, and place carved monuments over their dead. From that time forward history is based on records and enduring stone.

[40] This point is disputed by Mr. Chadwick, op. cit. 88.
[41] The name is discussed in *V.C.H. Derb.* i, 246 ; see also *Arch. Journ.* xiv, 102.
[42] Penda was at Cirencester in 628 ; Roman roads would have served him all the way.
[43] For details of the position see J. R. Green, *Conquest of Engl.* (1899), i, 223.

POLITICAL HISTORY

THE history of Staffordshire from the English invasion to the Norman Conquest is closely connected with the history of Mercia. Staffordshire was 'Mercia proper.'[1] Tamworth, though never the capital in the sense that Winchester was the capital of Wessex, was the royal city of the kingdom, and was the favourite dwelling-place of several Mercian kings; Repton in Derbyshire being their Westminster Abbey.

There are unfortunately no peculiarly Mercian chronicles of early date, and its history has to be pieced together from references in West Saxon and Northumbrian chronicles, and from charters and laws. Its founders were the Angles, apparently the latest comers of the Low German tribes who in the first century after Christ were living on the right bank of the Elbe near its mouth.[2]

Whilst some of the Angles were pushing up the Soar to what is now Leicester, and others settling in Derbyshire, more important bands were coming along the Fosse Way and up the Trent, who founded Tamworth and Lichfield. For some time their settlements seem to have been confined to the district round these two places and the upper Trent valley. West of this the wild moorlands checked their advance, and they gained from their dwelling on the borderland between Angle and Welshman the name of Mercians or men of the March.[3]

The origins of Mercian history are involved in great obscurity; all we know is that at the end of the sixth century the kingdom appears as a powerful state, but it has no distinctly recorded founder or date of origin.[4] In fact it grew from the union[5] of a large number of small and wholly independent principalities, in this differing from the other kingdoms.[6]

Crida, whose pedigree was traced from Woden, is the first Mercian chief mentioned in the documents that remain to us, and is conjectured by Henry of Huntingdon to have been the first king,[7] but Penda, who began to reign in 626, seems to have been the earliest who can claim the title without question.[8] Penda was a sturdy heathen, and came nearer to uniting the whole of England under one sceptre than any king before Egbert, but at last, on the banks of the Winwaed in 655, he was defeated by Oswy of Northumbria and killed.

[1] Stubbs, *Const. Hist.* (ed. 4), i, 123.
[2] Hodgkin, *Political Hist. of Engl.* i, 80. For further particulars on this subject see the article on 'Anglo-Saxon Remains.'
[3] Green, *Making of Engl.* 85.   [4] Freeman, *Norman Conq.* i, 25.
[5] As the name Mercia was extended to the whole of central England it must have lost its original signification.
[6] Freeman, *Norman Conq.* i, 26–7.   [7] *Hist. Angl.* (Rolls Ser.), 53.
[8] Turner, *Hist. of Anglo-Saxons*, i, 354 ; William of Malmesbury, *Gesta Reg.* (Rolls Ser.), 76.

His death was of great importance to Mercia, for it removed the great obstacle to the spread of Christianity in the kingdom, which had already begun in the marriage of Penda's son Paeda to Oswy's daughter.

After the victory of the Winwaed Oswy was virtually master of Mercia. His son-in-law Paeda was under-king of the portion of the kingdom south of the Trent, but he apparently kept Northern Mercia in his own hands.[9] Paeda did not enjoy even this limited authority for long, as next year he was murdered, and in 658 Oswy was expelled and Wulfhere reigned once more over an independent Mercia.

From the time of Wulfhere dates the bishopric of Lichfield. The first three Mercian bishops had no cathedral, no 'sedes,' they were missionaries; but St. Chad, the great bishop, whom Wilfrid recommended to Wulfhere, fixed his head quarters, and built a small church and monastery near the junction of Ryknield and Watling Streets in 669,[10] a centre which would give him easy access in every direction into his province.

The Mercian kings of the end of the seventh and the beginning of the eighth century are not of great importance, and do not concern our county history except that Ceolred, who died in 716, was buried at Lichfield,[11] but from his death dates the period of the greatest glory of the kingdom under the two long reigns of Ethelbald and Offa, when it seemed as if the consolidation of England was to be worked out by Mercia instead of Wessex, and as if Lichfield rather than Winchester or London would be the capital of England. But Mercia at the end of Ethelbald's reign sustained a grievous defeat at Burford at the hands of Wessex, and her supremacy over that kingdom then apparently passed away for ever.

His successor Offa, who reigned from 757 to 796, loomed more largely in the eyes of his European contemporaries than any previous king in Britain. Hadrian I, writing to Charles the Great, calls Offa 'rex Anglorum,' and Charles himself, in his famous letter, writes as 'the king of the Eastern Christians,' to the 'mightiest king of the Western Christians.'

Offa, like many of the Mercian kings, was fond of the fertile valleys of the Dove and the Trent; indeed, it was in such districts that nearly all the ancient towns that attained greatness were built, provided they also afforded means of defence and commanded the country around. Tamworth enjoyed all these advantages, and is called by Offa in a grant of land to Worcester Cathedral, dated 781, 'his royal palace.'[12]

Cenwulf, the successor of Offa, maintained the greatness of Mercia for a time, but in 827 the kingdom had to submit to Egbert, and though retaining her own kings, they were only under-kings who received their crowns from their West Saxon overlords.[13]

The kings of Mercia, under the overlordship of Wessex, continued to hold their Witans, and there is a record of one held at Tamworth in 840 by Berhtwulf on Easter Day, but the business transacted there did not concern Staffordshire.[14]

Between 872 and 875 the Vikings marched through Mercia, dethroned Burhred, who retired to Rome, and set up a puppet Ceolwulf in his stead.

[9] Hodgkin, *Political Hist. of Engl.* i, 173.
[11] Henry of Huntingdon, *Hist. Angl.* (Rolls Ser.), 111.
[13] Freeman, *Norman Conq.* (ed. 2), i, 40.
[10] Bede, *Hist. Eccl.* iv, 3.
[12] Birch, *Cart. Sax.* i, 334.
[14] Birch, *Cart. Sax.* ii, 4–5.

POLITICAL HISTORY

They settled at Repton in 874, and from there subdued the whole of the surrounding country,[15] destroying and plundering Tamworth and Stafford.

When the Treaty of Wedmore put an end for a time to this ruinous war, Watling Street may be taken as the practical boundary between the Danelaw and Alfred's dominion.[16] Staffordshire therefore was divided between the two, the northern and central portions going to the Danes, the southern to Alfred. How far did the Danes fill up the district assigned to them ? This unfortunately is a question which as yet we have not sufficient materials to answer definitely. Our best guide is that of place-names, the commonest Danish terminations being 'by,' 'thorpe,' and 'toft,' and according to this test the Danes hardly left any permanent trace in Staffordshire.

The contest soon broke out again. The Danes, thrown back from the Continent by a great defeat at Louvain, turned their attention to England with renewed vigour, and were assisted by their brethren of the Danelaw. A terrible internal struggle was waged all along the boundary, Watling Street,[17] and must have involved Staffordshire.

However, a deliverer was at hand. In 910 Edward the Elder met the Danes at Tettenhall,[18] and defeated them, and from this time the Viking host was steadily pushed eastwards. The chief credit for the conquest of Danish Mercia must be given to Edward's 'manlike sister,' Ethelfleda, the 'lady of the Mercians.' The daughter of a Mercian princess and married to one who was probably connected with the royal line of Offa, she is one of the most capable women in English history. After her husband's death in 911 she won the 'love and loyalty of the Mercian people in an astonishing degree and wielded the warlike resources of the Midland Kingdom with wonderful energy and success.'[19] Her plan of campaign was to build a 'burh' in the hostile territory and hold it against all comers till the surrounding country was entirely subdued.

In the year 913

> God granting, Ethelfleda, lady of the Mercians, went with all the Mercians to Tamworth, and built the burh there in the early summer, and before the following Lammas (Aug. 1) that at Stafford. Then in the year after this that at Eddisbury in the early summer.[20]

The short time occupied in the building shows that the burhs must have been of very elementary construction. The burhs at Tamworth and Stafford are an excellent instance of the military genius of this warlike woman, as they blocked the way along the Trent and Watling Street, which the Danes used in order to effect a junction with their Irish brethren at Chester.

Ethelfleda died at the Tamworth burh which she had built, in 918, and was buried at Gloucester.[21] Her precise relationship with her royal brother Edward is hard to define. She fought, made treaties, and governed with apparently entire independence, but she is always described as 'lady,' never as 'queen.' Probably Edward was her 'mund–bora,'[22] or protector, and

---

[15] *Angl.-Sax. Chron.* (Rolls Ser.), ii, 63. [16] Hodgkin, op. cit. i, 315. [17] Ibid. i, 309.

[18] *Angl.-Sax. Chron.* (Rolls Ser.), ii, 77. Symeon of Dur. *Hist. Reg.* 122 (Rolls Ser.), and Flor. of Worc. *Chron.* i, 120, say 911.

[19] Hodgkin, op. cit. i, 321.

[20] *Angl.-Sax. Chron.* (Rolls Ser.), ii, 78–9. Matt. Paris, *Chron. Maj.* (Rolls Ser.), i, 443, says she restored Tamworth and the tower at Stafford, no doubt referring to the fact that they had lain in ruins since 874.

[21] *Angl.-Sax. Chron.* (Rolls Ser.), ii, 81. [22] Hodgkin, op. cit. i, 322-3.

knowing her capacity allowed her the widest discretion, but not absolute independence.

In the midst of so much warfare it is pleasant to be able to turn for a moment to a work of construction in which the creation of the county of Stafford formed part. Mercia, during its existence as a kingdom, was arranged in five regions, none of which bore the name of shire, one of them being 'Mercia proper with its bishopric of Lichfield and its royal city of Tamworth.'[23] These five regions represent the early settlements out of which the Mercian kingdom was created by Penda and his immediate predecessors, and which Theodore of Tarsus arranged as dioceses before their several nationality had been forgotten. After the reconquest from the Danes they were rearranged as shires and named after their chief towns by Edward the Elder,[24] and in this they differed from the counties of Wessex, which keep to this day the names and boundaries of the principalities founded by the first successors of Cerdic.

In the year 924 Edward the Elder died and was succeeded by his son Athelstan 'the glorious,' who, shortly after he came to the throne, had an interview with Sihtric, the Danish king of the Northumbrians, at Tamworth.[25] There Athelstan gave him his sister in marriage, in return for which Sihtric probably promised to become a Christian, but he is said to have repudiated both wife and religion before his death in the next year.

Edmund his brother succeeded Athelstan in 940.

> In the first year of Edmund's reign Anlaf (Sihtric's son) after besieging Hamton without result turned his army towards Tamworth, and having laid waste the surrounding country met Edmund with his army. But there was no battle, for the two archbishops appeased both kings and prevented it, and peace was accordingly made.[26]

This peace lasted about a year, for in 943 Anlaf 'took Tamworth by storm and great slaughter was made on either side, and the Danes had the victory and led away great booty with them.'[27]

On Edmund's approach, however, they retired to Leicester, and in 944 Anlaf was driven out of Northumbria and appears no more on the scene.[28]

In 957 England was divided between Edwy and Edgar, owing to the dissatisfaction of the people with the former's misgovernment, and Mercia, including of course Staffordshire, was again separated from Wessex and given to Edgar,[29] but as Edwy died in 959 the arrangement was short-lived.

In 987 the Danes commenced a new series of invasions, and Mercia was ruled at this time by two men whose traitorous conduct is one of the puzzles of our history, Elfric and Edric 'Streona,' who did their best to render the resistance of England futile and the task of the Danes easy.

Staffordshire, however, seems for some time to have escaped the terrible ravages which the rest of the country now suffered, but in 1013 Edmund Ironside and Uhtred of Northumbria ravaged Shropshire, Cheshire, and Staffordshire, because those counties had refused to help them against the Danes.[30]

---

[23] Stubbs, *Const. Hist.* (ed. 4), i, 123.   [24] Ibid.
[25] *Angl.-Sax. Chron.* (Rolls Ser.), ii, 85.   [26] Symeon of Dur. *Chron.* (Rolls Ser.), ii, 93.
[27] *Angl.-Sax. Chron.* (Rolls Ser.), ii, 89.   [28] Hodgkin, op. cit. i, 340.
[29] Matt. Paris, *Chron. Maj.* (Rolls Ser.), ii, 460.
[30] Freeman, *Norman Conq.* i, 415, and Roger of Hoveden, *Chron.* (Rolls Ser.), i, 80.

In that year[31] the character of the Viking invasions changed, and a period of regular and systematic conquest under Sweyn and his son Canute set in. In three years Staffordshire changed kings three times : for in 1013 it submitted with the rest of England to Sweyn ; on his death, with the whole country, it reverted to Ethelred ; and in 1016, on the division of the country at Olney, it went with the rest of Mercia to Canute.

In the same year, just before the treaty, both Canute and Edmund harried, burned, and slew in the county.[32]

The career of the traitor Edric Streona was cut short by Canute, and he was succeeded as earl, for so the ealdormen were now called, of Mercia by Leofwine, who in turn was followed by his famous son Leofric. He died at Bromley in Staffordshire in 1057, and after Elfgar had been earl a few years Edwin, the last earl of Mercia, succeeded him some time between 1062 and 1065, and is of interest to us as many of his estates lay in the county.[33]

On his death the earldom of Mercia came to an end, and its last earl cannot be said to have dignified that end. For though he had high birth, a handsome person, and winning manners, added to the piety of the age, he was politically worthless.[34] When Harold Hardrada sailed up the Tyne he left the coast unguarded ; when Harold the son of Godwine was marching south to fight William he hung back. He was one of the first to yield to William, yet he rebelled against the Conqueror, though his heart failed him before a blow was struck ; while his second attempt was futile and ended in his assassination, according to the English account, by his own men.

His estates went into various hands, the king kept the lion's share, while many went to found the two palatinate earldoms of Chester and Shrewsbury.[35]

We have now reached ' the turning point of English history.' England seemed conquered by the battle of Hastings, but after a brief lull a series of isolated risings took place, which were beaten in detail by William.

In 1069, when the Danes and English took York, Staffordshire and Shropshire broke out in revolt, probably at the instigation of Edwin. This district must have been imperfectly subdued up to this time. Both town and county paid dearly for their outbreak, for William in his northward march conquered them ; and the huge confiscations, which were always great in proportion to the resistance to his rule, show that the patriotism of the Staffordshire men had led to a vigorous contest that was punished with merciless severity.[36]

In the next year occurred William's celebrated winter march from York to Chester, and, provoked by the stern resistance he met then, the neighbouring counties, including Staffordshire, were fearfully ravaged ; ' men young and old, women and children, wandered as far south as the abbey of Evesham in quest of a morsel of bread.'[37] It was probably at this time that, according to his custom, William built the castle in the town of Stafford, which was

---

[31] It should be mentioned that Holinshed fixes the scene of the opening of the massacre of St. Brice's Day at Houndhill, five miles from Tutbury.

[32] *Angl.-Sax. Chron.* (Rolls Ser.), 121.

[34] Freeman, *Norman Conq.* iv, 182.

[36] Freeman, *Norman Conq.* (ed. 4), iv, 282.

[33] Eyton, *Staffs. Domesday*, 32.

[35] Eyton, *Staffs. Domesday*, 32.

[37] Ibid. iv, 315.

destroyed before the end of his reign, and at the date of Domesday lay in ruins.[38]

The displacement of the original landowners of the county after the Conquest was very thorough, no doubt aggravated by the resistance of 1069 and 1070. At the time when the commissioners of the Domesday Survey visited the county something like half was woodland, and generally speaking it was thinly inhabited, incapable of ordinary taxation, and badly stocked. At this time the greatest landowners in the county beside the king were, first of all, Robert de Toeni, afterwards called de Stafford, who took his name almost certainly from Stafford, of which he was governor. All that he held in the county had belonged to its last Saxon earl, Edwin, and he was the largest lay owner. He was the younger son of Roger de Toeni, the hereditary standard-bearer of the Conqueror, but in spite of his descent and his great possessions he was not granted the dignity and power of an earldom. This Robert de Stafford was the founder of the great house of Stafford, whose descendants in the fifteenth century became dukes of Buckingham, and perhaps the greatest landowners in England. Next to him came Roger of Montgomery Earl of Shropshire, one of the four great palatine earldoms.[39] Then came William Fitz Anculf, the owner, among other fiefs, of Dudley Castle, of whom nothing is known except that his entire barony came into the possession of Fulke Paynel, who probably married Fitz Anculf's heiress.[40] Henry de Ferrers, who built Tutbury Castle, was one of the commissioners of the Domesday Survey. His estates were more compact than those of most of the great nobles, whose holdings were split up partly by the policy of the Conqueror and partly by the scattered nature of the lands of their Anglo-Saxon predecessors. Hugh de Montgomery, one of the sons of Earl Roger, and Richard Forester also held estates in the county.[41]

Some lands still remained in the possession of Saxon thegns, and ecclesiastical landowners had a goodly share, the Bishop of Chester being the largest, while the others were the abbots of Westminster and Burton, the French abbey of Saint Rémy at Rheims, and the canons of Stafford and Handone (Wolverhampton).

The castles mentioned at Tutbury and Dudley were most probably like other castles of this period, of very simple construction, and the name does not necessarily imply even the use of stone in their construction.

After its terrible experience in the early part of the Conqueror's reign Staffordshire had peace till 1102, in which year the great house of Montgomery was in arms against Henry I. Robert of Bellême, another of the sons of Roger of Montgomery, forestalled Henry's summons to answer for his share in Duke Robert's invasion the preceding year [42] by gathering an army of Welsh and Normans. With these he and his brother Arnold laid waste part of Staffordshire, and thence carried off many horses and other animals and some men into Wales.[43]

At this time we find Stafford Castle, evidently a successor of that which had so short a life in the reign of William I, in the hands of the king under William Pantulf as its governor ; and the castle, garrisoned by 200 men-at-

[38] Freeman, *Norman Conq.* iv, 318.

[40] *Coll. for a Hist. of Staffs.* (Salt Arch. Soc.), ix (2), 6.

[42] Davis, *Engl. under Normans and Angevins*, 124.

[39] Stubbs, *Const. Hist.* (ed. 4), i, 294.

[41] Eyton, *Staffs. Domesday*, chap. 4.

[43] Roger of Hoveden, *Chron.* (Rolls Ser.), i, 159.

arms, was a royal base of operations against Bellême,[44] whose castles of Bridgnorth and Shrewsbury were captured and he himself driven to Normandy. The downfall of this man, one of the worst examples of the turbulent Norman barons, was hailed in England with delight.[45] His life was spared, but his English domains, which included large estates in Staffordshire, were confiscated. The royal castle after this declined in importance, and like many others degenerated into a gaol, though it was occasionally dignified with the name of castle, even as late as the reign of Henry VIII.[46]

The government of Henry I, 'the Lion of Righteousness,' though strong and just, was severe, and the chroniclers of the time frequently bewail the taxation which was 'not so burdensome by its weight as by its regular and inevitable incidence.'[47]

From the report of the sheriff of Staffordshire it appears that the annual ferm of the county, that is the amount arising from the king's demesnes, territorial rights, and profits from judicial proceedings, was in the years 1129–30 about £127 16s. 7d. in ordinary or unpurified money. Before rendering his account the sheriff had to discharge the king's debts in the county by paying the royal benefactions to religious houses, providing for the maintenance of the stock on crown lands, the costs of public business, of provisions supplied to the court, and the travelling expenses of the king within his district.[48]

When doing so at Michaelmas, 1130, among the items with which the sheriff of Staffordshire charged the king is £4 10s. paid for mead and ale in supply of a royal corrody (allowance for food), showing that the king had recently visited the county.[49] The Danegeld, the next most important item in the sheriff's account, and the most unpopular—for out of it he probably made his greatest profit—amounted in 1130 to £44 1s., that is, 2s. per hide on 440½ hides, a large area of Staffordshire being ingeldable by prescription. The rate at which the county was assessed for this purpose works out at about one twenty-seventh of £1 to the square mile, a very low rate, as the normal rate per square mile was about one-seventh of £1. This, however, was not altogether an indication of poverty, especially when we allow for the large portion of ingeldable land, for the rich county of Kent was assessed at one-fifteenth, and it is almost certain that the assessment differed according to the polity of the ancient kingdoms out of which England had been formed.[50]

The most heavily assessed counties, for instance, were those of Wessex, and Shropshire, part of which belonged to Wessex, was twice as heavily assessed as its neighbour Staffordshire.[51] At Michaelmas, 1156, the ferm had increased considerably in amount, and among the deductions is £29 18s. for restocking all the royal manors in Staffordshire.[52]

In the wars of Stephen's reign the eastern half of England was nominally for the king and the western for Maud, but really the former controlled little more than the counties round London, and the latter Gloucestershire and the

---

[44] Eyton, *Staffs. Domesday*, 20. [45] Stubbs, *Const. Hist.* (ed. 4), i, 334.
[46] *Coll.* (Salt Arch. Soc.), viii (2), 8. The collections made by this society must be gratefully acknowledged as giving most valuable assistance to the writer of this article.
[47] Stubbs, *Const. Hist.* i, 339. [48] Ibid. 411.
[49] *Coll.* (Salt Arch. Soc.), i, 5. [50] Round, *Feud. Engl.* 95.
[51] Ibid. 96. [52] *Coll.* (Salt Arch. Soc.), i, 21.

neighbouring parts. The rest of the country was a scene of anarchy and feuds between rival nobles. Of the great men of Staffordshire Robert de Ferrers, the third and surviving son of Henry de Ferrers the Domesday commissioner, raised a body of men from the country round his castle of Tutbury and from Derbyshire to assist in defeating the Scots at Northallerton in 1138,[53] and for his valour was made an earl by Stephen. It should not be forgotten that the creation of earls by both Stephen and Maud was an expedient for strengthening their respective parties, and it is possible that the frequent changing of sides which marked the struggle may have been caused by the desire of these newly-created nobles to obtain confirmation of their titles from both competitors.[54]

One staunch supporter in Staffordshire Stephen had in the person of Robert Marmion, the lord of Tamworth Castle.[55] When the king was taken prisoner at Lincoln his estates were given by the victorious Maud to Sir William de Beauchamp, but Sir Robert was loyal in spite of adversity, and fighting against the Earl of Chester at Coventry met his death by a curious accident. Matthew Paris describes him as a warlike man,[56] who had expelled the monks of Coventry from their church and made a castle of it, and falling into one of the ditches which he had dug for its protection, he broke his thigh and was dispatched by a common soldier as he lay helpless.[57]

Ralph Paynel of Dudley, the son of Fulke Paynel, who is thought to have married Fitz Anculf's heiress, fortified the castle against Stephen, who besieged it, and 'having burnt the country around and taken a great booty of animals, he went on against Shrewsbury Castle.'[58] Gervase Paynel, too, Ralph's son, held Ludlow against the king.

The evils of 'uncurbed feudalism' during Stephen's reign of anarchy made the law and order enforced by Henry II additionally welcome. His activity in carrying out his reforms caused him to exercise a close superintendence over his officers, and between 1155 and 1157 he was three or four times in Staffordshire. In 1158 he came to Tamworth with a considerable train, among whom was Thomas Becket the chancellor, and they were the guests of Robert Marmion at Tamworth Castle. But the great measures which were the glory of Henry's reign found no favour with the baronage, who saw their own influence limited by them, and in 1173 they formed a vast conspiracy, finding in the discontent of the king's sons a sufficient pretext. The revolt, though unsuccessful in 1173, was renewed next year. But Henry had the support of the Church, the towns, the mass of the people, and the new official class, and by August the rebellion was over and the castles of the rebels were surrendered one by one with little resistance, among them being Tutbury.[59] Robert de Ferrers had assisted in the burning of Nottingham, and was then besieged by the Welsh at Tutbury, but on the approach of Henry's army he went to Northampton and there submitted to

[53] Dugdale, *Baronage*, i, 259.   [54] Stubbs, *Const. Hist.* i, 391.

[55] This Robert was the son of Roger Marmion, who had probably been given the forfeited estates of Robert Dispensator by Henry I.

[56] *Chron. Maj.* (Rolls Ser.), ii, 177.

[57] Dugdale, *Baronage*, i, 376. Round, *Feud. Engl.* 195, does not allow the disinterestedness of Robert Marmion; he says, 'in their rivalry for Tamworth the Marmions embraced the cause of Stephen, and the Beauchamps that of Maud, their variance being terminated under Henry II by a matrimonial alliance.'

[58] Flor. of Worc. *Chron.* (Engl. Hist. Soc.), ii, 110.

[59] Roger of Hoveden, *Chron.* (Rolls Ser.), ii, 65.

the king.[60] Gervase Paynel also took part in the rebellion, and for his share in it his castle of Dudley was demolished.[61]

In 1175 Henry was again in Staffordshire, and when at Lichfield on his way to Nottingham, pleas were held there by William Fitz Ralph, Bertram de Verdon, and William Basset in Curia Regis.[62]

The possessions of the crown all over England had been considerably diminished during the reign of Stephen, who had granted many estates in order to obtain the support of those whom he thus favoured, and none of Henry II's acts was more unpopular with the barons than his command that the royal demesnes bestowed by the late king should be restored.[63] The estates of the crown in Staffordshire in the reign of Henry II consisted of—

(*a*) Such manors as having been in the crown or in the Earl of Mercia before the Conquest remained in the crown at the date of Domesday, and came into Henry's hands as ancient demesne or ancient escheat, and composed his ferm of the county:[64] Trentham, Penkridge, Wednesbury, Walsall, Wigginton, Kingswinford and Clent, Tettenhall, Tarbeck, Alrewas, Bromley Regis, Rugeley and Cannock, Meretown, Wolverhampton, Willenhall, Bilston, Rowley Regis, Wolstanton, Penkhall, Leek. Between the date of Domesday and the accession of Henry II, Trentham, Wolstanton, and Leek had been given to the Earls of Chester, but the grants were revoked by Henry.

(*b*) Estates of ancient demesne or escheat which were never incorporated in the ferm of the county, but were given in charge to bailiffs, fermors, and trustees other than the sheriff: Borough of Stafford, Half borough of Tamworth, Kinver, Cannock and its forest, Newcastle-under-Lyme, Hopwas.

(*c*) Another kind of crown estate consisted either in the ferm of manors which had been severed from the king's demesnes and granted to fermors before the accession of Henry II, or in the extra values placed upon estates of ancient demesne or ancient escheat after his accession, these were: Brome, Stafford Mill, Stafford Smithy, Rowley Regis, Cradley Mill, Trentham Market, Walsall, (Clent, Kingswinford, Meretown had a collective ferm set upon them), Alrewas, a house in Stafford which had belonged to Walter the Provost, who had been outlawed in 1175 and his house seized by the sheriff as an escheat of the crown.

(*d*) Escheated 'tainlands' which were always waste, and in the king's hands because no one had wanted them.

At the same time the estates of the Earl of Chester in the county probably comprised the following: Chartley, Sandon, Eiford, Drayton, Pattingham, Leek, Endon, Rudyard, The Rushtons, Alton.[65]

From 1184 the see of Lichfield[66] was occupied by a man who, like many of the ecclesiastics of that age, was also a keen politician and man of affairs, Hugh of Nonant, who combined the parts of bishop, soldier, justiciary,

---

[60] Matt. Paris, *Chron. Maj.* (Rolls Ser.), ii, 297, says that in 1175 Tutbury was levelled with the ground by Henry's orders in revenge for the wrongs which its owner had often done.

[61] *Coll.* (Salt Arch. Soc.), ix (2), 8.

[62] Eyton, *Itin. of Hen. II*, 193.   [63] Stubbs, *Const. Hist.* (ed. 4), i, 489.

[64] This list is taken from *Coll.* (Salt Arch. Soc.), ii, 171.

[65] Major-General the Hon. G. Wrottesley in *Coll.* (Salt Arch. Soc.), i, 231.

[66] The name Lichfield for the see is used to avoid confusion ; it was frequently called the see of Chester and Coventry in the twelfth and thirteenth centuries.

and sheriff at various periods of his life. He was sheriff of the county from 1190 to 1194,[67] at a time when John strove to undermine the authority of his absent brother, which William Longchamp upheld. Staffordshire felt the effect of John's schemes, and the sheriff charged the crown with £9 2s. 6d. for defending the county against malefactors ; he was also granted £26 from the king's purse to preserve the peace.[68] The shrewdness of this bishop was equal to his activity ; he took advantage of Richard's insatiable desire for money to buy the estates of Cannock and Rugeley from him for 25 marks (£16 13s. 4d.), and they were added to the possessions of the see.

King John favoured Staffordshire with several visits, no doubt because the county was particularly loyal to him, also because he was fond of hunting in its forests.[69] In March, 1200, he came through Burton to Lichfield, where he spent two days ; in 1204 he was again at Lichfield for three days, and two years afterwards paid another visit, at which date he bestowed the first charter on Stafford, though he never visited that town.

A letter written by Thomas de Erdinton, sheriff of Salop and Staffordshire in 1215, to the king in answer to his question, who, and how many knights bore arms against him in the war, shows the state of parties in Staffordshire clearly. He tells the king that in the county of Stafford there were not any opposed to John at first except Robert Marmion (he incurred John's anger by this opposition so that his castle of Tamworth was ordered to be razed, but the order was not carried out), who still remains disaffected, and Hervey Bagot, who had made himself Sheriff of Staffordshire by means of the barons, but had accepted the king's peace at the hands of the Earl of Chester ; and also except two brothers of Hervey Bagot, who were still against the king in the following of Fulk Fitz Warin.[70]

Ranulph Earl of Chester, whom Dugdale calls 'the greatest subject of England of his time,' was one of John's chief supporters, though he was not afraid to rebuke him for his evil life.[71] For his services to King John William de Ferrers was confirmed in his earldom of Derby, and was also rewarded by many grants of lands. At the 'fair of Lincoln' in 1217 the newly-created earl and the Earl of Chester helped to overthrow the French party,[72] but in the rising of Richard Earl of Cornwall, in 1227, both these great barons joined him. The two earls, indeed, seem to have been great friends, and in 1217 they went a pilgrimage to Palestine together.

Ranulph of Chester was the last earl but one of his line, and his sister Agnes brought Chartley to the Ferrers family by marrying William de Ferrers.[73] On the death of Ranulph's nephew John the earldom came to the crown.

During the early years of Henry III Staffordshire played very little part in history, though the Bishop of Lichfield, Alexander de Stavenby, was a politician of considerable eminence. In the middle of the thirteenth century several catastrophes, due to natural causes, occurred in the county. On the night of 2 October, 1254, Burton was visited by a fire, but the amount of damage is not recorded,[74] and in the same year, about 20 November,

---

[67] Coll. (Salt Arch. Soc.), ii, 10. [68] Ibid. ii, 14. [69] Eyton, Antiq. of Shrops. ii, 185.
[70] Eyton, Antiq. of Shrops. x, 326. [71] Dugdale, Baronage, i, 42.
[72] Matt. Paris, Chron. Maj. ii, 541. [73] Dugdale, Baronage (ed. 1675), i, 45.
[74] Ann. Mon. (Rolls Ser.), i, 323.

great floods are recorded by which a large number of people of both sexes, old and young, and little children in their cradles, were drowned. In the next year an extraordinary hailstorm visited the valley of the Trent, followed by a whirlwind which levelled trees and buildings with the earth, and there was a universal destruction of hay by floods such as had not happened for many years.[75]

Through the writs of protection, issued to those who applied for them while employed in the king's service, we are enabled to obtain an authentic record of those Staffordshire tenants who fought in the various wars of the thirteenth and fourteenth centuries. These writs gave complete protection against all personal actions and against any pleas in the superior courts of law except pleas of dower and last presentation.

When Henry III invaded Brittany in 1230 such writs were issued to the following Staffordshire tenants :—[76] Ralph Basset of Drayton,[77] Ralph Basset of Weldon, William de Aldithele (Audley), Henry de Aldithele, William de Dustun, Hervey de Stafford,[78] Adam Mauveisin, Nicholas de Verdun, John Fitz Philip, William Basset, Roger de Somery,[79] Hugh de Oddingesele, Geoffrey de St. Maur, Ralph de Pexhale.

In 1253, during the suppression of the rebellion in Gascony by Henry III, the following had writs of protection in the county :—[80] John de Chetwinde, Ralph de Arderne, Walkeline de Arderne, Adam Mauveisin, William le Blund, Robert de Stafford, Peter de St. Maur, Adam de Brimton, Philip Marmion, Warinne Fitz Gerald, John de Kaumville, Geoffrey de Genville, John de Verdun, Richard de Alazun, Roger de Somery, Roger de Monhaut, William Hose.

In 1257 several Staffordshire tenants assisted the king against the Welsh, and others accompanied Richard Earl of Cornwall, who had been elected king of the Romans, to Germany. In the former expedition, when Henry went on to Chester, he left part of his army with Richard de Clare, who made a secret journey, with only one knight, to confer with Queen Eleanor at Tutbury Castle, where Eleanor is stated to have been staying instead of at Nottingham because she could not endure the smoke of the sea coal.[81]

We have now come to the great crisis of Henry's reign, when clergy and laity found a leader against his misgovernment in Simon de Montfort, and in the barons' wars that ensued Staffordshire was almost wholly against the king. Not more than three of the principal tenants of the county were on his side : Philip Marmion, the last of the male line of that family, whose daughter Jane married Sir Alexander de Freville, James de Audley and Roger de Somery ; while of the lesser tenants, only William Bagot of the Hyde, Adam de Brimton, William Wyther, and Hugh de Okeover adhered to the king. Against him were Robert de Ferrers, Hugh le Despenser the Justiciary of England, Ralph Basset of Drayton, Henry de Verdun, William de Handsacre,

---

[75] *Ann. Mon.* (Rolls Ser.), i, 336.

[76] *Coll.* (Salt Arch. Soc.), viii (1), 2 ; *Cal. of Pat.* 1225–32, p. 357.

[77] This Ralph Basset of Drayton is the one of whom Dugdale says he was first of the family in any way memorable ; *Baronage* (ed. 1675), i, 375.

[78] Hervey de Stafford was the son of Millicent, the daughter and heiress of Robert de Stafford who had married Hervey Bagot ; ibid. i, 613.

[79] Roger de Somery must have been the de Somery who, in 48 Hen. III, was allowed to crenellate Dudley Castle because he supported the king against the barons.

[80] *Coll.* (Salt Arch. Soc.), viii (2), 3 ; Pat. 37 Hen. III.   [81] *Ann. Mon.* (Rolls Ser.), iii, 203.

John Fitz Philip, Geoffrey de Gresley, John de Audley, Roger Bagot of Brinton, John de Swynnerton, Richard de Bromley, William de Rideware, Giles de Erdington, and many more.[82]

Against Robert de Ferrers Henry had a special grudge because he had married the king's niece, Mary of Angoulême, and yet was opposed to him. This was aggravated by Ferrers capturing Prince Edward and imprisoning him. In 1264 he defeated the royalists at Chester, but soon after Edward, his old opponent, laid waste his lands in Derbyshire and Staffordshire, and demolished his stronghold of Tutbury.[83] Such determined hostility brought about his own downfall and that of his family. In 1265 he was brought to trial, confessed, and was forgiven, yet with extraordinary infatuation he again raised an army and seized Chesterfield,[84] but was defeated, attainted, and his lands confiscated.

Immediately after the battle of Lewes, Earl Simon, acting in the name of Henry, appointed for the first time a 'custos pacis' in every county in England, who appears to have superseded the sheriff and wielded almost despotic power, the custos for Staffordshire being Ralph Basset of Drayton,[85] who at the battle of Evesham fell fighting against the king with Hugh le Despenser, Richard Trussel of Kibblestone, and William de Bermingham.[86] The last-named was a tenant of Roger de Somery, one of Henry's few supporters, and their being found on opposite sides shows that the feudal tie was severed.[87]

It is perhaps fitting that in the early years of the reign of the great legislator Edward I the history of Staffordshire should be concerned with a famous lawsuit, which not only is a good illustration of the litigation of the time, but was important in the annals of the county. In the second year of the reign Robert de Ferrers, the staunch opponent of Henry III, sued Edmund Crouchback, the late king's son, to whom all Ferrers' lands, with two exceptions, had been given, that he might redeem his lands according to the Dictum de Kenilworth.

This was an agreement drawn up between Henry and his tenants in chief during the siege of Kenilworth, by which those who had been disinherited might upon submission recover their estates, and was published on 31 October, 1266. In it was a special clause by which Ferrers was to pay seven years' revenue and give up his castles.[88] Edmund appeared and said that Ferrers could not claim the benefit of the Dictum de Kenilworth, since after it was passed he had offered of his own free will to redeem his lands and himself from prison for £50,000; an enormous sum when its present value is considered, and especially considering that the annual value of the Earl of Derby's estates at this time was put at £3,000.[89]

This sum was to be paid by the Quindene of St. John the Baptist, and if not paid then Edmund was to hold the land until it was paid, and he

[82] Coll. (Salt Arch. Soc.), viii (2), 5.   [83] Dugdale, Baronage, 263 ; Ann. Mon. (Rolls Ser.), iii, 230.
[84] Ann. Mon. (Rolls Ser.), ii, 370 ; Mosley, Hist. of Tutbury, 16. Robert de Ferrers, though hostile to the king, was not a loyal supporter of the barons ; Rishanger says of him, 'fidus nec Regi nec Baronibus'; Chron. and Ann. (Rolls Ser.), 13. In the summer of 1263 he marched about the country plundering and burning indiscriminately. He incurred the hostility of Simon de Montfort at Lewes and was imprisoned by him ; Engl. Hist. Rev. x, 31.
[85] Coll. (Salt Arch. Soc.), viii, 4.   [86] Ann. Mon. (Rolls Ser.), ii, 365.
[87] Coll. (Salt Arch. Soc.), viii, 6.   [88] Stubbs, Const. Hist. ii, 100.
[89] Dugdale, Baronage, i, 265.

produced the charter of Robert de Ferrers to that effect. Robert pleaded that this charter was signed by him when in prison under duress, and, therefore, could not invalidate his claim. However, Edmund's answer to this was that Robert after the execution of the charter had come before the king's chancellor and enrolled the same, and that an act so done could not be pleaded as the act of a prisoner. Robert was obliged to admit he had acknowledged the validity of his act before the chancellor, but he still maintained he had done it under duress, for the chancellor had come to him in prison with the charter in his hand, and he had acknowledged it under bodily fear; moreover, the chancellor had come to him privately and not as chancellor. But Edmund finally pleaded that as Robert did not deny he had acknowledged the deed, nor its enrolment, he could not appeal to a jury now, and the court found in his favour because they could not go behind the chancellor's rolls, especially when the said chancellor had quitted office and delivered up his rolls to the king, who had given them into other custody.[90]

Thus the bulk of the estates of this great family passed away from them into the hands of the house of Lancaster, and the title of earl disappeared with them, but John the son of Robert de Ferrers received again from the king the castle and honour of Chartley, and his family long flourished as Lords Ferrers, Barons of Chartley, until Anne, heiress of William Lord Ferrers, married Sir Walter Devereux, in the reign of Henry VI, and Chartley passed into that family.[91]

In 1275 the king cautioned Bogo de Knoville, Sheriff of Shropshire and Staffordshire, regarding his dealings with Llewellyn, Prince of Wales, who was at that time dreaming of driving the Saxon from Britain, and, consequently, refused to do homage to Edward I, a refusal that next year caused Wales to be invaded, and its conquest begun.[92]

When in 1282 the Welsh broke out into revolt and made their last bid for independence, many Staffordshire men were ordered to take the field at once, others were summoned to be at Worcester, the usual basis of operations against Wales, by Pentecost.[93] Among them were William de Aldithel, Roger de Somery, Geoffrey de Geneville, Richard Basset of Weldon, Richard de Harcourt, Theobald de Verdun, Nicholas the Baron of Stafford, and John Fitz Philip.

Edward was a great general, and neglected no preparations; no less than 310 carpenters and 1,000 sappers were to attend the king's army, of whom Staffordshire and Salop together contributed fifteen carpenters, and forty sappers, according to their population.

A proclamation was issued that markets were not to be held in Staffordshire and other counties until further orders, Chester being appointed temporarily as the sole market for Stafford, Lancaster, and Derby.[94] The careful preparations and sound strategy of Edward had their reward and the war was soon over. After a portion of the English troops had been cut to pieces in the Isle of Anglesey, among whom was Sir Thomas de Haughton, a Staffordshire knight, Llewellyn was surprised and killed near Builth in

---

[90] *Coll.* (Salt Arch. Soc.), vi (1), 63, from Coram Reg. Roll, Trin. 2 Edw. I.
[91] Mosley, *Hist. of Tutbury*, 29 ; Dugdale, *Baronage*, i, 265 et seq.
[92] Rymer, *Foedera* (orig. ed.), ii, 53.
[93] *Coll.* (Salt Arch. Soc.), viii, 10; Rymer, *Foedera* (orig. ed.), ii, 189. [94] *Coll.* (Salt Arch. Soc.), viii, 11.

December, David was executed at Shrewsbury in the following year, and with them fell Welsh independence.

In the rising of 1287 Staffordshire and Salop were ordered to array 500 footmen and no less than 2,000 sappers and wood-cutters[95] against the Welsh, and it was during this campaign that Nicholas the Baron of Stafford was killed by the walls of the castle of Drosselan falling on him.[96]

War in the Middle Ages was nearly always followed by demoralization in civil life, so we are not surprised to find in 1286 grievous complaints of many persons that many malefactors were overrunning the county and perpetrating robberies, homicides, and other enormities. The sheriff was therefore ordered to bestir himself to preserve order, and among other things to clear ' the passes' of the woods.[97]

In the famous expedition to Flanders in 1297, when Roger Bigod Earl of Norfolk refused either to go or hang, Staffordshire tenants mustered in great force, and the long Scottish wars having now commenced a fresh field was open for their warlike energies.

July 22, 1298, was the day of the battle of Falkirk, when Edward completely defeated William Wallace, and it was in this fight 'that the valiant Lord Rafe Basset of Draiton' said to the Bishop of Durham, who at the head of the second division hesitated to attack, ' My lord bishop, you may go and say mass,' and rushed himself upon the enemy,[98] dispersing the Scottish cavalry.[99]

But the stubborn Scots refused to recognize that they were beaten, and year after year Edward continued his efforts, in which he was aided mainly by levies from the more northern counties, Staffordshire performing its due share of service. Thus in 1300 the commissioner of array for the county, William de Stafford, was ordered to select 500 footmen and take them to Berwick-on-Tweed.

In 1301 writs were issued to all those tenants who held £40 in land. and the return [100] gives 835 for England exclusive of Durham and Chester; Staffordshire furnishing seventeen,[101] Salop eleven, and Devon making the best show with seventy-seven.

Besides these, a month earlier, John de Ferrers, Hugh le Despenser, Geoffrey de Caumville, Ralph de Grendon, Edmund Baron Stafford, and Theobald de Verdun, jun., were summoned.[102]

In 1306, the year when Scotland was offering a national resistance for the first time, Ralph Basset and Roger de Mortimer were arrested by the Sheriff of Staffordshire for leaving the king's army in Scotland without leave, and all their lands taken from them. However, their punishment was

---

[95] Rymer, *Foedera* (orig. ed.), ii, 345.

[96] *Coll.* (Salt Arch. Soc.), viii, 14.

[97] *Cal. of Close*, 1279–88, p. 434.

[98] *Coll.* (Salt Arch. Soc.), viii, 20.

[99] But it was not until the king brought up the archers and the third division of horse that the day was won. Fortescue, *Hist. of the Army*, i, 18.

[100] *Coll.* (Salt Arch. Soc.), viii, 22.

[101] The Staffordshire tenants holding £40 in land were John Doyley, Robert de Staundon, William de Stafford, Hugh de Blunt, William de la More, Richard de Draycote, Geoffrey de Gresele, Robert de Knytele, Robert de Tock, William Wyther, John Hamelyn, Ralph le Botiller, jun., Edmund de Somerville, Philip de Chetwynde, John Fitz Philip, Richard de Vernun, Henry Mauveysyn.

[102] The following Staffordshire tenants holding £40 in land were returned under other counties : John de Longford and William de Montgomeri under Nottinghamshire and Derbyshire ; Roger Basset and Henry de Erdington under Somerset and Dorset ; Robert de Stapleton, Roger de Morteyn, Walter de Aylesbury, and Ralph de Grendon, under Warwickshire and Leicestershire ; Adam de Brimpton, Robert de Halughton, and Walter Beisin under Salop ; John de Harecurt and Adam de Brimpton under Oxfordshire and Berkshire ; John de Wasteneys under Lincolnshire. *Coll.* (Salt Arch. Soc.), viii, 23–5.

of short duration, for in the next year they were pardoned at the intercession of the queen and their lands restored.

The year 1295 is one of the most important in English history, for it may be accepted as fixing finally the right of shire and town representation,[103] although there were for some years afterwards various anomalies which only illustrate the growth of the new system. To a Parliament summoned to meet at Westminster in 1290,[104] when two or three knights were summoned from each county probably to grant the king more money, Staffordshire had sent two representatives, William de Stafford and William de Mere, but from the model Parliament of 1295 must be dated the first regular members of Parliament as we understand them to-day.

To this came earls, barons, two knights chosen in the court of each shire by writs sent to the sheriff of the shire, and two citizens from every city or borough, chosen, like the knights, in the county courts. The archbishops and bishops brought the heads of their chapters, their archdeacons, one proctor for the clergy of each cathedral, and two for the clergy of each diocese.[105] To this 'inauguration of the representative system'[106] Staffordshire sent four members, two for the county, Henry de Creswall and Richard Caverswall, and two for the borough of Stafford,[107] William Reyner and John Beton.

The Parliament of 1296 was constituted in the same manner as its famous predecessor, but the returns are wholly lost, and in that of 1297, when two knights from each county were summoned, but no representatives from the cities and boroughs, the returns for Staffordshire are missing.

In 1298 the model of 1295 was reverted to, but though Stafford county sent William de Stafford and Henry Mauveysin, the borough made no return, and so for the next two or three Parliaments the borough of Stafford is sometimes represented and sometimes not. However, in 1304–5 the county for the first time sent six members altogether, two for the county, two for Lichfield borough, and two for Stafford borough.

The borough representation, however, in Staffordshire, as all over England, was irregular. In 1307 the county only was represented, whereas in 1311, 1312, and 1313 the county, Lichfield, and Stafford sent two members each, while in 1315 Lichfield drops out again, as in the next year did Stafford borough.[108]

Edward I, the great general, statesman, and lawyer, died 7 July, 1307, and on the accession of his worthless son we enter upon an era of cruelty, luxury, factions, foreign wars, social rebellion, and religious divisions. In the same year we find the king forbidding the holding of a tournament at Stafford, and the sheriff ordered to make a proclamation that no one is to hold a tournament without the king's special licence.[109] The reason in this instance is not given, but such displays were sometimes forbidden as tending to disturb the king's peace.

---

[103] Stubbs, *Const. Hist.* ii, 235.

[104] Close, 18 Edw. I, pt. vi, m. 8 *d.* To this Parliament thirty-seven English counties sent two members each, and this county representation was maintained until 1545. Lane Poole, *Historical Atlas*, notes on map xxiii.

[105] Stubbs, *Const. Hist.* ii, 132.   [106] Ibid. 133.

[107] *Parl. Accts. and Papers*, lxii (1), 6. In the same Parliament Worcestershire was represented by no less than sixteen members, Derbyshire by four, and Salop by six.

[108] Ibid. lxii (1).   [109] Rymer, *Foedera* (orig. ed.), iii, 76.

It was about this time that John de Somery, lord of Dudley Castle, took upon himself so great an authority in Staffordshire that no man could 'have law or reason by means thereof,' and he domineered there more than a king, so that no man could abide in those parts unless he well bribed John de Somery for protection or helped him in building Dudley Castle, and the said John beset men's houses in that county to murder them, and extorted large sums of money from men.[110] This John was the last of the male line of Somery; his sister Margaret married John de Sutton, and brought Dudley into that family.

In 1312, when the barons beheaded the hated Piers Gaveston on Blacklow Hill, several Staffordshire tenants were on their side. Edward was greatly enraged at his favourite's death, but was unable to exact any punishment on his executioners, for his army deserted him, and pardons were granted to all those implicated, among whom were[111]: William Trussell, Ralph de Grendon, Roger de Somerville, Nicholas de Audele, John de Swynnerton, Thomas de Ardene, Robert de Wolseley, Edmund son of Edmund Trussell, John d'Oddyngesels, Hugh de Meignell, Philip Hastang, Roger de Swynnerton, Nicholas de Longford.

The disastrous battle of Bannockburn was fought in 1314, a contest in which the number of the English troops has been much exaggerated, but we know that Staffordshire and Salop provided no less than 3,000 footmen equipped to proceed against the Scots.[112] Besides the foot-soldiers, the sheriffs of Salop and Staffordshire were ordered to furnish twenty carts with four horses, and send them to Berwick on Tweed, while twenty-nine of the chief men of the county, including the Bishop of Lichfield, followed the king to the unfortunate campaign, the chief absentee being Thomas of Lancaster, who, through his father Edmund Crouchback, now held the Ferrers estates in the county.[113] After Bannockburn, Edward was hard pressed for men, and at the Parliament at Lincoln, in which Lancaster was made president of the royal council, the lords and knights promised him a foot soldier from every rural township,[114] and the sheriffs were ordered to certify the towns or vills in each hundred. In answer to this the sheriff of Staffordshire returned the names of twenty-eight towns in Offlow Hundred, thirty in Cuttlestone Hundred, twenty-one in Totmonslow Hundred, forty-four in Pirehill Hundred, and twenty-five in Seisdon Hundred, a total of 148.[115] However, these men were never employed; Lancaster refused to join the army, and the summonses were countermanded. The commissioners appointed to make this levy were William Trussell, John Giffard of Chillington, and William Trumwyn, the last-named being also the Parliamentary representative with Robert de Tok at Lincoln when the levy was ordered.[116]

In 1315 the condition of England was miserable in the extreme, dearth and pestilence were added to the misfortune of an unsuccessful war, and to

---

[110] Dugdale, *Warwickshire* (ed. 1656), 538.

[111] *Coll.* (Salt Arch. Soc.), viii, 31; *Cal. of Pat.* 1313–17, p. 21 et seq.

[112] *Coll.* (Salt Arch. Soc.), viii, 32, where the total number of infantry is put at 17,500; but were not many of the orders sent to the sheriffs lost? See Oman, *Art of War in the Middle Ages*, 573.

[113] Stubbs says of him: 'His hatred for his cousin was a stronger motive than his ambition, or else he was a traitor to his country as well as his king. . . . The Scots spared his estates when they ravaged the North, his own policy towards them was one of supineness, if not of treacherous connivance'; *Const. Hist.* ii, 357.

[114] *Ibid.* ii, 356.

[115] *Coll.* (Salt Arch. Soc.), viii, 35; *Parl. Writs*, ii (4), 394.

[116] *Parl. Accts. and Papers*, lxii (1), ci

crown all came the king's constant demands for more money. We are not, therefore, surprised to find that certain of the people of Staffordshire refused to pay the twentieth granted to Edward, alleging that the said tax had been given the king under certain conditions, namely that he would observe the Great Charter, the Forest Charter, and other ordinances, and would have a perambulation of the forests conducted, and these things had not been done. The king professed great astonishment, as he had commanded the said ordinances to be observed in every particular. Apparently with a real desire to learn the truth of the matter, he issued a commission to make strict inquiry into it.[117]

At the end of 1321 Edward with unwonted energy resolved to attack the party of the great Earl of Lancaster, to whose ascendancy he could no longer submit. In reply Lancaster collected an army of about 30,000 men at Tutbury, one of his many castles, and his principal residence. On the king's approach, in order to prevent his crossing by the bridge at Burton on Trent to attack Tutbury, he erected defences on the east end of the bridge about 10 March, 1322. The vanguard of the king made an assault upon these, and was repulsed with loss.

A halt was called for a few days, and at a council of war it was decided to divert the enemy's attention by keeping up the attack on the bridge at Burton[118] and push on with the rest of the troops to Salter's Bridge, a few miles distant. However, before this was carried into effect a man who had suffered from the exactions of Lancaster, who had made the monks of Burton Abbey assist him with money and provisions, and quartered his soldiers on the inhabitants of the town, informed the king of a ford at Walton, by which he crossed. He was on the point of attacking when suddenly the younger Despenser leapt from his horse,[119] and prostrating himself before the king on the snow which then covered the ground, besought him not to unfurl his standard, for those whom he was about to attack were the nobles and lieges of his kingdom, and were not led by wise advice but excited by youthful ardour, and if the king's standard was unfurled universal war would lay waste the whole land, which could hardly be controlled in the king's time. Whatever might have been the effect of this curious speech, the day was already won, for in the meantime the vigorous attack on the bridge at Burton had engaged all the enemy's attention, and when the king was across the river he had almost surrounded Lancaster's army. They were seized with panic, and having set fire to part of Burton escaped in the smoke to Pontefract.[120]

At Tutbury the king captured some wounded who had been abandoned in the hasty flight, and remained there five days, ordering the arrest of Thomas of Lancaster and his supporters.[121] He then set out for Pontefract, where he heard the news of Lancaster's defeat at Boroughbridge, a defeat soon followed by his trial and execution. In these troubles several Staffordshire tenants fought against the king, among them James and John the sons of William de Stafford, William de Chetelton, Nicholas de Longford,

---

[117] *Rot. Parl.* (Rec. Com.), i, 449.   [118] Holinshed, *Chron. of Engl.* ii, 566.

[119] *Chron. of Edw. I and Edw. II* (Rolls Ser.), ii, 75, 267.

[120] Thos. of Walsingham, *Hist. Angl.* (Rolls Ser.), i, 164. A chest full of coins discovered in the River Dove in 1831 is supposed by Mosley (*Hist. of Tutbury*) to have formed part of Lancaster's treasure.

[121] Rymer, *Foedera* (orig. ed.), iii, 933.

William Malveisin, Richard de Stretton, John de Miners, Thomas Wyther, John de Swynnerton, William de Stafford, and the elder and younger Hugh de Audley.

On the other hand, for their loyal services, John de Somery, whom we have seen lording it over the county, and Ralph Basset of Drayton, were rewarded by grants of manors.[122]

Such rebellious conduct as that of Lancaster could only be followed by the seizing of his estates into the king's hands; but on the accession of Edward III an Act of Parliament reversed the attainder, and Henry the brother of Thomas succeeded to nearly all his vast possessions.[123] An inquisition taken at that time mentions the following in Staffordshire: Tutbury Castle, Tutbury, Rolleston, Barton, Agardsley, Marchington, Uttoxeter, Needwood Chase, Yoxall Manor, Rowley Park, Newcastle under Lyme, Keele.[124]

In 1333, when Edward was raising forces for the endless wars against Scotland, the greater part of the 1,000 foot soldiers to be raised from Salop and Staffordshire were to be archers, and it was by the bowmen's shafts that the battle of Halidon Hill was won and Bannockburn avenged. Edward III had profited by the tactical ability and experience of his grandfather, the first great encourager of the use of the long bow.

The writ summoning sixty hobelars[125] or light horsemen from the county in 1335 shows that the light cavalryman of the day was somewhat heavily armed. He was to have a horse, an aketone, or heavily-plated doublet, a bacinet, a 'pisam' or a 'colarettum,' steel gloves, sword, dagger and lance, or other arms.[126] They differed from the pauncenars in not having a habergeon or sleeveless coat of chain mail, and as a rule the hobelars did not carry lances. The heavy cavalry of the time was composed of the men-at-arms, so-called because they were covered with defensive armour from head to foot, while their horses after 1298 were also heavily protected. These men at arms were all squires and knights.

In 1336 the military equipment of the time is further illustrated in the arms demanded from the 2,000 men arrayed by Staffordshire in that year. Those having land or rent between £40 and £20 were to be provided with competent arms and horses according to the late proclamation of the king; those having £15 of land, or chattels to the value of 40 marks, with a hauberk, steel cap, sword, dagger, and horse; those with £10 of land or chattels to the value of 20 marks with hauberk, steel cap, sword, and dagger; those having 100s. of land with a steel cap, sword, and dagger, and lastly those having land between 40s. and 100s. with sword, bow, arrows, and dagger.[127]

At the commencement of the great war with France the English armies were raised by commissioners of array, who chose from each county a certain number of men-at-arms, archers, and other soldiers, and from the

---

[122] *Coll.* (Salt Arch. Soc.), viii, 43.
[123] Mosley, *Hist. of Tutbury*, 57, 58; Rymer, *Foedera* (orig. ed.), iv, 285.
[124] *Cal. of Inq. p.m.* (Rec. Com.), ii, 8.
[125] So called from the hobbies or ponies on which they rode.
[126] These men seem more heavily armed than the ordinary hobelar, whose arms are stated by Fortescue (*Hist. of the Army*, i, 28) to have been merely an iron helmet, aketon, gloves, and sword; *Coll.* (Salt Arch. Soc.), viii, 53. Bacinet, according to Littré, was a kind of bonnet placed under the helmet; colarettum, a gorget; pisam, a weight (?)
[127] *Coll.* (Salt Arch. Soc.), viii, 57

muster rolls of thirty-seven counties in February, 1339, we see that fewer and possibly better men were picked in that year than in the year of Bannockburn, Staffordshire furnishing 55 men-at-arms, 220 archers, and 220 other armed infantry.[128]

During the course of the war the system of indenture came into use by which the king bargained with his baron or knight, as the case might be, for the production of a certain number of men, in return for payments on the part of the sovereign. The men were freely enlisted, and better soldiers than the pressed men, and were largely recruited from old soldiers who pursued the trade of war because they liked it.

The sinews of war were provided by the Parliament, which in 1338 [129] granted Edward half the wool in the kingdom, amounting to 20,000 sacks. The commissioners appointed to collect the share of Staffordshire were two knights, Sir Robert Malveisin, and Malcolm de Wasteneys (who was also a member for the county in that year),[130] as well as five merchants, Roger Bride, Henry de Tytnesoure, Nicholas Reyner, Thomas the Goldsmith, and John le roter.[131] Many of the men of Staffordshire concealed their wool, and the king appointed William de Myners his sergeant-at-arms to inquire into the matter and seize the wool which had been hidden and send it to the ports named to receive it.

At Crecy in 1346 Staffordshire was well represented. Ralph de Stafford, who had been made seneschal of Aquitaine in the previous year, and at the siege of Aiguillon filled the breaches in the walls with wine casks full of stones,[132] had an eminent command in the van of the army under the Black Prince, and was one of those who made the famous report on the number of the French slain : eleven great princes, eighty bannerets, 1,200 knights, and 30,000 common soldiers.[133] Beside him served a great number of the foremost men in the county. In addition to the usual writs to the commissioners of array writs were sent to the mayors of the towns, and while London was ordered to supply 100 men-at-arms and 500 armed men, Lichfield provided fifteen men, Stafford eight, Tamworth four, and Newcastle under Lyme three.[134] The pay of the men who fought at Crecy seems very high allowing for the difference in the value of money ; an earl received 6s. 8d., a knight 2s., an esquire 1s., a mounted archer, a pauncenar, and a hobelar 6d., a foot archer 3d. per day, the Welsh spearman coming at the bottom of the list with 2d.[135]

About this time Tamworth was visited by one of the fires that were frequent in an era of wooden houses, and was so burnt that the great part of the people of the town described themselves as reduced to beggary, yet in spite of this calamity the tax gatherers demanded of them the full amount of their taxes, a harshness which they petitioned the king to mitigate.[136]

[128] Oman, *Art of War in the Middle Ages*, 593 ; Rymer, *Foedera* (Rec. ed.), ii (2), 1070.
[129] In this Parliament Stafford county and borough only were represented.
[130] *Parl. Accts. and Papers*, lxii (1), 123.
[131] *Coll.* (Salt Arch. Soc.), viii, 62. Nicholas Reyner and John le roter were members of Parliament about this time.
[132] Dugdale, *Baronage* (ed. 1675), i, 160.
[133] Ibid.
[134] *Coll.* (Salt Arch. Soc.), viii, 80.
[135] Fortescue, *Hist. of the Army*, i, 30.
[136] *Rot. Parl.* (Rec. Com.), ii, 189, where the date of the petition is 1347, yet in Rymer's *Foedera* (Rec. ed.), iii, i, 57, the king is stated to have ordered a new assessment in 1345 because the town had suffered from fire. And see *Cal. Close*, 1343–6, p. 605.

The return of the triumphant king and his nobles from their conquests at Crecy and Calais was naturally celebrated after the fashion of that age by jousts, tournaments, and other chivalrous festivities, and in April, 1348, Lichfield was selected as the scene of one of these rejoicings, which were celebrated with great splendour.

The prevailing dress for both ladies and gentlemen was a blue cloak with a white hood presented by the king, and the ladies wore various masks or visors.[137] Among those who were thus clothed from the royal wardrobe were Sir Walter Manny, John de L'Isle, Hugh Courtenay, John Grey, Robert de Ferrers, Philip de Spenser, Roger de Beauchamp, Miles de Stapleton, Ralph de Ferrers, and the Earl of Lancaster, while among the lady recipients were the king's daughter Isabella, the ladies Ulster, Juliers, Wake and Segrave, and Darcy. These ladies, with others of high rank, watched the king and seventeen knights joust with the Earl of Lancaster and thirteen knights, and it is not unlikely that here the incident took place which suggested to the chivalrous king the founding of the Order of the Garter.[138]

In May, 1349, the Black Death which had first appeared in England in the preceding year showed itself in Derbyshire, and for the next four months raged with fury throughout the kingdom.

At Poictiers in 1356, 'a battle far more hazardous and far better fought than that of Crecy,'[139] Staffordshire was represented by Edward le Despenser, James d'Audley, Sir Richard de Stafford, and Ralph Basset of Drayton, who was as doughty a knight as his ancestor who won fame at Falkirk. Sir James d'Audley and his four squires, two of whom, by name Dutton and Delves, were Staffordshire men, performed prodigies of valour, fighting in front of the army.[140]

For the expedition of 1359, which ended in the treaty of Bretigny, Staffordshire contributed forty to the number of mounted archers 'of the best and strongest in their counties, clothed uniformly,'[141] who were now superseding the hobelars, and were like the dragoons of the seventeenth century, rather mounted infantry than regular cavalry. One of the commissioners who drew up the treaty which ended the war was Ralph the great Earl of Stafford, a man renowned in war and peace, who had been created earl by Edward III, and was one of the original Knights of the Garter. He died in 1372. His son Hugh was worthy of him, and equally active in his country's business; in 1376, at the meeting of the Good Parliament, although he belonged to the court party, he was one of the four earls appointed with four bishops and four barons to confer with the Commons,[142] and was a member of the standing council which the Commons proposed and the king accepted.

When John of Gaunt in 1373 was smitten with the 'midsummer madness' which made him dream of conquering France and Castile he had Tutbury Castle, which had been neglected since the downfall of Thomas of Lancaster, prepared for his children and the 'queen of Castile.' It was one of the numerous castles, more than thirty in number, which this great prince held in England, and had come to him through his marriage with

[137] *Archaeologia*, xxxi, 118.
[139] Oman, *Art of War in Middle Ages*, 632.
[141] Ibid. 102.
[138] *Reliq.* xix, 87.
[140] *Coll.* (Salt Arch. Soc.), viii, 99.
[142] Stubbs, *Const. Hist.* (ed. 4), ii, 449.

Blanche, the heiress of the great house of Lancaster. Newcastle under Lyme was another. To each of his castles Gaunt appointed a constable who was responsible for its military efficiency, whose duty it was to provide it with artillery and bows and arrows, see that the walls were in repair, and superintend the new work of his master, the greatest builder of the age. In time of war no one could pass the gates without a mandate under the duke's seal, and in time of peace the constable might have the custody of civil prisoners, debtors, and other evil doers until the justice in eyre came on his circuit.[143] Needwood Chase was one of Gaunt's innumerable hunting grounds.

It was at this halcyon period in the history of Tutbury Castle that the famous minstrels' court and the king of the minstrels were instituted. For Gaunt did not spend much of his time there with his wife, as his attachment to Catherine Swynford had alienated his affections, and it was to distract the attention of his neglected wife as well as to satisfy her great love of music that the court was established. Indeed, it had become necessary, for Constance of Castile had introduced so many musicians, including some from her own land, that her husband appointed a governor over them with the title of king of the minstrels, and soon afterwards a court was established to hear plaints among them, which were carried out with strictness and regularity.[144]

The reign of Edward III cannot be dismissed without a reference to the great number of crimes of violence which the Plea Rolls and similar records of the time mention.[145] So frequent were they that a petition was made[146] to his successor in 1379 by the people of Staffordshire and other counties that men from Cheshire were continually coming by day and night in great numbers to make war, and riding through the county, robbing, burning, and ravishing, and ' suddenly beating and maiming divers men ' of the county, returning to the county of Chester without being arrested, so suddenly did they come and go, to the great mischief and annoyance of Staffordshire and the other counties. And because Cheshire was a palatine county and there was no forfeiture for such crimes done outside their county they did not fear to commit any misdeed, so that many men dared not dwell in their houses. In spite of complaints to Parliament these grievances had not been remedied, and the men of the said counties petitioned that these criminals should be restrained. The king promised in answer to remedy this state of affairs.

There is another petition in the same Parliament[147] from the men of Staffordshire as well as Herefordshire, Gloucestershire, Worcestershire, and Salop bearing equal testimony to the inefficiency of the law. Therein it is stated that Welshmen who had purchased lands in those counties came often with their kindred and friends in bands of from one to three hundred or more, armed and in warlike manner to kill, rob, and ransom, and take beasts, goods, and chattels, and convey them away to Wales, where the sheriffs and other officers of the king dare not exercise jurisdiction ; thus the said counties have been wasted, and in a short time would be utterly

[143] Armytage Smith, *John of Gaunt*, 218.   [144] Mosley, *Hist. of Tutbury*, 77.

[145] One of the grave evils at this period was that justices of assize acted in their own counties, and being friends or often relations of the local magnates, allowed them to set the law at defiance with impunity. Stubbs, *Const. Hist.* ii, 640. This was put an end to by statute in 1384 ; *Rot. Parl.* (Rec. Com.), ii, 334.

[146] *Rot. Parl.* (Rec. Com.), iii, 81.   [147] Ibid.

ruined. They therefore prayed that henceforth no Welshmen of pure blood, except those in the retinue of the king or his nobles, should purchase any lands in the said counties under pain of forfeiture. Their petition did not mend matters, for shortly afterwards the same incursions are complained of.

By the Great Revolt of 1381 Staffordshire, and the whole of the West Midlands from Gloucestershire to Derbyshire, seem to have been practically undisturbed. There was no more local disturbance than was common to all counties of mediaeval England when village ruffianism was a normal feature.[148] The figures returned by the collectors of the Poll Tax of 1381 give the number of people in the county over the age of fifteen as 15,993, but the figures are not to be relied on, being in many cases obviously manipulated.[149]

Let us turn for a moment from the wars, lawlessness, and murders of the time to the doings of men who were laying the foundation of better things. In the Parliament of 1355 Newcastle under Lyme was first represented by John de Blorton and Richard de Podmor ; the county sending Sir John de Draycote and Walter Verdoun, while Stafford borough sent Adam Rotour and William de Homeresleye ; Lichfield makes no appearance.[150] The like representation occurs from 1358 till 1370–1, when the borough of Stafford drops out.

To the Great Council, called at Winchester in June of the same year, the county, Stafford borough, and Newcastle under Lyme sent one member each as directed.[151] To the Parliament of January 1376–7 the county sent Sir Nicolas de Stafford and Adam de Peshale ; Newcastle, Richard Buntable and Thomas Thicknesse ; Stafford borough, Robert de Mersshe and Henry Prest ;[152] but next year the county only was represented. For many years after this Staffordshire was generally fully represented with the exception of the borough of Lichfield.

In 1398, after the *coup d'état* by which he overthrew the lords appellant, we find Richard II at Lichfield, where he kept Christmas with due solemnity,[153] and while there he issued a pardon to those Staffordshire men who had supported the lords.[154] In the next year he passed through Lichfield on his way from Chester to London, practically a prisoner in the hands of Henry of Lancaster, to deposition and death.

At the commencement of the next reign Lichfield was again the scene of important events. In July, 1402, upon hearing of Edmund Mortimer's defeat by the Welsh, Henry IV ordered the sheriffs of twenty-one counties to array and forward all their available forces to meet him at Lichfield by 7 July, and a few days before that the Prince of Wales had gone forward to Tutbury. From Wigmore southwards the defence of the frontier was entrusted to the Earl of Stafford, and north of Wigmore to the Earl of Arundel, who commanded the Staffordshire levies. However, these elaborate preparations came to nought, the weather was exceptionally bad, and the English host was driven from Wales without effecting anything.

---

[148] Oman, *The Great Revolt of* 1381, p. 142. [149] Ibid. App. ii.

[150] *Parl. Accts. and Papers*, lxii (1), 158.

[151] One member of each constituency who had attended the previous Parliament was summoned, but the member for Stafford borough must have been summoned for this Parliament only.

[152] *Parl. Accts. and Papers*, lxii (1), 196.

[153] Trokelowe, *Chron.* (Rolls Ser.), 224. [154] Rymer, *Foedera* (orig. ed.), viii, 40.

POLITICAL HISTORY

The ill success of Henry in Wales was in striking contrast to the success of the Percys at Homildon Hill, and was a decided factor in forming against him the great league of Northumberland and his son Hotspur, Douglas, Glendower, and Mortimer in 1403. Henry was at Lichfield on 11 July, on his way to Scotland to assist Northumberland, and probably there heard the news of the Percys' rebellion. He accordingly changed his plans, and resolved to strike a sudden blow at the rebels in the west, and from Burton on 16 July he ordered the sheriffs of several counties, including Staffordshire, to cause proclamations to be made that all lords, knights, esquires, and yeomen of their respective bailiwicks should hasten sufficiently armed to the king's person to resist Sir Henry Percy, and they were to arrest any person suspected of rebellion whom they might meet.[155] The king's commissioners to issue this proclamation in Staffordshire were the Earl of Stafford and Robert FrQunceys the sheriff. The king also wrote from Burton to the council in London for money, assuring them he was strong enough to overthrow any combination of his enemies, and then marched through Lichfield with all speed to Shrewsbury, evidently without waiting for the money or the men he had asked for when at Burton, and on the 21st the battle was fought, and Hotspur defeated and slain.[156] At the battle, in which the men of Cheshire fought gallantly for Hotspur, Edmund the fifth earl of Stafford and father of the first duke was killed fighting for the king.[157]

Staffordshire must have been, unlike Cheshire, overwhelmingly on the king's side, as the estates of the house of Lancaster had now come to the crown, and Stafford, the most powerful noble in the county, was loyal to the throne.

There is, however, an account of a fight which shows some difference of opinion, for the two knights Sir Robert Mauveisyn and Sir William Handsacre marching, the former to help Henry and the latter Hotspur, for Shrewsbury met not far from their own homes, and in the fight that followed Sir William was slain, and Sir Robert went on to meet his death at Shrewsbury.[158]

Four days after the battle Henry was at Stafford, and stayed at Lichfield from the 26th to 28th July on his way to Derby. In the summer of 1404 Henry IV, who, although only thirty-seven, seems to have already fatally impaired his original energy, retired to his northern castles and was at Tutbury in the middle of August, where he remained until the 21st, proceeding to Lichfield, where he had ordered a grand council to assemble.[159] From a list still preserved[160] it consisted of eight bishops, eighteen abbots and priors, nineteen lords and barons, and ninety-six representatives from the counties, the cities and boroughs not being represented. The situation to be faced was serious; in Wales the garrisons were clamouring for pay, as neither the king nor anyone else seemed to have any money,[161] the troops in Scotland were mutinous, and an invasion was expected from France. It was decided that the king should not go to Wales, but remain near Tutbury ready for

---

[155] Rymer, *Foedera* (orig. ed.), viii, 313 ; *Cal. of Pat.* 1401-5, p. 297.
[156] Wylie, *Engl. under Hen. IV*, i, 351.
[157] H. S. Riley, *Annals of Ric. II and Hen.* IV, i, 370.
[158] Shaw, *Hist. of Staffs.* i, 49–50, 179. Political differences were aggravated by a family feud.
[159] *Royal and Hist. Letters of Hen. IV* (Rolls Ser.), i, 433.
[160] Sir Harris Nicolas, *Ordinances of P.C.* (Rec. Com.), ii, 85. [161] Stubbs, *Const. Hist.* iii, 41.

emergencies till the Parliament which was summoned should meet at Coventry and writs were issued to the sheriffs to summon the forces.

Henry was perpetually in want of money, and at this juncture the Bishop of Lichfield, John Burghill, lent him the not very munificent sum of 100 marks.[162] Loans of this kind were of very little use, and the council issued an order from Lichfield suspending all payments of pensions and annuities from the Exchequer until the next meeting of Parliament, or until further orders.[163]

After this important council was dismissed Henry still remained in the north, and on 1 September left Lichfield for Tutbury, where he received two commissioners from Robert III, king of Scotland, and took an oath to observe the truce with him.[164]

To the Parliament which had been summoned to meet at Coventry in October, 1404, Staffordshire, like most of the other counties in England, sent no borough representatives; the members for the county were Sir Robert Fraunceys and Sir John Bagot.[165]

In 1407 we have a harrowing tale of the disorder wrought by war in the county. Constant attacks were made on the king's estates, the houses of his tenants broken into, the roads about Lichfield and Stafford were swarming with marauders, women and old men were waylaid and beaten, and one of the king's officers was attacked while collecting the taxes and stabbed to the heart.[166] The chief leaders of these riots were said to be Hugh de Erdeswyk, Thomas de Swynerton, John Myners and his two brothers Thomas and William.

In the second year of his reign the lawlessness of the county brought Henry V in person to Lichfield, where he remained two months hearing every kind of plaint. The number of assaults, woundings, robberies, and murders committed by gentle and simple is almost incredible. Occasionally the county was in a state of civil war owing to these private feuds, which were aggravated by the political dissension of the day, as shown by such presentments as the following :—Hugh Erdeswyk of Sandon and Robert his brother, with many other malefactors to the number of 1,000 men, had congregated to kill Sir John Blount and other liegemen at Newcastle under Lyme, and they kept the field arrayed as for war three days ; and on another occasion, members of the same family with a large body of men beat and wounded several of their neighbours, and would have killed them, but were prevented by a great posse of the county. In another case they entered the town of Newcastle and attacked the house of Sir John Boghay, and intended to kill him, because he had merely done his duty and presented them in the court leet, but he fortunately took refuge in a church and escaped them.[167] About the same time we find Edmund Ferrers of Chartley and others presented for giving liveries of cloth to various squires and yeomen contrary to the statute.

The question of livery [168] was one of the most important of the later Middle Ages, and the Statute Book is full of Acts on the subject. Livery

---

[162] Cal. of Pat. 1401–5, p. 407.
[163] Wylie, Engl. under Hen. IV, i, 462.
[164] Rymer, Foedera (orig. ed.), viii, 371.
[165] Parl. Accts. and Papers, lxii (1), 267.
[166] Rot. Parl. (Rec. Com.), iii, 630.
[167] Ibid.
[168] Livery (liberatio) originally meant the allowance in food and clothes given to the servants and officers of great households, but became restricted to the allowance of clothing only.

was granted by great lords to many besides their servants in order to swell the number of their adherents, who were only too glad to avail themselves of the protection of the powerful at a time when the law was for the rich. If a man wore a lord's livery the lord would 'maintain' his suit for him in the law courts, and liveries had also become the uniforms of factions.[169] Previous legislation having proved ineffective, a statute was passed in 1399 enacting that the lords might only give livery of cloth to their menial servants and officers, and 'them that be of their council,'[170] and it was clearly this statute[171] that Edmund Ferrers had broken.

We also find Staffordshire petitioning against another grievance common enough then. The royal courts were, as we have seen, ubiquitous, and were preceded by a crowd of purveyors seizing provisions and demanding services, but paying little or nothing ; 'Every old woman trembled for her poultry, the archbishop trembled for his household and stud until the king went by.'[172] In 1362[173] Edward III had renounced the right of purveyance except on behalf of the king and queen, and promised to make payments in ready money, but the promises were not kept. In 1406 Staffordshire with other counties complained that the purveyors of the king had taken cattle, sheep, pigs, corn, litter, and hay without paying, and the poor commons of the county had applied day after day to the treasurer of the king's household for their money, but only received 'sticks and tallies and promises to pay,'[174] to their utter destruction and ruin, so that they had nothing to live on and were becoming beggars. The king graciously answered that he was always willing that payment should be made by his purveyors, and they would find no fault in him in that respect for the future, and all the statutes previously made were to be observed.

At Agincourt the county was represented by many valiant soldiers,[175] the following barons and bannerets displaying banners :—Edmund Lord Ferrers of Chartley, Hugh de Stafford Lord Bourchier, and Sir John Blount. In the king's retinue were Sir John Gresley, Sir Thomas Gresley, Sir John Bagot, Ralph de la Pole of Newborough, John Chetwynd.

In the retinue of Lord Ferrers of Chartley were William Handsacre, William Draycote, Walter Yonge, John Bromshelf, and John Walker. These are described as 'lances,' that is, esquires or men-at-arms, and there were with them nine mounted archers.

In the retinue of Sir John Blount were Richard Stafford, Thomas Gifford of Chillington, Giles Gifford, Thomas Newport, and Robert Whitmore, men-at-arms.

In the retinue of Hugh de Stafford, lord of Bourchier in right of his wife, were Richard Hampton, Roger Snede, Nicholas Pershale, John Acton, and John Bromley, men-at-arms.

In the retinue of Lord Grey were John Cokayn, William Bromley, Thomas Fitz Herbert, and John Curson, men-at-arms.

---

[169] Stubbs, *Const. Hist.* (ed. 2), ii, 531 et seq.

[170] Livery of 'cloth' was distinguished from livery of 'company,' which was an imitation of the order of the Garter, whereby lords wore each other's badges out of compliment.   [171] I Hen. IV, cap. 7.

[172] Stubbs, *Const. Hist.* (ed. 4), ii, 423.   [173] *Rot. Parl.* (Rec. Com.), ii, 270.   [174] Ibid. iii, 592.

[175] This list was compiled by Maj.-General the Hon. G. Wrottesley from the Sloane MSS. 6400, Miscellanea, Treasury of Receipt $\frac{48}{9}$, and the French Roll of 3 Hen. V (Rec. Ser.). See also Sir Harris Nicolas, *Hist. of Battle of Agincourt*, names of dukes, erles, barons, &c.

In the retinue of Richard Earl of Warwick were Humphrey Stafford, William Burmyngham, Richard Curson, Humphry and Edmund Lowe, Thomas and Edmund Swynarton, men-at-arms.

With Sir William Bourchier were Sir Roger Aston and John Hampton of Stourton ; with Lord Talbot was Robert Erdeswick ; and William Trussell served with the Duke of Gloucester.

In 1421 Humphrey, then Earl of Stafford, was retained by indenture to serve the king in France, on the rupture of the Treaty of Troyes, with nine men-at-arms besides himself, and thirty mounted archers, taking for himself 6s. 8d. per day, for the rest of his men-at-arms twelve pence, and for his archers sixpence,[176] and supposing his men-at-arms were esquires, the scale of pay was the same as in the year of Crecy. In addition to their pay they were to have all prisoners they might take, except kings and kings' sons. In 1435 the number of his followers was more in accordance with his power and wealth ; he was retained to serve the king with 80 knights and 523 archers.

In 1453 the English were finally expelled from Southern France, and in this year the quota of archers demanded from Staffordshire was 173, Derbyshire sending 141, and Gloucestershire 424.

Commissioners were to be sent into every shire, except Cheshire, to assign the number of these soldiers which each hundred, city, borough, township, village, and hamlet should be charged with, whose inhabitants were to be compelled by distress, if necessary, to provide them. The archers were to be 'ready sufficiently and defensibly arrayed as belongeth to an archer,' to take sixpence a day as pay, and to serve six months from the time of their appearance.[177]

In the Wars of the Roses, which we have now reached, the main strength of the Yorkists lay in the south and east, while the north was Lancastrian. To a great extent the wars were merely a series of faction fights, fought out by the heads of the great families and their retainers, during which the greater part of the commonalty went on with their daily business, but the great mass of the people were in favour of the Yorkists for the plain reason that the triumph of that party would give them the order and settled government under which that daily business might be carried on.

Staffordshire was mainly Lancastrian. The Duchy of Lancaster had been merged in the crown on the accession of Henry IV, and Henry VI had granted it to Margaret of Anjou as part of her dower. Tutbury was the chief seat of the duchy, and most of the manors in the northern and eastern parts of the county were held under it. Moreover, the greatest landowner in the county, and perhaps in England, Humphrey, first Duke of Buckingham, was at first a Lancastrian, and so were the gentry who held under him ; but there were several of the great families on the Yorkist side, Wrottesley, Audley, Blount, Stanley, Sutton, Wolseley.

The Duke of Buckingham was the son of Edmund Earl of Stafford who was killed at Shrewsbury, and Anne the daughter, and eventually sole heiress, of Thomas Duke of Gloucester, the youngest son of Edward III. When only twenty-eight he was, in 1430, made constable of France, and in 1440 was created Duke of Buckingham.

---

[176] Dugdale, *Baronage* (ed. 1675), i, 165. [177] *Rot. Parl.* (Rec. Com.), v, 232.

In 1454 he is said to have had two thousand Stafford Knots, his badge of livery, made 'to what intent men may construe as their wits will give them.' [178] His estates at this time stretched all over central England, from Holderness to Brecknock, and from Stafford to Tonbridge. [179]

The political state of Staffordshire in these wars is clearly shown by the first commission of the peace, issued by Edward IV in 1461, in which the only Staffordshire names are Sir John Sutton of Dudley, Sir Walter Blount, John de Audeley, John Harpur, Thomas Everdon, Thomas Wolseley, Thomas Asteley, Walter Wrottesley, and Nicholas Waryng. [180]

In the commission issued by Richard III the same policy can be traced, for the only names of landowners of the county are John Sutton Lord Dudley, John Blount of Mountjoy, John Gresley, Richard Wrottesley, Humphry Persall, Nicholas Mountgomery, Ralph Wolseley, and John Cawardyne. [181]

After the battle of St. Albans in 1455 there was no chance of peace, and in September, 1459, York raised his standard on the Welsh border, and it was to join him there that Salisbury, the father of the kingmaker, with about 7,000 men, marched southward from Middleham Castle. Margaret had collected 10,000 men at Market Drayton under two Staffordshire peers, James Touchet (Lord Audley) and John Sutton (Lord Dudley), [182] the queen herself being at Eccleshall with Prince Edward. [183]

To the queen, when at Eccleshall, Lord Stanley, who had been raising men for the Lancastrians in Lancashire, promised to fight against the Earl of Salisbury, and his failure to carry out this promise, although he was at New-castle, within a few miles of the battlefield, was a chief cause of the Lancastrian defeat at Blore Heath, for which treachery the Commons impeached him. [184]

York had arrived at Ludlow, and the Lancastrian forces prevented Salisbury from joining him there.

On 22 September Salisbury took up a strong position on Blore Heath, three miles east of Market Drayton, his front protected by the Hempmill Brook, a tributary of the Tern, 'not very broad but somewhat deep.' 'In the early morning,' on the twenty-third, to quote Hall's account :— [185]

> He caused his soldiers to shoot their flights towards the Lord Audeley's company, which lay on the other side of the said water, and then he and all his company made a sign of retreat. The Lord Audeley suddenly blew up his trumpet and passed the water. The earl of Salisbury, who 'knew the sleights, stratagems, and policies of war, suddenly returned' and encountered Audeley when his forces were only partly across the water.
> 'The fight was sore and dreadful,' but in the end 'the earl's army so eagerly fought that they slew the Lord Audeley and all his captains, and discomfited all the remnant of his people.'

[178] *Paston Letters*, i, 265 ; Dugdale, *Baronage* (ed. 1675), i, 165.   [179] *Dict. Nat. Biog.* 'Stafford.'
[180] *Coll.* (Salt Arch. Soc. New Ser.), vi (2), 217.   [181] Ibid. 249.
[182] The peerage had practically originated in the writ summoning John Sutton to Parliament in 1440, though a predecessor had been summoned as feudal baron of Dudley. He had been wounded at St. Albans in 1455. He was a successful 'trimmer,' as, though a supporter of Henry, he gained Edward IV's favour, and derived grants of land both from Richard III and Henry VII. *Coll.* (Salt Arch. Soc.), ix (2), 68.
[183] *Paston Letters*, i, 282.
[184] *Rot. Parl.* (Rec. Com.), v, 369.
[185] Hall, *Chron.* (ed. 1809), 240. Holinshed's account is identical.

If Holinshed [186] is correct in saying that 2,400 were slain in this battle the fight must have indeed been 'sore and dreadful,' as allowing the usual proportion of wounded to killed, more than half the two forces must have been put *hors de combat*. Among the prisoners taken by Salisbury was Lord Dudley; on the other hand two of Salisbury's sons, pursuing the defeated enemy too far, were captured, but their father after his victory succeeded in effecting a junction with York at Ludlow.

The Duke of Buckingham, who had been wounded [187] by an arrow 'in the vysage' at the battle of St. Albans, where his eldest son was killed, did not remain quite loyal to Henry, no doubt recognizing the rising sun and fearing to lose his vast wealth. [188] However, on the whole he favoured the Lancastrians, and was with the queen in London in 1458 [189] at the 'loveday' between the two parties, and in 1460 received a grant of land from that party for his services. [190] He was slain just before the battle of Northampton in July of the same year. [191]

In 1470 Sir Walter Wrottesley, a staunch supporter of Warwick the kingmaker, probably lost his life in that cause. He was with Warwick and Clarence when they were on their way to join Sir Robert Welles, who had been defeated in Lincolnshire. Welles disclosed the conspiracy that these two had entered into, and on the king summoning them to answer this charge they fled; but Sir Walter was probably among those of Warwick's followers who were hanged at Southampton. [192]

During the Lancastrian period Staffordshire was until the Wars of the Roses well represented in Parliament; the county, the borough of Stafford, and Newcastle under Lyme generally sending two members each, but Lichfield is not mentioned. The last-named town was one of those that did not value highly the privilege of representation. In fact it was regarded more as a burden than a privilege, so that there was great difficulty in finding duly qualified members. The only men who were anxious to be elected were the lawyers, who 'saw the advantage of combining the transaction of their clients' business in London with the right of receiving wages as knights of the shire at the same time.' [193]

To the Parliament of 1414 held at Leicester, Stafford county sent two members, John Meverell and William Walshale, [194] the boroughs being unrepresented.

In the 'Parliament of bats' or bludgeons, summoned to meet at Leicester in February, 1425–6, where the parties of Gloucester and Beaufort met in hostile attitude, and Bedford arbitrated between them, [195] six members represented Staffordshire: the county sending Richard Lane of Bentley and Thomas Arblaster; Newcastle, Robert Wodehous and Henry Lilie; Stafford borough, Robert Whitegreve and William Preston. [196]

At the Parliament held at Westminster in 1455, when, after the battle of St. Albans, Henry was obliged to declare his enemies loyal, no returns have

[186] Holinshed, op. cit. ii, 251.
[188] Ibid. i, 335.
[190] Rymer, *Foedera* (orig. ed.), xi, 443.
[191] Hall, *Chron.* (ed. 1809), 244.
[193] Stubbs, *Const. Hist.* (4th ed.), iii, 407.
[195] Stubbs, *Const. Hist.* iii, 103, 387; *Rot. Parl.* (Rec. Com.), iv, 296–7.
[196] *Parl. Accts. and Papers*, lxii (1), 311.

[187] *Paston Letters*, i, 327.
[189] Ibid. 416, 426.
[192] *Coll.* (Salt Arch. Soc.), vi, (2), 227 (New Ser.).
[194] *Parl. Accts. and Papers*, lxii (1), 282.

been found at all for Staffordshire ; the same is the case in 1459 and 1460, doubtless owing to the confusion of the times ; while of the Parliaments of 1461 and 1462–3 no returns for any part of England have been discovered. Constitutional forms were in abeyance, and the regular machinery of government paralysed. From 1462–3 to 1483 Parliaments were only summoned irregularly.[197]

The part played in the reign of Richard III by Henry Stafford the second Duke of Buckingham, grandson of the duke killed before the battle of Northampton, and descended both on his father's and mother's side from Edward III,[198] was as important as from his lineage and wealth we should expect. He was the greatest of the old nobility, possessing lands in half the counties in England, including in Staffordshire the castle and manor of Stafford and the manors of Billington, Bradley, Tillington, Madeley, Eaton, Darlaston, Doddington, Stalbroke, Packington, Wigginton, Hartwell, Tittensor, and the fourth part of the manor of Blymhill.[199] He was married to Catherine Woodville, but regarded his wife's family as upstarts, and was naturally in return hated by them. On the death of Edward IV he threw all his influence upon the side of the Duke of Gloucester, and he was mainly instrumental in effecting the arrest of his own brother-in-law Lord Rivers, and Lord Grey, and obtaining possession of Edward V.

Gloucester was not lacking in gratitude for the support of the head of the old nobility, and he was invested with extraordinary powers in Wales and five of the English counties, made chief justice and chamberlain of the principality of Wales, and constable and steward of all the royal castles there, in the marches, and in the counties of Salop, Hereford, Somerset, Dorset, and Wilts.[200]

In Richard's coronation procession Buckingham's magnificence outshone everyone, his retainers all wearing his livery of the Stafford knot,[201] and immediately afterwards he was made steward of the honour of Tutbury and other Duchy of Lancaster estates in Staffordshire, and vast additions, by reason of his descent from the Bohuns, were promised to his enormous possessions.[202] Yet in a little while he was in revolt, why it is impossible to determine ; and after some hesitation, during which visions of claiming the throne for himself may have crossed his mind, he decided, with the connivance of his prisoner Morton, Bishop of Ely, to marry the earl of Richmond to Elizabeth of York, and place them on the throne.[203] His fall was terrible in its suddenness : the army he had collected dispersed in a few days, and he was a fugitive. He had been proclaimed a 'false traitor and rebel,'[204] his hiding-place was discovered, and on 1 November he was brought to Salisbury, where he was executed next day, and his vast estates confiscated.[205]

But the period of constant strife was nearly over. On 7 August, 1485, Henry Tudor landed at Milford Haven, and marched by way of Shrewsbury

---

[197] C. H. Parry, *Parliaments and Councils of England* under the above dates.

[198] His mother was Margaret, daughter of Edmund Beaufort, second Duke of Somerset, great-grandson of Edward III.   [199] Dugdale, *Baronage* (ed. 1675), i, 166 ; *Cal. of Inq. p.m.* (Rec. Com.), iv, 294.

[200] Dugdale, *Baronage* (ed. 1675), i, 169 ; *Dict. Nat. Biog.* Stafford.

[201] Hall, *Chron.* (ed. 1809), 375.   [202] Dugdale, *Baronage* (ed. 1675), i, 168.

[203] Dugdale, *Baronage* (ed. 1675), i, 169.   [204] *Rot. Parl.* (Rec. Com.), vi, 245.

[205] Hall, *Chron.* (ed. 1809), 395.

to Stafford, having by that time collected a considerable force. In the mean time Richard had entrusted the defence of Lancashire, Cheshire, and North Wales to Lord Stanley and his brother Sir William, and had taken up his head quarters at Nottingham. From Stafford Henry marched to Lichfield, and lay without the walls in his camp all night, entering the town next morning, when he was received 'with all honour like a prince.'

A day or two before, Lord Stanley with 5,000 men had been in the town, but evacuated it, being afraid to commit himself by any definite action, for he had been summoned both by Henry and Richard, and was as yet undecided. Henry left Lichfield and marched towards Tamworth, meeting on the way Sir Walter Hungerford, Sir Thomas Bourchier and others who joined him.[206] 'Divers other noble personages which inwardly hated King Richard worse than a toad or serpent,' also came to him now.

Hall [207] gives a quaint account of Henry's wandering away from his own army near Tamworth, perplexed as to the future conduct of Stanley, and passing the night in a small village, three miles from the head quarters of his force, much fearing least he should be captured by King Richard's scouts. However he was unmolested, and next morning after giving an excuse to his men for his absence, and riding through the streets of the town so that all could see him, he went to Atherstone, where he had an interview with the Stanleys, then either returned to Tamworth, or slept where he was, and next day was joined by his army and marched on to Bosworth. Shakespeare makes him return to Tamworth, where on 'the plain near Tamworth' [208] he makes his address to his troops.

Among those who died fighting for Richard at Bosworth was Walter Devereux, who had married Anne the heiress of William Lord Ferrers of Chartley, and had been advanced to the dignity of a baron under the title of Lord Ferrers.[209] Henry VII had the good fortune to enjoy a reign which, compared with those immediately preceding it, was peaceful and quiet, and he had leisure to enjoy the sport of hunting, of which he was fond. Needwood Forest was one of his hunting grounds, and he often brought his court to Tutbury for that purpose when on his way to Lathom House in Lancashire to see his mother the Countess of Derby.[210]

In 1512 Staffordshire was summoned to provide a contingent for war with France, Henry VIII having joined the Holy League ; and the Earl of Shrewsbury was directed to muster 'as many of our subjects able men for the war under the degree of a baron to do unto us service as be our own tenants, and other our subjects within our counties of Derby, Salop, and Stafford,' and those retained for the war were to have delivered to them tokens or badges to wear, but the expedition was a failure.[211]

The chief connexion of the county of Stafford with the political history of England during the reign of Henry VIII is furnished by the life of Edward, third Duke of Buckingham. In England, by the time of Edward I most of the feudal nobility of the Norman period had disappeared. In Staffordshire, as we have seen, Fitz Anculf was soon only a memory, and the great

[206] Hall, *Chron.* (ed. 1809), 413.   [207] Ibid.   [208] *Ric. III*, Act v, sc. 2.
[209] Dugdale, *Baronage* (ed. 1675), ii, 177.   [210] Mosley, *Hist. of Tutbury*, 132.
[211] Rymer, *Foedera* (orig. ed.), xiii, 337.

Ferrers family forfeited their estates after Evesham, the male line of the Earls of Chester came to an end with John Scot the last earl, and the Paynels in 1194 handed on their estates through a woman. In England, as a whole, between 1290 and the opening of the Wars of the Roses, many more great houses of the twelfth and thirteenth centuries had vanished ; and those wars exterminated so many noble families that by the time of Henry VII their power and wealth were concentrated in a few hands. Stafford, Nevill, Percy, Howard, and Berkeley, were the chief of these. Edward Stafford, the third Duke of Buckingham, had received back his father's lands on the accession of Henry VII, with whom he was high in favour, and this royal favour he retained at the beginning of the reign of Henry VIII. He accompanied Henry to the Field of the Cloth of Gold, 'fitting himself[212] with more splendour than any other nobleman.' The state he maintained was almost regal. But he was too great a man by descent, wealth, wide estates, and connexions to be allowed to live by his king. He was brother-in-law of the Earl of Northumberland ; his three daughters had married the Earl of Surrey afterwards Duke of Norfolk, the Earl of Westmorland, and Lord Abergavenny, and his son had married Ursula, sister of Cardinal Pole, grandson of George Duke of Clarence.

He was the mouthpiece of the old nobility for expressing their hatred of the upstart Wolsey, and it was to Wolsey he was betrayed. The charges against him when brought to trial were that he had listened to prophecies of the king's death and his own succession, and had expressed an intention to assassinate the king, a frivolous accusation, and probably untrue, but sufficient to get so dangerous a subject out of the way, and he was beheaded on Tower Hill, 17 May, 1521. On hearing of his death Charles V is said to have exclaimed, 'A butcher's dog has killed the finest buck in England.'[213]

The history of this illustrious house had of late been marked by a long list of calamities, the last four heads of the house had all met violent deaths as well as the eldest son of the first duke, and with the third duke the magnificence of the house departed for ever. His son Henry received back some of the family estates in Staffordshire and elsewhere, and in 1531 he was granted the castle and manor of Stafford.[214] In Edward VI's first Parliament he was member with Richard Forssett for the borough of Stafford,[215] and by that Parliament he was restored in blood and made Baron Stafford. This barony devolved at last upon Roger, who sold the dignity to Charles I for £800.[215a]

New names were now arising in Staffordshire, as all over England, and old ones springing into greater prominence, and from the family of Dudley came men who had a decided influence on the history of their country, an influence which does not redound to their credit.

Edmund Dudley, who with Empson is notorious for filling the coffers of Henry VII, was a representative of a younger branch of the Suttons of Dudley Castle, and was rewarded by Henry VIII for the vast stores of

[212] Dugdale, *Baronage* (ed. 1675), i, 170.
[213] Ibid. ; Burke, *Extinct Peerage*, Stafford ; Rupert Simms, *Bibliotheca Staffordiensis* ; *Dict. Nat. Biog.*
[214] Dugdale, *Baronage* (ed. 1675), i, 170.
[215] *Parl. Accts. and Papers*, lxii (1), 376.
[215a] G.E.C. *Peerage*, vii, 214.

wealth [216] which had been accumulated for him to squander by execution on Tower Hill. He had married his ward, Elizabeth daughter of Lord de Lisle, and their son was John, said to have been born near Okeover in 1502.

John Dudley was able, tactful, and resolute, and soon made his way to the front. In 1536 he was sheriff of Staffordshire, and about that time bought the Dudley estates from a member of the Sutton family.[217] Created Earl of Warwick and Duke of Northumberland, his ambition overleaped itself, and his design of bringing the crown into his own family is familiar to every one.[218]

He was the ablest man of his time, but unscrupulous; he supported the reformers for his own gain, but on the scaffold attributed the troubles of England to the quarrel with the Papacy.

His fifth son was Robert Dudley, Earl of Leicester, whose story is too well known to need repetition; he is chiefly connected with Staffordshire by the fact that about the time he married his third wife Lettice, countess of Essex,[219] whose husband he was suspected to have poisoned, he bought Drayton Basset, where he visited her; her son Robert, the second Earl of Essex, living conveniently near at Chartley.

In 1547 the county had to bear its share in the war against Scotland, and the Earl of Warwick was commissioned for the 'North partes,' including Staffordshire, to levy all and singular the king's subjects who were 'habill and mete for the warres,' whenever he should think fit, and to drill and arm them at his discretion. To carry out this commission effectually all justices of the peace, sheriffs, mayors, bailiffs, stewards, and constables were to obey his orders.[220]

In 1570 Pius V issued a bull excommunicating Queen Elizabeth and declaring her to be deposed from the throne, an act which placed the Roman Catholics in England in a most unenviable position, as Romanism thereby became identified with disloyalty. It also had its effect on the conduct of Parliament, which in 1571 enacted penal statutes against the Catholics and made assent to the Thirty-nine Articles obligatory. Yet John Giffard of Chillington, a 'prominent papist,' in the year when the Armada brought forth all the patriotism of the country, did as many Roman Catholics did, took the oath of allegiance to Elizabeth.[221] His fourth son, as we shall see, was one of Walsingham's tools for intercepting the correspondence of Mary Queen of Scots when at Chartley.

The intrigues of the Jesuits against Elizabeth provoked her to deal still more strongly with the recusants. In 1583 the sheriff of the county was ordered by Burghley and Walsingham to make an inventory of the property of Lord Paget at Beaudesert who was 'affected to the Romish religion;' and for favouring Mary his lands were forfeited. Elizabeth evidently had

---

[216] Henry VII after Bosworth had rewarded many of his followers by grants of land in Staffordshire, but the greatest change was in the reign of Henry VIII, who dissolved thirty-six religious houses in the county, and gave them to different persons; Harwood, *Erdeswick*, xi. The effects of the suppression of the monasteries are discussed in the Ecclesiastical and the Social and Economic Articles.

[217] Dugdale, *Baronage* (ed. 1675), ii, 216.

[218] Lord Guildford Dudley, the husband of Lady Jane Grey, was fourth son of the Duke of Northumberland.

[219] This lady, of vigorous character and wonderful vitality, lived until 1634, when she died at the age of 94. She was the great-niece of Anne Boleyn.

[220] *Acts of the P.C.* 1547, pp. 118–19.   [221] *Cal. of S.P. Dom.* 1581–90, p. 561.

good cause for watching the recusants in Staffordshire ; Thomas Morgan, Mary's most trusted agent, advised her 'if possible not to go out of Staffordshire which is altogether in her favour,'[222] and ' Ridworth ' (Ridware ?) is described as being ' a town where all are recusants.'[223]

In 1585 people refusing to attend church were disarmed, and later on the arms taken from such persons were given to the queen's good subjects ;[224] consequently fifteen recusants were formally disarmed, of whom Sampson Erdeswick of Sandon was one. The commissioners appointed to search for recusants displayed in some cases too much zeal, some of them having searched Sampson Walkeden's house at Stone in a manner which led to inquiry by the sheriff on the order of the council.

There is a list dated 1592[225] of recusants in the county divided into three classes, first those remaining at liberty, who were John Draicot of Painesley and Francis Gatagrea of Swynnerton, esquires ; William Stapleton of Bradley, John Stapleton of the same place, Philip Draicot of Leigh, Sampson Erdeswick of Sandon, William Maxfield of Mere, gentlemen ; secondly those imprisoned, Humphrey Cumberford of Cumberford, Erasmus Wolseley of Wolseley Bridge, Hugh Erdeswick of Sandon; and thirdly those at liberty upon bonds, John ' Jifford ' of Chillington, Brian Fowler of the ' Manor upon Sow.'

Queen Elizabeth visited the county in 1575 after her entertainment by Leicester at Kenilworth, from which place she came to Lichfield on 27 July, and thence went for some days to Chartley, whose owner, Walter Devereux,[226] had just sailed to Ireland.

Stafford made great preparations for her coming ; every house was newly painted, the streets gravelled, and the cross repaired.

She arrived on 8 August, and was met by the bailiffs on foot, who presented to her a cup ' two foote or more in height,' which she most lovingly received, ' saying most gracious favourable words,' which were duly responded to. She then passed on to the market-place, and pausing there, asked the cause of the decay of the town, and was told that the decay of ' Capping ' and the taking away from the town of the assizes were the chief causes. Elizabeth answered she would renew and establish better the statute relating to capping, and the assizes should be held there for ever. After this gracious promise, she passed on through the town to the castle, where she dined and ' sopted.'

The petition of the Stafford citizens to the queen on the matter of the capping statute was backed up by a letter dated 27 September in the same year from Lord Paget to Burghley, bringing to his recollection a petition of the poor cappers of Lichfield for the better execution of the statute for the wearing of caps, and commending the petitioners to his lordship's notice as the cappers were so poor.[227] Elizabeth kept her promise, for not long

[222] *Rep. on Salisbury MSS.* (Hist. MSS. Com.), iii, 148.
[223] *Cal. S.P. Dom.* 1581–90, p. 540.   [224] *Hist. MSS. Com. Rep.* iv, 330.
[225] Ibid. iv, 272.
[226] Walter Devereux, created Earl of Essex in 1572, was the grandson of Walter Devereux, Viscount Hereford, the grandson of Sir Walter Devereux, who had married the heiress of Lord Ferrers, and fell at Bosworth. The family of Devereux provided recorders of Lichfield for eight successive generations, probably a unique record. *Hist. MSS. Com. Rep.* xi, App. v, 122.
[227] *Rep. on Salisbury MSS.* (Hist. MSS. Com.), ii, 116.

afterwards we read that the statute was daily put in execution in all parts of the realm.[228]

We have now to narrate the part which Staffordshire played in the captivity of Mary Queen of Scots, the most romantic figure in English history.

In February, 1568–9, Mary arrived at Tutbury from Bolton,[229] having been transferred thither because of her many intrigues, in order that she might be in closer custody. Tutbury was at that time one of the seven mansions of George Talbot, the sixth Earl of Shrewsbury, who held it on a lease from the crown, and was used by him as a hunting box. His wife, the famous 'Bess of Hardwick,' owned two more in her own right, so that Shrewsbury was almost a king in that neighbourhood. As he was 'half a Catholic' and a nobleman of high rank and character, he seemed peculiarly fitted to be Mary's guardian.

It cannot be said, reading the provision made for Mary, that she was so badly treated, in spite of the house being poor. She was allowed two physicians who slept in the house, a large suite of more than fifty persons attended her, ten horses were provided,[230] and £52 a week was allowed for her maintenance.

She was not destined to stay at Tutbury long, for in the middle of March Shrewsbury received orders to remove her to Wingfield Manor, another of his mansions, and a great change for the better for the captive. In September Mary was taken back to Tutbury in order to be again in more strict custody, as Elizabeth had awakened to the danger of Norfolk's plot to marry Mary, who probably was all the time only using Norfolk as a tool whereby she might obtain her freedom.

Her second visit to Tutbury marked an epoch in her captivity, for hitherto she had been treated leniently; now her retinue was diminished and her actions more closely watched. She was at this time, indeed, the centre of plots against Elizabeth and her government which were backed up by Spain, and it was now that the conspiracy of the northern earls, Westmorland and Northumberland, came to a head, and they resolved to march and deliver Mary from Tutbury, an enterprise which failed miserably. If it had been resolutely carried out it might well have succeeded, as the earls got within fifty-four miles of the castle, a weak place and easily stormed. It was to suppress this rebellion that Walter Devereux Viscount Hereford raised a troop of horse, and for his services was created Earl of Essex.[231] The attempted rescue caused Mary to be hurried off to Coventry[232] with orders that if she tried to escape she was to be executed forthwith.

---

[228] *Acts of P.C.* 1577–8, p. 341. The evils arising from the decay of the trade of cap-making, which had been the subject of several Acts of Parliament, by the disuse of caps, had received attention in the statute 33 Eliz. cap. 19, some time before the queen's visit. By this every person, except maiden ladies, and gentlewomen, all noble personages, and every lord, knight, and gentlemen of the possession of twenty marks in land by the year, shall on Sundays and holidays wear on their head a cap of wool made in England by the cappers. The penalty was 3*s.* 4*d.* per day.

[229] *Cal. of Scot. Pap.* ii, 616.   [230] MSS. Mary Queen of Scots, iii, 41 ; *Cal. of Scot. Pap.* ii, 617.

[231] Dugdale, *Baronage* (1675 ed.), ii, 177. There are many letters from Mary at this time in the *Cal. of Scot. Pap.* iii. In one dated from 'Tutbury the ix of November, 1569,' to Cecil, she prays him to ask the queen to 'have pitie on our estait' as the writer is waiting on her 'loofing friendship' and has in no ways done anything to offend her, albeit the queen may be otherwise 'informit' by the false inventions of 'our enemies.'

[232] *Cal. of Scot. Pap.* iii, 9.

POLITICAL HISTORY

There is a letter from Mary dated from 'my prison at Tutbury, October 1st,' complaining of the severity shown to her servants, and that she was not allowed to receive any news from Scotland or France :

> instead of which they have forbid me to go out, and have rifled my trunks, entering my chamber with pistols, not without putting me in bodily fear, and accusing my people, rifle them and place them under arrest.[233]

As soon as the rebellion was over Mary came back to Tutbury,[234] where, to prevent her escape, among other precautions, the lock of her outer chamber door was removed so that her movements might be watched more closely. Next May she went to Chatsworth. In the beginning of 1585 the ill-fated queen arrived again at Tutbury from Wingfield, most reluctantly, as it was the most wretched of all her prisons in England, and when she arrived she found her rooms had been unoccupied since her last stay. The place was miserably furnished, the walls damp, doors and windows ill-fitting, and in a letter written at the time Mary thus describes it :—

> I am in a walled enclosure on the top of a hill, exposed to all the winds and inclemencies of heaven. Within the enclosure there is a very old hunting lodge, built of timber and plaster cracked in all parts; the said lodge, distant three fathoms or thereabouts from the wall, and situated so low that the rampart of earth behind the wall is on a level with the highest part of the building so that the sun can never shine upon it on that side nor any fresh air come to it . . . The only apartments that I have for my own person consists of two little miserable rooms so very cold that but for the ramparts and entrenchments of curtains and tapestry I have made it would not be possible for me to stay in them.

The garden for exercise was a potato ground 'fitter to keep pigs in than to bear the name of a garden,' and it need hardly be said that the sanitary arrangements were disgusting.[235]

The neighbouring gentry[236] lent her linen and bedding, otherwise she would have fared ill, as she was now a martyr to rheumatism ; and little pity could be expected from Sir Amyas Paulet, who was made her guardian in April.

Elizabeth apparently was not aware of the wretched condition of the place, for when she heard of it she wrote expressing her anger at the persons 'who had furnished Tutbury so basely, and thus given the Queen of Scots such just cause of complaint against her.'

When at Tutbury Mary was visited by Nicholas White, who discreetly advised that 'very few should have access to or conference with this lady, for besides that she is a goodly personage, she hath without an alluring grace, a pretty Scotch speech, and a searching wit clouded with mildness.'[237]

At the end of the year she was removed to Chartley, avowedly in answer to her own demands for a less rigorously unpleasant residence, but really that Walsingham might trap her.

Chartley was now in the ownership of the second Earl of Essex, then a very young man, whose consent to Mary's imprisonment there was not

---

[233] *Cal. of Scot. Pap.* ii, 682.
[234] Ibid. iii, 41.
[235] Strickland, *Letters of Mary Queen of Scots*, ii, 161.
[236] An order was sent to Thomas Gresley, sheriff of the county 7 Nov. 1584, to convey the household stuff of Lord Paget, who had lately been attainted, to Tutbury for the use of the Queen of Scots, but it was of indifferent quality, as the best had been sold ; Harwood (ed. 1844), *Erdeswick*, 532 ; and see *Cal. S.P. Dom.* 1581–90, p. 226.
[237] *Rep. on Salisbury MSS.* (Hist. MSS. Com.), i, 400.

asked, and who objected, when told it had already been decided upon, that the house was too small, and he wanted it for himself. It is described [238] ' as low and unhealthy, and the water surrounding it as of such depth as may stand instead of a strong wall,' and as having only one kitchen.

Here Mary's health was very poor, so bad that an advocate of Elizabeth's harshest measures wrote of her that she was ' so sickly and impotent her majesty thought it impossible she should be anyways able to annoy her or to do her any great harm.'

Walsingham was firmly convinced that Mary deserved death, and that her death was necessary for the safety of England. He knew that Elizabeth would not consent to her death unless she knew and could let the world know that Mary had been plotting against her. At Tutbury Mary had had no chance to plot because she was so rigorously guarded; at Chartley she was to have more scope, and the Babington conspiracy followed in the next spring.[239]

The plot was given ample time to develop, and it was not until August that the conspirators were seized, and it was then resolved to take stronger measures.

Mary's health had improved at Chartley, and one day Paulet proposed a visit to Tixall, a house belonging to Sir Walton Aston a few miles distant, to see a buck hunt. On their arrival a party of horsemen awaited them, who poor Mary hoped were her friends at last come to rescue her. But their leader rode forward with a warrant for her removal to Tixall, and the sending of her secretaries to London, and she was forthwith hurried into the house and kept there seventeen days. Paulet in the meantime hurried back to Chartley, ransacked all Mary's papers, and sent every scrap to Windsor for Elizabeth's perusal. This done Mary returned there.[240]

The conspirators were tried and executed in September, a commission was appointed to try Mary in October, and she was removed to Fotheringhay at the end of September.

In the year of the Armada letters were sent to the lords-lieutenant of several counties, including Staffordshire, for the training and mustering of soldiers,[241] and from the abstract of the certificate returned from the lord-lieutenant, the Earl of Shrewsbury, the following were the ' able trayned and furnished men in the county, ' reduced into bandes under Captaines, and how they were soarted with weapons' in April of that year.[242]

The ' ablemen' numbered 1,910, the ' furnished' 1,000; there were two companies of ' trained' men numbering 200 each, and one company of ' untrained' men of the same strength.

The captains of the two trained companies were Ralfe Sneade and Thomas Horwood, and Ralfe Sneade commanded the untrained.

[238] Morris, *Letters of Sir Amyas Paulet*, 94.

[239] Innes, *England under the Tudors*, 335. It was at Chartley that the Queen of Scots received and dispatched her letters in the false bottom of a barrel of beer which used to come every week from Burton; and these Giffard read and betrayed.

[240] Hosack, *Mary Queen of Scots and Her Accusers*, ii, 385 ; Morris, *Letters of Sir Amyas Paulet*, 250 et seq. Paulet gives us a glimpse of the wealth of the country gentlemen of the time : ' Sir W. Aston saith he hath upon the point of a hundred persons uprising and downlying in his house'; *Letters of Sir A. Paulet*, 98. Sir W. Aston was thanked for ' yielding his house' ; *Acts of P.C.* 1586–7, p. 210.

[241] *Acts of P.C.* 1588, p. 16.

[242] Harl. MSS. No. 168.

Each of the trained companies was armed thus :—

Men	Shott	Corsletts	Bows	Bills
200	85 cal.[243]	60	20	20
	15 mus.			

The untrained company was armed in a slightly different manner :—

Men	Shott	Corsletts	Bows	Bills
200	80	60	20	40

The cavalry consisted of the following :—Launces, 28; Light Horse, 50; Petroneles, 26.[244]

The levies summoned to resist the Armada were in a very bad state of discipline; Shrewsbury, the lord-lieutenant, complained to his deputy lieutenants that of the whole band of horsemen in Staffordshire only six were serviceable and furnished as they ought to be.[245]

It was the old tale enforcing the old lesson which the English have never learnt, that false economy in peace means extra risk and extra expense in war; as Leicester wrote to Walsingham: 'Great dilatory wants are found upon all sudden hurly burlies. If the navy had not been strong enough what peril would England now have been in.'[246]

Of these inefficient troops Staffordshire furnished the commander-in-chief, Leicester, a man with no military capacity, but he fortunately had at his elbow Sir John Norreys, the one experienced captain available.[247]

In the order of 27 June, 1588, to the county levies in England to be ready to go where directed at an hour's notice[248] Staffordshire is not mentioned, but in August of that year the county was ordered through the lord-lieutenant to furnish 400 foot, and share with Derbyshire in providing thirty-four horsemen to join the Earl of Huntingdon in the north, for the Spanish fleet was said to have landed men at Moray Firth.[249] In October again Staffordshire was one of ten counties which with London provided 1,500 voluntary soldiers to go to the Low Countries.[250] In 1596 Staffordshire shared with the counties of Warwick, Worcester, Gloucester, and Salop in providing 800 men to go to Calles (Cadiz) in the brilliant expedition of Howard, Essex, and Raleigh, the contingent being ordered to march to Plymouth under Sir Christopher Blunt.[251]

In 1599 and 1600 constant levies of men were made in the county for the wars in Ireland, a service which was evidently very unpopular, as many of the men deserted and their places were filled up with much difficulty, a task which the authorities were by no means ready to perform.[252]

Under Henry VIII and his three successors a number of old electoral boroughs were revived, and others newly summoned, mainly for the purpose

[243] Presumably 'cal' means calivers, which, according to Clepham (*Defensive Armour of Mediaeval Times and the Renaissance*, 225), means a 'harquebus or light musket, of a standard calibre, introduced into England during Elizabeth's reign, 4 ft. 10 in. in length.' The musket was making its first appearance at this time.

[244] Petronel, 'a kind of hand bombard fired by a horseman from a forked rest fixed on the saddle.' When not in use it hung suspended from the rider's neck; Clepham, op. cit. 219.

[245] *Hist. MSS. Com. Rep.* iv, 332.

[246] *Cal. S.P. Dom.* 1581–90, p. 513.   [247] Innes, *England under the Tudors*, 362.

[248] *Acts of P.C.* 1588, p. 137.

[249] Ibid. 231; *Hist. MSS. Com. Rep.* xii, App. iv, 259, which says thirty-six launces instead of thirty-four horse.

[250] *Acts of P.C.* 1588, p. 297.   [251] *Rep. on Salisbury MSS.* (Hist. MSS. Com.), vi, 206.

[252] *Acts of P.C.* 1599–1600 *passim*, and *Hist. MSS. Com. Rep.* xii, App. iv, 276, 279, 331, 333.

of creating votes in the interests of the crown, and the Parliamentary representation was practically set upon the basis which it retained till 1832.[253]

Lichfield, which had been unrepresented for 200 years, again sent two members in 1552–3, Mark Wyrley and William Fitzherbert, the county sending to the same Parliament William Devereux and Walter Aston ; Newcastle, Roger Fowke and John Smyth ; and the borough of Stafford, Edward Colborne and Francis Smith.[254] In 1563 Tamworth appears for the first time, and the county in all was represented by ten members.

These members sat for a considerable time, as this Parliament was repeatedly prorogued, partly on account of the plague which was then raging in London and Westminster,[255] and partly because under the Tudors it had become customary to resume business in repeated sessions with the same body of members.[256] The Parliament of 1572, to which the county again sent ten members, lasted eleven years. In 1601 a Northamptonshire gentleman, Robert Browne, was one of the members for Lichfield.[257] At the famous Parliament of 1621, which attacked monopolies, impeached Bacon, and entered in the journals of the House a protestation of their privilege to speak freely on all subjects, only to have it torn from the book by the king, Sir William Bowyer and Thomas Crompton represented the county ; William Wingfield and Richard Weston of Rugeley,[258] Lichfield ; Sir John Davis and Edward Kerton, Newcastle ; Matthew Cradock and Richard Dyott, Stafford borough ; Sir Thomas Puckeringe and John Ferrour, 'merchant of London,' Tamworth.[259]

In February, 1604, the government, alarmed at the result of the toleration they had granted to the Catholics, determined on sterner measures, and the result was the Gunpowder Plot, of which Holbeche House saw one of the closing scenes. The original conspirators, Catesby, Thomas Percy, Thomas Winter, Guy Fawkes, and John Wright, were no obscure fanatics, but gentlemen of name and blood, and if they had kept the secret to themselves the House of Lords would probably have been blown up. But they committed the fatal error of having too many accomplices, and determined that arms and men should be ready in the country to commence war as soon as Parliament was destroyed. Tresham betrayed the plot, and even then the conspirators would probably have escaped, but when they fled into the country, leaving Fawkes grimly sticking to his post, they raised open insurrection.[260] As they rode through the country on the morning of 5 November they found that the zeal of most of their supporters had cooled, and only a few score joined them. What followed may be told in the words of the sheriff of Worcestershire to the council. After describing how the rebellious assembly had broken into Lord Windsor's house at Hewell on 7 November, 'taking there great store of armour and artillery,' he relates how they passed that night into the county of Stafford unto the house of one Stephen Littleton, gentleman, about two miles distant from Stourbridge, 'whither we

[253] Lane Pool, *Hist. Atlas.* Notes on Map xxiii ; Gneist, *Hist. of Engl. Parl.* (ed. 3), 232.
[254] *Parl. Accts. and Pap.* lxii (i), 379 ; Shaw, *Hist. of Staffs.* i, 318.
[255] Parry, *Parls. and Councils of Engl.* 216.
[256] Gneist, *Hist. of Engl. Parl.* (ed. 3), 241.
[257] *Parl. Accts. and Pap.* lxii (i), 440.
[258] Afterwards baron of the Exchequer.
[259] *Parl. Accts. and Pap.* lxii (i), 453.
[260] Trevelyan, *Engl. under the Stuarts,* 96.

pursued, with the assistance of several gentlemen and the power and force of the country.'

> We made against them upon Thursday morning, and freshly pursued them until the next day, at which time about twelve or one of the clock in the afternoon we overtook them at the said Holbeche House, the greatest part of their retinue, and some of the better sort being dispersed and fled before our coming, whereupon and after summons and warning first given, and proclamation in his highness's name to yield and submit themselves, who refusing the same we fired some part of the house and assaulted some part of the rebellious persons left in the said house, in which assault one Mr. Robert Catesby is slain, and three others verily thought wounded to death as far as we can learn are Thomas Percy gentleman, John Wright and Christopher Wright, gentlemen ; and these are apprehended and taken, Thomas Winter, John Grant, Henry Morgan, Ambrose Rokewood, gentlemen, and six others of inferior degree. The rest of that rebellious assembly is dispersed.[261]

Percy, John Wright, and his brother died of their wounds, so that only Fawkes and Thomas Winter of the original five fell into the government's hands alive. In the meantime Fawkes, under dreadful torture in the Tower, was telling the council the whole of the plot, and it was not long before the plotters were tried and punished.

James I visited Staffordshire more than once ; his fondness for hunting attracted him to Needwood, where his favourite eminence for resting and looking at the scenery was called 'The King's Standing.'[262] In 1617 he visited Stafford, and was received most loyally, and in 1619, 1621, and 1624 he was at Tutbury, the scene of so much of his mother's misery.

In 1625 Staffordshire gentlemen were fined for their non-appearance at the coronation of Charles I to receive the order of knighthood, the qualification for which had been fixed in the reign of Henry VI at the annual income of £40, an increase from the £20 enacted by the Statute 'de Militibus.' The fines had been levied at the coronations of Edward VI, Mary, and Elizabeth, but not by James I.

The average fine imposed upon a defaulter in Staffordshire was £10, whereas the average fee for knighthood was between £60 and £70. So wide was the net cast that in Staffordshire a yeoman was summoned.

The coronation was on 2 February, 1625–6, but it was not until 1630 that decisive steps were taken to enforce the fines on defaulters residing at a distance from the capital, when special commissions were issued to prominent persons in each county, that relating to Staffordshire being addressed to Robert Earl of Essex, Walter Lord Aston, Sir Hugh Wrottesley, and Sir William Bowyer, kts., and Richard Weston, esq.

Another commission was issued on 12 February, 1630–1, and another on 9 June, 1631. Altogether about 260 gentlemen compounded, the compositions varying from £10 to £50, the former sum being that generally paid, and no doubt the far-reaching nature of these exactions helped to turn the country gentlemen against the king. The abolition of compulsory knighthood was one of the first Acts of the Long Parliament.[263]

In 1636 the Roman Catholics in the county felt the benefit of Charles' more lenient treatment of their co-religionists, to which he was urged by Henrietta Maria and the Archbishop of York. Wentworth and others were commissioned to lease to recusants in Staffordshire and other northern counties

---

[261] S. R. Gardiner, *What Gunpowder Plot Was*, 46–7 ; *Cal. S.P. Dom.* 1603–10, pp. 247, 255.
[262] Mosley, *Hist. of Tutbury*, 207.   [263] 16 Chas. I, cap. 20.

lands which had been forfeited for recusancy, and to compound with them for sums of money due by reason of the same offence.[264] This leniency gave great offence to the Puritans, but was nobly rewarded in the approaching Civil War by the Roman Catholics.

The same year the king visited Tutbury, and a proclamation was issued postponing Tutbury fair, the minstrels' court, and the bull-running from 15 August to 22 August, as the king would be there on the 15th, intending to spend five nights. The reason given for this was that a great confluence of people being attracted to such scenes there was in these times, when the plague was an ever-threatening enemy, great danger of infection.[265]

In the second Bishops' War in 1640 Charles called on Staffordshire among other counties for its quota of men, who were furnished him in the case of the infantry by the train-bands and by impressment ; the cost of their equipment and maintenance until they had crossed the borders of the county [266] was paid by the shire under the name of coat and conduct money, but many of the country gentlemen refused to pay it, and the crown, knowing its unpopularity, dared not prosecute them. The men were promised 8*d.* a day,[267] but owing to the chronic emptiness of the royal exchequer often went unpaid. The cavalry contingent from Staffordshire numbered sixty-nine cuirassiers and thirty-one light horsemen. The infantry, who in the previous year had been drawn chiefly from the northern counties, were now drawn from the southern, which had no traditional feuds with the Scots. Insubordination was rife, the men supplemented arrears of pay by plunder, and in Staffordshire, among other offences, they pulled down fences and burnt them.[268] An amusing letter from the deputy-lieutenants of the county mentions that it was necessary to put constables in charge of these defenders of their country, and even this precaution did not keep them within bounds. It is hardly necessary to say that these men on meeting the Scots ran like sheep.

In 1641 the king visited the county, and in the same year the Commons expressed their opinion that the recusants in it should be disarmed of all war-like weapons, but without violence.[269] No doubt this was directed against them as a body of men who were known to be loyal to the king. But though there were many recusants the great body of the people of the county viewed the king's policy with alarm ; in May, 1641, more than 2,000 of the knights, esquires, gentlemen, ministers, freeholders, and other inhabitants prayed the House of Lords to present to the king their loyal and humble desires that he would settle the militia question, and 'that he would lean upon the hand and follow the counsels of Parliament, and would send speedy succour to their brethren in Ireland.'[270]

On 10 January, 1642, Charles fled from Whitehall, and for the next eight months both sides with difficulty prepared for war a nation which

---

[264] Rymer, *Foedera* (orig. ed.), xix, 740. [265] Ibid. xx, 46.

[266] Fortescue, *Hist. of the Army*, i, 196. The train-bands were now composed exclusively of musketeers and pikemen, bows and bills having been abolished in 1596, and calivers a generation later (Firth, *Cromwell's Army*, 8). They were only drilled once a month, and treated their drills as ' matters of disport and things of no moment.'

[267] The ordinary pay of the infantry of the day, a labourer receiving from tenpence to a shilling. As money then went three times as far as it does now his pay was fair, but out of it he had to provide money for food and clothing ; Firth, *Cromwell's Army*, 189. [268] *Cal. S.P. Dom.* 1640, pp. 477–8.

[269] Ibid. 1641–3, p. 100. [270] *Hist. MSS. Com. Rep.* v, 23.

for fighting purposes had become utterly demoralized by peace. Charles at first tried to raise soldiers by commissions of array, and, this failing, by disarming the train-bands and giving their weapons to his volunteers. Parliament also made the same attempt to use the train-bands and failed.[271] As the train-bands had proved unreliable both sides began the war by voluntary enlistment, appealing for subscriptions of men and horses, and this was succeeded by issuing commissions to officers authorizing them to raise regiments, an infantry regiment consisting of 1,200 and a cavalry regiment of 500 men. The regiments raised for the king, unlike those of the Parliament, seem to have been equipped at the expense of their officers, and were raised from the districts where the colonel's estates lay, Lord Paget's, for example, being raised in Staffordshire.

The issue of the war was decided by two small minorities: 'The number of those who desired to sit still,' said Clarendon, 'was greater than of those who desired to engage in either party.' In Staffordshire, as in other counties, a neutral party was formed to oppose the entry of any armed party without the joint consent of king and Parliament, but these arrangements were short-lived. The Staffordshire Roman Catholics all fought for the king or remained neutral, as was inevitable; but most of the Protestant landowners fought against him. Many, like Sir Edmund Verney in Buckinghamshire, believed the war was on behalf of the bishops, for whom they had no love, and a considerable number of landowners were neutral, the sequestrations after the war making many men out and out Royalists who would not have been so otherwise.

A considerable amount of favour was, however, shown in these sequestrations, owing doubtless to bribery, the most signal instance of which was the case of Walter Astley of Patshull. He was stated to be a disaffected Papist, and had made his house a garrison for the king, for whom two of his sons had fought. An information was laid against him, but no proceedings taken, and he was eventually restored to the full possession of his estates.[272] Summing up the position of Staffordshire landowers in the Civil War, sixteen Roman Catholics fought for the king, and seven remained neutral. Of the Protestants twelve fought for the king, twenty were neutral, and no less than forty were against him. Mr. Firth [273] calculates that of the two Houses of Parliament thirty peers supported Parliament, eighty the king, and twenty were neutral; of the Lower House 300 were for Parliament, 175 for the king, and as there were about 500 members, this would leave a score or so neutral.

Comparing these sets of figures the country gentlemen of Staffordshire were more Puritan than the rest of England, for the House of Commons certainly represented that class more than any other in the reign of Charles I, a period when its character and public spirit touched its highest level. Indeed, it was composed of the pick of the country gentlemen, uncontaminated by court life, and with no idea of office-seeking, 'who brought to the counsels of England a directness of intention and simplicity of mind, the inheritance of modest generations of active and hearty rural life, informed by Elizabethan

---

[271] Trevelyan, *Engl. under the Stuarts*, 223; Firth, *Cromwell's Army*, 16, 17.
[272] *Coll.* (Salt Arch. Soc. New Ser.), vi (2), 330.
[273] *Cromwell's Army*, 69.

culture and spiritualized by Puritanism.'[274] The rural labourer remained neutral to the end, his uneducated mind not grasping constitutional questions. The tenant farmer followed his landlord, the yeoman in the east was for Parliament, in the north and west for the king ; the tradesmen as a rule were for Parliament.[275] Following the examples of other counties, Staffordshire associated with Warwickshire in order to combine into active resistance the scattered elements of the Parliamentary party over a considerable area,[276] but the king had many friends in the county and received very good recruits from it at the beginning of the war,[277] the association being opposed at once on the king's behalf by Colonel Hastings, a younger son of the Earl of Huntingdon, who was one of the first to raise a troop. Although most of the gentry were for Parliament, of the strong places and country houses more were garrisoned[278] for the king than for his foes. Lichfield declared for the king and raised a troop of horse ; Tutbury was garrisoned for him under Lord Loughborough ; so were Tamworth and Dudley Castle, the latter by Sir Thomas Levison. Eccleshall held out for him vigorously for a long time, the bishop, Robert Wright, helping in the defence, while other royal posts were Stafford Castle, Keele House, Patshull, Swynnerton, Bentley, Reynolds Hall. For the Parliament were Painsley House, Caverswall Castle, Burton, Rushall ; and Birmingham was hotly Roundhead.

Robert Devereux, the third Earl of Essex,[279] was from the first opposed to Charles's political and ecclesiastical policy, and in 1640 had first shown his hand by voting with the minority of the Lords who wished to refuse assistance to the king against the Short Parliament. Charles tried in vain to gain him over, and on 12 July, 1642, he was made general of the Parliamentary army, more on account of his character than his military experience ; but moral excellence in a military commander is not all-sufficient ; his tactics throughout the war were feeble, and culminated in the surrender at Lostwithiel. He had the good sense to resign before the second Self-Denying Ordinance, and died September, 1646.[280]

After Charles had unfurled his standard at Nottingham on 25 August, 1642, he withdrew to Derby, and then to Uttoxeter,[281] whence proceeding towards Stafford he and his staff passed Chartley Park, Essex's seat, which to the great chagrin of some of his officers was by the king's special mercy left untouched. At Stafford he was received loyally, and remained there a day or two before going to Shrewsbury. 'A more general and passionate expression of affection cannot be imagined than he received by the people of Derby, Stafford, and Shropshire as he passed.'[282] On the road from Nottingham to

---

[274] Trevelyan, *Engl. under the Stuarts*, 102.   [275] Ibid. 277.

[276] S. R. Gardiner, *Hist. of Gt. Civil War*, i, 90. Staffordshire afterwards was also associated with Shropshire and Cheshire ; *Hist. MSS. Com. Rep.* v, 72, 80. Clarendon says Shropshire, Cheshire, Warwickshire, Leicester, Derbyshire, and Northants associated with Staffordshire ; *Hist. of Rebellion*, vi, 274. This association must not be confused with the more famous Eastern Association.

[277] Clarendon, *Hist. of Rebellion*, vi, 22.

[278] The garrison system proved the ruin of the king. Living at free quarters they devoured the country side, and as long as there was anything left to plunder would never move to where they were really wanted ; Trevelyan, *Engl. under the Stuarts*, 245 ; Firth, *Cromwell's Army*, 26.

[279] He had been restored in blood and honour by Act of Parliament in 1604. His wife, Frances Howard, left him for Carr, afterwards Earl of Somerset.

[280] *Dict. Nat. Biog.* Robert Devereux.

[281] *Cal. S.P. Dom.* 1641–3, p. 390.

[282] Clarendon, *Hist. of Rebellion* (Clar. Press ed.), vi, 29.

Derby ' the lord Paget, who to expiate former transgressions ' [283] had raised a good regiment of foot, joined the king, and at Shrewsbury His Majesty was met by a great number of the gentry of the neighbouring counties, some of whom offered to raise levies for him at their own expense. Then Charles entered into negotiations with the Roman Catholics of Salop and Staffordshire, ' of whom there were a good number of very valuable men,' with the result that they advanced him between £4,000 and £5,000,[284] and shortly afterwards he wrote to Sir Edward Mosley, high sheriff of Staffordshire, requiring him to use his utmost industry with the well-affected in that county to persuade them to contribute horses, arms, ammunition, plate or money for his assistance.[285]

At the outset matters went in Charles's favour, and in the midland counties in February, 1643, he was steadily gaining ground. Lord Brooke was therefore chosen to redeem the day at the head of the force of the associated counties. He drove the Royalists out of Stratford and advanced to Lichfield, where a force had garrisoned the close, aided in their object by the walls of Bishop Langton. He at once commenced the siege, and stepping into the street to watch the effect of a cannon shot aimed across the pool, was shot through the brain [286] by a bullet, according to tradition, from the gun of one of the sons of Sir Richard Dyott, who with the Earl of Chesterfield commanded the cathedral garrison. The garrison were few in numbers, and ill provisioned, and in three days surrendered to Sir John Gell, who succeeded Lord Brooke. A contemporary broadside [287] printed in London makes the following comment on the shooting of Lord Brooke by Dyott :—

> to whom he had immediately before shewne mercy, by which we may see what their dealings would be with us and all true Protestants if they were peaceably entertained into the city, like snakes received into our bosoms we should be in continuall danger of an unexpected generall throat cutting or some bloody tragedy : the Lord have mercy upon us and keep us from being a prey to the wolf-like cavaliers and bloody-minded Papists.

The damage done during the siege, short as it was, to the cathedral at Lichfield, was immense, and the wanton destruction committed afterwards by the Puritans as bad. Even the records were destroyed, the gravestones stripped of their brasses, the tombs broken open and their contents scattered.

Lichfield was not to remain long in the hands of the Parliament, for its loss was felt by the Royalists as weakening the king's hold upon the midlands where it was most important he should be strong. The Earl of Northampton was therefore dispatched from Banbury to retake it, and met Sir John Gell at Hopton Heath. Of the battle that ensued it may be instructive to give an account written by either side : the Royalist account is as follows [288] :—After the surrender of Lichfield Stafford became the head quarters of the Royalists of the county, and against this Sir John Gell led his troops, flushed by the recent victory. But the Earl of Northampton [289] came to its aid, and Sir John

---

[283] William fifth Lord Paget had at first been against the king, and therefore made by the Parliament lord-lieutenant of Buckinghamshire ; Whitelocke, *Memorials*, 58. [284] Clarendon, *Hist. of Rebellion*, vi, 65.
[285] Mosley, *Hist. of Tutbury*, 220. [286] Gardiner, *Civil War*, i, 112.
[287] Now in Bodleian Library. [288] Clarendon, *Hist. of Rebellion*, vi, 278 et seq.
[289] Clarendon says of him : ' He was a person of great courage, honour, and fidelity, and not well-known till his evening, having in the ease and plenty and luxury of that too happy time indulged to himself with that license which was then thought necessary to great fortunes ; but from the beginning of these distractions, as if he had been awakened out of a lethargy, he never proceeded with a lukewarm temper ' ; *Hist. of Rebellion*, vi, 283.

Gell fell back to form a junction with Sir William Brereton, and then moved again towards Stafford. The earl marched to meet them with about 1,000 men, the forces of the Parliament being about double, and found them awaiting him at Hopton Heath ; he charged them at once and dispersed them, taking eight pieces of cannon ; but in the second charge the earl's horse was killed under him, and he was surrounded. He refused to surrender, and was killed fighting gallantly. After this Sir Thomas Byron, who commanded the Prince of Wales Regiment, attacked the enemy's infantry, but the approach of night and the fact that many coal pits made the ground unfavourable to cavalry caused fighting to cease. In the night the enemy decamped, the Royalists, much fatigued and harassed, and having no officers to direct them, for Lord Compton and Byron were both disabled, retired to Stafford the next day. Clarendon puts the Roundhead loss at two hundred killed, and the Cavaliers' at twenty-five.[290]

The Parliamentary story of the fight is given by Sir William Brereton.[291] On 19 March, about two o'clock in the afternoon, he joined Sir John Gell near 'Salt Heath,' and found the Royalists in much superior force, especially in cavalry, of whom, according to some, they had 2,500, whereas he only had 400 and some dragoons. He says the enemy came on with great resolution and in good order, and they fought till all their powder and bullet was spent, and then fell to with the butt-ends of their muskets. The Roundhead horse, however, gave way, was disordered, and routed. He estimates his infantry force at 500 men, who were attacked by the royal cavalry, and by the first volley did great execution. This drove them back, only to make a second desperate charge which was repulsed, and this decided the day. Sir William puts the enemy's loss at 600 dead, and his own at thirty ; and among the enemy's slain were Captains Middleton, Baker, Leeming, Cressitt Bagott, and Biddulph of Biddulph, 'a recusant in Staffordshire.'

Except with regard to the losses, the two accounts are not so divergent as many stories of battles written from opposing sides. The true account of the engagement seems to be that the Royalist cavalry drove the enemy off the field with their usual impetuosity, and pursued them too far. Brereton came up with fresh troops, and enabled those of the Puritans who were left to hold their ground.[292]

A letter[293] written by a Royalist who took part in the battle says that, besides those mentioned by Brereton, Captain Harvey and Ensign Bowyer, Lieutenant Greene and Cornet Hall were killed ; and Northampton's son, writing to his mother from Stafford on 22 March, confirms the story of the refusal of the Parliamentary generals to deliver up the body of Lord Northampton. Gell and Brereton also informed the son that his father's armour was so good that they could not kill him till he was 'downe and had undone his headpiece.'[294]

As Northampton had failed in the object of his expedition, the recapture of Lichfield, the battle must be taken as a Royalist defeat. Rupert was sent

---

[290] A contemporary letter published in London, now in the Bodleian Library, agrees in the main with this account.
[291] Shaw, *Hist. of Staffs.* i, 54. Shaw states that his account of the Civil War was derived from contemporary MSS. letters and papers which he had access to.   [292] S. R. Gardiner, *Civil War*, i, 123.
[293] Published in London by H. Hall, 1643, and now in the Bodleian Library.
[294] Letter of same year, also in Bodleian.

to do what Northampton had failed in, and on 3 April seized Birmingham, and on the 10th laid siege to the close and cathedral at Lichfield, which surrendered after eleven days' resistance. It was during this siege that Charles delivered his final terms, which asked too much for the Parliament to grant.

Soon after the battle of Hopton Heath, Stafford was captured by a very small force of Parliamentarians ; but the castle, under old Lady Stafford, refused to yield. The successor to Lord Brooke in command of the associated counties was the Earl of Denbigh,[295] who was appointed by Essex in June, 1643, and this command he laid down in April, 1645, in obedience to the Self-Denying Ordinance. He joined the Parliamentary cause against the wishes of many of his family, probably because he was convinced the cause was just. He seems to have done his best to alleviate the miseries of war, and inspired the feeling that his justice could be relied on for the redress of injuries. On the occasion of some differences between Denbigh and 'some of the country,' which caused his absence for a time, 4,000 Staffordshire men presented a petition to the House of Commons that the dispute should be ended and the earl sent down again amongst them, and letters of the time show that his return to his command was eagerly looked for.[296]

There is a letter written by Essex in the summer of 1643, throwing light on the feeling of the county at a time when all seemed going in favour of the king, in which he says that then a formidable army could be raised from the associated counties of Stafford, Warwick, &c., as the people were then willing to rise, both because they feared the landing of the Irish in Wales, and many Papists were flocking to that district ; but expedition was necessary, or the people would return to their former coldness.[297]

After Rupert had retaken Lichfield he left a garrison at Burton before returning to Oxford, which garrison was almost immediately captured by the troops of the Parliament, and they in their turn were driven out by the queen in July, 1643. Altogether, Burton changed hands six times during the war.

About this time the Duke of Newcastle 'came into our country,'[298] where he had considerable estates, miserably plundered it, raised great sums of money, and made many recruits.[299] Wootton Lodge, the house of Sir R. Fleetwood, one of the strongest places in the county, 'manned with such a company of obstinate papists and resolute thieves as the like were hardly to be found in the whole kingdom,' was captured by the Parliamentarians.[300] In September, 1643, Sir William Brereton laid siege to Eccleshall Castle, then garrisoned by 'the great cowstealers the lord Capell his forces,' who sent to Hastings at Tutbury for relief. Hastings at once came to their aid, but Brereton laid an ambush for him into which he was decoyed by an assumed flight, suddenly attacked, and driven back to Tutbury. Hastings was himself besieged in Tutbury Castle,[301] and the place would have fallen but for the dissensions which were rife in the Roundhead army at that time, each

---

[295] This was Basil Feilding, second Earl of Denbigh. His father was mortally wounded in Rupert's attack on Birmingham ; his brother, also fighting for the king, was killed at the second battle of Newbury.

[296] *Hist. MSS. Com. Rep.* iv, 255. [297] Ibid. 262.

[298] Firth, *Duke of Newcastle*, 144. [299] Shaw, op. cit. i, 57.

[300] Shaw, *Hist. of Staffs.* i, 57.

[301] The town appears to have been under the power of the Parliament, although the castle was held for the king. Mosley, *Hist. of Tutbury*, 224. An excellent example of the divisions of the time.

commander going his own way; the consequence was that the castle held out till 1646, when it surrendered to Brereton. On another occasion, as Hastings was marching from Ashby to Tutbury he was attacked by the 'valiant Moorlanders,' who routed his troops, killed 100, and took many prisoners.[302] As, however, they were unable to capture Tutbury, the Roundheads placed a garrison at Barton Blount, about four miles from the castle, to interrupt supplies and intercept its communications with the north, and in the plain between many a skirmish took place.

The general progress of the war in Staffordshire up to the end of 1643 may be summed up as follows: On 1 May in that year the whole of the southern and central portions of the county were mainly for the king, and the northern for the Parliament; by December, with the exception of a few isolated posts, only Lichfield and Tamworth and a small region round remained to Charles.[303]

In February, 1644, Captain Stone, one of the most prominent local Roundheads, with a small party marched against 'Pattishall' house, 'a popish garrison of the enemies,' strongly fortified, and seeing that the drawbridge was down, rushed in, and after some fighting took it, capturing Mr. Astley, the owner, two Jesuits, and about sixty or seventy officers and men.[304]

In May the Earl of Denbigh set out from Stafford with the intention of attacking Rushall Hall, then held by Colonel Lane, which had been captured by Rupert in the previous year, 'Mistress Leigh defending it gallantly with only her men and her maids'; and took with him two drakes, two sakers, and 'the Stafford great piece,' and among other troops the Stafford horse and the Stafford regiment of foot. The twenty-sixth of May was spent idly at Walsall and the 27th in preparing for the assault. Next day a small party of Royalists coming to Lichfield were beaten off, and on the twenty-ninth the bombardment of the house began, and was continued until 9 p.m. The church, too, which had been garrisoned by the Royalists, was battered, and preparations were made for an assault. The hearts of the Cavaliers, however, failed them, and the place was surrendered, the garrison being allowed to march out without their arms and be conveyed to Lichfield.[305]

In the same month the Committee of Both Kingdoms stated that Lord Newcastle's horse had done great damage in Staffordshire and Leicestershire, and recruited themselves to a great strength there, raising at least 1,000 horse and £10,000.[306] Like the rest of England the county suffered severely from the exactions of both parties; Uttoxeter in 1644 alone paid £158 towards the maintenance of the royal troops[307] at Tutbury, and in April of the same year Rupert plundered the town of Tutbury and stole forty of Hastings's own horses! But though there was much plunder the war was

---

[302] Shaw, *Hist. of Staffs.* i, 60; Mosley, *Hist. of Tutbury*, 223.

[303] See maps to S. R. Gardiner's *Hist. of Civil War, passim.* In the map of 23 Nov. 1644, the above two places hold out, with a dwindling district round them. In the map of 23 July, 1645, Tamworth has gone. These maps must be taken broadly, as many small places held out for the king after the country around was practically in the power of Parliament.

[304] Shaw, *Hist. of Staffs.* i, 70.

[305] *Cal. S.P. Dom.* 1644, p. 177–8, giving Denbigh's own account. According to the *True Informer* of 1 June, 1644, the force at Rushall was 'one of the most thieving garrisons of the Cavaliers in all that county,' and had perpetually robbed the carriers who came from London and other parts to Lancashire; Willmore, *Hist. of Walsall*, 317.

[306] *Cal. S.P. Dom.* 1644, p. 168.   [307] Mosley, *Hist. of Tutbury*, 224.

humane, no portions of England were burnt to deserts, towns were not reduced to half their size, villages did not disappear wholesale.[308]

In June, 1644, Lord Wilmot, the Earl of Northampton, and the Earl of Cleveland were sent to relieve Dudley Castle with a brigade of horse and 1,000 foot; but the fighting, judging by the losses incurred, must have been very mild; and in a letter written soon after, Lord Denbigh, describing the engagement, says he beat the Royalists, and in his force was a Staffordshire regiment commanded by Colonel Symon Rugeley and Major Pinkeney.[309]

In October, Stafford, where there was a magazine of importance, was in danger of treason within the walls, and Sir William Brereton, acting on orders of the Committee of Both Kingdoms, occupied it and secured the suspected persons.[310] Among them were Colonel Lewis Chadwick, Lieut.-Colonel Chadwick, and Captain-Lieutenant Hughes, who were sent away to Eccleshall Castle, and Captain Stone was appointed to take charge of the place.

In England the year 1644 was disastrous for the king, and but for the victory of Lostwithiel his cause would have been utterly ruined. In Staffordshire a list of the places held by the two parties in May, 1645, given by a Royalist officer, Captain Symonds, discloses a very different state of affairs from that at the commencement of the war. 'Eccleshall, Stafford, Russell [Rushall?] Hall, Chillington, Tamworth, Alton, Peynsley House, Caverswall House are,' he says, 'now in the hands of Parliament; Lichfield and Dudley Castle are held for Charles.'[311]

In May of that year the king was marching north to the defeat of Naseby, and on the sixteenth the prince's head quarters were at Wolverhampton; the king lay at Bushbury. On the twenty-second the royal army arrived at Stone, the king lying at the house of Col. Crompton, 'a rebel,'[312] and M.P. for the county 1646–1660.

On the twenty-fourth it reached Uttoxeter, and marched that day by Sir H. Bagot's house in the moorlands, 'a rebellious place.' Although in the enemy's country, the king was unmolested, Lord Byron having informed him that the troops of the Parliament upon the news of His Majesty's advance had retreated.[313] On the twenty-fifth they reached Burton, the king lying at Tutbury Castle, then under Sir Andrew Kniveton.

On 14 June came the crushing defeat of Naseby, the king losing all his infantry and all his munitions of war; but he brought off his cavalry nearly intact from the field,[314] and still had a force of all arms under Goring in the south-west.

The unfortunate monarch was at Lichfield,[315] one of the few places now left to him, on 15 June, and lay in the Close; and next day he marched to Wolverhampton, thence into Worcestershire, Herefordshire, Wales, and Shropshire, returning to Lichfield on 10 August, and having a skirmish with the enemy, from their post at Barton, near Tutbury on the thirteenth, in

[308] Trevelyan, *Engl. under the Stuarts*, 230.

[309] *Cal. S.P. Dom.* 1644, p. 236. Lord Denbigh in his account says the fight for three-quarters of an hour was 'very hot,' yet the losses he mentions are trifling. [310] Ibid. 195.

[311] Shaw, *Hist. of Staffs.* i, 72; Harwood, *Erdeswick*, xvi.

[312] Shaw, op. cit. i, 72; *Cal. S.P. Dom.* 1644, pp. 521–2, 534–5.

[313] Clarendon, *Civ. War*, ix, 32. [314] Trevelyan, *Engl. under the Stuarts*, 267.

[315] *Hist. MSS. Com. Rep.* vii, App. i, 451.

which the Royalists had the advantage ; [316] but on 24 September Charles saw from the walls of Chester the defeat of his last army at Rowton Heath.

The castle of Tutbury was one of the last places in the county that held out for Charles ; the strength of its position and the bravery of its garrison had defeated numerous attempts of the Roundheads to take it. But larger forces were concentrated upon it, and on 30 March, 1646, Sir William Brereton closely invested it, and after three weeks' gallant resistance Kniveton surrendered on 20 April, 1646,[317] and next year the castle was dismantled.

In May Charles took refuge with the Scottish army at Newark ; on 24 June Oxford capitulated, but it was not till 10 July that Lichfield's gallant resistance came to an end.

In 1648 Staffordshire saw the closing scene of the second civil war. Charles's chief hope was in the Scottish army, which under Hamilton crossed the border, advanced through Lancashire, and was cut in two by Cromwell at Preston, and finally crushed at Wigan and Warrington. The incapable Hamilton, with the wreck of his army, reached Uttoxeter on 22 August, and there his worn-out soldiers refused to go any further. Three days after he offered to capitulate to the governor of Stafford, but before they came to terms, Lambert, who had been left by Cromwell to conduct the pursuit, came upon the scene, and Hamilton surrendered to him on the terms that all were to be prisoners of war, 'having their lives and safety of their persons assured to them.'[318] This put the finishing touch to the destruction of the last hopes of the Royalists.

Three years later the connexion of the county with the Stuarts and their cause was again renewed. Charles was a fugitive from Worcester fight, and leaving behind him the small body of trusty adherents who had accompanied him at White Ladies, he took refuge in a wood called Spring Coppice on the Penderels' demesne, the family being tenants of the Giffards of Chillington.[319]

After his stay in Spring Coppice Charles put on rustic disguise at Richard Penderel's house and intended to cross the Severn at Madeley to take refuge with the loyalists in Wales. At midnight they reached the house of Mr. Wolfe, a Royalist gentleman residing at Madeley, who was informed of the rank of his guest, and as the hiding-places of the house had on former occasions proved useless, the king was placed in a barn among some straw. In the meantime Lord Wilmot had arrived at Moseley Hall, the owner of which, Mr. Whitgreave, had fought for Charles I. From there, on 5 September, Wilmot found means of communicating with Colonel Lane of Bentley, a staunch Royalist as we have seen, who waited on Wilmot that evening, and offered his house and services in the royal cause. Charles, unable to cross the Severn, came to Boscobel again and there sat in the famous oak all day on 6 September. The next day John Penderel and Mr. Whitgreave arranged

---

[316] Mosley, *Hist. of Tutbury*, 228 ; *Cal. S.P. Dom.* 1645–7, pp. 70–1.

[317] Mosley, *Hist. of Tutbury*, 229 et seq. In addition to the horrors of civil war Tutbury, Stafford, Lichfield, and other places in the county were 'grievously infected with the plague' at this time ; *Cal. S.P. Dom.* 1645–7, p. 520.

[318] Gardiner, *Civ. War*, iii, 448. On 22 Aug. the Committee of Both Houses told Cromwell they had written to Staffordshire and the neighbouring counties 'to send against the Scots all the force they can muster, and to endeavour to disperse and destroy them' ; *Cal. S.P. Dom.* 1648–9, p. 252.

[319] The above account is taken mainly from J. Hughes, *Boscobel Tracts*, Clarendon's narrative being inaccurate.

with Wilmot that he should meet the king that night at Moseley, whither he set out accompanied by the five Penderels and their brother-in-law, all well armed, Charles riding on Humphrey Penderel's mill horse, of whose roughness he complained. 'Can you blame the horse, my liege,' said the miller, 'to go heavily when he has the weight of three kingdoms on his back?' At Moseley he arrived safely, meeting Wilmot, and while there a party of Round-heads came in pursuit, but Mr. Whitgreave's self-possession foiled them. In the evening of 9 September the king went on to Bentley Hall, where, next morning, Colonel Lane converted his royal master into a serving-man with the intention of taking him to Bristol, and mounting his sister behind him the party rode off for Stratford, where they arrived safely, although the king rode right through some Roundhead horse on the way, and that night he slept safely at Long Marston, about four miles beyond Stratford. At the Restoration the Parliament granted Mistress Lane £1,000 to buy a jewel for this service,[320] and the king granted an addition to the arms of the family.

In the first Protectorate Parliament, summoned in September, 1654, in which the Conservative Puritans were in the majority,[321] several knights were ordered to be returned for each county, but few burgesses were summoned, and accordingly the county of Stafford sent three members, the Right Hon. Sir Charles Wolseley, bart., Col. Thomas Crompton, and Thomas Whitgreave; Newcastle sent Edward Keeling of Wolstanton; Stafford borough John Bradshawe, serjeant-at-law, who had presided at the king's trial; Lichfield sent Thos. Miners, and Tamworth was unrepresented. In the Parliament of 1656 the representation of the county was similar, Stafford borough sent Martin Noele of London, Newcastle Col. John Bowyer, Lichfield Thos. Miners.[322] In the Cavalier Parliament the county and the four towns each again sent two members, who, as it lasted until January, 1678–9, were subject to many changes.

The reign of terror which the infamous fabrications of Titus Oates brought upon the Roman Catholics found its victims in Staffordshire. At the assizes held in August, 1679, nine persons were accused of being Popish priests, two of whom were ordered to be removed to London, and five being 'violently suspected to be Jesuits' were to remain in custody till the next assizes that evidence might be accumulated against them. The remaining two, Andrew Bromwich and William Atkins, were indicted for high treason in taking orders beyond the sea, and afterwards coming into England and seducing His Majesty's subjects to their popish religion, it being fully proved against them both that they had said mass and administered the sacrament in the popish manner to the witnesses that gave evidence against them, whereupon, after a full hearing they were both found guilty.[323]

In the year 1715 Jacobitism seems to have been rampant in Stafford fanned by the zeal of the rector, who had 'by his uncharitable tenets and unchristian raillery so inflamed the minds of the unthinking that their insolence towards the Dissenters since his coming is almost unaccountable.'[324] He was also very industrious in promoting the interest of Mr. Sneyd, who

---

[320] Harwood, *Erdeswick*, 410.

[322] *Parl. Accts. and Paps.* lxii (i), 516.

[324] *Flying Post*, 8 Sept. 1715.

[321] Trevelyan, *Engl. under the Stuarts*, 307.

[323] *Domestic Intelligence*, 26 Aug. 1679.

had been a member of the last Parliament,[325] and was an unsuccessful candidate for that of 1714–15. The Pretender's health was openly drunk, and his birthday solemnized with ringing and other rejoicings.

His exhortations infuriated the mob to such an extent that on 7 July they began to pull down the Presbyterian meeting-house, that day being publicly kept in celebration of the late glorious peace of Utrecht with bonfires all over the town, in express contempt of the Whig government, and with the connivance of the magistrates. They continued at their work for a fortnight unhindered, and the sheriff of the county allowed a month to pass before he ordered a court to be summoned in the Shire Hall, and then only a small number of the rioters, in spite of positive evidence, were found guilty.[326] A better spirit was shown at the assizes when the grand jury agreed upon an address to the king expressing their abhorrence of the recent riots and promising to discover the authors. This satisfied the king so well that the lords of the Treasury were ordered to pay the high sheriff, Sir Oswald Mosley, £500 as a reward for the extraordinary expenses he had incurred during the riots, during which his conduct was so dilatory.[327] Doubtless the Hanoverian dynasty at this time had to walk warily.

In 1745 the invasion of the young Pretender again brought a Stuart to Staffordshire. When Charles's army crossed the border it consisted of 6,000 men, of whom 500 were cavalry, but the Highlanders soon began to desert in great numbers, and by the time they reached Penrith there were only 4,500 left.[328] Few recruits came to make good these losses, even Lancashire, devotedly Stuart by profession, was lukewarm in action. That so small and ill-disciplined a host could march into the heart of a powerful country unmolested was due to the gross military incapacity of the English generals and the extraordinary want of public spirit in the people, whose prevailing disposition was fear or sullen apathy, few being disposed to risk anything on either side.[329]

However, England recovered from the disgraceful panic that the Pretender's march had occasioned: Wade was with one army in Yorkshire, Cumberland with another cantoned from Tamworth to Stafford, and George II was gathering a third at Finchley. Early in December Cumberland's advanced guard was at Newcastle, with a small party of horse pushed forward. Charles's army divided into two columns, and Lord George Murray by a clever ruse deceived the duke, advancing to Congleton with his column, and driving before him the advanced party of horse some way on the road to Newcastle.

Cumberland, thinking Charles was marching for Wales, pushed forward to Stone with his main body, but Murray turned suddenly to the left and gained Ashbourne by a forced march, and then joining the prince, who had marched through Leek with his motley host, headed by a hundred pipers, entered Derby, where his officers insisted on retreat. Cumberland meanwhile had marched into Warwickshire to bar the way of the rebels to London, and there he received news of Charles's retreat. He immediately

[325] Ralph Sneyd of Keele and Henry Vernon of Sudbury were members for the county in the Parliament of 1713 ; *Parl. Accts. and Paps.* lxii (2), 33.
[326] *Flying Post*, 8 Sept. 1715.   [327] *Cal. of Treas. Paps.* cxci, 31.
[328] Stanhope, *The Forty-five*, 79.
[329] Lecky, *Hist. of Engl. in Eighteenth Cent.* i, 422.

turned northwards and went in pursuit through Lichfield, Uttoxeter, and Cheadle, ' over the most dreadful country.'[330] From Lichfield Cumberland wrote to Newcastle :—

> They march at such a rate that I can't flatter myself with the hopes of overtaking them, though I set out this morning in a march of at least thirty measured miles.[331]

It was to be some time before he caught them up.

The general feeling of the county in this rebellion seems to have been loyal to the Hanoverian dynasty. The country people cheerfully brought their horses to the duke's army, and when he was pursuing the Pretender the country gentlemen did the same,[332] nor does the invading army seem to have attracted any number of Staffordshire recruits worth mentioning.

Sir Richard Wrottesley, a staunch Whig and Hanoverian, armed his servants and tenantry for George II, and his father-in-law, Lord Gower, was raising forces on the same side in the north of the county, but the rebels retreated before they had a chance of proving their courage.[333]

Jacobites, on the other hand, like the Giffards and Astleys, in the same fashion as their fellows in the rest of England, ' spilt their wine more than their blood ' for the Stuart cause.[334]

No doubt their loyalty to the Stuarts was weakened by the fact that the Pretender had called the French to help him ; they were Englishmen first and Jacobites after, but the chief reason was perhaps that Walpole had given the country a long period of peace and prosperity. The estates of the country gentlemen had thereby increased largely in value,[335] and they were not likely to upset a rule which gave them so much benefit.

The early military history of the county has been set forth in the foregoing pages, and we will complete it by a brief account of the regular and auxiliary forces since the beginning of the eighteenth century.

In the year 1705 was raised the first regular battalion of infantry connected with Staffordshire, when Parliament, encouraged by the campaign of Blenheim, voted six new regiments, of which the one connected with this county alone, and originally known as Lillingston's Regiment, exists to-day.[336]

It did not partake in the glories of Marlborough's wars, for in 1706 it went to the West Indies, and is said to have remained there for sixty years, during which detachments served at the capture of Guadaloupe in 1759 and of Martinique in 1762.[337]

In 1745 it was, like the rest of the British forces at home and abroad, in a miserably neglected condition ; at St. Kitts not forty per cent. of the

[330] Contemporary Account of the Rebellion (Bod. Lib.), 63.
[331] Ewald, *Life of Prince Charles Stuart*, 184. [332] Contemporary Account as before.
[333] *Coll.* (Salt Arch. Soc. New Ser.), vi (2), 347.
[334] The chaplain at Okeover, Jeremiah Kitching, gives an amusing account of the exactions of the Pretender's troops : ' Upon Tuesday night we had five lay with us, and upon Friday night as they returned from Derby four lay with us and about seven o'clock at night came three horsemen and said they wanted armour and plundered the house and stables and barns and the church : and they have taken your best saddle trimmed with gold lace, and your lady's bridle and two other saddles . . . and upon Saturday morning came three ruffians . . . and pick the servants' pockets of their money and my silver tobacco box ' ! *Coll.* (Salt Arch. Soc. New Ser.), vii, 112.
[335] Morley, *Walpole*, 133. [336] Fortescue, *Hist. of Army*, i, 450.
[337] Lawrence Archer, *Brit. Army*, 317.

men were fit for service, their clothing was in rags, they had neither hats, shoes, cartridge boxes, nor swords.[338]

The regiment received its number of the 38th Foot in 1751, and was called the First Staffordshire Regiment in 1782.[339]

The long period of foreign service in the West Indies came to an end in 1765, but the 38th was one of the first regiments to be sent to America when war threatened. At the sanguinary combat of Bunker's Hill, out of 400 men present 150 were killed and wounded.[340] After sharing in the victory at Brooklyn and the capture of Fort Washington, the regiment[341] was stationed chiefly at New York and in Nova Scotia, and so missed most of the subsequent fighting, but the flank companies served at another capture of Martinique and Guadaloupe in 1794, and the remainder of the regiment shared in the disastrous retreat to Bremen.

After fighting at the Cape of Good Hope and in South America the 38th went to the Peninsula, and was at Rolica, Vimiero, and Corunna, then took part in the wretched Walcheren expedition, where it suffered dreadful losses from disease, and after recovering its strength went back to the Peninsula[342] and fought at Salamanca, Vittoria, San Sebastian, the passage of the Bidassoa, Nive, Nivelle, and Bayonne, and in 1815 this hardworked corps was summoned to join Wellington, but was too late for Waterloo.

After service at the Cape, in the Burmese War of 1822–6, and in the Ionian Isles, it served all through the siege of Sevastopol, including the Alma and Inkerman, and greatly distinguished itself at the attack on the cemetery in June, 1855.[343]

In the Indian Mutiny it fought in many actions and suffered severe losses at the capture of Lucknow, was in the Egyptian campaigns of 1882 and 1884–5, and served with gallantry in the South African War ; altogether a splendid record.

The next battalion in point of seniority is one now known as the first battalion of the North Staffordshire Regiment, formerly the 64th Foot, which was formed in 1758 out of the then second battalion of the 11th Foot,[344] which after being engaged in the capture of Guadaloupe in 1759, fought all through the American War, but was not in the Peninsula or at Waterloo.

The Persian War of 1856 then claimed its services, and thence the regiment was hurried off to help in quelling the Indian Mutiny, suffering considerable loss in the advance on Cawnpore under Havelock, Major Stirling being killed at the head of the regiment.[345]

In 1793 was raised the present second battalion of the South Staffordshire, the old 80th, by Lord H. Paget, nearly all the men coming from the Staffordshire Militia,[346] and its first service was in the inglorious campaign of the Duke of York in Flanders, where the regiment lost over half its strength in the retreat to Bremen.

On their way to join Abercromby in Egypt in 1801 part of the regiment was wrecked, and another detachment was again wrecked on their

---

[338] Fortescue, *Hist. of Army*, ii, 565.

[339] Lawrence Archer, op. cit. 316. A second battalion of the regiment was formed during the Peninsular War, which fought at Busaco and Badajoz, and was disbanded after the peace.

[340] Fortescue, op. cit. iii, 160.   [341] Lawrence Archer, op. cit. 316.   [342] Ibid. 317.   [343] Ibid. 318.

[344] Fortescue, *Hist. of Army*, ii, 300. About the same time Pitt made the daring experiment of raising two regiments of Highlanders.   [345] Lawrence Archer, op. cit. 449.   [346] Ibid. 319.

way from Egypt to India. There they remained from 1802 to 1818, during which time most of the recruits were derived from the Staffordshire Militia.

In the first Sikh War the regiment made up for missing the Peninsula and Waterloo by distinguishing itself highly at Moodkee, Ferozeshah, and Sobraon, but took no part in the Crimean War, and only reached India after the backbone of the Mutiny was broken, yet were in time to render valuable service as part of one of the flying columns in 1858. During the Zulu War a company of the regiment was nearly annihilated at the Intombi River.[347]

The last regular battalion now connected with the county to be formed was the 98th or Second Battalion North Staffordshire Regiment, raised at Chichester in 1824, which fought in the China War of 1841, the Punjaub campaign of 1846, the Indian Mutiny,[348] and also in the late war in South Africa.

The condition of the militia during the seventeenth and the greater part of the eighteenth century can only be described as disgraceful. Under the early Stuarts they were hardly called out once in five years for drill.[349] In 1745 the march of the Pretender with a few thousand irregular troops into the heart of England proved the utter incompetence of the constitutional force.

The great Chatham inspired the country with a new spirit, and in 1757, when England was fighting in all parts of the globe, among other measures of defence a new Militia Bill[350] was passed remodelling that force, but Staffordshire, instead of balloting for its quota, paid a fine.

However, in 1778, ' owing to warlike preparations in France becoming every day more considerable,'[351] the militia of the kingdom were embodied and Staffordshire furnished 560 men ready to ' march to such posts as shall be judged proper.'[352] Their colonel was Lord Paget, their lieutenant-colonel Sir John Wrottesley, and the other commissioned officers were a major, six captains, nine lieutenants, an ensign, and an adjutant.[353]

In order to establish the seniority of the various regiments for that year lots were drawn at the St. Albans Tavern in London by the lords-lieutenant or their deputies, and by this method Staffordshire came fortieth on the list.[354]

---

[347] Lawrence Archer, op. cit. 321.

[348] Ibid. 450.

[349] Fortescue, *Hist. of Army*, i, 194.

[350] 30 Geo. II, cap. 25.

[351] Military Entry Bk. No. 4, 148, P.R.O.

[352] Ibid. 148, 202. Clode, *Military Forces of Crown*, i, 48.

[353] The property qualification required for officers of the militia by 30 Geo. II, cap. 25, was :

For a colonel, an estate of the yearly value of £400   For a captain, an estate of the yearly value of £200
  ,, lieut.-colonel ,,   ,,   ,,   £300   ,, lieutenant,   ,,   ,,   ,,   £100
  ,, major   ,,   ,,   ,,   £300   ,, ensign   ,,   ,,   ,,   £50

Raikes, *Hist. Rec. of First Reg. of Militia*, App. E.

[354] From ' A List of Officers of the Militia of England printed in London, 1779,' now in Bodl. Lib. which also gives the pay as follows :—

	Full Pay			Subsistence					
	£	s.	d.	s.	d.			s.	d.
Colonel .	. 1	4	0	18	0	Sergeant .	. . .	1	0
Lieut.-Colonel .		17	0	13	0	Corporal .	. . .		8
Major .	.	15	0	11	6	Private .	. . .		6
Captain .	.	10	0	7	6	Drummers and Fifers,			
Lieutenant .		4	8	3	6	each .	. . .		8
Ensign .	.	3	8	3	0				
Adjutant .	.	4	0	3	0				

At the peace of 1783 the regiment, in common with the rest of the militia in the country, was disembodied, but in 1793[355] it was called out again owing to the declaration of war by France and not disembodied till the peace in 1802, which was short-lived, for the year 1803[356] saw England once more threatened by the ambition of Napoleon, so that in addition to the embodiment of the militia,[357] volunteers were raised all over the kingdom, being encouraged to serve by exemption from service in the militia and regular army.[358]

Staffordshire's share of the volunteers was represented by eight troops of cavalry with a total strength of 664, under the Hon. E. Monckton, and troops were also raised by Bilston, Uttoxeter, Stone and Eccleshall, Handsworth, Tamworth, and Walsall, the total number of cavalry for the county being 1,090.[359]

The infantry were raised locally by companies varying in strength from one company of eighty from Berkswick and Walton to six companies of eighty men each from Newcastle, the total strength of the foot being 5,425;[360] no artillery however was raised by the county.

England was deeply stirred by the insatiable ambition of Napoleon, and Lichfield alone in August of this year raised £2,193 for clothing and arming the volunteers within the city,[361] and six years before the firm of Robert Peel gave £10,000 to the ' voluntary contribution.'[362]

In 1805 George III, with whom the regiment, owing to its good conduct and excellent discipline while quartered at Windsor, was in high favour, conferred upon the Staffordshire Militia the title of ' King's Own,' and the facings were changed from yellow to blue.

In 1806 the Staffordshire Volunteers were included in the ' North Inland District.'[363] The strength of the cavalry was 872 men and 930 horses, but only 313 and 355 respectively were present at inspection, and of the infantry establishment of 5,440, only 3,521 were present.

Both infantry and cavalry were raised locally as in 1803, and of the former half are described as fit to act with troops of the line, two companies as ' deficient in discipline,' the rest as ' advancing in discipline.' None of the cavalry were considered fit to act with troops of the line, but were all described as advancing in discipline except the Uttoxeter troop, which was ' too few to judge of.'[364]

The militia remained embodied until the peace in 1814, and on Napoleon's escape from Elba were again called upon,[365] being disembodied in 1816. After Waterloo the militia was suffered to fall into decay until just before the Crimean War, when three battalions were embodied in Staffordshire.[366] The first went in 1855 to the Ionian Islands, where they remained

[355] Militia Muster Bk. 1793, in P.R.O.　　　　[356] Ibid. 1803.

[357] In 1803 the First Staffordshire Militia consisted of thirty-three commissioned officers and 838 non-commissioned officers and men, under Colonel Lord Uxbridge. Militia Muster Bk. 1803.

[358] Clode, *Military Forces of Crown*, i, 312.

[359] *Return of the Volunteers of the United Kingdom for* 1803, printed for the House of Commons.

[360] Ibid. The Commandant of the Caversall Moorland Company was the Rev. St. George Bowles.

[361] From a list of subscribers in ' Lichfield Elections.' A collection of contemporary MSS. and extracts in Bodl. Lib.　　　　[362] ' Lichfield Elections,' as above.

[363] *Return of Yeomanry and Volunteer Corps*, printed for House of Commons in 1806.

[364] Ibid. From 1793 to 1815 the Staffordshire Militia provided 100 officers and 4,000 men for the line.

[365] Militia Muster Bk. 1815, P.R.O.　　　　[366] Ibid. 1853.

until the next year ; the second did valuable garrison duty, and the third furnished nearly 1,000 trained men for the regular army.

In 1859 Staffordshire was one of the first counties to respond to the call for volunteers, and six companies were at once raised from Walsall, Longton, Hanley, Handsworth, Lichfield, and Wolverhampton ; and by the end of the next year forty companies of riflemen had been raised who were organized into five battalions, as well as one corps of artillery.

In the territorial organization of 1881 the South Staffordshire Regiment comprised the 38th Foot as first battalion, the 80th as second ; while the third and fourth battalions were composed of the First Staffordshire Militia, with three volunteer battalions.[367] The North Staffordshire Regiment was composed of the 64th and 98th Foot and the Second and Third Staffordshire Militia with two volunteer battalions ; and this arrangement of the county forces remained for five and twenty years unaltered.[368]

To the South African War, 1899–1902, besides the two regular battalions mentioned above, Staffordshire sent all four militia battalions, seven companies of volunteers, and one company of imperial yeomanry.

The list of members of Parliament for Staffordshire during the eighteenth century shows a constant succession of well-known county names : Wrottesley, Littleton, Bagot, Leveson-Gower, Dyott, Anson, Chetwynd, Paget, etc., for trade had made as yet little difference to the ascendancy of the old families.

In 1747 the elections at Lichfield and Stafford were marked by unusual rioting ; at the former place the Hon. R. Leveson-Gower polled 278 votes, and Thomas Anson, the brother of the great navigator, 272, the defeated candidates being Sir Lister Holt with 237 votes and G. F. Vernon with 229.[369]

An excellent example of the manner in which territorial magnates controlled elections at this period is given by the following agreement drawn up in October, 1765, between Lords Townsend and Weymouth respecting the Tamworth election :—

> In consideration of opposition to Thurlow upon the Manour interest being dropped by Lord Townsend, Lord Weymouth agrees that if Townsend and Mr. Luttrell will each give £500 towards the election, Lord Weymouth will provide a seat in the next parliament for any nominee of Townsend's.

Weymouth also agreed to fill up by his interest one half of the corporation with Townsend's friends.[370] Accordingly Edward Thurlow of the Inner Temple was elected for Tamworth in that year, and re-elected in 1770 on his appointment as Solicitor-General, and again in the next year when made Attorney-General,[371] a position which he occupied till raised to the House of Lords.

---

[367] *Army List*, 1881.   [368] Ibid. 1906.

[369] Contemporary MS. in ' Lichfield Elections ' in Bodleian Lib. The riots are thus alluded to by a contemporary rhymer :—

> ' At every meeting mobs arose,
> And freely dealt each other blows ;
> Highfliers quickly were brought down
> By a swinging knock o' the crown (!)
> In chanels weltring lay a squire,
> A lord perhaps flung in the mire.'
>
>   'The Lichfield Squabble,' in Bodleian Lib.

[370] *Hist. MSS. Com. Rep.* xi, App. iv, 401.   [371] *Parl. Accts. and Papers*, lxii (2), 131, 143.

In 1780 Richard Brinsley Sheridan, who although only twenty-nine had already written most of his famous comedies, began his long connexion with Stafford borough, a letter from the Duchess of Devonshire in his favour being of great service to him in the election.[372] His first speech in Parliament was in defence of a charge of bribery brought against him by his opponent Whitworth, and it was successful in its object.

Sheridan was re-elected in 1784, 1790, 1796, 1802, and in 1806 when appointed Treasurer of the Navy.[373] He was diligent in the discharge of his parliamentary duties, and an opponent of the Game Laws and, strange to relate, of gambling. In 1807 he was elected for Ilchester, but returned to his old love in 1812, and being unable to bribe the voters sufficiently was defeated, the successful candidates being Ralph Benson and Thomas Wilson.[374]

In 1790 Robert Peel of Bury, in the county of Lancaster, the father of the great statesman, was elected for Tamworth as an ardent supporter of Pitt, as being the great encourager of the commercial interests of England.

In the election of 1799, when Sir John Wrottesley was returned at the head of the poll for Lichfield with 295 votes, the opposite side asserted that this total was swollen by 125 'unconstitutional votes of annuitants, and of those granted burgages during the election.'[375] In Sir John's election address he is especially recommended as one 'who will see that the Charities of Lichfield are honestly and impartially applied. Therefore, my friends, be not imposed upon by the Black gowned tribe with young Hotspur at their head.'[376]

During the first quarter of the nineteenth century the county families maintained their position as parliamentary representatives, and though after 1832 many new names appear with increasing frequency, especially for the new boroughs, it was not until after the Reform Bill of 1867 that they were ousted from the ascendancy they had held so long.[377]

In July, 1830, Sir Robert Peel, then Home Secretary and leader of the House of Commons in the Wellington Ministry, was elected for Tamworth, but by November he was in opposition, the reforming government of Earl Grey having come in. In 1835, as Prime Minister, he issued his famous Tamworth manifesto, indicating the principles and reforms of which he approved, and Tamworth had the honour of electing him until his death in 1850.

By the great Reform Bill the county of Stafford was divided into two divisions, the northern and southern, each sending two members, and three new boroughs were created, Stoke-on-Trent and Wolverhampton with two members each and Walsall with one.[378]

In 1835, after a contest lasting three weeks, Mr. C. P. Villiers began that long connexion with Wolverhampton which only ended with his death in 1898. In his first address to the electors he pledged himself to oppose all restrictions upon trade, and declared himself 'a decided advocate of triennial parliaments and vote by ballot.'[379]

---

[372] *Dict. Nat. Biog.* Sheridan ; *Parl. Accts. and Papers,* lxii (2), 168.
[373] *Parl. Accts. and Papers,* lxii (2), 181, 194, 207, 221.
[374] Ibid. 264.
[375] 'Lichfield Elections,' Bodl. Lib. 92.
[376] Ibid. 55.
[377] See the lists in *Parl. Accts. and Papers,* lxii (2).
[378] *Parl. Accts. and Papers,* lxii (2), 345 ; 2 Will. IV, cap. 45.
[379] *Dict. Nat. Biog.* C. P. Villiers.

POLITICAL HISTORY

By the Reform Act of 1867 the county was freshly divided into three divisions with two members each, the northern, eastern, and western, while a new borough, Wednesbury, with one member, was created, and Lichfield lost one of its representatives.[380]

The first Parliament after the Act was distinguished in the county history by the strong representation of the brewing interest, Mr. M. A. Bass being one of the members for the eastern division of the county and Mr. S. C. Allsopp another for the same division in 1873, while Mr. Thomas Salt was elected for Stafford borough in 1869. In the same Parliament Sir William Henry Lytton Bulwer, afterwards Lord Dalling and Bulwer, was one of the members for Tamworth.[381]

By the Redistribution Act of 1885, Lichfield and Tamworth ceased to be represented as boroughs. Newcastle under Lyme, Stafford, and Stoke on Trent each lost one member.

On the other hand Wolverhampton gained one member, and the new boroughs of Hanley and West Bromwich were created with one member each, while the county was re-divided into the following seven divisions with one member each : Leek, Burton, Western, North-western, Lichfield, Kingswinford, and Handsworth.[382]

---

[380] *Parl. Accts. and Papers,* lxii (2), 485 ; 30 & 31 Vict. cap. 102.
[381] *Parl. Accts. and Papers,* lxii (2), 485.   [382] 48 & 49 Vict. cap. 23.

SOCIAL AND ECONOMIC HISTORY

IN the last two centuries Staffordshire has been transformed from a thinly-populated, poor, and mainly agricultural county, into one which is rich and densely populated, depending chiefly for economic prosperity on its mineral resources and the industries based on these. In the census returns of 1901, Staffordshire stands fourth on the list of English counties, but all the available evidence goes to show that in point of numbers and wealth this county ranked very low till the eighteenth century.

The Domesday Commissioners of 1085 found but few people dwelling there, and mention many isolated estates all over the county which they describe as 'waste lands.' It is estimated that there was only one villein, boor, or serf, to two hundred and fifty acres of actual surface.[1]

The assessment returns at various dates since give the same result, from the Subsidy Roll of 1332–3 onwards, including the assessment for a special aid made by Henry VII in 1503.[2]

Rather later, in the returns of a muster roll 20 July, 1573, it is said that the county is too poor to support the expense of training a large number of men,[3] and this is the general record till the middle of the eighteenth century.

It is easy to see why it remained poor for so long, despite its rich stores of mineral wealth, notably iron and coal, for up to the eighteenth century the conditions were unfavourable for the development and expansion of its industry and commerce.

It was only then that the use of coal for smelting iron became general, though Dud Dudley obtained a patent for his blast furnace for making iron by means of coal as early as 1639.[4]

Further, since there was no great demand for Staffordshire coal till the epoch of the Industrial Revolution, the mines were little worked till the eighteenth century, nor could they be worked effectively till the ingenuity of engineers had discovered a means of pumping the water from the pits.

Another great obstacle to industrial and commercial development was the lack of communication between this county and the rest of England. Nothing indeed is clearer than its isolation in mediaeval times, lying as it

[1] R. W. Eyton, *Dom. Studies, Staffs.* 1881, pp. 17, 21.
[2] *The Will. Salt Arch. Soc. Coll.* x, 79 ; and Thorold Rogers, *Hist. of Agric. and Prices,* iv, 89.
[3] *Cal. S.P. Dom.* 1547–80, p. 465.
[4] See his *Metallum Martis,* quoted by Stebbing Shaw, *Hist. of Staff.* ii, 8.

did far from London, cut off from easy communication with the continent of Europe, shut in on the north by wild tracks of moorland and limestone hills, with the thickly wooded Cannock Chase on the south and the Welsh mountains as a barrier in the western distance. For the numerous rivers of Staffordshire, though excellent for fertilizing purposes, were practically useless for navigation. The Trent only becomes navigable at Burton, and its distance at this point from the eastern sea makes it negligible as a ready means of communication. All the other rivers of any importance take an easterly direction, and there was thus no way of reaching the western coast by water until the cutting of canals in the eighteenth century. As to the roads, which are now excellent, the evidence goes to show that in the central part of the county they were good, but not elsewhere.

Dr. Plot, writing in 1686, says—

> the highways, owing to the gravelly nature of much of the soil, are universally good, except in the most northerly parts of the moorlands, where they are nearly impassable . . . and a little about Wednesbury, Sedgley, and Dudley, where they are necessarily worn by the carriage of coal.

He goes on to quote a remark of King James, who, speaking jocularly of this county, once remarked that it was 'fit only to be cut out into thongs to make highways for the rest of the kingdom.'[5]

But as the developing industry of the county was centred within these northern and southern parts, it was peculiarly unfortunate that the roads there should be so bad. The potters suffered much in the first half of the eighteenth century from the badness of the roads. Many of the materials for their manufacture had to be imported from outside the county, and these, as well as the finished goods for export, were conveyed by means of 'pot-wagons,' or on the backs of pack-horses. The roads are described as being narrow, with high banks at their sides, always, even in summer, soft and clayey, and full of deep ruts. In winter, the strings of pack-horses could scarcely get from place to place, and many a poor horse fell dead on the roadside, breaking, as it fell, the heavy load of crockery it bore on its back.[6]

Besides coal and iron, Staffordshire possesses other mineral resources in limestone, alabaster, salt, clays and marls for the rougher sort of pottery ware, and a certain amount of good building stone.

Its rock formation is of a kind to ensure a pure and plentiful water supply, owing to the porous nature of the new red sandstone which covers the greater part of the county. Besides this, the hill regions of millstone grit and carboniferous limestone which lie east of the northern coalfield are the source of innumerable springs of pure water, and the slope of the boundary hills such as Mow Cop and Cloud is such as to keep the streams well within the county. The millstone grit indeed and the coal measures throw off most of the 29 in. of annual rainfall,[7] though it is to be noted that the water drawn from the coal measures is contaminated, and therefore useless for purposes of consumption. Staffordshire gains a further supply from the limestone hills of Derbyshire, and it seems probable that the great underground reservoir of

---

[5] Rob. Plot, *The Nat. Hist. of Staff.* (1686), 110.   [6] Llewellyn Jewitt, *The Wedgwoods*, 170.
[7] The general average for the county, calculated from the rainfall returns covering a period of twenty years, is 29 in. For the north-west it rises to 33·12 in. whilst in the south-east it only reaches 26 in.

hard water beneath the town of Burton, and largely utilized for the making of beer, comes in part from that source.[8]

The limestone district in north-east Staffordshire does not get the full benefit of the streams that pass through it, owing to the porous character of the rocks, and to fissures through which much of the water disappears. A notable example of this may be seen in the Manifold valley, where the rivers Hamps and Manifold run underground for several miles of their course to reappear again together at Ilam.[9]

It was along the river valleys that the most important towns of mediaeval Staffordshire were to be found—Stafford, for instance, at the junction of several valleys encircled by small hills, Lichfield and Tamworth, respectively the centres of the ecclesiastical and political life of the old Mercian kingdom, Burton on the banks of the Trent, the seat of an ancient monastery dating back to the tenth century. Up to the eighteenth century the population was fairly evenly distributed over the county, with the exception of the barren moorland regions in the north and south. Its economic prosperity depended mainly upon agriculture, carried on chiefly in the well-watered fertile plain which lies between the northern and southern coalfields, and which is still largely an agricultural region.

At the present day the greater part of the population is found massed together in two great industrial regions, known respectively as the Potteries and the Black Country, in the neighbourhood of the two great coalfields. It is here that the large towns of modern Staffordshire are to be found, for Stafford is no longer ' the most considerable town in the county, with the exception of Lichfi ld,' as it was in the time of Defoe (1778).[10]

Of the four largest towns, judged by the last census return (1901), three, Wolverhampton, Walsall, and West Bromwich, are in South Staffordshire, whilst the fourth largest, Hanley, is, of course, the chief of the pottery towns, being a county borough, but it was unknown to mediaeval Staffordshire, save as an insignificant part of the ancient parish of Stoke upon Trent.

The situation of these North Staffordshire pottery towns is interesting and significant, showing that the manufacture of pottery has from very early times been the staple industry of the district. For though as towns they are of comparatively modern growth, they date back to early times as villages, and they are not situated along the outcrops of the main seams of coal, but extend in an almost continuous line from Longton in the south to Tunstall in the north along the outcrop of the quick burning coals, clays, and marls, which were once used in the manufacture of the coarse pottery of the early days, and are still used for making the ' saggers ' in which the ware is placed for firing in the ovens. Newcastle-under-Lyme is not, strictly speaking, within the Potteries, being situated on a wide strip of barren measures let down by the Apedale Fault between the pottery towns on the east and the

[8] H. Evershed, ' Agricultural Surv. of Staff.' *Journ. Roy. Agric. Soc.* (2nd Ser.), vol. v, 1869, p. 296.

[9] See Dr. Darwin's description of these rivers. *The Botanic Garden*, Part ii, Canto iii, 129 :—

' Where Hamps and Manifold their cliffs among   On beds of lava sleep in coral cells
Each in his flinty channel winds along,   And sigh o'er jasper fish and agate shells,
With lucid lines the dusky moor divides   Till where famed Ilam leads his boiling floods
Hurrying to intermix their sister tides.   Thro' flowery meadows and impending woods,
Three thousand steps in sparry clefts they stray   Pleas'd with light spring they leave the dreary night
Or seek thro' sullen mines their gloomy way ;   And mid circumfluent surges rise to light.'

[10] Defoe, *Tour through Great Britain* (8th ed.), ii, 358.

mining districts of Silverdale and Apedale on the west. Newcastle is therefore a residential rather than an industrial and manufacturing town, and may be regarded as a suburb for the whole of the pottery district.[10a]

The rainfall varies greatly in different parts of the county, being especially heavy in the hilly moorland regions of the north and north-east.

But, taken as a whole, the climate is too damp for corn growing, and both climate and soil are better adapted for pasturage, the central part of the county being composed largely of marls intermixed with a sandy, gravelly soil, found largely also on the borders of the southern coalfield. The rich alluvial deposit of the river valleys produces excellent grass, and even the limestone uplands produce, as Dr. Plot observed in 1686—

> a short but fine and sweet pasture, and large oxen. Much more [he adds] can they breed and feed cattle in the rich meadows that adorn the banks of Trent, Blithe, Terne, Churnet, Hamps, and Manifold, and more especially on the famous Dove banks.[11]

With the exception of a tract of light land round Stafford, and extending thence through Lichfield to Tamworth, dairy-farms are the rule, Uttoxeter being specially famous for its dairy produce, which is sent thence daily to London and other parts of the country.[12]

Corn is grown to some extent on the drift plain which lies to the west of the pottery coalfield, but more and more arable land is being turned into pasture, as corn becomes less and less profitable, and the demand for dairy produce increases with the growth of industrial populations in the districts adjoining the agricultural area.

The poverty of records for the period between the Domesday Survey (1085) and the opening of the twelfth century makes the student of social history in Staffordshire peculiarly grateful for any indication of the life of the people at this time. One very valuable record for a part of the county is to be found in the Burton Chartulary[13] containing the early surveys of the manors belonging to that monastic foundation, and a number of documents concerning the relationship between the monks and their tenants. The date of the surveys has now been conclusively fixed between the years 1100 and 1133,[14] whilst the other documents refer to times as late as the reign of Edward II.

The surveys show that the tenants on the Burton manors were divided into three main classes, consisting of those who paid rent for their land, and in addition performed certain fixed agricultural services; others who held their land in return for fairly arduous labour services, with food contributions and an occasional payment, such as 4d. at Martinmas; and finally a third class of cottars who held a cottage and a croft in return for one day's work per week on the lord's land. Among the last class may be placed the 'bovarii,' a few men on each manor who looked after the lord's oxen for the plough-team, and in return for these services possessed a cottage and a small plot of land.

[10a] W. Gibson, 'North Staff. Coalfield,' *Memoirs of the Geolog. Surv. of Engl. and Wales*, 1905, pp. 3, 229.

[11] Rob. Plot, *The Nat. Hist. of Staff.* (1686), 107.

[12] In Leland's day Uttoxeter was famous for its dairy produce. See his *Itin.* (3rd ed. Hearne, 1769), vii, 26, where he says 'the men of the town useth grazing, for there be wonderful pastures upon Dove.'

[13] *The Will. Salt Arch. Soc. Coll.* v, pt. i.

[14] *Engl. Hist. Rev.* xx, 275 et seq.; J. H. Round, *The Burton Abbey Surv.*

SOCIAL AND ECONOMIC HISTORY

There were no tenants paying rent alone without services, and none belonging to the class of wholly unfree cultivators, the 'servi' of Domesday Book.[15]

The smith often held his land in consideration of giving his services to the monks, but at Stretton he had the option of paying 12d. a year instead.[16]

A consideration of the surveys shows that on the Burton manors, as elsewhere, it was customary for the ordinary villein to give two days' work per week to his lord, and to perform a certain number of miscellaneous services. For instance, the villeins on the Wetmoor manor had to plough twice yearly, to reap for three days in August, to attend the hunt, do a certain amount of carting, to make contributions of fowls at Christmas and to pay certain dues, such as 8d. for the use of the lord's fold.[17]

The rent-paying tenant was free from the ordinary 'week-work,' but he too had a number of services to perform, e.g., to lend his plough twice a year, as at Branston, Stretton, and Abbot's Bromley, to attend the hunt, to keep up the fences, to reap in harvest usually for three days. Sometimes, as at Bromley, Wetmoor, Appleby, and Finden, to go where the abbot bade him.[18]

Sometimes the manor was farmed by a number of the tenants, as at Bromley,[19] who performed certain services however in addition to payment of rent, the abbot keeping the wood and the profits thereof in his own hands.

At Branston we get an example of a man holding 8 bovates of land and having seven men under him.[20] Very often one of the monks farmed the manor, as at Winshill, which Edric the monk farmed for £4 10s. per year, exclusive of the wood, hay, and certain lands reserved to the use and profit of the whole monastic body.[21] Not much is to be gathered from these surveys as to the progress of the villeins towards commutation of services for money payment, for while there are instances of men holding land for services who formerly paid rent, as at Stretton,[22] there are other cases in which the opposite holds good.

Later on, however, in the time of Henry III, we hear of an attempt of the 'customary tenants' to gain their freedom from servile tenure, but unfortunately they were not successful. The case came up for judgement at Westminster, and the record states that the abbot sued his tenants

> for customs and services due for the tenements they hold of him in Bromley, inasmuch as they held the tenements in villeinage, and owed villein services, viz., tallage once every year at his will, and merchetum for marrying their daughters and other services, and they owed tallage assessed at eight marks two years ago.

The marriage payment here, as elsewhere, seems to have been the distinctive mark of servile status, and the tenants of Bromley denied that they owed either this or the tallage, and asserted that they held their tenements by certain fixed services and a payment of 20s. at Christmas. The final verdict was not given till 1252 at Nottingham, when eight knights and eight freemen who formed the jury stated that all the tenants named, and their ancestors

---

[15] The analysis of the Domesday Survey for Staff. gives only thirty-three servi for the whole hundred of Offlow, fifty-seven for Seisdon, sixty for Cuttlestone, sixty-eight for Pirehill, and thirteen for Totmonslow (R. W. Eyton, *Dom. Studies, Staff.* 15).

[16] *The Will. Salt Arch. Soc. Coll.* pt. i, v (1), 19.

[17] Ibid. 26.

[18] *Engl. Hist. Rev.* xx, 284–6.

[19] *The Will. Salt Arch. Soc. Coll.* pt. i, v, 20.

[20] Ibid. 25. The usual holding was 2 bovates.

[21] Ibid. 24.

[22] Ibid. 19.

before them, held their tenements in villeinage, and gave merchetum for marrying their daughters, and every year they gave ' stud ' (tallage), sometimes more and sometimes less, at the will of the abbot, and that they owed all villein services.[23]

The monks, it may be noticed, showed a good deal of pious indignation at the presumption of their tenants, and complacently contrasted the pride of the latter with their own humility, illustrating and concluding their homily by the text, ' God resists the proud and gives His grace to the humble.' [24]

It is to be feared that the relations of the abbots and their tenants were never of the friendliest, for when in the early years of the fourteenth century the abbot was prosecuted in the hundred of Pirehill for ' fraudulently concealing and disposing of the goods and chattels of Thomas earl of Lancaster,' the jury gave the verdict against him, and the abbot, who denied the whole story to the king, maintained that the jury was a packed one, consisting of men evilly disposed towards him.[25]   Indeed, many instances might be given of the somewhat truculent behaviour of the abbots, not only towards their tenants but in their relations with the neighbouring landowners, with whom they were frequently in conflict.

From an old survey of Tutbury, made in Elizabeth's reign, we know that the services of the villeins here were not commuted for rents till the reign of Henry V (fifteenth century), and reference is made to the heaviness of these services as they were enforced by the founder of Tutbury Priory in 1080:

> Part of the lands of the priory (says the survey) were granted to his bondmen, for no freemen would take land with such villainous customs as were found in an ancient record at Tutbury (called the Cowcher, and made in the time of Henry V), viz. to mow the grass in the meadows, make the hay and carry it into the castle, and the arable land to plow it, sow it, harrow it and reap it, and carry it either to the lord's manor house, or to the said castle, at their own costs and charges.

They were also bound to divers customs, services, and carriages which at the making of the old Coucher were reduced to annual rents.[26]

From the available records we see that in the latter part of the thirteenth century the process of commutation was going on gradually all over the county, if not very rapidly.   From a number of ' extents of manors ' of the time of Edward I [27] we see that the services were always appraised in terms of money, and it may be concluded that it was sometimes convenient to accept money payment rather than labour, whilst the next step to a general substitution of money rents is not difficult.   For instance, the ' works ' of the customary tenants at Swinford are valued at 5s. each.   Again, in the manor of Sedgeley we hear of a great many services which the customary tenants *ought* to perform, such as mowing, reaping, carrying hay and wood, gathering nuts, and so on, but in each case they are valued in terms of money, and it is more than likely that the word ' ought,' which occurs in this and other records, points to an ideal of duty once regarded, but now repudiated.   This conjecture is the more likely to be true in the case of Sedgeley, inasmuch as it was, even at that date, a place of some industrial and commercial importance—for the same record speaks of four coal-pits, worth yearly £4, and of sixteen small shops.   Still the peasants of Sedgeley were as yet only struggling to be free,

[23] *The Will. Salt Arch. Soc. Coll.* pt. i, v, 64–5.   [24] Ibid. 65.   [25] Ibid. 4–5.
[26] Stebbing Shaw, *Hist. of Staff.* (1801), i, 45.   [27] *The Will. Salt Arch. Soc. Coll.* pt. ii, ix, 26–29.

for the record also speaks of the profit accruing from the 'market' of daughters, the special mark of servile status in those days.[28]

The examples cited refer to the eastern and southern part of the county. The state of affairs as it existed near the western border is illustrated by the record of a manor court held at Wrottesley in 1382, one year after the Peasants' Revolt.[29] Of the seventeen tenants four only were freeholders, six are described as 'holding in bondage,' and the rest were crofters or cottagers. Reference is made to a certain Hugh Roberdes who had lately died, leaving a daughter who had recently married with the permission of the lord. Yet all the tenants were paying rent for their holdings, despite the dependence of their position in some ways as shown by the lord's control over the marriage of their daughters indicated above.

References to the food contributions of tenants holding in bondage persist till quite late in manor rolls, even when the tenants are paying rent, e.g. at Rolleston in 1414.[30] In a list of receipts occurs the entry of 5s. 7½d. and fifty-three capons, the rent of tenants 'holding in bondage.' Again, in 1480, in a bailiff's account we hear of the contribution of capons or fowls by the Walsall tenants, and reference is still made at that date to their 'works,' though these were by that time commuted.[31]

At Barton, in the honour of Tutbury, in 1463 some tenants were still holding land in return for services alone,[32] so that it is clear that villeinage and its servile accompaniments died but slowly in this county. A fairly late example of the way the ordinary villein was tied to the soil occurs in the record of a 'Magna Curia' held at Wrottesley in 1401, in which the jury presented that John de Green, 'the native,' had left his home without his lord's permission, a serious offence in mediaeval times.[33]

Of the wild, barren, moorland region of North Staffordshire we know but little in early times; even now it is a thinly populated district, made up chiefly of scattered hamlets and villages, and containing scarcely any towns. In the fourteenth century, apart from the few villages in the region now known as the Potteries and those districts near the fertile banks of the Dove or its tributary streams, this part of the country had but little economic or social importance.[34]

With regard to the Peasants' Revolt of 1381, all the most recent researches have failed to discover that the Staffordshire peasants had any part in it, though we now know that the tenants on the bishop of Chester's manors in the Wirral were implicated.

This must not be hastily taken to prove that the grievances of the Staffordshire peasants were less severe than those of other counties; their failure to participate in the movement may be regarded, in part at any rate, as a result

[28] *The Will. Salt Arch. Soc. Coll.* pt. ii, ix, 29.
[29] Ibid. vi (New Ser.), pt. ii, 175.
[30] Mins. Accts. bdle. 988, No. 20.
[31] Ibid. bdle. 641, No. 10411.
[32] Ibid. bdle. 371, No. 6197.
[33] *The Will. Salt Arch. Soc. Coll.* pt. i (New Ser.), 184. There are in Staffordshire, as elsewhere, numerous instances of survivals of manorial courts, e.g. the case of Standon, where we have evidence of the holding of a court baron at least as late as 1750, and the record of fines levied on freeholders for various offences such as omitting to repair roads, ditches, and fences (Edward Salt, *Hist. of Standon* (1888), 137).

[34] As to the early condition of the villages in the Potteries see Meteyard's *Life of Josiah Wedgwood*, 101, where she affirms her belief that for three or four centuries after the Norman Conquest the liberty of establishing a pot-works on the waste, and of digging for clay and coal, was conferred by manorial lords in return for services, commuted later for rents.

of their geographical position—far from London and the eastern counties, and with little means of communication therewith. Besides, the reaction in favour of the ruling classes was so swift that the news of the rising probably only reached this county with the additional information that it had been put down by the most vigorous methods. Yet there is reason to suppose that the effects of the Black Death in depopulating the county were not quite so serious in Staffordshire as in some parts of England, and that, in consequence, the peasants here suffered somewhat less from the operation of the Statutes of Labour which had attempted, though vainly, to fix the rates of wages according to those which prevailed before the plague. There is a tradition that Wolverhampton was partially devastated by the disease,[35] and here and there in the records there are indirect references to its ravages.[36] It was of course most unlikely that this county should have escaped the pestilence, and the general scantiness of the ordinary judicial records at this time renders it dangerous to make serious general statements.

There is, however, a distinct statement on the matter in a letter directed to an official of the archdeaconry of Coventry and Lichfield in 1361, which points to the comparative immunity of the county in the second great visitation of 1361–2, if not in the earlier one of 1348–9.[37]

> The pestilence (says the letter) with which God is visiting the sins of the people, *has not yet come into this diocese*, but many other parts of the country are rendered empty by it! Prayer is therefore to be made in all churches for the staying of the Plague.

Certainly it was felt severely round about the Staffordshire borders, as appears from various entries in the Episcopal Registers. Thus in 1380 a request was made by the monks of Bordesley, in the diocese of Worcester, for the appropriation of the church of Kinver in the archdeaconry of Stafford, the abbot pleading poverty on the ground that his chief endowment is in land and agriculture, which bring in nothing through lack of labourers owing to the pestilence. He states that an unusual number of guests have visited the monastery, and that the cattle plague has further reduced his resources.[38]

As regards the commercial and industrial development of Staffordshire, it is quite evident that there was but little progress between the eleventh and the sixteenth century. We know that the county suffered considerably in the civil war of Stephen's day, being for some time in the campaign of 1153 the head quarters of Matilda's son Henry. In 1187–8 the sheriff reports that 84 hides of geldable land were so desolated that he could levy nothing on it. 'Lo it was near one-fifth of the geldable area of the county.'[39]

The growth of the towns was certainly late. From the Subsidy Roll of 1332–3 we see that Stafford, one of the ten fortified English towns mentioned in Domesday Book, comes first, with a contribution of £13 8s. 10d.[40] Lichfield is next on the list, and pays £12 ; the third town is Newcastle under Lyme, paying £10 13s. 4d., whilst Burton contributes only £8, and the other towns are inconsiderable, and come far behind.[41]

[35] F. Burleigh, *Hist. and Descriptive Guide to Wolverhampton*, 4.
[36] *The Will. Salt Arch. Soc. Coll.* vii, 38 ; ibid. xii, 98 ; ibid. xiv, 73.
[37] *Reg. of Bishop Robert de Stretton* (Lich. Epis. Reg.), printed in *The Will. Salt Arch. Soc. Coll.* viii (New Ser.), 99.
[38] *The Will. Salt Arch. Soc. Coll.* viii (New Ser), 141.
[39] Ibid. x.   [40] Ibid. x (1), 79–132.   [41] Ibid.

SOCIAL AND ECONOMIC HISTORY

From the Quo Warranto Pleas of 1293 we learn that Lichfield, Rugeley, Cannock, and Brewood possessed no market till the reign of Henry III, and the profits went, even then, to the bishop of Lichfield and Coventry.[42] The market at Wolverhampton also dates from this reign, as also does that of Stone.[43]

In a charter granted by King John to the burgesses of Stafford, that town gained the privileges of a free borough 'with freedom from toll, suits of shires and hundreds, and all other free customs of the free boroughs of England.'[44]

Tamworth also gained a charter of privileges in the reign of Edward III, though these were restricted to ' the men and tenants of that half the town of Tamworth which had been ancient demesne.'[45] In the same reign Walsall also gained a charter, giving the burgesses freedom from toll.[46]

The first city to obtain a charter of incorporation was Lichfield, in 1547. Stafford was incorporated two years later,[47] whilst Tamworth had to wait till 1560.[48] Newcastle gained its charter of incorporation in the reign of Henry VIII.[49] The other corporate boroughs of Staffordshire are of modern origin.

After the dissolution of the religious gild of St. Mary, which had hitherto managed the affairs of the town, the only town possessing a merchant-gild in the fourteenth century seems to have been Newcastle-under-Lyme, and the attempts of that city to carry out a policy of trade protection were unsuccessful. In an interesting case which came before the judges in 1279–80 the gild tested its powers of exclusive trading. It seems that a burgess of Stafford named William de Pykestoke had taken out a summons against certain burgesses of Newcastle-under-Lyme for carrying off and illegally detaining his chattels, viz. four ells of cloth. The Newcastle men admitted the fact, but in defence charged the said William with keeping a shop, cutting cloth, and selling wool and fleeces by the ell without having been received into the gild and contrary to the regulations of the gild granted to Newcastle by a charter of Henry III.[50]

Pykestoke on his part admitted that he was not a gild member, but pleaded that by virtue of the charter of King John making Stafford a free borough he ought to enjoy the liberty of free trade in Newcastle. He further asserted that he and other burgesses had enjoyed these privileges till a year ago, when their chattels had been seized as aforesaid.

After many adjournments a jury decided in favour of the Stafford burgesses, despite the regulations of the gild, and awarded them 40s. damages and the restoration of their chattels.[51]

We see therefore that the general civic protection of the middle ages was not so firmly established in Staffordshire as in many other counties, where it had the disastrous result of driving trade and industry to the country villages to the impoverishment and depopulation of the towns.[52]

[42] *The Will. Salt Arch. Soc. Coll.* vi (1), 244.   [43] Ibid. 249.
[44] Merewether, *Boroughs and Corporations,* i, 408, who gives reference Rot. Cart. 2 John, m. 7, but this is not printed by the Rec. Com.   [45] Pat. 4 Edw. III, m. 32.   [46] Ibid. 47 Edw. III, pt. 2, m. 35.
[47] Merewether, *Boroughs and Corporations,* iii, 2281.   [48] Ibid.
[49] *Staff. Constitutional Mag.* Feb. 1890, p. 303.
[50] *The Will. Salt Arch. Soc. Coll.* vi (1), 111.   [51] Ibid. 112.
[52] See *Trans. Roy. Hist. Soc.* vii (New Ser.), 1893, for acct. of the Mercers' Company, Lichfield, instituted 1624 by the town authorities, who were empowered by royal charter to regulate the trade of mercers, grocers, linen drapers, woollen drapers, silkmen, hosiers, salters, apothecaries, and haberdashers.

A HISTORY OF STAFFORDSHIRE

The industrial development of the county was no more rapid at this time than its commercial progress. Staffordshire played no part in the early history of the woollen industry in England; the Flemish weavers could not come so far inland as this to teach their craft; but some simple form of cloth-making there was here as in all parts of the country, and it is said that the wool trade was the staple trade of Wolverhampton until its decline in the sixteenth century.

The returns of the Poll Tax of 1379–81 show that there must have been a considerable manufacture of cutlery at Rugeley,[53] and reference has already been made to the coal-pits of Sedgeley, which, however, only brought in £4 10s. a year, so could not have been very extensively worked (between £40 and £50 of modern money).[54] Iron mines are also mentioned at Tunstall in 1361,[55] but we know that until the eighteenth century there was no important industrial development in North or South Staffordshire. It is believed that iron smelting was carried on at Uttoxeter in the thirteenth century and wool stapling in the fourteenth. The smelting of iron went on to some extent in other parts of the country, but it was as yet effected by means of charcoal, easily procurable in a county so well wooded. For the rest the return of the Poll Tax of 1379–81 for the hundreds of Offlow and Cuttlestone[56] shows us a miscellaneous population, shoemakers, smiths, carpenters, skinners, fullers, tailors, butchers, and a few weavers, with a very large proportion of agricultural labourers or husbandmen, about eighty-eight per cent. of the whole number, compared with twelve per cent. employed in trade and industry other than agriculture.

The records of the administration of justice in the manorial and other courts, including those of the forest, throw a good deal of light upon the life and customs of the people in mediaeval times. They show us a community mainly agricultural whose misdemeanours are chiefly connected with field and forest. There are innumerable fines for depasturing sheep and cattle, inclosing parts of the forest for purposes of cultivation, and throwing down fences on the lord's land, and so on.

In 1129 the men of Arley are amerced ten marks for lands of the forest taken by them unwarrantably into cultivation, but the king releases them from the penalty 'for that the debtors were poor.'[57]

After the passing of the Statute of Merton in 1235, which gave the freeholders the right to protest against encroachments of the lord on their pasture land, the Assize Rolls of Staffordshire are full of cases in which the tenant brings an action against the lord for this offence. The following case is only one of many of the kind :—'An assize if John Golde had unjustly disseised Milicent Basset of her common of pasture in five acres in Finchespath appurtenant to her free tenement. Verdict for Milicent.'[58] The fact that in most cases the tenants seem to have got favourable verdicts points to a rather general attempt on the part of the Staffordshire lords to ignore the rights of the freeholders in this respect. It is worth noting in passing that the Statute of Merton, which was really the first inclosure act, gave no

[53] *The Will. Salt Arch. Soc. Coll.* xvii, 186.
[54] Ibid. pt. ii, ix, 29.
[55] De Banco R. 405, Hil. 35 Edw. III, m. 299 *d.*
[56] *The Will. Salt Arch. Soc. Coll.* xvii, 61–205.
[57] Ibid. i, 8 ; Pipe R. 31 Hen. I.
[58] *The Will. Salt Arch. Soc. Coll.* vi (1), 50 ; Misc. Assize R. 55 Hen. III, Lichfield ; *also headed* Plea Rolls of reign of Edw. I, No. 1217. (The Rolls are *not numbered* in Salt.)

rights of protest to the villein or the inhabitants generally, hence much inclosure must have taken place to the injury of these people.

An interesting example of the summary method of dealing with 'manifest felons' occurs in the records of the Staffordshire Assizes in 1273.

> The jury of the hundred of Seisdon presented that Roger de Reyneyde was arrested upon suspicion of robbery and delivered to William —, Peter, etc. to convey him to Bridgnorth, and the said Roger escaped from their custody, and the said William and others followed him and cut off his head and brought it to Stafford. His chattels are worth 22d., and the jurors say he was a robber and a malefactor.[59]

The first mention of a jury in criminal matters occurs in 1204 at Lichfield,[60] and numerous entries show the corporate responsibility of the hundreds for crime in their midst.

Thus in 1174 we are told that nine murders in Offlow Hundred had been assessed by the itinerant justices at the rate of one mark each,[61] and next year the 'tithing' of Newbold was fined half a mark for the sins of one Brun of Newbold, an escaped felon whose chattels the sheriff had sold for five shillings.[62] Many examples might be given of the mediaeval custom of valuing the instrument of death, whether accidental or deliberate, and exacting the money from the owner or the locality implicated, as a payment or 'deodand' to the king. For instance, the vill of Weston upon Trent is chargeable 'for a sword with which John Gardyner had been feloniously killed by Stephen Benet of Creswalle—four shillings.' Likewise the vill of Leek has to pay 2s. 6d., the value of a horse which was the cause of death of a certain Adam, killed by accident.[63]

The number of private individuals who had the right to hang thieves on a private gallows in the fourteenth century seems to have been considerable, and included the priors of Stone, Trentham, and Lapley, as well as the abbot of Burton, whilst the claims of the bishop of Lichfield and Coventry, and of the dean and chapter of Penkridge, were under consideration at the time when Edward I made his famous inquiry into feudal jurisdictions in the interests of national justice.[64]

With regard to wages and prices of provisions in mediaeval Staffordshire the evidence is rather scanty, but there is enough to enable us to gather some general idea as to the changes in these between the eleventh century and the fifteenth, though not enough to warrant the drawing of any definite conclusions as to the local variations in the county. The rent of land was fairly steady during this time, and may be taken as 6d. per acre, rising to 8d. for specially good land, and falling to 4d. for poor soil.

At Tutbury in 1257 a quarter of wheat could be bought for 4s. 4d.[65] A little later, in 1294, it was sold at 3s. 4d. per quarter at Stafford;[66] at the same time a chicken could be bought for a halfpenny, and two oxen for 15s. at Wolverhampton.[67] In Berkeswich (Baswich) manor wheat varied from 3s. to 4s. per quarter in 1312.[68] About the same time a

---

[59] *The Will. Salt Arch. Soc. Coll.* iii, 18.
[60] Ibid. iii, 98.
[61] Ibid. i, 75; Pipe R. 21 Hen. II.
[62] Ibid. i, 76; Pipe R. 21 Hen. II.
[63] Ibid. xvii, 13; quoted in extracts from Plea R. Lichfield, East. 2 Hen. V.
[64] Ibid. vi (1), 243–9.
[65] Mins. Accts. 40–1 Hen. III, bdle. 1094, No. 11.
[66] Bailiff's Acct.; quoted in *The Will. Salt Arch. Soc. Coll.* vi (2), 71.
[67] Ibid. 72.
[68] MSS. pertaining to the D. and C. of Lichfield, N. 1.

thatcher's wages in Berkeswich did not rise beyond a penny, though a carpenter could earn 3d.[69]

By the middle of the fourteenth century in the reign of Edward III wages had risen considerably : a thatcher could earn 3½d. to 4d. per day, and other skilled labourers, such as carpenters and masons, rather more.

By the middle of the fifteenth century another rise may be seen, and from a considerable number of individual accounts the wages of an unskilled labourer may be calculated at 4d. per day, whilst masons, sawyers, and carpenters earned 5d. or 6d.[70] The average price of wheat for the whole country from 1260 to 1400 is estimated by Thorold Rogers at 5s. 10¾d. per quarter ; and from 1401 to 1540 one penny more,[71] and in estimating the purchasing power of the wages given above, it is usual to suppose the value of money in the fifteenth century to be twelve times as great as it is at present,[72] and 1s. per week was an ordinary estimate for the board of a workman.[73]

It is now recognized that the sixteenth century, though marked by glorious national achievements, was a period in which the mass of the people suffered considerably, and the inhabitants of Staffordshire were not exempt from the social distress of the time. The influx of silver from the South American mines (1540–1600), and the systematic debasing of the currency in the reigns of Henry VIII and Edward VI led to a great rise in prices, and the contemporary documents constantly refer to the dearness of provisions, and especially of corn. Unfortunately for the labourer his wages did not rise in proportion, so that his lot was often very hard at this time.

The dissolution of the monastic houses, of which there were thirty-six in Staffordshire,[74] meant inevitably, here as elsewhere, serious economic dislocation, for with the change of landlords came frequently change in the use to which the land was put, since the growing demand for wool for the expanding cloth industry caused many landowners to inclose for pasture land which had been formerly used for tillage.[75]

The tenants and labourers of the old monastic landowners in Staffordshire must inevitably have suffered by the change, even though there is good reason to suppose that inclosures were not nearly so widespread in this county as in many others. The report of the commissioners appointed to inquire into inclosures in 1517 shows that in this county, where the woollen industry had never been very important, there was no serious grievance. The total number of acres inclosed was slightly under five hundred (488¼ acres). Of these 118¼ acres were in the hundred of Cuttlestone, of which 85 acres only were for purposes of pasture, and none occurred before 1502. In Pirehill Hundred 100 acres had been inclosed, of which 60 were for a park and 40 for pasture, the earliest date of inclosure there being 1486. In Offlow Hundred 80 acres

[69] Mins. Accts. Edw. II, bdle. 1132, No. 7.   [70] Mins. Accts. Hen. VI, bdle. 369, No. 6179, &c.
[71] See Thorold Rogers, *Six Centuries of Work and Wages*, 330.
[72] Ibid. 539.   [73] Ibid. 329.
[74] Stebbing Shaw, *Hist. of Staff.* i, 51.
[75] Sir Simon Degge gives us some impressions of the evil results of the monastic dissolution. See, Sir Simon Degge, 'Observations on the Possessors of Monastery Lands in Staffordshire,' printed 1717, in Sampson Erdeswick's *Surv. of Staff.* He speaks of the 'Sacrilegious purchasers of this Age,' and asserts that the owners become bankrupt and sell, or else die without male issue, whereby their memories perish, and he adds, 'the next thing that hath been a great ruin to the gentry is their living and taking pleasure to spend their estate in London.'

had been inclosed, of which only twenty were for sheep farming, the dates of inclosure being 1510 and 1576. One hundred and sixty acres of inclosed land were found in the liberty of the Duchy of Lancaster, but the whole extent was for park land.

The fewest inclosures occurred in the Seisdon Hundred, 26 only, and only 3 of these for pasture. For Totmonslow Hundred there was no return. The total number of acres inclosed for pasture amounted to 148, whilst only 28 were inclosed for tillage, and the remainder was imparked. No cases of eviction were mentioned.[76]

Unfortunately there is no information for Staffordshire in respect to the Inclosure Commission of 1548.

The monks had, of course, been the great agents of charity before the dissolution of the monasteries in Staffordshire, and this event must have been one of the causes of the multitude of vagrants and beggars to which constant reference is made in the records of the time. And we know that the severe repressive measures adopted for solving this problem had to give place to more constructive and humane methods of dealing with the poor, methods which culminated in the great Act of 1601, which provided for the raising of a rate in each parish for relieving the impotent, setting the able-bodied to work, and apprenticing the pauper children to some useful trade.

As we have already seen, there is ample evidence of the poverty of the county at this time. In 1559 it is said to be weakened by sickness.[77] In 1593 there was a serious visitation of the plague in England, and more than eleven hundred are said to have died in Lichfield alone.[78]

We hear also of the decay of towns. For instance, when Queen Elizabeth visited Stafford in 1575 the burgesses complained of the decay of the town, and ascribed it to the depressed and dying state of the cap trade.[79]

Again, in an Elizabethan survey of Tutbury, the writer laments the general decay and depopulation of towns, and says that there ought to be more markets and fairs ' to make men more desirous to plant their habitations in these places.' [80]

Leland, who travelled through England in the years 1536–9, makes no mention of the Potteries. He describes Walsall as a little market town, and Burton as a place where ' there be many marbellers working in alabaster.' [81] As yet there is no mention of the great brewing industry, nor of the clothing trade, which, according to Defoe, was carried on there with great profit in 1778.[82]

The seventeenth century may be regarded as a time in which the way was prepared for the industrial developments of the eighteenth in Staffordshire. By 1639 Dudley had got his second royal patent for smelting iron with pit-coal instead of charcoal, and he was carrying on his experiments with considerable success at Sedgeley in spite of fierce opposition and jealousy on the part of the neighbouring iron-masters.[83] The discovery of this new process,

[76] See Inq. of 1517 (Inclosures and Evictions), ed. from Lansdowne MSS. i, 153, by J. S. Leadam, M.A. *Trans. Roy. Hist. Soc.* (New Ser.), vi (1892), 310, 314.

[77] *Cal. S.P. Dom.* 1547–80, p. 122.   [78] Stebbing Shaw, *Hist. of Staff.* i, 333.

[79] J. L. Cherry, *Stafford in Olden Times* (1890), quoting an old document.

[80] Stebbing Shaw, op. cit. i, 45. Tutbury paid £1 16s. 3d. to the subsidy of 1590. See Talbot Papers in Coll. of Arms, v, 218.   [81] Leland, *Itin.* (ed. Hearne, 1769), 26.

[82] Defoe, *Tour Through Great Britain* (8th ed.), ii, 365.

[83] Lord Dudley, *Metallum Martis*, 16, 17.

coming as it did at a time when the wood supply of Sussex, Surrey, and Kent was seriously diminished, was bound to lead eventually to great industrial developments in South Staffordshire where the coal and ironstone lay side by side. The manufacture of the iron into finished goods was also going on in the district. Henry Powle, who wrote an account of the iron trade in 1677, points out how the 'sow' iron made by the iron-workers in the Forest of Dean found its way up the Severn into the Staffordshire forges, and so to the workshops of Wolverhampton, Sedgeley, and Walsall, where it was made into the hardware goods for which the district was already becoming famous.[84] The nail trade had become localized in Staffordshire towards the end of the sixteenth century, and the cost of nails, so typical an item of mediaeval accounts, was now no longer credited to the village blacksmith. Since 1565, when Shutz, a German, introduced 'slitting mills,' which prepared the rods for the nailers, this industry steadily developed, and in 1584–5 a Bill was brought into Parliament to regulate the trade by statute, and to make nailing a separate employment in Staffordshire, Worcestershire, and Salop.[85]

Nail-making, which included the manufacture of nuts, bolts, rivets, and screws, was purely a domestic industry till the eighteenth century, and though the nail industry is now carried on largely in factories, there is still a considerable, though declining, amount of work done in the miserable little workshops that adjoin the homes of the nailers in the neighbourhood of Sedgeley and Dudley and in some other districts. The conditions of these people seem always to have been bad, their hours long, and their pay poor. In an ' Essay to enable the Necessitous Poor to pay Taxes,'[86] it was stated that nailers worked from four in the morning on Monday till late on Saturday night, receiving for their work 3s., or less if the iron were bad. In 1760 screwmaking began to be organized on the factory system, but little progress was made till the inventions of Whitworth in 1840, and the domestic system went on practically unchanged till 1861 in all other branches, despite numerous inventions between 1760 and 1841. The nut and bolt trade, now practically a factory industry, was the next to succumb, and at the present time only certain kinds of nails are made in domestic workshops, and chiefly by women, children, and old men.[87]

It is interesting to notice the relative wealth and importance of the Staffordshire towns at this time. In the assessment for ship-money, 1635, the whole county was assessed at £2,000. Lichfield contributed far the most, viz. £100 ; Walsall came next with a payment of £25 ; Stafford, not yet the seat of the boot and shoe trade, paid only £20 ; and Newcastle under Lyme £16.[88] The position of Walsall is interesting as evidence of the growing industrial prosperity of the South Staffordshire towns, and because it still stands second in the list of Staffordshire cities, though Wolverhampton and not Lichfield ranks first in point of population and general importance.

Two years later, and again in 1665, when the plague was raging in London, the Walsall authorities took the most serious precautions to preserve the immunity of their town, as may be read in an old record of the regula-

---

[84] W. A. S. Hewins, *Engl. Trade and Finance* (1892), 14, 15.
[85] Ibid. 16.   [86] Ibid. 17.   [87] Ibid. 19.
[88] J. Langford, *Staff. and Warw. Past and Present*, 429.

tions issued to the constable of Walsall borough.[89] Four sufficient house-keepers are to be appointed to keep out all strangers from entering the town unless they bring certificates that they do not come from infected places ; and ale-house keepers are to refuse all guests save under the same conditions. This was in 1637, but in 1665 the regulations are more detailed and rigorous, and are interesting as a specimen of sanitary precautions in an age not given overmuch to such things.[90] The first regulation says :—

> That if any carrier Shall for the future desperately adventure to travel to London untill it shall please God upon the removeall or good abatement of the Sicknes wee may goe with lesse danger and more Safety, and shall presume to come home to his owne house at Walsall, that his house shall be shutt upp for the space of one month at the least.

The other regulations are similar in intention, and provide for the whole body of citizens acting as special constables to keep out infected persons. The strictest prohibitions are also laid on the inhabitants as to the entertainment of the aforesaid carriers or any suspicious strangers, and nobody is—

> to receve any goods or wares brought down (by the carriers) before the same have been aired by the space of one month at the least, upon the payne of having their house shutt upp and to be other wayes proceeded against as dangerous persons and contemners of authority.

From a document in the Corporation Records at Stafford we learn that in 1646 there was a great visitation of the plague in that town, ' which by that meanes is now growne so poore, that unless some speedie course be taken for their relief, the meaner sort of people must of necessitie break out for want of sustenance.'[91]

As for the Pottery district at this time, its area was much the same as at present, but the population was scanty, probably not more than four thousand ; and it was distributed in small hamlets and villages separated by strips of wild moorland, with two or three potworks in each village, each giving occupation to about eight persons. Sometimes the family alone were sufficient to carry on the various processes of the primitive manufacture of that day, and the women of the family usually had the task of driving the loaded and panniered asses to the distant towns where they sold their pottery, and whence they brought back food and other household necessaries on the backs of their animals. As late as 1653 Burslem is described as a mere village, with few houses and a scanty population. Hanley was still smaller, and Stoke on Trent a small aggregation of thatched houses and two potworks gathered round the ancient parish church.[92]

The pottery industry had existed in some rude form in North Staffordshire from time immemorial, but though certain advances had been made in the seventeenth century, such as the discovery that glazing could be effected by salt in 1680, the manufacture of pottery was still in a primitive stage of development, was a purely domestic industry, and was confined chiefly to the making of common vessels of everyday use. No serious general advance was made indeed until the genius and industry of Josiah Wedgwood in the eighteenth century transformed a rude and primitive industry into an elaborate and beautiful art, and in so doing changed the social condition of a wide district and a large population.

[89] E. L. Glew, *Hist. of Borough and Foreign of Walsall* (1856), 119.   [90] Ibid. 120.
[91] J. L. Cherry, *Stafford in Olden Times*, 56.   [92] Meteyard, *Life of Josiah Wedgwood* (1865), i, 96–9.

Dr. Plot, writing in 1686, says :—'The greatest pottery they have in this county is carried on at Burslem, . . . where for making their several sorts of pots they have as many different sorts of clay, which they dig round about the towne . . . the best being found nearest the coale.'[93]

One of the chief articles made at Burslem was the long cylindrical butter-pot, made of coarse material and unglazed, which one may regard as the link between the industrial and the agricultural workers of Staffordshire, and symbolical of the dependence of the one upon the other.

Dr. Plot mentions this butter-pot incidentally in his description of the dairy industry in the limestone district and on the banks of the Dove,

> from which limestone hills and rich pastures and meadow the great Dairies are maintained in this part of Staffordshire, that supply Uttoxeter Market with such vast quantities of good butter and cheese that the cheesemongers of London have thought it worth their while to set up a Factorage here for these commodities. . . The butter they buy by the Pot of a long and cylindrical form made at Burslem in this County of a certain size.[94]

The main feature of the industrial revolution in England at the end of the eighteenth century was the widespread change from a system of domestic industry to one in which large numbers of wage-earners worked in large factories belonging to capitalist landowners, a change which brought with it a vast increase in the population of this country and a redistribution of population. It was made possible by the discovery and working of the great coalfields of northern and midland England, accompanied by a succession of important mechanical inventions, and completed by the application of steam to machinery as a motive power, in place of water, which had been used in the new factories that sprang up all over the country in the latter part of the eighteenth century. In 1750 Staffordshire was still one of the thinly populated counties, though since 1700 it had probably increased its population by 30 per cent.[95] Toynbee estimated its population in 1750 as 140 to the square mile compared with 862 in 1881. The inventions we are accustomed to connect most nearly with the industrial revolution are those associated with the textile industries ; these only indirectly affected Staffordshire by increasing the demand for coal and also for machinery, both needed in increasing quantities by the growth of the factory system made possible by these inventions. There were new cotton factories started at the end of the eighteenth century on the banks of the Dove and Trent, at Fazeley, Tamworth, Rocester, Tutbury, and Burton.[96] But it was the inventions in connexion with the mining and iron industries that made the industrial expansion of Staffordshire possible at this date, and especially the introduction of the new steam-engine of Watt and Boulton, first used at the engineering works at Soho, whence so much of the machinery of the factories was supplied. For though the coal had always been there, in Staffordshire, the mines had only been worked to a very slight extent ; hence neither the coal nor the iron industry could make much progress. The new engine was used not only to pump water out of the mines, but also to sink shafts to bring the coal up from the pits.

[93] Rob. Plot, *The Nat. Hist. of Staff.* (1686), 122.

[94] Ibid. 108–9. An Act of 1661 regulated the size of this butter-pot ; it was to hold 14 lb. of butter and to be made of material hard enough not to imbibe moisture ; it was, moreover, to be 14¼ in. high and 6½ in. in diameter.

[95] Toynbee, *Industrial Revolution*, 34–5.   [96] Pitt, *Agric. Surv.* (1796), 171.

The result was an enormous development in the output of coal in Staffordshire and the other coalfields of England, followed by an immediate revival in the coal and iron trades, which had greatly declined between 1737 and 1740.[97]

At the same time there was a series of important inventions affecting the manufacture of iron, and as a result all the various branches of the hardware trade received an immense impulse, and population grew rapidly in all the towns and manufacturing villages of the district.

In North Staffordshire a similar effect was seen in the mining and pottery industries. In the latter, great progress had been made under the influence and guidance of Wedgwood, especially since the introduction of china clay from Devon, Dorset, and Cornwall had led to the establishment of the porcelain manufacture in this county, and consequently to a vast extension of the pottery trade there.

Arthur Young, whose account of his northern tour through England was published in 1771, speaks of the rapid increase of the industry and its considerable export trade to Ireland, most of the European countries, America, and the East Indies, despite the great obstacles arising from the extraordinary difficulty of transporting the goods to the coast by means of wagons and pack-horses along the narrow clayey roads which led out of the county.[98]

The success of Brindley's effort in 1758 in making a canal for the Duke of Bridgewater's colliery at Worsley caused the progressive spirits among the North Staffordshire manufacturers, led by Wedgwood, to agitate for a similar enterprise in that district.[99] There was great opposition from the people of Newcastle, as they feared the traffic might be diverted from their town, to the detriment of their trade. But despite opposition the Grand Trunk or Trent and Mersey Canal was opened in 1777, and very greatly increased the trade of the Potteries, passing as it does through its chief towns, and connecting these with the centres of the salt industry of Cheshire and with the ports on the coast, notably Liverpool. Other canals followed in quick succession, chief among them being the Staffordshire and Worcester Canal, projected to unite the Severn with the Trent, and connected with the system now known as the Birmingham Navigation, which in its turn connects Birmingham with Wolverhampton, Bilston, and other centres of the iron and coal industry in South Staffordshire, so that this district presents a perfect network of canals with innumerable foundries, coal-pits, and other works clustered along their banks for convenience of transport.

Among other short branch canals may be mentioned one of eighteen miles which runs from Uttoxeter up the Churnet Valley till it joins the one at Caldon, and finally meets the Grand Trunk at Stoke on Trent.

About the same time that canals were being constructed all over Staffordshire, the turnpike roads were undergoing great improvement, firstly by means of Acts of Parliament which enabled tolls to be levied for their upkeep, and afterwards owing to the improved methods introduced by Metcalfe, Telford, and Macadam.

There was an early system of primitive railways in this county, in connexion with the mines, e.g. there was a system of wayleaves at Newcastle

[97] De Gibbins, *Industry in Engl.* (1906), 352–3.
[98] Arthur Young, *Tour through the North of England*, iii, 253.   [99] L. Jewitt, *The Wedgwoods*, 163.

under Lyme, where colliery owners paid as much as £500 per annum for leave to draw coal over the estates of landowners, and it is probable that in 1750 every important mine had its accompanying railroad, with wooden tram-lines at first, followed by iron ones after 1738.[100] Apart from these mineral lines no railroad passed through Staffordshire till the opening of the Grand Junction Railway in 1837, which connected London with Liverpool and Manchester by way of Birmingham, Wolverhampton, Stafford, and Chester. Others quickly followed, and to-day the chief lines running through the county are the London and North Western with its various branches, and the North Staffordshire Railway, incorporated 1846, which connects the Potteries with every part of the country, and which took over in that year the Trent and Mersey Navigation. The Great Western passes through only a part of South Staffordshire, whilst the Midland Railway skirts Staffordshire pretty closely from Tamworth to Burton.

By 1801 the industrial development of the county had produced a considerable effect upon the population. Burslem contained 6,578 persons, whilst Stoke on Trent, with Bucknall-cum-Bagnall chapelry, had a population of no less than 16,414.

In South Staffordshire the face of the county was being rapidly changed, and contemporary writers[101] bear witness to the rapid rise in population in many parishes in recent years. The parish of Handsworth is a good example of this. By 1801 its population had risen to 2,719, owing to its nearness to Birmingham and the establishment of various manufactures in its neighbourhood, notably the great manufactory of Watt and Boulton at Soho, already mentioned. A few years before Soho had been a barren heath upon the bleak summit of which, says Shaw, stood a lonely warrener's hut.[102]

The scattered parish of Sedgeley with its nine villages numbered 9,874[103] inhabitants, chiefly workers in coal and iron.[104] Wolverhampton, which in 1750 is estimated to have contained only 7,454 persons,[105] had now a population of 12,565,[106] and Walsall (Borough and Foreign) was not far behind with 10,399.[107] The borough of Stafford contained only 3,898 persons,[108] and Lichfield, including the Close, 4,842.[109] In the purely agricultural districts the changes in population were not very important.

The same period that saw the industrial changes in Staffordshire witnessed here as elsewhere the progress of a considerable agrarian revolution. Agriculture had changed very little since mediaeval times, and even the substitution of pasture for tillage which marked the sixteenth century appears to have been less considerable in Staffordshire than in many counties. Some improvements were made in the seventeenth century, such as the use of winter roots, learnt from the Dutch, and a greater interest was shown in artificial grasses. Still even these improved methods were not universally adopted, and it was not until the next century that any general and marked change took place.

The chief features of the agrarian revolution were the inclosure of the common fields, the consolidation of farms by capitalist landlords, the intro-

---

[100] J. Langford, *Staff. and Warw. Past and Present*, 59–60.
[101] Stebbing Shaw, op. cit. ii, 117, 134; Pitt, *Agric. Surv.* 174.
[102] Stebbing Shaw, op. cit. ii, 117.   [103] *Pop. Returns.*
[104] Stebbing Shaw, op. cit. 222.   [105] J. P. Brown, *The Offic. Guide to Wolverhampton.*
[106] *Pop. Returns.*   [107] Ibid.   [108] Ibid.   [109] Ibid.

duction of a system of rotation of crops, and the extension of what is known as artificial pasture by the more extended use of rye grass, clover, and sainfoin. The Staffordshire agriculturists had moved but slowly in the way of supplementing their natural resources, judging by the evidence of Pitt, who made an agricultural survey for the newly-formed Board of Agriculture, and reported on it in 1796. 'Upon the whole,' he says, 'to the eye of the intelligent agricultural stranger it would convey the idea of a county just emerging from a state of barbarism.' A want of initiative seems to have been general, and the farmers are said to suffer from 'want of education and reading, though they are not wanting in readiness to adopt established improvements.'[110]

A similar want of intelligence and adaptability in the agricultural labourer seems to be shown by the evidence of a farmer who had been successfully ploughing with Leicestershire ploughs, worked by ploughmen from that county. But when these men returned to their homes the ploughs were useless, 'for,' said he, 'they might as well have taken the ploughs with them, for Staffordshire men could not plough with them.'[111]

Pitt reported that the most considerable portion of the cultivated land was by that time inclosed, only about one hundred acres remaining in common fields, viz. at Stafford, Stone, Cheddleton, and Bloxwich.[112] Most of the inclosures date only from the beginning of the eighteenth century, though there is evidence of a certain number of small inclosures made in the early part of the seventeenth century in the neighbourhood of the Dove and near Needwood Forest, viz. at Rolleston, Uttoxeter, and Marchington.[113]

Shaw refers to the inclosure of the land round Wolverhampton, mostly effected at the opening of the eighteenth century, and describes the great productiveness of a certain tract of meadow which was nothing but a morass in the sixteenth century, and was known as the 'Hungry Leas.'[114]

The case of Elford parish, too, described by Mr. Bourne, and quoted by Pitt, is a good example of the beneficial results generally accruing from inclosure. 'The greater part of the parish of Elford,' says Mr. Bourne, 'was common field till 1765, when an Act was obtained for an inclosure. By inclosure rents have been trebled and the tenants are better enabled to discharge them. About five hundred acres out of nineteen hundred are in tillage, which we suppose bring as much grass to market as the whole parish did in its open state. The quantity of cheese made now in proportion to that made prior to the inclosure is more than three to one; the proportion of beef and mutton produced on the land is still greater, as much as ten to one, for though there were sometimes many sheep kept in the common fields, they were so subject to the rot that little or no profit arose to the farmer, or produce to the community. Respecting population there were, prior to the inclosure, fifty-seven houses; there are now seventy-six, and 360 inhabitants; the increase is not due to manufactures, merely to improved cultivation, which demanded more labour.'[115]

---

[110] Pitt, *Agric. Surv.* (1796), 26. [111] Ibid. 389.

[112] The period from 1760 to 1830 was remarkable for the great number of Inclosure Acts for this county passed by Parliament.

[113] *Rentals and Surv. Duchy of Lanc.* (Rec. Com.), 930, 991.

[114] Stebbing Shaw, op. cit. ii, 165.

[115] Pitt, *Agric. Surv.* 41.

The consolidation of small farms was not so extensive in this county as in some districts, farms being found of all sizes from 20 to 500 acres.[116] The value of estates varied greatly from that of the great nobleman or rich commoner worth £10,000 per annum to the holding of the forty shilling freeholder of historic fame.

The improvements in agriculture were, however, chiefly due to the moderate proprietors of 200 to 300 acres, or to the high-class tenant farmers, who had been the first to introduce new methods of cultivation and stock-breeding.[117]

The rental of farms at this time ranged from 10s. to 30s. per acre, but as a large part of the land was in a backward state of cultivation the average price would fall below 20s.[118]

'Few fortunes,' says Pitt, 'are made by farming, unless the farmer is connected with some other employment,' and he sums up the farmer's troubles as high rents and taxes, especially the poor rate and the malt tax, and the rise in the price of labourers' wages, and of the price of agricultural implements and other materials.[119]

This was, of course, the time of the French War, of Corn Laws, of great fluctuations in the price of wheat, and of a serious rise in the poor rate due largely to a short-sighted and demoralizing system of administration. These great fluctuations in price were welcomed by the capitalist farmers who could withhold their stock till prices rose, but the small farmer was often ruined by the low prices; yet rents went up steadily.[120] The average price of wheat per quarter rose from 43s. in 1792 to 75s. 2d. in 1795, and 78s. 7d. in 1796. In 1798 it had fallen to 51s. 10d., but rose next year to 69s., and in 1800 was as high as 103s. 10d.[121]

In 1796 a considerable part of the county was waste and unimproved land. Cannock Chase was still a wild heathery moorland tract, unsullied by the smoke of coke ovens. Part of the east side of Dilhorne Heath had been recently planted with potatoes which had produced excellent crops. 'In fine,' says Pitt, 'in this part of the moorlands the potato harvest is of great consideration, and the thirty thousand artificers and "yeomanry" there eat very little wheaten bread.'[122]

The wages of agricultural labour varied considerably in different parts of the county, being highest always in the neighbourhood of manufactures, but having increased within the last two years, according to Pitt, about 10 per cent., this being due to the cutting of canals, in which work a labourer could earn 2s. 6d. or 3s. per day without beer, compared with the 1s. or 1s. 6d. per day with beer, which is given as the average rate of an agricultural labourer's daily wages in 1796.[123]

Similarly, the recent erection of cotton-mills in various places had made it extremely difficult to get female farm servants without paying excessive wages. A dairymaid earned £3 10s. to £5 per annum at this time, and an under-dairymaid from £2 10s. to £3 10s.[124]

Admittedly the wages of the day labourer were inadequate to provide him with the necessary provisions at current prices. Beef and mutton could,

[116] Pitt, op. cit. 25, 26. [117] Ibid. 16–17. [118] Ibid. 26. [119] Ibid. 32. [120] Cunningham, *Hist. of Industry and Commerce*, ii, 477–9. [121] *Whitaker's Almanack*, 1906. [122] Pitt, op. cit. 129. [123] Ibid. 155–6. [124] Ibid. 156.

however, be obtained at from 3½d. to 4½d. per lb., and butter at 10d. to 1s. Fuel was, of course, plentiful and cheap, and it was usual for the ordinary farm labourer to get a load of coal weighing nearly three tons as part of his harvest pay. In the moorlands a good deal of peat was dug for fuel, and wood was still used to some extent for smelting purposes.[125]

It is interesting to compare the state of things in 1796 with that recorded nearly three-quarters of a century later in 1869.[126] In 1796 the amount of cultivated land was 600,000 acres, in 1869 it had fallen to 570,000. During the same period the meadow and pasture land had been more than trebled, rising from 100,000 acres to 340,000 acres, an increase which has continued, as the Agricultural Returns for 1904 show an extent of 438,220 acres to be under permanent pasture. An immense and unparalleled rise in manufacturing industries is recorded in 1869, accompanied by a rise in agricultural wages, and an occasional scarcity of labour, which might have been very serious but for the increase in pasturage.[127] A point worth notice is the greater equality of wages in various parts of the county at the later date, due to improved means of communication by railways and the development of manufactures. For instance, the local industries competing with agricultural labour in the Uttoxeter district, which is not a manufacturing area, included in 1893 all the following—winter work at the Burton breweries; an iron-foundry at Uttoxeter employing 400 hands; cotton mills in the Dove valley; brass and copper works at Oakamoor; collieries and a tape factory at Cheadle; and, finally, alabaster and gypsum works at Draycott in the Clay, employing 100 men, at an average wage of 18s. per week.[128]

At Uttoxeter itself the cottage accommodation is said to have been much improved since the growth of the ironworks, the increased population having led to a new demand for well-built cottages in place of the old insanitary ones, many of which were pulled down.[129] At Rocester, too, the cottages were found to be of good quality, many of them having been recently built by the owners of the large cotton-mills in the place.[130] The average weekly wages of an agricultural labourer in 1796, at the rate of 15s. for thirteen weeks and 10s. 6d. for the other thirty-nine, works out at 11s. 9¾d. per week, whilst in 1869 a married ploughman obtained 12s. per week, a house and garden, an annual load of coal, and often a potato patch in his employer's field, making, as Evershed computes, an average of 15s. per week.

Midway between these two dates, in 1834, the average wages of an agricultural labourer amounted to 10s. in winter and 12s. in summer,[131] whilst in 1892 the wages of the typical agricultural district of Uttoxeter are given as 15s. to 17s., compared with 14s. in the same district in 1867–70.[132] 'Compared with twenty-five years ago,' says Mr. Little, Senior Agricultural Commissioner, in 1893, 'wages are higher, food cheaper, hours of work fewer, and educational advantages greater.'[133] At the present time (1906) the

[125] Pitt, op. cit. 163. [126] 'The Agric. of Staff.' *Journ. Royal Agric. Soc.* (Ser. 2), v, (1869).
[127] H. Evershed, op. cit. 269.
[128] 'Rep. of Mr. Edward Wilkinson, Assistant Commissioner,' *Rep. of Poor Law Commissioners* (1893–4), vol. xxxv. [c. 6894, vi, 93]. [129] Ibid. 94. [130] Ibid. 95.
[131] *Rep. of Poor Law Commissioners*, 1834. App. B. 1, pt. 1, pp. 439a–46a.
[132] *Rep. of Labour Com.* iii, vol. xxxvii, pt. ii [c. 6894, xxv, 59].
[133] Ibid. 1893–4, Rep. iii, 159.

wages of an agricultural labourer in this district vary from 16s. to 18s. with the 4 lb. loaf at 4½d. to 5d.

A good deal of light is thrown on the social condition of the people in Staffordshire by studying its Poor Law administration in various periods. We do not know much of its early history after the passing of the great Consolidating Act of 1601, but here and there are indications of the difficulties experienced by the local authorities dealing with the care of the poor, and the need for special measures not laid down by the Act during times of special distress. For instance, in April, 1631, the justices of the peace for Stafford say they have adopted the measures directed by the ' Book of Orders ' for relief of the poor during times of scarcity of corn, viz. the enforcement of penalties in cases in which the fine was given to the poor, the sale of corn to the poor below market price, a compulsory reduction of the quantity of corn converted into malt, and the billeting of poor children on the inhabitants of the parish as apprentices.[134]   The justices add, however, that there are great abuses in Lichfield, Stafford, and Tamworth, corporate towns, into which they have no authority to enter. A little later on in the same year they say they have procured the maltsters and ale-sellers of Lichfield, Burton, and Tamworth to contribute certain sums to the relief of the poor.

The building of workhouses was slow in this county. The one established at Bilston in 1700 was the first in the district, being a two-roomed building belonging to one John Wooley of ' Ye Bull in Bilston ' : ' Ye inhabitants to have free liberty to place what poore persons they shall think fitt in yt part of my house wherein ye Widdo Bennett now is placed.' [135]

No workhouse was built in Walsall till 1717,[136] and Shaw writing in 1801 gives an unfavourable account of the Wolverhampton workhouse. He describes it as dark, dirty, and ill-ventilated, surrounded by a high wall which prevents the circulation of air, adding that whenever small-pox, measles, or malignant fevers make their appearance, the mortality is very great. In 1801 there were 131 inmates, of whom about sixty were children and the rest soldiers' wives with families, and others, either infirm, old, or insane. Those able to work made hop-sacks in a workshop provided by the parish, under a manufacturer who paid 1s. 2d. per head for every pauper above eight years old who could work, for which he was entitled to their earnings, which generally amounted to £80 per annum.[137]

In the year ending 1793 the average number of poor in the house was sixty-nine, and the expenditure on food 2s. 4½d. per week for each person.[138]

In Stafford there were other devices for dealing with the poor. In 1700—

> one John Higginson did offer to take upon himself the general care of the poor of the corporation and to pay the several sums allowed for their support, he being remunerated for his trouble to the extent of £5, and the money disbursed coming chiefly from the rent of a certain malt-mill.[139]

In 1735, however, a vestry meeting decided to set the poor to work in a house in St. Mary's churchyard and drew up a list of rules, which are

---

[134] *Cal. S.P. Dom.* 1631–3, p. 16.
[135] Old document quoted in *Hist. of Bilston* by G. T. Lawley (1893).
[136] E. L. Glew, *Hist. of Walsall* (1856), 59.
[137] Stebbing Shaw, op. cit. ii, 164.
[138] Ibid. 165 ; Eden, *Rep. of State of Poor* (1795), i, 655–78.
[139] J. L. Cherry, op. cit. 183.

interesting as a sample of eighteenth-century methods of poor law administration, and as a contrast to those of to-day. Among other rules was one which laid down that any pauper working for the whole day was to have half his daily wages for himself, and that others—

> subsisted in the House were to have two-pence out of every Shilling they gained. And that they who assist in the kitchen or wash-house shall be paid a penny, two-pence, or three-pence a week according to the nature of the business, and as their service shall deserve. But whosoever shall make an ill use of this money shall be denied the encouragement.

The inmates are to go twice to church on Sunday, but if found begging, loitering, or taking the opportunity to get drunk, or not returning in time, shall be expelled from the house, sent to the house of correction, or otherwise severely punished.

The pauper children were set to work at a very tender age in the school within the workhouse—

> where all children above three shall be kept until five, and then be set to spinning, knitting, or other such work as shall be thought most proper for the benefit of the parish. And the master or mistress who shall teach them to work shall likewise instruct such of them in reading twice a day, half-an-hour each time until they are nine years of age.

The children above three are to be up and at school by seven o'clock, or eight in winter, the rest to rise at five or seven o'clock, all going to bed at nine p.m. ' with the rest of the family.'[140]

In 1806 the borough workhouse is said to have been in a deplorable state, the poor, seventeen in number, being farmed out at 3s. 3d. per week per head, washing, soap, and firing included. The building was damp, dirty, and nearly tumbling down, with no special room for the sick, and four years before, when a fire broke out, twenty-two persons died out of forty-eight.[141]

The last years of the eighteenth century and the first decades of the nineteenth form an epoch in the history of Poor Law administration in this country. They were unfortunately marked by an incredibly rapid rise in the poor-rate, a great increase in the number of paupers, and a general demoralization of the working classes due to methods intended to be philanthropic but really disastrous to everyone concerned.

An Act of 1796 practically rescinded the workhouse test and enabled the poor to receive relief at their own houses [142] if they had an income which the justices deemed insufficient. The result in most counties was that the justices made a sort of by-law by which they pledged themselves to make up deficiencies in wages out of the rates, according to the price of bread and the number of children in the pauper's family. Naturally wages fell and the poor-rate continued to rise till in some districts it swallowed up the value of the land, and drove it out of cultivation.

From the report published in 1834 by the commissioners appointed to inquire into the working of the Poor Laws in England, a great deal may be learnt as to the state of affairs in Staffordshire, not only at that date, but in the period which preceded it. In this county the worst evils of the old unreformed parochial system were not so widespread as in the purely agricultural counties of the south and east. The assistant commissioner for Staffordshire

---

[140] J. L. Cherry, op. cit. 81, 82.   [141] Article in *Gent. Mag.* 1806, quoted by J. L. Cherry, op. cit. 83.
[142] Fowle, *Hist. of Poor Law,* 70–1.

reported a decrease in the total expenditure of the county since the appointment of ninety-seven assistant overseers and sixty select vestries in accordance with an Act of 1819.

The population during that time had risen steadily, but the rates, which amounted in that year to £155,309, fell to £133,701 in 1822, and to £107,634 in 1825, though they again rose in 1829 to £119,977, and amounted to £133,971 in 1832.[143]

The workhouses showed no trace of anything like a plan to prevent residence being an object of desire, and an entire absence of uniformity in management led the discriminating pauper to choose that which provided him with the best bill of fare, the kindliest governor, and the largest amount of freedom, added to the smallest modicum of work exacted.[144] Most of the workhouses suffered from inadequate classification of inmates, so that one might find able-bodied men, women and children, invalids and idiots, all herded together in a horrible community, in a sort of frowsy comfort of the most repulsive kind.[145]

At Tamworth the master of the workhouse was also the assistant overseer, vestry clerk, and police constable of the borough, and as there was no select vestry the parishioners of Tamworth seem to have troubled themselves very little as to the examination or audit of the accounts, one of them complacently remarking that 'they had always given satisfaction.'[146]

But some of the establishments were very well conducted, as at Walsall, where there were in 1833 fifty-three old men and women, and twenty children under ten who went to the national school under the charge of one of the aged paupers.[147]

In Lichfield there were three parishes besides the cathedral close, and a workhouse in each.[148] The governor of the workhouse in the 'Foreign' of Walsall was also the assistant overseer and farmed the poor under his charge at 3s. 6d. per head. He admitted with engaging frankness that the contract found him in wine and spirits for his table, and perhaps £20 or £30 besides. His salary as assistant overseer and collector of rates amounted to £120. 'Incidental expenses' came to £33 14s. 9½d., and overseers' journeys on parish business, such as removing paupers and litigation, amounted to about £40. In this workhouse idiots were allowed to wander freely among the rest of the inmates with dreadful results.[149]

The case of Lichfield Close was interesting and is quoted by the assistant commissioners as an illustration of the evils of the current system under the most unexceptionable management.

The close was extra-parochial, had its own authorities, maintained its own poor, was exempt from the county rates, and possessed its own workhouse. The rates were levied on the occupiers, two hundred inhabitants living in sixty houses. The poor-rate, which in 1816 amounted to £92, had risen in 1832 to £265.

In 1833 there were in receipt of weekly pay nine women and five men, formerly domestic servants, and ten children. One was an able-bodied man

---

[143] *Rep. on the State of the Poor Laws in Engl. and Wales* (1834), App. A, pt. i ; *Rep. on the Counties of Stafford and Chester,* vol. x, A. 265.

[144] Ibid. 265. [145] Ibid. 266. [146] Ibid. 271.
[147] Ibid. 266. [148] Ibid. [149] Ibid.

between forty and fifty, formerly coachman to the dean of Lichfield. He had a wife and three children and received 8s. per week and his house rent. The chapter clerk and the senior verger were the two overseers, being appointed to their office by the dean and chapter, who audited the accounts.[150]

Wolverhampton was another town which illustrated the evils of the existing system, under the best conditions. The parish was divided for the maintenance and support of the poor into the townships of Wolverhampton, Willenhall, Bilston, and Wednesfield, the chief of these being Wolverhampton with 24,732 inhabitants.

Since 1824, when the poor-rate was £3,637, it had gradually increased till it reached £5,477 in 1832, and was still increasing. Yet it had its good points, having a select vestry regularly and efficiently attended, a workhouse well and economically conducted, active and upright overseers, intelligent salaried assistant overseers, and, finally, a perfect system of keeping the parish books.[151]

As to the various forms of poor relief, the assistant commissioner reported that the system of relieving able-bodied labourers at their own homes had been extensively practised in Staffordshire; had received a considerable check since the order of sessions in 1818, which strongly discouraged the practice; but unfortunately was gaining ground once again.[151a]

Out of fourteen parishes and boroughs questioned, however, seven definitely said that the system was not now in use, Wolverhampton and Rowley Regis being honourably distinguished by the fact that the authorities there had never given allowances to the able-bodied in aid of wages.[152]

The Roundsman system (a system by which the parish sold the pauper's labour to the farmer and made up the deficit in his wages out of the rates) had gained but little ground in this county, but there were some examples of it. In the parish of Longdon, e.g., after great struggles the system was abandoned, in defiance of strong opposition from the farmers, who profited at the expense of the community. The road surveyors co-operated with the magistrates, and set to work the unemployed, with the result that the farmers were obliged to hire regular labourers at decent wages, and the surveyors soon had no more labour to deal with than was needed for the repair of the roads.[153] In some townships the system, under the name of 'house-row,' was said to be in use, and in a few the remuneration of labour was determined not by the value of the work done but by the size of the family.[154]

The question of the 'settlement' of paupers was one which had given rise to much trouble, injustice, and expense here as in other counties. For instance, in one township an item of £40 occurred as the cost of appeal to the last quarter sessions, and this when the whole amount of poor rate was rather less than £200. Servants were hired for fifty-one weeks instead of a year to prevent them from being chargeable to the parish.[155] Darlaston and Tamworth were cited as examples of the evils that might result from granting a 'settlement' by apprenticeship. The manufacturers of Tamworth had been in the habit of taking many apprentices for seven years, thus securing

[150] *Rep. on State of Poor Laws* (1834), as above, A, 269.   [151] Ibid. 269–70.   [151a] Ibid. 267.
[152] *Rep. on Poor Laws*, 1834; App. B 1, pt. iv, 39 *d.*; App. B 2, pts. iv, v, 213 *i*, 213 *k*.
[153] Ibid. App. A, 267.
[154] Ibid.   [155] Ibid. App. A, 268.

to them a settlement in the parish, and these children had come from London and various other parts of the country.

In course of time the numbers of those who had once been apprentices had become very great, and it was said that these people were constantly streaming in from Nottinghamshire and Lancashire to Tamworth, their place of legal settlement, to the great annoyance of that town and the burdening of the ratepayers. Tamworth had unfortunately been in the habit of giving relief in aid of wages, but was now discontinuing this practice. In Darlaston the distress had been so great that but for private charity the gross rental of the parish (£4,213 in 1815) would have been insufficient for the support of the poor.[156]

With the Poor Law Amendment Act of 1834 the evils of the old system were largely remedied. Rigorous control of parochial affairs by a central board, a uniform system of account-keeping and general administration, the grouping of parishes in unions with a common workhouse, and the establishment of the workhouse test for the able-bodied—these were some of the chief means by which reform was effected, and both expenditure and pauperism declined in Staffordshire as in all other parts of the country.

When the commissioners issued their fifth annual report in 1839 they recorded a great improvement in the state of things. New workhouses were completed and in operation at Burton on Trent, Stafford, and Walsall.

Others were being built at Leek, Newcastle under Lyme, Uttoxeter, and Wolverhampton, whilst old ones were in operation at Penkridge, Madeley, Seisdon, Stoke upon Trent, Tamworth, and Stone.[157]

The treatment of pauper children is now much improved, and very few are being educated in the workhouse itself. The only instance of this at present is the case of Newcastle under Lyme. Wolverhampton is an example of a town where the children are educated in poor-law schools, but under a separate administration from that of the workhouse. At Walsall, West Bromwich, and Lichfield they are taught in poor-law district schools, and in the other parts of the county they attend the ordinary elementary schools.[158]

By the middle of the nineteenth century Staffordshire had become thoroughly established as an industrial county, with an ever-increasing population and growing riches, and with the special social and industrial problems presented by such a densely-populated community.

The towns grew rapidly, especially in South Staffordshire—too rapidly for the provision of adequate machinery to cope with the new conditions as regards sanitation and decent living.

In the report of the Midland Mining Commission of 1843[159] there is a vivid description of the southern coalfield district and its inhabitants as it appeared at that time, a description which with some changes might hold good at the present day:

> In traversing much of the country included within the above-mentioned boundary of red sandstone [says the writer] the traveller appears never to get out of an interminable village, composed of cottages and very ordinary houses. In some directions he may travel for miles and never be out of sight of two-storied houses, so that the area covered by bricks and mortar must be immense. These houses for the most part are not arranged in

[156] *Rep. on Poor Laws*, as above, App. A, 271.
[157] *Fifth Ann. Rep. of Poor Law Commissioners* (1839), pp. 116–17.
[158] *Thirty-fourth Ann. Rep. of Local Govt. Board* (1904–5), p. 487.　　　[159] *Rep.* i, vol. xiii.

continuous streets, but interspersed with blazing rurnaces, heaps of burning coal in process of coking, piles of iron-stone, calcining forges, pit-banks and engine chimneys, the country being besides intersected with canals, crossing each other at various levels, and the small remaining patches of surface soil are occupied with irregular fields of grass or corn inter-mingled with heaps of refuse of mines, or from the slag of blast furnaces. Sometimes the road passes between mounds of refuse from the pits, like a causeway raised some feet above the fields on either side, which have subsided by the excavation of the minerals beneath. These circumstances in the state of the surface and the substrata, united to the clouds of smoke from the furnaces, coke hearths, and heaps of calcined iron-stone, which drift across the country according to the direction of the wind, have effectually excluded from it all classes except those whose daily bread depends upon their residence within these districts.

This separation of rich and poor, employer and employed, was one of the worst features of the district. In the parish of Sedgeley, e.g., which comprised a number of scattered but densely-populated villages, there were reported to be not more than four of the gentry in the whole district, nor a single resident independent proprietor.[160]

At Rowley Regis there was neither resident clergyman nor magistrate among 12,000 inhabitants; 8,000 were employed in mining or in some branch of the iron industry.[161]

At Kingswinford, again, the report says that

before the rapid advance of the miner the ancient gentry are being driven back and the sites of their mansions are only known by the names of the collieries and ironworks erected on them.[162]

The scarcity of clergy and churches throughout the district at this time is reflected in an expression of the day, ' as few as parish churches.' The people who seemed to be most wretched were the nailers, men, women and children working together in the little domestic workshops adjoining their miserable homes. Suffering from the evils of the middleman and the sweater, as they do in a minor degree to-day, they were also largely at the mercy of the truck system, now happily stamped out among them.

It is interesting to notice how the geological structure of the district affects the occupation of the people and, indirectly, their social condition. The nailers, as the report points out, are usually to be found everywhere along the line of junction between the Coal Measures and the Red Sandstone, and with any other formation, such as the limestone hills near Sedgeley.

The following description of a village of nailers in 1843 is given by Mr. James Boydell, managing partner of the Oak Farm Company Works in Lower Gornal :—

Lower Gornal is the dirtiest and most uncivilised village in the world, yet the people have the best hearts. The people are mostly nailers, and are a very rough set. Men, women and children work together, there is no comfort at home, and both men and women go to the public houses and drink and sing together.

As yet the machine-made nails were not competing with the hand-wrought article, but such competition was drawing near :

I fear great injury (says Mr. Boydell) will be done to our nailing population by an invention I saw yesterday in London, by which nails of excellent quality are made by pressure. This seems likely to reduce the cost of hand made nails considerably.

---

[160] *Midland Mining Com. Rep.* i (1843), vol. xiii, p. cli.
[161] Ibid. clii.   [162] Ibid. cli.

The writer then goes on to describe the sweating middle man :

> I will show you a man in Gornal who will offer to do work for me for nothing— a middleman of the worst description. He takes all trouble off the nailmaster's hands by taking the iron, giving it out to the nailers, and collecting the nails when made and he pays the money for them for the nailmaster. For this trouble he repays himself by co- ercing those he employs to buy his goods, for he sells beer, clothing, bread, butter, flour and meal.[163]

The year 1842 is remembered in Staffordshire as a period of great distress, owing to a great strike among the colliers. The immediate cause of the strike was notice of reduction in wages given throughout a considerable part of the district and the fear of such a reduction becoming general.[164] But there were deeper seated evils under which the miners of South Staffordshire were suffering, chief among these being the tyranny of the 'butties' or con- tractors who controlled the conditions of the workers, arranged their hours and methods of work and of payment, and generally came between the miners and mine-owners.

One of the grievances was the payment of wages in public houses, sometimes the property of the 'butty.'

Another great evil was the truck system, by which the miners were compelled to accept a large proportion of their wages in food at the shop of the mine-owner or the contractor, at prices much above the market rate. One woman who gave evidence before the commissioners described how she went for her husband's wages every Saturday, first going to the bailiff's office to see what was due, and then to the shop to buy the sixteen shillings- worth of food which must be procured for every twenty shillings received.

The differences in price of the various goods as sold at the mine-owner's shop and the Wolverhampton market respectively were given as follows :—

	Price at the Shop.	Price at Wolverhampton Market.
	s. d.	s. d.
Cheese	0 8 per lb.	0 5 per lb.
Bacon	0 8 „	0 5½ and 6d. per lb.
Salt Butter	1 0 „	0 9 per lb.
Sugar	0 8 „	0 7½ „
Tea	0 5 per oz.	0 3½ per oz.
Flour	2 2 per peck	2 0 per peck.

The butties were accused of deliberate recklessness of the lives of the workers, and the number of accidents and violent deaths was enormous, especially in the thick-coal districts of Dudley and West Bromwich. Yet there was in 1843 nothing in the shape of a hospital in the whole mining district, with the exception of the Wolverhampton Dispensary, which received a few indoor patients.[165] Lord Ashley's Act of 1842 did much to remedy these abuses, and the commissioners appointed to inquire into its working reported a great improvement in 1844.[166]

[163] *Midland Mining Com. Rep.* i (1883), vol. xiii, pp. v, vi.
[164] Wages had been steadily falling since 1837. For some years before 1837 the wages of men working in the thick coal seams were 5s. for bandsmen, 4s. 6d. for pikemen. In 1837 they stood at 4s. 6d. and 4s. respectively. In May, 1842, 4s. and 3s. 6d. ; 1843, 3s. 6d. and 3s. In the thin coal and ironstone mines, 2s. 6d. and 2s. *Midland Mining Com. Rep.* i, vol. xiii, p. cxiv.
[165] *Midland Mining Com. Rep.* i (1843), vol. xiii, pp. lx-lxii.
[166] Rep. of Seymour Tremenheere, *Rep. on Mines and Collieries*, 1844 [592], 54.

SOCIAL AND ECONOMIC HISTORY

During the period of the strike the Chartists had their head quarters in Bilston, and it can hardly be doubted that some of their more irresponsible orators worked on the credulity and ignorance of the miners and led them to hope for many material benefits as a result of gaining the 'Six Points' of the Charter. But all the evidence points to the fact that the Staffordshire miners were not, at this time, in the least interested in politics, the conditions of their lives were too narrow and restricted for that, and indeed to some persons this absorption in purely material and physical needs seems to have been regarded as a virtue. One employer of labour remarked, 'In general colliers are very peaceable men and do not trouble themselves about government ; so that they can get bread and cheese to eat I should never be afraid of colliers.'[167] From personal observation Dr. Tancred gives a like opinion as to the 'non-political character' of the South Staffordshire miners.

> No class of people, said he, are more totally devoid of any sort of political feeling than the South Staffordshire miners. Not one of the Six Points of the Charter could be made intelligible to them, and no orator could persuade them to listen for ten minutes on such a theme.[168]

The special grievances of the South Staffordshire miners hardly existed in North Staffordshire.

The truck system was practically non-existent, and the relations of the employers and their work-people appear to have been, on the whole, excellent, some having, in the late depression in the iron trade, continued to raise coal and ironstone at a loss, to keep their workmen employed. Moreover, the printed statement of reasons for the strike, delivered by the trade-unionists to the masters, related only to hours of work and wages.[169]

The North Staffordshire miners were largely piece-workers, and by means of their good wages and thrift, many of them had been enabled to build their own houses with gardens attached. Acting under the advice of the unionist leaders they had made a demand for an eight-hours' day at 3s., and ultimately 4s. per day, and nearly the whole of the 4,500 miners of North Staffordshire had struck work simultaneously, remaining idle for five or six weeks, after which time they returned to work at the masters' terms.[170] The wages of boys in the North Staffordshire mines in 1842 ranged from 4s. to 10s. weekly for boys from ten to eighteen.[171]

In some respects the conditions of work in the Staffordshire mines were much better than those in other parts of the country. For instance, women have never worked underground in this county, though girls and women were employed to a considerable extent at this time on the pit banks, and in helping to load and unload coal boats on the canal banks.

The evidence obtained by the commissioners showed further that throughout the whole of the collieries within the Potteries no young children were employed in mines, as they found plenty of work above ground in the pottery industry.[172]

---

[167] *Midland Mining Com. Rep.* i (1843), vol. xiii. p. cx. [168] Ibid. ; T. Tancred's Rep. vol. xiii, p. cx.

[169] Rep. of Seymour Tremenheere, *Rep. on Mines and Collieries* (1844), vol. xvi, 58.

[170] *Rep. on Mines and Collieries* (1844), vol. xvi, 59–60.

[171] *Children's Employment Com. Rep.* i (1842) [380], vol. xv, 154.

[172] S. Scriven, *Children's Employment Com. Rep.* i (1842), vol. xvii, App. 128. 'No young children were employed below. This I found to be the case throughout the whole of the potteries, they being occupied in the earthenware manufactures.'

The effect of the coal strike was, of course, widely felt among all the trades dependent on the coal supply, that is to say throughout the whole of Staffordshire. The distress was widespread, being increased by the fact that it occurred at the time when the hardware trade was suffering a severe check as the result of a money crisis in America. Rents remained unpaid, the homes of the workers were stripped of nearly all their possessions, riots occurred, and an enormous amount of outdoor relief had to be given. The poor rates went up rapidly, and the small shopkeepers suffered severely.[173]

The clerk to the Dudley Board of Guardians said that in his district the chief applicants for relief were whitesmiths, and chain and trace-makers; also glass-makers, who used to get £3 or £4 per week, and were now reduced to breaking stones and scraping the streets.[174]

The moral and intellectual condition of the children of the industrial classes in Staffordshire was deplorable. This is abundantly proved by the evidence given before the Commissioners in 1842–3. The provision of schools was wholly inadequate, and the attendance at such as existed was very bad, the children being taken away as early as possible to work in the iron, coal, and pottery industries.[175]

In South Staffordshire the evidence of many resident clergymen went to show that there was not provision for a quarter of the uneducated youth of the neighbourhood, and that a great number of children never attended school at all nor any place of worship.[176] At Bilston, for instance, with a population of twenty thousand, there were the following schools for the working classes :—Four ordinary day schools, two infant schools, two or three night schools, and two schools for girls where reading and sewing were taught. A British School was attempted but did not succeed, and the only other means of instruction consisted in a few Sunday schools.[177] Yet Bilston was admittedly better in many respects than the neighbouring town of Wolverhampton. 'Among all the children and young persons I examined,' says Mr. Horne, speaking of the Wolverhampton district, 'I found, with a few exceptions, that their minds were as stunted as their bodies, their moral feelings stagnant as the nutritive process whereby they should have been built up towards maturity.'[178]

These remarks refer specially to the children working in the various branches of the iron trade, where the physical condition was as bad as the moral and intellectual state of the young workers. In his report on the mining population of South Staffordshire Dr. Mitchell testifies to the excellent physique of the miners young and old, which compares favourably with that of the workers in the pottery industry in North Staffordshire. But he adds, 'whilst the physical condition and treatment of the boys are so satisfactory, it is to be lamented that as to the moral condition it is in some respects quite the reverse.'[179] The health and physique of the children and young persons working in the pottery industry was not invariably bad, but in some branches of the work the bad effect was very marked.[180]

---

[173] *Midland Mining Com. Rep.* i, 1843, vol. xiii, p. xxix.   [174] Ibid. App. 101.
[175] *Children's Employment Com.* 1842, Rep. i, App. vol. xvi, 23.
[176] Ibid. xvi, 26 and xiii, 142.   [177] Ibid. vol. xvi, 24, Dr. Mitchell's Rep. on S. Staffs.
[178] Ibid. App. Rep. ii, 1843, vol. xiv, 574, Mr. Horne's Rep.
[179] Dr. Mitchell's Rep. 1842, vol. xvi, *Rep.* i, App. 23.
[180] *Children's Employment Com. Rep.* ii, vol. xiii, 107–8.

SOCIAL AND ECONOMIC HISTORY

The moral and intellectual condition of the Potteries district appears, unfortunately, to have been but little better than that existing in South Staffordshire. Three-fourths of the persons who gave evidence before the Commissioner could neither read nor write, and on all hands were signs of moral degradation. 'I almost tremble,' says Mr. Scriven, 'when I contemplate the fearful deficiency of knowledge existing throughout the district, and the consequences likely to result to this increased and increasing population.'[181] The brightest spot in the county seems to have been that part of North Staffordshire which comprised the lead and copper mines of Ecton, and Deepdale, the brass and copper mines of Cheadle, and the coal mines of Cheadle and Rugeley. Here the workers, young and old, are described as being sober, industrious, and intelligent, the children well taught, healthy, clean, and tidy.[182] The conditions in the town of Leek, among the silk workers, seem also to have been exceptional.[183]

The system of employing pauper apprentices in the South Staffordshire mines was not extensive, though, in so far as it existed, it was undoubtedly bad, and the unfortunate children were often harshly treated.

In the years 1840, 1841, and 1842, forty-one pauper children were sent from seven unions to be apprenticed in mines. Twelve of these came from Dudley, and eleven from Wolverhampton ; of these, fourteen were only nine years old, six were aged ten, and the rest were between eleven and fifteen years of age. Their apprenticeship ended at twenty-one ; the premium was usually nothing, otherwise one or two suits of clothes.[184]

The condition of the numerous apprentices in the different branches of the hardware trade in South Staffordshire was a scandal. Some were bound by legal indentures, but the greater number were not, and were at the mercy of their employers till the age of twenty-one.[185]

At Willenhall, Sedgeley, and Wolverhampton the conditions of these children were found to be specially bad. The children were frequently shockingly deformed, stunted, and dirty, besides being badly nourished, and in rags. Wednesbury had the best record in the district as regards these pauper children, Darlaston and Bilston were fair. At Wolverhampton bad fish and diseased meat were specially bought for the consumption of the children,[186] and it was high time that the law interfered to protect them, as it subsequently did.

They began to work at the age of seven or eight, sometimes as early as six, and their hours of work were without limit save that ultimately set by human endurance.

Children, other than pauper apprentices, were, of course, largely employed in these domestic workshops, especially among nailers, where they worked with the rest of the family at the trade, earning from 2s. to 3s. per week, or, if young persons, from 4s. to 10s.[187]

---

[181] *Children's Employment Com. Rep.* ii, App. 1843, vol. xv, c. 10 ; S. Scriven's Rep. on the Staff. Potteries.
[182] S. Scriven's Rep. on North Staff. Mines, 1842, xvii, 134, 137.
[183] *Children's Employment Com.* ii, App. 1843, vol. xv, c. 18 ; see S. Scriven's remarks : 'On the whole, whether in the large establishments or small ones, in the private dwellings or public schools, I believe the children to be better clothed, fed, educated, and protected than any others in the same sphere of life that I have ever met with.'
[184] *Midland Mining Com. Rep.* i (1843), vol. xiii, pp. xl, xli (Dr. Tancred).
[185] *Children's Employment Com.* 1843, *Rep.* ii, vol. xiii [430], 26.
[186] Ibid. 80, 93, 94, 101, 104.   [187] Ibid. *Rep.* ii, vol. xiii, 93.

There is a description of Wolverhampton and its workshops at this time (1843) which gives some idea of the dreadful conditions of life which prevailed in this rapidly-developing industrial district, where population had increased with great rapidity with little or no attempt at control or regulation by the civic authorities in the interests of sanitation or morals.

> There are few manufactories of large size, the work being carried on in small work-shops, usually at the back of the houses, so that the places where children and great bodies of operatives are employed are completely out of sight, in its narrow courts, unpaved yards, and blind alleys. In the smaller dirtier streets, in which the poorest live, there are narrow passages at intervals of every eight or ten houses, and sometimes every third or fourth house; these are under three yards wide and about nine feet high, and they form the general gutter. Having made your way through the passage you find yourself in a space varying in size with the number of houses, hutches, or hovels it contains, all proportionately crowded. Out of this space other narrow passages lead to similar hovels, the workshops and houses being mostly built on a little elevation sloping towards the passage. The great majority of yards contain two to four houses, one or two of which are workshops, or have room in them for a work-shop. In process of time, as the inhabitants increased, small rooms were raised over the workshops, and hovels were also built wherever space could be found, and tenanted, first perhaps as workshops, then by families also. By these means the increasing population were lodged from year to year, while the circumference of the town remained the same for a long time, owing to the difficulty of obtaining land to build upon, as it was all the property of private individuals or of the church. As soon as land was obtained, Stafford Street and Walsall Street were built for the working classes, two of the largest and most disgraceful streets in the town.
>
> None of these houses have any underground drainage; there is often a common dunghill at one end, where everything is cast, more generally there is nothing but the gutter and passage into the street. The interiors of the dwellings are extremely squalid, containing little furniture, and are for the most part exceedingly dirty in every respect.[188]

On the other hand, while workshops of the small masters (locksmiths, &c.) were all of this kind, the large factories were usually placed in healthy situations and were fairly well ventilated.

The growth of the factory system, and the operation of the Factory Acts, accompanied by a regular system of inspection, has fortunately changed the old industrial conditions very much for the better, except in the lingering survival of the hand-wrought nail makers, whose little workshops round about Sedgley and Upper and Lower Gornal recall some part of the above description even yet.

In 1869 an Act was obtained by the Wolverhampton Corporation to enable them to deal effectually with such things as street management, sewerage, and police. Also, since 1875, an area of 16 acres in the heart of the town has been swept away, and its old dirty streets and noisome courts have been replaced by broad, well-paved, well-lighted roadways, with handsome buildings.

But it was small wonder that when a visitation of cholera came, as it did in 1832, and again in 1848–9, such towns as this fell an easy prey, and that the people were swept off in hundreds. In Bilston, e.g., the state of sanitation was, if possible, worse than at Wolverhampton. Here, as there, the people were herded together in narrow courts and alleys, while stagnant pools and heaps of filth were found on every hand, menacing the health and the very life of the inhabitants.

Yet in March, 1832, a public meeting decided that the health of the township was so good that nothing further need be done in the way

---

[188] *Children's Employment Com. Rep.* ii, 1843 [430]; Rep. of Mr. Horne, vol. xiii, App. 33.

of improving the conditions, nor of forming any sort of board to regulate sanitation.

In July the cholera attacked Tipton, and early in August appeared at Bilston. There were sixty cases in the first week, and many deaths. One hundred and forty-one died in the second week, and 309 in the third, out of a population of 14,500. Panic seized the community, factories were closed, business was at a standstill, and the pestilence swept everything before it.

So great was the misery and destitution caused that a subscription of more than £8,000 was raised from various parts of the country to alleviate the distress.[189]

Again, in 1848–9, cholera returned, and the whole county suffered severely, 2,683 persons dying out of a population of 608,716. Bilston headed the death-roll with 605 victims, and Willenhall came second, but a long way after, with 281. The other towns to suffer most were Newcastle under Lyme, Wednesbury, and Sedgeley, in each of which more than 200 persons died. Even yet Bilston remains a town of too many courts and alleys, needing to follow the example of its neighbour Wolverhampton in the sweeping away of some of its unsanitary areas.

The death-rate in the pottery towns was not nearly so high as in South Staffordshire ; this may be accounted for partially by the fact that the pottery industry was by this time organized on a factory system, and the standard of life and health was higher than in the densely-populated area of the iron district, with its domestic industries still flourishing. Not that the conditions of work in the Potteries at this time were by any means wholly satisfactory. Some of the more recent buildings, it is true, were large, well-ventilated, and light, but the majority of them were old buildings, gradually enlarged by adding room to room, and still remaining low, damp, dark, and unhealthy.[190]

There were at this time some thousands of apprentices employed in various branches of the pottery industry between the ages of thirteen and twenty-one, bound for seven years, but not usually by legal indenture, so that the masters had little control over them. The apprentice was usually paid one-fourth of a journeyman's wage in the first years of his apprenticeship, and in the later part two-thirds.[191]

From an indenture of apprenticeship of a certain Aaron Wood, apprenticed to Dr. Thomas Wedgwood in 1731, we learn something of the eighteenth-century conditions in this matter.[192] The said Aaron, having promised faithful and obedient service, is to be taught certain specified processes, to wit, the art of turning the lathe, handling, and trimming. His father is to provide him with food, lodging, and clothing, with the exception of an annual pair of boots bestowed by his master. Aaron is to receive 1s. per week for the first three years of his apprenticeship, 1s. 6d. for the next three, and 4s. in the seventh year, 'lawful money of Great Brittaine.' We also learn that at the conclusion of his apprenticeship he is engaged as a journeyman at the rate of 5s. per week for five years, and after that at the rate of 7s.

[189] G. T. Lawley, *A Hist. of Bilston* (1893), 172–93.
[190] *Children's Employment Com. Rep.* ii, 1843, Rep. of Sub-Commissioners, xiii, 35.
[191] Harold Owen, *The Staff. Potter* (1899), 46.   [192] L. Jewitt, *The Wedgwoods*, 66–7.

Arthur Young gives the wages of an apprentice as 2s. weekly for the first year, and a rise of 3d. weekly in each succeeding year. He also gives the current average wages of various classes of pottery workers, which vary exceedingly, from the wage of the grinder at 7s. to that of the painters, throwers, and handlers, who earned from 9s. to 12s. per week.[193] The general average for men in 1771 may be taken as 7s. to 12s., and for women from 5s. to 8s. per week.

As in the mining industry, so also in the 'potting trade,' the year 1843 marks something of an epoch. In that year trade-unionism, started first in 1824, revived again after its collapse of seven years previous, and its central committee began a campaign of reform directed against the special grievances of the trade. Foremost among these were the truck system and the allowance system; but the union was successful in putting an end to the former by taking proceedings against offending masters in the police courts.[194]

The allowance system, which had been going on unchecked for seven years, was an ingenious method of lowering wages by exacting from the journeyman an allowance of 2d. or even 4d. in the shilling.[195] Against this custom the union waged steady war, and finally put an end to it, having obtained the opinion of an eminent lawyer that the deductions thus made were absolutely illegal, and could be recovered in a court of law. Another grievance was the system of annual hiring at Martinmas, at which time the prices of labour were fixed for the coming twelve months, and the workman was bound to his employer for the same period, though he could be dismissed at the will of the master. This was not finally given up until 1865, however, when a month's notice on either side could terminate the engagement.[196]

A fourth cause of complaint only affected certain classes of workers, who complained that deductions were made from their wages for injury done to their work after it had left their hands. This grievance was a constant source of irritation for forty years, and it was not till 1871 that redress was obtained by the making of a special 'trade rule,' which laid down the general principle that deductions should only be made for injury or bad work proved to be the fault of the workman.[197]

Up to 1844 machinery had entered but little into the various processes of pottery manufacture.

When in that year it was rumoured that a machine had been invented to make a certain article, the potters began to fear the worst, and when one machine after another followed, something like a panic prevailed amongst them. Money was raised by the union to fight the evil, and a great emigration scheme was planned, whereby the surplus labour of the Potteries was to be transferred to the United States, and a certain number of men were sent out in advance to prepare the way and buy land. The whole thing was a fiasco; the funds of the union were drained to support the emigration society, and the union itself collapsed, only to be revived again in 1863.[198]

The effects of the introduction of machinery have been largely to increase production, and, especially in some departments, to displace the labour of men by that of women paid at lower rates. The number of women

---

[193] Arthur Young, *Tour through the North of England*, iii, 254–5.
[194] Harold Owen, op. cit. 54–5.　　[195] Ibid. 56–8.　　[196] Ibid. 61, 113.
[197] Ibid. 60, 131, 141.　　[198] Ibid. 78–105.

SOCIAL AND ECONOMIC HISTORY

employed before the use of machinery was comparatively small, but it subsequently rose to one-half the total labour employed.[199]

In the arbitration of 1891, the manufacturers asserted that though the prices paid for different articles had been lowered since the introduction of machinery, the wages of the men need not sink if they would but work a little harder. To this the operatives replied, with some justice, that though a man might be able to 'put on a spurt' occasionally, he could not be 'on the spurt' always.[200]

It is admittedly very difficult to arrive at any satisfactory estimate of the average wages in the pottery industry. Not only do the wages differ greatly according to the branch of industry, but

almost every reference to wages deals with the rate of pay for various articles, and any comparison made is that between prices paid for such an article, at different times, the question being further complicated by reference to shapes and sizes.[201]

It is possible, however, to quote the return of wages issued by the Potteries Chamber of Commerce in 1836 as paid at the principal manufactories. This return showed that in 1833-4 an average workman earned between 17s. and 21s. per week, a woman 6s. to 11s., and a child of fourteen from 3s. to 3s. 6d.[202] In 1836 the man's average wage had risen to from 21s. to 28s., the woman's to from 10s. to 15s., and the child's to from 3s. 6d. to 4s. 6d.[203]

In the various arbitrations before the joint board of masters and men established in 1868, the evidence of the two sides differed in their estimate of wages, and here again it is difficult to arrive at any general conclusion. In 1877 and 1879 the evidence indicated that the average rate of wages of a good workman fell below 30s., though the manufacturers quoted instances of a much higher rate. In 1891 wages were at about the same level, and a manufacturer supplied the following figures for 1900, as the minimum earnings of workmen working full time :—

Dish-maker	£1 15s.
Plate-maker	£1 10s.
Jiggerer of pails, &c.	£2 1s.
Basin-maker	£1 12s.
Saucer-maker	£1 9s.

Women's wages quoted by the same employer were as follows :—

Cup-maker	£1 0s.
Saucer-maker	£0 14s.

All these prices are calculated on the basis of a five per cent. advance obtained in 1900.[204]

As everyone now knows, the pottery industry is one of the trades specially dangerous to health, and has been carried on since 1891 under special conditions enforced by the Home Office.

Dust is the great enemy of the potter ; dust given off from the flint and lead used in the manufacture of the pottery. The flint dust being absorbed into the lungs produces bronchitis and phthisis, and the workers specially

[199] Harold Owen, op. cit. 322-3, quoting evidence before Arbitrations of 1877, 1879, 1891.
[200] Ibid. 314-15.   [201] Ibid. 317, 318.
[202] Ibid. 37-8.   [203] Ibid. 318.   [204] Ibid. 333.

liable to these are the makers of plates and cups, ware-cleaners, 'scourers' and 'turners.' The lead dust produces lead poisoning in various forms, and attacks specially the persons who mix the lead-glaze or dip the articles in the glaze, also colour mixers and majolica paintresses. The lead is also absorbed through the pores of the skin, and its fumes through the mouth and nostrils.

In the Factory and Workshop Act of 1891 special rules were laid down for the conduct of pottery workshops and for the safeguarding of the health of the workers. These regulations concerned the provision of special washing appliances, of effectual means, such as fans, for the removal of dust where necessary, and for the wearing of overalls and head coverings in certain processes ; meals were forbidden in workshops, and more stringent rules were laid down for the sweeping and cleansing of the work places. Something was effected by these special rules, but the result of an investigation made by Professor Thorpe and Dr. Oliver in 1898 revealed a very serious state of affairs. The returns of Mr. J. H. Walmsley, H.M. Inspector for the Potteries district, showed that in the three years 1896–8, 1,085 persons were certified as suffering from lead poisoning, and of these 607 were women and girls. It was quite clear that much of the evil could be prevented if the use of raw lead, then universal, were discontinued, and replaced by 'fritted' lead, admittedly far less injurious to the worker.

Since the Home Office rules of 1900 the use of raw lead has been abolished, except in a few special cases, and the Annual Report of the Factory and Workshops Inspectors for 1905 shows a considerable reduction in the number of reported cases of lead poisoning in North Staffordshire. In 1899 there were 204 ; next year the number fell to 165, and in 1901 to eighty-four.

In 1902 the lowest figure was reached, viz. sixty-six ; the next year the cases numbered seventy-five, and rose to eighty-four the next year, and in 1905 fell again to seventy-five.

Of the seventy-five, forty-six were cases of 'dippers,' and of these twenty-nine were women and girls.

The present figures for lead poisoning show a percentage of 1·5 of the total number of persons employed in the pottery industry compared with 9·4 in 1898.[205]

The lady inspectors, however, are of opinion that with a more intelligent and scrupulous observance of the special rules on the part of employers and workers alike, a still greater measure of improvement ought to be seen.[206]

In a minor degree, the workers in enamelling and tin-plate works also suffer from lead poisoning, and women are in this case also the greatest sufferers.

In the Returns for lead poisoning issued by the Board of Trade[207] for the eight months ending August, 1906, the china and earthenware manufacture was responsible for seventy-six cases, tinning and enamelling for eighteen only, and litho-transfer work for three.

Women play a very important part in the industrial economy of Staffordshire, especially, as we have seen, in the Potteries. No one passing

[205] *Ann. Rep. of Factory and Workshops Inspectors*, 1905, pp. 352–7.
[206] Ibid. 292.   [207] *Labour Gaz.* Sept. 1906, p. 283.

through one of the great pottery works can fail to be struck by the large number of women and girls employed.

Much of the work is done in groups, and both the work and the wages are interdependent. For instance, in a printing group two or three women and girls work with each printer. There is first the journeywoman transferrer who transfers the printed paper to the ware. An apprentice will then rub the pattern into the 'biscuit,' and finally wash the paper from the ware, leaving the pattern behind. The 'cutter' is the youngest of the party, her work being to fetch the print from the press and cut away all the superfluous paper, leaving the pattern on a long narrow strip ready for the transferrer.[208]

In a printing group described by Miss Collett in 1893–4, the printer received 28s. 3d., out of which he had to pay for gas; the journeywoman transferrer earned 11s. 3d., the apprentice 7s. 6d., and the cutter 5s.[209]

In many other processes girls are employed as assistants to men working the lathe for the cup-maker or the maker of plates. Other processes in which women and girls are specially employed are those of sponging, scouring, 'towing,' dipping, and painting. As their work varies, so does their rate of pay, which ranges from 5s. to 18s. and upwards per week. The paintresses, who have to serve a seven years' apprenticeship, are the best paid; they get about 2s. per week in the first year of their apprenticeship and afterwards one-third of their full ultimate rate of pay.

From statistics gathered by Miss Collett in 1893–4 it appears that the earnings of the greatest number of women and girls averaged from 10s. to 12s. per week, some earning more, some less than that amount.[210] At that time about four hundred women were said to be members of one or other of the men's unions. At the end of 1904 this number had fallen to 325, consisting chiefly of women in the printing group. In 1893 the Women's Trade Union League succeeded in forming a potteries' branch among women in that industry, but it did not flourish, and having in 1902 reached the low level of thirty members it was dissolved next year.[211]

The employment of so many married women in the pottery industry is an important factor in the social problem of a district where the atmosphere and surroundings are so grimy that the difficulty of keeping decent homes must be very great when the mother is at home all the day, but when she is at work, the effect on the homes of the people and the inevitable consequences in the health, feeding, and general up-bringing of the children are bound to be more or less serious, and when to these considerations is added the fact that this industry is one of the occupations dangerous to health, the outlook for the rising generation is somewhat disquieting.

In South Staffordshire women and girls work in enamelling and japanning works, especially at Wolverhampton and Bilston ; at saddlery and harness-making in Walsall, and in clothing factories here and elsewhere.

The enamelling and japanning trade is one which seriously affects the health of women, especially those engaged in the processes in which lead is used, notably that of brushing the lead powder from the tin plate.[212]

---

[208] C. F. Binns, *The Story of the Potter* (1898), p. 227.
[209] *Rep. of Labour Com.* 1893–4 [c. 6894, xxiii, p. 61]. [210] Ibid. 63.
[211] *Rep. on Trade Unions*, 1902–4, Board of Trade (Labour Dept.), 76–8.
[212] *Rep. of Labour Com.* 1893–4, xxiii, 83.

Since 1893 detailed rules have been issued by the Home Office similar to those in use in the pottery workshops, and these have done much to reduce the dangers to health.[213]

In Sedgeley, Upper Gornal and Lower Gornal many women and girls are engaged in the fast-declining hand-wrought nail trade, but every year fewer children are being brought up to the work. The hours are long and the wages poor—6s. or 7s. being an average weekly wage for an industrious woman. Some time ago the women in the Sedgeley district were formed into a union, but it has since died out, experience having proved once again how difficult it is to get overworked, ill-nourished, isolated home-workers to combine for a common object, even if that object is to improve the conditions of their own work, since they are lacking in both the physical and mental vitality necessary for successful union.

The only holiday or change these women allow themselves, apart from seasons of slackness, seems to be the yearly visit to the hop-districts, which many of them make in the hopping season, and which provides them with a change of scene and of occupation, if not a rest.

The wages of women in the harness trade averaged in 1893–4 from 9s. to 10s. per week, rising to 12s. in busy times, and this is a common weekly wage for industrial women. During the South African war the trade was good and wages better, but the present rate of wages seems to be about what it was in 1893. The motor-car industry has damaged this trade as it has also affected the saddlery trade, owing to the lessened demand for horses and horse equipments. The trade of Wolverhampton may thus be said to have gained at the expense of the women workers of Walsall.[214]

The work done by women in the saddlery industry largely consists in making suits for horses, either of kersey or blanketing, at the rate of about 4s. per suit. Working ten to twelve hours per day a woman can earn an average weekly wage of 13s. 10d., though she may get as much as 18s. some weeks. The chief drawback to this trade is its irregularity, and it has declined within the last fifteen years for reasons given above.[215]

In Leek, where the silk industry has been established since the seventeenth century, women work in the silk factories, earning in 1893–4 an average weekly wage of 11s. 6d.[216]

Compared with other industrial counties, Staffordshire does not show a large proportion of trade-unionists compared with its total population, despite the fact that one of its principal industries is mining, which is the most highly organized of all the industries. In 1892 it only stood twelfth on the list of English counties, with 4·49 per cent. of unionists to its whole population, and since 1900 there has been almost without exception a decrease in the membership of every trade union in the county. The North Staffordshire Miners' Federation is a striking example of this, having fallen

[213] From a widespread investigation in the Birmingham district, the average wages of japanners of eighteen years and over is estimated at 12s. 4d., with a maximum wage of 18s. and a minimum of 4s. among all workers. Probably the same rate may be taken to hold good for the South Staffordshire district, which closely adjoins the area investigated. E. Cadbury, M. Matheson, and G. Shann, *Women's Work and Wages* (1906), 315.
[214] *Women's Work and Wages* (1906), 83; *Rep. of Labour Com.* 1893–4, xxiii, 58.
[215] *Handbook of the Daily News Sweated Industries Exhibition*, 1906, pp. 84, 121.
[216] *Rep. of Labour Com.* 1893–4, xxiii, 135.

from a membership of more than eleven thousand in 1900 to rather less than half that number at the end of 1904. Within the same period at least five unions have been dissolved, including two associated with the Wolverhampton hollow-ware trade.[217]

Among the potters, unionism has never been very strong, the membership having never reached more than 10 per cent. of the total number of working potters. In the 400 earthenware manufactories of North Staffordshire 50,000 operatives were employed in 1901, of whom about 27,000 were males, but only 5,000 were enrolled members of the various branch unions, and these were chiefly males.[218]

It has been suggested that the fact that the potters are concentrated in one district has made them feel that a trade union is not so necessary as in other industries and with different circumstances. Doubtless, too, the old custom of fixing wages for the whole year at Martinmas has made it difficult to keep up interest in the union during the other parts of the year when the question of wages was no longer open to discussion.

Between the years 1868 and 1891 questions in dispute between the masters and the men were settled by the ' Potteries Board of Arbitration and Conciliation,' a body composed of representatives of employers and employed, which did excellent work in its time—calling in an outside arbitrator or umpire to give a final verdict on special occasions, notably in 1877, 1879, 1880, and 1891.[219]

With regard to methods of fixing wages, that of a sliding scale, according to which wages vary with the selling price of coal, has now fallen into disfavour, and wages are now arranged by means of conciliation boards composed of representatives of the masters and the men.

In the South-east Staffordshire and East Worcestershire district, after the great strike of 1874 which ended in the masters' favour, the system of a sliding scale was introduced. This was, however, abandoned in 1899 when a Wages and Conciliation Board was formed, which still decides on any changes made in rates of wages in the district. Similarly in that part of Staffordshire which belongs to the ' Federated Districts,' changes in rates of wages are arranged by a joint Conciliation Board, of which Lord James of Hereford is chairman.[220]

In North Staffordshire a sliding scale for colliers' wages has never been in use. A sliding scale was established in 1899 for blast-furnacemen, but the wages of those in South Staffordshire are regulated by the Midland Iron and Steel Wages Board.

With regard to the rates of wages in various industries in Staffordshire certain general tendencies may be indicated. The years between 1900 and 1904 were characterized by a general decline in wages in coal-mining, iron-mining, iron and steel manufacture, and building trades, and the wages in Staffordshire in these industries shared the general downward movement.

In the mining industry the period between 1894 and 1896 was one of declining wages ; then came a rise between 1897 and 1900, and another

[217] S. and B. Webb, *Hist. of Trade Unionism*, 413 ; *Rep. of Trade Unions*, 1902–4, Board of Trade Labour Dept. 6–27.

[218] Harold Owen, op. cit. 334.   [219] Ibid. 150, 160, 180, 234 et seq.

[220] *Rep. on Changes in Rates of Wages and Hours of Labour*, 1904, Board of Trade Labour Dept. 15.

fall, as described above, between 1900 and 1904. At the same time a comparison of miners' wages in the years 1888 and 1906 reveals an increase of 40 per cent. on the standard rates of that year.[221]

However, it must be remembered that wages and conditions of work vary considerably in different parts of the county. In the returns of the census of wages made by the Board of Trade in 1886, e.g., the weekly wages of a coal-hewer in the Potteries district were 25s. 5d. (piece-work).[222] But in the South Staffordshire district, excluding Cannock Chase, the weekly wages of a coal-hewer paid by the piece were as much as 28s. 5d.[223] At the present time it is admittedly difficult to give an approximate idea of the average earnings of a coal-hewer in the whole county. It has been computed at 6s. 6d. per day, with an average working week of four days, which makes the average weekly wage for the county 26s., which is of course sometimes exceeded.[224] But with Cannock Chase district the rates would be lower, as it is largely a house-coal district working badly in the summer.

Again, in the South Staffordshire and East Worcestershire district the wages of a coal-hewer are estimated at 5s. 9d. per day in the thick coal seams, the wages in the thin coal being slightly lower.[225] With a four days' working week this makes a weekly wage of only 23s.

Wages of course vary very much among different classes of workers in and about the mines, but the wages of the hewer have been taken as the most representative. The returns of the Census of 1886 give some other valuable wages statistics which may be compared with those of the miners.

Thus a 'general labourer' working underground in the Potteries district earned 18s. 3d. per week,[226] whilst in South Staffordshire he obtained 19s. 5d.[227] On the other hand, a horsekeeper in North Staffordshire could earn 22s. 9d.,[228] but in South Staffordshire he obtained only 19s. 1d.[229]

The wages of carpenters and bricklayers for the same date may be gathered from this return. A North Staffordshire bricklayer earned an average of 26s. 6d. per week ;[230] a South Staffordshire man 27s. 5d.[231] The wages of carpenters show less variation in the two districts, for whilst a carpenter working about the mine earned on an average 25s. 11d. per week in 1886, the southern workman's weekly average amounted to 25s. 10d.[232]

The more highly skilled workman would of course obtain more than this. At the present time (Oct. 1906) a skilled carpenter is paid at the rate of 8½d. per hour, which at the rate of ten hours per day for five-and-a-half days amounts to 38s. 11½d., but this would be a maximum wage and could not be counted on throughout the year. Rather more allowance for periods of slackness must be made in calculating the average wage of the skilled bricklayer, whose present rate of pay is 8¾d. per hour, which gives a maximum weekly wage of £2 0s. 1¼d., supposing him to work the same hours as the carpenter.

In 1886 boys working in or about the mines earned in North Staffordshire from 7s. 2d. to 14s. 6d. per week and in the south from 7s. 2d. to 14s.[233]

[221] Rep. on Changes in Rates of Wages and Hours of Labour, 1904, p. 104 ; and information obtained from Labour Department, Board of Trade.
[222] Return of Rates of Wages in Mines and Quarries, 1891, p. 19.   [223] Ibid. 21.
[224] Evidence from Secretary of Midland Miners' Federation, Oct. 1906.
[225] Evidence of South Staff. and East Worc. Amalgamated Miners' Association, Oct. 1906.
[226] Return of Rates of Wages in Mines and Quarries, 1891, p. 19.
[227] Ibid. 21.   [228] Ibid. 20.   [229] Ibid. 22.   [230] Ibid. 20.
[231] Ibid. 22.   [232] Ibid. 20, 22.   [233] Ibid.

SOCIAL AND ECONOMIC HISTORY

The return of 1886 shows that compared with the coal-hewers, engine-wrights, fitters, and boiler-makers earn a considerably greater weekly sum. In North Staffordshire the average weekly wage was estimated at 28*s.* 9*d.*, whilst in the south it was given as varying from 23*s.* 9*d.* to 51*s.* 8*d.*, but as comparatively few men received the higher pay, the average wage would probably work out at much the same rate as in the north.[234]

An analysis of the census returns in the period between 1801 and 1901[235] shows an enormous aggregate increase in the population of Staffordshire, which in the latter year stood fourth on the list of English counties. The greatest increase has of course been in the great industrial regions of North and South Staffordshire, the Potteries and the Black Country, and in the neighbourhood of the small Cheadle coalfield in the north.

But even in the agricultural districts there has been a rise in population in a considerable number of cases in the first half of the nineteenth century, though this has often failed to maintain itself. Bromley Regis is a case in point ; it had a population of 454 in 1801 which increased in the next forty years to 718, but has now fallen to 500.

The township of Salt and Enson, in the hundred of Pirehill, shows exactly the same number of inhabitants in 1901 as it did a hundred years ago, viz. 370, but in the year 1841 its numbers had reached 580. These are only two instances out of a good many similar ones which might be cited.

The growth of population both in the industrial and agricultural districts is due directly or indirectly to the industrial development of the county, and to the growth of railways during the last century.

Of the four most densely populated towns in the county three are in South Staffordshire, and one only, the smallest, in the north. During the century Wolverhampton, the most populous, has increased from 12,565 to 94,187 ; Walsall, the centre of the leather, saddlery, and harness trade, has risen from 10,399 in 1801 to 87,464 in 1901. The largest part of this rise in population is due to the growth of Walsall Foreign as it is called, as the township proper has only risen from 5,177 to 5,729 in the hundred years, though in 1851 it contained more inhabitants, viz. 8,761. West Bromwich contained, in 1801, 5,687 persons, compared with 65,114 in 1901. The population of Hanley county borough in 1901 was 61,599. Its growth cannot be tabulated so clearly as the other towns, as the town of Hanley is part of the ancient parish of Stoke upon Trent, and was not separately rated to the relief of the poor until 1894, and its population is not separately shown in the table given below.

The sum of the populations of the two townships of Hanley and Shelton in 1811, however, is estimated at about 9,968, but this is admittedly only approximately correct. During the nineteenth century many industrial villages have become towns, e.g. Burslem, which has risen rom 6,578 to 40,234, and Darlaston, which had a population of only 3,812 in 1801, and at the last census contained 15,386 inhabitants. The parish of Sedgeley is still made up of a number of scattered villages, but its numbers have gone

---

[234] *Return of Rates of Wages in Mines and Quarries,* 1891, p. 19. The weekly wages of a 'puddler' are given as 30*s.* in 1893. See *Rep. of Lab. Com.* 1893–4, xxxii (c—6894—x), 18.
[235] See Table of Pop. appended to this article.

up from 9,874 to 38,179 in the century. Willenhall, the home of lock and key makers, contained, in 1901, 21,438 persons, compared with 3,143 a hundred years ago. Bilston, with a population of 24,034, has more than trebled itself, and the population of Tipton has risen during the same period from 4,280 to 30,543.

The increase of the population of Tettenhall is only indirectly due to industrial development, as it is now the great residential suburb of Wolverhampton. The growth of Bushbury, however, another suburb, is accounted for largely by the engineering and electrical works established there. It is worth notice that the district round Wolverhampton has maintained its upward movement in population despite the fact that many of the ironworks which formerly employed so many workmen have latterly either been closed, or have migrated to the coast, e.g. to Newport, on account of the heavy cost of freight, a serious item of commercial expenditure at a time when foreign competition in the iron trade becomes increasingly acute.

Between Bilston and Sedgeley, and again between Walsall and Wolverhampton, considerable tracts of unsightly mounds and pits mark the sites of mines no longer worked, either because the coal has already been exhausted, or owing to the fact that the mines have become water-logged, and the cost of drainage is too great to allow them to be worked at a profit. The town of Wolverhampton is, however, still famous for the manufacture of tin, japanned, and galvanized goods, whilst other trades—such as the manufacture of bicycles and motor cars—have grown up during the last thirty years, and given employment to those who have been displaced by the extinction of other industries.

The case of Cannock is interesting as that of a town which began the nineteenth century with a tiny population of 1,359, which however reached 23,974 at the opening of the twentieth, having gained most of its increase since 1851, when coal was first dug on Cannock Chase.

In the agricultural parts of the county the population has in the main remained stationary or slightly decreased, this decrease being due partly to the inevitable drift of the countryman to industrial centres, and partly to the increase of pasturage and consequent diminution of the demand for agricultural labour. In the hundred of Seisdon, with the exception of two or three places, no decrease has taken place at all. In the north division of the hundred of Pirehill there has been none, and the slight decrease in the south division chiefly occurs in villages away from the track of the railways. The same remark applies also to the hundred of Cuttlestone.

The most sparsely populated, as it is also the most picturesque, region of Staffordshire is that elevated part of the county which comprehends the limestone regions extending for about forty square miles east of the Dove, and the adjoining tract of moorland with its sharp escarpments of millstone grit and its narrow valleys lying between the limestone and the coal measures. It is a district in which railways play little part, and is given up mainly to pastoral farming, carried on with difficulty in the more barren moorland region, but with greater success in the valleys and on the uplands of the limestone hills, which produce a short sweet grass good for pasturage. There has been some difficulty as to a market in this limestone district, but this should disappear now that the North Staffordshire Railway Company has opened up the beautiful valley of the Manifold by means of its light railway from Waterhouses to Hulme End.[236]

It is probable also that work may be renewed in the now disused copper and lead mines of Ecton, which have been worked since the seventeenth century, and were at one time exceedingly productive.

In that case the little hamlet of Ecton, which now contains about seventy persons, will become a much more important and populous place than it is at present.

The extensive copper mines at Oakamoor in the Churnet Valley account for the considerable population at Alton, which has risen from 818 in 1801 to 1,227 in 1901, and consists chiefly of the families of men concerned in some way in the mining industry there. Biddulph, again, in the moorland region of Pirehill Hundred, shows an increase of population from 1,180 to 6,247 in the century, a fact accounted for by the presence of coal in its neighbourhood.

In examining the census returns certain sudden rises in population are noticeable which demand some explanation. For instance the sudden rise of population in the country villages of High Offley, Church Eaton, Lapley, and Gnosall in 1831 is due to the presence of a number of workmen who were excavating the Birmingham and Liverpool Canal and settled here for a time.

At Leigh in 1851 the population was increased in a similar way, railway workers being in this case substituted for canal labourers. The increase at Whittington in 1881 is due to the establishment of a new military dépôt, whilst the rise noticed in 1861 in Hopton and Coton township is traceable to the enlargement of the county lunatic asylum and the building of a new one at Coton Hill. The sudden rise of population at Cheddleton in 1901 is due to the recent establishment of the county asylum in that parish. When the next census is taken the returns will probably show a large permanent increase of population in the parish of Cheddleton and the surrounding villages, as during the last few years a rich coalfield has been discovered within half a mile of this village, and the new colliery will probably be working shortly. The site of the main shaft is well placed for purposes of transport, being near a valley which runs direct to Wall Grange station and the canal. As valuable deposits of clay and ironstone have been found near the coal it is probable that at least three new industries may be established in the district, and the inevitable result of that will be the growth of an industrial community round about the colliery.

As there has been considerable poverty and lack of employment in the district recently, this new development is to be welcomed from an economic point of view, though from a different standpoint it is melancholy to see another beautiful bit of country given up to the sway of the blast furnace, the brick kiln, and the coke oven.

The traveller in Staffordshire, passing through this district, will find himself once again inverting a well-known motto of the Potteries: 'Out of dirt we make beauty'; and will reflect with a certain sadness how much beauty has in this county given place to dirt.

[236] This railway was opened in the summer of 1904, and worked for that year only by motor 'buses from Leek till the completion of the heavy railway from Leek to Waterhouses in 1905.

TABLE OF POPULATION, 1801 TO 1901

Introductory Notes

AREA

The county taken in this table is that existing subsequently to 7 & 8 Vict., chap. 61 (1844). By this Act detached parts of counties, which had already for parliamentary purposes been amalgamated with the county by which they were surrounded or with which the detached part had the longest common boundary (2 & 3 Wm. IV, chap. 64—1832), were annexed to the same county for all purposes ; some exceptions were, however, permitted.

By the same Act (7 & 8 Vict., chap. 61) the detached parts of counties, transferred to other counties, were also annexed to the hundred, ward, wapentake, &c. by which they were wholly or mostly surrounded, or to which they next adjoined, in the counties to which they were transferred. The hundreds, &c. in this table are also given as existing subsequently to this Act.

As is well known, the famous statute of Queen Elizabeth for the relief of the poor took the then-existing ecclesiastical parish as the unit for Poor Law relief. This continued for some centuries with but few modifications ; notably by an Act passed in the thirteenth year of Charles II's reign which permitted townships and villages to maintain their own poor. This permission was necessary owing to the large size of some of the parishes, especially in the north of England.

In 1801 the parish for rating purposes (now known as the civil parish, i.e. 'an area for which a separate poor rate is or can be made, or for which a separate overseer is or can be appointed') was in most cases co-extensive with the ecclesiastical parish of the same name ; but already there were numerous townships and villages rated separately for the relief of the poor, and also there were many places scattered up and down the country, known as extra-parochial places, which paid no rates at all. Further, many parishes had detached parts entirely surrounded by another parish or parishes.

Parliament first turned its attention to extra-parochial places, and by an Act (20 Vict., chap. 19—1857) it was laid down (*a*) that all extra-parochial places entered separately in the 1851 census returns are to be deemed civil parishes, (*b*) that in any other place being, or being reputed to be, extra-parochial, overseers of the poor may be appointed, and (*c*) that where, however, owners and occupiers of two-thirds in value of the land of any such place desire its annexation to an adjoining civil parish, it may be so added with the consent of the said parish. This Act was not found entirely to fulfil its object, so by a further Act (31 & 32 Vict., chap. 122—1868) it was enacted that every such place remaining on 25 December, 1868, should be added to the parish with which it had the longest common boundary.

The next thing to be dealt with was the question of detached parts of civil parishes, which was done by the Divided Parishes Acts of 1876, 1879, and 1882. The last, which amended the one of 1876, provides that every detached part of an entirely extra-metropolitan parish which is entirely surrounded by another parish becomes transferred to this latter for civil purposes, or if the population exceeds 300 persons it may be made a separate parish. These Acts also gave power to add detached parts surrounded by more than one parish to one or more of the surrounding parishes, and also to amalgamate entire parishes with one or more parishes. Under the 1879 Act it was not necessary for the area dealt with to be entirely detached. These Acts also declared that every part added to a parish in another county becomes part of that county.

Then came the Local Government Act, 1888, which permits the alteration of civil parish boundaries and the amalgamation of civil parishes by Local Government Board orders. It also created the administrative counties. The Local Government Act of 1894 enacts that where a civil parish is partly in a rural district and partly in an urban district each part shall become a separate civil parish ; and also that where a civil parish is situated in more than one urban district each part shall become a separate civil parish, unless the county council otherwise direct. Meanwhile, the ecclesiastical parishes had been altered and new ones created under entirely different Acts, which cannot be entered into here, as the table treats of the ancient parishes in their civil aspect.

POPULATION

The first census of England was taken in 1801, and was very little more than a counting of the population in each parish (or place), excluding all persons, such as soldiers, sailors, &c., who formed no part of its ordinary population. It was the *de facto* population (i.e. the population actually resident at a particular time) and not the *de jure* (i.e. the population really belonging to any particular place at a particular time). This principle has been sustained throughout the censuses.

The Army at home (including militia), the men of the Royal Navy ashore, and the registered seamen ashore were not included in the population of the places where they happened to be, at the time of the census, until 1841. The men of the Royal Navy and other persons on board vessels (naval or mercantile) in home ports were first included in the population of those places in 1851. Others temporarily present, such as gipsies, persons in barges, &c. were included in 1841 and perhaps earlier.

GENERAL

Up to and including 1831 the returns were mainly made by the overseers of the poor, and more than one day was allowed for the enumeration, but the 1841–1901 returns were made under the superintendence of the registration officers and the enumeration was to be completed in one day. The Householder's Schedule was first used in 1841. The exact dates of the censuses are as follows :—

10 March, 1801	30 May, 1831	8 April, 1861	6 April, 1891
27 May, 1811	7 June, 1841	3 April, 1871	1 April, 1901
28 May, 1821	31 March, 1851	4 April, 1881	

NOTES EXPLANATORY OF THE TABLE

This table gives the population of the ancient county and arranges the parishes, &c. under the hundred or other sub-division to which they belong, but there is no doubt that the constitution of hundreds, &c. was in some cases doubtful.

In the main the table follows the arrangement in the 1841 census volume.

The table gives the population and area of each parish, &c. as it existed in 1801, as far as possible.

The areas are those supplied by the Ordnance Survey Department, except in the case of those marked 'e,' which are only estimates. The area includes inland water (if any), but not tidal water or foreshore.

† after the name of a civil parish indicates that the parish was affected by the operation of the Divided Parishes Acts, but the Registrar-General failed to obtain particulars of every such change. The changes which escaped notification were, however, probably small in area and with little, if any, population. Considerable difficulty was experienced both in 1891 and 1901 in tracing the results of changes effected in civil parishes under the provisions of these Acts ; by the Registrar-General's courtesy, however, reference has been permitted to certain records of formerly detached parts of parishes, which has made it possible approximately to ascertain the population in 1901 of parishes as constituted prior to such alterations, though the figures in many instances must be regarded as partly estimates.

* after the name of a parish (or place) indicates that such parish (or place) contains a union workhouse which was in use in (or before) 1851 and was still in use in 1901.

‡ after the name of a parish (or place) indicates that the ecclesiastical parish of the same name at the 1901 census is co-extensive with such parish (or place).

o in the table indicates that there is no population on the area in question.

— in the table indicates that no population can be ascertained.

The word 'chapelry' seems often to have been used as an equivalent for 'township' in 1841, which census volume has been adopted as the standard for names and descriptions of areas.

The figures in italics in the table relate to the area and population of such sub-divisions of ancient parishes as chapelries, townships, and hamlets.

TABLE OF POPULATION, 1801—1901

—	Acreage	1801	1811	1821	1831	1841	1851	1861	1871	1881	1891	1901
Ancient or Geographical County [1]	749,602	242,693	290,595	344,838	409,480	509,472	608,716	746,943	858,326	981,013	1,083,454	1,234,533

PARISH	Acreage	1801	1811	1821	1831	1841	1851	1861	1871	1881	1891	1901
Cuttlestone Hundred—East Division												
Baswich, or Berkswich :—	6,971	1,096	1,111	1,376	1,329	1,438	1,623	1,555	1,335	1,378	1,327	1,457
Acton Trussell, with Bednall Chap. ‡	2,594	436	460	562	551	574	673	617	569	548	490	538
Baswich, Milford, and Walton Township †	2,013	443	416	559	546	626	704	660	549	606	625	704
Brocton Township †	2,364	217	235	255	232	238	246	278	217	224	212	215
Brewood [2]	12,152	2,867	2,860	2,762	3,799	3,641	3,565	3,399	3,237	2,948	2,667	2,535
Bushbury (part of) [3] :—												
Essington Township	3,054	369	540	605	598	623	644	976	1,065	1,295	1,368	1,670
Cannock :—	10,961	1,700	1,639	2,232	2,468	2,852	3,081	3,964	7,749	18,377	21,959	26,012
Cannock Township	8,010	1,359	1,143	1,563	1,771	1,932	2,099	2,913	6,650	17,125	20,613	23,974
Huntington Township	1,303	114	135	138	106	121	158	161	142	177	195	351
Wyrley, Great Township	1,648	227	361	531	591	799	824	890	957	1,075	1,151	1,687
Castle Church . .	3,933	563	566	1,118	1,374	1,484	2,315	3,362	4,746	5,923	6,384	6,455
Cheslyn Hay Extra Par.	819	443	486	548	648	774	876	1,177	1,431	1,799	2,066	2,560
Penkridge (part of) [4] :—	13,138	2,018	2,243	2,641	2,723	2,857	3,013	2,873	2,798	2,901	2,749	2,699
Coppenhall Chap.	907	83	92	108	100	119	91	88	95	86	109	90
Dunston Chap. .	1,448	208	214	234	272	250	259	275	268	279	257	262
Penkridge Township	10,783	1,727	1,937	2,299	2,351	2,488	2,663	2,510	2,435	2,536	2,383	2,347
Rugeley . . .	8,449	2,030	2,213	2,677	3,165	3,774	4,188	4,362	4,630	7,048	6,942	7,327
Shareshill ‡ :—	2,827	441	493	583	520	594	540	531	511	612	619	667
Shareshill . .	889	200	228	286	274	305	278	295	297	342	350	354
Saredon Township	1,938	241	265	297	246	289	262	236	214	270	269	313
Teddesley Hay Extra Par.	2,625	—	59	43	50	61	109	117	128	130	115	125

[1] *Ancient County.*—The County as defined by the Act 7 & 8 Vict. cap. 61, which affected Staffordshire to the following extent :—(1) *added to Staffordshire*, the part of Scropton and Foston shown in this Table (from Derbyshire) ; (2) *severed from Staffordshire*, the Parishes of Broom and Clent (to Worcestershire).

The area is taken from the 1901 Census volume. The population is exclusive of 3,045 militia in 1811, and 1,134 militia in 1821, who could not be assigned to their respective parishes. Dudley Castle Hill is said to be in Staffordshire ; it is not included in this Table. (*See* also notes to Sheriff Hales, Scropton and Foston, and Bobbington.)

[2] *Brewood* and *Forton.*—The populations in 1831 include 278 men in Brewood and 106 in Forton employed in excavating the Birmingham and Liverpool Canal.

[3] *Bushbury Ancient Parish* is situated partly in Cuttlestone Hundred—East Division, and partly in Seisdon Hundred—North Division.

[4] *Penkridge Ancient Parish* is situated in Cuttlestone Hundred—East and West Divisions.

Parish	Acreage	1801	1811	1821	1831	1841	1851	1861	1871	1881	1891	1901
Cuttlestone Hundred—East Division cont.)												
Wolverhampton (part of) [5] :—	3,632	349	422	443	422	490	474	561	546	564	608	653
Featherstone Township	504	48	52	49	34	34	37	54	61	76	51	51
Hatherton Township	2,015	248	299	320	320	378	368	415	420	426	468	507
Hilton Township	810	34	56	55	45	57	54	82	58	50	64	77
Kinvaston Township	303	19	15	19	23	21	15	10	7	12	25	18
Cuttlestone Hundred—West Division												
Blymhill ‡ . . .	3,024	475	513	604	566	633	622	591	608	503	532	522
Bradley † ‡ . . .	5,594	593	627	723	731	649	628	597	614	496	474	399
Church Eaton [6] ‡ .	4,283	784	804	829	922	743	654	643	638	655	616	587
Forton [6a] † . . .	3,746	566	607	702	904	764	741	729	649	541	576	520
Gnosall [7] † . . .	10,577	2,246	2,372	2,671	3,358	2,424	2,673	2,400	2,431	2,379	2,099	2,085
Haughton † ‡ . .	1,903	437	455	473	490	480	510	516	459	501	439	410
Lapley [8] ‡ . . .	3,542	759	746	916	1,042	952	962	828	779	744	767	742
Norbury ‡ :—	3,361	371	357	349	438	353	358	364	344	318	368	383
Norbury Township	2,102	215	224	220	257	210	218	217	205	212	236	258
Weston Jones with Loynton Township	1,259	156	133	129	181	143	140	147	139	106	132	125
Penkridge (part of) [8a] :—												
Stretton Chap. [9] ‡	1,615	257	243	255	268	272	303	273	260	233	224	245
Sheriff Hales (part of) [10]	2,907	616	809	876	914	688	698	650	656	621	522	485
Weston-under-Lizard ‡	2,438	101	275	296	257	297	248	275	325	284	316	301
Offlow Hundred—North Division.												
Alrewas :—	4,329	1,312	1,665	1,492	1,607	1,658	1,649	1,633	1,541	1,448	1,410	1,401
Alrewas † . . .	—	940	1,121	979	1,102	1,173	1,144	1,125	926	955	939	938
Fradley Township †	—	268	395	426	382	362	367	333	409	380	360	347
Orgreave Township †	—	104	149	87	123	123	138	175	206	113	111	116
Alrewas-Hays Extra Par.†	1,680	12	49	74	77	92	107	48	72	115	102	119
Bromley Regis [11] ‡	3,987	454	527	612	629	718	704	646	582	580	568	500
Burton upon Trent (part of) [12] :—	7,501	5,278	5,891	6,151	6,455	7,759	9,364	15,365	22,286	34,336	40,112	43,060
Branston Township	2,482	281	373	412	382	441	473	542	577	991	1,422	1,448

[5] *Wolverhampton Ancient Parish* is situated in (1) Cuttlestone Hundred—East Division, (2) Offlow Hundred—South Division, and (3) Seisdon Hundred—North Division.

[6] *Church Eaton.*—The increase in population in 1831 is attributed to the presence of a number of labourers employed in excavating the Birmingham and Liverpool Canal.

[6a] See note 2, *ante.*

[7] *Gnosall.*—The population in 1831 includes 197 men employed in excavating the Birmingham and Liverpool Canal.

[8] *Lapley.*—The population in 1831 includes 130 men employed in excavating the Birmingham and Liverpool Canal.

[8a] See note 4, *ante.*

[9] *Stretton.*—The 1821 population is an estimate.

[10] *Sheriff Hales.*—The remainder is in Salop (South Bradford Hundred—Newport division). The population of the entire Ancient Parish (except that of Woodcote Chapelry) 1811–31 is shown in Staffordshire.

[11] *Bromley Regis* includes the area and the population (1841–1901) of King's Bromley Hays, which was formerly Extra Parochial and became a Civil Parish under the Act 20 Vict. cap. 19.

[12] *Burton upon Trent, Clifton Campville,* and *Croxall Ancient Parishes.*—The remainder of these Parishes is in Derbyshire (Repton and Gresley Hundred).

TABLE OF POPULATION, 1801—1901 (*continued*)

Parish	Acreage	1801	1811	1821	1831	1841	1851	1861	1871	1881	1891	1901
Offlow Hundred—North Division (cont.)												
Burton upon Trent —(*cont.*)												
Burton, Extra Township †		716	872	910	910	1,193	1,289	2,849	7,025	12,582	15,140	16,455
Burton upon Trent Township †	3,772	3,679	3,979	4,114	4,399	4,863	6,374	9,534	9,450	9,348	8,212	7,370
Horninglow Township * †		272	297	341	391	852	815	1,968	4,750	10,717	14,513	16,930
Stretton Township	1,247	330	370	374	373	410	413	472	484	698	825	857
Clifton Campville (part of) [12a] :—	4,871	751	741	838	801	759	784	752	756	773	703	631
Clifton Campville Township [13]	3,347	362	362	627	369	341	337	328	329	494	462	402
Harlaston Chap. ‡	1,524	160	150	211	218	221	248	239	265	279	241	229
Haunton Township [13]	—	229	229	—	214	197	199	185	162	—	—	—
Croxall (part of) [12a] :—												
Oakley Township [14]	739	27	27	31	29	31	20	28	37	38	34	22
Edingale † . . .	900*	158	162	224	177	197	190	208	217	181	165	156
Hamstall Ridware †	3,124	349	428	455	443	391	471	440	382	383	316	305
Hanbury :—	13,108	1,622	2,130	2,516	2,448	2,483	2,535	2,638	2,605	2,411	2,541	2,462
Draycott in the Clay Township	1,930	288	384	498	461	431	411	484	492	451	491	525
Hanbury Township	3,288	424	493	493	546	553	566	543	514	537	631	521
Marchington Chap.	2,493	210	324	463	491	471	480	484	479	453	526	526
Marchington Woodlands Township	2,525	260	306	318	193	286	311	339	350	319	319	324
Newborough Chap.	2,872	440	623	744	757	742	767	788	770	651	574	566
Lichfield St. Chad (part of) [15] :—												
Curborough with Elmhurst Township †	2,080*	174	229	250	249	227	239	225	257	241	237	195
Lichfield St. Michael (part of) [16] :—	2,303*	198	201	181	208	196	225	238	228	331	424	425
Fisherwick Township	1,313	83	73	91	96	86	90	101	93	95	124	129
Streethay Township †	990*	115	128	90	112	110	135	137	135	236	300	296
Freeford Extra Par. [17]	—	—	—	—	—	27	23	9	41	—	—	—
Fulfen Extra Par. †	—	—	—	—	—	15	15	10	9	19	11	8
Haselour Extra Par.	586	33	42	49	36	29	22	27	21	29	42	49
Mavesyn Ridware ‡	2,486	486	548	598	576	531	523	462	467	473	391	438

[12a] See note 12, *ante*.

[13] *Clifton Campville* and *Haunton Townships*.—The 1801 populations are estimated. Clifton Campville Township includes the area and the population (1821, and 1881–1901) of Haunton Township.

[14] *Oakley.*—The 1811 population is an estimate.

[15] *Lichfield St. Chad Ancient Parish* is situated partly in Offlow Hundred—North Division, and partly in the City of Lichfield.

[16] *Lichfield St. Michael Ancient Parish* is situated in (1) Offlow Hundred—North Division, (2) Offlow Hundred—South Division, and (3) the City of Lichfield.

[17] *Freeford Hamlet* includes the area and the population (1881–1901, and probably in 1801) of the formerly *Extra Parochial Place of Freeford*.

TABLE OF POPULATION, 1801—1901 (*continued*)

Parish	Acreage	1801	1811	1821	1831	1841	1851	1861	1871	1881	1891	1901
Offlow Hundred—North Division (cont.)												
Pipe Ridware ‡ .	823	107	101	114	111	100	90	93	90	74	84	63
Rolleston :—	3,647°	646	700	869	866	797	918	956	1,079	1,140	1,196	1,303
Anslow, or Annesley Township †	—	200	225	270	302	278	297	348	393	383	398	370
Rolleston Township †	—	446	475	599	564	519	621	608	686	757	798	933
Scropton and Foston (part of) : [18]	142	—	—	—	—	15	15	17	47	98	85	100
Tamhorn Extra Par.	793	10	9	16	7	5	10	23	31	33	21	20
Tamworth (part of) [19] :—												
Syerscote Township [19]	483	23	—	41	34	46	48	37	42	43	40	36
Tatenhill :—	10,100	1,430	1,754	2,059	2,180	2,229	2,329	2,500	2,593	2,722	2,722	2,552
Barton under Needwood Chap. †		834	1,066	1,287	1,344	1,459	1,561	1,589	1,677	1,789	1,775	1,650
Dunstall Township †	8,458	177	157	184	204	180	187	240	249	267	246	279
Tatenhill Township †		286	372	426	475	435	450	519	517	493	506	472
Wichnor Chap.‡	1,642	133	159	162	157	155	131	152	150	173	195	151
Thorpe Constantine ‡	961	62	54	40	49	42	58	54	49	57	87	84
Tutbury † . . .	4,001'	1,004	1,235	1,444	1,553	1,835	1,798	1,982	2,149	2,306	2,057	1,974
Whittington [20] ‡ .	2,921	611	602	707	766	799	809	819	869	2,009	2,033	2,392
Yoxall [21] † . .	4,961	1,300	1,345	1,463	1,582	1,535	1,496	1,443	1,419	1,301	1,283	1,160
Offlow Hundred—South Division												
Aldridge :—	8,191	1,492	1,643	1,583	1,700	2,094	2,174	2,254	2,480	3,017	3,594	3,822
Aldridge Township ‡	2,939	736	847	820	841	1,007	1,173	1,179	1,418	1,890	2,206	2,478
Great Barr Chap. ‡	5,252	756	796	763	859	1,087	1,001	1,075	1,062	1,127	1,388	1,344
Armitage with Handsacre ‡	1,948	464	483	793	977	987	1,014	937	992	1,283	1,290	1,318
Canwell Extra Par.	347	36	28	24	24	27	27	43	47	38	78	52
Darlaston † . .	800	3,812	4,881	5,585	6,647	8,244	10,590	12,884	14,416	13,563	14,422	15,386
Drayton Bassett ‡	3,368	395	455	468	459	404	408	441	439	442	461	476
Elford ‡	2,024	383	397	424	483	434	468	461	453	426	373	363
Farewell † . . .	1,049°	165	165	202	200	203	189	209	200	218	182	224
Handsworth . .	7,752	2,719	3,027	3,859	4,944	6,138	7,879	11,459	16,042	24,251	35,066	55,269
Harborne . . .	3,420	2,275	2,612	3,350	4,227	6,657	10,729	16,996	22,263	31,517	44,105	64,713
Hints ‡	1,889	245	271	250	225	213	218	200	193	214	238	212
Hopwas Hays Extra Par.	354	—	—	3	2	4	6	2	6	5	6	5
Lichfield St. Michael (part of) [21a] :—	6,836°	888	965	977	1,042	1,079	1,149	2,712	5,950	7,733	8,787	9,884
Burntwood Township †	4,417°	582	659	675	731	749	781	1,634	4,525	6,241	7,113	8,195
Hammerwich Chap.	1,779	209	215	218	218	239	270	991	1,325	1,391	1,573	1,546
Wall Township†	640°	97	91	84	93	91	98	87	100	101	101	143
Longdon	4,545	909	1,017	1,115	1,147	1,183	1,148	1,220	1,359	1,366	1,338	1,342

[18] *Scropton* and *Foston.*—The remainder is in Derbyshire (Appletree Hundred). It is entirely entered in Derbyshire 1801–1831.

[19] *Tamworth Ancient Parish* is situated in Offlow Hundred—North and South Divisions, and in Warwickshire (Hemlingford Hundred—Tamworth Division). *Syerscote Township* is included with the part of *Tamworth Township* in Staffordshire in 1811.

[20] *Whittington.*—The increase in population in 1881 is attributed to the erection and occupation of a new military depôt.

[21] *Yoxall.*—The 1801 population is an estimate.

[21a] See note 16, *ante.*

TABLE OF POPULATION, 1801—1901 (*continued*)

Parish	Acre-age	1801	1811	1821	1831	1841	1851	1861	1871	1881	1891	1901
Offlow Hundred— South Division (cont.)												
Norton under Cannock	4,068	547	519	669	678	755	968	1,628	2,776	3,546	4,047	5,214
Ogley Hay Extra Par.	1,063	—	8	23	24	222	518	1,357	1,824	2,040	2,478	2,677
Rushall ‡ . . .	1,950	485	613	670	693	1,609	1,946	2,842	3,702	5,809	6,980	7,943
Shenstone . . .	8,543	1,309	1,378	1,699	1,827	1,962	2,043	2,131	2,224	2,488	2,681	3,043
Statfold . . .	455	27	25	29	41	45	38	26	55	61	53	21
Tamworth (part of) [21b] :—	5,901	2,699	3,156	3,860	3,881	4,156	4,454	4,656	5,005	5,529	6,154	6,781
Fazeley Township	2,084	905	1,165	1,477	1,433	1,510	1,690	1,720	1,698	1,793	1,867	1,887
Tamworth Township (part of) [21b]	150	1,123	1,327	1,636	1,711	1,797	1,915	1,989	2,351	2,589	3,208	3,806
Wigginton Township	3,667	671	664	747	737	849	849	947	956	1,147	1,079	1,088
Tipton, or Tibbington	2,171	4,280	8,407	11,546	14,951	18,891	24,872	28,870	29,445	30,013	29,314	30,543
Walsall :—	8,314	10,399	11,189	11,914	15,066	20,852	26,822	39,690	48,524	58,453	71,397	87,464
Walsall Borough Township	95	5,177	5,541	5,504	6,401	7,395	8,761	8,166	8,279	7,652	7,286	5,729
Walsall Foreign Township *	8,219	5,222	5,648	6,410	8,665	13,457	18,061	31,524	40,245	50,801	64,111	81,735
Wednesbury . .	2,287	4,160	5,372	6,471	8,437	11,625	14,281	21,968	25,030	24,566	25,347	26,554
Weeford ‡ :—	4,626	393	377	440	470	426	425	399	395	405	417	385
Weeford . . .	2,545	200	190	278	306	276	289	290	254	244	213	223
Packington and Swinfen Township	2,081	193	187	162	164	150	136	109	141	161	204	162
West Bromwich *	5,851	5,687	7,485	9,505	15,327	26,121	34,591	41,795	47,918	56,295	59,474	65,114
Wolverhampton (part of) [21c] :—	8,466	4,804	5,345	6,111	8,538	13,317	18,301	28,047	29,856	32,527	35,109	40,353
Bentley Township	1,448	96	103	99	104	428	380	346	323	337	355	357
Pelsall Chap. ‡ .	1,263	477	471	579	721	1,026	1,132	1,892	2,389	2,928	3,364	3,626
Wednesfield Chap.	3,688	1,088	1,248	1,468	1,879	3,168	4,858	8,553	8,998	10,801	12,024	14,932
Willenhall Chap.	2,067	3,143	3,523	3,965	5,834	8,695	11,931	17,256	18,146	18,461	19,366	21,438
Pirehill Hundred— North Division												
Adbaston ‡ . . .	4,638	407	536	596	601	610	591	593	562	539	568	533
Ashley ‡. . . .	2,821	605	616	729	825	853	896	870	903	806	797	725
Audley	8,727	2,246	2,618	2,940	3,617	4,474	5,180	6,494	8,955	11,505	12,936	13,918
Barthomley (part of) [22] :—												
Balterley Township	1,235	237	249	242	305	316	299	281	273	253	273	253
Betley ‡	1,463	670	761	932	870	884	882	850	826	821	827	837
Biddulph	5,671	1,180	1,460	1,666	1,987	2,314	2,683	3,468	4,769	5,557	5,290	6,247
Burslem	3,122	6,578	8,625	10,176	12,714	16,091	19,725	22,327	27,108	28,249	32,767	40,234
Drayton-in-Hales, or Market Drayton (part of) [23] :—												
Tyrley Township	6,589	581	607	726	737	750	784	814	800	766	721	689
Eccleshall :—	21,738	3,734	3,801	4,227	4,471	4,730	4,696	4,882	4,827	4,455	4,251	4,186
Chapel Chorlton Township ‡	1,983	247	268	331	386	365	384	484	475	380	373	387
Eccleshall Township	19,755	3,487	3,533	3,896	4,085	4,365	4,312	4,398	4,352	4,075	3,878	3,799

[21b] See note 19, *ante*.　　　　[21c] See note 5, *ante*.

[22] *Barthomley Ancient Parish.*—The remainder is in Cheshire (Nantwich Hundred).

[23] *Drayton in Hales,* and *Mucklestone Ancient Parishes.*—The remainder of both these Parishes is in Salop (North Bradford Hundred—Drayton Division).

TABLE OF POPULATION, 1801—1901 (*continued*)

Parish	Acreage	1801	1811	1821	1831	1841	1851	1861	1871	1881	1891	1901
Pirehill Hundred— North Division (cont.)												
Keele	2,613	904	944	1,061	1,130	1,194	1,232	1,062	1,052	1,048	1,090	1,080
Madeley ‡ . . .	5,864	945	1,018	1,166	1,190	1,492	1,655	1,940	2,387	2,457	2,904	2,909
Maer ‡	2,750	382	454	451	505	559	515	473	387	393	389	436
Mucklestone (part of) [23a] :	4,252	683	772	924	964	879	876	827	755	763	709	727
Norton in the Moors	4,141	1,480	1,761	1,983	2,407	2,891	3,327	4,393	6,902	8,870	9,919	12,180
Offley, High [24] ‡ .	2,761	523	548	569	759	658	786	883	865	811	787	627
Standon ‡ . . .	2,620	332	420	415	420	382	373	347	329	359	404	418
Stoke upon Trent :—	12,406	16,414	22,495	29,223	37,220	47,951	57,942	71,308	89,262	104,968	122,101	140,335
Stoke upon Trent *†	8,017	—	21,631	—	36,059	46,342	56,047	69,138	86,320	101,297	117,588	135,767
Bucknall-cum-Bagnall Chapelry ‡	4,389	—	864	—	1,161	1,609	1,895	2,170	2,942	3,671	4,513	4,568
Swynnerton . . .	6,481	648	893	832	791	961	946	880	876	778	880	811
Trentham † . . .	7,445	1,857	2,120	2,203	2,344	2,567	2,747	4,611	6,371	8,383	10,219	12,516
Whitmore ‡ . . .	2,015	234	291	302	281	367	377	345	332	311	318	308
Wolstanton * . .	10,816	4,679	6,990	8,572	10,853	16,575	22,191	32,029	41,824	47,216	50,885	57,994
Pirehill Hundred— South Division												
Barlaston ‡ . . .	2,184	349	396	462	514	591	617	637	733	821	782	744
Blithfield ‡ . . .	3,219	439	434	470	468	390	382	338	380	299	292	289
Bromley, Abbot's .	9,476	1,318	1,539	1,533	1,621	1,508	1,563	1,538	1,456	1,460	1,411	1,318
Chartley Holme Extra Parochial [25]	1,707	9	9	11	9	71	29	36	41	39	37	34
Chebsey ‡ :—	4,172	441	406	421	414	442	466	514	487	503	536	566
Chebsey . . .	2,853	379	358	377	377	401	448	472	436	467	462	503
Cold Norton Township	1,319	62	48	44	37	41	18	42	51	36	74	63
Colton †‡ . . .	3,692	545	484	569	675	672	652	629	657	678	645	677
Colwich :—	9,217	886	1,688	1,865	1,918	2,024	2,072	1,828	1,834	1,740	1,575	1,615
Colwich Township †	7,775	723	1,442	1,646	1,719	1,787	1,828	1,608	1,625	1,541	1,395	1,449
Fradswell Chapelry ‡	1,442	163	246	219	199	237	244	220	209	199	180	166
Creswell Extra Parochial‡	828	17	19	12	11	16	7	12	26	29	56	46
Ellenhall † . . .	1,801	256	251	287	286	280	320	300	261	231	238	207
Gayton ‡	1,515	273	261	284	296	291	264	249	237	236	221	180
Ingestre ‡ . . .	879	115	122	125	116	118	174	151	163	138	192	120
Milwich ‡ . . .	3,042	497	563	567	551	563	591	567	575	547	515	436
Ranton ‡	1,843	285	278	334	273	292	312	283	267	265	249	265
Ranton Abbey, Extra Par. †	748	14	14	11	17	28	18	13	2	12	6	13
Sandon ‡ . . .	3,574	516	480	513	558	586	556	590	576	513	472	458
Seighford ‡ . . .	4,741	841	866	851	898	903	851	808	781	756	793	947
Stafford St. Mary and St. Chad (part of) [26] :—	8,076	1,022	1,063	1,256	1,489	1,407	1,399	2,210	2,328	2,633	2,925	3,514
Hopton and Coton Township [27] †	3,711	336	332	517	642	464	468	1,174	1,216	1,392	1,707	2,225
Marston Chapelry †‡	1,487	99	100	96	119	178	206	345	490	664	623	779

[23a] See note 23, *ante.*

[24] *Offley, High.*—A number of men employed in constructing a canal present in 1831.

[25] *Chartley Holme.*—The boundaries were defined between 1841 and 1851; they were previously in dispute. Certainly too large an area taken in 1841.

[26] *Stafford St. Mary* and *St. Chad* is situated partly in Pirehill Hundred—South Division, and partly in the Borough of Stafford.

[27] *Hopton* and *Coton Township.*—The increase in population in 1861 is attributed to the enlarging of a County Lunatic Asylum and to the building of Coton Hill Lunatic Asylum.

TABLE OF POPULATION, 1801—1901 (*continued*)

Parish	Acre-age	1801	1811	1821	1831	1841	1851	1861	1871	1881	1891	1901
Pirehill Hundred— South Division (cont.)												
Stafford St. Mary and St. Chad (*cont.*)												
Salt and Enson Township †	1,677	370	391	439	533	580	534	509	470	427	435	370
Whitgreave Township ‡	1,201	217	240	204	195	185	191	182	152	150	160	140
Stone [28] *	20,509	5,373	6,270	7,251	7,808	8,349	8,736	9,382	10,387	13,155	14,066	14,233
Stowe [29] †	5,120	696	853	1,185	1,283	1,267	1,269	1,267	1,167	1,168	1,043	934
Tillington Extra Par. †	977	29	20	39	42	55	62	79	97	271	490	536
Tixall ‡	2,369	198	206	198	176	209	221	289	256	226	212	187
Weston upon Trent ‡	831	306	394	442	587	562	570	502	495	528	453	401
Worston Extra Par.	172	—	—	23	25	23	17	17	5	7	15	23
Yarlett Extra Par.	400	—	—	33	21	24	22	21	11	117	59	82
Seisdon Hundred— North Division												
Bushbury (part of) [29a]	3,520	488	603	624	677	886	988	1,075	1,218	1,770	2,252	3,389
Himley ‡	1,221	267	341	379	421	409	400	367	389	346	304	291
Kingswinford *	7,372	6,464	8,267	11,022	15,156	22,221	27,301	34,257	35,041	35,767	36,411	38,490
Penn :—	4,003	700	780	769	863	942	1,160	1,765	2,184	2,804	2,941	3,449
Penn, Lower Township	2,005	—	253	230	233	226	305	306	307	335	274	316
Penn, Upper Township	1,998	—	527	539	630	716	855	1,459	1,877	2,469	2,667	3,133
Rowley Regis	3,828	5,027	4,974	6,062	7,438	11,111	14,249	19,785	23,534	27,385	30,791	34,670
Sedgeley †	7,743	9,874	13,937	17,195	20,577	24,819	29,447	36,637	37,355	36,574	36,860	38,179
Tettenhall [30]	8,306	1,570	1,814	2,234	2,618	3,143	3,396	3,716	4,416	5,474	5,982	6,459
Wolverhampton (part of) [30a] :—	5,392	19,479	24,482	30,383	39,224	56,563	73,512	85,224	92,479	98,496	106,115	118,221
Wolverhampton Township *	3,525	12,565	14,836	18,380	24,732	36,382	49,985	60,860	68,291	75,766	82,662	94,187
Bilston Township	1,867	6,914	9,646	12,003	14,492	20,181	23,527	24,364	24,188	22,730	23,453	24,034
Seisdon Hundred — South Division												
Arley, Upper ‡	3,969	693	691	715	735	667	678	886	793	731	647	670
Bobbington (part of) [31]	2,189	381	366	393	426	396	385	401	396	373	345	303
Codsall ‡	2,994	589	739	903	1,115	1,096	1,195	1,204	1,313	1,398	1,436	1,452
Enville	4,986	799	746	842	766	814	807	850	793	773	715	645
Kinver ‡	9,011	1,655	1,668	1,735	1,831	2,207	2,872	3,551	3,194	2,842	2,160	2,176
Patshull ‡	1,824	160	142	144	132	117	112	194	208	193	234	222
Pattingham (part of) [32]	2,529	750	798	866	817	802	939	959	924	955	859	779
Swinford, Old (part of) [33] :—												
Amblecote Hamlet ‡	665	1,002	1,079	1,157	1,236	1,623	2,053	2,613	2,771	2,808	2,876	3,128

[28] *Stone Ancient Parish.*—The populations for 1801 and 1811 are estimated.
[29] *Stowe.*—The 1801 population is an estimate.   [29a] See note 3, *ante*
[30] *Tettenhall* is partly in Seisdon Hundred—South Division. None shown there.
[30a] See note 5, *ante.*
[31] *Bobbington Ancient Parish.*—The remainder is in Salop (Brimstree Hundred). It is entirely shown in Staffordshire 1801–1831.
[32] *Pattingham Ancient Parish.*—The remainder is in Salop (Stottesdon Hundred).
[33] *Swinford, Old, Ancient Parish.*—The remainder is in Worcestershire (Halfshire Hundred—Lower Division). The 1811 population for Amblecote Hamlet is an estimate.

SOCIAL AND ECONOMIC HISTORY

TABLE OF POPULATION, 1801—1901 (continued)

Parish	Acreage	1801	1811	1821	1831	1841	1851	1861	1871	1881	1891	1901
Seisdon Hundred —South Division (cont.)												
Trysull [34] ‡ . . .	2,951	529	491	539	562	541	559	610	583	567	554	553
Wombourn . . .	4,360	1,170	1,136	1,478	1,647	1,808	2,007	2,236	2,080	1,986	1,910	1,856
Woodford Grange Extra Par.[34]	199	—	—	14	18	14	8	13	11	8	8	15
Totmonslow Hundred— North Division												
Alstonfield :—	23,249	4,302	4,870	5,169	4,827	4,701	4,523	4,117	3,902	3,414	3,070	2,853
Alstonfield Township	2,938	573	654	677	649	654	681	651	562	471	476	438
Fawfieldhead Township	5,383	788	1,003	1,135	1,017	991	923	817	750	633	570	490
Heathylee Township	5,535	520	706	788	689	633	578	504	440	418	361	353
Hollingsclough Township	1,842	562	513	560	564	457	400	393	425	348	308	259
Longnor Chap. .	813	391	467	460	429	485	561	514	520	534	509	480
Quarnford Chap.	3,141	737	699	695	783	709	665	549	485	436	343	339
Warslow and Elkstones Township	3,597	731	828	854	696	772	715	689	720	574	503	494
Blore :—	2,257	239	164	351	354	333	299	320	302	279	235	250
Blore with Swinscoe Township ‡	1,885	203	164	288	299	273	241	248	224	217	178	176
Calton-in-Blore Township [35] †	372	36	—	63	55	60	58	72	78	62	57	74
Cauldon ‡ . . .	1,494	256	317	350	347	326	350	400	365	322	295	273
Caverswall † . .	5,262	756	900	1,082	1,207	1,505	1,581	3,046	4,082	5,109	6,125	6,880
Cheddleton [36] :—	9,176	1,174	1,392	1,525	1,664	1,824	1,877	2,050	2,098	2,056	1,973	2,766
Basford Township	7,017	209	243	282	300	349	367	428	370	1,832	1,772	2,562
Cheddleton and Rownall Township		775	952	1,061	1,167	1,285	1,294	1,374	1,502			
Consall Township	2,159	190	197	182	197	190	216	248	226	224	201	204
Dilhorne :—	3,776	1,083	1,184	1,409	1,510	1,579	1,615	1,573	1,536	1,637	1,770	2,160
Dilhorne ‡ . .	—	520	—	744	756	736	823	849	734	740	734	787
Forsbrook Township	—	563	—	665	754	843	792	724	802	897	1,036	1,373
Grindon ‡ . . .	3,274	388	403	455	431	404	381	371	381	364	350	355
Horton	4,975	752	794	942	970	942	967	1,046	1,159	1,201	1,216	1,295
Ilam †‡	3,006	177	177	253	210	244	233	243	206	207	228	171
Ipstones	5,697	1,204	1,235	1,425	1,384	1,370	1,292	1,904	1,673	1,417	1,351	1,340
Kingsley (part of) [37] :—												
Whiston Township	—	300	351	403	549	681	675	708	689	—	—	—
Leek (part of) [38] :—	31,819	6,710	7,368	9,035	10,663	11,648	13,207	14,232	15,474	17,138	18,641	20,001
Bradnop Township [39]	3,568	—	420	489	467	442	447	454	445	445	450	405
Stanley Township	5,453	734	766	113	118	122	108	1,241	1,370	1,560	1,759	1,884
Endon Chap. .				445	487	571	658					
Longsdon Township				350	398	405	428					
Heaton Township	2,689	343	346	391	402	430	405	396	361	328	371	359

[34] *Trysull* includes *Woodford Grange* in 1811.

[35] *Calton-in-Blore*, and *Calton-in-Waterfall*. The population of these two places included in that of *Calton-in-Mayfield* in 1811.

[36] *Cheddleton Ancient Parish.*—The increase in population in 1901 is due to the erection and occupation of a County Lunatic Asylum.

[37] *Kingsley Ancient Parish* is situated in Totmonslow Hundred—North and South Divisions. The entire area and population 1881–1901 are shown in the Southern Division.

[38] *Leek Ancient Parish* is situated in Totmonslow Hundred—North and South Divisions.

[39] *Bradnop* was probably included with *Onecote* in 1801.

TABLE OF POPULATION, 1801—1901 (*continued*)

PARISH	Acre-age	1801	1811	1821	1831	1841	1851	1861	1871	1881	1891	1901
Totmonslow Hundred—North Division (cont.)												
Leek (*cont.*)												
Leekfrith Township †	7,542	697	710	806	873	926	877	763	771	821	792	716
Leek and Lowe Township *†	2,722	3,489	3,703	4,855	6,374	7,233	8,602	9,057	10,127	11,486	12,783	14,224
Onecote Chap.[39a]	4,936	615	464	585	456	427	438	463	392	373	401	389
Rushton James Township	1,390	264	324	354	304	304	283	273	281	267	242	229
Rushton Spencer Township	1,860	294	362	359	337	350	355	358	330	341	339	315
Tittesworth Township †	1,659	274	273	288	447	438	606	1,227	1,397	1,517	1,504	1,480
Okeover †‡ . . .	874	42	60	69	62	67	61	61	65	81	81	67
Totmonslow Hundred—South Division												
Alton, or Alveton :—	7,619	1,633	1,898	2,170	2,391	2,390	2,326	2,250	2,235	2,621	2,757	2,889
Alton Township †	2,243	818	934	1,103	1,220	1,168	1,162	1,173	1,074	1,054	1,089	1,227
Cotton, Upper and Lower Township †	2,263	302	408	439	471	519	502	446	477	648	641	681
Denstone Township	771	192	217	230	250	231	232	241	263	441	537	550
Farley Township †	2,342	321	339	398	450	472	430	390	421	478	490	431
Bradley in the Moors ‡	677	75	83	84	75	72	64	43	50	51	65	69
Bramshall ‡ . . .	1,328	193	155	189	170	170	205	199	161	142	146	142
Cheadle *† . . .	6,793	2,750	3,191	3,862	4,119	4.399	4,681	4,803	4,492	4,724	4,884	5,512
Checkley † . . .	6,073	1,374	1,698	2,070	2,247	2,322	2,271	2,428	2,353	2,549	2,659	2,521
Croxden † . . .	2,644	293	263	258	272	293	260	224	191	181	209	209
Draycott in the Moors ‡	3,907	491	536	579	539	518	520	451	430	406	367	351
Ellastone :—	7,416	1,109	1,126	1,328	1,344	1,308	1,312	1,230	1,142	1,051	1,032	966
Calwich Township †	763	94	105	120	136	131	121	85	114	125	142	126
Ellastone Township †	795	294	285	350	361	351	384	384	327	280	274	268
Prestwood Township [40] †	450	80	80	88	77	68	74	55	63	47	46	39
Ramshorn Township [40]	1,509	} 402 {	130	152	130	142	118	118	112	101	82	85
Stanton Township	2,027		298	373	371	393	397	403	342	315	286	297
Wootton Township	1,872	239	228	245	269	223	218	185	184	183	202	151
Gratwich ‡	865	107	110	115	116	119	102	101	92	72	67	57
Kingsley (part of) [40a] †	4,769	673	787	917	867	873	890	1,332	1,196	1,832	1,935	2,283
Kingston ‡	2,037	276	335	355	368	339	326	312	278	280	252	223
Leek (part of) [40b] :—												
Rudyard Township and Manor	1,435	109	115	112	117	90	94	94	70	72	75	81
Leigh [41] ‡ :—	7,205	905	937	1,019	1,038	1,012	1,074	986	954	937	960	915
Leigh	6,223	842	868	947	956	926	965	902	866	866	883	853
Field Township	982	63	69	72	82	86	109	84	88	71	77	62
Mayfield :—	3,987	1,018	1,156	1,435	1,366	1,348	1,313	1,426	1,446	1,529	1,580	1,627
Butterton Chap. ‡	1,499	297	355	432	346	388	352	325	309	231	246	263

[39a] See note 39, *ante.*
[40] *Prestwood* and *Ramshorn.*—The 1811 populations for these places are estimates.
[40a] See note 37, *ante.*
[40b] See note 38, *ante.*
[41] *Leigh Ancient Parish.*—There were some labourers on railway works present in 1851.

TABLE OF POPULATION, 1801—1901 (*continued*)

PARISH	Acreage	1801	1811	1821	1831	1841	1851	1861	1871	1881	1891	1901
Totmonslow Hundred—South Division (cont.)												
Mayfield (*cont.*)												
Calton-in-Mayfield Township [41a] †	376	67	220	87	79	88	88	70	54	64	65	58
Mayfield Township †	1,859	626	581	890	913	847	844	1,005	1,061	1,215	1,252	1,291
Woodhouses Township	253	28	—	26	28	25	29	26	22	19	17	15
Musden Grange Extra Par. †	565	—	—	15	15	21	25	14	19	22	18	8
Rocester	2,537	899	873	1,037	1,040	1,146	1,185	1,175	1,341	1,220	1,288	1,413
Sheen ‡	2,893	362	414	429	366	402	395	427	458	419	364	347
Uttoxeter * †	8,973ᵉ	3,650	4,114	4,658	4,864	4,735	4,990	4,847	4,692	4,981	5,477	6,204
Waterfall :—	2,221	467	455	534	531	517	521	533	504	489	429	481
Calton-in-Waterfall Township [41a] †	596	—	—	73	81	71	76	65	73	74	75	75
Waterfall Township ‡	1,625	—	455	461	450	446	445	468	431	415	354	406
Wetton ‡	2,630	540	593	609	497	485	466	452	397	327	308	290
Lichfield City and Borough												
St. Chad (part of)[41b]	1,102	1,183	1,405	1,816	1,944	2,036	2,112	1,920	2,013	2,205	1,934	2,057
St. Mary	58	2,422	2,382	2,721	2,780	2,634	2,659	2,683	2,784	2,832	2,555	2,281
St. Michael (part of) [41c] :—	3,094ᵉ	1,037	1,123	1,424	1,636	1,977	2,076	2,162	2,412	3,242	3,276	3,546
St. Michael *	2,136	907	994	1,318	1,508	1,817	1,925	1,986	2,255	3,012	3,086	3,265
Pipehill Township [42] †	580ᵉ	95	110	92	111	110	126	156	137	177	144	181
Freeford Hamlet [42a]	378	35	19	14	17	50	25	20	20	53	46	100
The Close Extra Par. ‡	16	200	241	220	247	190	246	235	251	232	212	249
The Friary Extra Par.	11	—	—	—	20	14	9	8	12	9	9	7
Newcastle under Lyme Borough												
Newcastle under Lyme *	554ᵉ	4,604	6,175	7,031	8,192	9,838	10,290	12,638	15,538	16,838	17,805	19,147
Stafford Borough												
St. Mary & St. Chad (part of) [42b] * †	365	3,898	4,868	5,736	6,956	9,245	10,777	10,996	12,212	14,399	13,946	14,060

The following Municipal Boroughs and Urban Districts were coextensive at the Census of 1901 with one or more places mentioned in the Table :—

Municipal Borough or Urban District	Place
Amblecote U.D.	Amblecote Hamlet (Seisdon Hundred—South Division).
Biddulph U.D.	Biddulph Parish (Pirehill Hundred—North Division).
Bilston U.D.	Bilston Township (Seisdon Hundred—North Division).
Cannock U.D.	Cannock Township (Cuttlestone Hundred—East Division).
Rowley Regis U.D.	Rowley Regis Parish (Seisdon Hundred—North Division).
Tipton U.D.	Tipton Parish (Offlow Hundred—South Division).
Wednesbury M.B.	Wednesbury Parish (Offlow Hundred—South Division).
Wolverhampton M.B.	Wolverhampton Township (Seisdon Hundred—North Division).

[41a] See note 35, *ante*.   [41b] See note 15, *ante*.   [41c] See note 16, *ante*.
[42] *Pipehill* is partly in Offlow Hundred—South Division. None shown there.
[42a] See note 17, *ante*.   [42b] See note 26, *ante*.

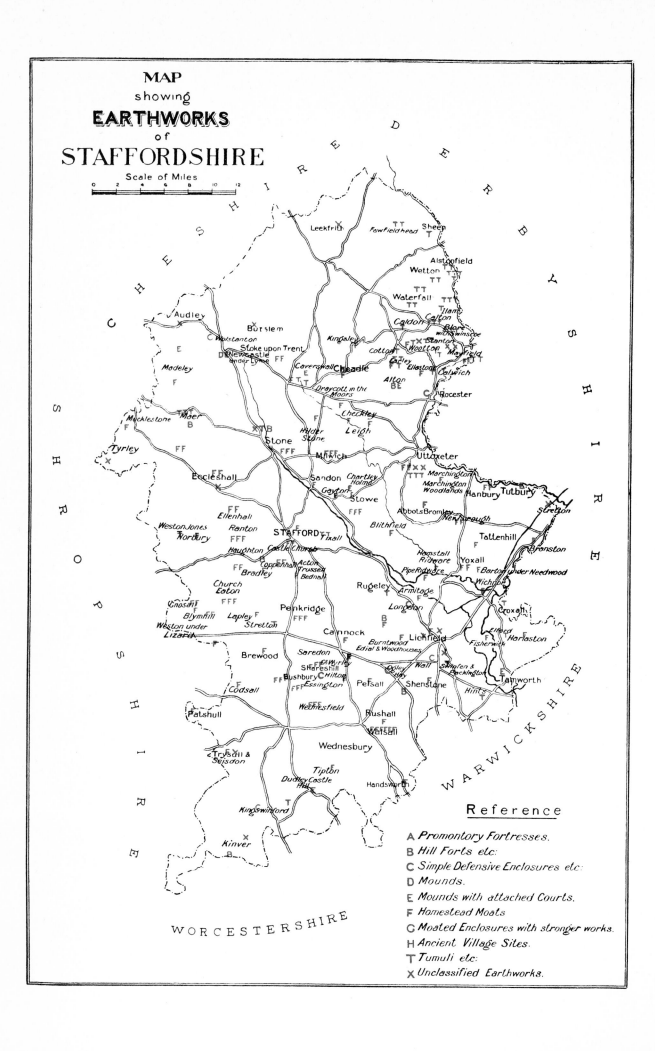

MAP
showing
EARTHWORKS
of
STAFFORDSHIRE

Scale of Miles

Reference

A *Promontory Fortresses.*
B *Hill Forts etc:*
C *Simple Defensive Enclosures etc:*
D *Mounds.*
E *Mounds with attached Courts.*
F *Homestead Moats*
G *Moated Enclosures with stronger works.*
H *Ancient Village Sites.*
T *Tumuli etc:*
X *Unclassified Earthworks.*

ANCIENT EARTHWORKS

The county of Stafford comprises an extent of some fifty-two miles in length and thirty-four miles in extreme width, containing in the whole about one thousand one hundred and seventy-one superficial miles. The surface varies in altitude from 150 ft. to 1,810 ft. above sea level. Rivers flow in its many valleys, measuring altogether an enormous length through lands of the richest character ; and its hills shape into the bossy forms which come of the gravels and new red sandstone, varied by the bare crags of the limestone rocks and the heathery moors and woods of its grit-stones.

Before, however, entering upon any description of the ancient earthworks of this county as they at present exist, reference to the writings of the early historians who dealt with the subject in their day should be alluded to. Camden, Gibson, Erdeswick, Harwood, Plot, Shaw, and others each recorded these works ; some of which have now disappeared. Many of the views of these early writers are by no means to be ignored, and their statements of facts are worthy of consideration.

One at least of the earthworks mentioned by Dr. Plot has now disappeared. At Wrottesley he says :—'There remained (in his day) either the foundation of some ancient *British City* or other fortification of great extent the whole containing in circuit about three or four miles lying part in Staffordshire and part in Shropshire.' So far as diligent and repeated search can now disclose there is nothing of this vast inclosure at present to be seen, nor has minute inquiry ended in information being obtained beyond the bare tradition of its existence. Placing the positions of the earthworks upon the map, it will be found that there is scarcely a parish within our borders which does not contain one or more of these features of remote or later date.

In the classification of these various works we follow the scheme formulated by the Congress of Archaeological Societies :—

Class A.—Fortresses partly inaccessible, by reason of precipices, cliffs, or water, additionally defended by artificial works, usually known as promontory fortresses.

Class B.—Fortresses on hill-tops with artificial defences, *following the natural line of the hill* ; or, though usually on high ground, less dependent on natural slopes for protection.

Class C.—Rectangular or other simple inclosures, including forts and towns of the Romano-British period.

Class D.—Forts consisting only of a mound with encircling ditch or fosse.

Class E.—Fortified mounds, either artificial or partly natural, with traces of an attached court or bailey, or of two or more such courts.

Class F.—Homestead moats, such as abound in some lowland districts, consisting of simple inclosures formed into artificial islands by water moats.

Class G.—Inclosures, mostly rectangular, partaking of the form of F, but protected by stronger defensive works, ramparted and fossed, and in some instances provided with outworks.

Class H.—Ancient village sites protected by walls, ramparts or fosses.

Class X.—Defensive works which fall under none of these headings.

It is difficult in the county of Stafford to follow strictly the above classification owing to certain peculiarities of types. For this reason all the camps on hill-tops have been placed under class B, and all the fortified mounds in the above classification divided into classes D and E have been grouped together.

Most of the plans have been taken from the Ordnance maps, which have been checked and measured approximately on the spot ; and some of the plans and all the sections have been produced from approximate measurements, and levelling taken on the sites. In every instance personal inspection has been made either by the writer or by surveyors in his employment.

The general position of the hill forts in relation to this county may be stated as follows:—In the extreme south-western corner of the shire is the fort on Kinver Edge ; at about forty miles in a direct line northward there is ' Berth Hill ' in the parish of Maer; at nearly a right angle to this, eastwards, is ' Bunbury ' in the parish of Alton, about eighteen miles distant ; at about twenty-four miles nearly due south from this, in the parish of Shenstone, is ' Castle Old Fort,' which is fourteen miles north-east from Kinver Edge. These four examples lie near to the boundaries of the shire. The remaining three, follow a winding diagonal line between ' Castle Old Fort ' and ' Berth Hill ; the first of these, ' Castle Ring,' being 7 miles from Castle Old Fort ; ' Bury Ring ' being 10 miles from ' Castle Ring ': ' Bury Bank,' in a direct line northwards, about 10 miles from Castle Ring, and about 5 miles from Berth Hill.

It will be noticed from this that for the whole width east and west of the county, and for 17 miles from north to south, the extreme north part has no example of the description termed the hill fort.

It would not be of any profit to speculate on the reasons which led to the placing of these forts in their actual positions, but it may be emphasized that those near the east and west boundaries lie in lines very nearly north and south, and that the two to the north run in line nearly due east and west, and also that the central area between the others is well covered by the intermediate forts. That this class of earthworks was for the purposes of succour and defence there can be no question. That collectively they form the means of safety over a given area is tolerably clear. They would seem to bear internal evidence that they all were constructed by the same people, for their main characteristics are strikingly alike. In every case their situation is on high ground from which full command is obtained, both of their immediate surroundings and of very extensive distant prospects. In fact, from each of them a panoramic view of vast extent is obtainable. In each a certain length of boundary abuts upon the upper edge of the steep slope of natural hills, the remaining boundaries are more or less circular in form, with the exception of that at Kinver Edge, which is distinguished as being rectangular ; thus, speaking generally, they are irregular in shape. The mode of their construction seems to have been as follows :—The site having been carefully selected with command and defence in view, and the size determined upon, the ground within the prescribed area was used for procuring by excavation the necessary materials for the inner vallum, in some cases mixed with rubble stone. The material so procured, with that from the fosses, was thrown up into screen banks along the lines of the adjacent steep slopes for about 6 ft. in height. On the other boundaries from one to three banks were thrown up with corresponding fosses of varying widths and depths. The magnitude of these walls and intrenchments was determined by the nature of the adjacent lands. Where they were flat and afforded easy approach to the fort, there the works of defence were multiplied; but where natural obstacles to approach existed in the shape of slopes or otherwise the works of defence were reduced to a minimum. But what these forts always afforded was an internal area of some acres in extent, but varying in size, inclosed within a well-raised vallum, effecting the exclusion from without of the inclosed area. On the outside of the inclosing wall were either the natural cliff-like slopes or the raised banks and sunk ditches, giving to those within the inclosure security from surprise and a very formidable defence against any invading foe. The tops of the walls it is considered had possibly the further defence of a stockade sloping outwards from the foot and making a solid barrier in addition to the walls and intrenchments. None of the intrenchments in this class of work were served with water as an aid to defence in the examples within the county.

Since the accounts given by the early writers on these earthworks very little has been added with regard to them, but the present writer did, in 1892, read a paper on the subject before the North Staffordshire Field Club, and also another at the congress of the British Archaeological Association held in York in 1891; and in the *Court Guide* for 1902 the subject was further referred to, when the main characteristics of the early forts were described as follows :—

1. Their situation is at a high level.
2. They command panoramic views, so that the surrounding country is everywhere within direct sight.
3. They are near to a water supply of stream or spring.
4. They make use of natural means of security to a full practicable extent by hugging the upper edge of a precipitous slope or cliff, and when this terminates fosses are dug and ramparts raised.
5. Their entrances are secluded and flanked by commanding mounds.
6. The surface of the inclosed area has been shaped by the removal of earth for the ramparts, and it forms a shelter and fortified space; the outlines are irregular and unsymmetrical.
7. The approaches are circuitous, secluded, and under view from the ramparts.

Their general aspect is that of a defended retreat safe in any direction from surprises of any kind and offering secure protection to a whole community, with its herds, flocks, and other belongings. These defensive forts in some cases have command of rivers, and in others lie upon their tributaries. The courses of rivers were, it must be remembered, commonly resorted to by the invader.

There still remains in this county strong evidence of Roman earthworks (class C), as may be seen in the remains of camps at Chesterton near to Newcastle under Lyme, at Barrow Hill near Rocester, at Longdon near Lichfield, and at Green's Forge west of Dudley.

The mound and mound and bailey type (classes D and E) of defensive earthwork is conspicuously present in this county, and exists at the county town of Stafford, and at Heighley, Newcastle under Lyme, Alton, Tutbury,

Chartley, Tamworth, and Dudley, and in a modified form at Caverswall, Eccleshall, and Lichfield.

Of the homestead moats (class F), which are numerous, it has been thought necessary only to give a tabulated list.

A tabulated list has also been given of the lows and other burial mounds.

In conclusion the writer has to tender his thanks to all those who have assisted him in his task, more especially to his son, the late Mr. Thomas Rickman Lynam, who worked for months in measuring and levelling, and who stood the trials of three years in the Royal Engineers in the South African war, but succumbed to the dread cold and wet of England's last spring.

HILL FORTS

(Class B)

ALTON : BUNBURY.—Of this fort Dr. Stebbing Shaw relates :—

> Near Alveton, or Alton, in the north-west borders of this county, upon a lofty situation in the lands of the Earl of Shrewsbury, there still remains near the lodge another fortress like that at Mere, only very much larger, which they call Bunbury. The form of it is irregular, being encompassed with a double, and sometimes treble trench, according to the situation required on the north-west and north-east sides, all the rest being naturally inaccessible, the whole including about an hundred acres . . . This work still remains very visible, and I was informed that an ancient sword was found very lately and sent to Sir Joseph Banks.

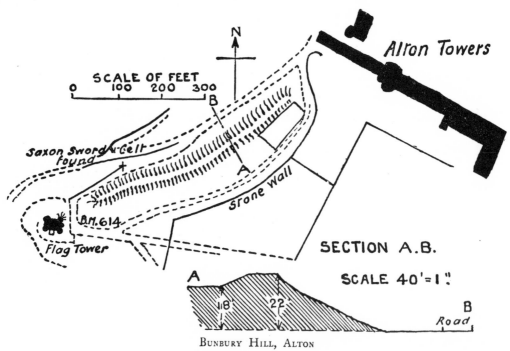

BUNBURY HILL, ALTON

Since the time of Stebbing Shaw the visibility of this fort has almost vanished, for part of it became the site of the far-famed Alton Towers and its sumptuous gardens. Happily a fragment of the hundred acres of the fort still remains ; its point of commencement starting immediately at the

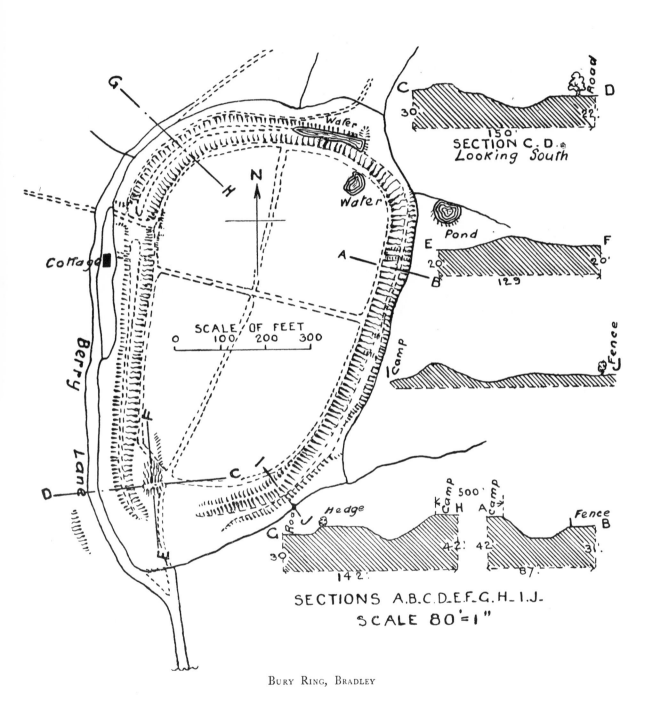

G

Water

N

H

Water

Pond

A

Cottage

B

Camp

SCALE OF FEET
0   100   200   300

C   I

D

Berry Lane

C

SECTION C. D.
Looking South

150'
30'
22'

E
F
20'
20'
129

Fence

Camp   500   Camp
K   H   A
Hedge
G   Road   J
30   142'   42'   42'   87'   31'
Fence
B

SECTIONS A.B.C.D.E.F.G.H.I.J.
SCALE 80'=1"

Bury Ring, Bradley

back of 'The Towers,' with a termination at the Flag Tower, and its banks and intrenchments may still be traced amidst the thickly studded and rugged woods and grounds. The foot of Bunbury Hill reached to the River Churnet, and barely outside its borders Alton railway station exists at the present time. This spot has had its marked features through long ages past and the valley here is unsurpassed for its natural beauty, and 'The Towers' on one side and the castle and monastery on the other render the landscape specially charming. The original hundred acres was chosen as the site of the fort when the hill was a barren waste.

BRADLEY.—BURY RING is in this parish at Billington, less than five miles to the west of the county town of Stafford, and only a few yards to the north of the main road between Stafford and Newport, Salop. It has been thought that this was the site of one of the three castles said to have been erected at Stafford, and it must be noted that there is one point in its construction which differs in an important particular from the usual type of these forts, namely that there is no inner vallum remaining except one short length next the inclosure which here bounds the edge of the intrenchment. Also it must be noticed that its general form is less irregular in shape; but having regard to its situation and general details of construction it may perhaps be concluded that it belongs to the period, and was the work of the same people that formed the class of forts of which we are now treating. It is placed on the top and side of a hill, roughly elliptical in form, surrounded by ramparts and intrenchments after the manner of the examples previously noticed (except as above pointed out), with a bastion of earth strictly guarding its simple entrance at its southern end, features all corresponding in character with this class. The intrenchments are deeper and broader than is usual. It would seem also that the present roadway on the west was originally another intrenchment. The inner extreme length is 250 yds., and width 158 yds., with an area of 7 acres. At the present time there is water within and outside the fort and Butterbank Brook is about half a mile away. The difference in this example, as pointed out above, may indicate a later date of construction. The nearest level on the main road between Stafford and Newport is 449 ft.

CANNOCK and LONGDON.—CASTLE RING, the next example to be noticed, is about $3\frac{1}{2}$ miles from Rugeley, and is situated in Beaudesert Old Park, within the area of the Cannock Chase Coal Field, one of the lodges of the present park being at its north-east corner. It lies less than half a mile north of Gentleshaw. The fort is five-sided : the two sides to the south-east and south-west are of equal length, the three other sides are of unequal length, that to the north being the longest, and that to the east the shortest. Each of the sides is practically straight in line, and they have rounded angles at their junctions both external and internal of the intrenchments. There are double ramparts and intrenchments on all sides, and to the east an additional set. The north side abuts upon the edge of a steep slope, the others face to open lands. The extreme length within the ramparts is 267 yds., the width 203 yds., and the area consists of $8\frac{1}{2}$ acres. There are indications of entrances in the north-east corner and on the south-west side, and a pathway now runs between these two points. The nearest level to the fort is given at 671·2 ft. The situation affords magnificent prospects, quite panoramic, and it is affirmed that no less than seven

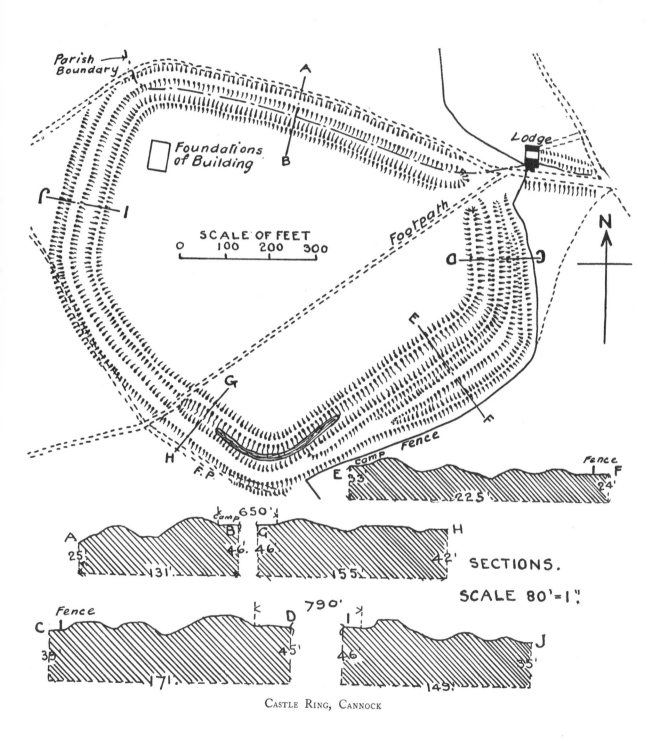

CASTLE RING, CANNOCK

counties can be seen from its summit. The geometrical form of the fort and its rounded angles seem to indicate that Roman hands have been concerned in its origin, but again the general character of the work is in accordance with the attributes of this class. The configuration of its outline tends to the conclusion that the claims of due fortification have been skilfully met.

KINVER EDGE.—In its situation this fort closely corresponds with the majority of its class. It is on a high level and commands most extensive views, the Malvern and other hills and intermediate country being clearly seen from it, and the usual protecting slopes largely prevail here ; but in the shape of

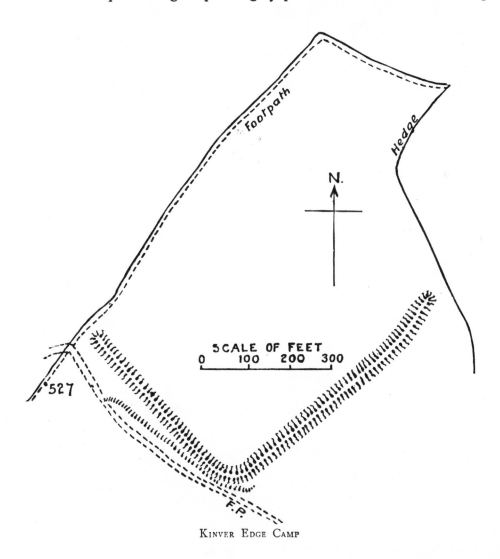

KINVER EDGE CAMP

its outline it is out of all conformity with the other examples. This may have arisen from the fact that its longest side, chosen for its usefulness, is a straight line following that of the natural 'edge' of the sloping hill to the north-west. The north-east side also is similar, thus causing a great irregularity in the general form of the fort. The south-west and south-east sides are also practically straight with a rounded corner at their junction, and apparently there was an entrance at the extremity of each of these lines. The south-west and south-east sides have a single line of vallum and fosse with slight indications of a former double line. The north-west line against the

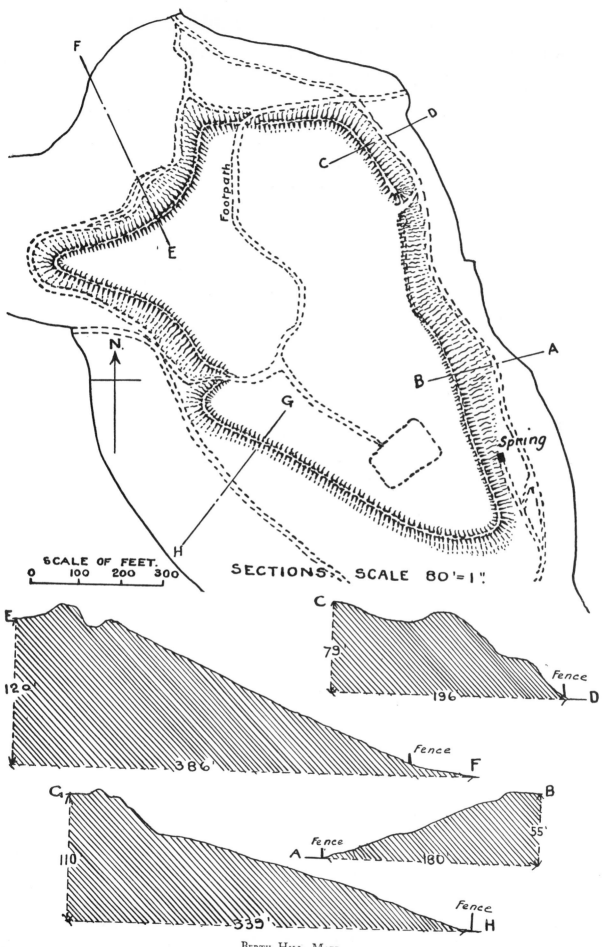

SCALE OF FEET.

0   100   200   300

SECTIONS. SCALE 80'=1".

E

120'

386'

C

79'

196'

Fence

D

Fence

F

G

110'

339'

Fence

B

55'

A

Fence

180'

Fence

H

N.

Footpath

Spring

BERTH HILL, MAER

339

slope of hill has a scarped inside vallum. The north-east side is edged by precipitous slopes. This side of the ramparts may have been scarped, and its irregularity of form exaggerated thereby.

The non-conformity of the general shape here would seem to suggest that the following of a hard and fast rule as to form is not always to be looked for, and that the advantages of site govern the shape to some extent.

The extreme internal length is 300 yds., and width 180 yds., with an internal area of 7½ acres. Its most striking feature is perhaps its apparent cornered safety of position, more than half its boundary being defended by natural means. The nearest given level is 463·2 ft., and it lies within about half a mile of the parish church.

LONGDON, see CANNOCK.

MAER.—BERTH HILL, formerly called Bruff or Burgh Hill, is situated less than two miles from Whitmore railway station on the London and North Western line between Stafford and Crewe. The nearest contour level on the 6-in. Ordnance map is 394 ft. To the south-west runs a road between Hill Chorlton and Blackbrook. Within a short distance to the north-east is the road between Whitmore and Market Drayton, and within this and the fort is 'Warhill,' and to the east 'Berry Hill' and 'Sandy Low.' There is an auspicious sound about these names, as also in 'Camp Hill,' about three-quarters of a mile to the north-west, about which the early histories indulge in pleasant theories.

The form of the fort is very irregular, being governed largely by the outline of the hill-top. It may be described as an irregular triangle with its base northward and apex southward. The north-west angle runs out to a sharp projecting promontory. The main entrance has been on the north-west side, with another entrance on the north-east side, the former at a high and the latter at a low level, both secluded and specially defended. The present site is wooded. The extreme length within the inner vallum is 355 yds., and the extreme width 225 yds., the area being 9 acres. The inner banks are all formed of a mixture of earth and rubble stone, and there is nothing in the nature of building stone now to be seen here. The acute-angled promontory on the north-west side, which is mounded, suggests a special military provision, commanding as it does long lengths of rampart, the two entrances, and a clear view of the immediate surroundings. Dr. Stebbing Shaw, quoting Plot, has this quaint description of the fort :—

> An old fortification in the Parish of Mere, commonly called the Bruff, probably a corruption of Burgh, fenced in some places with a double trench and rampire, the agger above the trench being partly made of stone and the whole of a very irregular form according as the figure of the hill would admit.

The water supply is from a spring within the boundaries of the fort, and its waters serve the present hall and village of Maer in bountiful measure. The little stream known by the name of 'Blackbrook' has its rise within about a mile of the fort, near the 'Wellings,' and with the River Tern delivers its waters into the River Severn, reversing the general flow of the rivers of this county, which is into the River Trent.

ANCIENT EARTHWORKS

SHENSTONE.—CASTLE OLD FORT is within 2½ miles of the Warwickshire border to the south-east, and 2½ miles from Watling Street on the north, and 3 miles from the Roman city of Etocetum or Wall, which is within 2 miles of the city of Lichfield. To the south of the fort is the Upper Stonnal road, the nearest level being 500 ft. The form of the plan of this fort follows others of its class, and may be likened to that of the longitudinal section or

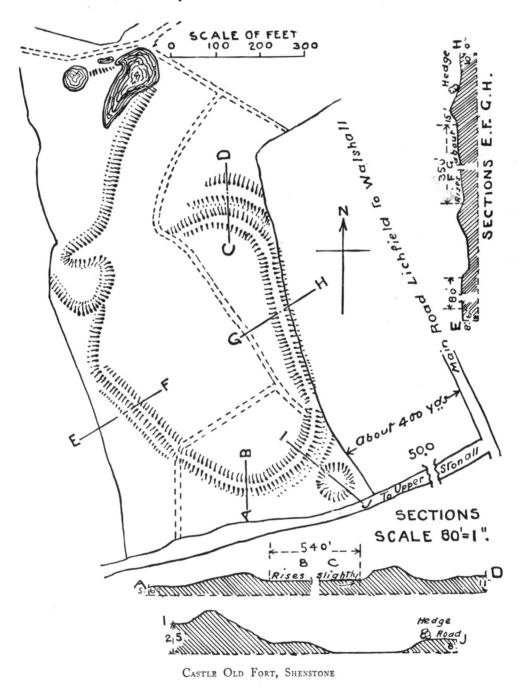

CASTLE OLD FORT, SHENSTONE

an egg, the broader end being to the north. The trace of symmetry in its outline follows that of 'Castle Ring.' Its extreme inner length is about 171 yds., and width 138 yds. The inner vallum is fairly complete except at the north-west end, and it would appear that there has been a second intrenchment throughout except perhaps on the west. The north-west

341

intrenchment has partly been removed. Here probably was the entrance with the usual bastion of earth on one or both sides of it, and the length of vallum possibly belonging to another branch of the fort, but this is only conjecture. There is a large and a small pool of water to the north of the fort. The fencing of the area somewhat encroaches upon the ancient work. The situation conforms only in a measure to that of the class in which it is placed, its altitude not being a very high one, and there is some absence of abutting steeply sloping ground. It may be that the duplicate defence, of which there is some indication, took the place of these characteristics, and of course the necessities of a particular site must always have been to the fore in the adoption thereof. The site is now woody, and cannot be recognized without close inspection.

STONE.—BURY BANK lies in the valley of the Trent at a point some 12 miles from its northern sources, and 5 miles south of Stoke-on-Trent, and 2 miles north of the ancient town of Stone, and here at Darlaston the valley and the swelling wooded hills present great natural charms, and amidst them 'Bury Bank' is planted. The road level to the east of it is given as 321·4, and that immediately to the south of it as 356·4. Its form may be called that of an irregular ellipse with the longer axis north-west and south-east, having an extreme length within the inner vallum of 239 yds, and an extreme width of 115 yds. The area within the inner rampart contains 3½ acres.

With the exception of a length to the north-west, steep slopes surround the works. The exact lines of the defences would seem to be not only governed by the contours of the ground, but also shaped after the rules of fortification. The ramparts and intrenchments are regulated by the necessities of defence. There is a well-defined entrance to the north-west shaped as it were into a specially defended barbican. In the opposite quarter to this entrance are indications of another entrance. In the midst of the inclosure there is in the southern part a raised mound which is remarkable as not occurring in any of the other Staffordshire cases of this class of fort. Whether its purpose was for military tactics, or as a place of sepulture it is hard to say; for this was the 'Royal Mansion' of King Wlferus who governed Mercia from 657 to 676, and according to the suggestion of Dr. Plot it may have been the place of his burial, or it is not beyond probability that this mound carried a wooden structure as a last resort for safety within the fort, and was in fact a prototype of the Norman keep. What however its special purpose was could only be determined by the work of the pick and spade, but this is hardly possible now as trees have been thickly planted over the fort within recent years. The present writer in 1892 had by permission a day's digging done, but without any satisfactory result. Robert Garner, F.L.S., in the supplement to his *Natural History of the County of Stafford*, writes :—

> The author was one of a party this year (1860) to open the large mound in the centre of the camp at Bury Bank; an attempt made to find the interments was unsuccessful, for at the base, in the centre, nothing was seen but a heap of stones, some bits of charcoal, and small fragments of bone.

It is a pity that these disregarded fragments were not preserved, for they strongly suggest interment. The inner vallum of the area was cut through at the time of the day's digging above mentioned, and its section showed its construction to be of earth and rubble stone. To the west of the mound

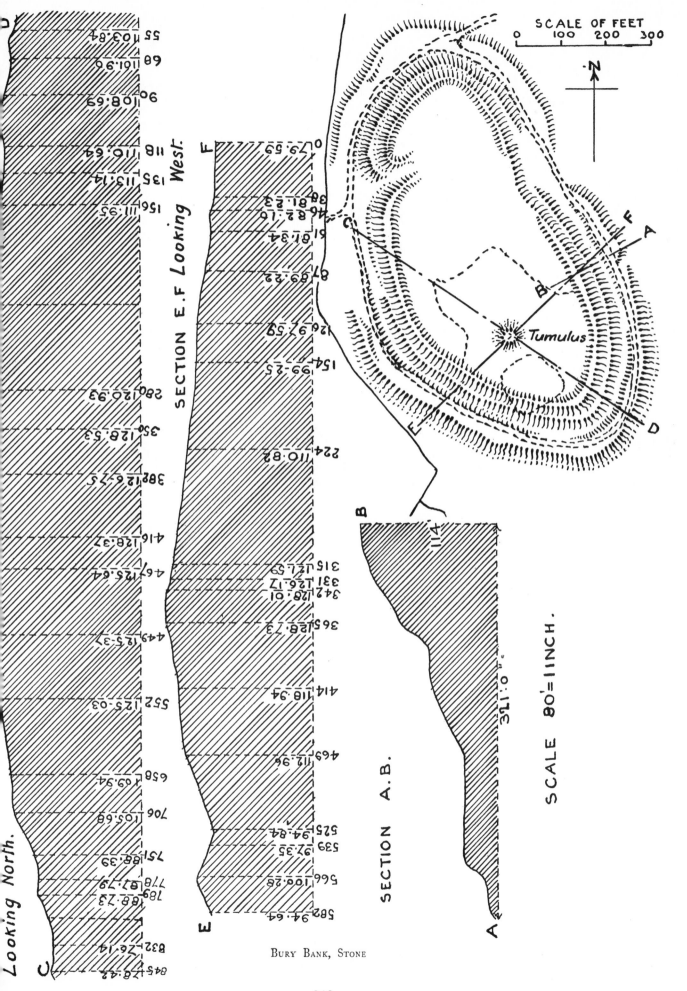

SCALE OF FEET

N

Tumulus

Looking North.

SECTION E.F *Looking West.*

SECTION A.B.

SCALE 80'=1 INCH.

BURY BANK, STONE

343

there was some appearance of the crown of a well, but no tangible proof of it could be established. Otherwise the nearest water supply would be the River Trent, some 300 yds. distant, though the natural conformation of the land to the north-west would bring water to the site. The property now belongs to the duke of Sutherland.

SIMPLE DEFENSIVE INCLOSURES

(Class C)

Chesterton, *see* Wolstanton.

Kingswinford: Green's Forge.—In this example there exists the most extensive remains of this class of camp in the county. It is more or

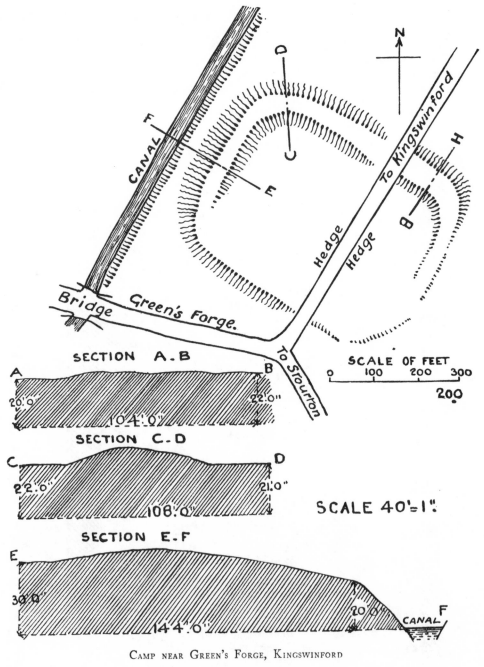

Camp near Green's Forge, Kingswinford

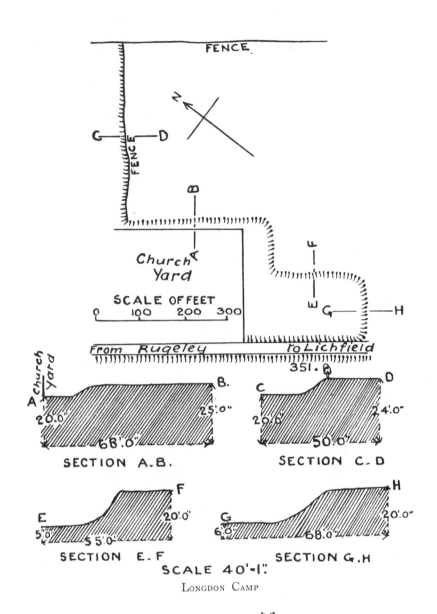

FENCE

N

G—D

FENCE

B

Church
Yard

A

SCALE OF FEET
0 100 200 300

F

E G——H

From Rugeley to Lichfield

351.0

A Church Yard   B.   C   D
20.0"   25.0"   20.0"   24.0"
          68.0"   50.0"

SECTION A.B.   SECTION C.D

E   F   G   H
          20.0"   20.0"
5.0'   55.0'   6.0'   68.0'

SECTION E.F   SECTION G.H

SCALE 40'=1".

Longdon Camp

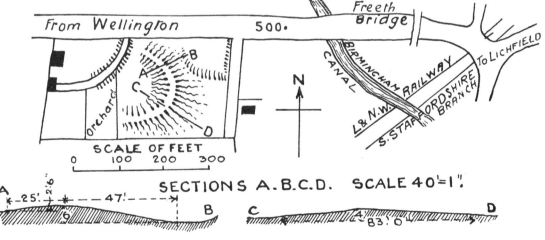

From Wellington   500.   Freeth
Bridge

B

Orchard   A
          C

D

SCALE OF FEET
0 100 200 300

N

Birmingham Canal

L & N.W. Railway

S. Staffordshire Branch

to Lichfield

SECTIONS A.B.C.D. SCALE 40'=1".

A ←25'→ 2'6" ←——47'——→   B   C   D
          6'   83.0'

Knaves Castle, Ogley Hay

less indicated throughout its full extent, and is quadrilateral in form with rounded angles, being 206 yds. in length and 160 yds. in width, containing an area of 6¾ acres. A stream runs within a short distance. A main road crosses it in a north-easterly and south-westerly direction. Its surrounding vallum has been disturbed and weathered away to some extent, and the general construction differs from its fellows in that the vallum is raised above the inclosed area, and its situation is at a low level, the nearest altitude being given at 200 ft. It is situated about seven miles to the south-west of Wolverhampton. There is no known Roman road to this camp.

LONGDON.—It is just possible to say that at Longdon there are indications of a Roman camp. They occur immediately to the south-east of the church, and consist at present of several short lengths of slopes from the plateau of the camp, which is on a high ground but without discernible boundaries, though faint traces of them may be seen. Like the other cases of this class the camp surfaces occupy the highest level—dimensions cannot be given, nor the area; the nearest level is stated at 351 ft. Longdon is halfway between Lichfield and Rugeley; there is a stream of water near to the site.

OGLEY HAY : KNAVES CASTLE.—The remains of this work are situated on Watling Street at the level of 500 ft., but they are very slight and near to the line of a roadway leading from the Watling Street.

ROCESTER.—BARROW HILL has but scanty remains consisting for the most part only of the north-west and south-east angles of the camp, but the sides are to some extent traceable along the boundaries. It is to be noticed here that contrary to the case in the hill forts the area of the camp itself has the highest ground, and the slopes run from its edges. This points to a material difference in the methods of construction and indeed of purpose. Though this camp is on an elevated site on the side of a hill its area is conspicuously open and not protected by the surrounding vallum as in the hill forts, indicating that the display of the camp was designed, rather than a sheltered obscurity, which suggests a marked difference of purpose. The situation is immediately above Barrow Hill on Dove Cliff, and about three-quarters of a mile north of Rocester and about eighteen miles from Chesterton. Its dimensions may be given as 147 yds. north and south and 167 yds. east and west, and its form rectangular with rounded angles and containing an area of 6¼ acres; the nearest stated altitude being 459 ft., and it commands very extensive prospects.

Immediately to the north of the camp is a tumulus or barrow—which no doubt gives name to the locality—whilst the camp is unnamed. The Ordnance map bears record that in 1872 Roman coins and pottery were found in the barrow, and in 1894 some fragments of Roman pottery and glass were disclosed on slight digging being made at the camp by members of the North Staffordshire Field Club by permission of Captain Dawson, the writer hereof being present. The River Churnet falls into the Dove near to Rocester.

SHARESHILL.—A small work in this parish, from its form and situation, has something of the appearance of a Roman origin. It is a square with

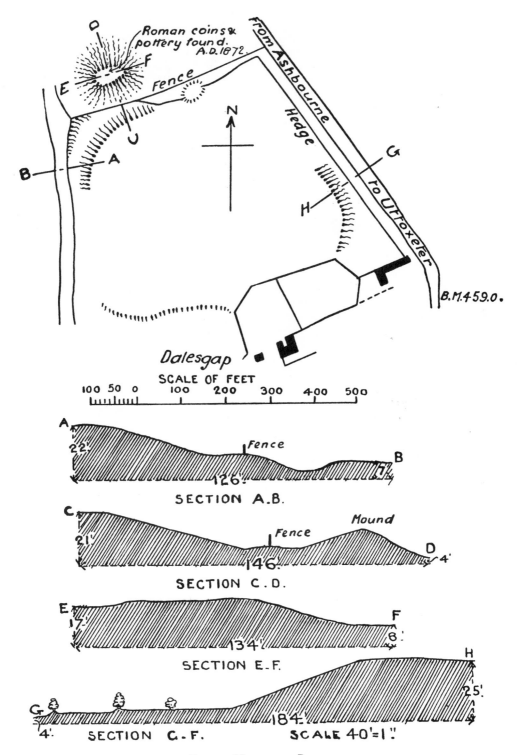

BARROW HILL, NEAR ROCESTER

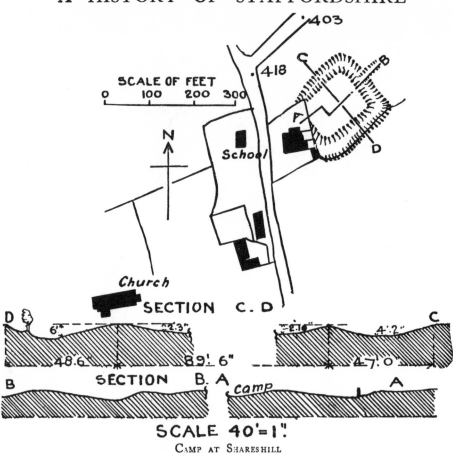

SCALE OF FEET

SECTION C. D

SECTION B. A

SCALE 40'= 1".

CAMP AT SHARESHILL

rounded angles, 191 ft. by 163 ft. over all, and is encompassed by vallum and fosse. The altitude is 418 ft.

WALL.—Camden and Plot both agree that the village of Wall is the Etocetum of the Romans, standing as it does at the crossing of Watling and Icknield Streets, about one mile and a half south-south-west of the city of Lichfield and being 32 miles from Wroxeter (Uriconium) on the west and 12 miles from Mancetter (Manduesedum) on the east with Pennocrucium and Uxacona between them. A plan and sections are shewn indicating the remains in relation to their present position. A further description will be found under the article on 'Roman Remains.'

WOLSTANTON.—CHESTERTON is within two miles north-west of Newcastle-under-Lyme. From the plan given of this camp or station it will be seen that it was almost a true square containing from 22 to 23 acres of area, two of the sides averaging 303 yds. long and the other two 289 yds. It is situated on elevated land at the height of 566 ft. above sea level, and its site commands the surrounding country for many miles distant. The surface of the camp is very little out of the level, but the present remains are only slight and are confined mostly to a part of its north-west side. There can be little doubt that the roadway to the north-east was originally a line of fosse. On the north-west side the fosse remains for some length in a very impressive form from its great dimensions. Its present south-west termination would seem to represent the position of the central entrance on this side. On the south-west and south-east sides there are indications on the site of the positions of the last-named boundaries, following the line of an old lane and the hedge as shown on the plan.

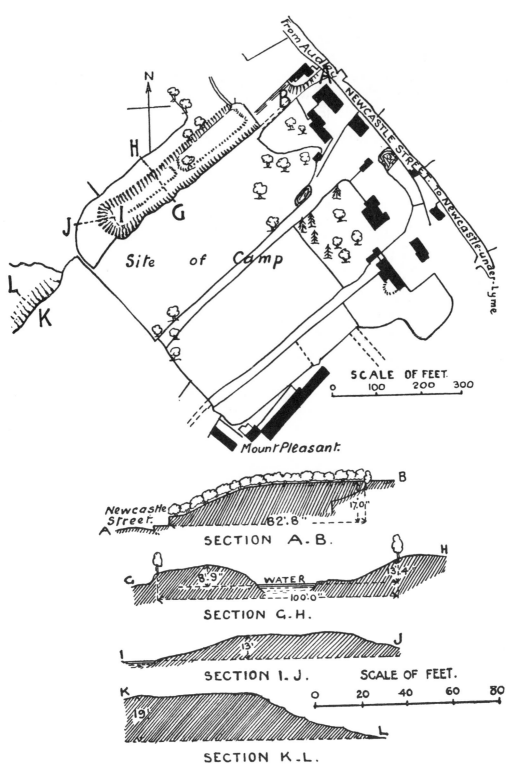

SCALE OF FEET.
0   100   200   300

SECTION A.B.

SECTION G.H.

SECTION I.J.

SCALE OF FEET.
0   20   40   60   80

SECTION K.L.

Camp at Chesterton, Wolstanton

349

MOUNDS AND MOUNDS WITH ONE OR MORE ATTACHED COURTS

(Classes D and E)

ALTON CASTLE stood upon the summit of a precipitous face of bare cliff rising from the valley of the River Churnet, and is said to have been built by Theobald de Verdun in the reign of Edward II. Its situation on the one side of the valley here with 'The Towers' on the opposite with their wooded slopes and long stretch of prospects in every direction give to this spot a truly beautiful aspect. With a sheer precipice on the north-west and

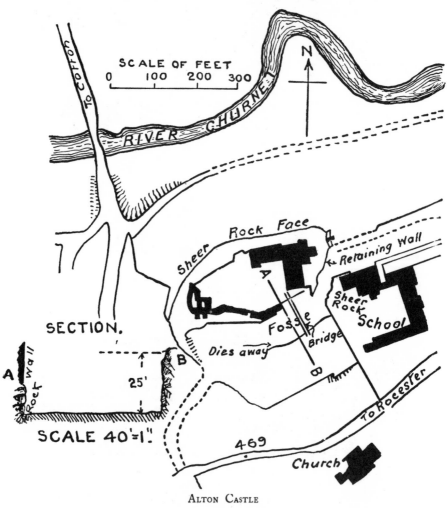

ALTON CASTLE

south-west sides the only other security called for was to the north-east and south-east, and here a great fosse some 19 yds. in width and 9 yds. in depth cut clear out of the rock, together with the precipitous face of rock on the valley sides, isolates the precincts of the castle from the neighbouring land. The approach from the valley was by a slope on the western side, well commanded from the castle walls, and the entrance was from the fosse near to the south-west corner of the great retaining wall which supported the castle area. It is not easy to define the form of the castle in consequence of the many alterations which have taken place ; but it would appear to have strictly met military exigencies, having generally a long oval outline.

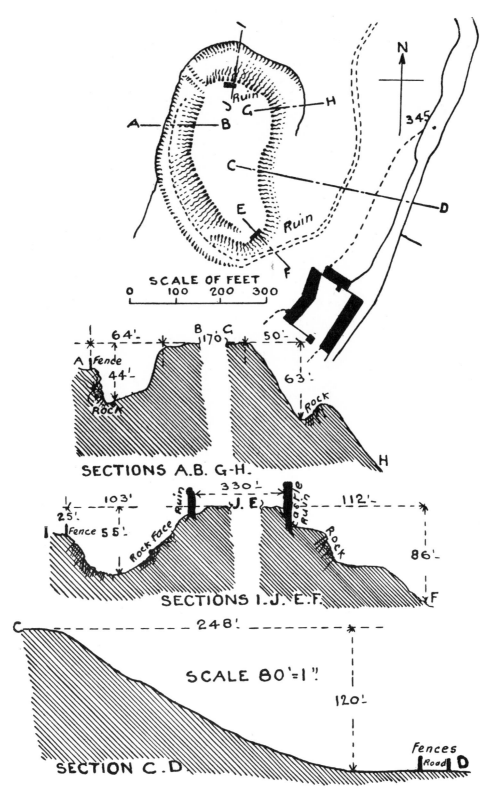

SCALE OF FEET

0   100   200   300

SECTIONS A.B. G-H.

SECTIONS I. J. E. F.

SCALE 80'=1"

SECTION C.D

Heighley Castle, Audley

The castle and the church are in close proximity to one another. The earthwork in this case, cut as it was through the solid rock, was of important character though not very extensive. Altitude 469 ft.

AUDLEY.—HEIGHLEY CASTLE is situated about 4½ miles westward of Newcastle under Lyme. It is on high ground at about the altitude of 345 ft. above sea level. The prospects from it are very extensive and embrace the view of the Church Stretton, Welsh and other hills. The site of the building was on a rocky hill which, however, was not formed by the raising of a mound but by the isolation of a peak by the hewing away of the surrounding rock and then forming out of the side of the hill a clear mound. At the same time there was constructed a fosse of great dimensions and stern aspect, being in places upwards of 30 ft. deep and of 50 ft. in width. It is said that the material from the excavation afforded stone for the masonry of the castle which was built by Henry de Audley in 1233. A stream of water passes near the foot of the castle. Heighley is now the property of the Lord Crewe. The plateau is of a pear shape, and the whole work contains an area of about 3¼ acres.

CAVERSWALL CASTLE is situated in the parish of Caverswall and stands to the north-west of the parish church. There are fragments of the lower masonry still remaining of William de Caverswall's work in the time of

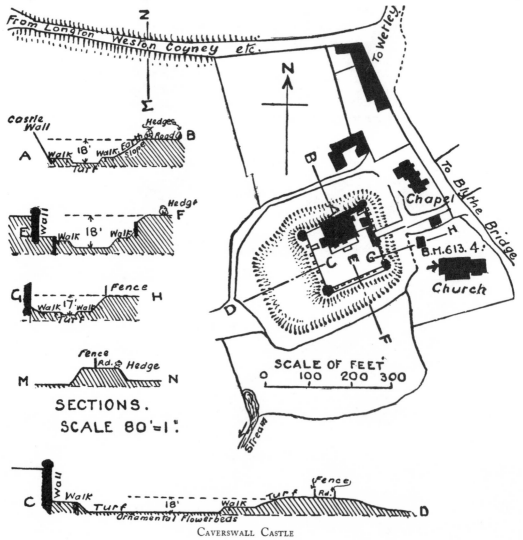

CAVERSWALL CASTLE

Edward II. It is not possible to say how much of the present dry moat belongs to the original castle. The situation is at an altitude of 613 ft., but assimilates to that of the church and village. The moat was entirely sunk from the natural surface of the land, and its sections have in recent years been moulded for the formation of the pleasure grounds. The River Blythe runs from north to south near to the house.

CHARTLEY HOLME.—CHARTLEY CASTLE stands on a wooded hill. Its earthworks consist of a mound and an inner and outer bailey separated by a fosse, the whole being surrounded by a double fosse. The main direction of the works is east and west, the mound being at the west end, which is brought to a slight angle. The length of the inner bailey is 83 yds., and the width 43 yds., partly inclosed by walls and bastions. The outer bailey is 66 yds. long by 60 yds. wide.

To the west of the castle is the site of a moated manor house to be noticed hereafter; and to the north of this is a very perfect quadrangular earthwork, 57 yds. by 31 yds. within the area, having fosse and vallum on the longer sides, and fosse only on the shorter. A brook skirts the work on the north. The altitude is 313 ft.

DUDLEY : CASTLE HILL.—This castle has in some respects the most commanding position of any within the county. It is situated on a high wooded hill rising from a valley far below its site, and encompassed by earthworks of greater magnitude than all others, and facing to a broad open country with the town of Dudley at its back. It presents a great promontory stern and predominant.

Within a central area a raised mound rises to a considerable height, affording a commanding position for the main part of the defensive works. As to the level of the site, section A B shows that in a horizontal length of 424 ft. there is a rise of 140 ft. At G H, with a length of 517 ft., the rise is 130 ft.; and at I J, with a length of 376 ft., a rise of 119 ft. These figures show the precipitous character of the works. The intrenchments measure in some places from 50 ft. to 60 ft. in width, and some 15 ft. in depth.

The natural hill must have required much labour to bring it into its present form. There are caverns beneath the hill, such as are found in Derbyshire and elsewhere. Its nearest altitude on the Ordnance maps is 700 ft.

NEWCASTLE UNDER LYME.—All that remains of this castle is a fragment of a mutilated mound of earth much lowered from its original height and reduced in area,

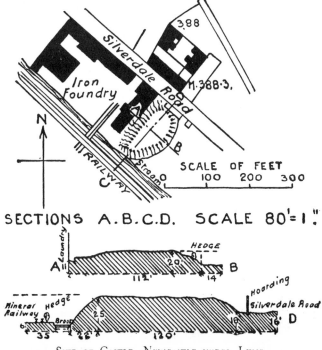

SITE OF CASTLE, NEWCASTLE UNDER LYME

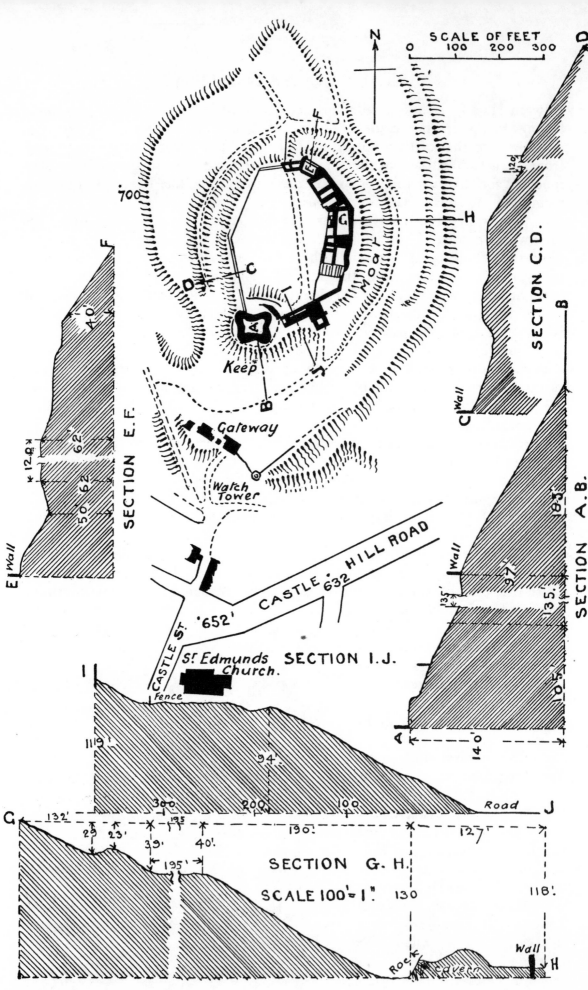

DUDLEY CASTLE

354

covering now a space of only about 150 ft. by 90 ft., and being not more than 20 ft. in height. It has been said it was originally built in a pool. Its situation is known as Pool Dam; though in the midst of the parish of Newcastle, Pool Dam was until recently in the parish of Stoke on Trent. The nearest altitude given in the Ordnance map is 388 ft.

STAFFORD.—Everyone passing this prominent feature of wooded hill and crowning towers rising from the low level of the flat meadows beneath it at Stafford, credits the building with hoary age, but this is not the actual case, for whatever may have been in the past the present building is of recent date; but of the mound on which the building stands more has to be said.

The earthwork consists of an oval mound with its axis north-east and south-west, measuring on the top 63 yds. by 50 yds. On its summit is a raised hillock of elliptical shape whereon the present building now stands. The height of the mound above the fosse is in places 35 ft. The entrance has been at the south-east, and duly defended. The slope of the mound starts from the plateau itself. The altitude is 476 ft. From the Anglo-Saxon Chronicle we learn that in 913 the Lady Ethelfleda built a fortress at Stafford.

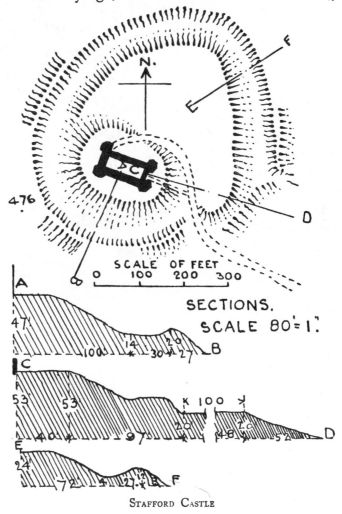

STAFFORD CASTLE

TAMWORTH.—According to the Anglo-Saxon Chronicle Lady Ethelfleda in 913 constructed a castle here. This was possibly a part of the present castle mound carrying some remains of Norman masonry, together with works of later dates which stand at the junction of the Rivers Tame and Anker. A mound here was essential for the establishment of anything in the way of defence of the place whenever and by whomsoever that might be required.

The town and castle were defended by the 'King's Ditch,' which was of great extent, and inclosed the parish church in the line parallel with the river, its ends terminating in bastions, whence two other sides ran down to the river which itself forms the remaining defence. At the present time the mound is, roughly speaking, circular with a table top of 37 yds. in diameter, and a base of 80 yds. in diameter, which, however, has in some places been

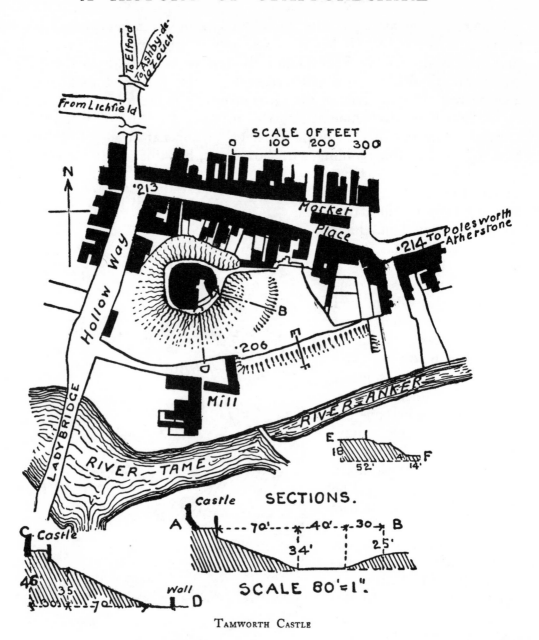

TAMWORTH CASTLE

much encroached upon. There is also a certain amount of proof that there were further works between the mound and the rivers.

This is a case of castle, town, and church within one protective fence, and with gates under authoritative control, the castle itself most probably having its own additional outworks. The altitude is 206 ft. above the Ordnance datum.

TUTBURY.—The castle owes its majestic situation to the hill on which it stands. Its strength of position is due first to its main boundary, lining with the upper edge of a precipitous cliff of about 180 yds. length, and next, to the immense sunken fosse circling the remainder of its boundary in places 95 ft. wide and 38 ft. deep, and running into the cliff at each of its extremities. Roughly speaking, the castle site is that of a semicircle with cliff across its diameter of 180 yds., and an extraordinary fosse skirting its circumference having a radius of 100 yds. This fosse has been dug through the hill of red

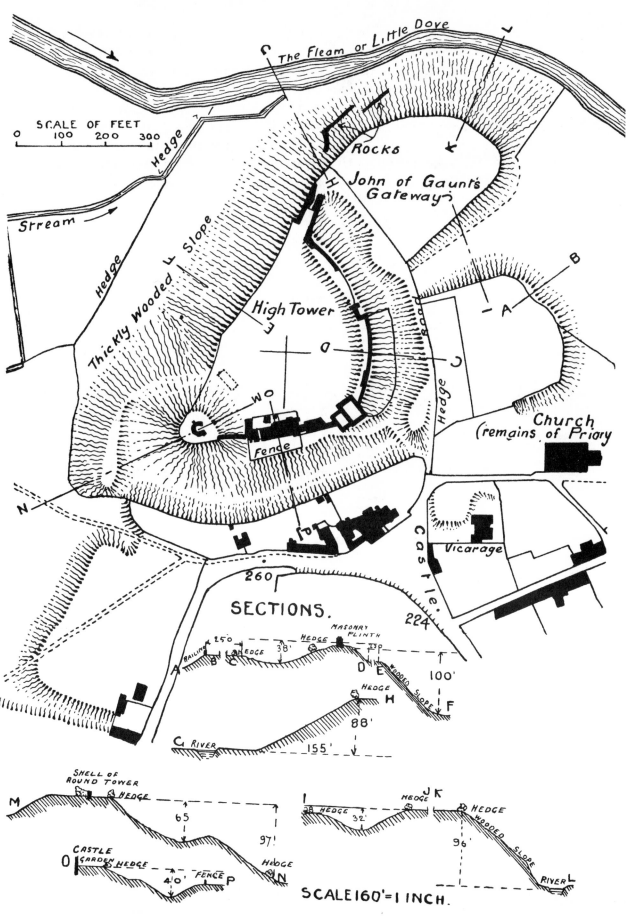

SCALE OF FEET
0 100 200 300

The Fleam or Little Dove

Rocks

John of Gaunt's Gateway

Hedge

Stream

Hedge

Thickly Wooded Slope

High Tower

Hedge

Church (remains of Priory

Fence

N

Vicarage

Castle

260

SECTIONS.

224

MASONRY PLINTH

RAILING 250   HEDGE   38'   HEDGE   130'

A   B   C   D   E   WOODED SLOPE   F

100'

HEDGE   H

88'

G   RIVER

155'

SHELL OF ROUND TOWER

M   HEDGE

65

97!

CASTLE GARDEN   HEDGE

O   HEDGE

40'   FENCE   P   HEDGE   O   N

I   HEDGE   HEDGE   J   K   HEDGE

32'   WOODED SLOPE

96

RIVER   L

SCALE 160'=1 INCH.

Tutbury Castle

357

marl associated with alabaster rock. At the south-west angle of the semi-circle a mound is raised as a site for a shell keep. To the north of this castle runs the River Dove flowing from west to east. On the east side of the fosse there is at present a fence, and to the east of this fence there are two plateaus or baileys of irregular squares of 100 yds., with slopes from their boundaries where not against the moat. Between these baileys there is a hollow formed by their two slopes, and it would seem that this was the main entrance, and that these two outlying works were for its protection. Its altitude is 260 ft.

HOMESTEAD MOATS

(CLASS F)

Ordnance Number	Parish	Name	Form	Dimensions (Outside Measurement)	Altitude	Situation, Notes, &c.
					Ft.	
XXXIX, 5	Abbots' Bromley	Bagot's Bromley	Rectangular; partly destroyed; two ponds, a hollow, and a monument within site; part wet	580 ft. by 340 ft.	400	On west side of road at Bagot's Bromley
XLIV, 11	Acton Trussell and Bednall	Manor Farm	Fragmentary; part wet; circular segment	615 ft. by 110 ft. (varying in width)	262	On west side of road at Acton, near Church
XLVI, 14	Armitage .	Handsacre Hall	Three sides of a square; wet; house on site	250 ft. by 240 ft.	265	Handsacre
XLVII, 9 & 5	Barton under Needwood	Blakenhall .	Square; altered in sundry places; wet	320 ft. by 320 ft.	235	On road between Barton and Yoxall
XXXVIII, 12	Blithfield .	Blithfield Hall	Single length . .	150 ft. long .	400	South-east of hall
XLIX, 7	Blymhill .	Brockhurst .	One side of square, and parts of two others; wet	200 ft., 150 ft., & 30 ft.	421	On road from Stretton to Gnosall
,,	,,	,,	Part of three sides	190 ft., 130 ft., & 140 ft.	411	On road from Stretton to Gnosall
XLIV, 5–6	Bradley .	Littywood .	Circular; part wet; house on site	650 ft. diameter .	400	1 mile north-east of Bradley
XL, 15	Branston .	Sinai Park .	Square; two sides disturbed; part wet; house on site	280 ft. by 280 ft.	300	1¼ miles north of Branston
LVI, 1	Brewood .	Hyde Farm .	Fragmentary; part wet	260 ft. & 290 ft.; 250 ft. by 100 ft.	400	½ mile south-west of Brewood
LII, 10	Burntwood, Edial and Woodhouses	Ashmore Brook	Fragment; wet; fed by stream	99 ft. by 25 ft.	400	North-west of Lichfield, 1½ miles on Farewell Road

HOMESTEAD MOATS (Class F)—*continued*

Ordnance Number	Parish	Name	Form	Dimensions (Outside Measurement)	Altitude	Situation, Notes, &c.
					Ft.	
LVI, 15	Bushbury .	Moseley .	Rectangular ; one corner enlarged ; wet	190 ft. by 140 ft.	459	½ mile south-west of Moseley
LXII, 3	,,	Showell's Farm	Square ; wet .	260 ft. by 260 ft.	400	1 mile south of Bushbury
LVI, 15	,,	Elston Hall .	Rectangular ; varied ; west side extended ; wet	260 ft. by 190 ft.	403	On road between Bushbury and Codsall
LI, 8	Cannock .	Ann's Well in Court Bank's Covert	Rectangular ; dry .	410 ft. by 250 ft.	600	About ½ mile south-west of Gentleshaw Church
XLIV, 3	Castle Church	Burton Manor	Rectangular ; with outlier ; dry	190 ft. by 145 ft.; 90 ft. by 50 ft.; outlier	333	1½ miles from Stafford South

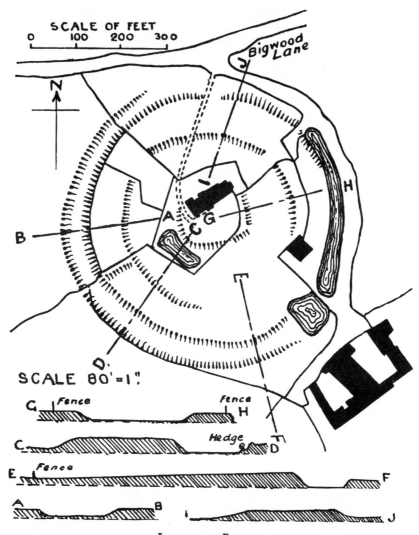

LITTYWOOD, BRADLEY

HOMESTEAD MOATS (Class F)—*continued*

Ordnance Number	Parish	Name	Form	Dimensions (Outside Measurement)	Altitude	Situation, Notes, &c.
					Ft.	
XXXVII, 14	Castle Church	South-west of Stafford Castle	Rectangular ; moat unusually wide ; dry	390 ft. by 350 ft.	299	1½ miles from Stafford on Newport road
XVIII, 7 & 8	Caverswall .	Weston Coyney	Rectangular ; part wet	240 ft. by 160 ft.	671	South of road between Caverswall and Hanley
XXXI, 14 & 15	Chartley Holme	Chartley Old Hall	Square ; on east side connected with a lake 600 ft. by 376 ft. ; wet	400 ft. by 400 ft.	311	North-east of Hall
XIX, 6	Cheadle .	Parkhall Farm	Rectangular ; one side and parts of two others wet ; also a second site	230 ft. by 190 ft.; second, 310 ft. by 180 ft.; part wet	549	1 mile north-west of Cheadle
XXV, 10	Checkley .	Blythe Wood, near Bittern's Dale	Rectangular ; dry ; three sets of intrenchments on the east side and two sets on the others	380 ft. by 440 ft.	500	2½ miles south-east of Draycott
XLIX, 4	Church Eaton	Shushions Manor	Fragmentary ; part wet	280 ft. . .	325	2 miles south of Church Eaton

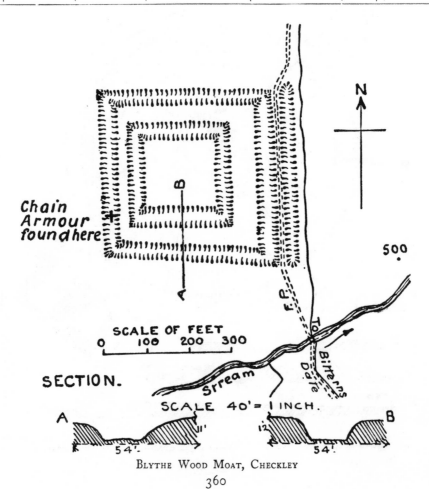

BLYTHE WOOD MOAT, CHECKLEY

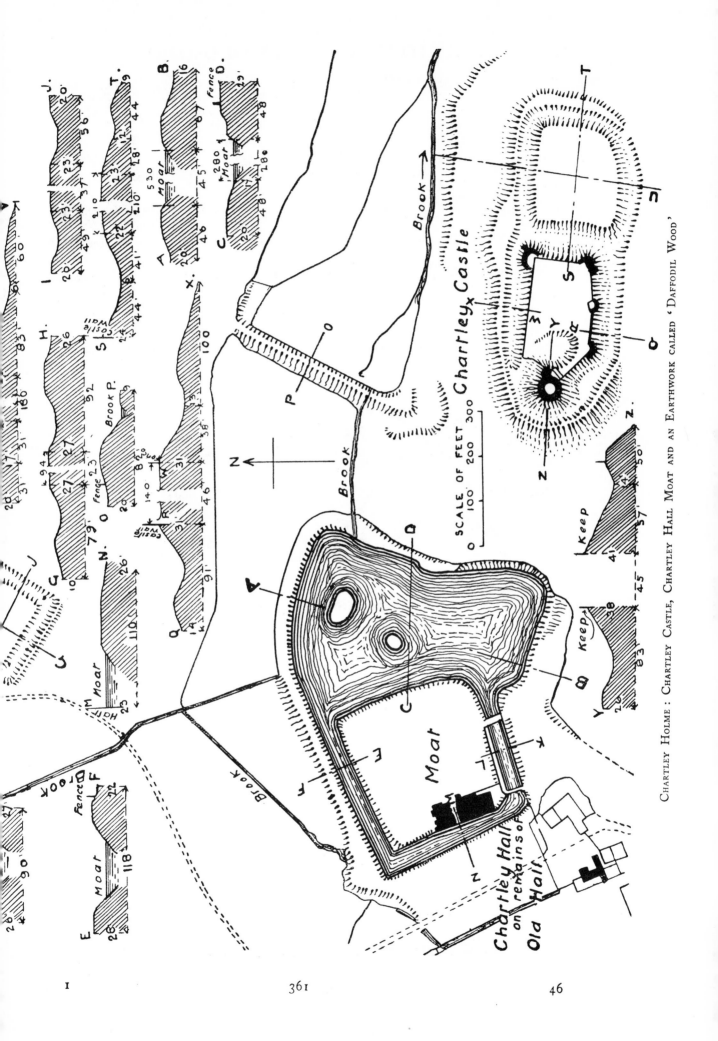

CHARTLEY HOLME: CHARTLEY CASTLE, CHARTLEY HALL MOAT AND AN EARTHWORK CALLED 'DAFFODIL WOOD'

HOMESTEAD MOATS (Class F)—*continued*

Ordnance Number	Parish	Name	Form	Dimensions (Outside Measurement)	Altitude	Situation, Notes, &c.
					Ft.	
XLIII, 15	Church Eaton	High Onn Manor	Fragmentary; three lengths; part wet and dry	260 ft., 400 ft., 420 ft.	436	1½ miles south-west of Church Eaton
,,	,,	Little Onn Hall	Rectangular; varied; wet	280 ft. by 190 ft.	378	1½ miles south from Church Eaton
LV, 12	Codsall .	Woodhall .	Rectangular; three sides; wet	210 ft. by 180 ft.	458	1 mile from Codsall on Albrighton Road
XLIV, 2	Coppenhall .	Coppenhall Gorse	Oval, with various outlying works; dry	450 ft. by 400 ft.	353	2 miles south-west of Stafford
,,	,,	Hydes Lea .	Fragmentary, with various outlying works; dry	Indefinite	420	2 miles south-west of Stafford

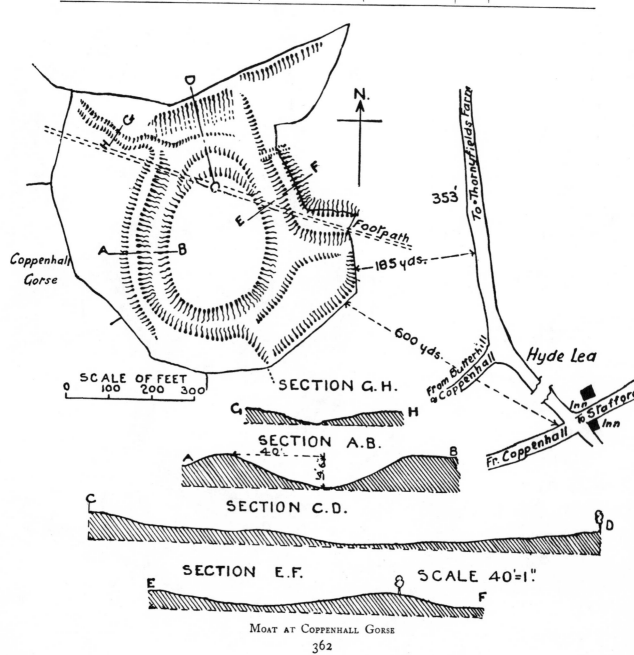

MOAT AT COPPENHALL GORSE

Ordnance Number	Parish	Name	Form	Dimensions (Outside Measurement)	Altitude	Situation, Notes, &c.
					Ft.	
XXXV, 6	Draycott in the Moors	Paynsley Hall	An inner ditch with banks, shewing one side and two returns ; also to south-east, two sets of ditches, 192 ft. long, with banks ; also two circular mounds between the outer and inner intrenchments, each 27 ft. in diameter ; also considerable fragments of intrenchments to the north-east and north-west.	200 ft. by 90 ft.	500	About 1½ miles from Draycott (South)
XXIII, 13	Eccleshall .	Charnes Old Hall	Irregular ; formed out of rectangle ; wet ; house on site	250 ft. by 200 ft.	400	½ mile east of Charnes
XXXVI, 3	,,	Wootton .	Fragment of irregular form ; dry	About 70 yds. in length	400	At Wootton, 1½ miles from Eccleshall
XX, 11	Ellastone .	Bentley Fold	Two sides of rectangle, and part of another ; wet	190 ft. by 190 ft.	351	Ellastone
XXXVI, 3	Ellenhall .	Old Hall .	Fragments of a square, connected with a pond ; dry	220 ft. by 180 ft.	378	Near church and road, between Ranton and Stone
XXXVI, 7 & 11	,,	Ranton Abbey	Part of two sides ; dry	400 ft. & 280 ft.	393	On road between Great Bridgeford and Littleworth
LVII, 13	Essington .	At the Hollies	Filled up in 1896	———	567	2 miles east of Bloxwich
LVI, 15	,,	West Croft Farm	Three sides of a square ; wet	170 ft. by 170 ft.	491	Off road between Wolverhampton and Shareshill, 3 miles north-east of Wolverhampton
LVI, 16	,,	Moat House	Filled up 15 years ago	———	550	———
XIV, 13	Farley . .	Moat House	Rectangular ; dry	160 ft. by 129 ft.	1,005	Near Cotton (north-east)
LIII, 13	Fisherwick .	Fisherwick . (figured in Plot)	Fragmentary ; circular segment ; dry	550 ft.	200	1¼ miles north-east of Whittington, near River Tame
XXXI, 13	Gayton .	Moat Farm .	Rectangular ; broken on north side ; part wet	260 ft. by 180 ft.	300	South of churchyard

HOMESTEAD MOATS (CLASS F)—*continued*

Ordnance Number	Parish	Name	Form	Dimensions (Outside Measurement)	Altitude	Situation, Notes, &c.
					Ft.	
XLIX, 1	Gnosall	Chatwell	Angle of square; water pit west; wet	160 ft. by 130 ft. water pit 160 ft. by 80 ft.	292	At Chatwell between Newport and Blymhill
XLIII, 3	„	Gnosall	Rectangular line of intrenchment to north-east; wet	170 ft. & 180 ft.	376	½ mile from Gnosall on Haughton road
XLIII, 6	„	Befcote Manor	Fragmentary; rectangular; part wet	330 ft. by 180 ft.	400	South of road between Gnosall and Morton, 2 miles from former
XXXIII, 9	Hanbury	Moat Farm	Fragmentary; rectangular; dry	240 ft. by 210 ft.	209	2 miles from Hanbury on Sudbury road
XL, 1	„	Woodend	Rectangular; part wet; now orchard	190 ft. by 210 ft.	437	¾ mile south of Hanbury
LXVIII, 12 and LXIX, 9	Handsworth	Perry Hall	Rectangular; with length of water 80 ft. wide down to River Tame; Hall is within site; wet	420 ft. by 240 ft.	343	½ mile north-east of Perry Bar
XLVI, 7	Hamstall Ridware	Near River Blythe (figured in Shaw)	Rectangular; dry	230 ft. by 210 ft.	215	At Hamstall Ridware
LIII, 11	Harlaston	Harlaston	Fragmentary; rectangular; one side missing; wet	280 ft. east, 280 ft. west, 380 ft. north	233	Adjoining churchyard
XLIII, 4	Haughton	Moat Farm	Fragmentary; wet	270 ft. & 130 ft.	348	West of churchyard
XLIII, 4	„	Booden Farm	Rectangular; much altered; house on site; part wet	470 ft. by 340 ft.	353	¾ mile south of Haughton
XXIV, 16	Hilderstone	The Hall	Rectangular; altered on south side, with extra bank on north side	400 ft. by 320 ft.	600	South-west of Hall
LVI, 8 & 12	Hilton	Hilton Hall Moat	Angular; fragment hall on site; wet	370 ft. & 240 ft.	500	Park Road from Shareshill to Bloxwich
XIII, 15	Kingsley	Glebe Farm	Fragment of a square; partly dry	320 ft. & 100 ft.	657	At back of house, which was vicarage
L, 5	Lapley	Old Manor House	Irregular remains; part wet	300 ft. & 200 ft. & 320 ft.	374	Lapley
XXV, 11	Leigh	Park Hall	Rectangular; wet	270 ft. by 260 ft.	500	½ mile north-east of Leigh Church on Tean Road
LII, 14	Lichfield St. Chad	Maple Hayes	Rectangular, with rounded corners; on south side is an angular intrenchment 56 yds. in length	193 ft. by 170 ft.	300	1¼ miles west of Lichfield, on Burntwood road

Ordnance Number	Parish	Name	Form	Dimensions (Outside Measurement)	Altitude	Situation, Notes, &c.
					Ft.	
XVII, 9	Madely	Manor ruins (figured in Plot)	Square, with moat and four shallow trenches, and angle moat ; part wet	340 ft. by 340 ft. angle moat 280 ft. by 140 ft.	379	North-east of ruins and within ¼ mile of Madeley Road station, on North Staffordshire Railway
XXXII, 15	Marchington Woodlands	Moat Springs	Square ; on skew ; wet	240 ft. by 240 ft.	300	⅛ mile north-west Marchington Woodlands, ½ mile south-east of Gorsty Hill
XX, 4, & XXI, 1	Mayfield	Old Hall	Irregular ; dry	Indefinite	600	North of Old Hall and and road adjoining
XX, 8	,,	Harlow	Oval	100 ft. by 85 ft.	600	West of Middle Mayfield
XXXI, 1	Milwich	Garshall	Square ; mound within arc, oval in form ; about 3 ft. high ; dry	260 ft. by 250 ft.	500	Near Oulton House, off road from Stone to Milwich
XXXI, 5	,,	Milwich Hall	Fragment ; wet	30 ft. by 25 ft.	424	South-east of Milwich Hall on road from Sandon to Uttoxeter
XXXI, 5	,,	Manor Farm	Fragment ; wet	132 ft. by 30 ft.	424	Off Sandon Road
XVI, 12	Mucklestone	Lea Head	Rectangular ; wet	190 ft. by 139 ft.	400	1¼ miles north-east Pipe Gate station, North Staffordshire Railway
XXXIX, 8	Newborough	The Hall	Square, varied by alterations ; wet	340 ft. by 340 ft.	374	At Newborough
XXXIX, 12	,,	Moat Hall	Rectangular, with second bank and ditch on south side ; part wet	380 ft. by 260 ft.	400	,, ,,
XXXVI, 10	Norbury	Norbury Manor (figured in Plot)	Rectangular ; wet	260 ft. by 220 ft.	326	On lane to Manor House
LXI, 1	Patshull	Burnhill Green	Three sides of a square ; part wet	115 ft. by 141 ft.	275	1 mile west of the Hall
LVII, 11	Pelsall	Moat Farm	Irregular ; wet	168 ft. by 80 ft.	494	At Pelsall
L, 7	Penkridge	Rodbaston Old Hall	Rectangular ; mound within site ; wet	340 ft. by 290 ft.	302	East of road from Penkridge to Wolverhampton, 1½ miles south of Penkridge
XLIV, 10	,,	Hay House	Rectangular ; one side house destroyed ; on site ; wet	230 ft. by 200 ft.	300	On road between Bradley and Penkridge, two miles north west of latter

HOMESTEAD MOATS (CLASS F)—*continued*

Ordnance Number	Parish	Name	Form	Dimensions (Outside Measurement)	Altitude	Situation, Notes, &c.
					Ft.	
L, 4	Penkridge	Pillaton Hall	Part oval, part straight	Oval 570 ft. by 380 ft.; straight 260 ft.	366	About 1½ miles south-east of Penkridge on Cannock Road
XLVI, 10	Pipe Ridware	The Hall	Two sides fed by streams from River Trent	240 ft. by 140 ft.	210	Pipe Ridware Hall
XXXVI, 11 & 15	Ranton	Broughhall	Fragmentary; rectangular; part wet	480 ft. by 300 ft.	451	On road between Gnosall and Ranton, midway
XXXVI, 8	Ranton	Ranton Hall	Remains rectangular; wet	340 ft. by 280 ft.	360	¼ mile from road between High Offley and Great Bridgeford, 1½ miles south of Ellenhall
XXXVI, 8	„	Extall	Three sides of a square; dry	230 ft. by 210 ft.	300	1 mile north-east of Ranton Hall, near junction of roads between High Offley and Ellenhall
LXIII, 7	Rushall	The Hall (figured in Shaw)	Fragmentary; one side and angles; dry	300 ft. & 100 ft. & 210 ft.	468	1¼ miles north-east of Walsall
XXX, 12	Sandon	Old Hall Moat (figured in Plot)	Rectangular; wet; to north-east are three fragments of moat	330 ft. by 312 ft.	412	East of church on road from Sandon to Fradswell
LVII, 5	Saredon	Black Lees	Rectangular; wet	150 ft. by 160 ft.	470	Near junction of roads from Bloxwich to Saredon and Great Wyrley
LVII, 5	„	„	Angle of bank	370 ft. & 320 ft.	470	Ditto, adjoining last
LVI, 3	Shareshill (detached)	Moat house bridge	Angular fragment; wet	140 ft. & 160 ft.	342	Near Staffordshire-Worcestershire Canal
LVIII, 15	Shenstone	Shenstone Park	There is an irregular rectangular area planted and bounded by water known as the Fish Pond. Also fragments of bank of two sides with water 40 ft. wide	350 ft. by 260 ft. & 200 ft. & 50 ft.	300	1 mile south-east of Shenstone
XII, 15, & XVIII, 3	Stoke upon Trent	Simfield	Rectangular	304 ft. by 178 ft.	600	South of Werrington Road between Ash Hall and Brookhouse
XVIII, 3	„	Hall Hill Farm	Rectangular; altered by mineral railway; dry	220 ft. by 200 ft.	543	Near Bentley Colliery on Longton and Adderley Green Railway

HOMESTEAD MOATS (Class F)—*continued*

Ordnance Number	Parish	Name	Form	Dimensions (Outside Measurement)	Altitude	Situation, Notes, &c.
					Ft.	
XXIV, 3	Stone . . .	Moat Farm, Hartwell	Part of square ; wet	300 ft. by 260 ft.	609	On road from Barlaston, near junction with Longton and Stone Road
XXX, 2	,,	Priory Farm	Rectangular ; fragments ; wet	180 ft. by 100 ft.	294	Near road between Eccleshall and Stone, and near junction with Stafford Road
XXX, 7	,,	Aston Hall .	Rectangular ; dry ; hall within site ; form much modified	Indefinite outline 410 ft. by 360 ft.	300	At Aston Hall, on road between Stone and Stafford
XXXVIII, 6	Stowe . .	Hixon . .	Fragmentary ; rectangular ; wet	160 ft. by 180 ft.	328	On road from Stafford to Uttoxeter, at junction of road to Weston
XXXVIII, 3	,,	Drointon .	Rectangular ; dry	330 ft. by 280 ft.	398	At Drointon
XXXVIII, 3	,,	,,	Square ; partly wet	120 ft. by 125 ft.	395	1½ miles on road from Stowe to Uttoxeter
XLVII, 1	Tatenhill .	Sherholt Lodge	Two sides of a square ; wet	180 ft. & 170 ft.	292	South of road from Yoxall to Burton-on-Trent

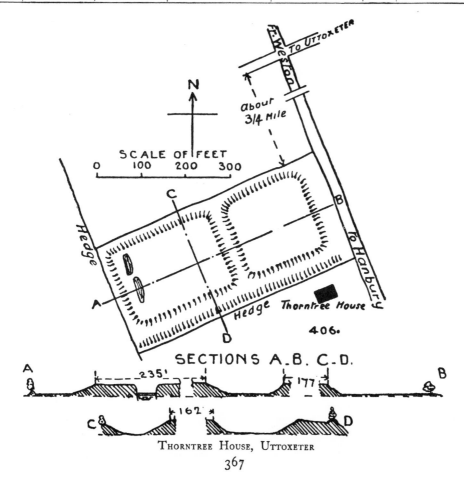

THORNTREE HOUSE, UTTOXETER

HOMESTEAD MOATS (Class F)—*continued*

Ordnance Number	Parish	Name	Form	Dimensions (Outside Measurement)	Altitude	Situation, Notes, &c.
					Ft.	
LXVIII, 5	Tipton	Ocker Hill	Rectangular ; one side and parts of two others ; house on site ; wet.	210 ft., 190 ft. & 110 ft.	452	1 mile south-west of Wednesbury
LXVI, 3	Trysull & Seisdon	Moat rough .	Rectangular ; dry ; planted	177 ft. by 143 ft.	400	1¼ miles west of Seisdon
XXXII, 5	Uttoxeter	Blount's Green	About square ; partly wet	230 ft. by 245 ft.	368	1 mile south-west of Uttoxeter, off Abbots' Bromley Road
XXXII, 10	,,	Thorntree House	Double moat .	230 ft. by 240 ft., & 280 ft. by 240 ft.	406	2 miles south of Uttoxeter, ¾ mile from Abbots' Bromley Road
LVII, 10	Walsall	Near Fishley Farm	Fragmentary ; short lengths of bank and ditch remaining, and some water	190 ft. by 120 ft.	500	1 mile to north-east of Bloxwich
LXIII, 10	,,	The Moat .	Rectangular ; three sides ; wet	330 ft., 200 ft. & 190 ft.	426	1 mile west of Walsall
LXIII, 12	,,	Moat Cottage	Rectangular ; dry	300 ft. by 290 ft.	588	1½ miles east of Walsall, on road to Sutton
LXIII, 12	,,	Near Wood End Farm	Rectangular ; three sides ; in part wet	180 ft., 120 ft. & 80 ft.	469	About 1 mile east of Walsall, near Moat Canal Bridge
LXIII, 14	,,	Bescot Hall	Rectangular ; with one length of double moat ; very perfect ; dry	300 ft. by 250 ft.; 190 ft. double length	399	1¼ miles south-west of Walsall, on road to Wednesbury
LXIII, 7	,,	Near Calderfields Farm	Circular .	260 ft. diameter.	483	1 mile east of Walsall
LXII, 4	Wednesfield .	Prestwood (figured in Shaw)	Rectangular ; wet	250 ft. by 190 ft.	500	1 mile north of Wednesfield
LXII, 4	,,	Ashmore Park Farm	Rectangular ; wet	270 ft. by 210 ft.	489	1¼ miles north-east of Wednesfield
LXII, 8	,,	Merols Hole	Angle fragment ; wet	130 ft. & 50 ft.	454	¼ mile south-east of Wednesfield
XLIX, 14	Weston under Lizard	Weston Park	Rectangular ; planted ; wet	118 ft. by 145 ft.	400	⅝ mile south of Watling Street
XLVII, 13	Wichnor	Wichnor	One side and parts of two sides ; part wet	320 ft. by 180 ft.	200	To south-west of Wichnor Church, south of canal
LVII, 2	Wyrley, Great	Moat Farm .	Rectangular ; fragment ; wet	210 ft. & 110 ft. & 140 ft.	426	On main road at Great Wyrley
XLVI, 8	Yoxall .	Near Mill Stream	Quadrant ; dry .	300 ft. by 110 ft.	226	Yoxall
XLVI, 4	,,	Longcroft Hall	Fragmentary ; wet	305 ft. & 75 ft.	274	¾ mile north-east of Yoxall

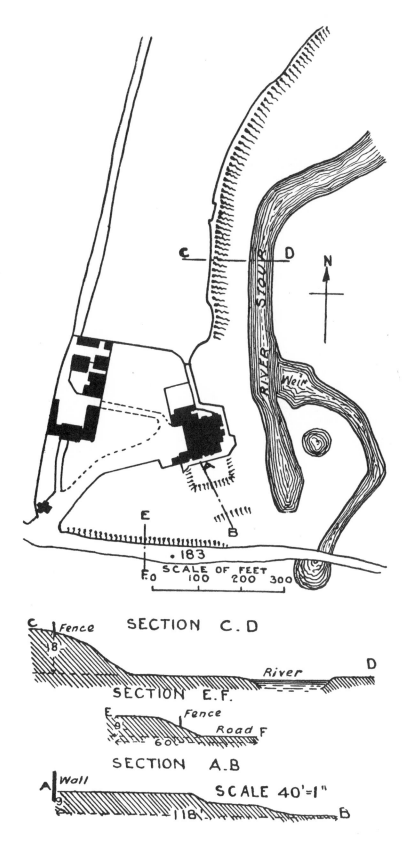

SECTION C.D

C Fence

River D

SECTION E.F.

E Fence
Road F

SECTION A.B

A Wall SCALE 40'=1"

B

STOURTON CASTLE, KINVER

MISCELLANEOUS EARTHWORKS

(Class X)

ECCLESHALL.—The defensive earthworks here would seem to have been a broad and deep moat, square in form, inclosing a quadrangular area, whereon the castle stood with a strong stone retaining wall supporting the isolated inclosure, with an arched bridge across the moat for the approach to the castle. Much of the retaining wall remains and also a fine angle tower of nine sides. The bridge across the moat seems to have been central on the south side, which would give a length of 280 ft. east and west for the building area, and 170 ft. north and south. The River Sow is in immediate connexion with the site. Recent dealing with the grounds and surrounding waters has much modified the character of the earthwork. The nearest altitude on the Ordnance map is 300 ft.

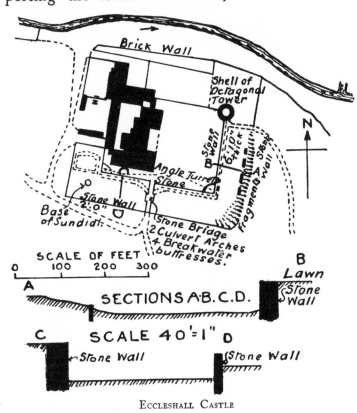

ECCLESHALL CASTLE

LICHFIELD.—The close and city were fortified with fosse and wall and towers as at Eccleshall. The lower part of the north-east tower still remains, and the eastern fosse bounds the palace grounds, and remains of the northern wall still exist in the palace and other gardens.

KINVER : STOURTON.—Here there are two lines of earthworks, one against the road to the south of the castle running east and west and the other following the line of the River Stour running north and south, but these may have been occasioned by the construction of the road and as flood-banks against the river. There are also slopes and banks to the south-east of the present house, but there is nothing about them indicating that they are of ancient origin. Stourton is said to have been fortified for the king at the commencement of the Civil Wars.

TYRLEY.—This is at present the site of a farm-house, and there are no definite remains of earthworks.

Besides the foregoing there are other earthworks enumerated in the following table, of which only a very general account can be given by reason of their indefiniteness both as to their extent and character.

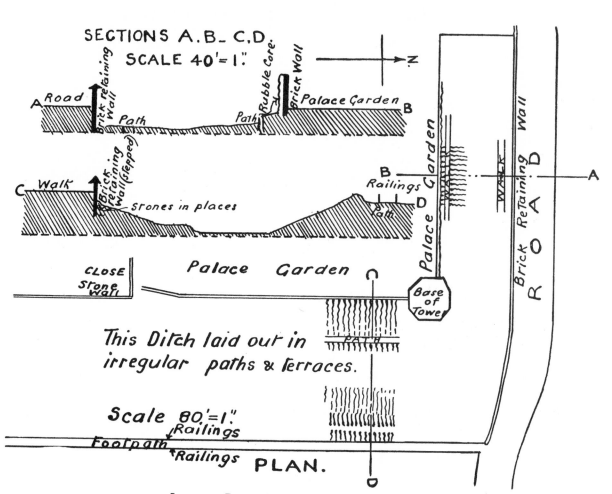

LICHFIELD DITCH, EAST AND NORTH OF CATHEDRAL

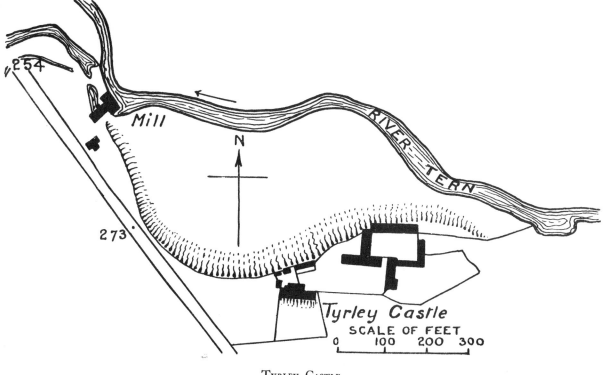

TYRLEY CASTLE

MISCELLANEOUS EARTHWORKS (Class X)—*continued*

Ordnance Number	Parish	Name	Form	Dimensions	Altitude	Situation
VI, 15	Audley . .	Bunker's Hill	Length of curved intrenchment	120 yds. & 306 yds.	Ft. 488 & 441	Linley Wood
LXIV 5	Barr, Great .	Round Hill .	Roughly circular .	400 ft. N. & S. 370 ft. E. & W.	500	Bourne Vale. This mound has been planted within the memory of man. It has no indication of defence, has not been tested by excavation and appears to be wholly of sand and is possibly of natural formation
XII, 10	Burslem . .	Abbey Farm	A length of ditch and bank	63 yds. & 63 yds.	500	Near Biddulph Valley Railway at Abbey
IV, 13	Leekfrith .	Lower Haddon	A length of ditch with bank	217 yds.	1,000	143 yds. from road between Rushton Spencer & Meerbrook
LII, 11	Lichfield, St. Chad	Prince Rupert's Mound	Rectangular . .	34 yds. by 25 yds.	319	North-east of Beacon Street
LII, 15	Lichfield, St. Michael	Barrow Cop Hill	Circular . . .	310 ft. diam.	300	About 1 mile south-west of Lichfield
XX, 4, & XXI, 1	Mayfield .	The Cliffs .	Terraces . . .	406 yds. varied	600	¼ mile north of Upper Mayfield
XX, 8	„	Hollow Lane	Series of terraces .	160 yds.	600	¼ mile west of Middle Mayfield
XXIV, 14	Stone . .	Mottley Pits Terraces	Various, straight, and curved	Covering a large area	459	¼ mile north-east of Stone railway station
XLI, 1 & 5	Stretton, (near Burton upon Trent)	Vicarage .	Irregular, with right angle corners	330 ft. by 130 ft. and varying	178	Adjoins Vicarage
LXVI, 3	Trysull and Seisdon	Abbot's Castle Hill	Running length .	About 2 miles	454	1 mile west of Seisdon
XXVI 10 & 14	Uttoxeter .	Hill House Terraces	Rectangular . .	420 ft.	400	West of Hill House, Stramshall
XXVI, 10 & 14	„	Cottage holding	„	120 ft. by 90 ft.	358	North-east of St. Michael's Church, Stramshall
XX, 3	Wootton .	Raddle pits .	Lines of trenches .	166 yds.	900	½ mile north of Wootton

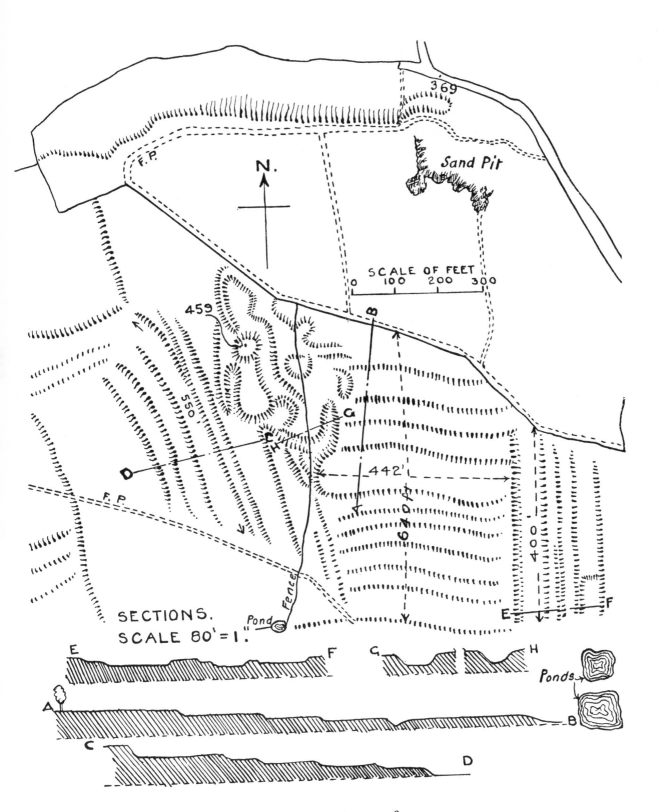

SCALE OF FEET
0   100   200   300

SECTIONS.
SCALE 80'=I.

MOTTLEY PITS TERRACES, STONE

373

EARLY BURIAL MOUNDS, OR LOWS

These burial mounds occur in every part of this county, but more frequently than elsewhere on the northern moors, and generally, but not always, at high levels. Their sizes and shapes vary. Excepting the exploration carried out by Thomas W. Bateman and his assistant Samuel Carrington very little has been done in that direction.[1]

The prolific results of the diggings of the above-named explorers have found a place in the public museum of the town of Sheffield.

The deposits in the Sheffield Museum represent nearly the whole of what has resulted from the opening out of the ancient burial mounds of the county. It is remarkable that the northern moorlands, the highest parts of the county, should be crowded with these memorials of the pre-historic dead, emphasizing their doings on earth and signifying their faith in a future. Looking at the number of them, localized so thickly though spread over centuries, it would almost appear that the heights of the hills were specially chosen as places of sepulture by those living far and near.

Ordnance Survey Sheet	Parish	Name	Form	Dimensions	Altitude	Situations, Finds, Notes
					Ft.	
IX, 8	Alstonfield .	Narrowdale Hill	Oval	Diam. 52 ft. by 43 ft.; 5ft. 6 in. high	1,000	½ mile east of cross roads at Gateham Farm
IX, 8	,,	Gratton Hill	Kite-shaped . .	42 ft. by 34 ft. ; 4 ft. 9 in. high	1,194	1 mile north of Alstonfield
XIV, 4	,,	Ilam Tops Low	Circular . . .	Diam. 80 ft.; 8 ft. high	1,103	¼ mile from Ilam Tops Farm
IX, 16	,,	Stanshope pasture Hall dale	,,	Diam. 47 ft. 6 in.; 8 ft. high	900	¾ mile south-east of Stanshope
IX, 11	,,	Steep Low .	Irregular . . .	93 ft. by 39 ft. ; 15 ft. high	1,000	½ mile north-west of Alstonfield
IX, 12	,,	Pea Low .	Circular . . .	Diam. 140 ft. ; 6 ft. high	1,000	½ mile north of Alstonfield
XIV, 12	Blore with Swinscoe	West of Blore	Oval	Diam. 63 ft. by 27 ft. ; 4 ft. high	1,000	½ mile west of Blore
XIV, 11	,,	Dun Low .	Circular . . .	Diam. 89 ft. ; 6 ft. 6 in. high	1,000	Near Waterings Farm to west
XIV, 12	,,	Lady Low .	Rectangular . .	60 ft. by 48 ft. ; 3 ft. high	700	¼ mile north of Blore Hall

[1] Thomas W. Bateman was well known to fame, but Samuel Carrington, the village schoolmaster of Wetton, a moorland parish wherein he opened very many burial mounds, has scarcely ever been heard of, but he was truly a man of science, well versed in botany, geology and archaeology. After a life of extraordinary usefulness was ended he was buried in the churchyard of Wetton, and under the auspices of Sir Thomas Wardle, the members of the North Staffordshire Field Club erected a fitting memorial over the place of his burial from the design of Mr. G. G. Scott, jun.

EARLY BURIAL MOUNDS, OR LOWS—*continued*

Ordnance Survey Sheet	Parish	Name	Form	Dimensions	Altitude	Situations, Finds, Notes
					Ft.	
XIV, 9	Caldon . .	Crow Low .	Circular . . .	Diam. 70 ft. ; 7 ft. high	1,000	Within 1 mile from Caldon Station
XIV, 7	Calton . .	Cart Low .	,,	Diam. 80 ft. ; 6 ft. high	900	North-east of Water-fall and Calton Lane
XIV, 11	,,	Near Lower Calton Green House	,,	Diam. 91 ft. ; 8 ft. 9 in. high	1,088	South-east of cross roads, Green Lane, and back lane
XIV, 11	,,	,,	,,	Diam. 58 ft. ; 4 ft. high	900	At rear of Lower Calton Green House
XX, 12	Calwich .	Calwich Low	,,	Diam. 103 ft. ; 3 ft. high	518	¼ mile north of Cal-wich Abbey
XVIII, 12	Caverswall .	Swan Bank Cookshill	Circular . . .	Diam. 139 ft. ; 10 ft. high	600	North-west Cavers-wall Excavation made through each direc-tion and at foot—nothing found
XVIII, 7	,,	Weston Coyney	Irregular . . .	Diam. 100 ft. by 120 ft.; 20 ft. high	700	North-west of cross-roads, Hilderstone to Leek and Caverswall to Hanley
XIV, 13	Cotton . .	Near Ribden Clay Works	Circular . . .	Diam. 88 ft. ; 7 ft. high	1,075	¼ mile north-west from Moat House near Cotton.
LIII, 2	Croxall . .		,,	Diam. 117 ft. ; 18 ft. and 29 ft. high	200	South-east of Church-yard against River Tame
LIII, 14	Elford . .	The Low .	,,	Diam. 69 ft. ; 49 ft. high	231	Near roadside Tam-worth to Burton
XX, 6	Ellastone . .	Gid Low .	,,	Diam. 86 ft. ; 11 ft. high	600	In park north of Wootton Lodge
XX, 5	Farley . .	Beelow Hill .	,,	Diam. 38 ft. ; 2 ft. high	852	Near road between Farley and Cotton
XX, 1	,,	Near Three Lows Cottage	,,	Diam. 83 ft. by 71 ft. ; 4 ft. 6 in. high	1,044	South-west of Leek and Ashbourne Road
XIV, 14	,,	Wardlow .	,,	Diam. 78 ft. ; 8 ft. high	1,211	200 yds. south-west of Wardlow
V, 10	Fawfieldhead	North of the Low	,,	Diam. 97 ft. 6 in.; 8 ft. 6 in. high	900	Off Hulme Lane
V, 10	,,	North-west of the Low	,,	Diam. 104 ft. ; 6 ft. 6 in. high	956	,, ,,

EARLY BURIAL MOUNDS, OR LOWS—*continued*

Ordnance Survey Sheet	Parish	Name	Form	Dimensions	Alti-tude	Situations, Finds, Notes
					Ft.	
LVIII, 16	Hints . .	Elford, Golds Clump	Circular . . .	Diam. 175 ft.; 30 ft. high and Diam. 180 ft; 19 ft. high	400	Elford Low Farm. Near Watling Street Hints between Tamworth and Lichfield
XIV, 4	Ilam . . .	Beechenhill .	„	Diam. 47 ft.; 4 ft. high	1,000	¼ mile north of Beechenhill Farm
XIV, 11	„	Musden Low	Circle disturbed .	Diam. 105 ft.; 4 ft. high	1,182	½ mile north-west of Waterings
XIV, 11	„	Musden Low north-west	Circle	Diam. 74 ft.; 6 ft. high	1,182	North-west of last
XIV, 11	„	Musden Low south	„	Diam. 50 ft.; 4 ft. high	1,180	⅛ mile north-west of Waterings
LXVII, 14	Kingswinford	Barrowhill .	Circular . . .	Diam. 99 ft.; 30 ft. high	500	East of Pensnett Churchyard
XXIII, 1	Maer . .	Camphills .	„	Diam. 51 ft.; 5 ft. high	600	600 yards north of King's Bank
XXIII, 1	„	„	„	Diam. 49 ft.; 7 ft. high	600	230 yds. north-west of King's Bank
XXIII, 1	„	King's Bank .	„	Diam. 130 ft.; 20 ft. high	600	Camp Hills north of Whitmore and Market Drayton Road
XX, 8	Mayfield .		Oval	Diam. 107 ft. and 78 ft.; 3 ft. high	600	¼ mile north-west of Middle Mayfield
XX, 8	„	The Rowleys	„	Diam. 145 ft. by 125 ft.; 11 ft. high	500	North-west of Red House on Ellastone and Mayfield Road
XLV, 7	Rugeley . .	Etchinghill .	Circular, irregular	Diam. 328 ft. by 63 ft.	454	Natural hill scarped
V, 10–11	Sheen . .	Brund Lane	Circular	74 ft. diam.; 13 ft. high	900	⅔ of a mile west of Sheen Church
XX, 3	Stanton . .	Over-low	„	Diam. 90 ft.; 6 ft. high	800	⅔ of a mile west of Stanton
„	„ . .	Scrip Low	„	Diam. 92 ft.; 10 ft. high	800	About ¼ mile west of Stanton village
XXIV, 9	Stone . . .	Saxon Low	Irregular	Diam. 241 ft. by 315 ft.; 38 ft. high	500	Near Hill Top Farm ⅓ mile from Trentham Road
L, 6	Stretton (near Penkridge)	Rowley Hill	Circular	Diam. 65 ft.; 3 ft. high	317	Planted 1½ miles east of village; ¾ miles north of Watling Street

Ordnance Survey Sheet	Parish	Name	Form	Dimensions	Altitude	Situations, Finds, Notes
					Ft.	
LVIII, 15	Swinfen and Packington	Offlow . .	Indistinct but traceable	Too indefinite for measurement	367	⅛ mile north-east of Watling Street on Lane to Whitehouse Farm
XXXVII, 12	Tixall . . .	Blackheath Covert	Circular	Diam. 120 ft. ; 9 ft. high	294	North-west of road from Ingestre to Stafford
XXXVIII, 9	,, .	Lower Hanyards	,,	Diam. 65 ft. ; 6 ft. high	400	South of road from Ingestre to Stafford at Lower Hanyard Farm
XXXII, 6	Uttoxeter .	Toothill .	,,	Diam. 85 ft. ; 6 ft. high	441	Marchington road ⅛ mile from junction of Brookhouse Lane, planted
XXXII, 2	,, .	,,	,,	Diam. 140 ft. 14 ft. high	300	Off Wood Lane ½ mile from junction with Bridge Street
,,	,, .	,,	,,	Diam. 64 ft. ; 5 ft. high		Woodlane near railway and river.
XIV, 2	Waterfall .	Waterfall Low	,,	Diam. 60 ft.; 8 ft. high	1,000	Within an inclosed plantation north-east of Waterfall 330 yds. east of Slade Lane
,,	,, .	South of Oldfield Farm	Oval	Diam. 89 ft. & 69 ft. ; 5 ft. high	1,141	Off Slade Lane between Grindon and Waterfall

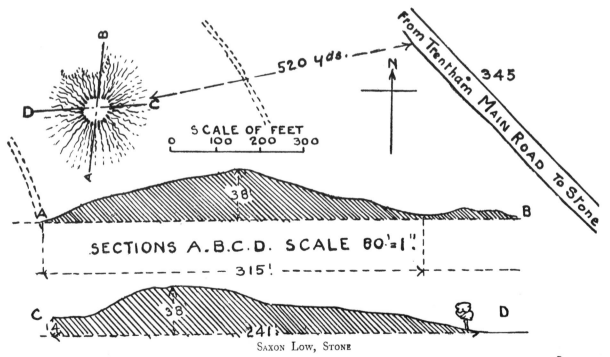

SAXON LOW, STONE

EARLY BURIAL MOUNDS, OR LOWS—*continued*

Ordnance Survey Sheet	Parish	Name	Form	Dimensions	Altitude	Situations, Finds, Notes
					Ft.	
XXXV, 8	Weston Jones	Gregory . .	Oval	Diam. 180 ft. by 150 ft. ; 8 ft. high	300	¼ mile north-east of Weston Jones
IX, 11	Wetton . .	Gateham, south-west	Kite-shaped . . .	Diam. 55 ft. by 60 ft. ; 4 ft. high	1,221	⅜ mile from Gateham
,,	,, . .	Adjoining last	Circle	Diam. 42 ft. ; 4 ft. high	1,221	,, ,,
XIV, 15	,, . .	Wetton Low	Circular	Diam. 69 ft. ; 10 ft. high	1,010	¼ mile south-east of Wetton
IX, 6	,, . .	Ecton Low .	Oval	Diam. 76 ft. by 85 ft. 6 ft. high	1,000	¼ mile east of Ecton Bridge
XX, 2	Wootton . .	Three Knowls on Weever Hill	Circular	Diam. 82 ft. ; 7 ft. high	1,185	One mile north-west of Wootton
,,	,,	One undefined	,,	Diam. 75 ft. ; 9 ft. high	1,183	¾ mile north-west from Wootton

INDEX

OF THE

PARISHES IN WHICH EARTHWORKS ARE SITUATED WITH THE LETTER OF THE CLASS TO WHICH THEY BELONG

ANCIENT EARTHWORKS

INDEX (*continued*)